The Finder (Chapter 5)

control+tab or control+I (in list view)	Chang... columns left to right (add shift key to cycle right to left)
command+J	Open View Options
command+B	Show/hide window toolbar for active window
command+shift+C/H/I/A/F	Go to Computer/Home/iDisk/Applications/Favorites (respectively) in active window (a new window will be opened if necessary)
command+shift+G	Bring up "Go to Folder" dialog in active window (a new window will be opened if necessary)
command+[or command+]	Go back or forward in window view history
command+W	Close active Finder window (add option to close all)
command+F	Bring up Find dialog
command+K	Bring up Connect to Server dialog
command+E	Eject/unmount selected disc/volume

Open/Save Dialog Shortcuts (Chapter 5)

tab	Switch between browser and text fields
arrow keys, page up/down	Navigate in browser
command+shift+A/C/F/H/I	Change directory view to Applications/Computer/Favorites/Home/iDisk (respectively); iDisk will be mounted if necessary.
command+N	Create new folder in the current directory
command+D	Change directory view to Desktop

The Dock (Chapter 6)

command+tab or command+shift+tab	Cycle through active applications. (You can quit or hide applications as you cycle through them.)
command+option+D	Toggle Dock auto-hide on/off

Applications including the Finder (see Chapters 6 and 7)

command+H	Hide current application (add option to hide other apps)
command+M	Minimize active window to the Dock (add option to minimize all windows for the active application)
command+` or command+shift+`	Cycle through current application's windows

Screenshots (Chapter 7)

By default, screenshots are saved to the Desktop in PDF format; add the control key to any of the below to copy to the clipboard instead.

command+shift+3	Full screenshot
command+shift+4	Crosshair to allow selection of screenshot area
command+shift+4, then spacebar	Camera to capture specific screen object

Mac® OS X Power Tools

Dan Frakes

San Francisco · London

Associate Publisher: Joel Fugazzotto
Acquisitions Editor: Ellen L. Dendy
Developmental Editor: Brianne Agatep
Production Editor: Dennis Fitzgerald
Technical Editor: James Bucanek
Copyeditor: Cheryl Hauser
Compositor: Jeffrey Wilson, Happenstance Type-O-Rama
Proofreaders: Emily Hsuan, Darcey Maurer, Nancy Riddiough, Monique van den Berg
Indexer: Ted Laux
Cover Designer, Illustrator: Richard Miller, Calyx Design

Library of Congress Card Number: 2003100045

ISBN: 0-7821-4192-7

Manufactured in the United States of America

10 9 8 7 6 5 4 3 2 1

To Jennifer, for being everything to me.

Acknowledgments

(Or: The people I've remembered to thank, which is not necessarily everyone whom I should have thanked.)

Specific Thanks

First, I couldn't have done this without the Sybex team: (in order of appearance) Ellen Dendy, Joel Fugazzotto, Brianne Agatep, Dennis Fitzgerald, and Cheryl Hauser. I can't thank them enough for approaching me to do this book, and for guiding me through the process of writing it. (Brianne's significance in the latter category was beyond measure.) And to the rest of the Sybex staff who shepherded the book through the writing, editing, and production processes so that you could be reading it right now: thank you, thank you, thank you.

Along those lines, I also want to thank my agent, Neil Salkind. If the Sybex team held one of my hands through this process, Neil pulled me along by the other. He and the StudioB staff made writing the book easier by worrying about contracts, payments, and the like, so that I didn't have to.

I of course want to thank Chris Pepper, who wrote the first and second drafts of Chapter 15 (Utilizing Unix). Due to several unexpected events, the book fell a bit behind schedule; Chris stepped in and took Chapter 15 off my hands, helping to ensure that we made our publishing deadlines. He did a great job squeezing an immense amount of information into one chapter, and was very responsive to feedback and questions. I consider myself to be fairly knowledgeable about Unix, but I learned some very cool things from his writing. I'm sure you will, too.

I also want to thank James Bucanek, the book's technical editor, for all his hard work in both catching my mistakes and commenting on my content (not to mention the time he spent trying every single procedure in this book!). His feedback improved the book significantly. I just hope he's available the next time, as well.

General Thanks

Since they rarely get thanked in places like this, I want to publicly express my gratitude to the people at Apple—top to bottom—without whom there wouldn't be this amazing thing called the Mac. They may not be perfect, but they get pretty darned close most of the time. Similarly, thanks to Mac software developers for keeping the pantry stocked with cool and useful products. Anyone who says the Mac platform doesn't have a lot of great software must not be looking very hard.

I would also be remiss if I didn't mention the thousands of Mac users with whom I've talked and exchanged e-mail over the years. Your support, questions, and knowledge have kept me at this longer than I ever would have imagined.

Special Thanks

Although he didn't have a direct role in this book, I want extent my warm thanks to Ted Landau, who over the past few years has become not only a mentor and a sounding board, but also a good friend. Many of my writing opportunities can be traced back to Ted's faith in my abilities. I look forward to many more years of friendship and collaboration.

I also want to send my best wishes to UCLA's GSE&IS ETU. I blame them for getting me into this business. :-)

Final Thanks

Finally, my deepest gratitude and appreciation goes out to Jennifer, without whose support I never would have started this project, and without whose presence I may never have finished it.

Contents

Introduction

(Or: The part of the book most people never read, but really should.)

When Sybex first approached me about writing a book called "Mac OS X Power Tools," I kept thinking about power drills, circular saws, and other shop machinery. But the more I thought about it, the more I realized how appropriate the title was to the content of the book I wanted to write.

Power tools, in the world of hardware stores, serve two purposes: (1) to let you do something that you wouldn't ordinarily be able to do; and (2) to help you do things that you *can* do, but do them faster, more precisely, and with much less effort. Looked at in this light, the title of the book is actually quite fitting, as I plan to show you how to do things with Mac OS X that you probably don't know how to do, and to help you *better* do the things that you know how to do already.

That being said, my goals are twofold. First, as I mentioned, I want to show you *how* to do things. Things you already know how to do, but want to do better, faster, or more efficiently; things you always wished you could do, but didn't know how; and things you never even thought about doing, but once you learn will make you think "Wow, that's cool!"

I'll do this in a number of ways. I'll answer questions that don't get answered anywhere else. I'll show you how to take advantage of features in OS X that are easily accessible but rarely fully understood or utilized. I'll show you how to access features of OS X that *exist*, but are hidden or not immediately obvious. Finally, I'll show you third-party software solutions that do all of the above, and also provide new and unique features and functionality.

My second goal, which may actually be a bit loftier, but more important, is to help you learn how to *think* about doing things in OS X. Through the background principles I provide on each topic, and the examples I use to demonstrate those principles, I hope to give you a better understanding of the operating system itself—how it works, why it works, and what you can do with it. After learning the basics, and seeing some of the things you can do, you should have a good feel for the kinds of things that are possible (or at least a better idea of where to look to see if they are).

Who Should Read This Book

The overall theme of *Mac OS X Power Tools* is to help proficient users become power users. However, the problem with using a word like *proficient* is that it's such a broad term—its meaning varies depending on who is using it. To some people, being able to turn your computer on, type a letter, and print it is enough to be considered a proficient user. To others, being proficient means possessing the ability to troubleshoot computer problems, install new software and hardware, and take advantage of more advanced features in applications and the operating system. I say that both of these definitions are accurate, and I've written this book to appeal to both sets of users (and anyone in between).

Again, the "power tools" analogy is fitting. Someone who's never seen a screwdriver, much less used one, would probably be a bit intimidated by a power drill (not to mention feeling clueless as to how to go about using it). Yet someone who's used a screwdriver—even just a few times—will probably deduce what a power drill with a screwdriver bit could be used for, and may even be willing to try using it. What's more, in the hands of an accomplished handyman (or woman), that power drill can do some pretty amazing things.

So it is with *Mac OS X Power Tools*. If you've never touched a computer before, this book probably isn't for you. But everyone else—whether they consider themselves a beginner or a more advanced user—should find a good deal of content that is understandable and appropriate.

The tips, tricks, and solutions I present vary in both their utility and their accessibility. Some will amaze the beginner but will be old hat to experts. Some will be useful to everyone, whereas others will be applicable (and interesting) mainly to more advanced users. Some chapters, by the very nature of their subject matter, will be more or less technical in nature than others. For example, the chapters on the Finder and Dock (Chapters 5–6) are much less technical—although no less useful—than the chapter on Unix (Chapter 15). If something is too basic for you, feel free to move on to more advanced topics; likewise, if something confuses you, come back to it later—you may find that it makes more sense as you learn more about OS X.

All this is to say that if you're the least bit comfortable with a computer, you'll be able to handle this book, and that even those who already consider themselves to be "power users" will find a lot of stuff here that they didn't know.

What This Book *Isn't*

I've tried to give you a good idea about what this book *is*, but I should also make clear what this book *isn't*.

First, it isn't a troubleshooting book. Although in Chapter 14 I cover a number of maintenance tasks you can perform to keep your Mac humming along, and throughout the book I discuss a few of the most common issues users experience with OS X, the truth is that including substantial content dedicated to troubleshooting would have taken space away from topics that address the book's focus. Granted, understanding how OS X works is the best "first step" you can take towards knowing how to fix it when it doesn't work; in that light, after reading this book you should be a better troubleshooter than when you first picked it up.

However, I wanted to concentrate on how to make your Mac work *better*, rather than how to get it working when it doesn't. If you're looking for a book on troubleshooting, the best one out there, in my opinion, is *Mac OS X Disaster Relief* by Ted Landau (although I'm biased, since I wrote part of it). It's also one of the best books on the market at explaining the intricate details of the OS. In addition, Apple's Knowledge Base has a helpful article on troubleshooting OS X at `http://docs.info.apple.com/article.html?artnum=25392`.

Second, as I mentioned earlier, this is also not an "absolute beginner" book. I've tried to make this book accessible and useful for many types of users, from beginners to power users, so I've tried to bridge the usual gap between "learning OS X" books and "tips and tricks for OS X" books. I touch on the basics the first time I mention each topic, and then move on to more advanced info. However, I assume that you've used a computer before, even if for just a little bit, and that you're familiar with the basics: turning it on, opening a folder or document, using menus in applications, dragging files around, etc. If you're not comfortable doing these types of things, I recommend spending a bit more time with your Mac before you dive in. If you want some recommendations for books to get you started, my favorites are *Mastering Mac OS X* by Todd Stauffer and *Mac OS X: The Missing Manual* by David Pogue. Both take you through the most basic of basics, but also delve into more advanced topics when you're ready.

Third, this isn't a hardware book; it's a book about the operating system and software that is Mac OS X. There may be occasions here and there where I point out certain hardware features that are (or are not) supported on various Mac models, but that's about it. I won't spend time talking about your Mac's hardware, how to install new hardware, and how to fix hardware problems.

Finally, this book isn't comprehensive—and I mean that in a *good* way! If you don't see a way to do something in this book, that doesn't mean it can't be done. Likewise, if you do see a way to do something, that doesn't necessarily mean it's the *only* way to do it. There are a lot of other ways to get more out of OS X, and that's the beauty of it. I've simply tried to put together what I feel is a great collection of information, tips, tweaks, and software gems that will help you get the most out of your Mac. If I'm lucky, the background and ideas you get from this book will inspire you to think of even better ways to accomplish the things you need to do. Websites like `http://www.macosxhints.com/` are filled with new tips and information on a daily basis.

How to Use This Book

1. Open book to desired page.
2. Read.
3. Buy more RAM.

But seriously, before you dive in, I'd like to briefly talk about the assumptions I make in this book, the book's organization (which is a bit untraditional), and conventions used in the text. Taking a few minutes to read this section will make the book much more useful. (By the way, I'm serious about the RAM thing—the best thing you can do for your Mac running OS X is to buy more RAM for it.)

Assumptions I Make

As I mentioned above, I'm assuming that if you're reading this book you've used a computer, and I hope Mac OS X, before—at least enough so that you can understand the basics. For example, I'm assuming that you know how to restart your computer, how to use the CD drive, how to connect the keyboard, etc. I'm also hoping that you've become at least somewhat familiar with the Mac OS interface. Overall, I'm simply assuming that you've got a Mac that is up and running and that you feel comfortable using it for most basic functionality. Making this assumption lets me spend less time explaining the most introductory topics—which generally take a good deal of space—and more time on the cool stuff. It also lets me structure the book a bit differently, as I explain in the next section.

Second, I'm assuming that you're connected to the Internet—that your ISP or network administrator has provided you with the information you need to connect, and that you've used Apple's setup assistant to enter that information. (If you knew enough about Internet settings and access to figure everything out yourself, even better.)

Finally, a small number of the procedures in the book assume that you've installed the Mac OS X Developer Tools. I talk about how to do this in a bit; rest assured that it's very easy to do if you haven't already.

How the Book Is Organized

Most computer books start out by telling you how to open folders, how to access menus, how to launch applications, and other "this is how to use a computer" topics. Some start out with detailed instructions on how to install the OS. Because I'm assuming you're already familiar with such basic actions, and you've already got OS X installed, I'm able to forego the discussion of the most basic topics, and replace the traditional topic order with one that I think is more appropriate given the focus of *Mac OS X Power Tools*.

Part I starts with an in-depth discussion of user accounts, permissions, and file and folder organization in OS X. As a Unix-based operating system, understanding OS X is much easier if you understand these topics, and *mastering* OS X requires it. You're free to read the book's chapters in any order that you like, but I urge you to read Chapter 1 first. In the remainder of Part I, I show you how to understand and use OS X's various system settings, how to use and abuse the startup and login processes, and how to install system software and applications, from both Apple and third parties.

Part II focuses on actually *using* your Mac: the Finder, the Dock, applications, and the Classic Environment.

Part III looks at networks and the Internet, including sharing files, connecting to other computers (locally and remotely), and printing.

Part IV deals with more advanced topics: system security, maintenance and administrative tasks, and taking advantage of OS X's Unix base.

I've also included a couple of useful appendices. The first talks about OS X versus OS 9, including ways to make the transition easier, tips for switching back and forth (if that's something you need to do), and ways to get some of your favorite OS 9 features in OS X. The second appendix focuses on setting up and using multiple volumes and disk partitions in OS X.

To make it easier for you to find information, I've provided both a general index and a list of software mentioned in the book. The software listing is actually in two parts. The first part, included at the end of the book, is a list of my 50 favorite utilities and add-ons (at the time of this writing, at least). The second part actually resides on the book's website (`http://www.macosxpowertools.com/`), and includes every software title mentioned in the book, along with links to get more information and/or to download each. (Note that software titles are also listed, with page references, in the main index.)

Finally, the book's website also features some supplemental material that simply wouldn't fit in the print edition.

Conventions Used in the Book

To make the content of *Mac OS X Power Tools* easier to read and understand, I've used a number of standardized conventions in the book's text and interface. Below is a summary of those conventions for you to use as a reference. Some may seem obvious as you read them here, but in the context of topical discussion they'll help make clear exactly what I'm talking about.

"Tip Tables"

As you may know, or will soon find out, OS X is a true multi-user operating system, with different *levels* of users (normal, administrator, and root), each of which has different abilities. (I cover user levels and abilities in detail in Chapter 1.) As a result, some ways of using, configuring, and customizing OS X can be performed by any user, but some can only be performed by admin users (or the root user). In addition, some ways of customizing and configuring OS X affect *all* users of the computer, whereas others affect only the particular user making the change.

Although these user levels and configuration possibilities make OS X incredibly flexible, they can also make a book such as this confusing, since a particular user may or may not be able to take advantage of a particular tip or example, and if they can, the results of that procedure may end up affecting other users of the same computer unintentionally.

In addition, although most ways of working with OS X can be accomplished via a graphical user interface (GUI)—pointing and clicking the mouse and typing in dialogs—some require the use of *Terminal*, OS X's command-line interface to its Unix subsystem. (I'll talk more about Terminal throughout the book, and I dedicate much of Chapter 15 to it). Some users love the fact that they can use Terminal; others hate it. I hope by the time you finish this book, you'll—at the very least—respect it for what it can do, but in the meantime, you may want a "heads up" if you need to use it.

For all of these reasons, I decided to implement what I call *tip tables*. At the beginning of each section, example, or procedure, I provide a table that looks something like this:

User Level:	any or admin
Affects:	individual user or computer
Terminal:	yes or no

The *User Level* field tells you, up front, whether or not the procedure or topic can be undertaken by any user of a computer, or just by an administrator. The *Affects* field tells you whether or not any change you make using the content or instructions that follow affects just your user account, or the entire computer (all users). Finally, the *Terminal* field tells you whether or not you'll need to use Terminal in order to take advantage of the cool info I present in that section. (If a procedure or tip doesn't include a tip table, you can assume that the tip table for the higher-level section applies.)

As far as I know, *Mac OS X Power Tools* is the first book on OS X to take this approach; I hope it encourages others to do the same, as I feel it clears up one of the most confusing issues surrounding the customization of OS X.

Note, Tip, and Warning Boxes

Throughout the book you'll see text boxes that provide additional information. These boxes contain *tips*, *notes*, and *warnings*; here is an example of each, along with its significance:

TIP Tips point out additional functionality or options relating to the topic being discussed, or tell you how you can use the preceding or surrounding content in other ways.

NOTE Notes present interesting information or further resources about the topic being discussed.

WARNING Warnings point out *very* important information that you should know and consider about the topic being discussed. A failure to read and heed such warnings could result in unexpected behavior or, in some situations, data loss.

What's a Sidebar?

Sometimes a topic doesn't quite "fit" anywhere else in a chapter, but is still important enough to include in the book. In these situations, I discuss the topic in a *sidebar* that looks suspiciously like what you're reading right now.

Terminology for Actions

In many sections of the book, I explain how to perform specific actions in OS X (often using step-by-step instructions). To avoid confusion, I've tried to be very consistent in the terms I use, especially when referring to parts of OS X's user interface. Although most of these actions should be obvious, there are a few situations where distinctions are important:

Choose refers to menus and menu items. For example, I might tell you to choose the Open command from the File menu. In addition, I use the ➢ symbol to guide you through a menu. For example, the phrase "choose File ➢ Open in the Finder" means than you should switch to the Finder, click on the File menu, and then choose the *Open* item.

Select refers to selecting files in the Finder, selecting files or items in lists, or selecting items in pop-up menus. If I tell you to "select a file" in a Finder window, it means you should click on that file to highlight (select) it. If you open the Displays panel of System Preferences, you'll see a list of available resolutions for your display; select one by clicking on it. Finally, many dialogs in OS X include pop-up menus—when you click on these items, a menu of options pops up. If I tell you to "select your preferred printer from the Printers pop-up menu," it means to click on the pop-up menu next to the word Printers, place your mouse cursor over your preferred printer, and click the mouse again to select it.

Press refers to keys on the keyboard. For example, if I tell you to press return, that means you should press and release the return key on the keyboard. If I tell you to *hold* a key *down* as you complete an action (click or move the mouse, type a letter, etc.), it means you should hold that key down until the action is complete.

Finally, *click* refers to clicking the mouse on an interface element. For example, if a dialog box has a button for "OK," I'll tell you to "click the OK button" or "click OK." In addition, if I tell you to *control-click*, it means you should hold down the control key as you click the mouse. *Shift-click* means to hold down the shift key as you click the mouse. And so on…if you see *click* presented with any keyboard keys, you should hold them down as you click the mouse.

Typefaces

To distinguish between the standard text of the book and text that refers to special content, I use special typefaces for the latter:

- *New or key terms are presented in standard italics.*

- `Filepaths (discussed below) are presented in this typeface.` *`If a filepath requires user input (for example, the user's username), it will be italicized.`* `URLs are also presented in this typeface to distinguish them from surrounding text. When typing a URL into your browser, include only the text in this typeface.`
- **Text that the user needs to type into a dialog or other text field, precisely as it is presented, is generally bolded.** ***Similar text that requires the user to provide information (such as their name or a filename) is italicized.***
- **`Commands or input that the user must type into Terminal are presented in this typeface.`** ***`If a command requires user-provided information (a username or filename, for example), that section of the command is italicized.`***
- `Examples of Terminal output (text that is presented to you by Terminal after entering a command) are presented in this typeface.`

As a side note, most interface elements (names of menus, buttons, check boxes, etc.) are presented in standard text; however, if there is a chance that an interface element's label might be confused for regular text, I enclose it in quotations. For example, the label Save is fairly clear, but the phrase "Add to list" may not be; the latter is enclosed in quotes.

Miscellaneous

In addition to the conventions mentioned in the previous sections, here are a few other miscellaneous standards I use throughout the book:

- I use the terms *folder* and *directory* interchangeably.
- Macs have always come with a single-button mouse, but for a number of years now, Mac users have been able to hold the control key down as they click the mouse to get a *contextual menu* (in the Finder or from within applications). This is commonly referred to as *control-clicking*. However, Mac OS X supports multi-button mice, which means if you've purchased a mouse that has more than one button, you can use the left-most button for standard clicks, and the right-most button for contextual menus without installing any additional drivers. This is known as *right-clicking*. Because some users will have the stock Apple mouse, and some will have a third-party mouse, I use the phrase *control/right-click* to indicate that you can use either the control key or the right-most mouse button.
- A *pathname* is the formal name for the path you would take to get to a file from the top level of your computer's file system. For example, if you want to access a file inside your personal documents folder in OS X, the pathname would be `/Users/`*`username`*`/Documents/`*`filename`*. (Did you like how I used those typefaces I was just telling you about?) The beginning / signifies the top level of your hard drive, and each subsequent / signifies a sub-folder.

- When typing text into Terminal, or into most interface fields, the case of that text matters. For example, as you'll see later in the book, typing **/Users** is not the same thing as typing **/users**. So be sure to pay attention to case when I instruct you to type something.
- One of the most confusing things about writing books where you try to instruct the reader to type text into Terminal or any other command-line interface is that it's often difficult for the reader to figure out *exactly* what they should be typing. Is a period part of the command, or is it just punctuating a sentence? Is a command on two lines because it's actually two different commands, or was it just too long to fit on one line? To avoid such confusion, I conclude *every* command-line input with **<RETURN>**. Anything preceding this marker is part of the command, on a single line, and anything after this marker is not part of the command. (In addition, when a line of code or a Terminal command is too long to fit on a single line in the book, I use the symbol ➥ to indicate that two or more lines here in the book are actually *continuations* of a single line or command.)
- Although Mac OS X Power Tools is generally focused on OS X 10.2 and later, many of the tips and much of the information apply to earlier versions of OS X, as well. In addition, if information applies to only a specific version or versions of OS X, I'll indicate this information in the text. For example, if I mention "10.2.2" or "10.1.3" it means I'm referring specifically to that particular version. However, if I say 10.1.*x* it means all variants of version 10.1—10.1.0, 10.1.1, 10.1.3, etc. Likewise with 10.2.*x*, and so on.

Installing Apple's Developer Tools

Apple has a set of software tools, applications, documentation, and support files that they provide—for free—to encourage people to develop software for OS X. They call this package the Developer Tools. I mentioned earlier that the OS X Developer Tools are required for some of the tips and procedures I describe in the book. The truth is that they're only required for a very small proportion of the exercises I show you, so if you don't install the Developer Tools, you'll be fine. However, because you might want to take advantage of those tips, and because installing the Developer Tools provides you with a number of very useful tools that you can't get anywhere else, I highly recommend it. (Don't be intimidated by the term "Developer Tools"—there's nothing scary about them, and they're very easy to install.)

There's a good chance that you already have the Developer Tools installer and don't even know it. Check the CDs that came with your Mac or (if you bought OS X separately) that came with OS X. If one says "Developer Tools," you've got 'em. Insert the CD, double-click the installation package, and follow the instructions. If OS X was pre-installed on your Mac, you should check to see if you have an `/Applications/Installers` folder; if you do, double-click the file called `Developer.mpkg` to install the Developer Tools.

If you don't already have the Developer Tools, you can download them at no charge by signing up for a free Online Developer membership at `http://developer.apple.com/membership/online.html`. Once you've signed up, you can log into the Developer site and follow the links to download software. Unfortunately, the download is pretty darned big, so if you have a slow Internet connection, I'd start the download before you go to bed so it will be finished when you wake up in the morning. When it's complete, double-click the downloaded image and follow the instructions to install. (I talk more about installing software in Chapter 4.)

(Actually, it's a good idea to sign up for a free Online Developer account even if you already have the Developer Tools CD, because Apple periodically releases updated versions.)

Software Mentioned in the Book

Throughout *Mac OS X Power Tools*, I introduce you to a good deal of software, from both Apple and third-party vendors. These products tend to be *my* favorites for the tasks at hand; I don't guarantee that you won't like something else better, but you can rest assured that I've tried out almost every option available at the time of this writing and presented you with what I feel is the cream of the crop. Occasionally, when two products do things differently enough that I feel it's more a matter of preference than quality, I'll point out a couple of titles so that you can choose for yourself.

Whenever I mention a product, I provide you with a URL to get more information about it (or to download it). However, as you surely know if you've spent much time on the Web, URLs change, and a few of the URLs included in this book are probably going to have changed by the time you read it. If the URL for a product isn't working, I recommend using one of the OS X software websites such as `http://www.versiontracker.com/macosx/` or `http://www.macupdate.com/` to get an updated URL. Both sites let you search for software by title, and will provide you with a link to the developer's website and, usually, a download link.

NOTE When I describe a particular software title, keep in mind that my comments are based on the product at the time of this writing; software is updated regularly, so there's a chance that a feature I say doesn't exist actually does by the time you read this (or vice versa). In fact, one of the exciting things about OS X is that new and updated titles are being released on a daily basis!

Shareware, Donationware, etc.

Some of the software I cover is commercial—software you have to buy to use. Other titles are *freeware*—the developer has released the software for your use at no charge. However, a good deal of software falls under the categories of *shareware* and *donationware*. Shareware are titles that allow you to use them for some set amount of time (e.g., 15 days or a month) in order to evaluate them. If you find that you use them, you're expected to pay for them (using the procedures the developer has provided, usually through a secure payment system like `http://www.kagi.com/`). Sometimes payment gets you additional functionality, as well. *Dona-*

tionware is similar to shareware, except that the software is fully functional when you download it, and instead of requiring a payment, the developer asks for a donation if you find the software useful.

As a former shareware author/developer myself, I can't stress enough how important it is to actually *pay* for the software you use. Shareware and donationware developers generally do what they do because (1) they love to do it; and (2) the traditional software distribution systems are prohibitively expensive. Yet neither of these reasons means they don't deserve to be paid for their work. The quality of many shareware/donationware titles is comparable to, or even better than, that of "commercial" software you would buy in a box at a store. In addition, in my experience, many shareware/donationware developers provide better support to their customers than many commercial developers do. Getting paid not only rewards them for what they've done; it also encourages them to keep going.

Basically, if you end up trying out a piece of software I mention in the book, pay for it (or, in the case of donationware, donate a little something). It's good for the developers, it's good for the Mac platform, and it's good for your software karma.

NOTE After trying out so many software titles, I've come up with a few suggestions for developers for improving the way they distribute OS X software. Check out the book's website to see if you agree.

Tools Used to Write the Book

While I'm on the topic of software, I wanted to mention a couple of tools I've grown incredibly fond of over the past seven months. I generally don't spend much time thinking about writing tools. Or if I do, I'm thinking about them only because of all the problems they cause (as was the case with the word processor used to write this book). However, I used two new tools in the writing of *Mac OS X Power Tools* that truly enhanced the creative and organizational process. First, the content database DEVONthink (`http://www.devon-technologies.com/products/devonthink.html`) made organizing and searching through the daunting amount of information I collected and created for this book far easier than I thought possible. Second, the outlining app OmniOutliner (`http://www.omnigroup.com/applications/omnioutliner/`) has over the past seven months become my new "writer's best friend." It's not only a great outline *creator*; it's also an amazingly flexible outline *editor*, which was especially important as I changed the way I organized the book at least once a week. If you're a writer, I encourage you to check out these two tools.

In addition to these new tools, like most Mac writers I'm grateful for Snapz Pro X (`http://www.ambrosiasw.com/`), the OS X version of the venerable screenshot standby. OS X has some impressive screenshot capabilities (which I discuss in Chapter 7), but they're no match for Snapz Pro X's feature set and flexibility.

Errors, Feedback, and Contact Info

The book's editors and I have endeavored to weed out errors and inconsistencies, and I hope we've been successful. However, a fact of life in publishing is that minor errors sometimes slip through. In addition, each time Apple releases an update to OS X, there's a chance that something that worked before no longer does, or that a specific functionality works a bit differently. If I find any errors or the need for clarification, I'll post them on the book's website, `http://www.macosxpowertools.com/`. In fact, just to be on the safe side, you should check the website before you dig in, to see if any important information has been posted. If you actually *find* an error, please let me know about it by sending an e-mail to `errors@macosxpowertools.com`.

I also welcome feedback from readers: what you like about the book, what you dislike, what you'd like to see more of (or less of), and any suggestions you might have for a future edition. Feel free to send any comments to `feedback@macosxpowertools.com`. I can't guarantee a response; however, I do guarantee that your feedback will be read and appreciated.

Finally…

I wrote *Mac OS X Power Tools* because I love the Mac OS and the things it can do. I probably spend far too much time figuring out exactly what those things are, but I'm excited at the chance to pass on some of this knowledge to you. I hope that you have as much fun reading this book as I did writing it.

—Dan Frakes
`http://www.danfrakes.com/`

Part I

Setup, Startup, and (In)Stalling

CHAPTER 1

The Power of Permissions: Understanding Users and Unix Organization

(Or: What the heck are user accounts and privileges, and how do I use them to my advantage?)

It may seem odd to start a book about becoming a power user of Mac OS X with such boring topics as user accounts, file organization, and privileges. After all, you're in this to learn cool tips and tricks, not to learn about the boring guts of the operating system, right? Yet when it comes down to it, if you don't understand these topics, you'll never become the master of your Mac. In addition, in my experience working with users of OS X (especially those users who have come to OS X from previous versions of the Mac OS), one of the most frustrating—and common—issues they have is dealing with permissions (such as error messages telling them they can't do what they want to do because they "don't have permission"). This means that some of the most useful tips and tricks relate to permissions and user accounts.

In addition to gaining a better understanding of these issues, in this chapter you'll learn how to create and customize user accounts and groups, how to work with permissions, and how to use NetInfo Manager. You'll also learn about root access and the root account.

The Basics: Permissions, Accounts, and File Organization

Because of its Unix heritage, Mac OS X is a true multi-user operating system from the ground up. Yet some people have used Mac OS X for many months without fully realizing what this means—as the only user of their Mac, they press the power key and it simply boots up and runs, much like a Mac running OS 8 or OS 9. To many other users, a multi-user OS just means that several people can use the Mac without sharing the same Documents folder and preference files.

The truth is that the multi-user architecture of Mac OS X offers so much more than separate Documents folders. It is a powerful system of files, folders, and volumes, with varying degrees of access to those items given to individual users. Everything from setting preferences to installing software, from opening files to emptying the trash, is affected by this system; as a result, OS X provides levels of security and flexibility heretofore unseen on the Mac platform. Understanding the concepts of user accounts and privileges, and understanding the file structure of Mac OS X, are the first steps towards becoming a true Power User. In fact, understanding these topics is vital to mastering many of the topics discussed later in the book.

Because these issues are important, and because Mac OS X accommodates so many different levels of users, I'm going to start at a more basic level in Chapter 1 than in subsequent chapters, to ensure that I thoroughly explain these concepts. Consider this chapter the foundation on which you'll build your power user skills.

Permissions Explained

Users of Mac OS 9 and earlier may remember setting up File Sharing privileges—when File Sharing was enabled, each "shared" file had a set of privileges, set manually by the user sharing it, that told the OS which remote users could access it. Since Mac OS X is based on Unix, it inherits the Unix system of file *permissions* (also called *privileges*). This system is similar to File Sharing privileges, except that in OS X *every* file and folder has a set of permissions (some set by users, most set by the OS itself), and these permissions apply to everyone, whether they are connecting remotely or sitting in front of the host computer. To put it simply, OS X keeps track of which users can open each document, folder, or application, and which users can edit each individual file. (In OS X, the terms "open" and "edit" are actually called "read" and "write.")

You can see an example of permissions by selecting a file in the Finder (a document in your Documents folder is a good one to choose), and then selecting File ➢ Get Info. In the resulting Info window, you'll see a section called Ownership & Permissions. Clicking the disclosure triangle will expand this section to show the permissions given to this file. The Info window for a document from my Documents folder is shown in Figure 1.1.

The owner of the file is me, *frakes* (the "Me" after the user name tells you that the owner is the current user), and I have read and write access to the file. You also see two other sets of permissions: *Group* and *Others*. In addition to an owner (the user who controls access to the file — generally the person who created it), every file belongs to a group, which is simply a defined subset of all users who have their own access privileges to the file. The group is automatically set to the default group for the owner—in this case, *staff*—and set to Read only.

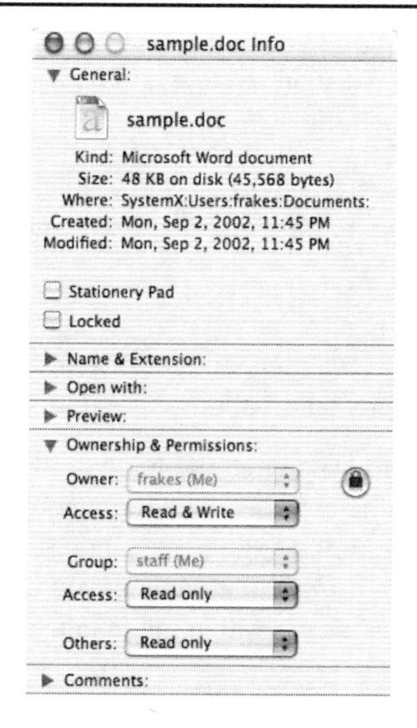

FIGURE 1.1: The Get Info: Ownership & Permissions window for `sample.doc`

These settings can actually be changed to provide certain other users with a particular level of access, without opening up such access to everyone. (I'll talk more about groups and group access later in this chapter, but for now just remember that they are there; they can be extremely useful once you learn how to use them.) Finally, the Others permission setting is used to set privileges for users who are neither the owner of the file nor part of the group assigned to the file; think of this as "everyone else." The default setting for others is Read only. (See "What Permissions Really Mean" for more info on the various levels of access.)

NOTE Mac OS X permissions are not enforced under Mac OS 9. If you reboot into OS 9, you're free to do anything you want, to any file you want—and so is anyone else.

Understanding what permissions *are* isn't too difficult; comprehending *how* they work and *why* they work the way they do can be quite confusing. The first step towards that goal is understanding user accounts.

What Permissions Really Mean

Read & Write sounds cute, but what does it really mean? Here's a rundown of what the different permissions levels mean for different types of items:

File

Read & Write You can open the file to read it or edit it or you can make a copy of it. If the enclosing folder allows it, you can also move it (deleting a file is considered moving it).

Continued on next page

Read only You can open the file to read it, and you can make a copy of it (the copy will acquire Read & Write status). If the enclosing folder allows it, you can also move the file.

No Access You cannot open or edit the file. However, if the enclosing folder allows it, you can make a copy of the file or move it. You can still see the file, provided you have Read access to the enclosing folder (next item).

Folder

Read & Write You can open the folder, and edit the contents of the folder (copy items to it, move items out of it, duplicate items within it, rename items within it, etc.).

Read only You can open the folder and view its contents, and you can make a copy of the folder (the copy acquires Read & Write status). If the enclosing folder allows it, you can also move the folder. You cannot add to or remove its contents, or rename any of its contents. However, you can (if you have access) change the permissions or ownership of files/folders within the folder.

No Access You cannot open the folder (and, therefore, you cannot view its contents).

Write only (Drop Box) This permission level applies only to folders; an example is `~/Public/Drop Box` (see "Understanding User Accounts" for more info on such folders). If you have Write only access to a folder, you can add items to it, but you cannot open the folder to view its contents. This is where the term "Drop Box" comes from—all you can do is drop files/folders in, like a postal mailbox.

Application

While an application in Mac OS X looks like a single file, it is actually a folder containing application support files; the technical name for this type of folder is a *package*. (See Chapter 4, "Installation, Inc.," for more info on packages.) When you double-click a package (or select it and choose File ➢ Open in the Finder), the application is launched. Because of this type of organization, permissions on an application work much like permissions on a regular folder:

Read & Write You can launch the application and view the application package contents (by control-clicking on the application and selecting Show Package Contents from the resulting contextual menu). You can also edit the package contents (copy items to it, move items out of it, duplicate items within it, etc.), and move the application/package and its contents (including deleting it/them).

Read only You can launch the application and view the application package contents, and you can make a copy of the application (the copy retains the Read only status). You cannot edit/change the application package's contents. If the enclosing folder allows it, you can move the application/package or edit its contents.

No Access You cannot launch the application, nor can you view its package contents. You can only see the application itself if the enclosing folder provides you with Read access.

Understanding User Accounts

Mac OS 9 and earlier were essentially single-user operating systems. Sure, Mac OS 9 had the less-than-perfectly-implemented Multiple Users feature, but it was just that—less than perfect. Mac OS X is a *true* multi-user system, meaning that whether you realize it or not, you're no longer the only user of your machine. In this section, I'm going to explain what "multiple users" means in a practical way: how files and folders are organized, what users do and don't have access to, and more.

User Accounts and File/Folder Organization

At the topmost level of your Mac OS X hard drive (this is called the *root* level of the drive), you'll see a folder called `Users`. This folder contains all user-level files for all users of your computer. Within this folder, each user has their own individual folder, the name of which is their "short" username (I'll talk more about short and long usernames in a bit). This folder is called the user's *home* folder or directory, and is generally identified with the abbreviated pathname `~/`. Thus, on my computer, my home directory is located at `/Users/frakes` (Figure 1.2). Within each home folder are several folders that were automatically created when the user account was created: Desktop, Documents, Library, Movies, Music, Pictures, Public, and Sites. In addition, a user's home folder can also contain any other files and/or folders the user has placed there.

The important thing to note about home directories under OS X is that with the exception of the Public and Sites folders (which are accessible by other users), files, folders, or applications stored inside your home folder are for your eyes only, and unless you explicitly change their permissions, no one but you will be able to edit them, or even view them. Your user folder is yours and yours alone. In fact, the Desktop that you see is actually a folder called `Desktop` within your user folder. Each user has their own Desktop, so anything you save or copy to the Desktop will be visible and accessible only to you.

FIGURE 1.2:
A typical home user folder

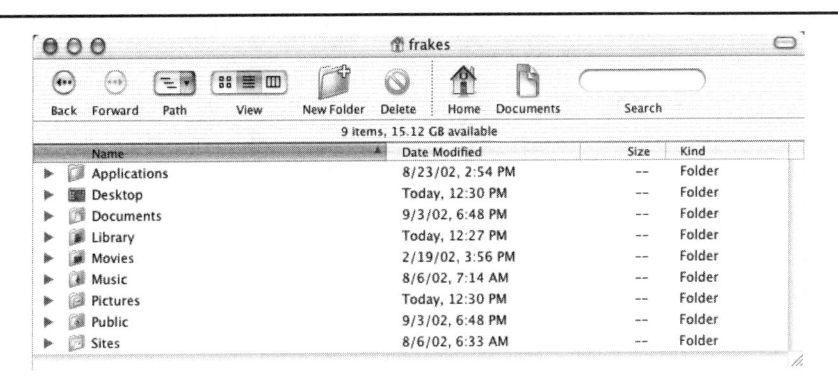

However, user folders aren't just for security. They also provide an enormous amount of flexibility between users. In addition to documents, folders, and applications, user folders also store each user's preferences (in `~/Library/Preferences`). This means that any settings or changes you make to your Mac—your desktop picture, your e-mail account information, your web browser bookmarks—will apply only to you, allowing each user to customize OS X to best serve their own needs. When you log in, the OS uses your preferences and restores the environment to exactly the state it was in when you last logged out. This is important to note because it means that as you go through this book, many of the neat tricks and customizations you find will only apply to your personal account, thus preventing you from annoying or disrupting other users.

NOTE When I said that all preferences apply only to the user who set them, that wasn't *entirely* true. There are a few exceptions to this rule; for example, network settings apply to all users, and therefore can only be changed by an administrator. I'll talk more about which settings are system-wide in Chapter 2, "Sensational Setup."

Dissecting the Contents of Your Home Directory

While your home directory (`/Users/`*`username`*, or the more common designation of `~/`) contains any files, folders, or applications that you personally place there, it also includes a number of folders that were automatically created when your account was created. Here's a quick list of what each of these folders is for:

Applications This folder may or may not exist in your home folder. Some application installers create it during the installation process, but OS X does not create it by default. I'd suggest creating it yourself it if doesn't exist, as any applications that you install here will be available *only* to you. If you have an application that you need to use but you don't want other users of your computer to be able to access, install it here. (In order to have it created automatically, edit the new user template as explained at the end of this sidebar.)

Desktop This is your personal Desktop. If you open this folder, you'll notice that its contents are exactly the same as the items visible on your Desktop. In Mac OS X, each user has their own Desktop, and anything placed on the Desktop is actually placed inside this folder.

Library This folder contains many of the support files and resources used by the OS when you are logged in to your account. Any preferences, system add-ons, fonts, and other files and information used *only* by your account are located here. See "Why Are There So Many Copies of So Many Folders?" later in this chapter for more info.

Continued on next page

Movies OS X creates this folder as a convenient place to store any movies you create with iMovie.

Pictures In addition to being a convenient place to store photos, your iPhoto library is stored in this folder.

Public This folder and its contents are viewable and readable by all users, both local and remote. In addition, inside the Public folder is a folder called Drop Box—this folder provides others with Write only access, meaning they can place files in this folder for you, but cannot open the folder or view its contents. (I go into much more detail about the Public folder in Chapter 10, "Stellar Sharing Strategies.")

Sites This folder is where you store documents you wish to make available via Mac OS X's built-in web server. More details about this feature are also contained in Chapter 10.

Editing the New User Template

When you create a new user, the contents of the new user's home directory include, by default, the folders listed here. However, you may want an Applications folder, or some other folder, to be created by default. The contents of a newly created home directory are dictated by the folder templates located at `/System/Library/User Template`. Inside this directory are home directory templates, one for each language supported by your installation of OS X (`English.lproj` is the template for English). If you open one of these template folders, you'll see the standard folders in a new home directory. Any changes you make to the contents of this directory will be reflected in any new user account. For example, to have an Applications folder created by default, create a new folder here and change its permissions to owner: system, Read & Write; group: wheel (a default Unix group that includes admin users and the root user), No Access; others: No Access. (Note that to create a new folder here, you'll need root access, which I'll talk about later in the chapter.)

User Levels

As I previously mentioned, every user of Mac OS X has their own account. Each of those accounts has one of two levels of access: normal and administrative.

Normal users Normal users have full access to their own user folder and to other users' Public folders. They can also launch applications located in the `/Applications` directory, and can change user-specific System Preferences (Desktop picture, views, Dock settings, as well as their own account password). However, that's basically the extent of their access. Outside of their own user folder, they have only Read access (except for other user folders, for which they have no access at all). In fact, a normal user cannot even create a folder or save a document outside of their own home folder.

Admin users Admin users do not have complete run of the house, but they are much less limited than normal users. Admin users can install new applications in the `/Applications` directory, can change system-level System Preferences (Network, Accounts, Sharing, Software Update, etc.), can install fonts and other system add-ons, can create folders and save documents almost anywhere on the drive, and can use system-level utilities such as Disk Utility and NetInfo Manager. The first account created under Mac OS X (the one you created when you first installed OS X) is an admin-level account by default, since every Mac OS X computer must have at least one administrator.

You can view user levels in the Accounts panel of the System Preferences application (Figure 1.3). We'll talk more about the use of this panel when we talk about creating and editing user accounts later in the chapter.

FIGURE 1.3: User levels, as shown in the Accounts panel of System Preferences

Despite having a higher level of access, even admin users cannot access other users' private folders, nor can they make changes to certain system-level folders (such as much of the System folder at the root level of the hard drive)—at least not without help. Although I said that there are only two levels of accounts in Mac OS X, this is technically not true. There is a third level of access in Mac OS X called *root* access that has complete control over everything, regardless of permission or location. However, you cannot simply assign root privileges to particular accounts; Mac OS X actually has a separate *root account* (disabled by default, for obvious security reasons). In order to gain root access you must log in as the root user. I'll talk much more about the root user, as well has how to temporarily gain root access from an administrator account, later in this chapter.

It is important to understand the differences between these levels of access, as many of the tips discussed in this book require admin access, and some require at least temporary root access. As I mentioned in the Introduction, I've noted the level of access required for each procedure.

Other Uses for User Accounts (besides Other Users, That Is)

User Level: admin
Affects: computer
Terminal: no

At this point you may be saying to yourself "OK, I'm the only user of my computer, and I have admin access by default, so why do I need to know about user accounts?" That's a good question. In addition to the importance understanding user accounts and permissions has for fully understanding OS X as a whole, there are several reasons I recommend creating other users accounts that have little or nothing to do with multiple users:

Troubleshooting While Mac OS X is incredibly stable, the truth is sometimes things go wrong. When you experience a computer problem, the first step you should take towards finding a solution is *always* to narrow down the possible causes. In Mac OS 9, you held the shift key down to start up without extensions; if your Mac then worked fine, you had isolated the problem to a startup file conflict. In Mac OS X, because each user account has a different set of preferences, support files, and startup/login files, the first thing you want to do is to find out if your problems are caused by your account or by a larger system issue. A helpful way to do this is to create a new account (now, before you have problems), name it something clever (I call mine "Trouble"), and then never use it…until you have a problem. If that happens, log out of your own account, log back in under your troubleshooting account, and see if the problems are gone. If they are, you've just isolated your problem to something in your own account (`~/Library` files, Login items, etc.), and that's where you should start looking for the cause. If the problems still exist, then the cause is system-wide.

TIP I recommend that you give your troubleshooting account admin access as discussed later in the chapter. If you ever find yourself in an emergency where you need admin access but you can't log into your normal admin-level account, having an extra admin account can be a lifesaver.

Testing Software If you're an aspiring power user, chances are that at some point you've downloaded "beta" software (or even—*gasp*—"alpha" software). In other words, you've tried out software that isn't quite ready for prime time. Although a lot of beta software is very stable, some isn't, and you may have experienced crashes or other problems. Even if you're not that brave, at some point you may have installed software just to check it out, and later decided that you didn't really like it, but you couldn't figure out how to get rid of all the support files that the software installed. My approach to these situations is to create an extra user account just for testing out software. You can run the alphas, betas, and "just curious" software from this account until you've either decided you want to use it in your main account or decided you want to get it off your Mac as soon as possible. Whatever you decide, your personal account—the important one you can't afford to screw up—should be unaffected.

Guests We've all had a friend who needs to borrow our laptop to type up a report, or asks to use our computer to do their taxes, or is just hanging out and wants to browse the Web. We let them (because we're nice people, of course), but the next time we sit down at our computer we find that our Desktop is a mess, or our application preferences have been changed, or, worst case scenario, an important document was accidentally deleted! A great solution is to create an extra account, call it "Guest" (or something a bit more clever), and then set it up for just these situations. I've got my guest account configured with limited access (see "Creating User Accounts" later in the chapter) and with just the essentials in the Dock: web browser, word processor, spreadsheet, etc. You can even set up the account with no password so that anyone visiting or borrowing your computer can simply click on the "Guest" icon at login and be on their way.

Remote access and file sharing In addition to allowing others to use your computer locally (sitting in front of it), user accounts also control who can access your Mac remotely (over the Internet, via your home or office LAN). If you want someone to be able to access files on your computer, that person must have a user account on your computer—even if they will never use the computer in person. (I'll talk more about remote access and file sharing in Part III, "The Internet, Networking, Sharing, and Printing.")

As you can see, "multiple users" doesn't necessarily mean "multiple people using the computer." I hope these suggestions will get you thinking about other ways to take advantage of the security and flexibility provided by multiple user accounts.

Why Are There So Many Copies of So Many Folders? (OS X File/Folder Organization)

I previously discussed the flexibility that user accounts provide, especially in providing a way for users to customize their individual computing environments. However, this versatility also creates new challenges that are not present in single-user operating systems. For example, what if you or another administrator of your Mac wants to install a system add-on or utility, and wants the effects or features of that software to be applicable to *all* users? Or, at the opposite extreme, what if some software needs low-level access to the operating system and needs to ensure that nosy users don't remove installed files?

Fortunately, the way Mac OS X is organized provides solutions to these dilemmas. Unfortunately, this organization can be quite confusing for the user (even for experienced users). If you truly want to master Mac OS X, understanding how files are organized is just as important as understanding permissions and user accounts; many of the tips and tricks discussed in this book require that you be familiar with OS X's file system. With that in mind, I'm going to explain the various folders and folder levels and their purposes.

Domain/Directory Levels

If you've done any digging around on your OS X hard drive, you've most likely discovered a number of "identical" folders in different places. In reality, these similarly named folders are not identical; in fact, they serve different, but parallel, purposes. This parallel structure is due to the fact that Mac OS X has three different levels of system and user support, called *domain levels*. These three levels are called the *system*, *local*, and *user* domains. Each of these domains provides a different level of support, and a different degree of access to its files and folders; a summary of each follows.

System The system domain is represented by the directory `/System` at the root level of your hard drive. The contents of this folder (which are effectively the contents of `/System/Library`, as that is the only folder contained in `/System`) comprise the entire operating system. With a few exceptions, everything inside was installed by the Mac OS X installer or by Apple updaters (those exceptions being a few third-party installers that require very low-level access to the OS). The contents of this folder are protected by the OS and are not easily modified—and for good reason: modifying files in the `/System` directory is the easiest way to screw up your OS! If you want to witness this security in action, try deleting a file or folder, such as `/System/Library/Keyboard Layouts`. (Go ahead, try to drag that folder to the trash, I'll wait….) You'll receive an error message that says, "The operation could not be completed because this item is owned by root." Unless you have root access, most of the `/System` directory is off-limits. Think of `/System` as the foundation of the OS—you can remodel what's on top of it, but you don't want to start messing with it unless you really know what you're doing.

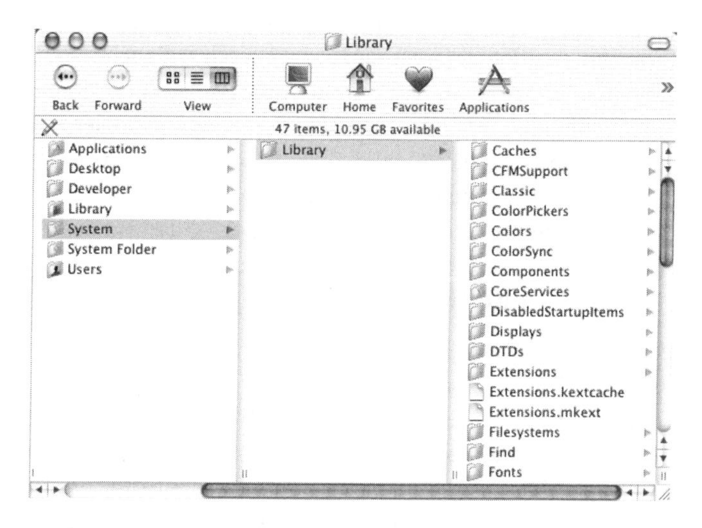

Local The local domain is represented by the `/Library` and `/Applications` folders (at the root level of your hard drive). These directories provide a way for administrators to provide resources to *all* local users of the computer. You'll notice that the contents of `/Library` look similar to the contents of `/System/Library`. Whereas almost everything inside`/System/Library` is installed by the OS X installer, `/Library` is largely populated by support files and system add-ons installed by administrators or software installers. The `/Applications` folder contains any applications you or another administrator have installed there; much like the resources in `/Library` are available to all users, the applications installed in `/Applications` can be used by all users. While the contents of these two folders are not modifiable by a normal user, any administrator can make changes.

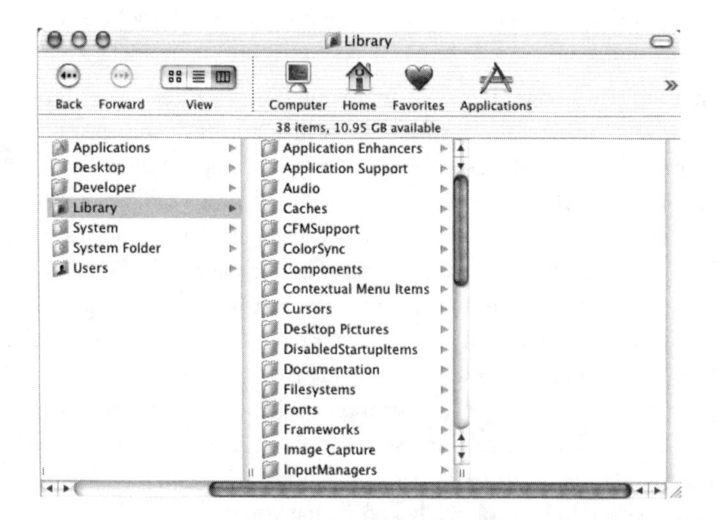

User The user domain is represented by each user's home folder (`~/`). As described in the sidebar "Dissecting the Contents of Your Home Directory," each user folder has its own `Library` and `Applications` directories (referred to by the paths `~/Library` and `~/Applications`). While support files and other resources located in the `~/Library` folder work in much the same way as files located in `/Library` and `/System/Library` (and the folders inside `~/Library` look very similar to those in the other two Library directories), those in `~/Library`, the user-level directory, are available only to the *particular* user whose user folder contains them. Likewise, if a user creates their own `Applications` folder as suggested earlier in the chapter, any applications installed in `~/Applications` will only be available to that particular user.

Files generally get installed in `~/Library` or `~/Applications` for two reasons. First, when an admin decides that they want to make certain files or applications available only to themselves or to a particular user, the administrator will install files in their own or a particular user's directory. Second, recall that a normal user cannot modify any folder outside of their home directory. Thus, if a normal user wants to install an application, system add-on, or other `/Library`-level file, they must use their own `~/Library` and `~/Application` directories.

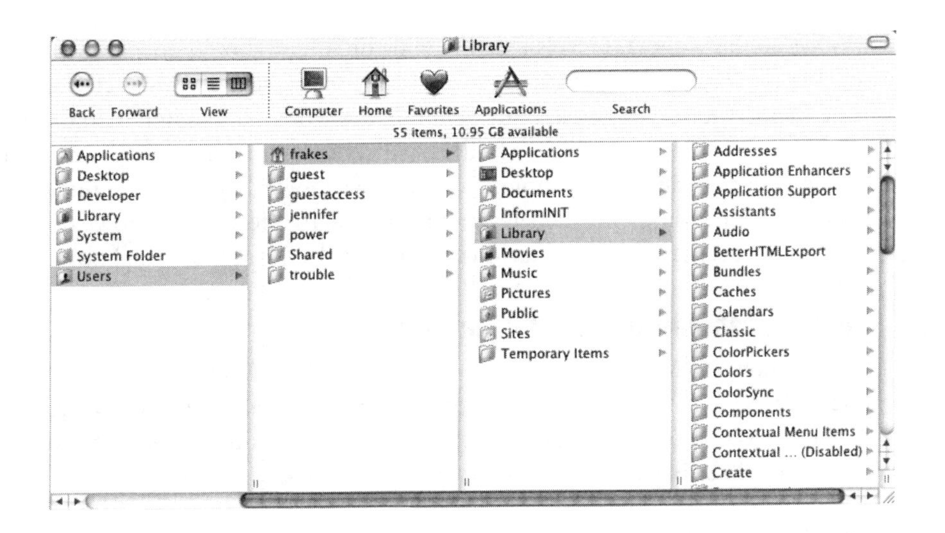

NOTE There is actually a fourth domain level in Mac OS X, the *Network* domain. If you are connected to a network (most likely a local area network, or LAN), a central server can host this Network domain, and the corresponding `/Library` directory. This `/Library` directory can contain resources and support files available to all users on the network. However, as such a configuration is rare for the average user of Mac OS X, and the presence of such a Network domain does not really affect the discussion at hand, I'm not going to spend much time on it.

A good example of a group of parallel folders that illustrates the concepts discussed in this chapter is the way Mac OS X stores fonts. Fonts that are installed by the Mac OS X installer are stored in `/System/Library/Fonts`. Fonts installed by applications or by administrators for use by all users are located in `/Library/Fonts`. Fonts installed by a single user, or by an administrator for use by only a single user, are located in `~/Library/Fonts`. All users can take advantage of fonts stored in `/System/Library/Fonts` and `/Library/Fonts`, but user-level fonts (those stored in their own `~/Library/Fonts`) are only accessible by the user in whose `~/Library` directory the fonts are located.

Another good example of parallel Library folders is folders that hold preference files. The folder `/Library/Preferences` contains system-level preference files that affect all users, such as login window prefs, sharing and firewall prefs, power management prefs, and serial numbers for applications available to all users. These preferences generally require administrative access to change. Each user also has their own `~/Library/Preferences` folder, holding all of their own preference files. This system is actually quite powerful, as it allows for both personal and system-wide preferences. (You'll notice that there are relatively few preference files in `/Library/Preferences`; this is a testament to how much of OS X is configurable by each user individually.) Also note that there is no `/System/Library/Preferences` directory. This makes sense if you think about it, as `/System` shouldn't be modified.

What do these domain levels mean to you? First, you should now have a better idea of how OS X keeps track of single-user versus all-user versus system-level files. But perhaps more important for this book, understanding these domains should help you understand how changes you make to files or folders will affect your own user account, other user accounts, or the system as a whole. You also now know where to put something or edit something depending on which accounts you wish to affect. This knowledge will come in handy as you experiment with various tips and tricks throughout the book.

The Man behind the Curtain: NetInfo

If you've come to Mac OS X from earlier versions of the Mac OS, you may be wondering where OS X stores all of its info on users, user accounts, and the like. The answer is a file called the NetInfo database. Since we'll be working with this database at various points, it's helpful to talk briefly about what it is, what it does, and how to work with it.

What Is NetInfo?

NetInfo is a central, system-level database (meaning it cannot be modified without administrator or root access) that stores network and administrative information. This data includes information on all user accounts (usernames, file locations, group memberships, etc.), groups, access levels, network domain information, file sharing services, printer info, and more. Basically, any kind of network-related data (remember, in Mac OS X, even local accounts are "network-related") is stored in the NetInfo database.

The information in the NetInfo database is stored hierarchically: a root NetInfo domain contains various directories, and each directory can contain further directories or properties, which are the actual settings stored in the database. For example, the "real name" for my user account, "Dan Frakes," is stored in a property in the NetInfo database called *realname*, located at: `/users/frakes/realname`. Note that while NetInfo paths look very much like file paths (`/Users/frakes/`), they are not the same. They simply look similar because both NetInfo and the Mac OS X file system are organized hierarchically.

Some of the info in the NetInfo database is maintained by the system and is accessible and edited via other methods (user accounts, for example, are set up via System Preferences, as explained later in the chapter). However, certain information, such as groups and group membership, is only configurable by editing your NetInfo database. How to do this is our next topic of discussion.

TIP NetInfo is actually a pretty complicated system, too much so to go into more detail here. However, Apple has provided a rather thorough description of it in the form of a document called *Understanding and Using NetInfo*. You can download the PDF file from `http://docs.info.apple.com/article.html?artnum=106416` or `http://www.apple.com/server/pdfs/UnderstandingUsingNetInfo.pdf`.

Working with NetInfo

The NetInfo database is physically located at `/var/db/netinfo/local.nidb`, but you can't access the database in the Finder without root access. So how do you work with it? There are actually two ways: Terminal and NetInfo Manager. Of course, given the importance of the data managed by NetInfo, both methods are only available to an admin-level user.

WARNING Making changes to your NetInfo database can have drastic consequences. The information stored in the database is vital to your Mac's operation, and making changes to items you aren't familiar with can cause problems such as not being able to access files or not being able to boot up your computer. Before making any changes to NetInfo, you should back up your NetInfo database as described in "Backing Up and Restoring the NetInfo Database."

Terminal

You can access and edit your NetInfo database from the command line using the Terminal application (`/Applications/Utilities/Terminal`). In fact, OS X has a built-in Terminal command for doing so: `niutil` (which stands for NetInfo utility). Using this command you can create, rename, and delete NetInfo settings, as well as find out current settings. We'll actually use this command later in the book (see Appendix B).

However, although using Terminal to edit your NetInfo database is fast and convenient if you know exactly what you want to do (including exactly which property you wish to modify), it's not very intuitive for those who are not experts in the various directories and properties managed by NetInfo. A better solution can be found in the NetInfo Manager application.

NetInfo Manager

The NetInfo Manager application (`/Applications/Utilities/NetInfo Manager`) provides a graphical interface to the NetInfo database. It allows you to quickly view current database settings, and—with administrative access—to change, add to, or delete settings. While all of the possible things you can do with NetInfo Manager are beyond the scope of this book, I want to briefly show you how it works in general, since we'll be using it at various points in the book to do NetInfo-related things.

To use NetInfo Manager, you simply launch it like any other application. If you simply want to *view* settings, you can dig right in. However, if you want to *edit* settings, you need to authenticate by clicking the "Click the lock to make changes" button at the bottom of the window. You will be asked for your username and password; assuming your user account has admin privileges, entering your username and password will give you temporary Write access to the NetInfo database (remember what I said about backing up your database before making any changes).

I mentioned previously that the NetInfo database is hierarchical in its organization; the NetInfo Manager window reflects this organization. In fact, if you've ever viewed windows "by Column" in the Finder, or used the expanded view in an Open/Save dialog, the top half of the

NetInfo Manager window should look familiar. In Figure 1.4, I've navigated to the NetInfo directory for my own user account, `frakes`. You can see the root level of the database in the left window (/), and all of the directories located at the root level in the middle window. I've selected the `users` directory, which provided me with a list of all users on my Mac. Selecting my username provides me with a list in the bottom window of all the properties associated with my account.

Some of the properties listed should make sense (*realname* is my "full" name, *hint* is my password hint, *home* is the location of my home folder). On the other hand, some probably don't mean much to you right now. That's normal—we'll talk about some throughout the book; others you may never care about. What's important is to see how NetInfo Manager lets you view and work with the database.

If you want to edit a value, you simply double-click it (provided you've authenticated as described here). The field will become an editable text field, and you can type in the new value. If you really know what you're doing, you can even add properties, values, and directories. When you're finished, you simply select Domain ➢ Save Changes. Or, if you decide that you want to discard any changes you made, you can instead select Domain ➢ Revert to Saved.

FIGURE 1.4: User account settings in NetInfo Manager

At this point, I encourage you to simply click through the various directories in NetInfo Manager to get a feel for how it is organized and what types of information are stored in the NetInfo database. Unless you're already familiar with NetInfo, do not make any changes yet; later in this chapter you'll get your first taste of actually working with the database.

NOTE You'll notice in Figure 1.4 that there are quite a few users listed. Only four of those users (frakes, jennifer, power, and trouble) are actually user accounts set up in the Accounts panel of System Preferences. The rest are system-level accounts used by the operating system for various tasks and purposes, and are present on all Mac OS X computers. You generally do not want to make changes to these accounts.

Backing Up and Restoring the NetInfo Database

Because making changes to your NetInfo database can have such drastic consequences, you *never* want to make changes without first making a backup of the database itself. The steps here show you how to back up your NetInfo database, and how to restore it, if necessary.

Backing Up the NetInfo Database

User Level: admin
Affects: all users
Terminal: yes

Although NetInfo Manager supposedly allows you to make a backup of your database from within the application (Management ➢ Save Backup), many users have found this method to be problematic; sometimes it works, sometimes it doesn't. To make matters worse, sometimes you get an error, sometimes you don't—and the error doesn't necessarily correspond with whether or not it works! I've found that a much more reliable way to backup your database is using Terminal:

1. Launch Terminal (`/Applications/Utilities/Terminal`).
2. At the prompt, type the following (all on one line, preserving all spaces as indicated; case is important in Terminal, so make sure you copy case correctly):

```
cd /private/var/db/netinfo <RETURN>
sudo cp -R  local.nidb local.nidb.backup <RETURN>
```

3. When you are prompted for a password, type your normal account password (you must be an admin user, of course).

The *cp* command copies the database `local.nidb` to a new file in the same directory called `local.nidb.backup`; since the database is actually a directory of files, the *-R* option tells `cp` to copy the directory and all files within it. The `sudo` command—which asked for your password—provides you with the temporary root access needed to be able to write a new file to that directory. (You'll learn more about `sudo` in "Getting to the Root of It," later in this chapter.)

Now you've got a backup copy of your NetInfo database. It's a good idea to use this procedure each time you make changes to NetInfo. In fact, if you're not the type to back up your computer regularly, it's also not a bad idea to back up your database after adding, deleting, or modifying user accounts, since such changes are actually editing the NetInfo database. (If you're not the type to back up regularly, you also need to read Chapter 14, "Mac OS X Maintenance and Administrative Actions," as soon as possible.) If you're especially cautious, you can name the backup files differently each time you make changes to the database (*local.nidb.backup1*, *local.nidb.backup2*, and so on) so that you have a backup of each generation of changes. (If you don't back up to a new, differently named, copy each time, make sure you delete the previous backup copy before backing up again; you can do so using the following command in Terminal: `sudo rm -R /var/db/netinfo/local.nidb.backup`.)

Restoring Your NetInfo Database from a Backup

User Level: admin
Affects: all users
Terminal: yes

If you spend a lot of time working with NetInfo, there's a chance that at some point you'll make a mistake, or the database will become corrupt, or, for lack of a better explanation, your NetInfo database will just get screwed up. When this happens, you might see funny things like home folders not being where they should be, or you may not even be able to boot the computer—you never see the login screen. At this point, you'll be glad you made that backup, because the first step you should take in fixing things is to restore your NetInfo database from a reliable copy.

To do this, you need to boot into what is known as *single-user mode*. Single-user mode is a limited way of working directly with the file system of Mac OS X without actually logging in as a user. What you see in single-user mode looks a lot like what you'd see in a Terminal window—text on a black screen. The benefit of single-user mode is that in most cases you can use it even if you can't boot up or log in to OS X. (Even if you can log in, you should still use single-user mode to restore your NetInfo database, since the current database is in use when you're logged in and cannot be replaced).

1. Reboot or start up your Mac; immediately press and hold command+S. You'll see a bunch of text scroll by, until you see the following:

   ```
   Singleuser boot -- fsck not done
   Root device is mounted read-only
   If you want to make modifications to files,
   run '/sbin/fsck -y' first and then '/sbin/mount -uw /'
   localhost#
   ```

2. If you're having problems, the first thing you should always do when booting into single-user mode is run `fsck`, which is OS X's built-in disk utility. Type the following at the prompt: **`/sbin/fsck -y <RETURN>`**

If you get an error that the file system was modified, run the command again; keep running it until you get a message that everything is OK. (The fsck utility will be discussed in more detail in Chapter 14.)

3. In order to access files on your boot volume, you need to mount the disk. Type the following command (note the space between uw and /): **/sbin/mount -uw / <RETURN>**
4. Use the mv command to rename the "bad" database from local.nidb to local.nidb.bad:

```
cd /var/db/netinfo <RETURN>
mv local.nidb  local.nidb.bad <RETURN>
```

5. Use the mv command again to rename the backup database local.nidb (all one line):

```
mv local.nidb.backup local.nidb <RETURN>
```

Note that if you're restoring from another backup with a different name, you should replace *local.nidb.backup* with the actual name of your backup database in the command above.

6. Restart your computer by typing **reboot <RETURN>.** This command tells the computer to finish any disk writes that are in progress, and then restarts the machine.

When you reboot, OS X will use the newly restored NetInfo database.

The Last Resort: Rebuilding the NetInfo Database

User Level: admin
Affects: all users
Terminal: yes

I hope you never have to use this tip, because if you do, it means something has gone horribly wrong with NetInfo. However, the truth is that, well, it can happen. Sometimes the NetInfo database gets corrupted so badly that your Mac won't even start, and you either didn't make a backup, or your backup itself is damaged. In this scenario, your only hope is to wipe out the existing NetInfo database and tell Mac OS X that you want to start from scratch. Here's how:

1. As in the instructions for restoring your database, start up in single-user mode (command+S at startup).
2. At the localhost# prompt, use fsck to ensure that your drives are in good shape: **/sbin/fsck -y <RETURN>.** If you receive a message that your file system was modified, run fsck again, as many times as is necessary to get the message that your disk is OK.
3. To mount the boot disk so that you can access the files on it, type the following (note the space between uw and /): **/sbin/mount -uw / <RETURN>**
4. Type the following commands:

```
cd /var/db/netinfo <RETURN>
mv local.nidb local.nidb.deleted <RETURN>
rm /private/var/db/.AppleSetupDone <RETURN>
reboot <RETURN>
```

The first command changes the name of the corrupt NetInfo database to `local.nidb.deleted` (so that OS X won't use it when you reboot). You could have deleted it using a different command in Terminal, but by renaming it you'll still have a copy in case it turns out the problem wasn't a corrupted NetInfo database. The second command deletes a file the operating system uses to keep track of whether or not you ran the initial account setup process. Once you delete that file, Mac OS X thinks that you need to set up your initial account again, and will launch the Setup Assistant the next time you boot into OS X.

5. When your computer reboots, the setup assistant will ask you to set up a "first" user account. Be *sure* to provide the *exact same* short username you used for your original admin account (the one you generally use that has administrator privileges). This will cause Mac OS X to match your "new" account up with your existing user folder and all corresponding permissions. You may also need to go into the Users pane of System Preferences and re-create any other users you previously created (see "Creating User Accounts" in the next section). Again, be sure to use the *exact* same short usernames the original accounts used.

NOTE More info (and more advanced info) on recovering and replacing the NetInfo database can be found at `http://docs.info.apple.com/article.html?artnum=107210` and `http://www.westwind.com/reference/OS-X/NetInfo-recover.html`.

Mastering Permissions and Accounts

By now you should have a pretty good handle on the way Mac OS X organizes files, accounts, and permissions. While much of the book from here on out is oriented towards showing you how to *do* things, doing most of those things will be easier, and understanding *why* and *how* you're doing them will be easier, now that you understand the underlying structure. The rest of this chapter will provide some hands-on opportunities, as I discuss everything from creating and editing user accounts to creating groups and using group permissions, from working with the root account to dealing with permissions problems.

Creating, Editing, and Deleting User Accounts

When you first installed Mac OS X or first booted your Mac, you were asked for a name and password; whether you realized it or not, you were actually creating your first user account. That account was automatically given administrative access and, if your first Mac OS X installation was 10.2 (Jaguar) or later, was set to *auto-login* (meaning you're not prompted for your name and password at startup). Since that time, you may have continued to use your Mac as the sole user, in which case you're in the market for some additional user accounts like those mentioned in "Other Uses for User Accounts." Or you may have already set up other accounts for family or coworkers, in which case you want to know more about the options available to you (especially since OS X 10.2 and later have provided a number of additional account options over 10.1.x). In this section I'm going to explain how to create new accounts, edit existing accounts, and delete unwanted accounts. Even if you've already created accounts in OS X, you may find some of the details and tips interesting.

Creating User Accounts

User Level: admin
Affects: individual users
Terminal: no

In order to create a new user account in Mac OS X, your own account must have admin access. You create new user accounts using *Accounts* panel of System Preferences; in the Accounts panel, you select the *Users* tab. (In versions of OS X prior to 10.2, Users was a separate preference panel.) To add a user, simply click the New User… button (you may be asked to authenticate before you can make any changes; if so, enter your username and password). A new user account info window will drop down (Figure 1.5) and you will be asked to complete the fields presented:

Name The user's full name.

Short Name A short version of the user's name; this will also be the name of their user folder in `/Users`.

New Password The password you give the new account. If the account is for another person, they will be able to change it.

Verify Enter the password a second time to verify it; if this field and the Password field do not match, you will be asked to type both over again until they match.

Password Hint (optional) You can supply a hint for the given password in case the user forgets it. This hint will be shown only if you've selected the Show password hint… option in the Login Options tab.

Picture You can choose a login picture for the account. If you have selected to display the Login window as a list of users (via the Login Options tab), each user's account will be represented by their full name and the picture selected here. You can choose a picture from the list, or you can choose your own custom picture by browsing your hard drive or dragging the picture to the window.

Allow user to administer this computer If checked, the new user will have full admin access. Use this option sparingly and only with people you trust to do the right thing (and not to do the wrong things) with such access.

Allow user to log in from Windows If you have Windows Sharing set up (for more details see Chapter 10), checking this box will allow the new user to connect to your computer from a Windows computer.

FIGURE 1.5:
Creating a new user account

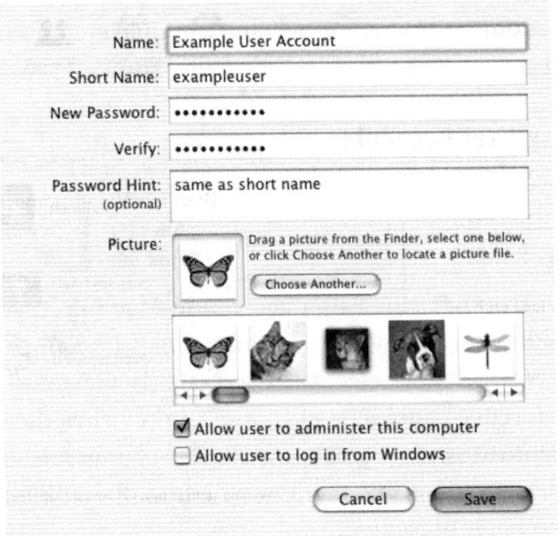

NOTE In versions of OS X prior to 10.2, the short username was limited to eight characters or less in length, and those characters were limited to a relatively small character set. However, in OS X 10.2 and later the short username can actually be up to 255 Unicode characters, greatly expanding both the length and the variety of possible characters that can be used (and making the term "short username" a bit of a misnomer). That said, since you're going to be typing your short name quite often (dialog boxes, file paths, etc.), I recommend keeping it a *short* name, and using characters that are easy to type. I also recommend avoiding punctuation, especially spaces, in short usernames, as they can cause problems.

When you've finished, click the Save button to create the new user account. You'll notice that a new user account is visible in the Accounts window, and, if you check, you'll find that a new folder has been created in `/Users`, with the new user's short username as its title . If you log out, the new user (or you) can then log in under the new account.

There is one other thing left to do before the new account setup is complete. If the new user is *not* an admin user, you can also choose to restrict the user's abilities. To do so, click on the Capabilities… button. A new window is presented with a number of options (Figure 1.6). While most are self-explanatory, a few deserve a bit more attention.

Use only these applications If this option is selected, you can control which applications in `/Applications` the user can access; which utilities in `/Applications/Utilities` the user can access; which OS 9 applications in `/Applications (OS 9)` the user can launch (if that folder is present on your Mac); and any other applications located elsewhere (*Others*). You can choose to allow or disallow each category, or you can click the disclosure triangle next to a category to select particular applications. In addition, you may find that some applications aren't listed; to add them to the list, click the Locate… button at the bottom of the window and browse your hard drive to find them. (This is also a good way to add applications stored on other partitions or volumes.)

Simple Finder This option lets you provide extremely limited access along with a very simple interface (for children or users who are not very comfortable with computers). The Desktop will be completely empty (it will not even show the hard drive). The Apple menu will be limited to just two commands: Sleep and Log Out… The Dock will include only the Trash, the Finder, and three folders: My Applications, Documents (for saving documents), and Shared (the Shared user folder, for saving or opening shared documents). Clicking one of these folders in the Dock brings up a window in "button" mode—documents and applications are represented by large icons, and a single click opens or launches them. The contents of My Applications is defined by you, the administrator; when you select the Simple Finder option, the Use only these applications option in the Capabilities window changes to Show these applications in My Applications folder. Just as you could limit the applications available to a user in standard Finder mode, selecting applications here lets you choose whether or not the user even sees them. Finally, if you've allowed the user to open System Preferences, only a few of the panels will actually be accessible: the *Personal* panels, as well as *Sound* and *Universal Access*.

NOTE The applications displayed in Simple Finder mode's My Applications window are actually aliases inside the folder `~/Library/Managed Items/My Applications` (inside the home folder of the affected user, not the administrator). When an admin enables an application for the user, OS X automatically places an alias to that application in this folder; likewise, disabling an application will result in the alias being removed.

FIGURE 1.6: Limiting the capabilities of a new user

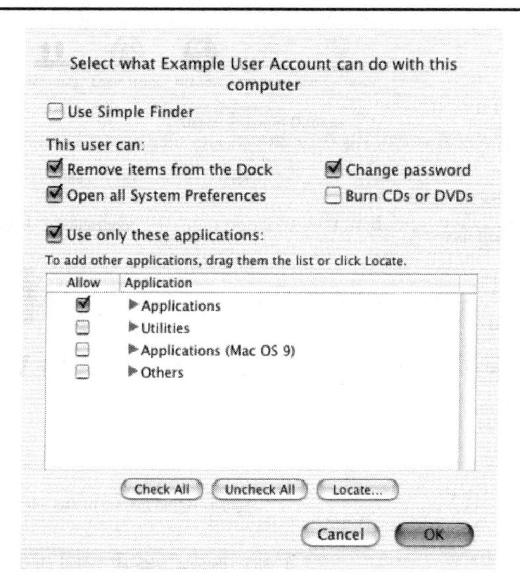

Editing User Accounts

User Level: admin
Affects: individual users
Terminal: no

Editing user accounts is also done using the Accounts panel of System Preferences. You simply select a user account, and then click either the Edit User... button or the Capabilities... button, depending on whether you want to edit the account itself or the user capabilities for that account. However, while this System Preferences panel is available to all users, how much of an account's settings can be modified depends on user level:

Normal users Assuming an administrator has not limited their capabilities (as previously described), normal users can edit their password, their password hint, and their login picture. They cannot change their own capabilities, nor can they change their Name or Short Name.

Admin users Users with admin status can edit all capabilities of other users, as well as every field in the Edit User… window except for Short Name.

NOTE Once you've created an account, its short name cannot be changed easily. Since the short name is not only a login name but also a directory name (the name of the user's home folder), the OS makes it difficult to change. If you'd like to edit the short name of a user account, see "Why Did I Ever Pick That Name?" later in this chapter.

Deleting User Accounts

User Level: admin
Affects: individual users
Terminal: no

At some point you may want to delete a user account. Perhaps the user is no longer employed at your company, maybe your friend or relative doesn't use your computer anymore, or maybe you've just been creating new accounts as an exercise as you've been reading this chapter. For whatever the reason, the need sometimes arises to wipe an account off of your computer.

Like creating and editing user accounts, deleting a user account starts in the Accounts pane of System Preferences. However, it doesn't end there. Since each account has its own home folder replete with settings, documents, and any other files or applications the user placed or saved there, deleting a user account runs the risk of losing anything inside that user's home folder. Luckily, as you'll see in a moment, OS X has a mechanism for avoiding this potentially problematic situation.

To delete a user account, first select the user you wish to delete and click the Delete User… button. As soon as you do so, a window will pop up asking if you're sure this is what you want to do. It also tells you that if you do delete the account, the contents of that user's home folder will "be put in a file in the Deleted Users folder" (Figure 1.7).

FIGURE 1.7:
Deleting a user account

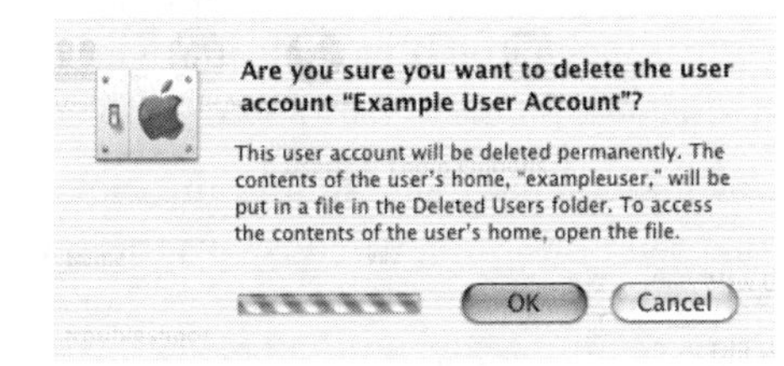

When you click OK, the account will be removed from the list of accounts. But what about that new file the warning box told you about? In the Finder, navigate to the `/Users` directory; in addition to the home folders of the user accounts that still exist on your computer, there is now a new folder, `Deleted Users`. Inside, you'll find a disk image called *`deletedusername`*`.dmg` (it's not actually called that, of course; *`deletedusername`* is the name of the user you just deleted). If you double click the file, Disk Copy will launch and mount the image in the Finder. The mounted disk contains the contents of the deleted user's home folder, so you, as the administrator, can copy any documents or files you or the previous user wish to preserve, burn to CD, or drop in another user's Public folder. Once you've done this, you can unmount the image, then trash the image file itself. At that point, the entire user account is gone forever.

Unfortunately, even though you can delete the image file, you can't delete the `Deleted Users` folder from the Finder, as it is technically owned by the root account. If you're a neat freak like me, and you really want to get rid of that folder, launch Terminal and type the following command (make *sure* you've checked the folder and you don't want anything inside, as this command will permanently delete it and any contents): **`sudo rm -rf '/Users/Deleted Users' <RETURN>`.** You'll be asked for your password; enter it and hit return. The folder is gone for good!

NOTE In OS X 10.1.x, deleting a user account doesn't provide the same nice, neat "disk image" solution; instead, OS X renames the user's home folder *username Deleted*, leaves it in the `/Users` directory, and transfers ownership of the folder to an administrator (you choose which one). The administrator who gains ownership should then go through the Deleted user folder and save or delete the contents as needed. However, just as you can't delete the *Deleted Users* folder from the Finder in OS X 10.2 or later, you cannot delete the *username Deleted* folder in 10.1.x. The Terminal command to do this is: `sudo rm -rf '/Users/`*`username Deleted`*`' <RETURN>`, where *username Deleted* is the name of the folder you wish to delete.

Getting to the Root of It: The Root Account

I mentioned in "User Levels" that in addition to normal user accounts and admin user accounts, there is a third user level, root. (The root account is also often called the *superuser*; while there is technically a difference between the two, for most intents and purposes they are one in the same.) While you can have as many normal and admin accounts as you like, you can only have one root account and it's called just that: root. You can't edit it or delete it; the most you can do is turn it on or off—and only if you have admin access. While it's possible to log in as the root user, you *definitely* don't want to do so unless you have a specific reason to.

Why all the limitations? Quite simply, the root account is too powerful. It is unhindered by permissions; it can move, edit, delete, copy, trash, view, and open at will. (More accurately, the root account in OS X *honors* permissions, but can change them without restriction, meaning the root account can do as it pleases quite easily.) While this is helpful at times when you need to do something you don't normally have the ability to do, it's also extremely dangerous. The root user can view the contents of all user folders. It can add to, edit, or remove contents of `/System`. In fact, it can even (accidentally or on purpose) move the entire `/System` directory to the trash. Do you really want to have that much power? I sure don't, and I don't recommend you do, either, at least not on a regular basis.

In addition, if you do decide to enable the root account, for all the reasons I mentioned previously, you *really* don't want to make it easy to log into. First, anyone who walks up to your computer could log in as root if they found out your password. Second, even if your Mac is physically secure from unsavory characters, if it's connected to the Internet and you have any sort of remote access or sharing enabled, anyone in the world with Internet access who discovers your password will have *full* access to your computer. Needless to say, neither of these situations is good. Have I impressed on you enough why root access is a bad idea? If so, then you're ready to learn how to use it.

There are actually three ways to gain root access. You can temporarily gain root access in Terminal from an admin account in order to issue commands as the root user. You can temporarily launch applications as the root user from any admin account. Finally, you can enable the root user account and actually log into your Mac as root.

Temporary Root Access in Terminal: *sudo*

User Level: admin
Affects: NA
Terminal: yes

If you need to do something in Terminal that requires root access, there is a command called `sudo` (short for *switch user and do* or *superuser do*), only available to admin-level users, that provides temporary root access in the Terminal. Any commands you issue via the `sudo` command will be free of the restrictions that your user account usually has. There are actually a couple of ways to use the `sudo` command.

Run a Single Command Using *sudo*

By preceding a Terminal command with `sudo`, you actually run that command with root access. Before the command executes, you will be asked for your password (enter your personal account password) to authenticate. This is a useful procedure for moving or deleting a file that is owned by root. If this sounds familiar, it should—we used it earlier when we deleted

FIGURE 1.8: Using `sudo` to execute the `rm` (remove) command on a protected file

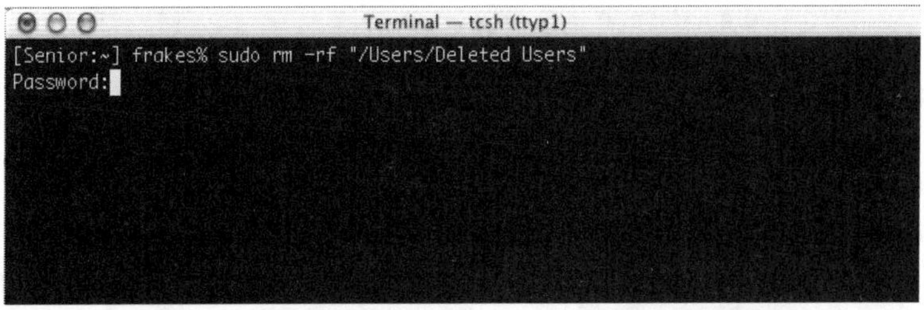

```
Terminal — tcsh (ttyp1)
[Senior:~] frakes% sudo rm -rf "/Users/Deleted Users"
Password:
```

FIGURE 1.9: Running a Terminal session as root using `sudo -s`

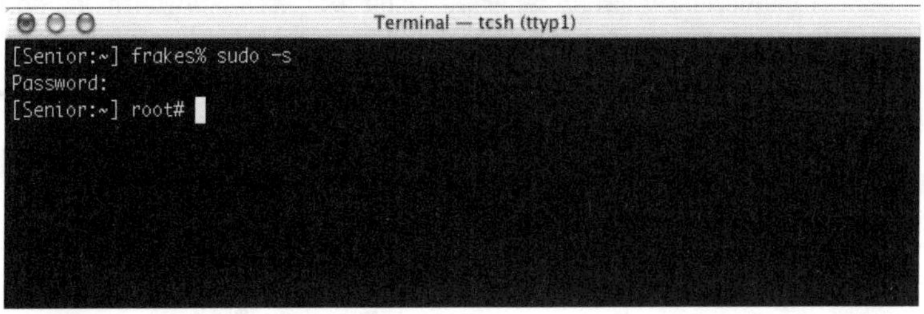

```
Terminal — tcsh (ttyp1)
[Senior:~] frakes% sudo -s
Password:
[Senior:~] root#
```

the `Deleted Users` folder (Figure 1.8). The `sudo` command actually has a built-in "authentication timer"; once you've entered your password to authenticate the `sudo` command, you can continue to issue commands using `sudo` without being required to provide your password. However, once you've stopped using the `sudo` command for about five minutes, your authentication period expires, at which point you'll be back to your old, boring self.

Run an Entire Terminal Session as *sudo*

If you know you're going to be using a lot of commands that might need root access, you can tell Terminal to maintain your temporary root access until you exit the session. To do this, type: `sudo -s` <RETURN>. You will be asked for your password (enter your personal account password). Once you have authenticated your account, you will have root access until you end your session (by typing `exit` <RETURN>). What you will notice is that after issuing the `sudo -s` command, instead of your Terminal prompt using your username, it will now say `root#` (Figure 1.9).

Sudo Caution (not Pseudo Caution)

Because you have so much power when using sudo, make *sure* you type what you mean to type. Word processors can correct typos; Terminal can't. Terminal interprets commands literally; if you accidentally mistype something, and the mistyped command still works, it will be executed. Take, for example, the Terminal command we used earlier:

```
sudo rm -rf '/Users/Deleted Users' <RETURN>
```

Continued on next page

This command can also be written as:

```
sudo rm -rf /Users/Deleted\ Users <RETURN>
```

I'll talk more about this in Chapter 15, "Utilizing UNIX", but for now, you'll have to trust me that the two are the same. Now, suppose that you accidentally type:

```
sudo rm -rf / Users/Deleted\ Users <RETURN>
```

Notice the space between `/` and `Users`? Terminal notices, and the resulting command will erase your hard drive. I'm not kidding.

The moral of the story is: when using root access in Terminal, don't mistype. Or use `rm -ri` instead of `rm -rf`; the former will ask you to confirm each file it attempts to delete.

Temporarily Running Applications as Root

User Level: admin
Affects: NA
Terminal: yes/no

There are times when you'll want to do something using an application—edit a configuration file in a text editor, move a file or folder using a file utility—that you don't have the privileges to do from your own account. Because the only way, or the easiest way, to do these tasks is from within an application, you can't (or don't want to) use Terminal. You might think that the only way to do this is to enable the root account and then log in as root. But fortunately, OS X provides a way to temporarily run individual applications as root. You will still be logged in under your personal account, but the application itself will behave as if it is being run by the root account.

While it's possible to do this from Terminal, I much prefer using two of my "essential" OS X utilities: Snard (shareware, `http://www.gideonsoftworks.com/`) or Pseudo (shareware, `http://personalpages.tds.net/~brian_hill/`). Snard provides a menu (either in the menu bar or in the Dock) that does a number of useful things, one of which is opening an application as root (Figure 1.10). You choose Open App As Root… from the menu, navigate to the application you want to use, and then provide your username and password to authenticate as root.

Pseudo is a one-trick pony, but it does that trick very well. You can drag an application onto the Pseudo icon in the Finder or the Dock. You can also launch Pseudo, which provides you with a convenient launch window (Figure 1.11), or you can choose File ➢ Launch… from within Pseudo. Finally Pseudo lets you create Launch Documents that open a particular application as root when double-clicked. I have several of these documents for various applications I use frequently as root.

As an example of when this type of functionality might be useful, some advanced users customize the configuration of the built-in Apache web server in Mac OS X. One of the

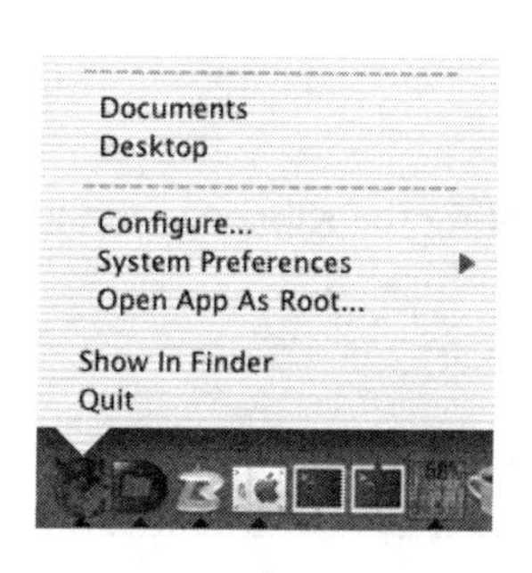

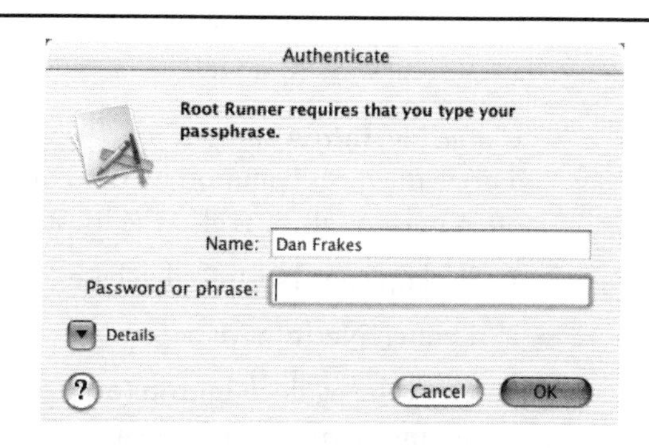

FIGURE 1.10: Using Snard to launch (left) and authenticate (right) an application as root

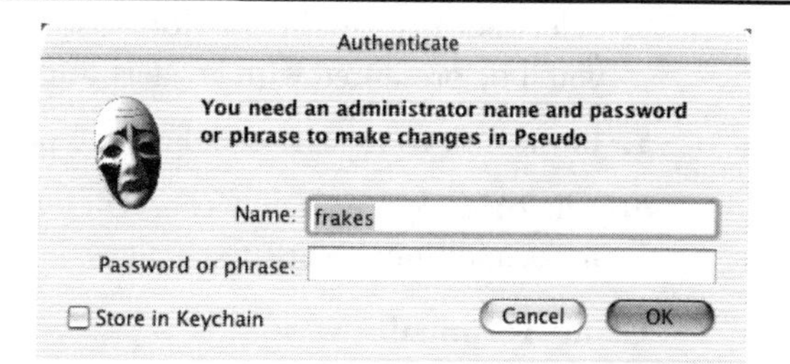

FIGURE 1.11: Using Pseudo to launch (left) and authenticate (right) an application as root

files used to do this is `/private/etc/httpd/httpd.conf`. This text file is owned by root, so even an admin user cannot edit it. Yet by launching a text editor, such as OS X's TechEdit or the commercial BBEdit Lite (`http://www.barebones.com/products/bbedit_lite.html`), as root, the file can be edited and saved.

As another example, many software installers ask for your admin-level username and password when you launch them. What is happening is that you are actually authenticating the installer to allow it to run as root so that it can install files where it needs to.

TIP Although you need the username and password of an administrator to launch an application as root, you can do so from any account, normal or admin. For example, if a normal user wants to run a software installer that requires authentication, you can actually type your username and password to authenticate it, even though you aren't logged into your account.

Enabling/Using the Root Account

User Level: admin
Affects: NA
Terminal: yes/no

If you can't do the things you need to do using the methods I've already covered, and you've read all my dire warnings, and you still want to enable the root account, here's how. (To be fair, there are a few tips in the book where it's either necessary or just easier to use the root account. I just want the seriousness of doing so to sink in.) Like many things in OS X, there are several ways to do it.

Using NetInfo Manager

This is the most common method of enabling the root account, and the one you'll see most often in tutorials. It is also the most straightforward.

1. Backup your NetInfo database (of course!).
2. Launch NetInfo Manager.
3. Click the padlock button (or choose Security ➢ Authenticate) to authenticate; enter your admin username and password.
4. Select Security ➢ Enable Root User; if this is the first time you've enabled the root user, you'll be presented with an alert warning you that there is currently no root password.
5. In the new root password dialog, type a new root password, then retype it.
6. The root account is now enabled, but you'll see a dialog that you must re-authenticate to make additional NetInfo changes.

Using Terminal

You can also enable the root user account via Terminal. While it's probably the quickest way, you're still working in terminal rather than the GUI of NetInfo Manager.

1. Launch Terminal (or open a new session window if Terminal is already running).
2. Type **`sudo passwd root <RETURN>`.** This command actually tells Mac OS X to change the password for the root account.
3. You may see the following prompt:

   ```
   Password:
   ```

   You should enter your personal (admin-level) user account password here; this is simply authenticating the `sudo` command.
4. You'll then see another set of prompts:

   ```
   Changing password for root.
   New password:
   Retype new password:
   ```

   Here you should type your new root account password, then type it again to verify it.
5. The root account is now enabled; you could actually go into NetInfo Manager to verify this.

Using the Mac OS X Install CD

You can actually use the OS X Install CD's *reset password* feature to enable the root user. You would most likely use this method if your computer is having severe problems that you can only fix by logging in as root.

1. Insert the OS X CD and start up/restart your Mac while holding down the C key (this forces your computer to boot from the CD).
2. Once the OS X Installer appears, select Installer ➢ Reset Password.
3. Select the hard drive or volume that hosts the copy of Mac OS X under which you wish to enable the root account.
4. Select System Administrator (root) from the pop-up menu.
5. Enter a new root password, then enter it again to verify.
6. Click the Save button, quit out of Password Reset and Installer, and restart your computer.
7. The root account is now enabled.

Logging In as Root

After you've enabled the root account, you'll probably want to do something really silly like… oh, logging in as root (just kidding about the "silly" part). To log in as root, first log out of your current account (or start up the machine if it's not already booted). At the login screen, depending on your settings in the Login Options tab of Accounts preferences, you'll see either a list of users, or a name and password field. If you see the name and password field, type in **`root`** as the username and the new root password you just created in the password field. If your computer is set up to show a list of users, the last user should now say Others… Clicking that button will give you a name/password window that you can use to log in.

WARNING If you plan on logging in as the root user, I *highly* recommend that you set up your desktop and other appearance settings in the root account so that they look *very* different from your personal user account (such as using a bright red Desktop). This way you will have an obvious indicator of when you are logged in as root (and hopefully a reminder of the unfettered power you have and how much trouble you could cause yourself).

Switching to Root for an Entire Terminal Session

If you've enabled the root account, you can actually log into a Terminal session as the root user. To do so, type: **`su`** **<RETURN>**. You will be asked for a password; instead of your admin-level account password, this is the root account's password. Once you've provided it, you will be logged into Terminal *as* the root user until you end that session (type **`exit`** to return to your normal account in Terminal). For most users this method is identical to using `sudo -s` as described earlier except that the root user account itself must be enabled to use `su`. The main difference between in terms of what you can *do* is a small subset of advanced Terminal commands that can only be executed from the root account. If you have enabled the root account, logging into Terminal as the root user makes these commands available to you.

TIP

If you ever get confused as to what account you're logged into inside Terminal, type **whoami <RETURN>**. Terminal will respond with your current account name (generally *username* or *root*).

It is important to point out that when you use this method, although your home folder in the Finder is still `/Users/yourusername`, your home folder in the current Terminal session is instead the root account's home folder, located at `/private/var/root`.

I Forgot My Root Password!

So you've enabled the root account, but you seem to have forgotten the password. Fortunately (or unfortunately, if you're security-conscious), Apple has made it relatively easy for an admin-level user to reset the root account's password. Here are the two easiest ways to do so:

1. In Terminal, type **sudo passwd root <RETURN>**. If you haven't used sudo in the last few minutes, you'll be asked for your password to authenticate. Once the command runs, you'll see the following text:

```
Changing password for root.
New password:
Retype new password:
```

   Type your new root password, then retype it to verify (if you don't type exactly the same thing, you'll have to do it over).

2. Boot from the Mac OS X Install CD. Once the OS X Installer appears, select Installer ➢ Reset Password.

What Do You Mean I Don't Have Permission? Working with Permissions

Now that you thoroughly understand permissions, it's time to actually work with them. In this section I'll talk a bit about default permissions, changing and setting permissions, and, finally, how to deal with permissions problems.

Default Permissions

At this point you know what permissions are, but you may be wondering how a file or folder *gets* its privileges in the first place. Files and folders created by the OS are given various permissions based on where they are installed and the purpose of the enclosing folder (see "Why Are There So Many Copies of So Many Folders?" earlier in this chapter). However, for files created by users, the answer is much simpler. Files are owned by the user who created them (with Read & Write access), inherit the group of the enclosing folder, and provide Read-only access to other users.

Creating a file means saving it to disk, whether that's by saving a new document from within an application or by downloading a file from the Web. This act of creating is the key—*moving* a file from one folder to another retains its original permissions, but *copying* the same file changes its permissions, as illustrated by Figure 1.12.

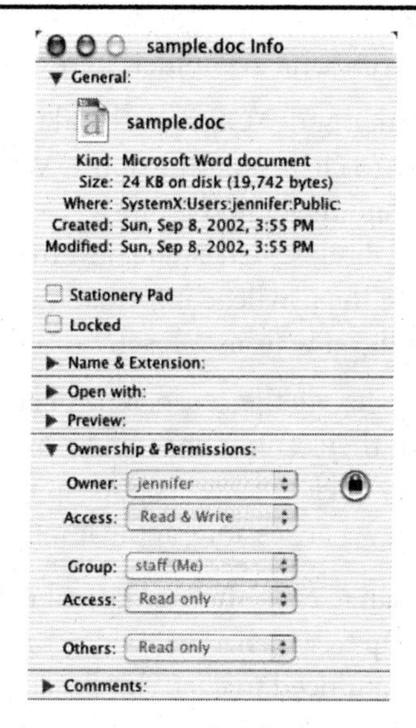

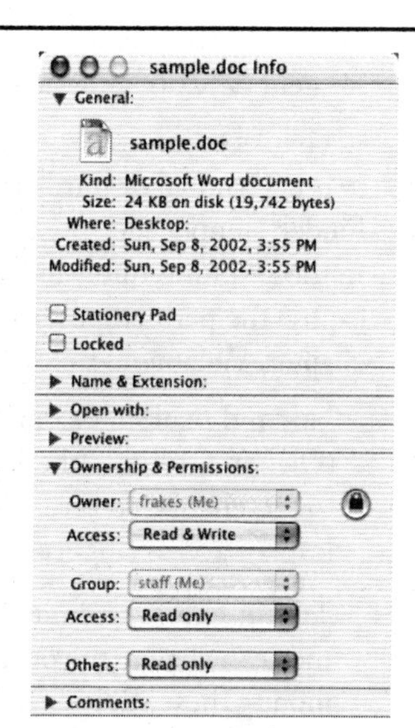

FIGURE 1.12: A file's permissions change when it is copied

The original file was created by jennifer in `/Users/jennifer/Documents`, then moved by jennifer to `/Users/jennifer/Public`. Since I (as an "Other") had access to read the file, I copied it from jennifer's Public folder to my own Desktop. As you can see, the file's owner changed when I copied it. This change is important because it illustrates that if you don't want other users to be able to access your files, you need to put those files in a folder others cannot view (Read), or you need to change permissions to give other users No Access.

NOTE Non-boot volumes (additional hard drives, separate drive partitions, removable disks, etc.) act, by default, as "shared" volumes. This means that they are visible and editable by all users, just like the Shared user folder (Read & Write access for everyone). If you want to restrict access to the volume, or to files/folders on the volume, you'll need to manually change the appropriate permissions.

Changing Permissions

User Level: admin or normal
Affects: certain users
Terminal: no

There are a number of reasons why you might want to change the permissions on a file, a folder, or even on a volume. Most users will at some point want to open up access to a file or folder so that others can use it, or restrict access to it so that no one else can view or open it. In addition, if you're an admin user, you'll inevitably be faced with a situation where you need to open, edit, move, copy, or delete a file or folder, but you can't because you "don't have permission." Admin users often find themselves in this position when they want to delete a file or folder, or when trying to work with files or folders in a location where they are generally not allowed (in the `/System/Library` folder, for example).

Thanks to improvements in the Finder under OS X 10.2 and later, there's no longer a need to use Terminal or third-party utilities to change permissions—you can do it all right from the Finder. Simply click the file or folder and then choose File ➢ Get Info (or press command+I). In the resulting Info window, click the disclosure triangle next to Ownership & Permissions to expose the permissions pane. You'll see the privilege information we talked about earlier in the chapter. What you can do here depends on your user level.

Normal users Normal users can change the access *level* of all three privilege categories (Owner, Group, Others). However, they cannot change the owner or group a file belongs to. To change an access level, simply click the Access pop-up menu and choose the desired level of access (Figure 1.13). The new permissions apply immediately.

Admin users Admin users can change everything a normal user can change; in addition, they can change the owner and group to which a file, folder, or volume belongs. In order to modify these additional fields, you first need to click the closed padlock icon; the first time you do this you'll be asked to enter your username and password in order to authenticate your account. Then simply click the Owner or Group field and choose the desired owner or group from the pop-up menu. As a security precaution, if too much time has passed since the last time you authenticated, after making the change you'll be asked for your name and password again. (This extra security exists to prevent an ill-intentioned passerby from giving themselves access to your entire system if you step away from your computer.)

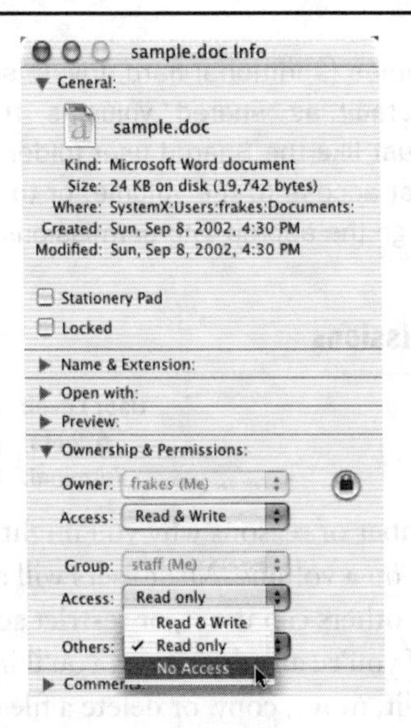

FIGURE 1.13: Changing the level of access *Others* have for a file

If you select a folder in the Finder and use the Get Info command, you'll see one additional option in the Owners & Permissions pane: a button that says "Apply to enclosed items..." Clicking this button will apply the *permissions* you've set for the folder to all items within that folder. I emphasized the word permissions because it does *not* propagate any changes you made to the owner or group settings. If you'd like to make such changes to the entire contents of a folder, you'll need to use Terminal.

Throughout the book, you'll find lots of places where I mention changing permissions. For example, file sharing, remote access, system security, and Finder troubleshooting are all topics that are privilege-related, and all may require you to use the Get Info window to change permissions. In fact, in just a few pages I'll be talking about groups and group permissions. Suffice it to say that being familiar with permissions and how to change them will serve you well, not just for the rest of this book, but in everyday use.

NOTE You can use Terminal to change permissions, via the chown, chgrp, and chmod commands. In addition, although it's no longer necessary to use third-party utilities to change permissions, there are still a number of other file properties that can be easily changed only by using such utilities—I'll talk more about those topics in Chapter 5, "Finagle Files and Foil Finder Frustration."

When Privileges Go Bad: Permissions Problems

User Level: admin
Affects: all users
Terminal: no

There are a number of situations where you'll find that a file, a folder, or multiple files or folders have obtained incorrect permissions. Symptoms of such faulty privileges can include printing problems; problems launching applications (even if they've been installed in `/Applications`); problems connecting to the Internet; an inability to work with a file that you should be able to access; or slow system performance. A couple of specific examples are "type –192" errors when using Disk copy, and "type –108" errors when printing. Some of the causes for these types of problems are software installers that incorrectly change permissions; files' being moved, created, or installed while booted into Mac OS 9; disk problems or file corruption; or something as simple as user error (i.e., "oops, I didn't mean to change that"). Regardless of the cause, you'll want to change the permissions to the correct ones in order to set things right.

For individual files for which you know the correct privileges, the solution is as simple as opening a Get Info window and choosing the correct values (as described in "Changing Permissions" section). However, at times you'll find more serious permissions problems: multiple files with incorrect permissions, or system-level files for which you have no idea what the "correct" permissions should be. In these situations, more drastic action is needed. Luckily, Apple has provided the solution for these problems and, unlike in of OS X 10.2 and later, has included the tools both on your Mac OS X Install CD and right on your computer in the form of a new and improved Disk Utility application.

To repair permissions while booted into OS X, launch Disk Utility from the Finder (`/Applications/Utilities/Disk Utility`) and click on the First Aid tab in the main Disk Utility window (Figure 1.14). Select your Mac OS X volume in the disk/volume panel on the left, and then click the Repair Disk Permissions button in the First Aid panel on the right. You may be asked for your admin username and password for the process to proceed. This process will reset *all* system files and Apple-installed software to their original and correct permissions (which will probably take a while, especially on large volumes with lots of files). The only caveat to such a repair is that some third-party software installers purposely modify the file privileges of system-level files. If these altered permissions are necessary for the third-party software to work, you may experience problems with that particular third-party software.

Although Apple recommends repairing permissions when booted into OS X, if a permissions problem is preventing your Mac from booting at all, you can also repair permissions from the OS X Install CD. To do so, reboot your computer from the CD (hold down the C key during startup). When the Installer screen appears, choose Installer ➢ Disk Utility. Run Repair Disk Permissions normally, and when it is finished, quit Disk Utility and then quit the Installer; this will restart your Mac.

FIGURE 1.14: Using Disk Utility to repair permissions

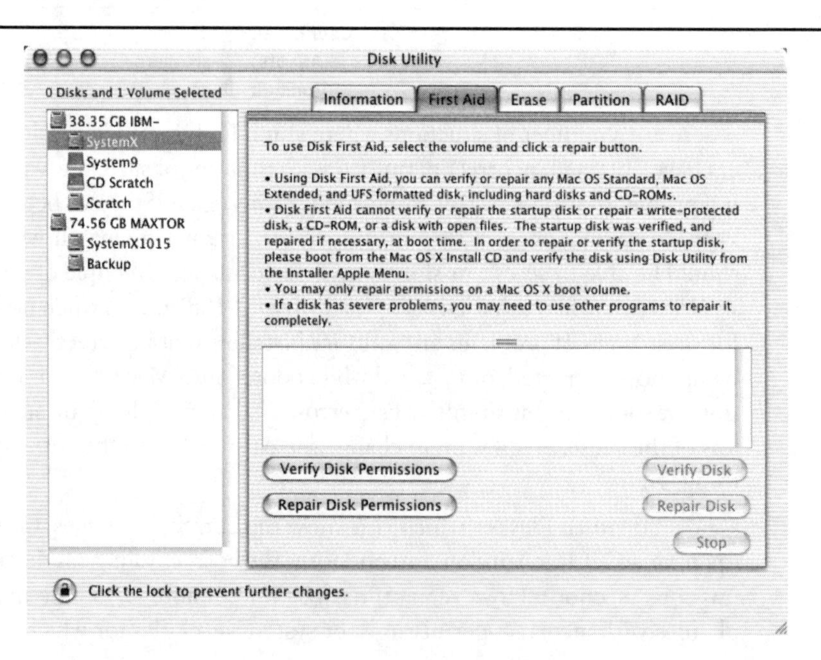

NOTE In versions of OS X prior to 10.2, Disk Utility did not include the repair permissions option. For these versions of the OS, this functionality is provided via Apple's Repair Privileges Utility, which must be downloaded. You can find more information about this utility, and download it, from `http://docs.info.apple.com/article.html? artnum=106900`.

How to Give Permission to More Than One Person (but Not *Everyone*): Groups

Imagine the following scenario: you have a document that you want both you and your spouse to be able to access and edit. However, you don't want your kids to be able to open or edit it. How would you do this? Obviously you'd want to place the file in a location where your spouse could get to it, such as your own Public folder or the Shared user folder. However, here's where the dilemma begins. If you don't provide access to the file to Others, your spouse can't access the file. If you open access to Others, your spouse can access it, but so can your kids. Hmm…you could change ownership of the file to your spouse, but then you would no longer be able to access it. If only there was a way to provide Read & Write access to you and your spouse, but restrict everyone else to No Access. The good news is that there *is* a way—groups. The bad news is that Mac OS X doesn't make groups easy to use. Lucky for you, you bought this book, because I'm going to show you how.

In the discussion of permissions, I explained that every file or folder has three sets of permissions: *Owner*, *Group*, and *Others*. I also mentioned that groups—called such because they are simply groups of user accounts—are a way to create a subset of users, and to give them access that is different from the access given to Others. If you provide a certain level of file access to a group, each member of that group inherits the group's permissions. Anyone not in the group (and who is not the owner of the file) will maintain the level of access given to Others. Each user can belong to any number of groups, and groups can both overlap or be completely independent.

For example, in a large company, you could have groups for the *finance* department, the *IT* office, and the *marketing* group. Another group (*employees*) could contain all the people in all of these groups, while a group called *executives* might contain only the heads of each department. In fact, this concept of groups is exactly how most file servers and large corporate networks keep track of users and user access.

Thus, if we return to the family example I gave, you can create a new group called "Parents" and include your own user account and that of your spouse. You would then give the group Parents Read & Write access to the file in question, and restrict Others to No Access. Finally, you would place the document in a location where your spouse could access it, such as your Public folder.

TIP Although you can give a group of users access to a file, remember that they must be able to *view* that file to use it. Thus if you give a group of users Read & Write access to a spreadsheet, but that spreadsheet is located inside your home folder (and is not in your Public folder), no one in the group will be able to access because your home folder is off-limits. Thus you must place the file in a "public" location such as your Public folder or the Shared user folder. (For more information on the Public and Shared folders, see Chapter 10)

Unfortunately, as I mentioned, OS X doesn't make creating groups very easy. In the sections that follow, I'll explain how to create new groups of users, then I'll talk about editing group permissions.

Creating a Group

User Level: admin
Affects: several users
Terminal: no

Apple's solution for creating and editing groups in OS X is NetInfo Manager. While this method isn't the most intuitive process, it works. You can also create and edit groups using the excellent donationware, SharePoints. I'll explain both methods here.

Creating a Group Using NetInfo Manager

To create a group using the "official" method, we come back to NetInfo Manager. Use the following steps to create a new group called Parents (no, the actual users in this example are not parents yet, but let's pretend for a moment that they are).

1. Open NetInfo Manager, then authenticate (click the padlock and enter your admin account password). You *did* backup your NetInfo database, didn't you?
2. In the second column of the browser pane of NetInfo Manager (the / level), click *groups*.
3. Although you could create a new group from scratch, it's much easier to simply copy another group and modify it. In the groups column to the right, select *guest*, and then click the Duplicate icon in the toolbar (the icon that looks like two folders). You will get an alert box asking you if you really want to duplicate the directory. Yes, you really do.
4. A new group is created called *guest copy*. Select this new group.
5. In the bottom (Property and Value) pane, double-click *guest copy* in the Value(s) column to edit the name of the group. For this example, we'll name it *Parents* (Figure 1.15).
6. Double-click the number for *gid* (*gid*, also seen as *GID*, stands for group ID)—since every group must have a unique group ID number, and our group currently has the same gid as the "guest" group, we need to change the gid to something different from all other gids. You could go through each group, write down each gid, and then choose one that isn't in use, but since user-created gid numbers are expected to be in the range of 100 to 199, it's easier just to

just start with 151 and work up from there. (You could start with 101, but if you or another user has already created a group or groups, you might stumble over an existing GID).

7. Next you want to add users to the group. Select the Property *users*, then choose Directory ➢ Insert Value. This inserts a new user value called `new_value`, highlighted for editing. Type in the *short* username of the user you wish to add to the group. You can use the Insert Value command as many times as you need to add all of the users you wish to include in this group.
8. When you've finished adding users, choose Domain ➢ Save Changes to save the changes you made. The group's name will change from *guest copy* to *Parents*.

You can repeat this process as many times as you want in order to create new groups. In addition, you can edit groups (or edit the users in a group) in the same way. To delete a group, you simply select the group name, then click on the Delete button in the toolbar (the large icon that looks like a "No Parking" sign). To delete a user from a group, you would simply select the group, then select the username in the users property, then choose Edit ➢ Delete.

NOTE When you give a user admin access, you are actually telling the OS to add that user to several special groups, including *admin* and *wheel*.

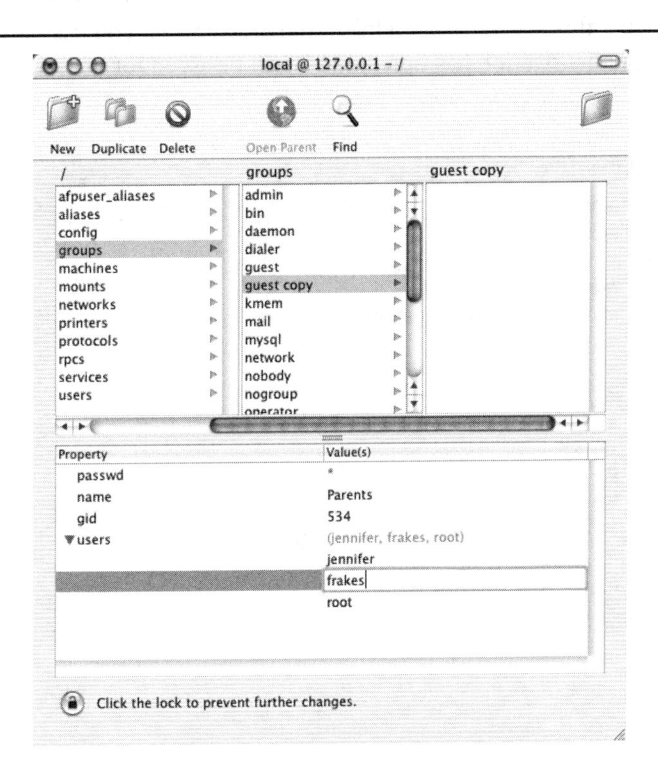

FIGURE 1.15: Creating a new group, *Parents*, in NetInfo Manager

Creating a Group Using SharePoints

An easier way to create and edit groups is to use the excellent SharePoints, `http://www.hornware.com/sharepoints/`. You can use it as either an application or as a System Preferences pane. In Chapter 2 we'll talk about installing and using Preference panes, but for now we'll use the application (both the application and the Preferences pane work the same).

1. Launch SharePoints, then authenticate (click the padlock and enter your admin account password). Yes, you should still back up your NetInfo database before using SharePoints, since it edits your database.
2. Click the Groups tab in the SharePoints window.
3. In the Group text entry field, enter the group name (for our example, Parents).
4. In the GID (group ID) field, enter the GID you wish to use for this group. Before you do, though, notice the Get Next GID button to the right. Unlike creating a group in NetInfo Manager, where you have to figure out or guess a good group ID number, SharePoints does the work for you—clicking this button automatically enters the next available GID into the field. Go ahead, click it (Figure 1.16).
5. To create the new group, click the Add New Group button; you'll be presented with an alert box asking if you're sure you want to create the new group. Sure you do, so click Yes. (At this point, if you didn't authenticate when you first launched SharePoints, or if your authentication has timed out, you'll be asked for your admin username and password.) The new group appears in the group list.

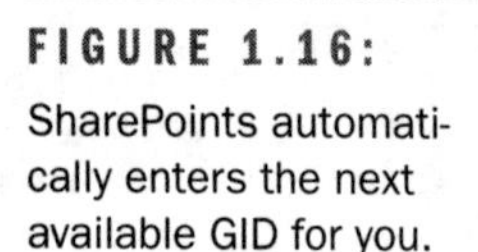

FIGURE 1.16: SharePoints automatically enters the next available GID for you.

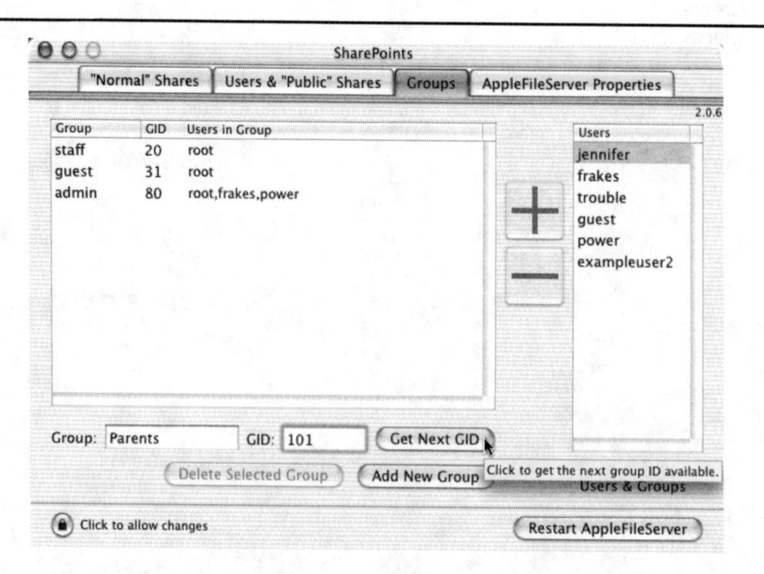

6. Now that your group exists, you need to add users to it. In the group list on the left, select the new group (Parents, or whatever you used for your new group name). In the Users list on the right, select a user by clicking the username, or select multiple users by clicking multiple usernames while holding down the command key. Then click the large plus (+) button to add the users to the group. The users will appear in the Users in Group column.
7. In order to make the changes stick, you must click the Update Group button (previously the Add New Group button). This will save your changes.

Repeat this process to create multiple new groups. You can also edit groups in this same window. To delete a group, select the group and then click the Delete Selected Group button. To simply remove users from a group, select the group on the left, select the usernames on the right, and then click the large minus (–) button to remove them.

Now you're an expert at users and groups in Mac OS X. Well, almost. Before you can proudly wear your "Users and Groups Xpert" button, you need to learn how to work with group permissions.

Changing/Setting Group Permissions

User Level: owner of a file/folder
Affects: users in the group
Terminal: no

When a file is created, the owner is set to the user who created it, and the group it belongs to is generally set to *staff*. If you look at the staff group in NetInfo Manager or SharePoints, you see that the members of the group are…well…root. This is a bit misleading, because in reality, every user is a part of the staff group. This means that since the default permissions for the staff group is Read only, if you move a document from your user folder to a publicly accessible folder, anyone can open that document. (What's more, the default permissions for Others is also Read only.) But since you generally keep private documents in your private home folders, this isn't too much of a problem. It's when you move documents to publicly accessible folders that you want to restrict access, and where group permissions become important.

Fortunately, with the release of OS X 10.2, changing group ownership and group permissions is an area where Apple has made things much easier than in previous versions of the Mac OS. In fact, changing group ownership and group permissions is built into the Finder itself. However, and I consider this unfortunate, only an admin user can change group ownership.

Select a document in your home folder (I'll use `sample.doc` as an example), and choose File ➢ Get Info. In the Info window, click the disclosure triangle next to Ownership & Permissions to expand the permissions area. Most likely, you'll see that the Owner is set to your username with Read & Write permissions, and the group is set to staff with Read only permissions. You'll also see that you can change the permissions for Owner, Group, and Others by simply selecting the appropriate access level from the pop-up menus. However, the Owner and Group names are inaccessible.

As I mentioned, if your account does not have admin access, you cannot change the Owner and Group. However, admin users can click the padlock button to unlock these fields. For example, I can change the Group owner of `sample.doc` from staff to our new group, Parents (Figure 1.17), and provide that group with Read & Write access, while limiting to Others to No Access. When I make the change, I'm asked for my admin username and password. After I enter it, the change is made and `sample.doc` now belongs to the Parent group. It's really that simple. Now I can move `sample.doc` into the Shared user folder or my Public folder inside my home folder, and only the members of Parents will be able to access it; other users else will be able to see that it's there, but they won't be able to open it or copy it. (Note that non-admin users can also click the padlock to unlock it, but since they will not be able to provide an admin username and password, any changes they make will not stick.)

TIP

In OS X 10.1.5 and earlier, it simply wasn't possible for a user—even an admin user—to change group ownership or permissions without using Terminal or a third-party utility. For those who are still using version 10.1.5 or earlier and want to change group permissions, I recommend the excellent shareware utilities BatChmod (`http://macchampion.com/arbysoft/`), FileXaminer (`http://www.gideonsoftworks.com/filexaminer.html`), File Buddy (`http://www.skytag.com/filebuddy/`), or XRay (`http://www.brockerhoff.net/xray/`). XRay's interface is the closest to the Finder's Get Info window, but all are excellent utilities. I'll talk about all of them elsewhere in the book.

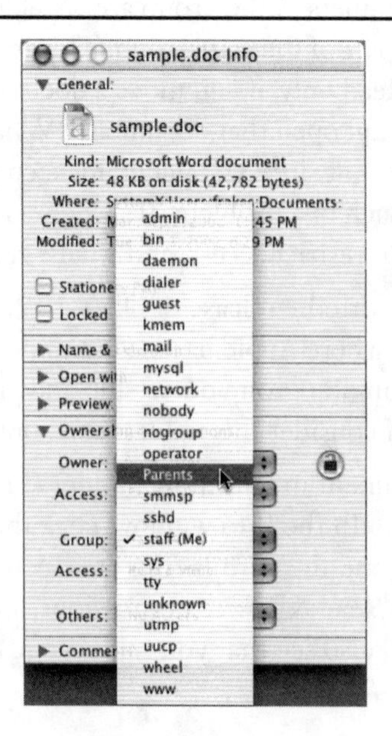

FIGURE 1.17: Changing the Group for a file using the Finder's Get Info window

Unfortunately, there is currently no way to assign a file to multiple groups in Mac OS X; if you need to give two or more groups of people access to a file (but don't want to open access to "everyone"), you'll need to create a new group that includes all of the users from those groups.

Why Did I Ever Pick That Name? (Changing Your Short Username)

I mentioned in the section on editing user accounts that although you can easily change your full username, it's very difficult to change your short username once you've created an account. This is generally a good thing, as it avoids potential problems with things such as folder locations, permissions, and group membership. However, although the OS discourages changing the short username, it is actually possible. I suspect that Apple will provide a way to easily change the short username in a future version of Mac OS X, but for now, the following procedures are how you have to do it.

There are actually two ways to change the short username. Any admin user can perform the first method; the second, which is a bit shorter, requires actually logging in as the root account. You could do this in Terminal, as well, but this is one case where you want to give extra special thanks that NetInfo Manager exists.

Changing the Short Username without Logging In as Root

User Level: admin
Affects: individual user
Terminal: yes

If you don't have the root user enabled, or you're uncomfortable logging in as root, this is the way to go:

1. Open NetInfo Manager, then authenticate (click the padlock and enter your admin account password). You *did* backup your NetInfo database, didn't you?
2. In the "/" column of the browser pane of NetInfo Manager (the / level), click on "groups."
3. In the groups column that appears, select wheel.
4. In the bottom (Property and Value) pane, click on the disclosure triangle next to users (this will reveal the user accounts in the wheel group).
5. If the short username you wish to change is listed here, double-click it in the Value(s) field; change it to the new short username. (If the username you're changing isn't a member of this group, skip this step and go to Step 6.)
6. Back in the browser pane, in the same column as groups, select users (if you made any changes to wheel, it will ask you if you want to save them when you click a different directory—yes, you want to save them).
7. In the users column that appears to the right, select the name of the user you want to change.

8. In the bottom (Property and Value) pane, change every instance of the old short username to the new short username (Figure 1.18). Generally, these are `_writers_passwd`, `name`, `_writers_picture`, and `home` (change **`/Users/oldusername`** to **`/Users/newusername`**), but it's possible to have more, depending on the account. If *realname* has the same value as *name*, it's because the account uses the same name for both short and long usernames.
9. In the browser pane, again click groups (yes, you want to save the changes you made to the user).
10. In the list of groups to the right, select admin.
11. In the bottom (Property and Value) pane, click on the disclosure triangle next to users (this will reveal the user accounts in the admin group).
12. If the short username you wish to change is listed here, double-click it in the Value(s) field; change it to the new short username. (If the username you're changing isn't a member of this group, skip to Step 13.)
13. If you've created any other groups that include this user account, you'll also want to change the short username in those groups as you did with wheel and admin.
14. Choose Domain ➢ Save; quit NetInfo Manager.

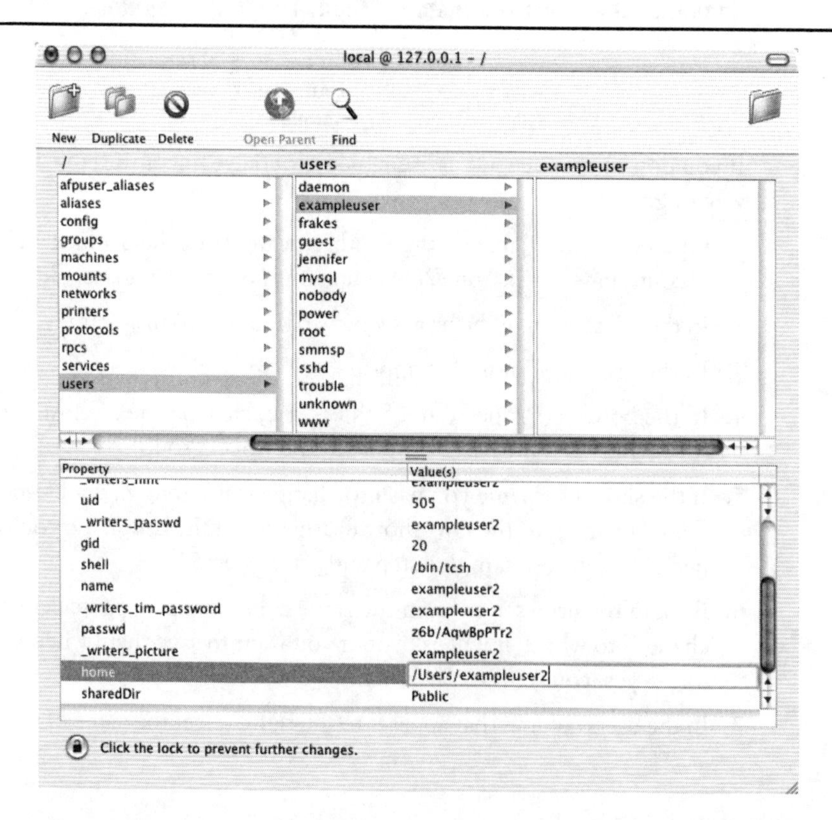

FIGURE 1.18: Changing the Short Name of *exampleuser* to *exampleuser2*

15. Open Terminal, and type the following command:

```
sudo  mv /Users/oldshortusername /Users/newshortusername <RETURN>
```

You'll be asked for your password to execute the command. This changes the name of the appropriate user folder from the old short name to the new short name.

16. Still in Terminal, type the following command:

```
cd /Users/newshortusername/Library/Keychains
sudo  mv oldusername newusername <RETURN>
```

This command renames the user's keychain so that it works properly with the new username.

17. If you ever use Web Sharing, type the following command in Terminal (if you don't use Web Sharing, skip to Step 19):

```
cd /etc/httpd/users <RETURN>
sudo mv oldshortusername.conf newshortusername.conf <RETURN>
```

This updates the Web Sharing configuration for the user account.

18. If you use Web Sharing, open the file you just renamed (`/etc/httpd/users/`*`newshort-username`*)—since it's owned by root, you'll have to use a text editor such as BBEdit Lite via Pseudo, as described earlier in this chapter—and change the line

```
Directory "/Users/oldusername/Sites/"
```

to

```
Directory "/Users/newusername/Sites/"
```

This tells the Mac OS X web server where the user's web documents folder is at; if the user is actually using a different location for their personal web server documents (you'll know if you are), then edit this file appropriately.

19. The short username of the account should now be changed. Phew! If you are actually logged in as that user, you should immediately log out and back in.

Changing the Short Username by Logging In as Root

User Level:	root
Affects:	individual user
Terminal:	no

If you've enabled the root user, you can log out, then log back in as root and use the following procedure. It's a bit quicker, and doesn't require Terminal, but does exactly the same thing as the earlier instructions:

1. Open NetInfo Manager, then authenticate (click the padlock and enter your root account password). You *did* backup your NetInfo database, didn't you?
2. In the "/" column of the browser pane of NetInfo Manager, click on groups.
3. In the groups column that appears, select admin.

4. In the bottom (Property and Value) pane, click on the disclosure triangle next to users (this will reveal the user accounts in the admin group).
5. If the short username you wish to change is listed here, double-click it in the Value(s) field; change it to the new short username. (If the username you're changing isn't in this group, skip to Step 9.)
6. Back in the browser pane, in the same column as admin, select the wheel group (yes, you want to save the changes to admin that you just made—it will ask you when you click a different group).
7. In the Property and Value(s) pane, click the disclosure triangle next to users (this will reveal the user accounts in the wheel group).
8. In the Value(s) column, click the short username you want to change; change it to the new short username.
9. Back in the browser window, in the same column as groups, select users (yes, you want to save your changes).
10. In the new users column to the right, select the name of the user you want to change.
11. In the Property and Values pane, change every instance of the old short username to the new short username. Generally, these are `_writers_passwd`, `name`, `_writers_picture`, and `home` (change ***/Users/oldusername*** to ***/Users/newusername***), but it's possible to have more, depending on the account. If *realname* has the same value as *name*, it's because the account uses the same name for both short and long usernames.
12. Choose Domain ➢ Save; quit NetInfo Manager.
13. In the Finder, go to the `/Users` directory. Change the name of the appropriate user folder from ***oldshortusername*** to ***newshortusername***.
14. In the Finder, go to the `/Users/`*`newshortusername`*`/Library/Keychains` folder. Change the name of the Keychain document from *`oldshortusername`* to *`newshortusername`*. This renames the user's keychain so that it works properly with the new username.
15. If your computer ever uses Web Sharing, go to the `/etc/httpd/users` directory in the Finder. Change the name of the appropriate document from *`oldshortusername`*`.conf` to *`newshortusername`*`.conf`. This changes the Web Sharing configuration for that user account. (If you don't use Web Sharing, skip to Step 17).
16. Open the file you just renamed (`/etc/httpd/users/`*`newshortusername`*) and change the line

    ```
    Directory "/Users/oldusername/Sites/"
    ```

    to

    ```
    Directory "/Users/newusername/Sites/"
    ```

This tells the web server where the user's web documents folder is located. If the user is using a different location for their web server documents, edit this file appropriately.

17. The short username of the account should now be changed. Log out of root. Log back in using your own account.

Apple has actually posted a set of instructions for changing the short username of an account. However, I personally am not a fan of Apple's instructions for four reasons:

- They *require* you to log in as root; there is no option to follow their instructions without enabling the root account.
- Apple's instructions hadn't been updated for Jaguar, so they were inaccurate due to changes made to the OS between 10.1.5 and 10.2.
- Rather than actually changing a user's short username, Apple's procedure has you create a new user, transfer everything from the old user's account to the new user's account, and then delete the old user. I find this to be messier than simply changing a user's actual short username.
- Apple's instructions do not take into account any group memberships the user may have that need to be updated, nor does it take into account any files or folders throughout the OS, but not in the user's home directory, that may be owned by the user—important if the user is an admin.

All that said, if you'd like to use, or just peruse, Apple's own instructions visit `http://docs.info.apple.com/article.html?artnum=106824`.

Create a No-Password Account

User Level: normal or admin
Affects: individual user
Terminal: no

If you're the *only* user of your machine—or don't have any reason to keep others out of your account—you may find it convenient to not have a password. Anytime you're asked for your password you can simply press Return rather than having to type in a password. This can be especially convenient if you're an admin user, since you'll be asked for your password whenever you make system-level changes and many times when you install software.

Before I explain how to do this, I should include a serious caveat: If your account is an admin-level account and you're either *not* the only user, or you're running *any* remote services (as described in Chapters 10 and 11), you should *always* have a password. An admin account without a password is the worst security risk possible. Anyone who walks up to your computer or connects to it over a network or the Internet can do pretty much anything they want, including enabling the root account and changing your personal account password so that you can no longer log in.

NOTE Keep in mind that if you're the only user of your machine, unless you've created an extra non-admin account your account will have admin access.

You can't remove the password from your account from the My Account preference pane; you have to use the Accounts pane. Click your user account and then click the Edit User... button. Enter your current password, then leave the New Password and Verify fields blank. When you click the OK button, you'll get a dialog warning you about not setting a password (Figure 1.19); click Ignore to continue. Your account now has *no* password, and you can simply hit the return key, or press the OK button, whenever you're prompted for a password.

FIGURE 1.19:

OS X warns you if your account does not have a password.

NOTE Some Mac OS updates require a non-blank password; if you've set your password to be blank and you want to install an OS X update, you should first change your password to a non-blank one using Accounts preferences. After the install is complete you can change your password back to its previous (blank) state.

Moving On...

Hopefully at this point you thoroughly understand the concepts of users, groups, file permissions, and Mac OS X's file organization. While these may not be the most exciting topics, they provide the basis for nearly everything else you'll do in the rest of the book. Having a good handle on these issues means you're ready to start getting into the fun stuff. We start with setup and preferences.

Chapter 2

Sensational Setup

(Or: Making your Mac work the way you *want.)*

As someone who's been using Mac OS X for a while now, you've probably used the System Preferences utility to customize your OS X preferences, and you've probably changed a few settings in applications, or maybe even in the Finder. Even if you just started using Mac OS X, you had to set up a few things when you first started your Mac (remember the Setup Assistant?). However, chances are there are still many settings you don't know exist, a few you don't quite understand, and ways of setting them up you've never even thought of.

System Preferences: Beyond the Basics

Most of the ways you can customize Mac OS X's built-in features can be found in the System Preferences application (`/Applications/System Preferences`), easily accessible from the Apple menu (Apple Menu ➢ System Preferences). Whereas in Mac OS 9 you had a folder full of individual control panels, System Preferences provides you with a smorgasbord of settings, all in a single window (Figure 2.1).

Each icon and name represents a topic-specific collection of settings that you can customize; if you click an icon, the window will present that group of settings to you for editing. For example, click the Desktop icon and System Preferences will present you with system settings that relate to the appearance of your Desktop. Each of these topical collections of preferences is called a *panel* or *pane* (the two terms are used interchangeably).

While many settings throughout System Preferences are self-explanatory, many others are not; in addition, some options are less than obvious—unless you know to look for them, you might never even know they exist! For this reason, I'm going to spend a good deal of this chapter covering the System Preferences application, the various panels within System Preferences, and how to best take advantage of them. Although any user can access any pane, some sets of preferences are only modifiable by admin users; when I discuss each pane, I note the access level required to change settings. I'll also include ways to expand the number of options Mac OS X provides.

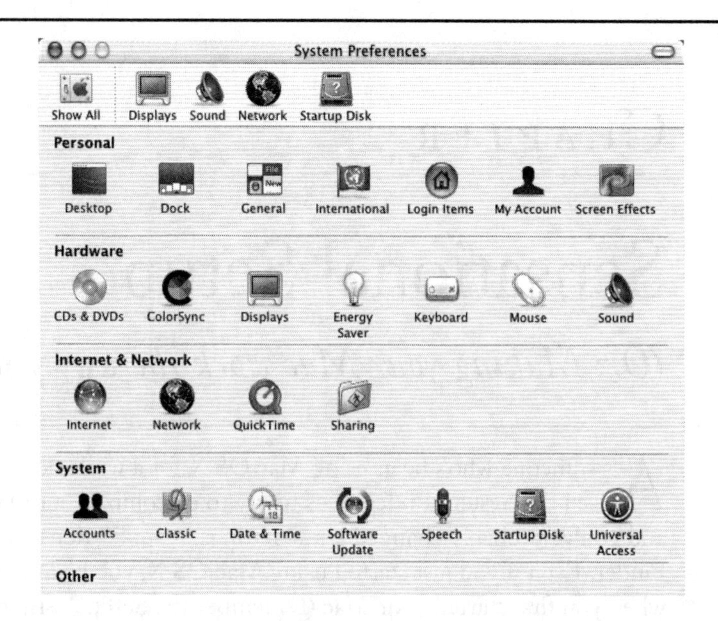

FIGURE 2.1: The System Preferences application

In addition, I'm going to talk about how to add preference panes to System Preferences, how to change preferences that aren't contained in System Preferences, and how to find and edit preference files directly.

The System Preferences Application

As I already mentioned, System Preferences is actually an application. When you launch it (either by selecting System Preferences from the Apple Menu, by clicking on the System Preferences icon in the Dock, or by manually launching it from your `/Applications` folder), you see it in the Dock just like any other application. It then provides you with groups of related preference settings, each represented by icon and name (e.g., Desktop, Displays, Mouse, Sound). However, as an application, it also provides you with other options than what you first see when you launch it.

View Alphabetically or by Category

By default, the various preference panes are arranged in categories that signify what part of your Mac they modify: Personal, Hardware, Internet & Network, System, and Other. (I'll talk about each of these categories, and the individual preference panels within them, in a bit.) While these categories can be helpful for some users, others are accustomed to looking for files alphabetically. Luckily, System Preferences provides that option, as well: select View ➢ Show All Alphabetically, and the categories disappear; the panes are then listed in alphabetical order.

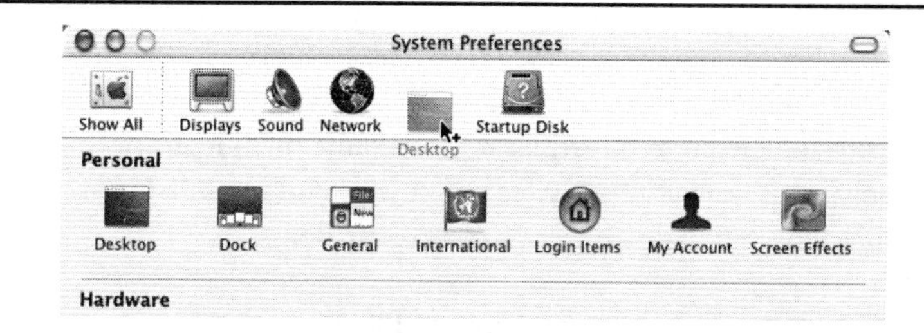

FIGURE 2.2: Adding a preference pane to the toolbar

Access Preference Panels Directly

If you'd rather not deal with icons at all, you can select any preference pane from an alphabetical list by choosing the appropriate panel name from the View menu. If a System Preferences window is already open, it changes to the appropriate pane; if you've closed the main System Preferences window, a new window appears with the chosen pane. This is also a helpful tip to use when switching between preference panes. Rather than having to click the Show All icon, and then choose another pane, you can simply choose the pane you wish to switch to and skip the middle step.

Pick Your Favorites and Customize the Toolbar

As you read this book, you'll find that most Mac OS X applications allow you to customize the toolbar—the area at the top of an application's window—and System Preferences is no exception. You can choose your favorite preference panes, and you can change how the toolbar appears.

Pick Your Preferred Panes

You'll notice that a few preference pane icons appear in the area to the right of the Show All icon. This area (the toolbar) in System Preferences is intended to be a place for you to put your most frequently used preference panes for easy access. To add a pane, simply select its icon from the main window and drag it to the toolbar; it will be added wherever you drop it (Figure 2.2). If you drag the icon between two existing icons, they'll spread apart to accommodate the new one.

You can also rearrange your favorites in the toolbar by dragging them left and right; again, the other icons will move apart to let you place each icon where you want it.

If you decide you no longer want a particular pane in the toolbar (or you want to remove one of the default items that was there from the beginning), simply drag its icon from the toolbar down into the main window area. You'll see an animated puff of smoke to indicate that it has been removed from the toolbar (it will still be available from the main pane window, of course).

Customize the Toolbar's Appearance

Here's one of those hidden features I was talking about. In the upper right of the System Preferences window is a clear, capsule-shaped button (often called the "toolbar widget"). You may have clicked this button and discovered that it collapses the toolbar so that only the main list of preference panes is visible. However, it does more that just that. Command-click on the button, and you'll find that it cycles through various toolbar views: large icons and text; small icons and text, large icons only, small icons only, large text only, and small text only. This is a very handy feature if you tend to put a lot of your favorite panes in the toolbar, since you can make the icons or text smaller.

Other Ways to Access Preference Panes

One major difference between changing system-level preferences in OS X and changing them in OS 9 is that in OS 9 you could go to the Apple Menu and select the appropriate control panel directly; in OS X, you have to first open System Preferences, and *then* choose the set of preferences you wish to modify. Fortunately, enterprising software developers have provided solutions for this minor inconvenience. In addition, you can even create your own solution with a bit of work.

Access from the Apple Menu

User level: admin to install, normal to modify
Affects: one or more users
Terminal: no

Users who have moved to OS X from OS 9 probably find themselves looking for control panels in the Apple Menu, sometimes even after weeks or months of use. Apple provided quick access to System Preferences in the Apple Menu, but, unfortunately, didn't provide the convenient sub-menu of settings panes you might expect. That can be easily fixed with the excellent shareware FruitMenu (`http://www.unsanity.com/`), which provides you with a System Preferences sub-menu (Figure 2.3). FruitMenu actually does *much* more than this, and I'll talk about it in several other places in the book.

Access from the Menu Bar

User level: admin to install, normal to modify
Affects: one or more users
Terminal: no

In addition to accessing individual preference panes from the Apple Menu, it's also possible to access them from a separate menu in the menu bar. My favorite utility for doing this is the shareware Snard (the menu version, `http://www.gideonsoftworks.com`), which provides a comprehensive menu with lots of features (again, one I'll talk more about later). One of those features is a hierarchical System Preferences sub-menu, sorted either alphabetically or by category. The freeware Menuprefs (`http://ksuther.dyndns.org/software/`) is another good choice, dedicated to doing nothing else but providing an elegant (and configurable) Preference Pane menu in the menu bar.

FIGURE 2.3:

FruitMenu provides a System Preferences sub-menu in the Apple Menu.

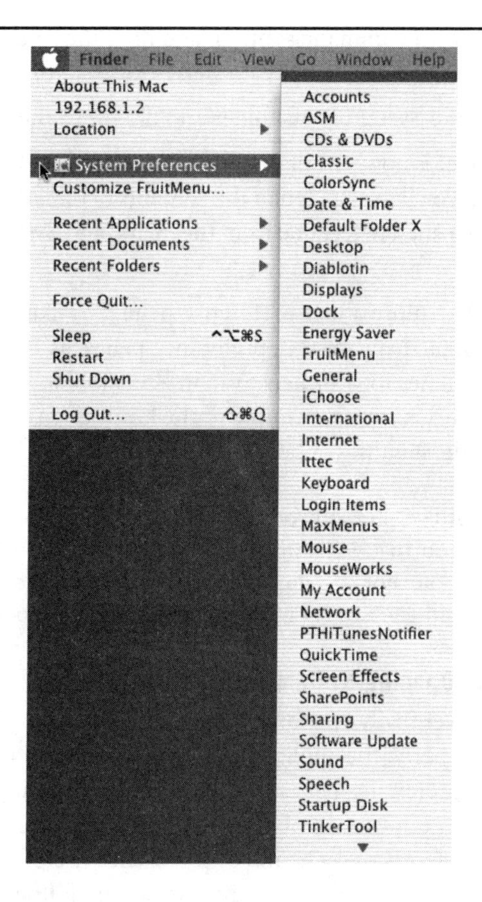

Access from the Dock

User level: any
Affects: individual users
Terminal: no

While there used to be a number of utilities, called Docklings, that provided a System Preferences menu from the Dock, most of them no longer work—Apple discontinued support for Docklings as of OS X 10.2. However, it is still possible to get such a menu from the Dock. One way is by using the Dock version of Snard (the utility I mentioned in the previous section). But a free, though less elegant, method is also within your reach.

1. In the Finder, create a new folder (File ➢ New Folder, or shift+command+N) inside your user folder, and call it *System Prefs*.
2. Open the `/System/Library/Preference Panes` folder.
3. Select all of the files inside the folder (they should all end in `.prefPane`).

4. Hold down command+option, and drag the selected files into your newly created System Prefs folder. This will create aliases for each of these files in the System Prefs folder.
5. Select the System Prefs folder and drag it to the right side of the Dock.

The folder is now part of the Dock; if you click and hold on the folder in the Dock, or control-click on it, you'll get a menu of the contents of the folder, which just so happen to be all of your preference panes. Select one from the menu, and System Preferences will immediately open to that pane.

I'll explain more about preference pane files like these later in the chapter. In addition, if you've installed any custom preference panes, as I discuss later in the chapter, you'll need to add their aliases to your new System Prefs folder, as well. But I'm getting ahead of myself. For now, this is just an example of the kinds of customization you can do in Mac OS X with a little understanding of how things work and a bit of creativity.

NOTE Now that I've showed you the manual method to do this, I'm going to tell you that you don't need to do it that way—instead you can download the freeware Dockprefs (`http://ksuther.dyndns.org/software/`), by the same people who provide Menuprefs (mentioned earlier). For more on Dockprefs and Dock customization, see Chapter 6.

Problems Opening System Preferences?

You may eventually encounter a situation where the System Preferences application doesn't behave properly: the application refuses to launch; it crashes when you launch it; it launches but some preference panes don't appear, or some appear more than once; or the application just behaves oddly. One of the most common reasons for this sort of behavior is a corrupt System Preferences cache file or preference file. If you find yourself having such problems, quit System Preferences, and then delete the following two files:

- `~/Library/Caches/com.apple.preferencepanes.cache`
- `~/Library/Preferences/com.apple.systempreferences.plist`

There's a good chance that the next time you launch System Preferences the problem will be gone.

Now it's time to talk about the preference panes themselves. I've divided them into categories to mirror the default display of System Preferences (on an English-language system, to be perfectly accurate; on non-English systems they are arranged differently).

The Personal Preferences Category

Apple calls this category of preference panes "personal" because they include preferences that only affect your personal account. I find this name a bit misleading, however, because it implies that changes made in the panes not included in this category affect more than just your account; in fact, most of them do not. Nevertheless, most of those included here do seem to be personal in their nature.

Desktop

User level: any
Affects: individual user
Terminal: no

The Desktop pane provides you with the ability to change the background of your desktop. You simply select a folder of images from the Collection pop-up menu, and then click one of the pictures in the preview list to change your Desktop to that image. You can choose from one of the folders of images Apple has provided, your own `~/Pictures` folder, or any other folder of images on your hard drive (by selecting Choose Folder…). OS X supports many different file types for Desktop backgrounds: JPEG, GIF, TIFF, PICT, even PDF files. Finally, by clicking the Change picture: box, you can choose to have your desktop picture changed automatically every login, every time from sleep, or at predefined time intervals. If you have multiple monitors attached, you will get a screen for each display to allow you to have different Desktop settings for each.

TIP To quickly access the Desktop preferences, control-click anywhere on the Desktop and select Change Desktop Background from the contextual menu.

There is also a hidden option here. If you select an image that is smaller than your screen (generally from a folder of your own choosing), you'll get a pop-up menu to choose whether the picture should be tiled across the entire screen; displayed at normal size in the center of the screen; fill the screen using its current aspect ratio; or stretched to fill the screen, not necessarily preserving its width/height ratio.

TIP If you select a custom folder for Desktop pictures, only photos at the top level of that folder will appear as options in the preview window; OS X will not look inside sub-folders.

Adding Permanent Folders to the Collection Menu

User level: admin
Affects: all users
Terminal: no

If you frequently choose your own folder of pictures, the most recently used folder will remain in the Collection pop-up menu. However, once you choose another folder, the previous custom folder is removed and the new folder takes its place. What if you want to add your own folders to the Collection menu and have them remain there permanently?

The Apple Background Images (the default images) are actually JPEG image files located at `/Library/Desktop Pictures`. The images included in the Collection menu are the folders of images installed by Mac OS X into that directory (Abstract, Nature, etc.). You would think that by simply creating a new folder inside, it would add that folder to the Collection menu. Unfortunately, it's not that easy. You actually need to edit a hidden file inside the Desktop preference pane itself, and you need root access to do it. While it's possible to edit this file with a text editor, we're going to use the developer tool Property List Editor, located at `/Developer/Applications/Property List Editor` (here's where installing the Developer Tools comes in handy).

First you're going to back up the existing file:

1. In the Finder, navigate to `/System/Library/PreferencePanes/DesktopPictures.prefPane`.
2. Control-click on `Desktop Pictures.prefPane`, and select Show Package Contents from the contextual menu.
3. In the resulting window, navigate to `/Contents/Resources`.
4. Copy the file `Collections.plist` to your user folder (option-drag it to copy it).

Now that you have a safe, unmodified backup of the file, we're going to edit the original to include a new folder. For this example, I'm going to include a folder called "Shared Desktop Pictures," located inside the Shared user folder.

1. Quit System Preferences if it is running.
2. Using your favorite utility, open Property List Editor as root (as described in Chapter 1).
3. In Property List Editor, select File ➢ Open… and navigate to `/System/Library/PreferencePanes/DesktopPictures.prefPane/Contents/Resources/Collections.plist`. Open this file.
4. You'll see a window with a Property List; the only one listed is Root. Click the disclosure triangle next to Root to display the properties contained in it. The resulting properties are the selections in the Collection menu in the Desktop preferences pane. You can click each property's disclosure triangle to see the various properties contained within it. We're going to create a new property for our folder.
5. Click Root, then click the New Child button in the toolbar. A new property will be created, probably with the number 0 as its name. In the Class column, select the menu for line 0 and choose **`Dictionary`** (Figure 2.4).
6. Click the disclosure triangle next to line 0. (Don't worry if you don't see anything after doing this; there's nothing there yet.) Highlight property 0, and click the New Child button. Change the name of the new property from New item to **`identifier`** (double-click the field if it isn't already editable). Make sure the Class is **`String`**. Change the value of the property to **`Shared Pictures`** (or whatever you would like to name your new collection—this is the name as it will appear in the Collection menu).
7. Click the line you just edited, and then click the New Sibling button in the toolbar. This will create another property at the same level as the previous one. Change the name of the property to path, make sure its Class is String, and change the Value to the path to the folder of pictures (in my case, **`/Users/Shared/Shared Desktop Pictures`**).

FIGURE 2.4:

Creating a new property in the Desktop Pictures Collections menu

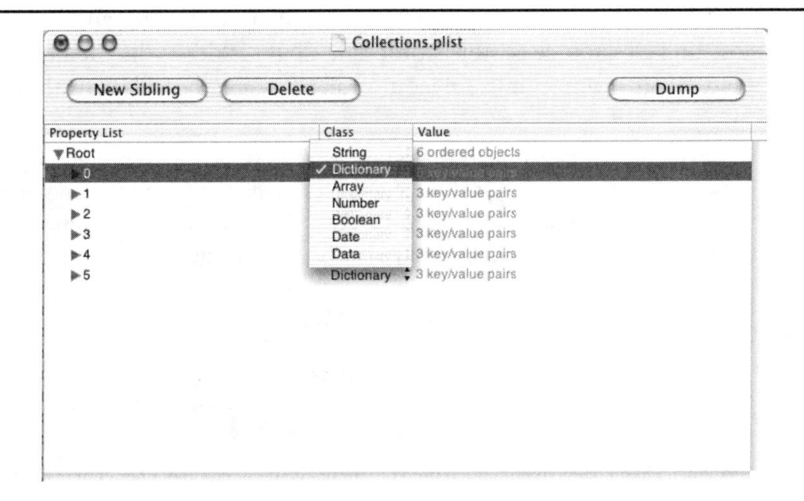

WARNING If you add a folder to the Collections menu, you're actually altering the Desktop preferences pane. Therefore, the new folder must be accessible by *all* users; don't use a folder inside your home folder.

8. If you'd like to see the Fill/Stretch/Center/Tile menu for the pictures in this collection, add one more sibling (click the path property and click the New Sibling button). Change the name to **`showScalingPopUp`**, make sure it's a String class, and change the Value to **`YES`**.
9. When you're done, choose File ➢ Save to save your changes.

The next time you launch System Preferences and select the Desktop pane, your folder of images will be listed in the Collection menu. You can add and remove pictures at will, making this one of the most convenient ways to get quick access to custom images.

Using iPhoto Albums as a Revolving Desktop

User level: any
Affects: individual user
Terminal: no

As I mentioned earlier, you can choose any single folder of images on your computer and then click the Change picture box to have OS X automatically rotate your Desktop between the pictures in that folder. Albums you've created in iPhoto would seem to be the perfect match for such a feature… except that iPhoto stores your pictures in myriad folders, all with incomprehensible names, inside the `~/Pictures` folder. In addition, OS X will only use pictures present at the top level of any selected folder, so since iPhoto stores photos in many different sub-folders, it wouldn't work even if you knew which top-level folder to choose.

Luckily, when iPhoto creates an album, it creates a new folder for that album (using the album name as the folder name) inside `~/Users/`*`shortusername`*`/Pictures/iPhoto Library/Albums`, and places aliases to each photo in the album inside. If you want to use one of your albums for a rotating Desktop, select the appropriate album folder in the Albums directory, and you'll be up and running with your latest vacation album doing the slideshow thing on your Desktop.

NOTE If you have a newer Mac that supports the Quartz Extreme graphics technology of OS X 10.2 and later, when Desktop pictures change they'll fade in and out beautifully. On older Macs, the pictures will simply switch. To find out if your video card supports Quartz Extreme, check out `http://www.apple.com/macosx/jaguar/quartzextreme.html`.

Rotate Photos from Multiple Folders

User level: any
Affects: individual user
Terminal: no

While Mac OS X by itself doesn't allow you to rotate Desktop photos from multiple locations, and it doesn't browse sub-folders for enclosed pictures, you can do these things quite easily with third-party software. My personal favorite is the freeware ChangeDesktop by Brian Bergstrand (`http://www.classicalguitar.net/brian/software/changedesktop/`). In addition to doing everything Mac OS X's Desktop preference pane can do, it allows you to pick any number of folders full of pictures and enable or disable them from the rotation at will. It also lets you "publish" your desktop picture to the web or any FTP server, and has extra options for things like iPhoto archives. Even better, it also provides the option to add a menu item to the menu bar for easy access.

There is actually one more, really cool, Desktop tip that I have to tell you about, but I'm going to save it until I talk about the Screen Effects preferences.

Dock

The Dock pane is where you customize the appearance and behavior of the Dock. Because I dedicate an entire chapter to the Dock (Chapter 6), and because my editors don't want me to repeat myself too much, I'm going to simply refer you to that chapter for all the nitty-gritty.

General

The General pane of System Preferences is a bit of a hodgepodge of settings. The settings here are ones that don't seem to fit anywhere else. Most are fairly self-explanatory: the colors of buttons and menus, the color for highlighted text, the behavior and look of scroll bars. However, a few deserve a quick mention, and a couple others can actually be modified to a greater extent than the General panel would have you believe.

Number of Recent Items

The Number of Recent Items settings actually refer to the Recent Items… sub-menu in the Apple Menu. The numbers here are the settings for how many recently used applications and documents, respectively, show up. You can also clear the menu by choosing Apple Menu ➢ Recent Items ➢ Clear Menu.

Get Better Scroll Arrows

In the General preferences pane, you're given two options for the scroll bar arrows. One option is "At top and bottom," which really means one on each end (up arrow at the top of a vertical bar, down arrow at the bottom, left arrow on the left side of a horizontal bar, right arrow on the right). The other option is "Together," which actually means up/down arrows together and left/right arrows together, with both sets grouped in the bottom-right corner of each window.

I don't know about you, but I'd prefer to have a combination of the two—left/right grouped together on both the left and the right, and up/down grouped together at both the top and the bottom! In fact, this layout is actually an option in the Mac OS, but you don't have any way to access it—or do you?

Actually, you do, and this will be my first mention of one of the best utilities available for OS X, TinkerTool (freeware, `http://www.bresink.de/osx/`). What makes TinkerTool unique is that it really doesn't do anything other than allowing you to access existing options, preferences, and features of Mac OS X that, for whatever reason—most likely a fear of confusing new users—Apple has decided to hide. Using TinkerTool, you can choose to have scroll arrows "Together at both ends" (Figure 2.5).

You'll find that as you read through the book, I mention TinkerTool many, many times.

FIGURE 2.5: Using TinkerTool to improve your scrollbar arrows

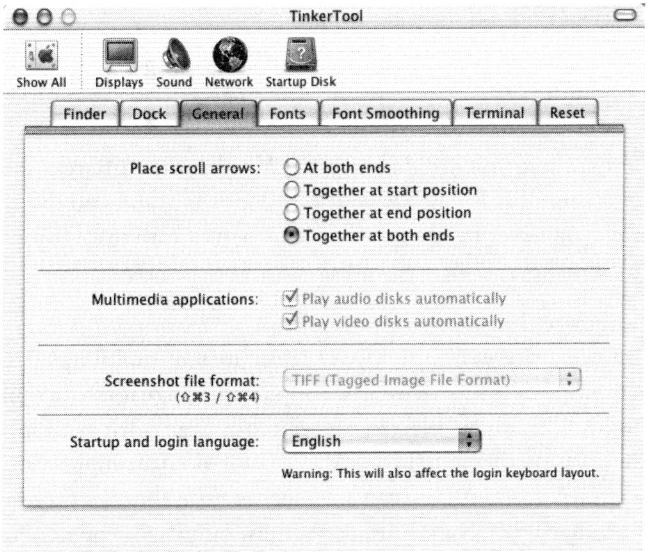

Better Font Smoothing

One of the reasons Mac OS X's Aqua interface looks so beautiful is that text is anti-aliased, which means that rough edges are smoothed out. However, since not all monitors (or eyes) are created equal, what looks smooth to one person might look blurry to another. In addition, the smaller the font, the more difficult it is to read if it is smoothed too much—at some point, different for everyone, "smooth" becomes "blur." The font smoothing area of General preferences lets you decide how much smoothing of fonts you want OS X to do, and at what size text you want it to stop smoothing altogether.

Beginning with OS X, Apple has made the setting for smoothing style easier by including examples: Standard is recommended for CRT monitors, while Medium is best for Flat Panel displays. However, you may not want to take Apple's recommendation as law—I actually find that I prefer the Standard setting for my flat panel displays. You should test the different levels of smoothing on your own system until you find the best one for you. Likewise, change the font size setting until you find the one that makes larger text smooth while maintaining the readability of smaller text.

If you really just hate font smoothing altogether, luckily there's TinkerTool. In TinkerTool's Font Smoothing tab, you'll find settings to disable font smoothing altogether.

TIP Font smoothing actually requires a good chunk of processing power. If you have an older Mac, you may find that it feels faster if you turn off font smoothing for as many sizes as possible or if you disable it altogether using TinkerTool.

International

User level: any
Affects: individual user
Terminal: no

Here's where you decide how your Mac handles different languages, character sets, and punctuation. If English is your only language, and you live in the United States, you may think you never need to touch this group of settings. However, there are a few neat things to be found here, even for English-speaking Americans.

Language Tab

Unfortunately, while the Mac OS itself may be multilingual, many applications are not, or if they are, they don't necessarily support the languages you'd like them to. In earlier versions of the Mac OS, if you selected a foreign language, such as Spanish, for your preferred language, there was no way to tell your Mac what to do if an application did not provide language support. In Mac OS X, you can actually *prioritize* your languages. First, click the Edit… button in the Languages tab and check only those languages you understand or want to keep as options (it's actually pretty amazing how many are there!). When you click OK, the Languages window will now only list those you selected. Here's the neat part: rearrange them in your preferred order, and Mac OS X will use these languages (in the Finder and in applications) in that order, provided applications support them. For example, if you select Español, Italiano, and English, in that order, the next time you launch an application, OS X will check to see if that application supports Spanish; if it does, it will run as a Spanish-language application. If not, OS X checks to see if it supports Italian, and so on down the list until a supported language is found.

The bottom of the Languages window provides you with an opportunity to select text behavior (sorting, case, dictionaries, etc.) for each type of script supported by Mac OS X. For example, if you select Roman script, the Behaviors pop-up menu will present all the possible behaviors (in this case, languages) supported for that script. Choose the one that is the most appropriate for the language you use with your Mac.

Date, Time, and Numbers Tabs

Different countries, and sometimes even different regions within a country, use various methods for writing the day and date, the time, and even numbers. Mac OS X has many formats built-in, and you can select these from the Region pop-up menu of each tab. In addition, you can customize each, or create your own using the settings in each tab's window. The small shaded area at the bottom of each window provides an example of how your selected preferences will look.

NOTE In pre-Jaguar versions of OS X prior to 10.2, the only place you could switch between 12-hour and 24-hour clock formats was in the International preferences. Many users complained that this setting belonged instead in the Date & Time preferences. Apple responded by putting the setting in Date & Time and leaving it in International, as well. This is, as far as I know, the *only* non-administrative setting in all of Mac OS X that can be changed via two entirely different preference panes.

The Numbers tab even lets you choose the currency symbol and whether you want to use Metric or Standard (U.S.) measurement systems.

Input Menu Tab

If you use multiple languages on your Mac, you may find that at different times you need access to non-English keyboard layouts. If you select more than one language in this tab, an input menu (that looks like a sheet of paper with text) will appear in the menu bar that lets you quickly switch between keyboard layouts.

In addition, in what is a very cool of OS X 10.2 and later feature, if you select Character Palette, the input menu will include a new item, Show Character Palette. Choosing this item will show the new palette as a window that floats over the top of other applications (Figure 2.6). You can view characters from any input type, and characters are grouped by type. You can then insert the chosen character into any text field (or add it to your "favorite" character list if it's one you access frequently). The disclosure triangle at the bottom shows you the font(s) the character is available in, the Unicode code for the character, and examples of related characters.

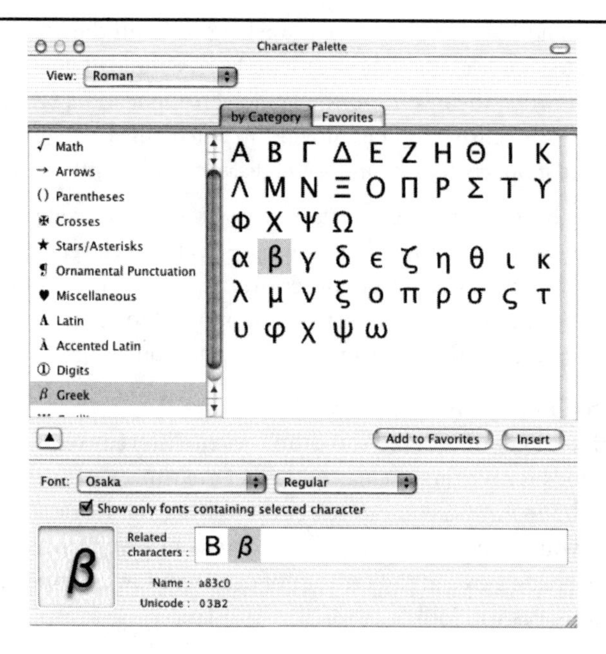

FIGURE 2.6: The Character Palette lets you choose any character in any font.

All in all, this is a great feature that most people never realize exists.

Login Items

The Login Items pane allows you to automatically launch applications and open documents at login. I cover this preference panel in detail in the next chapter when I discuss the login process.

My Account

User level: any, if not limited by an admin
Affects: individual user
Terminal: no

Using this pane, each user can change their login picture (by choosing a picture from the list, by clicking the Choose Another… button to navigate to a picture, or by dragging a picture onto the picture field), as well as their password. In addition, by clicking the Edit… button next to My Address Book Card, they can edit their personal address book entry.

I briefly mentioned this pane in Chapter 1 when I discussed user accounts. If you are an admin user and you decide to edit a user's account in the Accounts pane of System Preferences, you're basically editing the exact same things as the user themselves would edit via My Account. In addition, you can limit each user's access to this pane via the Capabilities… button in Accounts; you can choose to prevent them from accessing this preference pane at all, or just from changing their password.

Screen Effects

User level: any
Affects: individual user
Terminal: no

This preference pane controls one of Mac OS X's "almost useless but very cool" features: the screen saver. I say *almost useless* because the truth is that nowadays most screens don't suffer the same "burn-in" effect that spurred the development of screen savers 10 or 15 years ago. I say *very cool* because OS X's screen saver takes advantage of the graphics technologies of OpenGL and Quartz to allow for some very cool effects.

In the Screen Effects tab (yes, Apple used the same name for one of the tabs as they did for the panel itself—making tech writers everywhere pull their hair out), you can select a screen saver, configure it, and then test it. If a screen saver can be configured, the Configure button will bring up an options screen. The Test button simply shows you a full-screen example of what your configured screen saver will look like (simply moving the mouse or pressing a key will make it go away). If you're an admin user or a normal user with access to all preference panes, you can also open the Energy Saver preference pane by pressing the Open Energy Saver button.

The Activation tab lets you decide how much idle time (no mouse or keyboard activity) you want before the screen saver starts. In addition, while the screen saver will normally disappear as soon as you move the mouse or keyboard, you can require that your account password be used to get rid of it. While this isn't foolproof security, it's at least a good way of making sure that others don't access your account (without requiring you to log out) when you're not sitting in front of your computer.

Finally, the Hot Corners tab gives you two options that most people don't seem to use but that can be quite useful. If you click on a corner checkbox repeatedly, it will cycle through a check symbol, a minus symbol, and a blank box. The check means that if you place your cursor all the way in that corner of the screen, the screen saver will start immediately. This is useful if you've enabled password protection on the screen saver and are about to step away from your desk, or if you need to quickly hide the screen. The minus means that if you place the cursor in that corner, the screen saver will never start up, even if your computer is idle for longer than your preferred time. This is a great feature if you're doing something, like watching video on the Web, that doesn't require any mouse/keyboard input—otherwise the screen saver would start up while you were watching.

TIP When I talk about system security in Chapter 12, I'll show you how to *immediately* lock your screen behind a password-protected screen saver, regardless of your settings here.

In addition to the stock features of the Screen Effects pane, you can also use the screen saver as a very nice slide show application, add custom screen savers, and even animate the Desktop.

Use Screen Effects as a Slide Show

User level: any
Affects: individual user
Terminal: no

One of the built-in screen saver modules is called Pictures Folder. This saver takes images from the top level of your `~/Pictures` folder and presents them as a slide show. However, you can customize this slide show in many ways using the Customize screen. You can drop a folder of images onto the Slide Folder icon, or select one by pressing Set Slide Folder. You can also configure the Display Options to control cross-fades, zooms, cropping, position, and slide order. In addition to being a neat screen saver, you can use this screen saver to show off pictures to friends and relatives (and watch them be impressed by the stylish transitions Mac OS X is capable of).

TIP If you or someone you know has a .Mac account (formerly iTools), and has published a public slide show (I'll talk more about that in Chapter 7), you can instead select the .Mac saver, which is exactly the same as the Pictures Folder saver except that it accesses .Mac slide shows over the Internet. Simply click the Configure button, and then enter the person's .Mac member name in the appropriate field. If you've entered more than one .Mac slide show, you can select which ones you want to view by checking or unchecking the box next to each in the Configure window.

Install New Screen Savers

User level: any
Affects: individual user or all users
Terminal: no

Mac OS X comes with a good variety of screen savers, some simple, some quite impressive. However, there are many other good screen saver modules floating around the web that you can install, and doing so is quite easy.

1. Quit System Preferences.
2. Find a screensaver you want to install (if you don't have any yet, check out "Fave Savers" below, or do a search for "saver" on Version Tracker (`http://www.versiontracker.com/macosx/`) or MacUpdate (`http://www.macupdate.com/`)The name of the file should end in .saver.
3. If you're a normal user, or an admin user who only wants the screen saver to be available for your personal use, drop it in `~/Library/Screen Savers`. If you're an admin user and you want the new screen saver to be available to all users, drop it in `/Library/Screen Savers`.

The next time you launch System Preferences, the new module will be available in the Screen Effects pane.

Fave Savers

There are many, many third-party screen savers available on the 'net—a search on Version Tracker will give you eight or nine pages of results. I've included below a short list of what I think are especially worthy screen saver modules.

Marine Aquarium (http://www.serenescreen.com/). The most incredible screen saver I've ever seen, it provides a photo-realistic saltwater aquarium complete with 20 species of tropical fish and a starfish that crawls up the glass. It's not free, but it's well worth the $20 just to impress your friends.

Euphoria (http://s.sudre.free.fr/Software/Euphoria.html). A beautiful OpenGL screen saver with futuristic "plasma" effects (my description, not the developer's).

Galaxy (http://www.epicware.com/macosxsavers.html). Displays a very realistic image of a rotating galaxy. Check out their other screen savers while you're there.

Helios (http://spazioinwind.libero.it/tpecorella/uselesssoft/software.htm). Another good one hard to describe. Check out their other savers, too.

Old Glory (http://www.apple.com/downloads/macosx/icons_screensavers/oldgloryscreensaver.html). If you're a patriotic American, this is a must. Even if you're not a patriotic American, you'll still be impressed by the realistic animation.

Time Ballz (http://www.xscreensavers.com/timeballz/). Everyone needs a clock screen saver; this is my favorite.

ScriptSaver (http://homepage.mac.com/swannman/FileSharing1.html). A unique module that launches the AppleScript of your choice when it activates.

Create Your Own Slide Show Savers

The Pictures Folder module will cycle through the pictures in your `~/Pictures` directory. But what if you want to create your own slide show of pictures? You can do it very easily.

1. Create a new folder.
2. Copy any pictures you want in the slide show into the folder (you can even use aliases to the pictures if you like).
3. Rename the folder ***name*.slideSaver**, where ***name*** is the name you want to appear in the Screen Effects list of modules. You'll be asked if you're sure you want to use the `.slideSaver` suffix; yes, you really do.
4. Drag the new folder into one of the `/Screen Savers` folders described in the previous tip.

The next time you launch System Preferences, your new slide show will be listed in the Screen Effects pane; you can even use the Configure screen to choose the presentation options.

TIP You can also create a new slide show screen saver by dragging a folder of images onto `/Library/Image Capture/Scripts/Build slide show`. This handy little app will create a new module called `Recent Photos.slideSaver` inside your personal `~/Library/Screen Savers` directory (you can rename it something more meaningful in the Finder).

Animate the Desktop

User level: any
Affects: individual user
Terminal: no

Have you ever liked a screen saver so much that you wished you could watch it even while you were working? Evidently someone at Apple has. OS X 10.2 and later includes the ability to enable any screen saver module as not just a window, but as your *entire* Desktop—you can even choose the incredible Marine Aquarium and see fish swim across your Desktop. Instead of selecting a Desktop picture, you simply enable what are called Desktop Effects. You can do this using Terminal, or using a third-party utility.

Using Terminal

1. Open System Preferences and select the screen saver you want to use as your Desktop in the Screen Effects pane. My favorite is the Galaxy saver I mentioned in "Fave Savers."
2. Open Terminal and type **/System/Library/Frameworks/ScreenSaver.framework/Resources/ScreenSaverEngine.app/Contents/MacOS/ScreenSaverEngine -background & <RETURN>** (all on one line).

This will start the Desktop Effect using the screen saver you selected. Terminal will also present a number after you enter the command. This is the process ID (PID) of the command (it will be different each time). To *stop* Desktop Effects, simply type **kill *PID* <RETURN>.**

Using Third-Party Utilities

A number of utilities can enable Desktop Effects. My favorite at the time of this writing is the shareware xBack (`http://www.gideonsoftworks.com/xback.html`). It provides a universal menu in the menu bar that allows you to start and stop Desktop Effects, as well as the ability to quickly choose which saver to use.

NOTE Desktop Effects are only possible if your video card supports Quartz Extreme. In addition, they are very processor intensive, so if you're doing work that requires a lot of processing power, you're better off with a Desktop picture instead.

The Hardware Preferences Category

The Hardware category of System Preferences is filled with settings that affect how users interact with the Mac's hardware. Unless their accounts have been restricted by an admin, normal users can access every pane, and can change settings for all but the Energy Saver screen (which can only be used by admin users).

Bluetooth

User level: any, if not limited by an admin
Affects: individual user
Terminal: no

The Bluetooth pane lets you configure your settings for OS X's new short-range, wireless networking system. The panel only appears if you have a Bluetooth adapter or other Bluetooth hardware connected to your Mac. I'll talk more about setting up this pane in Chapter 9.

CDs & DVDs

User level: any, if not limited by an admin
Affects: individual user
Terminal: no

In this panel each user can decide what they want OS X to do when they insert different kinds of media. For example, when you insert a music CD, you have several options. You can have OS X automatically open iTunes for you; you can have another application launch (perhaps another audio program or player); you can tell the OS to run an AppleScript; or you can tell it to do nothing, and the CD will simply mount in the Finder. The AppleScript option is the most intriguing, because with a little bit of practice using AppleScript, you can do things you never imagined. For example, you could create a script that does the following: opens iTunes, converts all of the songs on your CD to MP3, copies all the track names from the CD, opens an existing document in TextEdit that contains a list of all your MP3s, pastes the names of the tracks into the document, saves the document, quits TextEdit, then ejects the CD. Writing such a script is beyond the scope of this book, but this example shows you that even such an apparently simply preference pane such as CDs & DVDs can be quite powerful.

ColorSync

User level: any, if not limited by an admin
Affects: individual user
Terminal: no

ColorSync is a technology designed to ensure consistent and accurate color between color devices (digital cameras, scanners, displays, printers, etc.). If a document doesn't have an embedded profile, you can choose the profiles you would like to be used as defaults here. In addition, in the CMMs tab, you can choose which color matching method you want ColorSync to use when it attempts to match colors.

Displays

User level: any, if not limited by an admin
Affects: individual user
Terminal: no

The Displays pane allows you to change the performance of your CRT or LCD display: resolution, brightness, color depth, and refresh rate (for CRTs). You can also choose whether or not to show a menu for display settings in the menu bar (click the Show displays in menu bar box). Via the Color tab, Displays also allows you to select or create a Display Profile to be used for ColorSync.

In addition to these features, on PowerBooks and iBooks another button appears in this panel, called Detect Displays. Clicking this button tells your Mac to check whether or not an external display is connected, and, if so, to enable video to it. This is very useful for connecting your laptop to an external monitor or video projector. Another nice feature on newer PowerBooks and iBooks is the ability to change the screen brightness without opening System Preferences. On these laptops the F1 and F2 keys serve double duty as dimmer and brighter, respectively.

TIP To quickly access the Displays pane of System Preferences, hold down the option key and press one of the brightness keys on your PowerBook or iBook or the brightness button on an Apple display. System Preferences will appear with the Displays pane already selected.

TIP If you have an older Mac, choosing Thousands of colors instead of Millions can decrease the load on your video card and squeeze a little more performance out of OS X.

Energy Saver

User level: admin
Affects: all users
Terminal: no

The Energy Saver panel lets you decide how frugal your Mac is with electricity (on all Macs) and battery power (laptops). On a desktop Mac, the settings in the Sleep tab are pretty straightforward. You can set your system to automatically sleep after a certain amount of inactivity (and set the display for a different time, if desired). You can also choose to have the hard drive sleep (which simply means it will stop spinning) whenever you aren't using it. The Options tab provides you with settings that allow your Mac to wake from sleep when your modem detects an incoming call (for faxes or dial-up remote access); to wake from sleep for certain types of network administration access; and to automatically restart after a power failure.

TIP In OS X 10.2, Apple removed the time setting for hard disk sleep; whereas in earlier versions of OS X you could choose the length of inactivity after which the hard drive would spin down, in 10.2 you simply get a toggle to "Put the hard disk to sleep when possible" (which defaults to 10 minutes of inactivity). You can actually set the length of the inactivity trigger using Terminal. The command is `sudo pmset -x spindown minutes`, where *x* should be *b* for battery settings, *c* for AC adapter settings, or *a* for both (all), and *minutes* is the number of minutes of inactivity before the hard drive spins down. So to set the hard drive spindown time to always be five minutes, you'd type `sudo pmset -a spindown 5` <RETURN>.

If you're using a PowerBook or iBook, the Energy Saver panel looks significantly different and has a few additional features. At the bottom of the window is a check box to show the status of your battery in the menu bar; if this is checked, a battery icon appears in the menu bar. (Clicking the battery icon in the menu bar provides you with a menu to choose how you want the indicator to appear.) The bottom of the window also includes a text description of the current energy saver settings and the status of the battery.

By default, the laptop version of Energy Saver has only one other setting, the Optimize Energy Settings pop-up menu, which has several preset combinations of energy settings: Highest Performance maxes out processor and hard drive performance and screen brightness, but leads to shortened battery life; Longest Battery Life provides the lowest overall level of performance, but provides the best battery life; DVD Playback optimizes the settings for watching DVDs; and Presentations provides good processor performance and prevents the screen from sleeping (even if you're running off of the battery), but saves some battery life by allowing the hard drive to spin down. By selecting Automatic, OS X will automatically change settings for you depending on whether you're using the AC adapter or the internal battery, as well as whether or not an external display is attached. You'll also see a setting called Custom; when this is chosen, you can create your own set of Energy Saver settings, using the Show Details button.

If you click Show Details, you'll see a Sleep tab that is almost identical to that of a desktop Mac (Figure 2.7). The Option tab is also identical, with the exception of one additional setting, Processor Performance (or Reduce Processor Performance on some laptop models). Highest performance (or Reduce Processor Performance Off) requires more power and is best used when your PowerBook or iBook is using an AC adapter; reduced performance (or Reduce Processor Performance On) reduces the processor speed to conserve battery power.

You won't be able to crunch numbers as quickly, but your batteries will last longer. Again, on laptops all the settings in the Energy Saver preference pane are configured automatically based on your chosen preset in the Optimize Energy Settings pop-up menu. In fact, if you make changes manually, the preset will change to Custom and your changes will be applied to the Custom configuration.

TIP On most Macs and PowerBooks, you can put your computer to sleep immediately and completely, fan and all, by pressing command+option+eject.

Unfortunately, one of the neat features found in Mac OS 9's Energy Saver control panel—the ability to have your computer boot up automatically at a certain time—is no longer present in OS X. This is probably because Apple sees OS X as an operating system that is meant to be "on" all the time and just "asleep" when not in use. However, this auto-startup functionality is actually a hardware feature, so on Macs that can boot into OS 9, set the Energy Saver control panel to your desired startup time, and then boot back into OS X; the auto-startup setting should still work.

Ink

User level: any, if not limited by an admin
Affects: individual user
Terminal: no

This panel lets you set your preferences for the built-in handwriting recognition abilities of OS X 10.2 and later. It will only be visible if you have a tablet or other writing device that is compatible with Ink connected to your Mac. I'll talk more about Ink in Chapter 7.

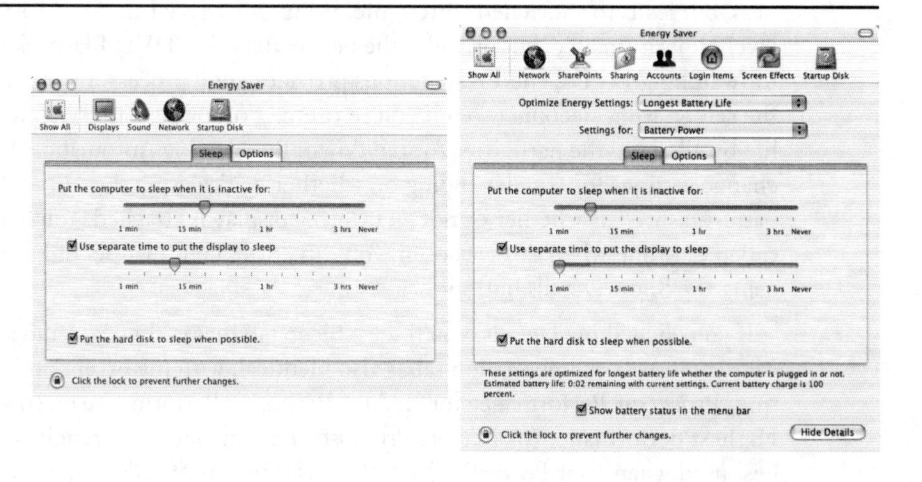

FIGURE 2.7: Energy Saver on a desktop (left) and a laptop (right)

Keyboard

User level: any
Affects: individual user
Terminal: no

While the main Settings tab of Keyboard preferences merely allows you to set the key repeat rate (how often a character is typed when you hold it down) and the delay until repeating begins, it's the second tab, Full Keyboard Access, that most users never take advantage of. By checking the box next to "Turn on full keyboard access," you can actually set up your Mac so that you can access almost anything using the keyboard. You can choose whether to use the Control key along with the function keys, letter keys, or custom keys that you choose (fn+control on PowerBooks and iBooks). For example, I have my desktop machine set to use the function keys. If I want to choose a different style for this paragraph as I'm typing it in Word, I simply press control+F2 to enable the menu bar, press the right arrow a few times to get to the Style menu, then use the down arrow to highlight the style; pressing the return key selects it.

Combined with OS X's ability to switch applications using command+tab (more on that in Chapter 6), you can do pretty much anything without using the mouse. This functionality comes in handy more than you might think. I've even had a few situations where my mouse stopped responding, but I was able to finish what I was doing by using full keyboard access.

TIP In Mac OS 9, iBook and PowerBook users could use the Keyboard control panel to eliminate the need to press the fn key (i.e., instead of pressing control+fn+function, you could simply press control+function). Unfortunately, OS X does not provide this option; however, many users report that changing the setting in OS 9 causes OS X to use the OS 9 setting. (In fact, on some Macs, other OS 9 Keyboard settings may also apply.)

Mouse

User level: any
Affects: individual user
Terminal: no

On a desktop Mac, the Mouse preference pane is about as basic and self-explanatory as they come. However, on a laptop, a few more options appear. The Mouse tab offers an additional setting for scrolling speed, and a new Trackpad tab appears (Figure 2.8). The most useful settings in this tab are those under the "Use trackpad for:" heading. You may not realize it, but you can avoid using the trackpad button at all—you can tap the trackpad instead. If you have the Dragging box checked, a tap on the trackpad followed immediately by a drag functions just like holding down the trackpad button while you move your finger across the trackpad (at times a difficult maneuver). Finally, in what amounts to a document saver for those of us who tend to drag our thumbs when we type, you can tell OS X to ignore the trackpad while you're typing. (In fact, you can disable the trackpad completely when a mouse is plugged in.)

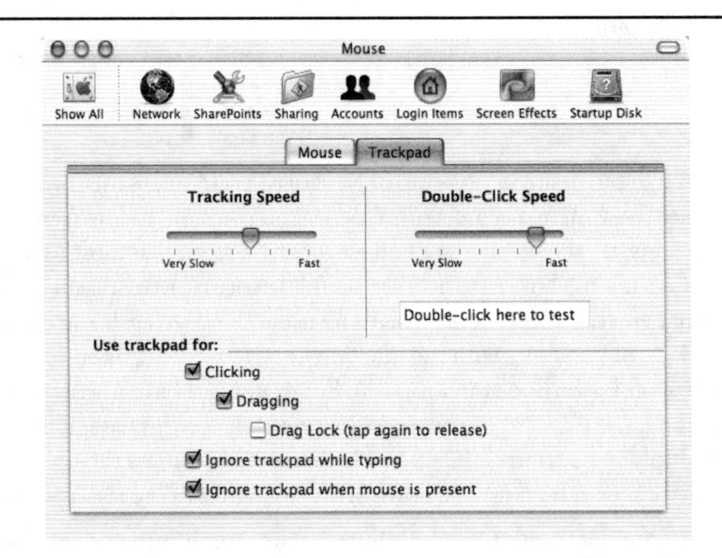

FIGURE 2.8:
Additional "Mouse" options for PowerBooks and iBooks

Sound

User level: any
Affects: individual user
Terminal: no

In the Sound Effects tab of the Sound preferences panel you can change your alert sound, the system volume, and the alert volume. You can also turn interface sounds on or off (e.g., the sound OS X makes when you move a file to the trash), and choose whether or not an alert beep is played when you press the up/down volume keys on your keyboard. Finally, you can choose to show a volume menu in the menu bar. The other two tabs, Output and Input, allow you to choose the device used for sound output and input, respectively; if you only have a single device for each, these two tabs aren't of much use. As straightforward as these settings might seem, I've got a few ways to spice them up.

TIP To quickly access the Sound pane of System Preferences, hold down the Option key and press one of the volume Control keys on your PowerBook, iBook, or Apple Pro Keyboard. System Preferences will appear with the Sound pane already selected.

Temporarily Silence the Keyboard Volume Keys

User level: any
Affects: individual user
Terminal: no

If you generally prefer to receive audible feedback when you change the volume using the keyboard, but there are times when you need such changes to be silent, check the box to "play feedback." When you need quiet, hold down the Shift key as you change the volume, and feedback will be temporarily silenced. Conversely, if you have disabled feedback, you can hold the Shift key down when you press one of the volume keys to temporarily activate audible feedback.

Control the Alert Volume Using the Volume Control Menu

User level: any
Affects: individual user
Terminal: no

If you choose to show the volume menu in the menu bar, you may not realize that you can control both the overall volume *and* the alert volume with it. To control the overall system volume, simply select the volume from the menu. To change the alert volume, hold down the option key when you click on the volume menu; any change you make will only apply to the alert volume.

Add Additional Alert Sounds

User level: any
Affects: individual user or all users
Terminal: no

If you get tired of the alert sounds available in the Sounds Effects tab of Sound preferences, you can actually add your own. The only requirements are that the sound file must be in AIFF format, and the name of the file must end in `.aiff` (`.aif` won't do). You can download AIFF files from the Internet, or you can make your own using tools such as QuickTime Player (if you've upgraded to QuickTime Pro) or the excellent freeware SoundHack (`http://www.soundhack.com/`). You can even convert other sound formats to AIFF using these tools.

Once you've got yourself some good AIFF files, place them in `/Library/Sounds`, where they'll be available for all users. (You'll need admin access to place files in `/Library`, of course.) The next time you launch System Preferences the new files will be available in the Sound Effects window. Individual users can also put AIFF files inside `~/Library/Sounds`, and they will only be available to each particular user.

Change the "Volume Change" Sound

User level: admin/root
Affects: all users
Terminal: no

When you change the volume on your Mac, PowerBook, or iBook using the keyboard volume keys, you get feedback in the form of a unique alert (it almost sounds like a bubble popping). If you'd rather use some other sound for this (an AIFF sound, of course), it's possible to change it. Not easy, but possible. You can make such a move in Terminal fairly quickly, but in this case I prefer doing it using File Buddy (`http://skytag.com/filebuddy/`), an excellent file utility that, among its many features, lets you move files using the familiar open/save dialogs.

1. Launch File Buddy as root (using one of the procedures discussed in Chapter 1).
2. Copy the original sound file for safekeeping. Select File ➢ Move.
3. Navigate to `/System/Library/LoginPlugins/BezelServices.loginPlugin/Contents/Resources/` and select the file `volume.aiff`.
4. In the subsequent dialog (the destination), select the folder you'll be using to store the original sound file, and click Move.
5. In the Finder, rename your *new* AIFF sound file `volume.aiff`.
6. In File Buddy, select File ➢ Move... again, and select your *new* `volume.aiff` file.
7. Chose the destination folder (the long path in Step 3) and click Move to move the new sound file into its new home.
8. Log out and then log back in. The new sound should now be fully functional.

TIP If you've enabled root login as described in Chapter 1, you can simply log out, then log in as root to move the files described here. Just make sure you immediately log out and then back in using your regular account.

Enable the Visual Beep

User level: any
Affects: individual user
Terminal: no

This technically isn't a "sound" issue; in fact, it's not even a setting located in Sound preferences. However, since it's directly related to system alert sounds, I thought I should mention it here. There are plenty of times when you don't want your computer to make noise (e.g., when you're in a meeting or class); at these times you may use the mute button to suppress any such sounds. On the other hand, you still want to be aware of system and application alerts (especially the ones that don't come with a dialog box). The solution can be found in the Universal Access panel (discussed later in this chapter). In the Hearing tab, simply check the box next to Flash the screen whenever an alert sound occurs. Even when alert sounds are muted, you'll still see the visual "flash" on the screen.

The Internet & Network Preferences Category

The Internet & Network Preferences provide the interface for all network- and Internet-related settings, including Sharing and QuickTime. QuickTime actually seems like the kid who's doing his own thing, but with Apple's increased emphasis on Internet media (streaming video and audio) this was probably the most appropriate category in which to place it. Most of the panes in this category will be discussed in much more detail in later chapters, so I won't say much about them here.

Internet

User level: any, if not limited by an admin
Affects: individual user
Terminal: no

This preference pane provides .Mac, e-mail, and web-related settings. I'll discuss it in detail in Chapter 10.

Network

User level: admin for most settings
Affects: all users
Terminal: no

I discuss network settings and the Network preference panel in Chapter 10.

QuickTime

User level: any, if not limited by an admin
Affects: individual user
Terminal: no

Although the QuickTime panel of System Preferences has a number of settings, they're actually much simpler than they appear at first. In fact, many of the settings are rather self-explanatory, so I'll simply talk about those that aren't. The Plug-In tab controls the QuickTime plug-in, not any other QuickTime functionality; any changes you make here only affect the functionality of web browsers that have the QuickTime plug-in installed. The MIME Settings… button lets you select which types of downloaded media files the QuickTime plug-in should handle for you.

The Connection tab lets you choose your connection speed to optimize QuickTime for that speed. A few words of advice: don't try to choose a setting faster than your actual connection; instead of speeding things up, it will actually slow down Internet media, since your connection won't be able to handle the increased amount of data that QuickTime will attempt to download. In the same tab, under Transport Setup… you generally shouldn't make any changes here unless you know exactly what you're doing or are told to do so by your network administrator.

The Music and Media Keys tabs are generally not used unless you have installed alternative MIDI music synthesizer files or need to enter access keys for secured media. If you do either of these things, you'll be told exactly how to configure them.

Finally, the Update tab lets you check for new versions of third-party QuickTime add-ins, or new versions of the QuickTime software itself. Click the Update Now… button to check for new version, or simply leave the "Check for updates automatically" setting enabled to have QuickTime watch for updates for you.

TIP The functionality of QuickTime's Update feature is independent of the Software Update preference pane (discussed later in this chapter and in Chapter 4).

Sharing

User level: admin
Affects: all users
Terminal: no

I talk about Sharing preferences in various other chapters of the book. You use this panel to access settings for Rendezvous and Internet Sharing (Chapter 9); File Sharing and OS X's built-in web and FTP servers (Chapter 10); Remote Login (Chapter 11); Printer Sharing (Chapter 12); and OS X's built-in Firewall (Chapter 13).

The System Preferences Category

Whereas the General panel is a hodgepodge of *settings* that don't seem to go anywhere else, the System category is a bit of a hodgepodge of *preference panes*. Some of them (Accounts, Date & Time, Startup Disk, Software Update) are certainly "System-related," and affect all users but others (Speech, Universal Access, Classic) provide user-level preferences that have little to do with the OS as a whole. However, since they aren't really "personal" and they certainly aren't related to hardware, Internet, or networking, it seems that "System" is probably the best place to stick them.

Accounts

User level: admin
Affects: specific users
Terminal: no

I covered most of the Users tab of Accounts preferences in detail in Chapter 1. (I'll talk more about the Login Options tab in Chapter 3 when I discuss login options.) However, there is one option I didn't cover completely, and that's the Set Auto Login setting. By selecting a user and clicking on Set Auto Login…, you're presented with a name/password dialog (with the selected user's name already entered). If you provide the user's password, that user's account will be set to log in automatically (without requiring a password); in effect, it's as if that user was the only user on the computer. The downside to this option is that if you want to set an account other than your own to auto-login, you need to know their account password.

NOTE To temporarily override the auto-login option (e.g., to allow another user to log in), restart your Mac, and hold down shift+option when the boot panel (the white box with the blue Apple icon) appears. Release the keys when the login window appears.

Classic

User level: any, if not limited by an admin
Affects: individual user
Terminal: no

This preference panel provides the interface for Classic Environment settings. I'll cover it, and much more related to Classic, in Chapter 9.

Date & Time

User level: admin for some settings
Affects: individual or all users
Terminal: no

The Date & Time preference pane really has two functions: (1) to allow an admin user to set the computer's date and time, using the first three tabs; and (2) to allow individual users to control the menu bar clock/calendar, using the fourth tab.

Getting the Time Right

If you're an admin user, you can choose the time zone in the Time Zone tab by either selecting a city in the Closest City menu or by clicking in the general area of your location on the map. In the Network Time tab, you can choose to synchronize your computer's time with a network time server. If you choose this option, you should choose the closest time server from the NTP Server menu; if you know the address of another network time server, you can click in the Server field and type it in manually. Clicking the Set Time Now button will connect to the server and set the time.

I mention the Date & Time tab last because it only lets you change settings if you have *not* chosen to use a network time server. If that is the case, you can simply click today's date in the calendar, and type in the current time above the clock.

TIP For a slightly more entertaining way to change the time, click the clock's hour, minute, or second hand and drag it around the clock face.

When you're done making changes, you'll be asked to save them, or to revert to the previous settings.

A Better Date & Time

Although you can customize the menu bar clock using the fourth tab, I prefer to uncheck that option and use the BYOC (bring your own calendar) approach. The donationware PTHClock (`http://www.pth.com/PTHClock/`) provides not only a clock that can be customized to a much greater degree than OS X's built-in menu bar clock (color, font, position, tool tips, etc.), but also a convenient drop-down calendar (Figure 2.9) that can be accessed by either clicking or double-clicking (depending on the user's preference).

FIGURE 2.9:

PTHClock provides a convenient drop-down calendar.

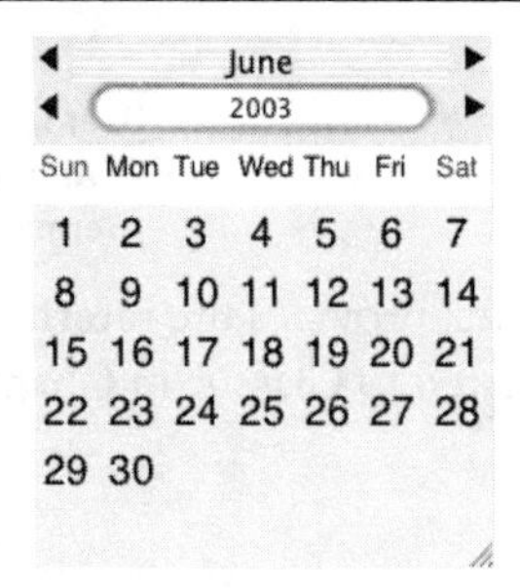

Software Update

User level: admin to install updates
Affects: all users
Terminal: no

The Software Update pane allows you to check, manually or automatically, for updated Mac OS X software. I discuss this panel extensively in Chapter 4.

Speech

User level: any, if not limited by an admin
Affects: individual user
Terminal: no

This preference panel actually provides the settings for three different sets of independent services. They're grouped together because of the common link of speech.

Speech Recognition

Speech recognition in Mac OS X is nowhere near perfect, but it's at the least entertaining, and for some uses it can actually be quite effective. In the Speech Recognition tab, you can turn the feature on and off (and if you use it often, you can choose to have it start up at login). The Helpful Tips button is actually quite useful; give it a try. If you really want to see all the things you can do, out of the box, using speech recognition, click the open Speakable Items Folder for a list all the different possible commands (I counted 76 on my iBook), including commands for Mail and Internet Explorer.

The Listening tab lets you choose when your computer will listen for commands, and whether or not you have to call your computer by name (a name which you get to choose). I highly recommend clicking on the Volume… button to calibrate your microphone—I couldn't get my iBook, Junior, to understand a thing until I discovered that the gain on the internal microphone was set much too high.

Finally, in the Commands tab you can choose to have your computer respond to all commands, or just certain categories (and whether or not you need to speak the commands exactly). I would choose the "exact wording" setting just to be safe. I once said "document" thinking that the iBook would know I wanted to open a document—it thought I had said "Log me out." The result wasn't quite what I had intended.

Default Voice

Many applications support text-to-speech, meaning you can have your Mac read text from within the application. In addition, when using the Spoken User Interface features, your Mac can speak interface text. The only thing this tab does is let you select the voice used for such functionality (but this can be overridden in the Spoken User Interface settings), and choose how fast it reads the text to you.

Spoken User Interface

The Spoken User Interface functionality of OS X adds additional feedback options for alert dialogs and certain text. The Talking Alerts section simply provides options for the computer to read alert dialogs (warnings, error messages, etc.). The items in Other spoken items, on the other hand, are a bit more broad. You can have your computer speak highlighted text (from within any application, including the Finder) by pressing a key combination, or simply have your Mac read aloud any dialog text if you hold the cursor over it for more than a second or two. However, my favorite feature is the ability to announce when an application requires your attention. I often have multiple applications running, and often they're doing things in the background. Some applications will beep when they're done with a task, but often I'm not even sure which application beeped at me. With this option selected, when I'm burning a CD in the background and it finishes, the computer gently interrupts me to tell me that Disk Copy requires my attention.

Startup Disk

User level:	admin only
Affects:	all users
Terminal:	no

In the Startup Disk preference pane, admin users can select the startup volume, and even the specific OS X system or OS 9 System Folder on that volume, that will be used the next time the computer boots up. I'll talk more about this preference panel in Chapter 3 when I talk about startup, and in Appendix B when I talk about multiple volumes.

Universal Access

User level:	any
Affects:	individual user
Terminal:	no

Designed for users with difficulties seeing, hearing, or using the keyboard and/or mouse, Universal Access provides special features that help make computing more accessible under Mac OS X. However, even if you don't have such difficulties, there are useful features to be found here.

Seeing

The Seeing tab provides two helpful features to those with various vision impairments. The first is zoom functionality, which allows you to zoom in on a particular part of the screen. Once zoom mode is enabled, command+option++ zooms in, and command+option+– zooms out; you can move around the screen while zoomed. If you check the Allow Universal Access Shortcuts box, you can actually turn zooming on and off by pressing command+option+8 (not *, as the instructions seem to indicate)—thanks to OS X's impressive graphics engine, most text and graphics look clear and legible even when enlarged. There are other zoom options available here, but it's hard to describe the effects they have; the best thing to do is just experiment with them until you find the combination that is most effective for you.

The second visual enhancement available is to change the color table of your display(s). You can choose to switch to grayscale mode (this is actually the only way to get a grayscale display in Mac OS X), or you can invert the screen completely (Switch to White on Black), which some people find easier to read (Figure 2.10). Note that although the default "inversion" color table is black/white, by inverting the screen and then changing the Colors setting in Displays preferences, you'll see a "color negative" display instead.

TIP If you check the Allow Universal Access Shortcuts box, you can invert the screen at any time by pressing control+option+command+8. Pressing these keys again will also change it back. If you like to read text white-on-black, this is a great way to quickly switch.

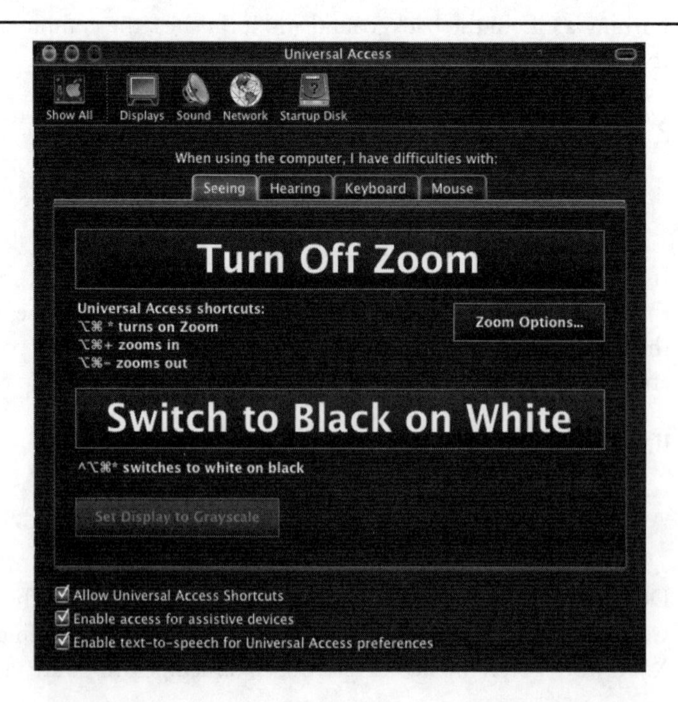

FIGURE 2.10: Inverting the display from Universal Access preferences

Hearing

I mentioned under the Sound preferences pane that you could flash the screen whenever a system alert occurs; this is where you change that setting. Even though I have perfect hearing, I still use this setting; sometimes I have my iBook muted, and sometimes at home my speakers are turned off, so I find the "visual beep" very helpful. There is also a link here (Adjust Sound…) to the alert sound volume control in Sound preferences.

Keyboard

If you have trouble pressing multiple keys at once (for example, pressing shift+x to get X, or command+S to save a document), you can enable sticky keys, and any modifier keys (control, shift, option, command) you press will be "held" until you press a non-modifier key (or until you press the modifier again, or the escape key to cancel). Each held modifier is displayed on the screen.

If you have trouble accidentally pressing keys, you can enable a delay (and choose the length of that delay) between pressing keys and when the key is accepted. This way, only keys you purposely hold down for longer than that delay will be accepted (you can also set how long the delay is before a keypress is accepted).

Mouse

For users who have trouble using a mouse or trackball, you can turn on Mouse Keys, which allows you to control the cursor with the keypad. Together with full keyboard access (discussed in "Keyboard" in the Hardware section above), you can control almost anything on your Mac using the keyboard—this can be very useful even if your only "difficulty" is simply a broken mouse.

Keys Used by Mouse Keys

Apple provides Mouse Keys functionality, but they don't tell you *which* keys to use for which function. Here's the list of keys and their actions:

Press Option five times Turn Mouse Keys on/off

1–9 (up, down, left, right, diagonal) Move the cursor

5 Click the mouse button

0 Hold down the mouse button

On PowerBooks and iBooks, in order to use Mouse Keys you need to use the Function (fn) key in combination with the overlaid numeric keypad on the keyboard. Since the Sticky Keys function does not work for the fn key, you need to press the "num lock" key (generally F6) to enable full use of the overlaid numeric keypad without needing to hold down the fn key.

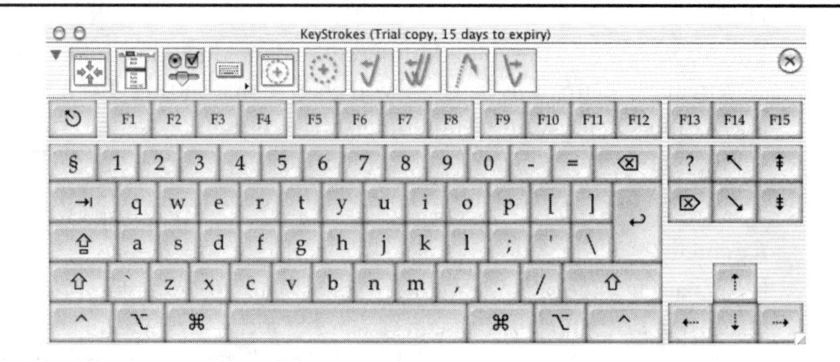

FIGURE 2.11: KeyStrokes provides an on-screen keyboard for accessibility.

Other Settings

At the bottom of Universal Access preferences are three other settings. Allow Universal Access Shortcuts allows you to enable or disable the Seeing, Keyboard, and Mouse assistance by pressing modifier keys repeatedly. Enabling access for assistive devices allows other software or hardware to access the services provided by Universal Access. Finally, the last setting allows text-to-speech to work from within Universal Access preferences.

On-Screen Keyboards

Unfortunately, at the time of this writing Mac OS X does not provide an on-screen keyboard solution, a necessity for a good number of limited mobility individuals. However, if you or someone you know is in need of such functionality, KeyStrokes (`http://www.assistiveware.com/keystrokes.html`) provides it, including enhanced mousing features and word prediction (Figure 2.11).

The Other Preferences Category

At the bottom of the System Preferences window is another category called "Other." If you've never installed any preference panes of your own, or any applications that installed them, your Others group may be empty (in fact, the Others category probably doesn't even appear). However, the reason this category exists is that eventually you *will* install another preference pane, and the Others category is where any preference pane that was not installed by Mac OS X will be listed. The question then becomes "How do I install other preference panes?"

Installing Other Preference Panes

User level: admin or normal
Affects: computer or individual user
Terminal: no

There are many third-party preference panes available for Mac OS X, and they're very easy to install. The folder `/Library/PreferencePanes` hosts panes available to all users, and `~/Library/PreferencePanes` is where individual users install panes for their own personal use. (The stock

OS X preferences panes are located inside `/System/Library/PreferencePanes`, but you shouldn't put any others there.) Every preference pane is actually a file package—with a name that ends in `.prefPane` to indicate its purpose—and simply placing it in the appropriate folder will make it fully functional. (Some preference panes are distributed via installer applications; the installer actually places the pane in one of the above folders for you, usually after asking if you want it installed for everyone or just your own account.)

As an example, I suggest something cute and simple like MooSB (`http://homepage.mac.com/nima/FileSharing.html`). This pane basically makes your computer "moo" at you when you plug in, or unplug, a USB device. Simple, informative…what more could you ask for? (Actually, MooSB does a lot more, as you'll see once you have it installed. If you like farm animals, you'll be quite pleased.) Once you've downloaded MooSB—or whatever preference pane you're trying to install—make sure its name ends in `.prefPane` (that means it's really a preference pane). Installing it is easy:

1. Quit System Preferences if it is currently running.
2. Drop the preference pane into `~/Library/PreferencePanes` for your own use. If you're an admin user, you can instead place it in `/Library/PreferencePanes` if you want all users to be able to use it.
3. Launch System Preferences, and the new pane should be listed in the Other category, ready for you to check out (Figure 2.12).

FIGURE 2.12: System Preferences' *Others* category after installing a new preference pane

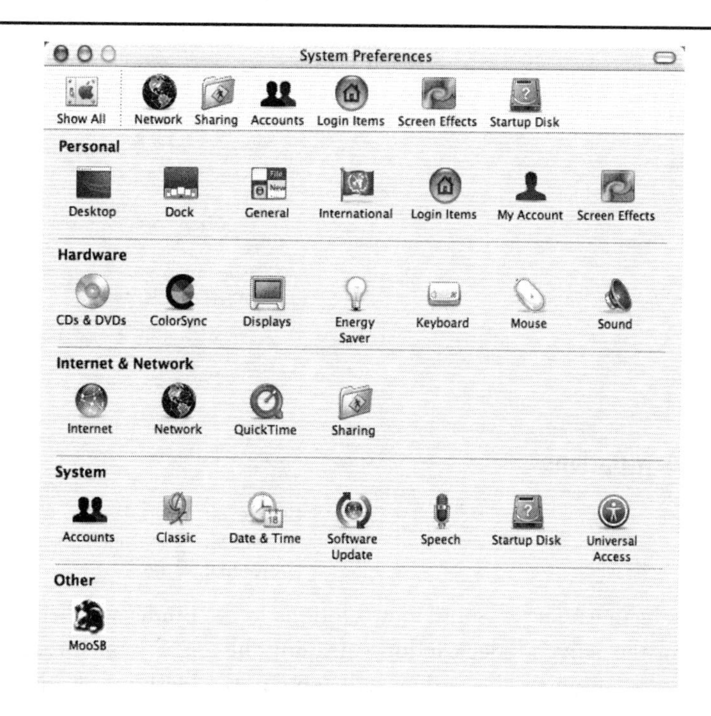

Finder Preferences

There are actually two other groups of system-related preferences in Mac OS X that are not located in the System Preferences application, both relating to the Finder: the Finder's own preferences and View Options for windows.

Finder Preferences

User level:	any
Affects:	individual user
Terminal:	no

The Finder in Mac OS X is actually an application; as such, its preferences are accessed via Finder ➢ Preferences, rather than from the System Preferences application (see "Application Preferences"). Selecting this menu item brings up the Finder's own settings dialog (Figure 2.13). All of the options here relate to how the Finder displays and accesses files; I cover these settings in detail in Chapter 5.

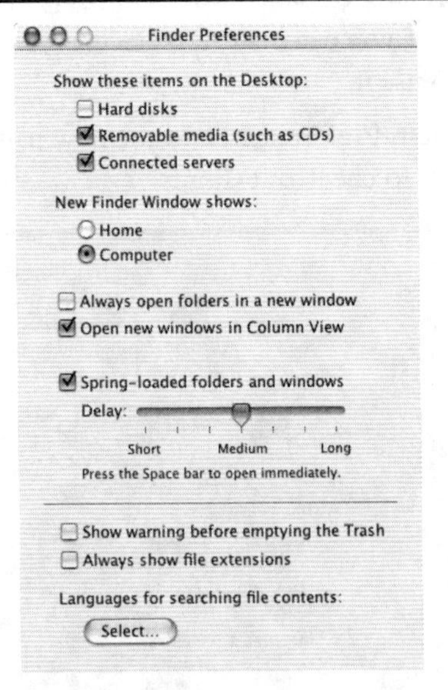

FIGURE 2.13: The Finder preferences window

View Options

User level:	any
Affects:	individual user
Terminal:	no

Selecting View ➢ Show View Options in the Finder will bring up the Finder's view settings for the active Finder window (meaning the one you most recently clicked on; if no open windows are active, the settings will apply to the Desktop). In this window you can control the appearance of that window (icon size, icon layout, window background, etc.), and you can also choose to have your settings applied to all windows rather than just the chosen one. The options here are covered thoroughly in Chapter 5.

Application Preferences

Most system-wide preferences are found in either the System Preferences application or in the Finder's two settings panels, discussed above. However, individual applications generally have their own, application-specific, preference interfaces. Luckily, the way you go about changing and customizing those settings is fairly consistent across the OS.

How Do I Access Application Preferences?

In previous versions of the Mac OS you might find the preferences for an application located in the Edit menu, the File menu, the Help menu, or even the Apple Menu. In Mac OS X Apple has standardized on a consistent location for preferences—in the Application menu, named so because it is always titled the same as the frontmost application—and strongly encourages developers to place their application's preferences menu item there.

This means that if you want to change the setting in an application that has a preferences dialog (not all applications do), you'll almost always be able to do so by going to *Application* ➢ Preferences (where *Application* is the name of the active application). Knowing this rule actually clears up a bit of confusion as to why the Finder preferences are in the Finder menu instead of in System Preferences. The Finder itself is actually an application, so by putting its settings dialog under Finder ➢ Preferences, Apple is simply being consistent.

However, despite this consistency, there is one set of preferences that are not modified from an application's preferences dialog, and that's toolbar settings.

Customizing Toolbars

Most applications written specifically for Mac OS X, and some applications originally written for Mac OS 9 but converted for use with OS X (called "carbonized" applications, after Mac OS X's "carbon" application environment), take advantage of OS X's new custom toolbars. I'll use Mac OS X's Mail application as an example; you can launch Mail and follow along if you like. (Even if you don't use Mail, you can still launch it just to play around with the toolbar.)

Changing the Toolbar Display

User level:	any
Affects:	individual user
Terminal:	no

We actually changed the toolbar display once before, when we covered the System Preferences application. The good news is that the same trick works in any Mac OS X application that uses the Aqua toolbar. Simply press the command key and click the toolbar widget in the upper right corner of the window, and the toolbar display will rotate between different combinations of icons, text, and icon and text size. Choose the one you want, and the application will always use that setup. (In case there is any confusion, your preference will only be used for Mail; you get to choose your preferred display for each application separately.)

Customizing Toolbar Contents

User level: any
Affects: individual user
Terminal: no

By default, the Mail toolbar has nine commands (Delete, Reply, Reply All, Forward, Compose, Mailboxes, Get Mail, Junk, and Search). These are the ones the developer (Apple, in this case) decided are probably the most useful to the average user. However, many more commands are available, and you don't even have to keep the ones that are already there. Simply control-click anywhere in the toolbar, and you'll get a contextual menu that provides you with the same display options you configured above. However, it also allows you to immediately remove a toolbar item, and it gives you the option to Customize Toolbar. That's the big one.

When you select Customize Toolbar, a sheet will appear containing a whole bunch of other toolbar items (Figure 2.14). Much like you did earlier in the chapter when you dragged your favorite preference panes to the System Preferences toolbar, you can simply click on an item and drag it to the toolbar. It will become another button for you to use.

FIGURE 2.14: Customizing the Mail toolbar

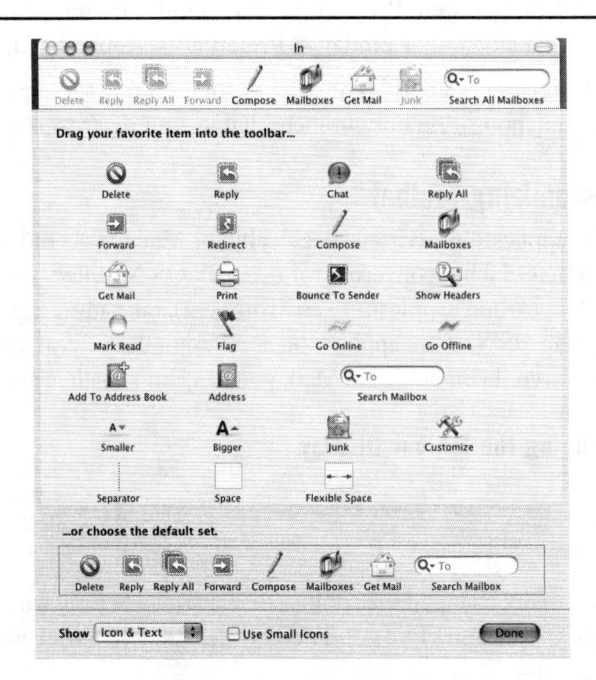

You can remove items you don't use much by dragging them from the toolbar into the item sheet, and you can rearrange items in the toolbar by dragging them left or right. If you decide you liked the toolbar better the way it was originally, just drag the default set, found at the bottom of the sheet, to the toolbar, and it will be as good as new. When you're finished, click Done and your newly customized toolbar is ready for use.

This friendly toolbar interface, consistent across most OS X–native applications, is one of the best features of Mac OS X that many users never realize is available. In fact, even the Finder has customizable toolbars, and I'll spend time in Chapter 5 explaining how to get the most out of them.

Working with Preference Files

Whenever you make a change to a setting, whether it's a Mac OS X setting or an application-specific setting, that change is stored somewhere on your computer. Apart from a few system-level settings that are stored in your computer's low-level memory, preference settings are stored in preference *files*. Each application or preference pane has its own preference file to store its own settings. Generally, the only way users interact with these preference files is via the System Preferences application and application-specific preference dialogs. However, at times you'll want to access these files directly. In this section, I'll talk about why and how.

Where Are My Preferences?

Much like everything else in Mac OS X, there are several locations for preference files. User-specific preferences files—those that affect only a particular user—are located in `~/Library/Preferences` and are only modifiable by that user. System-wide preferences—those that affect all users—are located in `/Library/Preferences` and can only be changed or edited by an admin user. For example, the settings for your Mac's firewall are located here, and only an admin user can use the Sharing pane of System Preferences or manually edit the preference file itself.

In Chapter 1 I mentioned how Mac OS X's file organization provides for flexibility in allowing each user to customize their own computing environment. The location of preference files is a prime example of this organization.

Editing Preference Files Directly

Although you can access most system- and application-specific settings via System Preferences or application preference dialogs, there are often other settings available for which there is no interface provided. In older versions of the Mac OS, there was no easy way to access such features. However, in Mac OS X Apple has encouraged developers to use a standard preference file format, one that uses plain text and a well-known formatting code. What this means for you is that it's actually possible to open most preference files in a text editor such as OS X's Tech Edit or BBEdit (`http://www.barebones.com/products/bbedit_lite.html`), make changes, save the file, and immediately see the changes in action.

That said, while it's possible to directly edit a preference file, that doesn't necessarily mean it's easy to understand it. Luckily, there are some excellent applications that allow you to view and edit preference files using a clear and relatively comprehensible interface. If you performed the earlier procedure to add additional folders to Desktop preferences' Collection menu, you've already used one, Property List Editor. The other good one is the freeware PrefEdit (`http://www.bresink.de/osx/PrefEdit.html`), from the same guy who gave us TinkerTool. As an example of the power of these utilities, I'm going to show you how to turn off one of the Finder's most annoying (in my humble opinion) features—zooming rectangles.

WARNING If a setting exists, but the developer has not provided you with an easy way to access it, there is often a good reason! Be sure you know what you're doing before you edit any preference file, and be sure to make a backup copy of the file beforehand; if you experience problems after making a change, you can revert to the backup copy.

Turn Off Zoom Rectangles by Editing Finder Preferences

User level: any
Affects: individual user
Terminal: no

When you open a window in OS X, you see a "zooming" rectangle that expands the window until it reaches its full size; the window also "zooms" down when you close it. While this is a neat effect, after a while it starts to bug me a little bit—I just want my windows to open or close quickly and let me work. Unfortunately, the Finder preferences dialog doesn't let me change this behavior. This is one of the hidden preferences I mentioned, and we're going to change it using PrefEdit.

1. Make a copy of the file `~/Library/Preferences/com.apple.finder`. This is your backup.
2. Launch PrefEdit. By default it shows all of the preference files in your personal Preferences folder on the left.
3. In the list of preferences, select `com.apple.finder`. In the middle window a list of all the settings contained in the file will appear.
4. Since the setting doesn't officially exist, we're going to create it; in the Contents box, select Logical from the "Type to add" pop-up menu. In the Key field, type **`ZoomRects`**. Click the Add button. You've just created the Zoom Rectangle setting in the Finder's preference file. (Note: I happened to know what the setting was called; you can't just make up names for them.)
5. In the list of settings in the middle column, scroll down and select it (*ZoomRects*). The value for that preference will show up in the column on the right, and a description of

the preference, along with its contents (the setting) appear at the bottom of the window. Unless you've previously used another utility to change this setting, it should say Yes.

6. In the Contents area, click on No (Figure 2.15).
7. Select File ➢ Update all values to save your changes.

Note that although we just created the ZoomRects setting, you could have also edited an existing setting by selecting it in the middle column and then changing its value.

In order for the changes to take effect, you need to relaunch the Finder. You can log out and then back in, or you can force quit the Finder (by selecting Apple Menu ➢ Force Quit, then selecting Finder), which will automatically relaunch. Your Finder windows should now open quickly and smoothly without the zoom effect. Note that we could have changed this setting using TinkerTool, but that would have spoiled all the fun of this exercise.

FIGURE 2.15:

Changing a Finder setting using PrefEdit

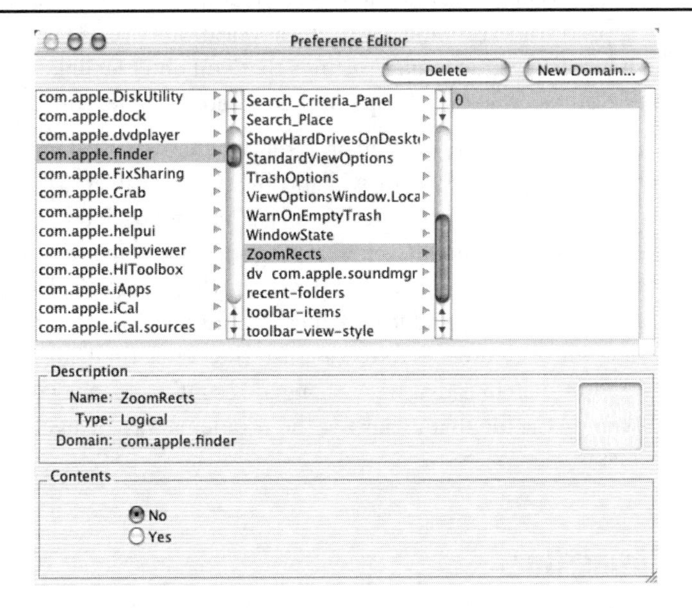

TIP You can launch PrefEdit as root/admin (described in Chapter 1) and use it to edit system-level preferences in `/Library/Preferences`.

How Can a Preference Be Wrong? Troubleshooting Preference Files

Preferences files are subject to the same risks as any other data stored on a hard drive. They can be deleted or changed accidentally, and they can simply become corrupt and fail to work. Here are a few quick tips on how to keep your preference files working, and to keep the bad ones from causing you too much grief.

Back Up Your Preferences

I'll talk a good deal more about backing up in Chapter 15, but suffice it to say that if you keep a safe and recent backup of your `~/Library/Preferences` folder, you'll always be prepared if something goes wrong with a preferences file, or if you accidentally delete or edit one and want the original back. You can simply quit the affected application, place the backup copy back in your Preferences folder and you're good to go.

Moving Preferences Files to Find Problems

If you're having trouble with a particular application, the first place to check is the preference file for that app. Quit the application, locate its preferences file in the `~/Library/Preferences` folder (preference files generally have the name of the application in their name), and move the file to the Desktop. Re-launch the application and see if the problem is gone; if it is, the problem was most likely a bad preferences file. A new one was created when you re-launched the app, so you can simply go to the application's preferences dialog and set things up again. Or, if you had very complex settings that you don't feel like re-entering, you can simply restore an older, working copy of the preferences file from a backup.

If you can't find the specific preferences file for the offending application, or if you're having more general system-wide problems, you can actually move your entire `~/Library/Preferences` folder to the Desktop. Log out and back in—if the problem still exists, it wasn't caused by a bad preferences file. If it's gone, it was due to one of the files in your Preferences folder. You'll need to manually figure out which one it is. Move your Preferences folder back, and then start making educated guesses about which is the culprit. A good first step to take is to view your Preferences folder as List, then click the Date Modified column to sort by date. Concentrate on files that were changed recently, or since you started having problems, since most likely the file that is causing the problems was changed around the same time your problems began.

Moving On...

Understanding settings and preference files is a valuable skill, especially as you perform some of the tips and tricks explained later in the book. You'll find yourself working with preference files, and even manually editing some, several times before all is said and done.

Now that you've got most of your settings the way you want them, let's talk about getting the most out of the startup and login processes. You'd be surprised how much you can do before you even start working.

Chapter 3

Subjugating Startup and Leveraging Login

(Or: Mastering startup and login to save time and frustration.)

You've most likely booted up your Mac many, many times; if you've been using OS X for a while, you may have even set up a few applications to launch at login. However, there's a lot more going on during startup and login than you're probably aware. The startup system is chosen, code is loaded, services are started, and the login process is executed. Like much of Mac OS X, each of these actions and processes can be customized. In this chapter, you'll learn more about the startup and login processes, how to tailor them to your preferences and uses, and how to take advantage of special startup options.

The Boot Process

When your Mac starts up, you see the gray Apple startup screen, then the white "Mac OS X" window (called the boot panel) on a blue background, and then the login screen. After logging in, you finally see the familiar Mac OS Desktop. (If your Mac is set to auto-login, you never even see the login screen.) However, between the time you hit the power button and when you see the Desktop, a lot of things go on in the background. While it's not vital for you to know these processes inside and out, background on them will be useful later in the chapter as we discuss ways to customize startup. The following is a summary of what happens at startup, in the order the events occur:

BootROM is activated The BootROM is firmware built into your Mac's hardware. Its purpose is to initialize and test your computer's hardware and to choose an operating system to boot into. Assuming you've chosen a Mac OS X volume to boot from, the process proceeds as described below. (*Open Firmware*, which I'll talk about later in this chapter, is part of the BootROM.)

BootX runs BootX is a utility that loads the core of Mac OS X (the *kernel*), as well as any *kernel extensions* (drivers that interact directly with the kernel to provided added functionality; these files are generally located in `/System/Library/Extensions`). You see the gray Apple image on the screen. BootX then loads the systems for data, I/O (input/output), and messaging, and mounts the file system. At this point your computer is officially "booting" Mac OS X.

System initialization occurs Officially called the "BSN init process," system initialization does four things:

- Checks for certain startup options such as single-user mode or CD booting (both discussed later in this chapter)
- Runs the system initialization scripts (located at `/etc/rc.boot` and `/etc/rc`)
- Launches the loginwindow application, which is responsible for displaying the login window and managing user-level processes
- Continues to run in the background, cleaning up system-level processes that terminate

The final step of the `/etc/rc` script is to launch Mac OS X's `SystemStarter` utility (located at `/sbin/SystemStarter`). This utility launches the various services that allow Mac OS X to function properly, as well as any services (from both Apple and third-party vendors) that provide additional, system-level functionality. Apple's startup items are located in `/System/Library/StartupItems`; third-party vendors generally install their startup services in `/Library/StartupItems`. (You're probably thinking, "Hey, there's that multi-domain file organization I read about in Chapter 1!" If so, you're correct.) Note that SystemStarter is a Unix utility that cannot be launched in the Finder; if you ever need to use it, you have to use Terminal to access it.

NOTE You can get all the gory details of the boot sequence from Apple's official developer note on the topic: `http://developer.apple.com/techpubs/macosx/Essentials/SystemOverview/BootingLogin/`.

If you've ever opened the Process Viewer utility and seen processes you didn't recognize, this is a big source of them. Most of the things launched by SystemStarter are processes that don't show up anywhere other than Process Viewer or other utilities that reveal system-level processes.

If the above seems a bit complicated and geeky, don't worry. None of it is necessary for you to use, and enjoy using, your Mac. However, later in the chapter I give a few cool tips that deal with the boot process; you'll definitely have a better understanding of the "why" and "how" behind them having read this section. Now it's time to talk about how to customize the process.

Choosing a Startup Volume or System

The most obvious way you can tailor the startup process to your needs is by choosing the boot volume and/or the copy of the Mac OS you want to use to boot your Mac. You can do this via System Preferences or using the keyboard at startup.

The Startup Disk System Preferences

User level: admin
Affects: all users
Terminal: no

The Startup Disk pane of System Preferences is where you choose both the drive and the operating system on that drive you wish to boot into at startup. When you select this panel from within the System Preferences application, Mac OS X checks all mounted/connected volumes (including NetBoot servers) for viable operating systems—on the newest Macs, it looks for bootable versions of Mac OS X; on older Macs, it looks for both Mac OS X and Mac OS 9 System Folders. During this process you'll see the spinning "beach ball" wait cursor. When it has finished, you'll be presented with a list of all versions of the Mac OS that you can choose for your startup system (Figure 3.1). Select the OS you want to use, and either click the Restart… button, close System Preferences, or switch to another preference pane. You will be asked if you want to save your change, or (if you clicked the Restart button) if you want to save the change and restart.

FIGURE 3.1:

The Startup Disk pane of System Preferences

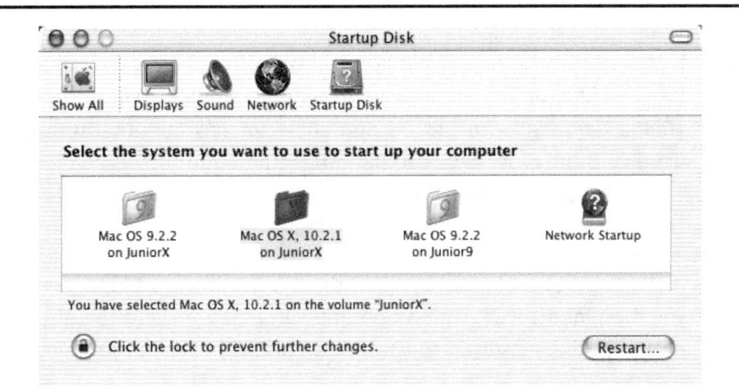

You'll notice that in Figure 3.1, the volume JuniorX actually has two available operating systems to boot into: Mac OS 9.2.2 and Mac OS X version 10.2.1. This illustrates how a single volume can contain multiple valid operating systems. I could also choose to boot into Mac OS 9.2.2 from the volume Junior9. The final option, Network Startup, is visible but does not list any version of the Mac OS because none is available for network booting right now. However, even if OS X isn't currently able to find a bootable system on your network, it still lets you choose Network Startup. If you do so, the next time you restart your Mac, it will first search for a NetBoot server to start from; if it can't find one, it will revert to the OS it most recently used.

Choosing a Boot Volume at Startup

In addition to using System Preferences, you actually have three other ways to select a boot volume at startup: you can use the keyboard to access the built-in Startup Manager, to boot directly from a CD-ROM, or to bypass previously chosen settings and boot from the most recent OS X volume.

Using Startup Manager

User level: any, unless restricted by Open Firmware
Affects: all users
Terminal: no

On recent-model Macs, holding down the option key at startup will bring up the Startup Manager utility. Your computer will search for all *volumes* that contain a bootable Mac OS (9 or X) system; the search can take a while, especially if you're connected to a network, but when it is completed, you'll be presented with a set of iconic buttons, one for each bootable *volume* (two are shown in Figure 3.2). If the icon for a volume has a blue "X" on it, selecting that volume will boot your Mac into OS X; selecting a volume with a blue and white Mac OS "happy face" will boot your Mac into OS 9. After you select a volume, simply click the right arrow to continue the startup process. If you need to rescan for volumes (e.g., if you've subsequently attached an external hard drive, or connected to a network), click the circular arrow.

TIP If you use the Startup Manager utility to choose a boot volume, you'll notice that it often takes a *long* time before you can actually select a volume and click the continue button. This is because your Mac is searching for any connected network volumes that could be used to boot your Mac. You can stop this search by holding down the mouse button until you see the spinning cursor stop.

TIP If you need to eject the CD/DVD drive from Startup Manager, press command+. (period); if you then insert a CD with a bootable OS that you want to select as your boot OS, be sure to click the rescan button to cause it to show up as an option.

I emphasize the term *volume* in the previous paragraph because unlike the Startup Disk pane of System Preferences, which allows you to select from multiple bootable operating systems on each volume, the Startup Manager utility only shows a *single* OS per volume—the one most recently used to boot up your Mac. In other words, if you have a volume that contains Mac OS X and Mac OS 9, and you most recently used that volume to boot into OS X, that volume will only show up once on the Startup Manager screen, and will only be selectable as a Mac OS X boot volume. You can see this difference by comparing Figure 3.2 (Startup Manager) with Figure 3.1 (Startup Disk in System Preferences); the same computer was used in both examples. The volume *JuniorX* has two bootable systems, Mac OS X and Mac OS 9, but whereas both are selectable in Figure 3.1, only OS X is an option in Figure 3.2. Note that the term *volume* means any hard drive, removable disk, or partition. (See Appendix B for more info on volumes and partitions.)

FIGURE 3.2:

The Startup Manager utility

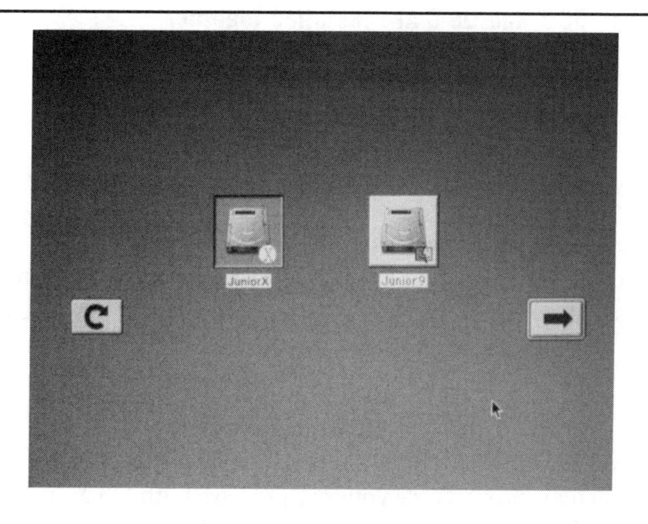

NOTE Macs that can take advantage of the Startup Manager include all iBooks; PowerMac G4 models with AGP graphics slots (including the G4 Cube); PowerBooks with FireWire ports; iMacs with slot-loading CD drives; and any Macs produced after these models. On earlier Macs, the option key does not invoke Startup Manager.

One other difference between using Startup Manager and System Preferences is that the volume you choose in Startup Manager is only used as the boot volume for that *particular* startup. The next time you restart/start up, the volume/system chosen in Startup Disk preferences will be used. In other words, Startup Disk settings in System Preferences remain until you change them; selections made in Startup Manager only affect the current startup.

Booting from a CD or DVD

User level: any, unless restricted by Open Firmware
Affects: all users
Terminal: no

There are times when you may want to boot from a CD or DVD that contains a bootable OS (a Mac OS installation CD, a disk utility CD, etc.). If your Mac is already up and running, you can simply insert the disc and use the Startup Disk pane of System Preferences to select it. However, if your Mac isn't running or if it won't start up because of some kind of problem (or if you just don't want to use System Preferences and make the CD selection "permanent"), you can force it to boot directly from the CD/DVD. Simply place the CD/DVD in the drive, and hold the C key down at startup. If you need to eject the drive to insert the CD, hold down the eject key on your keyboard (F12 on non-Apple keyboards), or the mouse button, until the drive opens.

When OS X and OS 9 Are Installed Together

User level: any, unless restricted by Open Firmware
Affects: all users
Terminal: no

If you have a single volume with both Mac OS X and Mac OS 9 (the default installation on new Macs), and your Mac is one that can boot into OS 9, there's one other trick you can use, but it's a very specific trick that only works in one specific circumstance. If you last booted into OS 9 *and* you want to instead boot into OS X, you can hold the X key down at startup; this boots you into OS X *and* changes the Startup Disk preferences to Mac OS X, making the change "permanent." You can't press the 9 key to do the opposite, and it doesn't let you change boot volumes; it doesn't do anything else at all. But if you need to boot into X in these particular circumstances, it's a handy tool.

As you read the different options for choosing a startup system, you may have noticed that if you only have a single volume, and have both OS X and OS 9 installed on it (or two copies of OS X or OS 9), it's a bit tricky to switch between the two without starting up your Mac, and then using System Preferences to switch. This situation is one where partitioning your hard drive comes in handy, as each partition is considered a different volume, allowing you to install a different OS on each. I'll talk more about partitioning in Appendix B.

Once you've chosen a startup volume/system, the computer begins booting into that OS and the boot panel appears. Here's how to make it appear the way you want it to.

Customizing the Boot Panel

The *boot panel* is the white and gray striped box with the blue Apple logo that appears at startup; you see it in between the initial grey Apple screen and the login screen. As it is displayed, you also see text that indicates the various system services that are being loaded. This is all well and good, but many users really don't care; they'd rather have a screen that illustrates their individuality (these are the same people that changed their startup screen under OS 9). It turns out that you can change both the image used for the boot panel, and the text displayed during boot (called the boot strings).

Changing the Boot Panel Image

There are two ways to change the boot panel image. You can either change it manually, or you can use one of several third-party utilities. But first you need to find or make a boot panel image. If you're the creative type, you can make your own in any photo or graphics application. The size of the image should be approximately 350 pixels wide by 265 pixels high (and you should make sure that you leave room in the bottom half of your image for the progress bar and boot strings). Your new image should be in PDF format (if your graphics application cannot save as a PDF file, you can use OS X's Preview application to convert your image to PDF). Or, if you want to take advantage of one of the many replacement boot panels already out there, check out `http://www.resexcellence.com/user_X_boot.shtml`. Once you've got your new boot panel image, you can choose how to install it.

NOTE Changing the boot panel only changes it for the specific Mac OS X volume on which you make the change. If you have multiple Mac OS X volumes and want a custom boot panel on each of them, you'll need to follow the procedures below for each volume.

Changing the Boot Panel Image Manually

User level: admin/root
Affects: all users
Terminal: optional

The default boot panel image is located in `/System/Library/CoreServices/SystemStarter/QuartzDisplay.bundle/Resources/BootPanel.pdf`. In order to replace it with your new boot panel image, you'll need to use `sudo` in Terminal or launch a utility like File Buddy as root (as discussed in Chapter 1). I'm going to use Terminal below, but you can use File Buddy to copy and move files as we did in Chapter 2.

1. Rename your new boot panel image **`BootPanel.pdf`**.
2. Launch Terminal and back up the default boot panel image to your Desktop:

   ```
   cp /System/Library/CoreServices/SystemStarter/QuartzDisplay.bundle
   ➥/Resources/BootPanel.pdf ~/Desktop/BootPanelBackup.pdf <RETURN>
   ```

   (There are two spaces in that line: one after the `cp` command, and one between the first `.pdf` and ~.)
3. Using the path to your new boot panel image, copy it to the location of the original image; since the location to which you're copying it is located in `/System`, you need to use the `sudo` command:

   ```
   sudo cp NewImagePath /System/Library/CoreServices/SystemStarter
   ➥ /QuartzDisplay.bundle/Resources/BootPanel.pdf
   ```

   (There are three spaces in that line: after `sudo`, after `cp`, and after *`NewImagePath`*.)

   You will be asked for your account password for the copy to proceed. It will automatically replace the original (which is why we made a backup in Step 1).
4. Restart your Mac to see the new boot panel image (see the example in Figure 3.3).

FIGURE 3.3:
The default (left) boot panel image, and a custom image (right)

Changing the Boot Panel Using Visage

User level: admin
Affects: all users
Terminal: no

Although the previous procedure is fairly simply, an even easier way to change your boot panel image is using Sanity Software's shareware Visage (`http://www.stanford.edu/~keaka/`). As a preference pane, you need to copy Visage to the appropriate `/Library/PreferencePanes` folder as discussed in the previous chapter. Once installed, Visage provides a graphical interface to changing the boot panel image, as well as changing many other boot and login characteristics. I'll discuss this excellent utility more in the next section when I talk about changing the boot strings, and later in the chapter when I talk about customizing the login process.

WARNING In addition to modifying the boot panel, it is possible to customize the *boot image*, the grey Apple logo on a grey background that you see immediately after pressing the power button (before you see the boot panel). However, to do this you must actually modify the BootX utility described at the beginning of this chapter. I do not recommend doing this, as any mistake or file corruption could render your Mac dead in the water, necessitating a full reinstall of Mac OS X. However, if you're feeling brave and want to try this on your own, you can check out (`http://www.ryandesign.com/jagboot/`) for a detailed tutorial on how to modify the boot image. The website also provides a utility, StartupSyringe, that will automate the process for you, and another similar utility, MacBoot, is available from `http://ittpoi.com/cci.html`. Hello Jaguar (`http://www.fishbacksw.com/`), does the same thing except that it replaces the gray Apple logo with the old Happy Mac image from earlier versions of the Mac OS.

Customizing the Boot Strings

User level: admin
Affects: all users
Terminal: no

In addition to changing the boot panel image, you can also modify the boot strings, which are the bits of text that appear in the boot panel as services are started (e.g., "Starting Apache web server," "Starting Core Services," and "Starting NetInfo"). Why would you want to change these strings? I can think of two reasons: first, because it can be fun to have your own little snippets of text appear; second, because you can use this functionality to identify your computer should it ever be stolen or lost. I'm going to use the latter as the basis for the following tutorial.

If you have a PowerBook or iBook, you've probably been concerned at some point about it getting stolen or lost—I know I have. When I was running Mac OS 9, I would create a custom startup screen that contained my name, phone number, and e-mail address so that anyone starting up my laptop would immediately see who owned it. Under OS X, I can use the boot strings to accomplish the same thing. I simply change the boot strings from their default state to the text strings that I want to appear at startup. I use Visage, discussed in the previous section.

1. Launch System Preferences and select the Visage pane.
2. Click on the Boot Strings tab.
3. Click the padlock button at the bottom of the window to authenticate using your admin username and password.
4. In the boot strings window, double-click on a boot string to edit it; when you're finished, hit return, or press the tab key to move to the next string.
5. Restart to view your new and improved boot strings!

TIP Since the boot strings go by incredibly fast during the boot process, you'll want to use multiple boot strings for each line of info you want to be readable at startup. I chose to show just two bits of info—my name and my e-mail address—so I put my name in half of the boot strings, and my e-mail address in the other half (Figure 3.4).

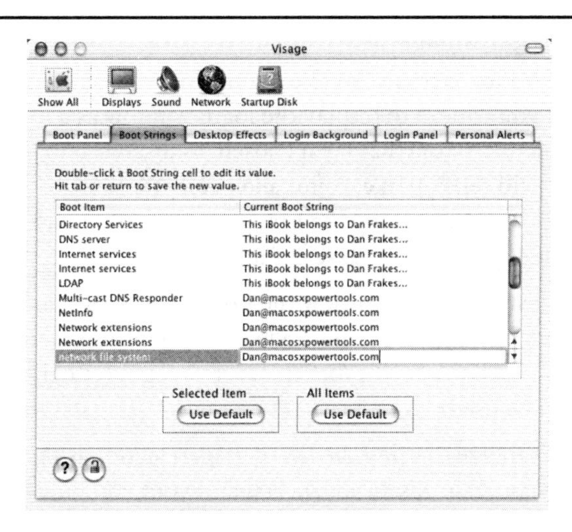

FIGURE 3.4: Editing the boot strings to identify an iBook's owner at startup

You could even use a picture of yourself (using the previous tip on replacing the boot panel image) to have a completely customized boot panel that identifies you and tells anyone using your laptop how to contact you. If you ever change your mind and want to go back to the default boot strings, simply click the Use Default buttons: the Selected Item button returns the current boot string to its default value and the All Items button returns *all* boot strings to their default values.

The Login Process

Once the boot process is complete, the Mac OS X login screen appears (assuming you don't have your account set to auto-login, of course). The login window is where users log in by selecting an account and then entering the password for that account. Although the login screen and window look rather simple, there are a number of ways in which you can customize them.

I discussed creating accounts in Chapter 1, and I talked about configuring the Users tab of Accounts preferences in both Chapters 1 and 2. However, login-related settings are configured in two other places in System Preferences: the Login Options tab of Accounts preferences and the Login Items pane.

Login Options in Accounts Preferences

User level: admin
Affects: all users
Terminal: no

If you launch System Preferences and click on the Accounts pane, you'll see the familiar Users tab; however, if you click on the Login Options tab you get a few extra options that we haven't yet discussed; all of these options require admin access.

Display Login Window as:

The first option is to display the login window as either "Name and password" or "List of users." If you choose to display the login window as a list of users, each user's username and custom picture (if one has been chosen, as discussed in Chapter 1) will be displayed. Clicking on a user will select that account and present a password box to log in as that user. (You can also select a user by typing the first few letters of the username; once the username/picture is highlighted, press return to select it.)

If you instead choose to view the login window as names and passwords, you will simply be provided with two blank fields: one for account username, and one for account password. Users will have to provide *both* in order to login (either the short username or the long username can be used).

The advantage to using the list of users selection is that it is easier and more convenient for users to login. The disadvantage is that if your computer is publicly accessible, showing user accounts at startup means that a malicious user already has half of what he or she needs to gain access to your computer (the username) and only needs to figure out a password. I personally use the list of users on my home computer, and the name and password setting on my laptop.

Hide the Restart and Shut Down Buttons

The second option is to "Hide the Restart and Shut Down buttons." Having these options (restart and shut down) available at login is convenient in a secure environment, such as your home. However, as I discussed earlier, you can choose the startup volume using the keyboard; a malicious user could use the restart button and then boot your Mac from an OS 9 volume, or from a system install CD, and change passwords or even wipe out your hard drive. Thus, on a laptop or publicly accessible computer, you may want to disable them.

Show Password Hint after Three Attempts to Enter a Password

Finally, you can choose to show password hints after three failed attempts at entering a password. You set up a hint when you created your account; other users can create and edit their hints in the My Account preference pane. Hints are helpful if you have a hard time remembering your password. However, again, if your Mac is at risk of someone trying to gain access, hints help not just you and your legitimate users; they also help the hacker.

The Login Items System Preferences

User level: normal
Affects: individual user
Terminal: no

Whereas the Login Options tab of Accounts preferences provides system-level login options, each user has their own Login Items preferences pane. This pane basically provides two options: to have an item (application, folder, file) opened automatically when the user logs in and, in the case of applications, to have the application hidden in the background after it is opened (so as not to clutter up the screen).

To choose an item to be opened at login, open the Login Items preference pane, and then drag the item into the window; alternatively, click the Add… button and navigate to the item in the file browser. To remove an item, click the item to select it, and then click the Remove button or hit the delete key on the keyboard. Finally, to automatically hide an application after it is launched, check the Hide box to the left of the item's name (the Hide check box has no effect on documents or folders). The next time you log in, these items will be launched or opened as soon as the Finder appears.

Login Items are actually a very useful feature, as you can log in and have your favorite applications waiting for you to use when login is complete. You can also open documents, or even folders that you tend to access frequently (Figure 3.5). (In Chapter 12, I'll even show you how to use Login Items to automatically connect to servers at login.) In addition, you

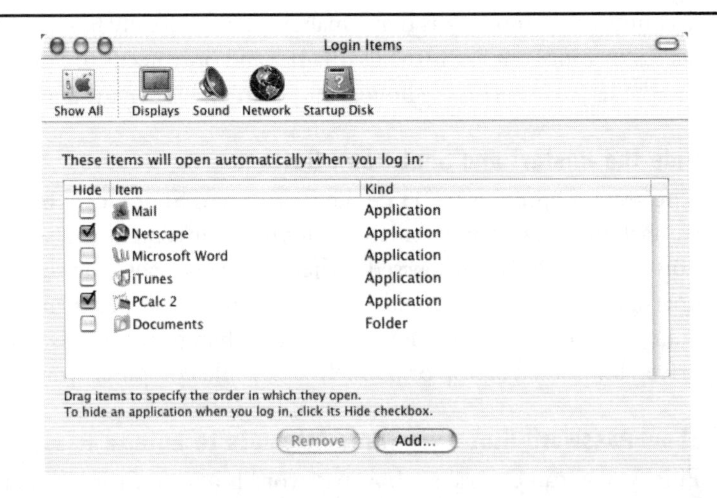

FIGURE 3.5: Using Login Items to automatically open frequently used items

can change the order that items are opened by dragging them up or down in the Login Items window; some applications prefer to be opened earlier or later, or perhaps you want to open a certain spreadsheet *before* you open other documents that link to it.

NOTE You may notice a few Login Items that you never set up yourself; this is normal. Some Mac OS X applications require background processes in order to function properly and use the Login Items feature to start those processes. In addition, some applications will ask you if you want them to run at login; if you say "yes," you're basically giving them permission to add themselves to the Login Items list. If an item appears in your Login Items list and you didn't put it there, be sure you know what it does before you remove it.

If you used Mac OS 9 before moving to OS X, Login Items probably remind you of startup items; they are very similar. In fact, you can actually use the Mac OS 9 method if you prefer; that's the next tip.

Using OS 9-Style "Startup Items" instead of Login Items

User level: normal
Affects: individual user
Terminal: no

Under Mac OS 9, if you wanted items to be launched at startup, you placed them, or aliases to them, in the Startup Items folder inside the System Folder. If you prefer this method to Mac OS X's Login Items preference pane, you should download the freeware Login Items Engine from Northern Softworks (`http://www.northernsoftworks.com/`). You simply drop the Login Items Engine in the `/Applications` or `~/Applications` folder. At the next login, a folder called Login Items will be created in your home directory. You can treat this just as you would an OS 9 Startup Items folder—drag items in or out as you desire; anything inside will be opened at login. (The Login Items Engine will add itself to the Login Items preference pane; you should leave it there for it to work properly.)

Customizing the Login Screen

Earlier in the chapter I showed you how to customize the boot panel; you have just as much flexibility in changing the login screen. You can change the appearance of the login background, the login window logo, and the login window title.

Changing the Login Background

User level: admin
Affects: all users
Terminal: no

By default, the login background (the screen you see behind the login window) is Apple's Classic Aqua Blue image; you can view this image at any time from within the Desktop System Preferences (it's in the default Apple Background Images collection). However, this image can get a bit, well, boring after so many logins. You can spice up the login screen with any background picture you like. The only caveat is that the image must be in JPEG format (JPEG image names generally end in `.jpg`); you can use Apple's Preview application or the excellent Graphic Converter (`http://www.lemkesoft.com/`) to convert pretty much any graphics format to JPEG.

The easiest way to change the login background is to again use the handy Visage preference pane. Simply click on the Login tab then click the Import button in the Manage Background Collection box. Navigate to your JPEG image and add it to your collection (you can add multiple images by repeating the process). Any image you add to your collection will be available from the pop-up menu in the Current Login Screen Background box. Select your new background from the menu, enter your username and password when prompted, and the next time you log in, the boring blue background will be replaced by your new, stylish one. (You can click the Preview button in Visage to see what it will look like without logging out.) Select Pick Randomly from the menu to have Visage randomly choose a background at each login.

Changing the Login Window Logo and Title

User level: admin
Affects: all users
Terminal: no

In addition to choosing a different login background, you can customize the actual login window itself. Specifically, you can change the graphic at the top of the window (the login panel logo) and the graphic text in the middle of the window (the login panel title). You can create your own logo and title graphics; most common graphic formats are acceptable: TIFF, GIF, JPEG, and even PDF files will work. (The title doesn't have to be text, by the way; it can be any image or graphic.) When creating images, the login panel logo graphic should be 63 pixels wide by 77 pixels high, and the login panel title graphic should be 143 pixels wide by 34 pixels high.

Like the login background, the easiest way to change the login window logo and title is using Visage. Click on the More Login tab and import your logo and title graphics using the respective Import buttons. Then select your favorite logo and title (see Figure 3.6) using the respective pop-up menus. The next time you or any other user logs in, the custom login window will be displayed (you can click the Preview button to get a sneak peak without logging out). If you're curious, the default login panel graphics are located in `/System/Library/CoreServices/SecurityAgentPlugins/loginwindow.bundle.Contents/Resources/`

TIP You can also add a text banner to the login window by editing the file `/Library/Preferences/com.apple.loginwindow.plist` as root. Immediately after the first occurrence of <dict>, add the following two lines:

```
<key>LoginwindowText</key>
<string>banner text</string>
```

Managing Startup/Login Options

In Mac OS 9 and earlier, you could control what startup files (extensions, control panels, startup items, etc.) loaded at startup—manually, by moving them in and out of particular folders, or automatically using utilities such as Extensions Manager or Conflict Catcher. Generally the reason for doing this was to solve startup conflicts, to reduce the potential for such conflicts, or simply to reduce the amount of RAM used by the OS.

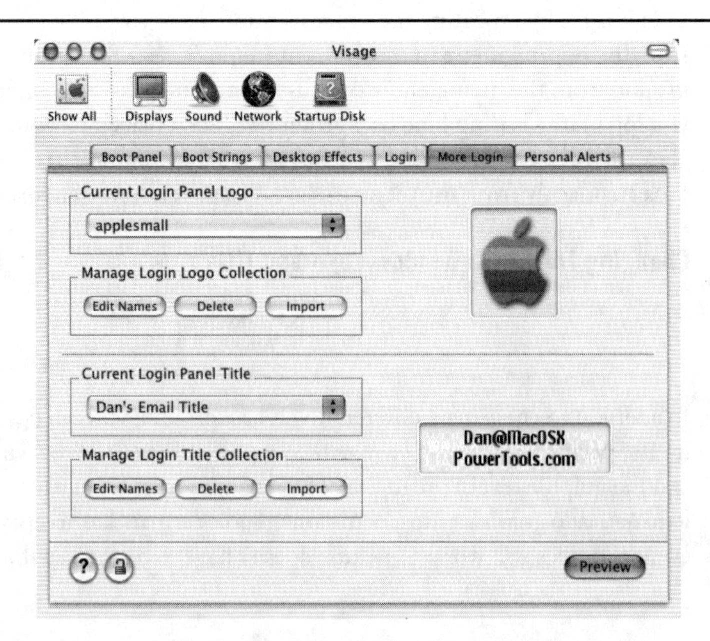

FIGURE 3.6: Customizing the login window using Visage

In Mac OS X, extensions, control panels, and startup items have been replaced by kernel extensions, preference panes, and login items. Only kernel extensions actively modify the "guts" of the operating system, so to speak, so the chances for major conflicts have been reduced considerably. In addition, the amount of RAM used by most "startup" files is minimal, and because of OS X's superior memory management, the gain from deactivating such files is much less than it was under OS 9.

Nevertheless, there are still valid reasons to activate and deactivate services and system add-ons in Mac OS X. For example, you may find that a particular screen saver causes System Preferences to crash. Or you may want to turn system-wide startup items, such as the Apache web server, off "permanently" so that other admin users cannot enable Web Sharing. Or perhaps font conflicts are causing problems with applications or even the OS itself. A bit later in the chapter I'll talk about preventing the loading of *any* kernel extensions, login items, etc., by holding down the shift key at startup. However, you can also manage files on an individual basis. You can do this manually, or using a utility that automates the process.

NOTE In this section the phrase "login items" refers to files loaded by Mac OS X at startup and login such as preference panes, fonts, screen savers, and sounds, and is different from the files, folders, and/or applications each user adds to the Login Items pane in System Preferences (discussed earlier in the chapter).

Managing Startup/Login Items Manually

User level: any
Affects: depends on user level
Terminal: no

Managing files such as preference panes, screen savers, fonts, etc., is actually quite simple. As discussed in Chapter 1, each type of file must reside in a specific location in order to be loaded by the OS. Fonts, for example, must be in `/Library/Fonts` (for fonts available to all users) or `~/Library/Fonts` (for user-specific fonts). Preference panes must be located in `/Library/PreferencePanes` or `~/Library/PreferencePanes` in order to appear in the System Preferences application. Third-party, system-level startup items must reside in `/Library/StartupItems`. Thus in order to prevent a particular item from being loaded and used at login, you simply need to move it out of the appropriate folder—for example, if a font isn't located inside one of the fonts folders at login, it won't be available to users or the OS.

One way to deactivate files and still keep some semblance of order is to create a matching folder in the same directory as the enclosing folder that includes the word "Disabled" in its name—for example, create a new folder called "PreferencePanes (Disabled)" inside `/Library` and use this folder to store system-wide preference panes that you want to disable.

If you've got a good grasp on user accounts and file organization at this point, you know that an admin user can modify system-wide files, and thus can affect all user accounts; individual users can only manage items in their personal `~/Library` folder.

NOTE As mentioned in Chapter 1, each of these types of files (preference panes, fonts, screen savers, etc.) also has its own folder inside /System/Library. The files located in these folders were installed by Mac OS X, and should generally not be moved. In fact, the only way to move them is via root access. Luckily, they are rarely a cause of problems.

WARNING As discussed earlier in this chapter, there are also a few other types of startup/login processes: system-level startup processes provided by the OS that start during BootX, startup items/processes provided by third-party vendors that are launched during BootX (but after the system's own processes), and login processes. Unless you're an experienced user who is sure of what you're doing, I would discourage you from trying to disable these services.

Although managing startup and login items is fairly easy, it's a bit of a pain if you do it frequently since every type of file has its own folder, and every such folder exists on two or three levels (`/System/Library`, `/Library`, and `~/Library`). A much easier way to manage such files is using a utility such as Diablotin.

Managing Startup/Login Items Using Diablotin

User level: any
Affects: depends on user level
Terminal: no

If you find yourself enabling or disabling startup and login files often, or if you just don't want to bother mucking around in all the various Library folders, you definitely want to check out the excellent freeware preference pane Diablotin (`http://s.sudre.free.fr/Software/Diablotin.html`). It provides a consolidated view of all installed startup/login files, including fonts, preference panes, and system-wide startup items, and allows you to easily disable or enable them.

After installing Diablotin, simply launch System Preferences and choose the Diablotin pane. In the list of items on the left, you can click the disclosure triangle next to any category of files and see all the files of that type you've installed. Items with a library icon (three books) are located in the `/Library` directory (and thus available to all users); those with a user icon are located in the current user's `~/Library` folder. Clicking on an item's name in the Diablotin window provides you with information about that item (including the version number) in the information box on the right (Figure 3.7). To disable an item, uncheck the box next to its name and icon; to enable it, check the box. If you want to enable or disable items in `/Library`, you'll need to authenticate using your admin name and password (click the padlock at the bottom of the window).

NOTE When you disable an item in Diablotin, it is simply being moved to a newly created Disabled folder, just as you would have done using the manual procedure described in the previous section. Enabling an item from within Diablotin moves it back to the "active" folder.

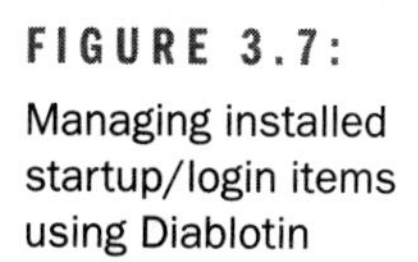

FIGURE 3.7:
Managing installed startup/login items using Diablotin

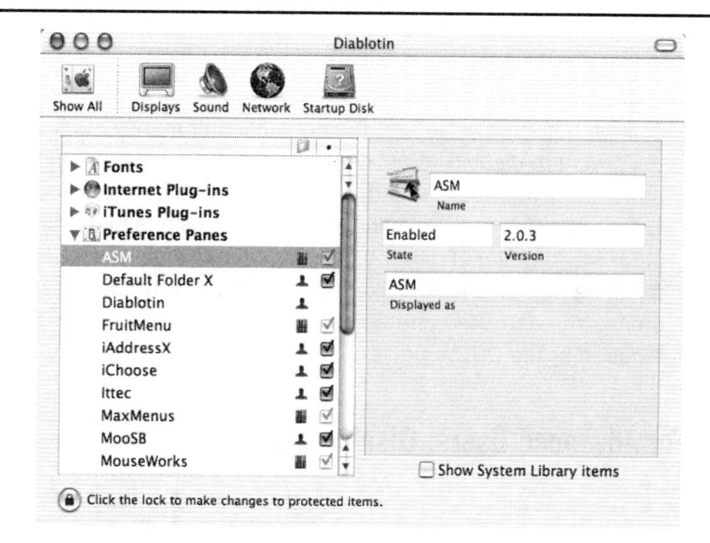

One common cause of minor problems in OS X is when a preference pane is accidentally installed twice—once in `/Library/PreferencePanes` for all users and again in `~/Library/PreferencePanes` for the current user. This can be especially risky if the two copies are different versions (i.e., an older one and a newer one). Diablotin makes it easy to find such duplication by listing such items next to each other; you can then simply disable one of them.

TIP If you see a file in Diablotin that you want to remove from your Mac completely, control-click on the file's name. Select Show in Finder from the contextual menu and the file will be presented in a Finder window, from which you can drag it to the Trash.

Checking the box next to Show System Library Items will include files located in `/System/Library` in the list. As mentioned in the warning a few pages back, you generally don't want to be changing these files; however, viewing the list this way does let you see the files provided by Apple (those with the OS X icon next to them) next to the files provided by other vendors (those with the library or user icons).

Changes you make in Diablotin (or changes made manually, for that matter) take effect at different times, depending on the type of file. Changes made to fonts or other application-specific files take effect the next time you launch each application that uses them. Changes made to preference panes generally take effect in two steps:

1. The preference pane itself appears in or disappears from System Preferences the next time you launch System Preferences.
2. The effects of the preference pane, if any, will be disabled or enabled the next time you log in.

Changes made to startup items take effect the next time you restart your Mac (since they load before the login window loads).

WARNING One type of startup file that Diablotin doesn't manage is kernel extensions. It's rare that you'd want to disable kernel extensions unless one of them is causing a startup problem; however, if you ever have that need, the shareware MOX Optimize (`http://fly.to/infosoft`) allows you to manage kernel extensions much like Diablotin lets you work with other startup files. From the MOX Optimize menu, select Mac OS X Options, and in the resulting window click the Extensions button. From the pop-up menu, select Kernel Extensions. You can then enable or disable each extension. Keep in mind that many are required by the OS, so be *very* careful what you turn on or off.

For Advanced Users: Disabling Services

User level: admin
Affects: all users
Terminal: no

I mentioned earlier that you probably don't want to disable System Library items, especially those in `/System/Library/StartupItems`, as some are essential for normal system functionality. However, advanced users may have system services that they simply don't use—and don't plan on using—and that they want to disable. The advantage of disabling services is that the OS takes up less RAM and processor resources (however, as I mentioned earlier in the chapter, such gains are likely to be small). If you decide you want to disable such services, you could use Diablotin, but instead I recommend the freeware utility Boot Config (`http://cs.northwestern.edu/~josha/bootconfig.htm`). Launch Boot Config and click on a startup item, and you'll quickly understand why I prefer this utility—in the Description box at the bottom of the window you see two important pieces of information (Figure 3.8). The first is a summary of what services or objects are currently depending on the selected service to be active; if there are any, you don't want to disable it. If you've selected a "core" service (one that is generally required by the OS for standard functionality), the box will also include a message that states "WARNING: Core startup item!" You generally do not want to disable these types of items, but experienced users may have a reason to do so. To disable a startup item, uncheck the box next to it, then restart. Boot Config moves the disabled service to a new folder, `/System/Library/DisabledStartupItems`, where it won't be launched at startup. If you later change your mind and want to restore a service, use Boot Config to enable it, then restart.

One other caveat: if you disable a service, make sure you don't try to use it inadvertently. For example, if you disable Apache, don't try to turn Web Sharing on in Sharing System Preferences, since Web Sharing uses Apache. The result could be a crash.

FIGURE 3.8:

Using Boot Config to configure startup services

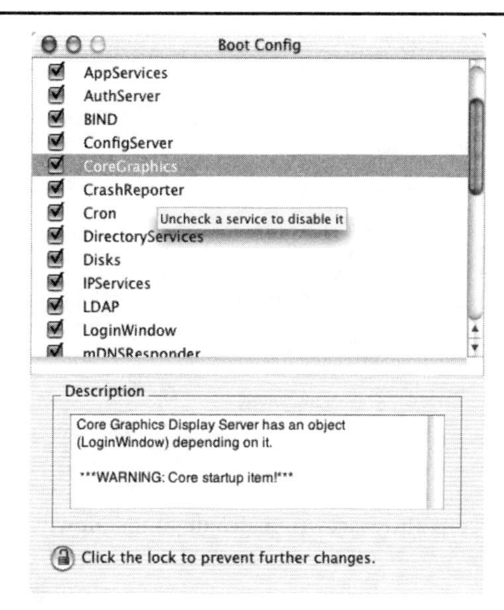

Stopping and Restarting Startup Processes

I've discussed how to set up Login Items for individual users and how to manage system-level startup processes and items. However, one thing I haven't mentioned is how to stop services and processes that are already running, or how to start services that you disabled at startup or stopped manually. These aren't things most users will need to do very often, if ever, but you'll know how to do both after reading this section.

The various startup and login services discussed throughout this chapter can be broken down into three basic categories: Mac OS X system-level services, located in `/System/Library/StartupItems` and launched by SystemStarter at the end of the boot process; third-party system-level services, located in `/Library/StartupItems` and launched by SystemStarter immediately after the OS services; and user-level (and user-specific) login items, listed in the Login Items pane of System Preferences and launched when the user logs in.

You can view active processes, and figure out whether they are system-level or user-level, using Apple's Process Viewer application, located at `/Applications/Utilities/Process Viewer`. After you launch Process Viewer, selecting User Processes from the Show: pop-up menu provides you with a list of all user-level processes that were launched at or since login (Figure 3.9). Selecting Administrator Processes shows all system-level processes, most of which were launched by SystemStarter during the boot process. (To see what many of these processes do, check out `http://www.westwind.com/reference/OS-X/background-processes.html`.)

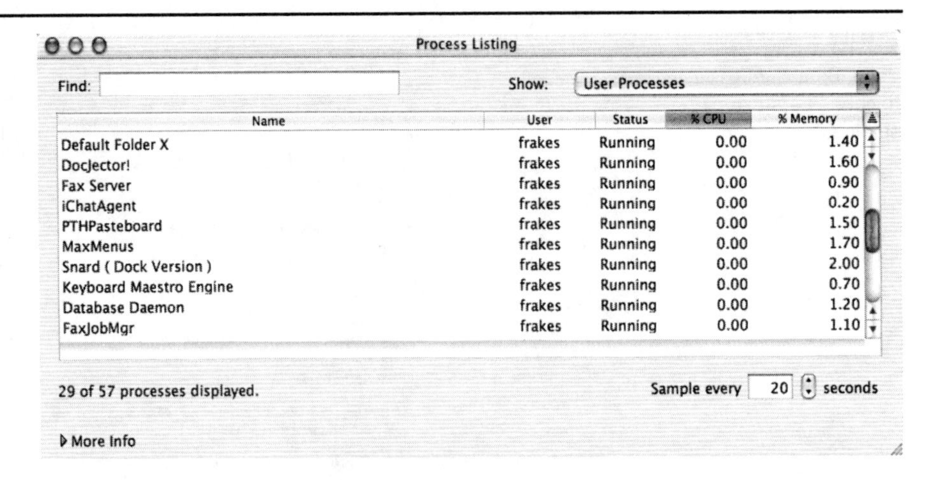

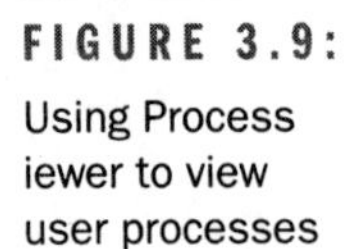

FIGURE 3.9: Using Process iewer to view user processes

How to stop and start processes depends on whether they are user-level or system-level processes.

NOTE Process Viewer actually shows *all* processes and applications, not just startup processes (especially if you select "All Processes" from the Show: pop-up). However, it's the easiest way to view processes by user level.

Stopping and Restarting User-Level Processes

User level: normal
Affects: individual user
Terminal: no

Most user-level login items are simply applications; they show up in the Dock and can be quit just like any other applications. Others are background applications or daemons, which means that they don't show up as regular apps; however, you can stop them by selecting them in the User Processes view of Process Viewer, then choosing Processes ➢ Quit Process. (Reasons for quitting applications vary, of course, and the scope of why you might want to quit various applications or processes is too big for this chapter; let's just say that troubleshooting is a frequent motivation.)

Starting or restarting such applications is also fairly easy. If you know where the original application resides, you can just double-click it to launch it again. However, some of these applications are difficult to find. For example, if you use Microsoft Entourage as your e-mail/calendar program, the reminders that pop-up for appointments, to-do items, etc., are provided by a background application called Microsoft Database Daemon, located inside the Microsoft Office folder. If you find that this application is not running and want to launch it, you have to track it down, which can be a real pain. If you find yourself in this situation, the easiest solution is simply to log out and log in again. Since these processes are all user-level and launch at login, they will all be started anew when you log in. And since you're not rebooting, it's a pretty quick fix.

Stopping and Restarting System-Level Processes

User level: admin
Affects: all users
Terminal: yes

System-level processes are a bit trickier than user-level processes; luckily, most users won't need to interact with them very often. However, if you find yourself needing to stop a system-level service, or if you had previously disabled such a service (as discussed earlier in the chapter) and want to start it again without having to restart, OS X allows you to use SystemStarter to do it.

I mentioned SystemStarter when I explained the boot process; I also mentioned that SystemStarter is the utility that loads services in the two `/StartupItems` folders at startup. What I haven't yet mentioned is that Apple has made SystemStarter available in Terminal as a way for admin users to start, stop, and restart individual services or all startup services at once. It uses a fairly simple command format:

```
sudo SystemStarter action service <RETURN>
```

where *`action`* is either `stop`, `start`, or `restart`, and *`service`* is the path to the service you wish to act on. The `sudo` command will ask for your account password to authenticate you as an admin user. For example, if I wanted to stop the SSH service (described more in detail in Chapter 12), I would simply type:

```
sudo SystemStarter stop /System/Library/StartupItems/ssh <RETURN>
```

(Try saying that ten times fast.) If I had previously disabled SSH (for example, using Boot Config as explained earlier in the chapter), and had just re-enabled it and wanted to start it without restarting my computer, I could simply type the following into Terminal:

```
sudo SystemStarter start /System/Library/StartupItems/ssh <RETURN>
```

SSH would be started just as if it had been loaded at startup. You can also restart a service that is already running by using `restart` in place of `start`.

You can do a few other useful things with SystemStarter. If you don't specify a particular service, SystemStarter will perform the action on *all* startup items. (A word of warning: don't try this with the `stop` action, or you'll be forced to reboot your Mac when all of the login services are stopped.) If you specify the `-x` option, SystemStarter will only load Apple-provided startup services; for example:

```
sudo SystemStarter -x restart <RETURN>
```

will stop all currently running services and restart just those provided by Apple with Mac OS X. Third-party items will not be restarted. This can come in handy when trying to figure out if third-party services are causing problems. Finally, you can execute these commands remotely if you have Remote Login enabled in Sharing System Preferences. I'll talk more about this in Chapter 12, but the gist of it is that you can take advantage of SystemStarter to troubleshoot a problematic computer remotely.

TIP Apple has actually provided a few scripts that perform some of the most common SystemStarter actions. Located in `/System/Library/SystemConfiguration/Kicker.bundle/Resources`, these scripts can be run from Terminal, or via a Telnet/SSH session: `restart-AppleTalk`, `restart-lookupd`, `restart-NetInfo`, and `set-hostname`. If you use the `-g` option with SystemStarter's `restart` action (`sudo SystemStarter -g restart`), you'll actually see the boot screen appear, even though you're already logged in!

Special Startup Options

In addition to the ways you can customize the boot and login processes, a few special startup options are available. They all do slightly different things, but because they don't fit neatly into any particular category of functionality, I'm grouping them here.

Single User Mode: Command+S

User level: any, unless restricted by Open Firmware
Affects: all users
Terminal: yes

If you hold down command+S at startup, you'll be presented with a bunch of code (white or yellow text on a black screen) in what looks like Terminal. What you're seeing here is called *single-user mode*, and the text you're seeing is basically BootX (discussed earlier in this chapter) in all its glory. After it's done its thing, you're presented with a command-line prompt. At this point you can run `fsck`, the built-in disk utility (discussed more in Chapter 14) or work directly with Terminal commands (and thus files on your hard drive).

WARNING Single-user mode gives anyone with command-line experience pretty much unlimited access to your system. For this reason it's definitely a security risk. If you want to be super-safe, I'll show you how to prevent unauthorized single-user mode access when I discuss Open Firmware protection in Chapter 13. (I mention Open Firmware later in this chapter, as well.)

To exit single-user mode, type `exit` <RETURN> to continue the startup process and proceed to the login screen, `reboot` <RETURN> or `shutdown -r now` <RETURN> to restart your Mac and start up normally, or `shutdown -h now` <RETURN> to shut down your computer.

Verbose Mode: Command+V

User level: any, unless restricted by Open Firmware
Affects: NA
Terminal: no

Holding down command+V at startup puts you into what is called *verbose mode*. During BootX, verbose mode is identical to single-user mode; however, instead of stopping when BootX finishes and presenting you with a command-line prompt, verbose mode continues through the boot process until the login screen appears. Basically, you skip the boot panel and its status messages (in fact, if you watch the text that goes by in verbose mode, you'll see the same messages).

Verbose mode lasts until the next shutdown or restart; if it is invoked at startup, the next time you shut down, you'll see a textual report of the shutdown processes.

"Safe" Startup or "Safe" Login: Shift

User level: any, unless restricted by Open Firmware
Affects: all users or individual
Terminal: no

Former Mac OS 9 users will remember that if you held the shift key down at startup, your Mac would boot using a bare-bones system with no extensions, control panels, or other startup files loaded (including items in the Startup Items folder). The shift key in Mac OS X performs a similar trick; however, it does so in three parts, each independent of the others.

If you hold down the shift key immediately after the boot process starts and release it after you see the gray screen with the dark gray Apple (hold it until the "spinning" progress indicator appears), you'll enter what Apple calls *safe mode*. In safe mode, your Mac starts up with only essential kernel extensions and services, and ignores the kernel extension cache it normally uses to speed up the startup process. As a bonus, this procedure also automatically runs OS X's built-in disk check/repair utility, `fsck`, to ensure that your boot volume is free of problems. Safe mode can be a very effective tool for troubleshooting major startup issues, especially those caused by kernel extension problems.

NOTE How does OS X know if a kernel extension is "essential" or not? Inside every kernel extension package (viewable by control-clicking on the kernel extension and selecting "Show Package Contents" from the resulting menu) is a text file at `/Contents/Info.plist`. Essential files have a "key" variable called *`OSBundleRequired`* included in the text of this file. (I'll talk more about packages in Chapter 4.)

If you have your Mac set to auto-login, holding down the shift key *after* you see the boot progress panel (the white panel that shows which services are loading—I showed you how to modify this earlier in the chapter) *until* you see the standard login window prevents auto-login. You'll have the opportunity to login normally, or to allow another user to login.

Finally, if you hold down the shift key from the login screen until you are completely logged in (until you can actually start using the Finder), no personal login items (those listed in the Login Items pane of System Preferences) will load, and any Finder windows that were left open during your previous session will be closed. This "safe login" affects only the user currently logging in, and is a nice trick to figure out if one of your Login Items is causing problems.

These three procedures are independent of one another: you can do one, two, or all three, in any combination. The only caveat is that if you *don't* want to take advantage of all three, the timing is a bit tricky. For example, if you want to *permit* auto-login, but suppress login items, you have to wait until the instant you see your Desktop appear on the screen, and then press the shift key. If you want to use safe mode, but allow auto-login, you need to release the shift key as soon as you see the gray boot screen.

Once you've used safe mode and/or safe login to isolate a problem, you should restart and let your Mac start up normally to ensure that all necessary kernel extensions and services are loaded.

Accessing Terminal at Login: Console Login

User level: any, unless restricted by Open Firmware
Affects: NA
Terminal: yes

There are times when you need or want to use Terminal to work with files or to fix a problem. However, what if the problem you're trying to fix prevents you from logging in? Or what if you you're not logged in, and you want to quickly use Terminal without having to log in, launch Terminal, complete your task, and then log out again? The solution to both of these problems is to log in as "console."

NOTE Logging into console is different than entering single-user mode at startup. Single-user mode is accessible to anyone, and no startup services are loaded; whereas console login requires a valid OS X user account and, since it occurs after the boot process, includes all of OS X's startup services.

1. If your Mac is currently shut down, press the power button to start up.
2. If you had your login set to show "Name and password," skip to the next step. If you have your login window set to display the "List of users" (login pictures and usernames), click the Others… user—it should be the last icon listed—and press return to bring up the name and password dialog. If Others… is not an option, press option+escape, then click on any user. This should present you with the Name and Password fields.
3. In the Name field, type **>console** (including the > character) and press return (you don't need to enter a password). You'll be presented with what looks like a Terminal window, but it will have taken over the entire screen. You're now working directly with the command-line.
4. At the login prompt, enter your username and press return.
5. Enter your account password when prompted.

You're now logged into your computer, but without the user interface. You have the same access as if you had booted into OS X normally. When you're done doing what you need to do, type **exit** and press return; you'll be logged out and the login window will reappear. You can use console login as often as you like, and in fact I frequently use it to do quick things that don't require a full login.

NOTE The "console" you use for login is different from Mac OS X's Console application. "Terminal" would probably have been a better name for Apple to choose for login (or "Console" a better name for Terminal), since console login is very similar to working in Terminal.

Open Firmware: Command+Option+O+F

User level: admin
Affects: all users
Terminal: yes

Open Firmware is part of your Mac's BootROM, discussed at the beginning of this chapter. It controls your computer for the short period between hardware initialization and the processes controlled by BootX. As such, it is in the unique position of controlling *all* access to your Mac. There are two situations where Open Firmware can come in handy for the average user. First, if you have a CD or DVD that simply won't eject no matter what you do, typing **eject cd** in Open Firmware will *force* your Mac's built-in CD or DVD drive to eject. Second, and more significant, Open Firmware allows you to prevent access to any of the special startup options discussed above, as well as *any* of the methods of choosing a startup volume or system discussed earlier in this chapter. By setting an Open Firmware password, only a user (presumably you) with that password will be able to access any of these functions, thus closing a good number of Mac OS X security loopholes (booting into OS 9, booting off of a CD, accessing single-user mode, etc.). I'll explain how to set up an Open Firmware password in Chapter 13.

NOTE You can invoke Open Firmware at startup by pressing command+option+O+F; however, unless you have a very specific reason to access Open Firmware, there's not much to do or see. Simply type **mac-boot** and press return to continue booting up, or type **shut-down** and then return to shutdown.

Moving On...

We're almost ready to get down and dirty with the everyday use of your Mac. However, we've got one more topic to cover first, and that's installations. Since a lot of the exercises and tips we'll be doing for the rest of the book entail installing third-party software, and you may need to install (or uninstall) software, understanding installations is an important skill to have. Plus you never know when you'll have to install or reinstall the OS, or parts of it.

Chapter 4

Installations, Inc.

(Or: Mastering Mac OS and third-party installations.)

When you first took your Mac out of the box, it came with most of the things you needed to be a fairly functional member of the computer-using public: e-mail client, web browser, word processor—maybe even the AppleWorks or Microsoft Office suite of applications. However, at some point you had to (or will have to) install other software, whether it's commercial software, games, or even shareware or freeware you've downloaded from the Internet. In addition, you may want to (or, unfortunately, *need* to) reinstall software that came with your computer. Finally, there are sure to be times when you have to undertake the (sometimes daunting) task of *un*installing software.

Since you're already using Mac OS X, I'm going to talk first about installing applications and third-party software, including system add-ons. Then I'll talk about Mac OS X and Apple software installations and updates, and uninstalling software. Finally, I'll show you how to transfer your files from one computer or hard drive to another and support some "unsupported" computers and peripherals.

Installation Basics

If you've ever decided to take a curious trip around your hard drive, you've surely discovered that Mac OS X includes tens of thousands of files, organized in hundreds and thousands of folders and sub-folders. If you're a former user of Mac OS 9 or earlier, the sheer number of files that are present is enough to make you wonder if upgrading to OS X was such a great move. However, the truth is that despite the large number of files, OS X and its applications are organized in a fairly logical manner. Understanding the basics of application and system software organization will help you better understand installations (and installation troubleshooting).

Where Are Things Installed?

I spent a good amount of time talking about OS X's file and folder organization in Chapter 1, but I'm going to briefly revisit this organization as it relates to software installation.

Mac OS X The bulk of files and folders in most computers running Mac OS X is made up by the operating system itself. Because of the sheer number of files installed by Mac OS X, explaining the location and purpose of each and every file would take more space than this entire book! Thus, for the sake of this discussion, I'm going to generalize a bit. Core OS-related files are installed inside the directory `/System` at the root level of your hard drive. Support files are located in `/Library`, as well as in a few invisible folders at the root level, such as `/usr` and `/sbin`. (I'll talk more about invisible files in Chapter 5, "Finagle Files and Foil Finder Frustration.") I've already mentioned a few such files in the preceding chapters, and you'll work with a number of others before the book is through.

Applications I discussed Mac OS X's "parallel" folder structure in Chapter 1; application location is another example of parallel folders. Applications are generally located in `/Applications` (for all users) or in `~/Applications` (for individual users). Although applications can technically be installed anywhere, there are good reasons to limit them to these folders—see "Moving Installed Applications" later in the chapter for more information.

NOTE As discussed in Chapter 1, the `~/Applications` folder (within each user folder) isn't created automatically, so each user will need to create it within their own folder if they want to take advantage of it.

Many applications also require support files. These files are often located within the application itself (see "Packages," later in this chapter); however, this is not always the case. Inside `/Library` (for all users) and `~/Library` (for individual users), you'll most likely find a folder called `Application Support`, inside which you'll find folders containing support files for various applications. Applications may also store fonts, contextual menus, help files, and other necessary files inside specialized folders in the `/Library` directories. In addition, as mentioned earlier in the book, applications save their preferences inside `/Library/Preferences` and `~/Library/Preferences` (again, depending on whether the preferences apply to all users or if each user has their own preferences). Finally, if an application requires a low-level startup item that needs to be active at startup (such as the backup scheduler used by Dantz's Retrospect backup application), it will most likely be located in `/System/Library/Startup Items`.

If you're running Mac OS X on a computer that previously ran Mac OS 9 or earlier, you may also have a folder at the root level of your hard drive called Applications (Mac OS 9). This is where applications that were previously installed under Mac OS 9 are stored. You may be able to run many of these applications using the Classic Environment (see Chapter 8, "Clobbering Classic").

Utilities Utilities are actually just applications, and there really is no official way to differentiate between an application that is a utility and one that isn't—I generally think of utilities as applications that do something *to* your computer (fix it, alter its functionality, etc.), or help you *monitor* your computer (e.g., Network Utility lets you monitor network traffic). Mac OS X has a special folder *inside* `/Applications` called `Utilities`. This folder contains all of the utilities that are installed by OS X (e.g., Terminal, Disk Copy, Network Utility), as well as any utilities installed there by third-party installers or placed there by users.

System add-ons You can alter or enhance the way Mac OS X works in many ways. We've discussed a few (screen savers and preferences panes) already in the book. However, where these add-ons reside depends on the *type* of add-on. I go into more detail about these locations in "Adding Add-ons," later in this chapter.

Unix software In addition to software written for Mac OS X, many command-line applications are pre-installed by Mac OS X. You can also install many other Unix applications yourself. I'll talk much more about installing Unix software in Chapter 15, "Utilizing Unix," but for now I'll just briefly mention that a good number of command-line Unix applications are located in the invisible `/bin`, `/sbin`, and `/usr` directories. Many of these applications are used regularly by Mac OS X itself, and many others are accessible to you via Terminal.

Packages

If you previously used a Mac running Mac OS 9 or earlier, you'll remember that when you installed an application, you generally also installed various other files needed by that application. Sometimes these files were conveniently located in the same folder as the application itself; however, they were often scattered across your hard drive—some in the Extensions folder, some in the Control Panels folder, some in various other locations depending on the application.

This made for a very messy hard drive, and for potential problems. An application could stop working as a result of seemingly innocuous actions such as:

- Moving the application from its original location
- Moving an application around within its *own folder*
- Accidentally moving or throwing away an essential support file (which could be easy to do because an application's folder was often littered with support files)
- Accidentally moving or disabling support files such as System extensions

Mac OS X makes some impressive strides towards eliminating this type of situation by using what are called *packages* (technically called *bundles*, but since Apple has taken to calling them packages, I'm going to do so as well). A package is actually a folder of files that acts like a single file. For example, an application package is a folder that contains an application and its support files; however, the package looks and behaves like an application—double-clicking it doesn't open the folder; rather it launches the application inside. An installer package is a folder that contains all the files and/or resources needed for a particular software installation; double-clicking on this kind of package launches Mac OS X's Installer utility.

FIGURE 4.1:

The contents of the *Mail.app* package

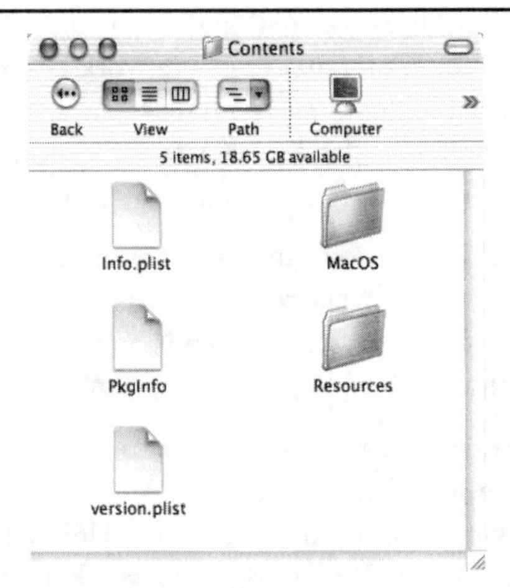

File packages have a number of advantages. Most importantly, as I'll discuss shortly, is that they make installing new applications much easier. But in addition, they also make it less likely that a user will accidentally move or delete files needed by applications, and they make it easier to move applications and other types of packages around (including deleting them when you want to).

To see a package in action, navigate to `/Applications`, and locate the `Mail` application. If you hold the control key and click on Mail (or right-click if you have a multi-button mouse), you'll be presented with a contextual menu. Select Show Package Contents from the menu. You'll be presented with a new Finder window with a folder called Contents. Inside that folder are the actual contents of the Mail package (Figure 4.1). If you dig into the `Resources` folder, you'll even see the various TIFF graphic files used by Mail for buttons and toolbars.

There are actually several types of package files. If you have chosen to view files extensions in the Finder (via Finder preferences), you'll recognize some packages by their file extension: installer packages end in `.pkg`; application packages end in `.app`. Files that end in `.bundle`, `.framework`, and `.menu` are a few other examples. All of these are examples of bundles of files that appear in the Finder as a single file.

It's possible to create your own packages, but you really don't want to do it unless you're familiar with all of the types of files that need to be included; if you're not, you'll be left with a package that doesn't do anything. For more information on packages, check out `http://developer.apple.com/techpubs/macosx/Essentials/SystemOverview/AppPackaging/`.

WARNING If you remove the file extension (`.app`, `.pkg`, `.bundle`, etc.) from the name of a package or bundle, it will no longer function properly; likewise, if you add a package extension to the name of a normal folder or file, it will become a package, but will not function like one. In fact, you may not be able to easily get your folder back. So be careful with file extensions. (See Chapter 5 for more information on file extensions.)

Getting a List of Files in an Installer Package

User Level: any
Affects: NA
Terminal: no

If you're really interested in the contents of a particular installer package (or even if you just want to see such a list once, so that you never have to wonder again), a neat little AppleScript called QuickBom (`http://homepage.mac.com/bhines/applescripts.html`) will show you. Drop a `.pkg` file onto the QuickBom icon, and QuickBom will create a new TextEdit document with a list of every file inside the package, organized by file path. (QuickBom is actually an AppleScript interface for the Terminal command `lsbom`, but automates the process.)

Moving Installed Applications

Throughout the rest of this chapter I'll be talking about how to install (and uninstall) software, including applications, system software, and system add-ons. However, before I do so, I want to quickly talk about moving files, including applications.

Many users (including myself) like to keep their hard drive neat and organized. For example, under OS 9 I liked to create a folder called Internet inside my Applications folder and put any Internet-related applications inside. However, this isn't such a good idea under Mac OS X, which can be quite strict when it comes to file location. As you might expect, system-related files only work properly when they are installed in the correct location. However, because of permissions issues and even software updater issues, many other files must also be in particular locations.

For example, I mentioned earlier in this chapter that applications should be located in `/Applications` or `~/Applications`. There are a few reasons for this organization. First, the permissions on these folders are set to provide the appropriate users with access to applications. If an application was installed in `/System/Library`, for example, only the root user would be able to use it; by installing applications inside the Applications folders, all users (or particular users, in the case of `~/Applications`) can use them. Second, some applications are written so that they *must* be located in one of the Applications folders; if they are not, they won't function properly. Third, many utilities that provide quick access to applications only do so for applications located inside these folders. (We'll discuss some of these utilities later in the book.) Fourth, Mac OS X maintains a database of installed applications, and updates it automatically whenever it detects a newly installed application; however, it only does this for applications that reside in the official Applications folders. This database is used, for example, whenever you double-click a file to open it. Finally, in my opinion, it simply makes your computer more organized and easier to use if applications are conveniently located in the Applications folders.

In addition to these reasons, in the case of Apple's own applications (those installed with Mac OS X), there is an even more persuasive argument for keeping them where they were originally installed: the Mac OS X software updaters will sometimes *only* update software that is located in its original location. For example, if you move the Mail application out of the

`/Applications` directory, or even just inside a sub-folder within `/Applications`, a Mac OS updater (an update to Mac OS X, or an application-specific updater), may not update the Mail application. Sometimes the updater will look for Mail in its original location, and when it doesn't find it there, it will either do nothing, or will install a new package of files where Mail should be. This package will *look* like a new Mail application package, but will only contain the files that were supposed to be updated within the Mail package. In other words, it will be incomplete and will not function. Apple claims that as of OS X 10.2.3 this is no longer an issue; however, I've still seen reports of it occurring.

So in general, it's best to leave applications where they were originally installed. If, like me, you hate the idea of opening `/Applications` and having to slog through files just to find the application you want to use, you'll appreciate Chapter 5, and the Online Bonus Chapter "Furthering Finder Frustration." I'll spend a good deal of time talking about other ways to access applications and files.

Installing Third-Party Software

So you're tired of using TextEdit for all your word processing, or you want to try a new web browser. Or maybe you read about a cool system add-on that makes it easier to access your files. Whatever the reason or need, you'll eventually want to install software that didn't come with your Mac. In this section I'm going to talk about the various ways in which you can install third-party software, along with a few tips on how to do it better. (If you've already installed quite a bit of third-party software, this section might be a bit elementary. However, I recommend that you at least skim along—you still might find something new.

There are generally three ways to install software in Mac OS X: via an installer application, using an installer package, or by simply copying the application to your hard drive. Which method you use is actually up to the software developers, as they decide how they want to distribute their software. But before I talk about each of these methods, I want to mention the ways in which software is distributed under Mac OS X.

How Software Is Distributed

Whereas five to ten years ago most software was distributed via floppy disk, today most commercial software is distributed via CD or Internet download, and shareware and freeware is distributed almost exclusively via the Internet. Software on CD is fairly easy to access, as you simply put the CD in your computer and either run an installer or copy files to your hard drive. However, downloading software poses a few unique challenges, mainly slow transfer speeds and the fact that Macintosh resource forks (file contents unique to Mac files) do not always transfer correctly over the Internet. Software downloaded from the Internet generally comes encoded and compressed in a format that reduces file size and preserves file contents.

Previous users of Mac OS 9 are most likely familiar with the StuffIt compression format (these files usually ended in `.sit`), which has historically been the most common compression format for Mac-related downloads. By double-clicking a StuffIt-encoded file, the StuffIt Expander application launched and expanded the file. This format is still common under Mac OS X, and StuffIt Expander is pre-installed with OS X. Windows users are more likely to be familiar with the `.zip` format (often called Zip files). Because of OS X's Windows compatibility, Zip files are becoming more common on the Mac platform. Finally, due to Mac OS X's Unix underpinnings, several Unix file compression formats are also becoming more common on the Mac platform; you'll recognize these types of file by their file extensions: `.tz`, `.tar`, `.gzip`, `.gz`. Luckily, all of these files can be decoded/decompressed using StuffIt Expander. You can simply double-click them, and StuffIt Expander will launch and do its thing. In the rare cases where this doesn't work, you can simply drag the compressed file onto the StuffIt Expander application (inside `~/Applications/Utilities`).

One increasingly common file type that you may find yourself downloading (or that may appear once you've "unstuffed" one of the file formats mentioned above) is the `.dmg` format. This type of file is called a *disk image* because it is actually an image of a mountable volume. If you double-click a `.dmg` file, Apple's Disk Copy utility will launch and "mount" the disk on the Desktop just like a CD, Zip disk, or external hard drive. You then open the disk to access its contents (which can be an installer, an installer package, or files and folders). When you're done with the disk, simply drag it to the Trash to "eject" it (unmount it). You can then throw away the original disk image file, or save it for later use or backup.

TIP If a file ends in `.dmg` and double-clicking it doesn't launch Disk Copy, you have three ways to get it to open properly. You can drag the `.dmg` file onto the Disk Copy application (`/Applications/Utilities/Disk Copy`). You can also launch Disk Copy manually, then select File ➢ Mount Image…; browse to the image file and click Open. The image will be mounted on the desktop. Finally, you can select the `.dmg` file in the Finder, then select File ➢ Get Info. In the "Open with" panel, select Disk Copy from the pop-up menu. The next time you double-click the image file, it will be mounted by Disk Copy.

Once you've got your software ready to install, how you proceed depends on how the developer has provided it.

Installer Applications and Packages

Installer applications and installer packages work similarly; both use an application to place files and folders in the appropriate places on your hard drive. They tend to be used when software requires that files be placed in various locations around your hard drive, so as to reduce the chances that the user will place something incorrectly (and to just make things easier on us users).

Although not as common as they were under Mac OS 9 and earlier, software installers are still used for some software under OS X. There are several different brands of installers (from companies like MindVision and Installer Vise), and some companies (such as Microsoft) actually build their own; however, they all work in a similar manner: you double-click the installer application, and it installs the software.

Some installers will require you to authenticate (provide an admin-level username and password), especially if the installer needs to copy files to `/Library` or `/System/Library`. In the case of application installers, most automatically place applications in the default location of `/Applications`. However, some will give you the option of choosing where the application itself is installed; if you want to limit use of the application to just your own user account, make sure you choose `~/Applications` as the location for installation. Finally, if the installer is installing any system add-ons, you may be asked to decide whether the add-on affects all users or just you; see "Adding Add-Ons," later in this chapter for details.

Installer packages work much like installer applications do; you simply double-click them, and follow the instructions on-screen. The major difference is that instead of using their own installation software, installer packages use Apple's Installer utility (`/Applications/Utilities/Installer`). When you double-click on an installer package, Installer launches, and uses a script contained within the installer package to install files in the appropriate locations. Installer will usually ask you to select a destination volume for the install (Figure 4.2); if you have multiple volumes/partitions, select the one you are currently using as the startup disk (that is, unless you really want to install the software onto another volume). Once installation is complete, you can either quit Installer, or you'll be asked to restart your computer.

TIP When using Apple's Installer utility, it's often possible to see a list of files that are going to be installed. Once you get to the Select a Destination screen, select File ➢ Show Files to be presented with a window that lists all the files about to be installed, including the exact location into which each will be copied.

FIGURE 4.2: The Select a Destination screen in the Installer utility

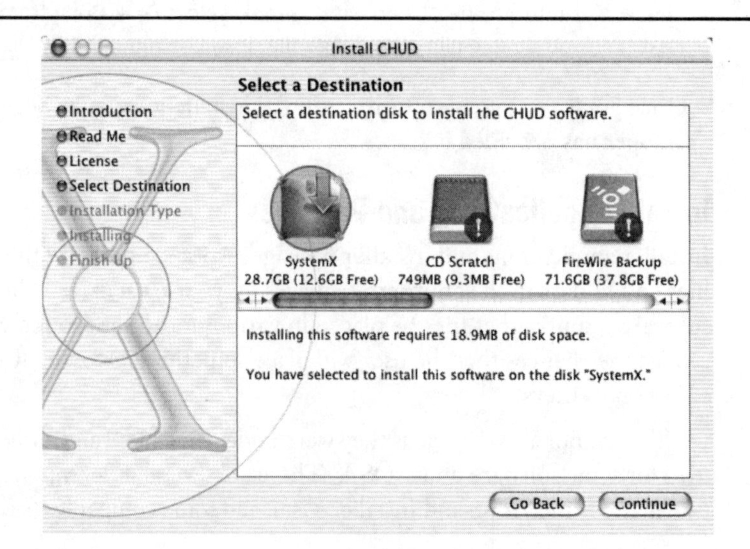

Installers are intended to make installation as easy as possible, and for the most part they do just that. However, the downside of installers and installer packages is that because they do everything automatically, it's often harder to *remove* the software that is installed. I'll talk about that later in the chapter (in "Uninstalling Software").

Do I Really Need to Restart after the Installer Is Finished?

Some installers or installer packages will require that you restart your computer after installation is completed. This is often the case when software has been installed that needs to be loaded by the OS at startup. For example, Dantz's Retrospect backup system requires a startup item called RetroRun for automated backups; the only way to ensure that this software is running is to restart so that it loads at startup. Another time a restart may be required is if the installed software replaced an earlier version that was already running. For example, a utility that alters Open/Save dialogs most likely loads code into memory that affects the way Open/Save dialogs are displayed. Updating the utility software doesn't necessarily *un*load the old code from memory. So to avoid problems that might arise from having both old code and new code running at the same time, the installer either suggests or requires that you restart after installation.

Some installers quit all running applications and don't give you any option other than restarting; however, such installers are becoming rarer under OS X. Most that require a restart will let you finish up tasks in other applications, then switch back and click the Restart button. If you really don't want to take the advice to restart, you can usually force the installer to quit without restarting. Select Force Quit… from the Apple Menu, select the installer in the resulting list of applications, and then click the Force Quit… button. However, keep in mind that there is usually a good reason for an installer to require a restart, so if you use this tactic, I still recommend restarting as soon as possible.

Drag-and-Drop Installing

Earlier in the chapter I talked about OS X's packages. One major advantage of packages is that they make installing software extremely simple. Rather than requiring a software installer to copy files to various locations on your hard drive, a package allows software to be distributed as a single "file" (remember, it only *looks* like a single file) that can be copied by the user to the hard drive. You simply mount the CD or disk image (`.dmg` file) in the Finder, and then drag the software package from the CD or image to the appropriate location on your hard drive.

The only thing that's a bit tricky about drag-and-drop installations is *where* to put the software. Luckily, most developers include a ReadMe file that includes detailed installation instructions. By now, because of how many times I've talked about it in this chapter, you should know exactly where to place applications. The other common type of file you might download is a system add-on (preference panes, screen savers, etc.). Because these can go in a number of different places, I'm going to talk about them separately later in the chapter.

TIP

Being a power user doesn't mean you can ignore the documentation that comes with software. As boring as some of them might be, you should *always* read the ReadMe files, or browse through the installation/system requirements sections of software manuals. They often contain important information about installing and/or using the software, and not reading them could get you into trouble (due to incompatibilities, requirements, or other issues). A couple minutes of reading could save you a few hours of headaches!

Beware the Cache

There is one caveat you should know about installing applications via drag-and-drop, and it has to do with the caching of application code. As part of OS X's memory management system, when you first launch an application its code is cached into memory. One benefit of this caching is that if you quit the application, the next time you launch it, it will launch much faster. However, this caching can backfire when you replace the original application with a newer version, because sometimes OS X simply uses the cached code instead of launching the new version.

For example, say you've been using the shareware graphics application Graphic Converter. As you're surfing the web, you find that a new version of Graphic Converter has been released. You download the new version, quit the old version and move it to the Trash, and replace it with the new one. However, when you try to launch the new one, you find—because of its appearance, or by going to the "About Graphic Converter" item in the application menu—that it appears to be exactly the same as the old version! What's happening is that OS X sees that you're launching Graphic Converter, and simply uses the application code it has cached in memory.

Sometimes cached application code gets purged from memory as you use other applications, and sometimes it just doesn't happen (in other words, it's not a consistent thing). When it does happen, the easiest solution is to simply restart your computer; luckily I've found that this phenomenon doesn't occur very often.

Adding Add-Ons

In addition to applications, utilities, and system updates, you can also install software that changes how Mac OS works. I mentioned a couple of them in Chapter 2—namely screen savers and preference panes—but there are actually a number of other types. Most of these add-ons are provided without installers; that is, you'll have to drag and drop them into the correct locations manually.

System Add-On Locations

In order to function properly, system add-ons need to be installed in very specific locations that differ depending on the type of add-on. Below is a list of the most common system add-ons you'll encounter, what they do, and where they are installed. As discussed in Chapter 1, in all of the examples below, items in `/Library` will be available to all users, whereas those in `~/Library` will only be available to that specific user.

Contextual menus As you've already seen in some of the exercises we've done in the book, contextual menus (often called "right-click" or "control-click" menus) are everywhere in Mac OS X. They're call *contextual* menus because the contents of the menus change depending on the *context* in which the menu is activated. You can add to the functionality of contextual menus by installing contextual menu plug-ins. I'm going to provide some examples of excellent plug-ins in Chapter 5, but regardless of the plug-in, to work properly it must be located in `/Library/Contextual Menu Items` or `~/Library/Contextual Menu Items`.

Fonts Fonts are available all over the web, on CDs you can purchase, and some users even create their own. In order to be available to applications, they should be located in `/Library/Fonts` or `~/Library/Fonts`. (Fonts installed in your Classic System Folder will also be available in OS X—I'll talk more about that in Chapter 8.)

Internet plug-ins Internet plug-ins such as Flash, Shockwave, and Windows Media provide additional functionality to web browsers. In past versions of the Mac OS, each browser had its own plug-in folder; in Mac OS X, there are universal plug-in folders that can be accessed by all browsers. These are `/Library/Internet Plug-Ins` and `~/Library/Internet Plug-Ins`.

Preference panes As I discussed in Chapter 2, third-party preference panes will be accessed by the System Preferences application when they are located in `/Library/PreferencePanes` or `~/Library/PreferencePanes`.

Printer drivers and PPDs Although Mac OS X contains drivers for many printers, printer vendors and other developers can add support for other printers by installing drivers in `/Library/Printers` or `~/Library/Printers`. (I'll talk a lot more about adding printer support in Chapter 12, "Printing Practicalities.")

Screen savers I talked about using third-party screen savers in Chapter 2. Any screen saver file located in `/Library/Screen Savers` or `~/Library/Screen Savers` will be available to the screen saver pane of System Preferences.

There are other types of system add-ons that can be installed, but these are the ones that you're most likely to encounter. How do you install them? Read on.

Installing System Add-Ons

Like applications, system add-ons are installed manually or via an installer application. However, you have other options, as well, such as third-party add-on managers. In addition, because system add-ons often affect the way the OS operates, there are times when installing an add-on requires a restart, or at least a logout/login.

FIGURE 4.3:

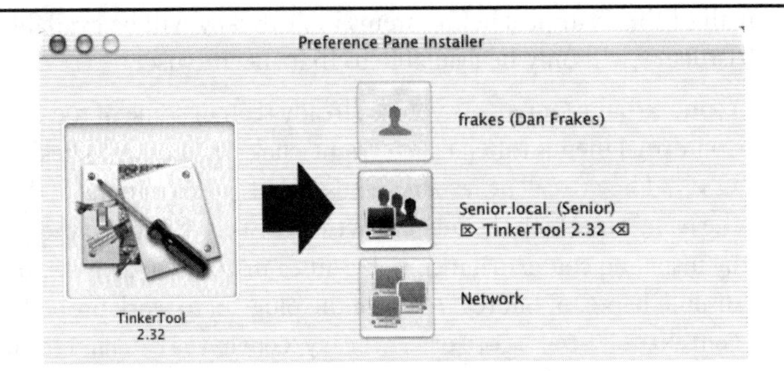

The TinkerTool preference pane installer asks whether you want TinkerTool to be installed for the current user or for all users. (It also has an option for network installation.)

Installing System Add-Ons Manually

User Level: user or admin
Affects: individual user or all users
Terminal: no

In my experience, the vast majority of system add-ons—whether commercial, shareware, or freeware—are installed manually: you download them over the Internet, and manually copy them from a disk image, or from your downloads folder, into the appropriate location. As I described in the previous section, where you move them depends on the type of add-on; again, be sure you read the ReadMe file that comes with the file to be sure.

Installing System Add-Ons Using an Installer

User Level: user or admin
Affects: individual user or all users
Terminal: no

Although a large number of add-ons require manual installation, some do come in the form of an installer application. Sometimes this is because the add-on requires that multiple files be installed in multiple locations; other times it's simply because the developer preferred to provide an installer. One thing such add-on installers generally have in common is that they ask you whether you want the add-on to affects all users or just your own user account. As I explained above and in Chapter 1, this decision affect whether it is installed in `/Library` or `~/Library` (Figure 4.3).

Installing System Add-Ons Using Alfred

User Level: user or admin
Affects: individual user or all users
Terminal: no

Another method for installing system add-ons is to use a third-party add-on/plug-in manager such as the shareware Alfred (`http://www.inferiis.com/products/alfred/`). Although one of the main purposes of Alfred is to manage add-ons and plug-ins (much like Diablotin, which I talked about in Chapter 3), it also has the very cool ability to automatically install system add-ons for you. To install a system add-on, simply drag it onto the Alfred icon in the Finder (or, if it is already running, in the Dock). In Figure 4.4, I've dropped a preference pane, DeskEffects, onto Alfred. Alfred presents a window telling me that the file is a preference pane and will thus be installed in one of the `Preference Panes` directories. It also gives me the option of installing DeskEffects for just my account (User), all users (Local) or even to the core operating system (System, and, of course, not recommended). Clicking User and then the Install button installs the preference pane into the appropriate folder (in this case, `~/Library/PreferencePanes`).

Alfred also has some other useful features worth mentioning here. It actually installs files based on rules. For example, the Preference Pane rule says that if a file ends in `.prefPane` and has a file type of `BNDL` (I'll talk more about file types in the next chapter), then it should be installed in the `PreferencePanes` directory inside one of the `Library` folders. What is interesting about this approach is that you can create your own rules. For example, after I install software, I like to keep the `.dmg` file handy in case I need to install it again or want to install it onto a different computer. I have a folder on one of my hard drives where I keep these archived `.dmg` files. I've created a rule in Alfred that says if a file ends in `.dmg`, to move it to my archive of installers. After I've installed software from a disk image, I drag the `.dmg` file onto Alfred and it automatically files it away for me.

Finally, much like Diablotin, Alfred lets you manage system add-ons such as preference panes, screen savers, fonts, and contextual menu items. Select Window ➢ Rules for a list of all types of files you can manage. Select a type of file and click the Manage button to see a list of all files of that type installed on your Mac. You can then enable or disable individual files. Although the change is immediate, sometimes a restart or logout/login will be necessary for the results of the change to take effect.

FIGURE 4.4:
Using Alfred to install system add-ons

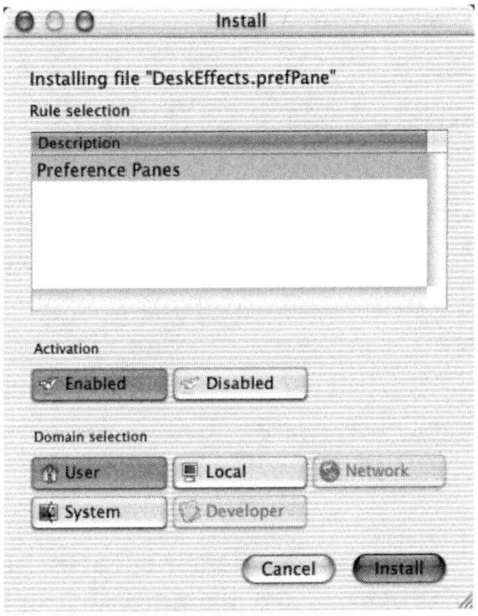

Logout/Login or Restart?

When you install, activate, or deactivate system add-ons, you're generally changing the way the system behaves, or its capabilities. In the case of screen savers, the change is immediate—a new screen saver will be available the next time you open System Preferences (you may need to quit System Preferences, and then launch it again, if it was running when you made the change). However, in the case of add-ons that change the way your Mac works, such as contextual menu plug-ins and certain preference panes, in order to gain the added functionality the software provides, you'll need to log out and then back in or, in the case of certain add-ons that affect the startup process itself, to restart your computer. Generally the ReadMe file that accompanies the software, or the installer, if the software used one for installation, will tell you when this is necessary.

Installing Mac OS and Apple Software

In some cases, installing software from Apple, such as applications and OS updates, works just like installing third-party software. However, most of the time you'll install Apple software using OS X's Software Update application, or a Mac OS X installer CD. In this section, I'm going to show you how to get the most out of Software Update, then talk briefly about installing Apple software manually, and finally get into the nitty-gritty of installing (and reinstalling) Mac OS X itself.

NOTE Whenever you install an update to Mac OS X itself, I recommend running the Repair Disk Permissions feature of Disk Utility (described in Chapter 1) immediately afterwards. Many users have found that doing so after installing an update to OS X avoids problems and provides better performance.

Bending Software Update to Your Will

Apple first introduced Software Update in Mac OS 9; some people used it regularly, others never even realized it existed. However, in Mac OS X, Apple has designed Software Update to be *the* way for users to keep their OS and Apple-provided application software up to date. This is a very good thing, in my opinion. Apple has always released minor updates to the operating system, or new versions of applications, on a fairly regular basis; however, in the past, many users were never even aware that such updates were available. Only people who actively kept track of software updates—from websites, mailing lists, or newsgroups—would know about every new release.

NOTE Although Software Update generally updates only Apple software (Mac OS X and applications like iTunes, iMovie, and iPhoto), a few non-Apple applications that are installed with Mac OS X, such as Microsoft's Internet Explorer, are also sometimes updated via Software Update.

FIGURE 4.5: The Software Update pane of System Preferences

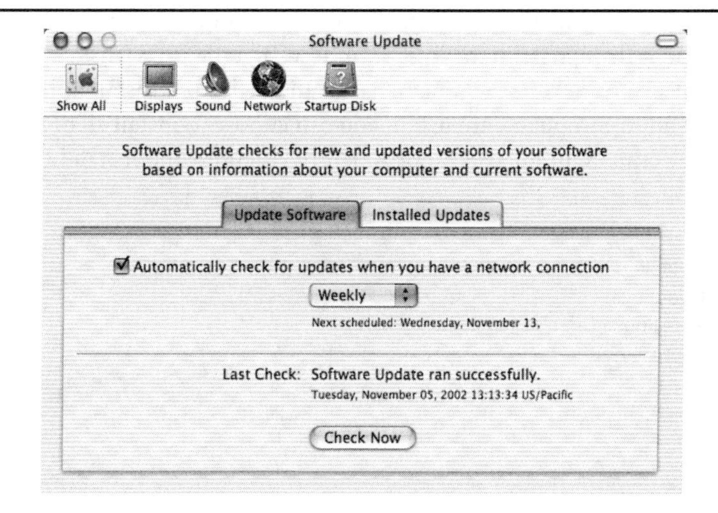

With Software Update, your computer will check for updates for you, either on a regular schedule or when you get the urge to tell it to. It's a great system in that it allows everyone, from the new computer user to the web-surfing veteran, to keep their software up to date.

Using Software Update

User Level: admin (usually)
Affects: computer
Terminal: no

Although there is actually a Software Update application located in `/System/Library/CoreServices`, Software Update is, in a more general sense, a system that Mac OS X uses to check for, and install, updates. You control this system from the Software Update pane of System Preferences; specifically, from the Update Software tab (Figure 4.5). You can choose to manually check for available software updates by clicking the Check Now button, or you can have your Mac do it for you at regular intervals by checking the "Automatically check for updates when you have a network connection" box. You then choose an interval (Daily, Weekly, or Monthly) for how often you want the check to be executed. (If your interval comes and goes, and you haven't been connected to the Internet, it will wait until the next time you're connected.) Whether you choose to check manually or on a schedule, when a check is executed, your Mac will examine the Apple-provided software (OS and applications) installed on your computer, and then contact Apple's software update servers and compare what you have to what is available. If all of your software is up to date, the Software Update preference pane will give you a message to that effect.

However, if newer versions of software are available, the Software Update utility is launched and provides you with a list of available updates, including the name of each update, the version number of the software that will be installed by each update, and the size of each update (Figure 4.6). Clicking on an update in the top window will provide you with details about the update in the lower window. If you want to install an update, check the Install check box next to the update name, then click the Install button at the bottom of the window. If multiple updates are listed, you can choose to install all of them, or just some of them, by selecting multiple check boxes before you press the Install button.

FIGURE 4.6:

Updates available via the Software Update application

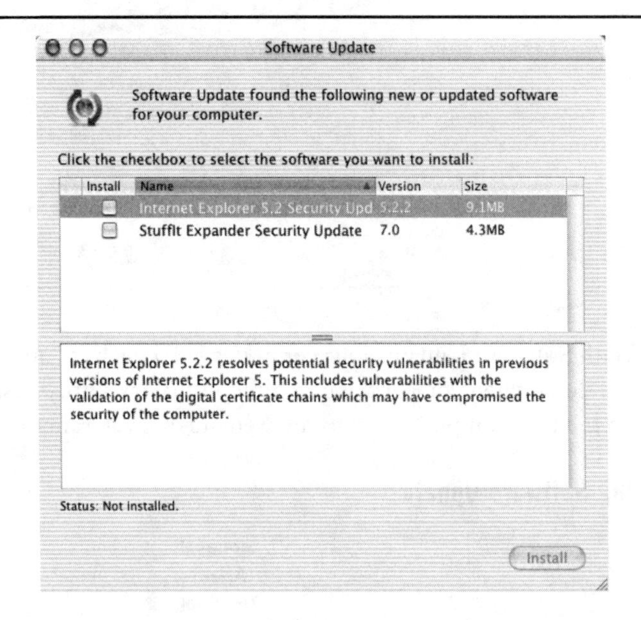

TIP If you're on a dial-up connection, keep an eye on the size of an update in the System Update window. Since each update you choose to install must first be downloaded over the Internet, larger updates will take a long time to complete. If you also have access to a broadband connection, you may want to wait and install larger updates when you're connected via broadband. If not, you can always connect before you go to bed, or when you're not going to be using your computer for a bit, and choose to update then.

Since most of the updates installed by Software Update are system-related, once you click the Install button, you'll probably be asked to provide your admin username and password. The update will then be downloaded (you'll see a progress bar at the bottom of the window letting you know the status of the download) and installed. (A nice feature: you can work in other applications while the update is proceeding.) Once the installation is complete, you can quit the Software Update application, unless the update requires that you restart your computer. However, unlike Mac OS 9, under Mac OS X you don't have to restart immediately; you can switch to other applications and finish up your work before restarting.

TIP The Software Update pane of System Preferences keeps a list of the updates you've installed using the Software Update system. Click on the Installed Updates tab to see a complete list. In addition to using Software Update as described here, you can also use it when logged in to your computer remotely. I'll show you how to do that in Chapter 11.

Telling Software Update You *Don't* Want to Install a Particular Update. Ever.

User Level: any
Affects: NA
Terminal: no

When you check for updates, you'll often come across an update that you don't care much about. For example, if you installed support for multiple languages when you first installed Mac OS X, every time a language update is released, it will show up in the Software Update window. This is good if you use the language, but what if you don't? Why should you have to waste your time (and bandwidth) downloading and installing it?

The solution is actually quite easy. Select the update in the Software Update window, and then select Update ➢ Make Inactive. (You can select more than one update at once by holding down the command key and clicking on each unwanted update.) The update(s) will vanish, never to bother you again.

The "inactive" updates are actually still there; in fact, if you look at the lower right corner of the Software Update window, you'll see the text "Inactive Updates: #" with the number of updates you've chosen to hide. If you ever decide that you really do want to install one of them, or you just want to see what you've hidden, select Update ➢ Show Inactive Updates, and they'll once again be visible. To make an inactive update "active" again (so that you can install it), select it and then select Update ➢ Make Active.

Saving/Downloading a Software Update for Future Use

User Level: any
Affects: NA
Terminal: no

Although Software Update is a convenient and easy-to-use system, some people just don't like automatic installations; these manual types (and I admit that sometimes I'm one of them) would rather download the updater on their own and do the installation themselves. In addition, some people (and I'm *definitely* one of these) like to have an archive of updates (on CD or removable volume) that they can keep handy in case they ever need to reinstall something or update another Mac without having to access the Internet. These groups of people would generally have to go to Apple's software updates Website (`http://www.info.apple.com/support/downloads.html`) and download updates manually.

There are two problems with this approach. The first is that software updates are usually available via Software Update at least a few days, and sometimes weeks, earlier than via Apple's Website. The second is that while Software Update only lists updates that are appropriate for your particular computer, Apple's Website lists every update available for any computer with any version of the Mac OS. In other words, knowing which ones to download isn't always easy.

Thankfully for both groups of people, you can use Software Update to get updates right away, and to only get those that are needed by your computer. And it's very easy to do. You just check for updates using Software Update as you normally would; the Software Update application will launch and show you the list of available updates. To download an update (or multiple updates) manually, check the install box(es) for the update(s), but instead of clicking Install, select Update ➢ Download Checked Items to Desktop. Software Update will download the update(s) normally, but instead of installing, it will save the selected update(s) to the desktop. The Status of each downloaded update will be listed as "Not installed, downloaded." You can still install it from Software Update, but now you also have a copy on your hard drive.

NOTE In OS X 10.2 and later, you can only use the Download Checked Items to Desktop feature on updates that have not yet been installed. Once you install an update, it will no longer appear in the Software Update window. If you happen to be using Mac OS X 10.1.x, you actually download an update *after* you install it (by selecting it and choosing Update ➢ Save As...).

One advantage of having an archive of update installers is that if for some reason an update fails, or you need to reinstall an update, Software Update won't be able to help—once you install something from Software Update, it won't be available for reinstallation. However, if you have a copy of the update installer available, you can manually install the update yourself.

"Software Update" for Third-Party Software?

If you think Software Update is a godsend for keeping your OS and Apple-provided software up to date, you may also appreciate the various services out there that perform similar functions for third-party software. These services generally use a similar system to Software Update: An application that runs on your Mac inventories all the software installed on your computer; it then periodically connects to a central database over the Internet, and checks to see if newer versions of software are available. You can then choose to download and/or install the updates.

The most popular update services for Mac OS X are VersionTracker Pro (`http://www.versiontracker.com/`), Update Agent (`http://www.insidersoftware.com/`), and Update-Radar (`http://www.ricciadams.com/programs/updateradar/`). They work a bit differently, but all provide similar functionality. Check out the features of each to see which is better for you.

Installing Apple Software Updates Manually

There are times you may need to (or want to) install Apple software updates from downloaded update installers, rather than via Software Update. Installing Apple OS and application updates manually works exactly like installing any other software manually—you just double-click on the installer package or installer application, and follow the instructions. However, unlike some third-party software installers, you are rarely given an option to choose where Apple software and updates are installed. In addition, one caveat you need to keep in mind when installing Apple updates manually is that they often must be installed in a certain order.

In What Order Do I Install Updates?

One disadvantage to installing updates manually—especially updates to the OS itself—is that if you have multiple updates to install, it's often difficult to figure out which should be installed first, second, etc. Order can be very important, because later updates often require software installed by earlier ones in order to update successfully (and they often give no warning when they aren't successful).

When you use Software Update, the issue of update order is taken care of automatically. However, if you're not using Software Update, you have to figure it out on your own. One way to do so is to Get Info on update packages and installers in the Finder (not disk image files, but the packages and installers contained *in* the disk images). You can often figure out when an update was released by looking at its Modified date, and use those dates to figure out the order to install updates (oldest first, newest last).

Unfortunately, for those updates that are not provided on disk images (they are downloaded directly as packages or installer applications), some web browsers set the Modified date as the date of download. Fortunately, Apple has provided a web page that lists the available updates to OS X 10.2: `http://docs.info.apple.com/article.html?artnum=75421`. This page doesn't list application updates, but installation order isn't as important in the case of applications. (Apple also has a similar document for updates to Mac OS X 10.1, which also includes updates to Mac OS X 10.1 applications: `http://docs.info.apple.com/article.html?artnum=106713`.)

Restoring Selected Software and Installing *Parts* of Updates

There are times when you may need to "get back" some of the software that came with your Mac. Or, you may need to get a copy of a single file or group of files installed by Jaguar or by an updater. In any of these cases, you're trying to *restore* software or get it from a source that generally makes retrieval difficult. Here are a few procedures you can use to get the software you need, depending on what exactly it is you're trying to get.

Using Software Restore CDs to Restore Selected Software

User Level: admin
Affects: computer
Terminal: no

Every Mac manufactured in the past few years has included a set of Software Restore CDs. These CDs are designed to allow the user to restore their hard drive to the original, "factory-fresh" state. (The instructions on how to do this are included on the Software Restore CDs themselves, so I won't go into that here.) But what if you don't want to erase your hard drive and start over? What if you just need a copy of iTunes because you accidentally deleted the copy you had? It's actually not too difficult, especially if your computer came with OS X pre-installed.

If Your Computer Shipped with OS X 10.2 or later Installed

If your computer is one of the Macs that shipped with OS X 10.2 or later pre-installed, you're lucky, because the version of Software Restore that comes with these computers is *much* better than the one that came with older computers—for two main reasons. First, and most importantly, it doesn't require you to erase your entire hard drive. And second, you can tell it exactly which applications or files you want to restore; you don't have to install everything.

Using this version of Software Restore is quite simple, and rather self-explanatory. You boot up normally, insert the first Software Restore CD, and launch the Software Restore application on the CD. You're given the option to install everything, or to just install certain items; once you decide what to install, it installs your choices. If you've installed anything that requires you to restart, you do so; after that, you're done. Simple. Unfortunately, not everyone has this version of Software Restore.

If Your Computer Shipped with an Earlier Version of the Mac OS

If your computer did not ship with OS X 10.2 or later installed, it came with either Mac OS X 10.1 or an earlier version of the Mac OS, and you purchased and installed 10.2 or later yourself. In this case, the Software Restore CDs that came with your computer are much more limited than the ones previously described. On these CDs, Software Restore has only a single mode of operation: erase your hard drive and restore everything that was on the hard drive when your computer was new. Clearly this isn't a great solution, especially if you just want to restore a single application or a few desktop patterns. Luckily there's a way to retrieve selected files or applications.

1. Make sure your hard drive has 2–3 GB of free space available on the hard drive (if it doesn't, you can't use this procedure, unfortunately).
2. Create a new folder on your computer (the Desktop is a convenient location) and name it something relevant, such as "Restore."
3. You should have a set of Software Restore CDs (generally three or four); insert the first CD. (Make sure you're using the Software *Restore* CDs, not the Software *Install* CDs.)

4. Open the Configurations folder on the CD. Inside, you'll find a disk image; copy that image to the folder on your computer.
5. Repeat this procedure for each Software Restore CD. Each will have a disk image inside the Configurations folder; copy all of these disk images to your hard drive (they must all be copied to the same location).
6. Launch the Disk Copy utility (`/Applications/Utilities/Disk Copy`).
7. Drag the first disk image (Disc 1) onto the Disk Copy window or onto the Disk Copy icon in the Dock (you can tell Disk Copy to skip the "checksumming" stage). This will mount the disk image on the Desktop; it will most likely be named "Macintosh HD."
8. Open the disk image and find the software you want to retrieve. Simply drag it from the disk image to the appropriate place on your hard drive.
9. Unmount the disk image by dragging it to the Trash (or selecting it and selecting File ➢ Eject).
10. After you're finished, you should run the Repair Disk Permissions feature of Disk Utility as described in Chapter 1. The reason is that when Mac OS X is installed, system-related files and applications are given specific permissions. When you copy files over manually, the permissions are often not set correctly. Running Repair Disk Permissions ensures that permissions are set correctly.

WARNING If your Mac shipped with an earlier version of the Mac OS (OS 9, Mac OS X 10.1, etc.), and you later installed a newer version, you should not use this method to retrieve files or applications that were updated by the newer version of the Mac OS. For example, if your Mac came with Mac OS X 10.1.5, and you later purchased and installed OS X 10.2, do not use this method to get a copy of iTunes or TextEdit. You should instead read the next section, "Installing *Parts* of an Update, System, or Software Install," to get the version of iTunes or TextEdit that came with 10.2. You can still use this tip to get third-party software, such as a game or other application, that originally came with your computer but did not come with 10.2.

Installing *Parts* of an Update, System, or Software Install

What if your computer didn't come with OS X 10.2 or later (you bought it and installed it yourself) and you want to reinstall an application or file installed with the newer OS? In this case you wouldn't be able to use the procedures described in the previous sections, since your Software Restore CDs don't contain the newer version. Or, what if you want to reinstall a single file or package from the Mac OS 10.2.3 updater (such as the Mail application package), or from some other installer package? Or, what if you want to reinstall a particular part of OS X (such as printer drivers) without having to run the entire installer?

Many of these types of files are located inside installer packages of the type I discussed earlier in this chapter. In fact, the Mac OS X installer itself is actually many different installer packages grouped together for installation. It's possible to use the View Package Contents feature of the Finder to browse the contents of an installer package, but without knowing where to look, where to install the pieces, and how to properly set permissions, this isn't a very easy task.

Luckily, third-party developers have provided solutions to this dilemma. There are currently several utilities for working with packages, including OS X Package Manager, ReView-Pkg, and Pacifist. Pacifist (`http://www.charlessoft.com/`) is my current favorite. By dragging an installer package onto the application's icon (or the Pacifist window if it is already running), Pacifist presents you with a list of software included in the package, and gives you the option of installing individual items.

This is a good place to provide an example of what you can do with Pacifist. I mentioned earlier in the chapter that if you move any of Apple's OS X applications from their original location, Apple's Mac OS X updaters will not update these applications correctly. When I installed OS X 10.2, I accidentally moved the Mail application inside another folder. When I used the Mac OS X 10.2.2 updater, it was unable to update Mail. So I was left with Mac OS X 10.2.2, except for Mail, which was still stuck at an older version. I could have run the entire OS updater again, but an easier solution was to use Pacifist to update just Mail. Here's how to do it:

1. Launch Pacifist.
2. Mount the Mac OS X 10.2.2 Update disk image in the Finder.
3. Drag the `MacOSXUpdate10.2.2.pkg` package onto the Pacifist window.
4. Pacifist will present you with a list of the package's contents; click the disclosure triangle next to `Applications` to see the applications contained in the package. You'll see `Mail.app` as one of the options (Figure 4.7).

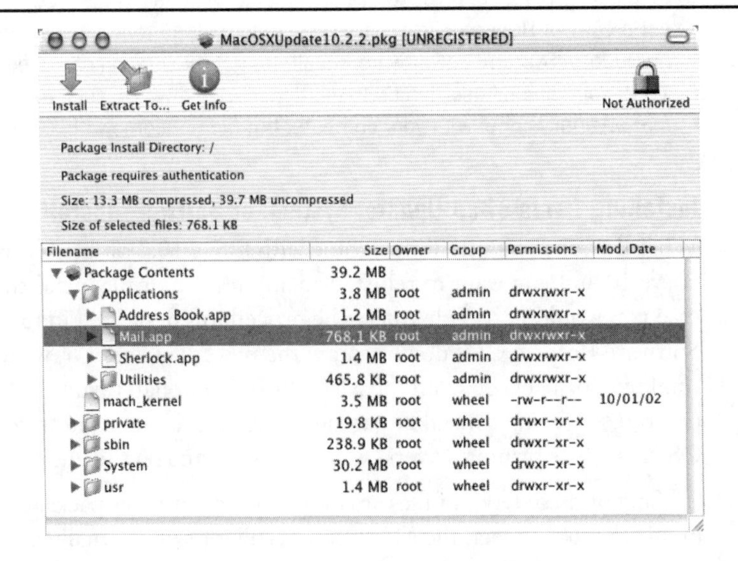

FIGURE 4.7: The contents of the Mac OS X 10.2.2 updater package as viewed in Pacifist

5. Select `Mail.app`. If you click on the Get Info button, you'll see some information about the Mail application, including where it will be installed and the permissions that will be set for it.
6. Click the Install button to install the Mail application in its default location. Pacifist will confirm the action, and then ask you for an admin username and password. (You can also choose to save the application elsewhere, using the Extract To… button, but I recommend using the Install command.)
7. Pacifist will then present a dialog telling you that Mail already exists, and asking you what to do: stop, leave the original application alone, replace it, or update it. Click the Update button and Pacifist will update the Mail application. (If I had instead been extracting the full Mail application from the OS X installer CDs, I would have clicked the Replace button. If no previous version existed, I wouldn't have seen this particular dialog; Pacifist would have simply installed the application.)

NOTE If you want to extract/install items from the Mac OS X installer CDs, when you open the CD in the Finder it may appear as though there are no packages on the CD. The reason is that all of the installer packages are located in a hidden folder on the CD, `/Volumes/Mac OS X Install Disc 1/System/Installation/Packages`. (If you have a single DVD, the path will be slightly different.) You can get to this folder by selecting Go ➢ Go To Folder… in the Finder and typing in this path. You can also access these packages by opening a new Finder window, selecting View ➢ as Columns, and then navigating to the Packages folder. You can then drag individual packages onto Pacifist to view the files installed by each. (Most of the key System-level files are contained in `BaseSystem.pkg` and `Essentials.pkg`.)

Updating/Reinstalling the Entire OS

User Level: admin
Affects: computer
Terminal: no

If you buy a new Mac, it comes with the latest version of Mac OS X pre-installed; if you want to install Mac OS X on a new hard drive, you just insert the OS X Install CD or DVD, run the installer application, and select the new hard drive when asked for the installation destination. However, what if you want to install a newer OS X over an existing Mac OS X installation (e.g., version 10.1.x or earlier)? The OS X installer includes an "upgrade" option, but many users have reported problems when using this option; if your current installation has any problems, those problems will likely still exist, and possibly be worsened, by installing a newer OS X on top. Or, what if you're having serious problems with your current OS X installation and want to just reinstall and start over? Chances are you've got accounts set up and personal data and preferences that you don't want to lose.

FIGURE 4.8:
The Archive and Install option of OS X 10.2 and later

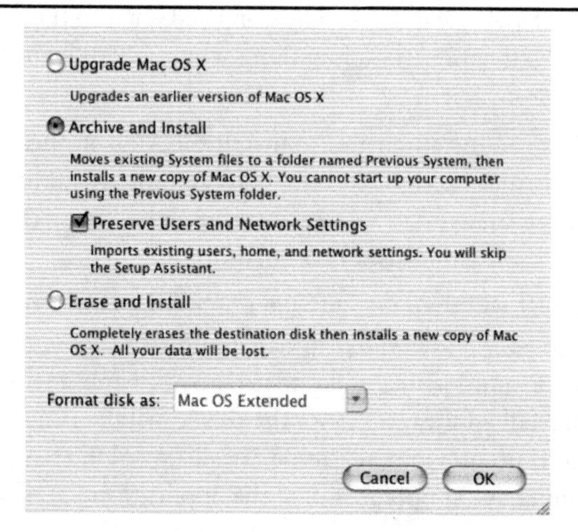

The installers for Mac OS 9 and earlier provided users with the option of a "clean install"—a new System Folder was installed, but your previous System Folder was preserved. This was considered a good way to get a "safe" system, and then gradually transfer over any preference files and system add-ons, rather than simply dumping a new system on top of an older one (especially bad when the old system was having problems). Users of Mac OS X waited a long time to get similar functionality, and OS X 10.2 and later finally provide it—and do it one better.

OS X's version of the clean install is called "Archive and Install," and is available from the OS X installer's Options screen (Figure 4.8), which appears immediately after you've chosen a destination for installation (in this case, presumably the volume that already has OS X on it). When you choose the Archive and Install option, all of the files from your existing OS X installation (whatever the version of that installation may be) are moved into a new folder at the root level of your hard drive called Previous Systems. OS X is then installed as if the hard drive has no operating system. In addition, the installer moves any third-party applications that you had previously installed into the new `/Applications` directory, saving you the trouble of reinstalling them.

A second option, called Preserve Users and Network Settings, (Figure 4.8) is where the newer installer really shines. This option retains all of your user accounts, files, and settings, as well as your system-wide network, Internet, and dial-up settings. When the installation is complete, you can restart your computer and boot into your new copy of OS X without missing a beat. The login screen will appear with all of your user accounts available, and you can connect to the Internet immediately upon logging in.

If you're reinstalling OS X 10.2 or later, or installing it over a previous version of Mac OS X, I highly recommend these two options, as such an installation will likely be more stable than an "Update" install, and will get you up and running much faster than an Erase and Install, or even just an Archive and Install (which would still require you to set up all of your accounts and network settings).

NOTE The Archive and Install option is only available from the full install CDs for OS X 10.2 and later. It is not available from OS X "update" CDs—the free update CDs Apple provides for users who buy a new Mac or copy of OS X after a major release (10.2, 10.3) is announced, but before it's available. I've seen mentions on the web of a procedure (unsanctioned by Apple) to turn the update CD into a standard installer that provides these options, but otherwise users with update CDs will have to simply use the "Update" install.

However, despite the advantages of an Archive and Install, even with the Preserve Users and Network Settings, there is still some cleanup that needs to be done to get your Mac running as it was before the install.

Restoring Other Files after an Archive and Install

User Level: admin
Affects: computer
Terminal: no

Although the previous procedure preserves your user accounts and network settings, and even your installed applications, there are a good number of system-level files that didn't get transferred over to your new installation of OS X. You may want or need some of these if you want your new system to have the same functionality as your old system. Some examples are system-level system add-ons and plug-ins, and application support files.

At the root level of your hard drive, you'll find a folder called Previous Systems. If you open this folder, you'll find a sub-folder called Previous System 1 with contents that mirror the files and folders at the root level of your hard drive: Applications, etc, Library, mach, mach.sym, System, Users, and var; you may also have a folder called Developer. These files and folders are simply the previous contents of your hard drive—your old Mac OS X. While you'll eventually throw many of the files inside these folders away, some are things you may want to transfer over to their corresponding locations in your new installation of OS X. Follow the guidelines below to decide what to move from the "Previous Systems 1" folder to the corresponding location in your new OS X installation (and what to leave).

NOTE Note: If you attempt to move a file or folder from your "Previous" system to your new OS X installation and get an error that you don't have the right privileges, you may need to use the Finder's Get Info command to change them (as described in Chapter 1). Just be sure that after you move the items, you change privileges back to their original values. An easier way to move restricted files without changing permissions is to use a utility such as SkyTag Software's File Buddy (`http://skytag.com/filebuddy/`), which allows you to move files and folders using root/admin access.

mach, mach.sym These files have been replaced by updated versions; you can safely ignore them.

Developer If you're upgrading from an earlier version of Mac OS X, the developer support files in this folder are not compatible with the newer OS X; you should leave this folder and its contents here. If you're reinstalling the *same* version of OS X, you can either move the "Previous" Developer folder to the root level of your hard drive, or leave it here and install a fresh copy of the Developer tools.

Applications All of your previously installed applications and utilities have been moved from this folder to the new Applications folder at the root level of your hard drive. In fact, the only files you will find inside this folder are older versions of Apple-provided applications, all of which have been replaced by newer versions in the new Applications folder. The same is true of the Utilities sub-folder. The lone exception is if you had previously moved files or folders inside the AppleScript folder under your previous Mac OS X installation; if you did, they will still be inside the archived AppleScript folder, and you will need to manually move them to the new Applications folder.

Users As explained previously, the OS X installer moves all user folders from the archived Users folder to the new OS X Users directory— except for one. For some reason the Shared user folder does not get transferred. If you had previously placed files in the Shared user folder, you'll need to manually move them from the archived Shared folder to the Shared user folder in your new Users directory. (Make sure you copy the contents of the folder and not the entire folder.)

Library This is the most complex folder to deal with because of the mix of older Apple-installed files that you don't want to transfer over and newer user- or application-installed files that you do. Luckily, again, the OS X installer does a few things for you. It moves the Application Support, iTunes, and PreferencePanes folders, as well as the contents of the `Preferences` directory, into the new `/Library` folder. However, many applications install other support files in this folder, and other files, such as contextual menu plug-ins, browser plug-ins, and Services are installed here for system-wide use. If you decide to manually reinstall applications, support files, and third-party add-ons from scratch (some people do), then you can ignore this folder. However, if you want to retain the full functionality of your previously installed software, going through this folder is the only way to do it. Note that because of privilege issues, when you drag files from the archived Library folder to the new Library folder, some files will copy while others will be moved; this is normal.

The first step is to look for any folders that exist in the archived Library folder that don't exist in the new Library folder. It's safe to simply drag these over wholesale. Dealing with the rest of the folder is a bit more tedious. You'll need to open the new Library folder and the archived Library folder side-by-side and compare the contents of each sub-folder. Files that exist in the old Library but don't exist in the new one can be moved over—some examples are fonts and Internet Plug-Ins. On the other hand, don't replace files or folders that already exist in the new folder—chances are these are newer versions—without first checking the version numbers and/or creation dates on each (using the Finder's Get Info command). A few folders warrant special consideration:

- Don't transfer the contents of `/Library/Caches` from the archive to the new `/Library`. OS X will recreate these files as needed.
- In the `/Library/Receipts` archive, only copy over receipts that were clearly installed by third-party software (e.g., FaxSTF, Windows Media Player). If you're unsure about an item, leave it—these aren't vital.
- If you were previously running a web server off your Mac, but were using the system-level web directory rather than your user-level web directory, be sure to transfer any custom contents of `/Library/WebServer/Documents`.

If you installed a new OS X over a version of OS X prior to 10.2, the following three tips apply:

- The folder `/Library/ColorSync/Scripts` in the archive corresponds to the new directory `/Library/Scripts/ColorSync`.
- In OS X 10.2 and later, Apple has replaced some of the available login pictures with new ones. If you'd like to retain all of the pictures from Mac OS X 10.1.x, make sure you move the appropriate files and folders—specifically the Cheetah and Orangutan files and the Landscapes and X Images folders—from the old `/Library/User Pictures` folder to the new one.
- Before transferring any files from `/Library/Printers`, try setting up your printer—there's a good chance support for your printer already exists in the new version of OS X. The exception is if you had previously installed FaxSTF, in which case you should transfer over the `/Library/Printers/SmithMicro` folder.

System This folder can largely be ignored, as it is rarely modified by users or applications, and the new OS X System directory contains newer versions of almost everything. One exception occurs if you've customized sendmail (Mac OS X's built-in Unix mail server); if so, carefully check the contents of the archived `/System/Library/StartupItems/Sendmail` folder. You may need to move some of these files over (and you will probably need to change permissions or use File Buddy or another utility to do it).

etc and var These two "folders" are actually aliases to folders within the invisible `/private` directory in your archived OS X folder. Most users can safely ignore them. However, for a few users (you'll know if you're one of them) there is important information contained in a few subfolders:

`/etc/crontab` If you've made changes to cron, this file is important.

`/etc/hostconfig` If you've set up sendmail on your Mac, this file is important.

`/etc/httpd.conf` If you've manually edited your Apache configuration, you'll want to move this file over.

/usr/local Some Unix software packages (MySQL, CVS, ViaVoice) install files in this directory. Unless you plan to reinstall these packages, you will need to move their support files to your new /usr/local directory.

/var/log This folder contains archives of system-level log files. If they're valuable to you, copy them over.

/var/mail Again, if you've set up sendmail on your Mac, the contents of this folder are important.

/var/root If you previously enabled the root user in Mac OS X, this is the root user's user folder, and contains the Desktop, Documents, and user-level Library directories (as well as any other files/folders that may have been created or saved to the "home" folder when logged in as root).

Kernel Extensions One other type of file that the OS X installer does not move into your new installation of OS X is kernel extensions (located in /System/Library/Extensions). And with good reason, since they interact with the OS at a very low level and incompatibilities can cause major problems. If you're not sure which kernel extensions to move over, a safer approach is to simply reinstall them using the original installer. Examples of applications that install kernel extensions include USB Overdrive, Kensington Mouseworks, and other utilities that affect input devices.

Once you've used these guidelines to transfer files over from the archived system to your new OS X installation, it's a good idea to restart your computer and then login. You'll need to set up your printer(s) again, but apart from that there should be minimal additional setup necessary. Once your Mac has been running smoothly for a few days, you can delete the Previous Systems folder and its contents; note that some of the remaining files may have permissions that prevent you from doing this without changing some permissions; in order to delete the folder, select it in the Finder, and use the Get Info command to give yourself read and write privileges. Click the "Apply to Enclosed Items…" button to change the permissions of everything inside the folder. You can now drag it to the Trash.

NOTE If you installed a newer version of OS X over an older version, it's possible that some of your older software doesn't work with the new OS. If one of these applications was previously set up as a Login Item, it will launch at login just as it did before, which can cause problems. To fix this, press the shift key just after the login/startup screen, and hold it down until after the Finder loads—this will prevent all Login Items from loading. You can then remove the offending Login Item from the Login pane of System Preferences and then log out and back in.

After installing Mac OS X, especially when you've performed an Archive and Install, it's a good idea to run the Repair Disk Permissions feature of Disk Utility to ensure that all system-level files have the correct privileges.

NOTE If you're reinstalling the same version of OS X you previously had installed, remember to also reinstall any updates to OS X that have been released, since your OS X installation CDs/DVDs are most likely not the latest version.

Forcing Apple Setup to (Re-)Run after an OS Install

User Level: admin
Affects: computer
Terminal: yes

The first time you startup your Mac in OS X, the Apple Setup utility begins and walks you through the setup process. Afterwards, you never see it again. However, if you've reinstalled the entire OS and *want* it to run to make setup a bit easier, here's the quick and dirty solution: launch Terminal and type **`sudo rm /private/var/db/.AppleSetupDone`** **<RETURN>**. Restart your Mac, and the Apple Setup Utility will run at startup.

Uninstalling Software

At some point you'll want to remove software that you've installed. You may have tried out some software that you didn't like, or you may want to free up some disk space or clean up some clutter. Whatever the reason, uninstalling software is one of those things that everyone ends up doing at some point. Here's how to do it right.

Uninstalling Mac OS Software

It's rare that you would want to uninstall part of the Mac OS; more importantly, it's generally not a good idea. However, there are a few things installed by OS X, such as language files, that you may not want or need. In addition, if you've installed the OS X Developer Tools, you may decide down the line that you no longer want them (they take up quite a bit of space). Here's how to get rid of them.

Removing Unwanted Language Support

User Level: admin
Affects: computer
Terminal: no

Unless you specifically tell the OS X installer not to, it will install support for a wide range of languages; if your Mac came with OS X, language support files were already installed. While it's neat that your computer supports so many languages, if you're like most people, you probably use only one, or perhaps two, languages. Yet these language support files take up *hundreds* of megabytes of space on your hard drive. You can regain this space by removing language support

FIGURE 4.9:
Monolingual lets you remove extra language support

files for languages you never use. It's possible to do this using Terminal, but it's much easier to use one of the many utilities that have sprung up since Mac OS X was released. My favorite is the sponsorware Monolingual (`http://homepage.mac.com/jschrier/`). Launch Monolingual, and you're presented with a list of languages supported by Mac OS X (including non-American English variants) (Figure 4.9); check the boxes next to those you wish to remove, then click the Remove button. You'll be asked for an admin username and password, and will be asked if you *really* want to remove these localization resources. If you do, they'll be removed just like that.

If you want to get any of these files back, you either need to use a utility like Pacifist, as described earlier in this chapter, or you need to reinstall OS X, so be sure you really want to remove them!

Removing the OS X Developer Tools

User Level: admin
Affects: computer
Terminal: yes

I recommended in the Introduction that you install the Mac OS X Developer Tools, as some of those tools are very useful for some exercises in this book. However, if you ever decide that you want to get rid of them, you can't just throw away the `/Developer` folder; the Developer Tools installer actually installs files in several other locations on your hard drive. Luckily, one of the files inside the `/Developer` folder is a script that uninstalls all Developer Tools files. To run the script, launch Terminal and type **`sudo /Developer/Tools/uninstall-devtools.pl`** **<RETURN>**. Enter your password when prompted, and the script will do the rest.

Uninstalling Third-Party Software

Most third-party software can be uninstalled without consequence. However, some are easier to uninstall than others. Here are a few methods for removing software, easiest first. Besides deleting the software itself, most applications and system add-ons also create preference files, usually with the name of the software in the name, in either `/Library/`

Preferences or ~/Library Preferences. Although it won't do you any harm to keep these files, you can delete them if you want to completely remove any trace of a piece of software.

Manually Deleting Software

User Level: normal or admin
Affects: user or computer
Terminal: no

If a particular piece of software was installed via drag-and-drop, chances are it can be removed via drag-and-drop (as in, drag it out of its folder and drop it onto the Trash). If the software was installed by an admin user into /Applications, /Library, or another system-level directory, only an admin will be able to delete it; if the software was installed by a user into the user's home directory, only that user will be able to delete it.

Uninstalling Packages Using OS X Package Manager

User Level: admin
Affects: computer
Terminal: no

I discussed installer packages earlier in this chapter. In addition to being a convenient way to install packages, most well-behaved installer packages also leave behind a "guide" to make removing them easier, in the form of an installation receipt in /Library/Receipts. All you need is a package uninstaller such as DesInstaller (http://krugazor.free.fr/software/desinstaller/DesInstaller.php) that can read these receipts.

When you launch DesInstaller, you're presented with an empty window with five buttons; click the left-most button to list all the installed packages in the DesInstaller window (Figure 4.10). (Unfortunately, DesInstaller's buttons aren't labeled very well; you can reveal a button's function by holding the cursor over it for a few seconds.) The second button from the left opens and closes the package content drawer; when the drawer is open, double-click on a package to view the files that were installed by that package. The third button lets you create a an archive of a package before you uninstall it (in case you change your mind later); however, these archives require running scripts in Terminal in order to reinstall, so they aren't the most convenient backups. Finally, the fourth button is the "uninstaller" button that lets you remove an installed package; select the package you wish to uninstall and click this button—after authenticating, it's gone. (The button all the way on the right lets you create a queue of uninstalls, so that you can remove packages in batches.)

WARNING You can actually uninstall Apple-provided software packages using DesInstaller. For individual applications like iTunes, iSync, etc., this is OK, but I don't recommend doing this for other items unless you know exactly what you're doing. Removing things like Essentials.pkg or BaseSystem.pkg will leave your Mac in an unusable state and require you to reinstall Mac OS X!

FIGURE 4.10:
Selecting a package to uninstall with DesInstaller

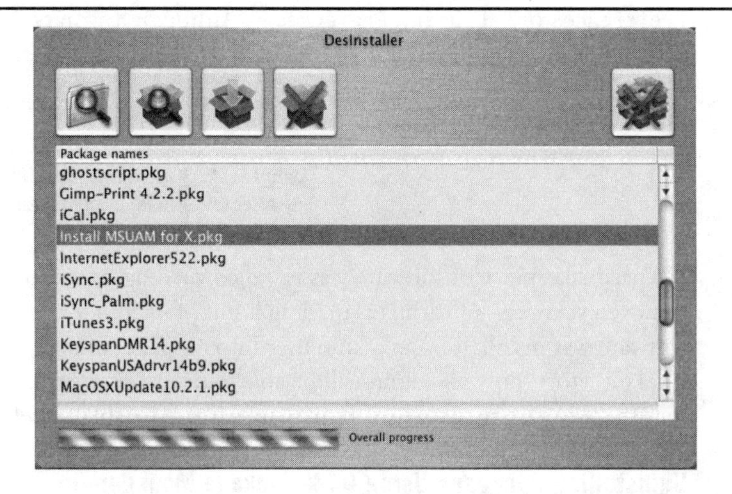

Taking Advantage of Installation Logs

User Level: usually admin
Affects: computer
Terminal: no

Some software is neither self-contained, nor does it provide a convenient receipt to tell a utility such as DesInstaller how to remove all of its pieces. For these types of software, you'll have to find all the pieces and delete them manually. If you're lucky, the software installer will have left an installation log somewhere on your hard drive. If so, you can use this log to locate all of the files that need to be deleted for a complete removal of the software.

For example, the following is part of the installer log from Symantec's Norton Solutions (which was saved inside the Norton Solutions folder in `/Applications`):

```
Created the Folder: Senior:Applications:Norton Solutions:
Created the Folder: Senior:Library:Application Support:Norton Solutions Support:
Created the Folder: Senior:Library:CFMSupport:
Created the Folder: Senior:Library:Documentation:Help:LiveUpdate Help:html:
Created the Folder: Senior:Library:Documentation:Help:Norton Help Scripts:
Created the Folder: Senior:Library:Documentation:Help:Norton Utilities Help:
Created the Folder: Senior:Library:Preferences:Norton Utilities Preferences:
Created the Folder: Senior:Library:StartupItems:NortonMissedTasks:
Created the Folder: Senior:Library:StartupItems:NUMCompatibilityCheck:
Created the Folder: Senior:Library:StartupItems:TrackDelete:
Created the Folder: Senior:Library:StartupItems:VolumeAssist:
Created the Folder: Senior:System:Library:Extensions:DeleteTrap.kext:
Created the Folder: Senior:System:Library:Extensions:symfs.kext:
Created the Folder: Senior:System:Library:Extensions:SymOSXKernelUtilities.kext:
```

Using this log, I could find each installed file and folder and delete it (although because some files and folders were installed in restricted directories, I'd need to use a utility such as XRay to delete them).

Using Third-Party Drive Cleaners

Finally, if none of the above methods is successful, there are also a number of third-party utilities that comb your hard drive for files and folders related to various applications and software packages, and then give you the option to remove them. However, most of these utilities simply search by creator codes, file types, and file extensions (topics I cover in more detail in the next chapter), meaning they aren't really doing much more than you could do yourself using OS X's Find utility (also covered in the next chapter). In addition, because they tend to rely more on educated guesses about some files than on receipts and installation logs (which are both fairly reliable), there's a greater chance a file or document that shouldn't be deleted will be accidentally. If you're suspecting that I'm not really a big fan of these types of utilities, you're right.

Transferring Mac OS X between Computers or Hard Drives

In my experience with users and participating in online forums and mailing lists, one of the most common questions that users of Mac OS X seem to have is "How do I copy my Mac OS X installation from one hard drive/computer to another?" Users generally fall into one of two categories: (1) people who have bought a new (larger) hard drive and installed it in their Mac, and want to move everything over from their old hard drive to the new one; or (2) people who have bought a new Mac and want to copy Mac OS X and all their files and software over from their old Mac to the new one.

The good news is that Mac OS X is, for the most part, hardware independent. That is, the same OS X that runs on a PowerBook also runs on an iBook and a G4 tower. That means that you can copy Mac OS X, and all installed software and files, directly from one computer to another, and it should boot up and function properly.

The bad news is that unlike Mac OS 9, where you could simply connect a drive or another computer, select all your files, and copy them over using drag-and-drop, Mac OS X requires some special tools. The Finder doesn't always copy invisible files properly (and there are lots of them in OS X), and because of permissions issues, it's difficult to make sure that *all* files are being copied.

This is one of those situations where Terminal can do something you can't do in the Finder. Terminal provides you with all the tools you need—specifically, commands that copy every single file, preserving permissions and file properties—to successfully copy an entire Mac OS X volume. However, most users don't want to learn the list of commands that it takes to do such a copy. Once again, a third-party developer has come to the rescue; in this case, Mike Bombich, whose Carbon Copy Cloner utility (`http://www.bombich.com/software/ccc.html`) puts a friendly face on the process. Here's how you use Carbon Copy Cloner to transfer your hard drive's contents to another hard drive, or to another computer.

Transferring Mac OS X between Hard Drives

User Level: admin
Affects: computer
Terminal: no

I recently got a new hard drive (a nice 80GB one), and installed it in my G4 tower; the original hard drive (a 20GB model) was getting a bit cramped. I wanted to transfer the contents of my original drive (Mac OS X, applications, documents, the works) to the new drive, and then use the new drive as my main drive. Using Carbon Copy Cloner, the process was a snap. Here's how to do it:

1. Make sure your destination volume has enough space for the contents of the source volume. If the destination volume already has an operating system on it, you should probably delete it before copying the source volume onto it. If you have valuable files on the destination volume, you should place them in a folder, named Saved Documents or something similar, until the copy is completed.
2. Launch Carbon Copy Cloner.
3. In the Source Disk box, select the source volume (the one you want to copy *from*) from the pop-up menu.
4. In the Target Disk box, select the destination volume (the one you want to copy *to*) from the pop-up menu. (Figure 4.11) If you want Carbon Copy Cloner to only replace files that exist on the target disk with identical names and paths, select the "Don't remove files from target" (yes, the description is a bit confusing); if you want it to delete any item on the destination volume that has a similar name to an item on the source disk, select "Remove like-named items." If you're installing onto an empty volume, you don't need to worry about these two settings.
5. In order to make your new drive a fully functional (bootable) copy, check both boxes in the Bootability options section.
6. If you *don't* want particular items to be copied (e.g., old folders you no longer care about), you can select them in the Items to be copied window and then click the Delete button.
7. When you're ready to copy, click the Clone button. You'll be asked to authenticate using an admin username and password, after which Carbon Copy Cloner will proceed to copy the entire volume, re-create all necessary links, and "bless" the volume so that it can function as a bootable volume. Carbon Copy Cloner will notify you when the copy is done.
8. Open System Preferences, click the Startup Disk icon, and select the new volume as your startup disk. The next time you restart, the new drive will be the boot volume. You can then erase or remove the original drive.

FIGURE 4.11:

Using Carbon Copy Cloner to copy a Mac OS X volume

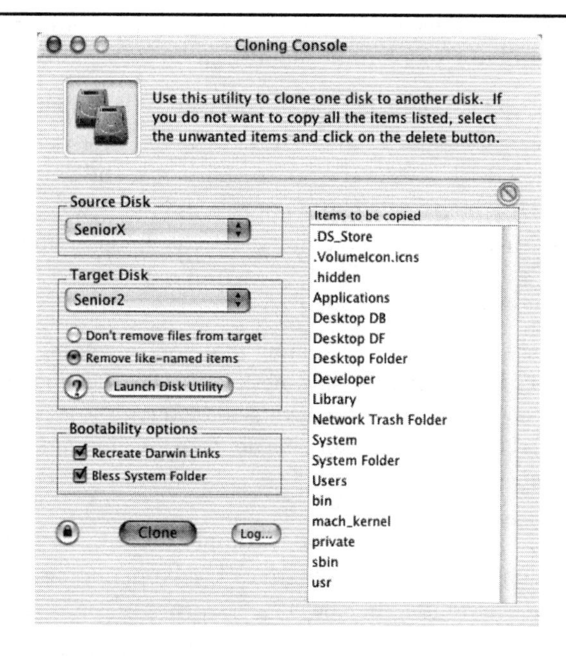

Transferring Mac OS X between Computers

User Level: admin
Affects: computer
Terminal: no

Similar to installing a new hard drive, many users who buy a new Mac want to transfer their existing Mac OS X installation to the new computer so that they can pick up right where they left off using their new hardware. You can use Carbon Copy Cloner in exactly the same manner to do this, but first you have to connect the new computer to the old one. Given that most computers supported by OS X have a FireWire port, the easiest way to do this is to use FireWire Target Disk Mode. You'll need a FireWire cable to do this, which should be available at any computer or electronics store.

1. With the new computer turned off, connect the FireWire cable to a FireWire port on each computer.
2. Boot up your old computer normally if it's not already running. Login to an admin account.
3. On the new computer, hold down the T key on the keyboard, and press the power button to start it up. Keep holding the T key down until you see a FireWire symbol on the screen. At this point your new computer's hard drive will be mounted on your old computer's Desktop as a FireWire hard drive.

4. If you don't need any of the files on the new computer's hard drive, you can actually erase it using the Disk Utility application.
5. Launch Carbon Copy Cloner on your old computer, and follow the instructions in the previous section, "Transferring Mac OS X between Hard Drives." (Select your old computer's hard drive in the Source Disk box, and your new computer's hard drive in the Target Disk box. If you chose not to erase the new computer's hard drive because you wanted files that came installed on it, click the "Don't remove files from target" option in the Target Disk box.)

NOTE In this example, I'm assuming that your old computer has a recent version of OS X installed, and you're simply moving your OS X installation to your new computer. If your older computer has an older version of Mac OS X installed, you'll probably be better off to simply copy over your user files and use the copy of OS X that is already installed on your new computer.

6. When the clone operation is complete, drag your new Mac's hard drive to the Trash to unmount it from your old Mac's Desktop, unplug the FireWire cable, and then press the power button on the new Mac to turn it off.
7. Press the power button on the new Mac again to boot it up normally (using the installation of OS X you just copied over, including all accounts and settings). It should boot up and behave exactly like your old computer.
8. Give your old Mac to a needy school :)

Supporting "Unsupported" Stuff

I'm not going to spend too much time on this topic, but I wanted to point out that just because a certain Mac model or a certain third-party peripheral/accessory isn't "officially" supported by Apple, doesn't mean your computer is relegated to the scrap heap. Third-party developers have provided some novel solutions that let you use Mac OS X on unsupported hardware, and peripherals that aren't officially supported by Apple or the peripheral's manufacturer. Here are a few examples:

XPostFacto A freeware solution that allows you to install Mac OS X on a number of unsupported Macs. For instructions, downloads, and a list of Macs that are compatible with XPostFacto, go to `http://eshop.macsales.com/OSXCenter/XPostFacto/`.

Sonnet PCI X Installer A commercial product from Sonnet Technologies that allows you to install Mac OS X on many computers that have been upgraded with Sonnet processor upgrade cards. For a list of supported computers and processor cards, visit `http://www.sonnettech.com/downloads/osx_upgrade_sw.html`.

USB Overdrive X Although you can connect any USB pointing device to your Mac's USB port, most devices require some kind of driver in order to function properly. Unfortunately, some USB peripheral manufacturers haven't provided drivers for Mac OS X. USB Overdrive X is a shareware driver that works with almost any USB pointing device, allowing you to use mice, trackballs, joysticks, gamepads, etc., that don't currently have drivers. See `http://www.usboverdrive.com/`.

Gimp-Print Although Mac OS X includes drivers for many printers, many other printers, including some very popular older printers, aren't currently supported. However, you can take advantage of Mac OS X's open source printing subsystem to provide printer drivers for a wide range of printers. I actually discuss the Gimp-Print drivers in depth in Chapter 12. See `http://gimp-print.sourceforge.net/`.

SWIM 3 Floppy Driver If you have an early beige G3 Mac or a PowerBook G3 Series that came with a floppy disk drive, you're surely aware by now that the floppy drive is not supported by OS X. The SWIM 3 driver allows you to use the floppy drive under OS X. Note that this driver only works with pre-installed floppy drives; it doesn't work on third-party floppy drives. Visit `http://www.darwin-development.org/floppy/`.

WARNING Remember, "unsupported" means just that—if something goes wrong, Apple won't help you, nor will most other software vendors. So use these types of hacks at your own risk.

Moving On...

Installing and uninstalling software are some of the most mundane tasks you can perform on your Mac. Yet they're also some of the tasks that users find the most mystifying. Hopefully this chapter has helped you become both more familiar with these processes and better equipped to take advantage of them.

At this point I've discussed some of the major conceptual topics that surround OS X, and covered a bunch of the possible setup and startup options available to you. These topics—permissions, accounts, preferences, startup/login, and installing software—really form the basis of mastering Mac OS X, as many of the topics and tips we cover in the rest of the book will involve some combination of the skills and knowledge you've gained. Now that you've got a handle on these topics, it's time to start talking about the ways you use OS X every day, and how to do those things better, faster, easier, and cooler. Part II will cover such topics as the Finder, the Dock, applications, and the Classic Environment.

Part II

Files, Finders, Docks, and Apps (including Classic)

Chapter 5

Finagle Files and Foil Finder Frustration

(Or: How to bend the Finder to your will.)

No matter what you use your Mac for—word processing, e-mail, surfing the Web, graphics, multimedia, games, business—you spend a lot of time working with files. Creating files, accessing files, editing files, copying files, moving files, saving files, everything you do on your computer is file-related. It follows that working with files is an area where becoming an expert can save you time and frustration. However, most Mac users take advantage of only a small percentage of the Finder's functionality. In this chapter I'm going to cover files and the Finder from top to bottom: understanding attributes to setting up settings, working with windows to finding information, customizing contextual menus to optimizing Open/Save dialogs.

In addition to the topics I cover in this chapter, a large part of working with files is accessing them quickly (especially applications). Mac OS X's Dock is Apple's solution to this need, but there are many other alternatives as well; I talk about the Dock and Dock alternatives in Chapter 6, "Develop a Dynamite Dock."

NOTE Be sure to check out the Online Bonus Chapter, available at `www.sybex.com` and `http://www.macosxpowertools.com/`; it's full of much more Finder-related info that just wouldn't fit in the book.

File Basics

Before you can master the Finder, you need to master files. Fortunately, doing so isn't too difficult. However, a few topics deserve your attention, as understanding them will become extremely valuable the deeper you get into using your Mac.

File Types, Creator Types, and File Extensions

For years, one of the biggest "incompatibilities" between the Mac OS and other operating systems had to do with how the respective operating systems determined what *kind* of file a particular file was. The Classic Mac OS used two different codes—the creator code and file type—attached to the file. The creator code was a four-letter code that identified the application with which a file should be identified. (MSWD was the creator code for Microsoft Word, for example.) The file type indicated what kind of file a particular file was (APPL was an application, WDBN was a Word document, etc.).

Windows and Unix-based systems, on the other hand, use three-letter codes appended to the end of filenames to determine each file's purpose and type. For example, in Windows, any file that ends in `.exe` is an application, and any file that ends in `.doc` will open in Microsoft Word.

The reasons for these different approaches are too complex to get into here; I point them out here because under Mac OS X, Apple has attempted to make many files, especially documents, more cross-platform–compatible. Files created in or used in Mac OS X generally have file extensions like `.doc`, `.txt`, and `.app`. However, because so many Mac users also interact with users of older versions of the Mac OS, Apple had to ensure backwards-compatibility as well.

What this means for you is that under Mac OS X, some files have creator and type codes, but no file extensions; some have no creator/type codes but do have file extensions; some have both; and, believe it or not, some have none of the above (these files are bound to the application that created them or first opened them). In addition, each setting can be changed by the user (as I'll talk about in a bit).

Understanding and Changing File Associations

User Level: normal or admin
Affects: individual user or computer
Terminal: no

Given all these possible settings, when you double-click on a document, how does Mac OS X know how to open it? The answer is that OS X uses a hierarchical model for associating documents with applications. The best depiction I've seen of this model is actually in the Type, Creator & Extension panel of the utility XRay (`http://www.brockerhoff.net/xray/`). In Figure 5.1 I've used XRay to get information on a sample text file. The vertical arrow on the left side indicates how OS X determines what application will be used to open the file if you double-click it.

The first thing checked is whether or not the file has been explicitly bound to an application. If no specific application has been set, the creator code is checked (Mac OS 9's creator code). If there is no creator set, OS X then looks at the file's three-character extension. If no file extension exists, OS X looks for a type code (Mac OS 9's file type)—if one exists, the OS checks to see which application files with that type code are generally opened with. Finally, if none of this data exists (if all of these fields are blank in XRay), double-clicking the file brings up a dialog asking what application you want to use to open it.

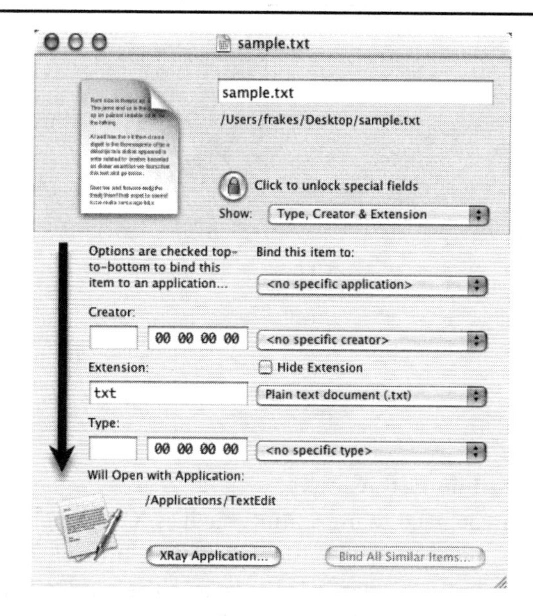

FIGURE 5.1: A document's application associations in XRay

Just as XRay provides the best view for understanding the various identifiers a file can have, it is also my favorite for changing these identifiers. You can click on the pop-up menu next to any option to select a specific application to associate with the document; to select an application from which the creator code should be taken; to select a file extension; or to select an application from which the type code should be taken. Once you've made your changes, you need to choose File ➢ Save Changes. If you've changed the "Bind this item to" setting, you can also click the "Bind All Similar Items..." button to bind all documents with similar settings to the chosen application.

The XRay window for an application looks slightly different than the one for a file window (Figure 5.2). Although it still has an Extension field (which is empty in the example shown here), and a Type field (which is set to APPL here, indicating this is an application), the other two fields differ. The top pop-up menu lists all extensions "claimed" by this application, and the second menu lists all file types claimed by it. In other words, if you double-click any document with an extension and/or file attributes listed in these menus, it will be opened in this application, unless you have specifically set another application to open files with those characteristics.

WARNING Although it's generally OK to change file types, creators, extensions, and bindings for documents (especially when you really want to change the application a document is opened in), be careful when changing these variables for other types of files. In Mac OS X, most application and system support files are identified *only* by their file extensions. For example, if you remove the `.app` from the end of an application name, it may no longer function as an application.

FIGURE 5.2:

An application's Type, Creator & Extension window in XRay

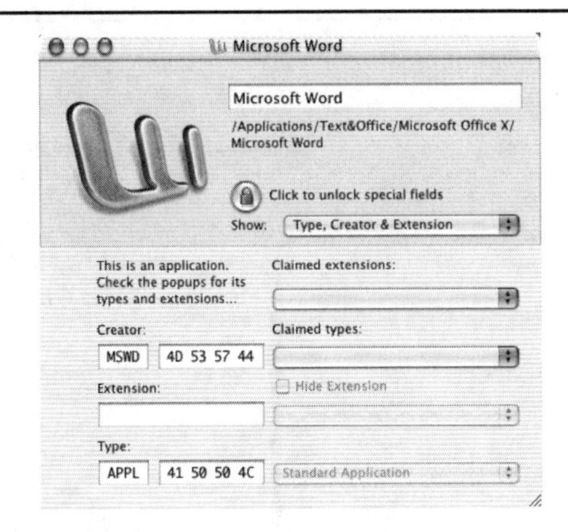

Changing File Extensions

Although you need to use a utility such as XRay to change a file's file type and creator code you can change a file's extension in the Get Info window for the file (see the next section for details), or in the Finder. To change it in the Finder, simply select the file, press return to edit the file's name, and add, edit, or delete the appropriate extension. However, be sure you know what you're doing here—simply changing a file's extension does not actually change the *file* in any way. For example, changing a Word document's name from `document.doc` to `document.txt` won't convert it to a text document; it will still be a complex Word document that will look pretty ugly opened in a text editor. Likewise, changing a graphic file's name from `picture.tiff` to `picture.jpg` won't actually change the file from a TIFF file to a JPEG file. In addition, as I'll explain later when I talk about Finder Preferences, just because a filename doesn't show an extension in the Finder doesn't mean it doesn't have one. For this reason, I recommend using the Get Info window to change file extensions.

TIP

If you don't have the "Always show file extensions" box checked in Finder Preferences, changing a file's extension will bring up an alert window asking you if you're sure you want to change the extension. The default button is to keep the original extension, which means you can't just press the return key to get on with your work. However, you can press the escape key to quickly dismiss the dialog and accept the change.

One more point about file extensions: if you've chosen to show file extensions in Finder Preferences (I talk more about that in the next section), extensions will be visible for all files that have them. However, if you've chosen *not* to show file extensions in the Finder, don't expect *all* extensions to disappear. The reason is that each file has its own hide/show extension setting. If this setting has not been used, the file will obey the Finder Preferences setting; however, if it has been set (by you, by the developer, by another user), the file's own setting will override the Finder's setting. I point this out because it's very easy—too easy, in my opinion—to add a file extension to a file that's already got a hidden one.

The Get Info Window

I talked about the Finder's Get Info window several times in Chapter 1 when I discussed changing file ownership and permissions. However, you can view and edit quite a few other bits of info in the Get Info window's other panels. Here are a few tidbits about these panels.

TIP The Get Info window in Mac OS X 10.0 and 10.1 was actually a dynamic window called the Show Info Inspector—you could only have a single Show Info window open, and it changed to reflect the info for whatever Finder item you clicked on. Due to user feedback, Apple changed the Get Info window to its current OS 9-like implementation—each item gets its own Get Info window, and you can open as many windows as you like. If you prefer the inspector version, press the option key and File ➢ Get Info changes to File ➢ Show Inspector.

The General Panel

The General panel is the default view of Get Info windows. For all types of files and folders, it shows you the item's icon and name; the kind of file (taken from the file's type code, or, if one doesn't exist, from the file extension); the size of the file; the location of the file; the creation date and time; the date and time the item was last modified; and whether or not the item is locked. You can toggle the Locked status on and off; on (locked) means the item cannot be modified or deleted.

In addition, the General panel provides other information depending on the file type. Get Info windows for documents include a Stationary Pad option. When checked, the document becomes a sort of template—if you open the file, a copy is made and opened instead, leaving the original untouched. Get Info windows for applications include information on the application's version number and (usually) developer. Finally, when you Get Info on a volume, the General panel provides information on the volume format, capacity, and the amount of space used and available.

The Name & Extension Panel

The Name & Extension panel simply provides a way for you to edit the item's name and extension. Although you can change an item's extension in the Finder, it is preferable to do it here or using a third-party file utility, because (as I mentioned earlier) sometimes the Finder doesn't show the true extension.

You can also choose to show or hide a file's extension in this panel; this setting takes precedence over the setting in Finder Preferences to show or hide extensions.

The Open with Panel

The Open with panel is only present for documents; it lets you choose an application with which to open the document. As I mentioned earlier, if you choose an application in this panel, the setting overrules any other application association, such as creator type, file type, or file extension. If you click the Change All... button, the setting will be applied to all documents with the same characteristics as the current file.

The Content Index Panel

This panel is only present for folders and volumes. I discuss it in detail later in the chapter when I talk about finding files by content, but it basically allows you to index the content of volumes and folders, and to see when the most recent index occurred.

The Preview Panel

The Preview panel is virtually identical to the Preview column in Finder windows viewed as columns. It exists for all Get Info windows, but its contents differ depending on the type of file. For any kind of item but a document, the Preview panel is simply a larger version of the item's icon. However, for document files, the Preview icon often provides you with a helpful preview of the file's contents (Figure 5.3). Note that not all documents take advantage of the Preview function; Word documents, for example, simply show a document icon.

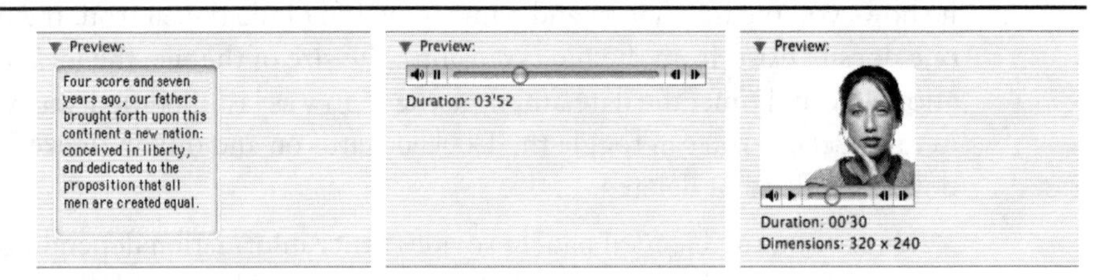

FIGURE 5.3: The Preview panel for (left to right) a text file, an MP3, and a QuickTime movie

TIP When previewing a music or video file, you can click the volume icon to change the volume. If you press shift as you change the volume, you can force the volume to play *much* louder. For some reason, this trick only seems to work in the Preview panel of Get Info or the Preview column of Finder windows (it doesn't work in applications).

The Memory Panel

The Memory panel only appears for *Classic* applications—applications written specifically for Mac OS 9. As I'll talk about in Chapter 8, "Clobbering Classic," Classic applications will run in Mac OS X's Classic Environment, but still use OS 9's memory management system. The memory panel shows the suggested, minimum, and preferred memory allocations for each Classic app (and allows you to edit the minimum and preferred amounts as needed).

The Languages Panel

The Languages panel only appears for applications; it allows you to disable supported languages in an application, and re-enable them later. If you've done any digging around inside application packages, you know that language support is usually contained inside the `/Contents/Resources` directory of a package. If you select a language in this panel and then click the Remove... button, a new directory, `/Contents/Resources Disabled`, is created, and the resources for the selected language are moved there. This doesn't save any hard drive space, nor does it affect how fast the application loads or runs. However, if you change your OS language to Spanish, for example, but have removed Spanish from an application's Languages panel, the application will not play along with the rest of the Spanish-speaking system. The only reason I can see for using this feature is if an application's language files are causing problems. If you need to re-enable a language that you've removed, click the Add… button and navigate to the Resources Disabled folder inside the application package to find it.

The Plug-ins Panel

The Plug-ins panel works just like the Languages panel, but is only shown for applications that support the standard Mac OS X plug-in architecture (iMovie is a good example). You can remove plug-ins, and later add them back in if desired. If one of your plug-ins is misbehaving, this solution is much easier than having to dig into the package contents of the iMovie application. This is also a convenient way to add third-party plug-ins to applications like iMovie.

The Comments Panel

Finally, all documents, folders, applications, volumes, etc., have a Comments panel. You can use it to type in any sort of comment about the file that you like. I never use this panel, but I know people who type each application's serial or registration number into its Comments field.

NOTE Even though Mac OS 9 also has a Comments field in its Get Info windows, those comments, and Mac OS X's, are not transferable. I talk more about this problem in Appendix A, "A Tale of Two Systems."

Other File Attributes

In addition to the standard attributes I just discussed, files in OS X also have other attributes that aren't as accessible (and aren't used very often by most users). A few, such as the SetUID, SetGID, Sticky bits, and the immutable flag, are fairly esoteric and beyond the purview of this book. However, one, invisibility, is fairly common, and another, labels, is available only by installing third-party software.

Invisibility

Invisibility is actually a pretty important file attribute in OS X. The OS uses invisibility to hide the many files—used by the system but typically not by the user—that would otherwise clutter folders and volumes. Invisibility is also used to hide files that shouldn't be deleted or moved by the user.

There are three ways a file becomes invisible in OS X. The first is the *invisible bit*. A file with the invisible bit enabled won't be visible in the Finder. Although you can't enable/ disable the invisible bit from the Finder's Get Info window, it's fairly easy to do using a third-party utility such as XRay, FileXaminer (`http://www.gideonsoftworks.com/filexaminer.html`), or File Buddy (`http://www.skytag.com/`). All of these utilities have a simple check box that lets you toggle the invisible bit; note that once you toggle the bit, you generally have to relaunch the Finder for the actual visibility to change. (You can do this by selecting Force Quit… from the Apple Menu, and force quitting the Finder; it will relaunch automatically.)

Although it's easy to make a visible file *in*visible, making an invisible file visible is a bit tougher—because you have to access the file, and it's, well, invisible. There are a number of utilities available that allow you to find or view invisible files, but for me the easiest way to find an invisible file is to use the Finder's Find tool. I talk about this tool in more detail later in the chapter, but for now, just choose File ➢ Find… in the Finder. In the Find window, select the location to search using the "Search in" pop-up, select "visibility" from the "Add criteria…" pop-up, and then select "off" from the pop-up next to "visibility." If you know the name of the file, type it into the "file name contains" field; otherwise leave that field blank. Click the Search button and you'll get a window with a list of all the invisible files that match your criteria. Find the one you want, and drag its icon from the results window onto one of the file utilities mentioned above. You can then disable the invisible bit. Whew!

NOTE If you've installed the Developer Tools, you can also change visibility using the `SetFile` command in Terminal, but it's not as quick and easy; however, Terminal does have the advantage of ignoring the invisible bit, so if you list a directory's contents in Terminal, all files will be visible, even those that are supposed to be invisible.

The second way a file becomes invisible in Mac OS X is if it begins with a period (.). If it does, the Finder hides the file. Although you can change an item's file extension in the Finder, you can't add a period to the beginning of its name to make it invisible—the Finder simply won't let you do it. However, you can drag it to your favorite file utility and change the name there.

If you want to remove the period from a filename to make the file visible, you need to use a technique like the one listed above to access the file; then drag it to your favorite file utility and change the name from within the utility's file info window.

The final way a file becomes invisible is via a text file called `.hidden`, located at the root level of the startup volume (and, of course, invisible due to the period at the beginning of its name). Any file or folder included in this file will be hidden from view in the Finder. Although it's technically possible to edit this file to include your own files or folders (or to remove files from the file to make them visible), I wouldn't do it, because the `.hidden` file is created by the OS. First, you might change something you shouldn't, and second, the next time you install a major system update, the file has a good chance of being replaced by a newer version. If you really want to view the file just to see what its contents look like, use the Finder's Find tool again, this time searching for files whose name is "`.hidden`" and whose visibility is off; when the search is complete, drag the `.hidden` file from the results window onto the TextEdit application.

Labels? You Bet

One of the extremely popular file attributes present in Mac OS 9 and earlier but missing in Mac OS X (at least at the time of this writing) is the Finder label. Users could label files and folders using various colors in order to categorize and identify them.

If you're one of the many users who have bemoaned the lack of labels in OS X, you can get them back using the shareware Labels X (`http://www.unsanity.com/haxies/labels/`). Labels X is a preference pane that provides the ability to apply labels (colors) to files and folders via a contextual menu—control/right-click on a file, select a label, and you're back to OS 9.

In addition, Labels X also adds a Label column to windows in list view, allowing you to sort file lists by label (one of the things I used labels for the most in OS 9). Finally, if you apply a label to a file in OS X, it transfers over if you boot into OS 9, and vice versa—so if you did a lot of file labeling in OS 9, and those files are still on your computer, you'll be pleased to find out that all of your previous labels show up in OS X when Labels X is installed.

Finder Preferences and View Options

In Chapter 2, I covered the System Preferences application, which provides access to most Mac OS X settings. However, the Finder has a few settings of its own that aren't located in System Preferences.

Finder Preferences

User Level: any
Affects: individual user
Terminal: no

The job of the Finder is to provide you with an interface to manage files, folders, and applications. If you're wondering why the preferences from the Finder aren't located in System Preferences like other Mac OS X settings, remember that the Finder is an application, just like your e-mail client, your word processor, and your web browser. (The main difference is that Mac OS X knows to always keep the Finder running, so if it crashes or if you force quit it on purpose, it will automatically relaunch.) As such, the Finder's preferences are located exactly where you'd expect to find them in any other application: in the Finder's application menu.

When the Finder is active, select Finder ➢ Preferences.... You'll be presented with the Finder Preferences dialog (Figure 5.4). Although some of the settings are fairly straightforward, a few deserve more detailed descriptions. Some of the features mentioned here won't be discussed until a bit later in the chapter; however, since the Finder preferences are so central to working with files and folders, I wanted to mention them up front.

FIGURE 5.4:
The Finder's Preferences dialog

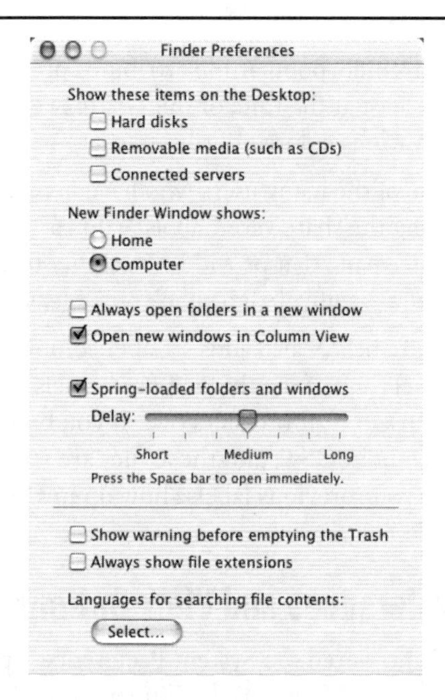

Show these items on the Desktop In Mac OS 9, every connected hard drive, every mounted server, and every mounted removable media (CD, floppy disk, DVD, MO disk, etc.) showed up on the Desktop. To access a volume, you double-clicked it. This was great for easy access, but not so great for Desktop clutter. For example, on my old computer, I had three hard drives, each divided into multiple partitions. After inserting a CD, mounting a couple remote servers, and mounting a disk image or two, I often had 10–15 volumes mounted on my Desktop! In Mac OS X, you have the option to show or not show particular types of volumes on the Desktop, in any combination. I personally choose to always show Removable media and connected servers, but sometimes I hide hard disks to keep my Desktop a bit neater.

New Finder Window shows Because of Mac OS X's multi-level (System/Local/User) file organization, many users can get by without ever leaving their home folder (~/). In fact, for many beginning users, trying to find their home folder from the root level of the hard drive would be a challenge. The New Finder Window shows preference allows you to choose what directory is displayed when a new Finder window is opened. When set to Home, the window opens automatically to the user's home directory; when set to Computer, the window opens up to the Computer view, which is simply a list of all mounted volumes and the Network icon.

TIP If you unchecked any items under "Show these items on the Desktop," I recommend setting "New Finder Window shows" to Computer so that you'll be able to easily access mounted volumes, disks, servers, etc., by opening a new Finder window.

Always open folders in a new window This setting is a bit confusing, since it only applies to certain window view options. As I'll talk about later in the chapter ("Working with Windows"), Mac OS X's Finder windows have three options for viewing files: icon view, list view, and column view. In icon view and list view, if you want to view the contents of a folder, you double-click it (or select it and choose File ➢ Open). By default, Mac OS X will open the folder in the *existing* window; in order to open the folder in a *new* window of its own, you have to hold down the command key as you open it. By checking this box, you change the default behavior so that opening a folder opens it in a new window.

TIP If the "Always open folders in a new window" box is checked, there's no way to open a folder in an existing window. However, if you hold down the option key as you open a folder, the existing window will close as the new one opens. It's not exactly the same, but at least you're left with only a single window.

Open new windows in Column View By default, new Finder windows will be presented using the most recently used view option (icon, list, column). However, if this box is checked, new Finder windows will *always* be presented in column view. Note that this setting only applies to new Finder windows created by choosing File ➢ New Finder Window (or pressing command+N) in the Finder; a window opened by double-clicking a volume or folder it will inherit the view of the previous folder, or will open in the view last used for that volume or folder.

Spring-loaded folders and windows I'll be talking about spring-loaded folders and windows a bit later in the chapter ("File and Folder Finesse"), but in a nutshell, if you drag a file or folder over a volume or folder icon in the Finder, and hold it there, eventually the volume or folder will open, revealing its contents, so that you can place the dragged file or folder inside a sub-folder of that volume/folder. This setting lets you choose the length of the delay before the volume/folder opens.

Show warning before emptying the Trash If this item is checked, when you choose Finder ➢ Empty Trash (or press shift+command+delete), you will be presented with a dialog asking if you're sure you want to empty the Trash. Unchecking this option means that the Trash will always be emptied immediately, without the dialog appearing.

TIP If you have "Show warning before emptying the Trash" checked, but you want to bypass the warning for a single emptying, you have three options: (1) You can hold down the option key as you choose Finder ➢ Empty Trash; (2) you can press shift+option+command-delete; or (3) you can control-click (or right-click if you have a multi-button mouse) on the Trash icon in the Dock, and select Empty Trash; using this method, you will never receive the confirmation dialog, no matter what your setting is in the Finder Preferences dialog.

Always show file extensions Earlier in this chapter I talked about file extensions (the `.xxx` extension to a file's name that indicates what type of file it is), and how you can choose to show or hide a file's extension—assuming it exists—on an individual basis using the Get Info window. However, what about files that haven't explicitly been set to show or hide their extensions? By default, Mac OS X hides the file extensions for these files. If you select this option in Finder Preferences, files extensions will be shown for all files with extensions that have not been explicitly set to hide them. (That sounded a bit convoluted, but that's because it's a bit of a convoluted setting.) I personally prefer to show file extensions, because it prevents me from adding an extra extension (for example, naming `sample.rtf` `sample.rtf.rtf`). However, many users dislike seeing file extensions at all; it's more of a personal preference than anything else. Just remember that if you do not have this preference selected, a filename may actually have an extension that is hidden.

Languages for searching files contents As I'll discuss later in this chapter ("File and Folder Finesse"), Mac OS X allows you to not only search for particular files, but to search for words or phrases *within* files. It does this by indexing words found inside each file's contents. By clicking the Select… button, you can choose what languages Mac OS X uses when indexing file contents. Unselecting languages that you (and your documents) don't use will speed up the indexing process and reduce the size of your file content indexes.

View Options

User Level: any
Affects: individual user
Terminal: no

The other major Finder-related settings are found in the View Options dialog, accessible by choosing View ➢ Show View Options. These settings let you control how icons are arranged, what information is provided with filenames, and other settings related to file display. However, this dialog is contextual, meaning it changes depending on which window is active in the Finder and how that directory is being viewed (it also floats on top of any and all Finder objects). Because the View Options window changes based on the current view, I'll talk about the specific options in the View Options dialog when I talk about the Desktop ("The Desktop and the Desktop Folder") and window views ("Working with Windows").

Now that we've talked about Finder options, it's almost time to talk about working with files and folders. However, since you access these items via the Desktop and Finder windows, I'm going to first give you some background and tips for working with the Desktop and windows.

The Desktop and the Desktop Folder

The Desktop is one of the busiest areas of any Mac. Since it's the easiest place to get to quickly, and you can (almost) always see it, many people use it as a place to put frequently used items, work in progress, and even permanent files and folders. If you've chosen to show mounted volumes on the Desktop, you also use it to access those volumes. Here are a few tips to help you get to it more easily and make it work better for you.

Where/What Is the Desktop *Really*?

If you're a veteran of Mac OS 9 or earlier, you probably know that the Desktop was actually an invisible folder called Desktop Folder at the root level of the hard drive. If you had multiple hard drives, each of them had their own Desktop Folder. These Desktop Folders were shared by all users.

In Mac OS X, because each user has their own Desktop, the Desktop is handled a bit differently. It's still a folder; however, *each* user has their own Desktop folder, located at `~/Desktop` (I actually mentioned these folders in Chapter 1). If you look at your own Desktop folder, you'll find it contains everything that is visible on the Desktop of your computer (except mounted volumes, of course).

NOTE If you actually see a folder called Desktop Folder at the root level of a volume when running Mac OS X, it's because that volume was used under Mac OS 9 or earlier. (Perhaps you booted your computer into OS 9, or used your computer in Target Disk Mode on a computer running OS 9.)

TIP If you boot into Mac OS 9 and need to access something on your Mac OS X Desktop, remember that it won't appear on your OS 9 Desktop. You need to navigate to `~/Desktop` to find it. Likewise, if you put something on your Desktop under OS 9 and later boot into OS X, it's not easy to access that item. I'll talk more about this situation in Appendix A, "A Tale of Two Systems."

View Options for the Desktop

User Level: any
Affects: individual user
Terminal: no

If you select the Desktop (by clicking anywhere on it), and then choose View ➢ Show View Options, the View Options window will appear (it will say "Desktop" in the title bar), and will present you with options specific to the Desktop (Figure 5.5). You can choose the size of Desktop icons, ranging from tiny (16 × 16 pixels) to huge (128 × 128 pixels). You can also choose the text size of Finder labels (file names, item info, etc.), as well as choose whether you want those labels to appear below or to the right of Finder icons.

The "Snap to grid" setting, if checked, keeps Finder icons arranged in a neat grid; you can drop an icon anywhere, and it will instantly snap to the closest grid space.

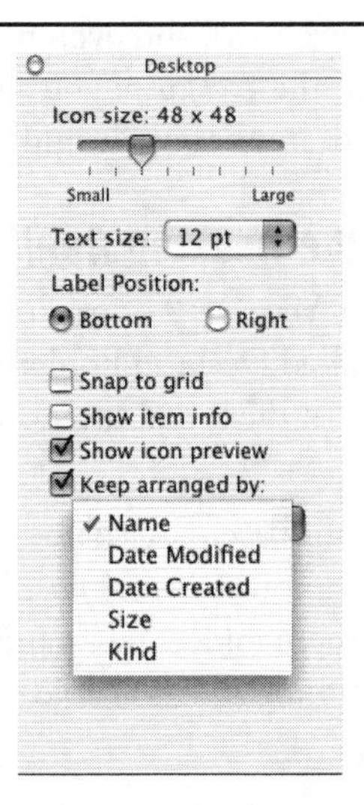

FIGURE 5.5: View Options for the Desktop

TIP If you *don't* select the "Snap to grid" option, you can still make Desktop icons snap to the invisible grid; drag an icon (or icons) to the approximate area you want them to be, but before you release the mouse button, hold the command key down. When you release the mouse button, the icon(s) you have moved will automatically position themselves as if "Snap to grid" was enabled. (Conversely, if you enable "Snap to grid," the command key will temporarily disable it for the current drag.)

"Show item info" provides additional info about an item directly below the item's name; the actual info provided differs depending on the item. For volumes, you'll see the total space used on the volume and the free space remaining; folders will show the number of items (files or folders) at the root level of each folder; info on graphics files will include the dimensions of the picture (in pixels); and movie and sound files will be listed with the length of the movie or sound.

If you select "Show icon preview," any graphics files (GIF, JPG, TIFF, etc.) that contain an icon preview will use those icons instead of their default file type icons.

NOTE Normally, when you select an item in the Finder, its icon becomes shaded; however, if you select "Show icon preview," a side effect is that this shading no longer occurs for items with icon previews. As a result, you cannot tell if such an item is selected in the Finder. Unfortunately, there is no way around this at the time of this writing.

Finally, "Keep arranged by" allows you to keep files and folders arranged by name, kind, date modified, date created, or size (always in ascending order), so items with a filename or type that starts with "A," older items, and smaller items will be listed first. Note that if you've checked "Keep arranged by," and you've also selected to show mounted volumes on the Desktop (in Finder Preferences) the boot volume will always be listed first, followed by other mounted volumes, then files and folders.

Accessing the Desktop (Especially When It's Hidden)

User Level:	any
Affects:	individual user
Terminal:	no

I'm sure you've been faced with this situation before—you need to open a file you've placed on the Desktop, but you can't see it because of all the windows that are open. Although the Desktop is extremely handy in terms of providing quick access to files, one of the biggest obstacles most people experience in using the Desktop for this purpose is that it is often obscured by Finder and/or application windows. Fortunately, under OS X there are many ways to get around this obstacle. I've included a few here. (These methods are useful even when the Desktop isn't obscured; I use a couple of them as my regular method of accessing Desktop files and folders.)

Note that unless otherwise noted, the tip table for this section applies to all of the following tips.

Hiding Everything but the Finder

If you're trying to get to the Desktop, but you have a number of application windows open, you can just hide all applications except for the Finder. There are actually two ways to do this: if the Finder is active (the current application) hold down the command and option keys and click the Finder icon in the Dock. All other applications will be hidden. If another application is active (frontmost), you can use the same procedure, or you can hold command+option and click anywhere on the Desktop itself to get the same results.

Hiding Everything Including Finder Windows

The only drawback to the method I just described is that if you have a number of Finder windows open, they won't be hidden (so they may still obscure the Desktop). You can minimize each Finder window to the Dock by clicking the yellow minimize button in the top left corner, or you can minimize all Finder windows at once by holding option as you click any window's minimize button.

However, that's a bit of a pain. Instead you can use the donationware Show Desktop (`http://www.everydaysoftware.net/`). When launched, the Show Desktop icon appears in the Dock just like any other application. When you click it, it will hide all running applications, and has a preference to automatically minimize all Finder windows, as well. Shift-click the Show Desktop icon in the Dock and all windows and applications will be revealed again.

Accessing Desktop Contents Directly

If your goal isn't necessarily to view the Desktop, but to simply access files or folders that reside there, you can do so in a number of ways without having to hide or close Finder and application windows. Here are a few quick solutions.

FIGURE 5.6:
Accessing the Desktop folder in the Dock

Accessing Desktop Contents from a Finder Window

In terms of accessing files and folders that reside on the Desktop, the first thing to remember is that the Desktop is simply a folder, just like any other folder in Mac OS X. Because of this, you can easily access its contents in any Finder window. Simply navigate to your home folder, and open the folder named `Desktop`. Any file or folder on your Desktop resides in this folder, and you can perform any actions on them here that you could by accessing them on the Desktop itself.

Accessing Desktop Contents from the Dock

As I'll discuss in more depth in Chapter 6, you can place any folder in the Dock and access its contents easily. If you put the previous tips and this one together, you'll see that you can actually put your Desktop folder in the Dock. To do this, simply navigate to your home directory in the Finder and then drag the folder `Desktop` to the Dock (you'll have to drag it to the right of the Dock's divider line). You'll then see an icon in the Dock that looks like the Desktop.

If you click and hold on the Desktop icon in the Dock (or control/right-click), a menu will pop up, listing the contents of the Desktop folder (which are simply any items sitting on your Desktop) (Figure 5.6). Selecting an item will open it directly. If any of the items are folders, you'll notice an arrow next to their names, indicating a hierarchical menu. Thus from this menu you can open any file on the Desktop, as well as any file within any folder on the Desktop.

Accessing Desktop Contents Using MaxMenus

User Level: normal or admin
Affects: user or computer
Terminal: no

Along the same lines as the previous hint, numerous third-party add-ons allow you to easily access the contents of the Desktop. My personal favorite is MaxMenus (`http://www.proteron.com/`), which lets you create multiple menus, each with different contents. After you've installed MaxMenus, you can easily create a menu for the Desktop:

1. Open System Preferences and select the MaxMenus preference pane; click on the Menus tab.
2. Choose where you'd like the menu to appear from the Choose Menu pop-up. I personally use the Lower Right setting, as it's closer to the Dock where the mouse cursor tends to be a lot anyway, but another of my favorites is the "Menubar empty area," which lets me click on any empty area of the menu bar to access my custom menu.
3. In the list of available items on the right, click Desktop and drag it to the menu items list on the left (Figure 5.7).

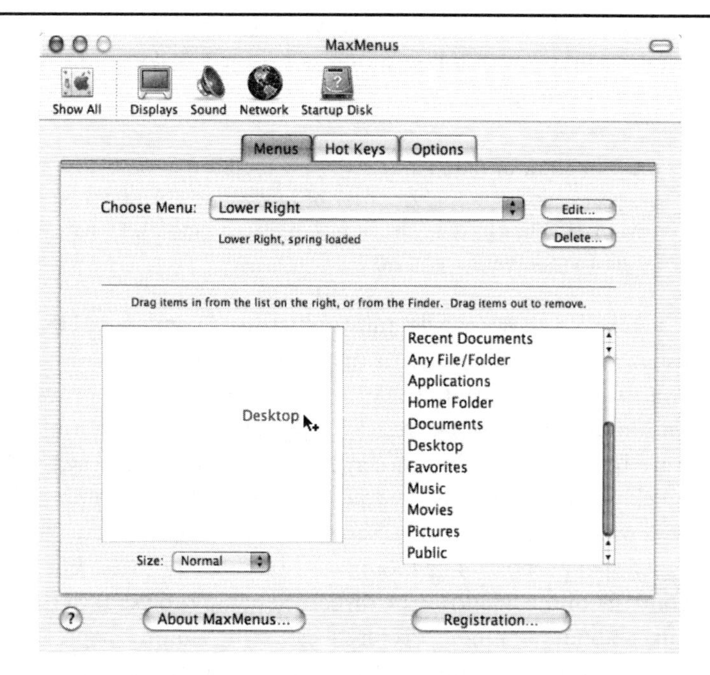

FIGURE 5.7: Creating a Desktop menu in MaxMenus

4. You can choose extra options for the menu by clicking the Edit… button next to the Choose Menu pop-up. For example, you can change the color of the menu symbol that will appear in the specified corner of the screen, and you can choose to access the menu by a simple mouse click, a combination of keys and the mouse, or via a keyboard combination.
5. When you're finished, close System Preferences. Your new menu will be accessible in the corner (or menu bar area) you've chosen.

Now that we've covered the Desktop, let's talk about Finder windows.

Working with Windows (Finder Windows, not Microsoft Windows)

People use the Finder every day without thinking much about it. This is even more the case when it comes to Finder windows—apart from moving things around on the Desktop, any interaction you have with the Finder is via Finder windows. Yet these windows are one of the areas where most users are taking the *least* advantage of the built-in power and flexibility of Mac OS X. In this section, I'm going to show you how to do some new things and how to do some of the things you already do even better.

The Toolbar

Mac OS X introduced a new feature to Finder windows, the toolbar. Although it may not always be visible, every Finder window has a toolbar, and these toolbars provide an incredible amount of functionality to Finder windows. Open a new window in the Finder, and you can follow along as I show you some of the ways you can use the toolbar to your advantage.

TIP You can show or hide Finder window toolbars in several ways. You can click the toolbar widget in the upper-right corner of any window. You can select View ➢ Show Toolbar to view the toolbar (or View ➢ Hide Toolbar to hide it). Finally, you can press command+B to toggle the toolbar on and off.

Figure 5.8 shows the default toolbar for a window in OS X 10.2.x (if you've already customized your toolbars, yours may look a bit different). The back and forward buttons allow you to quickly return to the previous folder you were browsing or (if you used the back button) to return to the "next" folder, respectively. (If you've ever used the back and forward buttons in a web browser, these work the same way.) The View buttons allow you to quickly switch between window views: icon, list, or column (I'll talk about the different window views shortly). The separator line simply divides the toolbar visually; it has no functional purpose. The Computer, Home, Favorites, and Applications buttons change the contents of the window (the directory being browsed) to the Computer view (which I talked about in "Finder Preferences" earlier in the chapter), your home directory, your favorites folder (`~/Library/Favorites`, which I'll talk about in "File and Folder Finesse," later in this chapter), and the Applications directory, respectively. Finally, the Search field allows you to search the contents of the current directory for a file or folder; I'll talk more about using the Search field later in this chapter.

However, just because this is the default toolbar for Finder windows doesn't mean you're limited to this configuration.

Customizing Finder Toolbars

You can customize Finder toolbars in two ways: by using Mac OS X's built-in configuration tool, and by manually adding items to it.

FIGURE 5.8: The default Finder window toolbar in OS X 10.2.xs

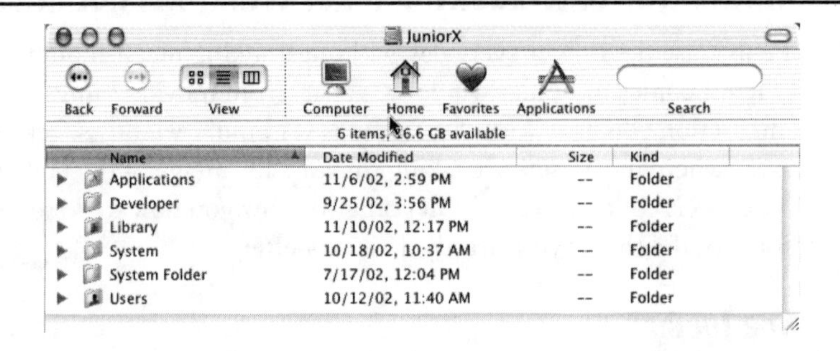

Customizing the Toolbar Using Mac OS X's Customize Toolbar Feature

User Level: any
Affects: individual user
Terminal: no

Although Apple has chosen a default toolbar configuration for you, Mac OS X includes an impressive configuration tool that allows you customize Finder toolbars any way you like. To access this tool, open a new Finder window and choose View ➢ Customize Toolbar… or shift-click the toolbar widget in the upper-right corner of the Finder window. (The toolbar must be visible first, so be sure to show it before you try to customize it.) You'll be presented with the Customize Toolbar dialog (Figure 5.9).

At the top of the window is your toolbar's current configuration; the middle section of the window contains all of the standard toolbar items you can place in the toolbar. To include an item in the toolbar, drag it from the items section and drop it on the toolbar. Existing items will move out of the way to allow you to place it exactly where you want it. You can also change the arrangement of toolbar items by dragging them left or right (again, the other items will move out of the way). In order to remove an item, drag it from the toolbar and drop it in the middle section of the configuration window. Note that if you've added more items than will fit in the current width of the window, once you close the Customize Toolbar dialog, you'll see a double arrow symbol on the right side of the toolbar. Clicking this symbol will give you a menu of all toolbar items that won't fit in the current window's toolbar. (You can also simply resize the window so that it's big enough to view all toolbar items.)

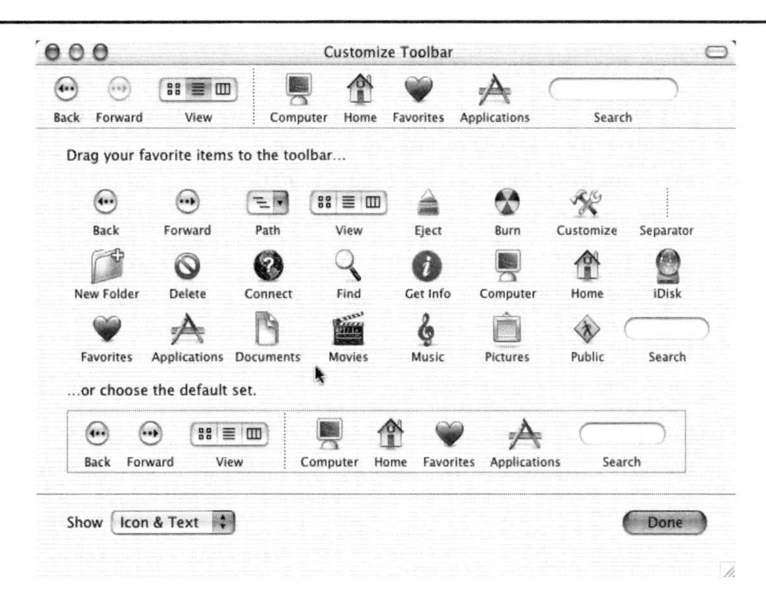

FIGURE 5.9: The Customize Toolbar dialog

TIP Toolbar configurations apply to *all* Finder windows, not just the current window. They don't apply to application windows. However, many applications that use Mac OS X-style toolbars also provide customization options. You can usually access these options by pressing command+shift and clicking the toolbar widget, or from a Customize Toolbar menu item. Some applications also allow you to control-click or right-click in the toolbar itself to bring up a toolbar customization menu.

Although most of the available toolbar items are fairly self-explanatory, a few deserve a quick explanation:

Path The path item allows you to see the path to the current folder, and browse any directory in that path. For example, if you're currently viewing your home directory, clicking the Path item will show you the full hierarchy of your home directory (`Computer Name`, `Volume Name`, `Users`, `username`); you can select any of these items to switch the window to that directory.

Eject If you're browsing the Computer list (the list of all mounted/connected volumes) in a window, selecting a volume and clicking this toolbar item will unmount/eject that volume. This is the same as choosing File ➢ Eject.

Burn If you're creating a CD or DVD using Mac OS X's built-in disc-burning capabilities (more on that in Chapter 7), selecting a mounted CD-R, CD-RW, or DVD-R and clicking this item will burn the disc. This is the same as choosing File ➢ Burn Disc....

Customize This item simply accesses the Customize Toolbar window. I showed you two other ways to access this window earlier: shift-click on the toolbar widget or choose View ➢ Customize Toolbar....

Separator The separator item allows you to insert a vertical line to divide the toolbar into sections. It doesn't "do" anything, but judicious use of separators can make for a more organized toolbar. For example, I put navigation items on the left, then a separator, then quick-access items (Home, Computer), then another separator, then my own custom items.

New Folder This item creates a new folder in the directory you're currently browsing. It works exactly the same as choosing File ➢ New Folder.

Delete If you select an item in a Finder window and then click this button, it will move the selected item to the Trash. It is the same as choosing File ➢ Move to Trash.

Connect This item brings up the Connect to Server dialog (which I discuss in Chapters 10 and 11). It is the same as choosing Go ➢ Connect to Server....

Find Clicking this item brings up the Finder's Find dialog. It is the same as choosing File ➢ Find....

Get Info Selecting an item in a Finder window and clicking this item is the same as choosing File ➢ Get Info.

iDisk Clicking on this toolbar item connects to and mounts your iDisk, using the username and password in the .Mac tab of Internet System Preferences. (I'll talk more about these settings in Chapter 9.) You can also access this same command by choosing Go ➢ iDisk.

Computer, Home, Favorites, Applications I covered these earlier when I talked about the default toolbars; however, I want to mention here that they each have their own menu item in the Go menu, along with their own keyboard shortcuts.

Documents, Movies, Music, Pictures, Public These items simply switch the directory being browsed in the current window to the appropriate folder inside your home directory.

You'll notice that some of these items are simply other ways to do things that the Finder already has menu items for. Personally, I consider using too many of these items to be a waste of toolbar space unless you use them frequently. In addition, most of them also have keyboard shortcuts (which are listed next to each command in Finder menus). The reason I mention this here is that in the next section I'm going to show you how to add your own items to the toolbar, and you may want to save some toolbar space for them.

Finally, after you've chosen which items to place in your toolbar, the bottom section of the window includes a pop-up menu to choose how you want to view toolbar items: as an icon with text, as an icon only, or as text only. Note that if you select the text-only view, the View item will become a menu rather than three buttons, and the Search field will no longer be visible (clicking search will bring up the Finder's Find dialog).

TIP If you ever get bored with the default icons of standard toolbar items, you can actually change them. Although you could do it manually, the shareware Toolbar Icon Changer (`http://www.tedpearson.com/index.php?page=software`) does it for you, quickly and painlessly. You can even create your own replacement icons using the instructions included with the utility. The shareware CandyBar, which I talk about in the Online Bonus chapter, performs a similar function.

Customizing the Toolbar with Your Own Items

User Level: any
Affects: individual user
Terminal: no

In addition to the standard toolbar items, you can also add your own items to Finder toolbars. Folders, files, applications, servers—anything that has an icon in the Finder—can be placed in the toolbar. To do so, simply drag the item's icon into the toolbar and place it where you want it to appear. To remove a custom toolbar item, drag it out of the toolbar.

NOTE Although you can manage both custom and standard toolbar items from the Customize Toolbar window, you can also move and/or remove them from any Finder window's toolbar. However, the procedure needed to move or remove an item depends on whether it's a standard item or a custom item. To change a custom item's location in the toolbar, simply drag it left or right; to remove the item, drag it out of the toolbar. For standard items, you must hold down the command key while dragging the item left or right or out of the toolbar.

Custom toolbar items behave just as they do in any Finder window or on the Desktop. Folder icons work just like the Home, Applications, and Documents items—clicking one will change the current window to the folder selected (as if you'd double-clicked the folder in the Finder to view it). When you click a file's toolbar item, the file is opened (the application needed to open the file will be launched, if necessary), just as if you had double-clicked the file in the Finder. Finally, when you click an application icon in the toolbar, the application is launched, just as if you'd launched it in the Finder. However, the real beauty of folder and application icons in the toolbar is that they support drag and drop. If you drag a file onto a toolbar application icon, it will be opened in that application. If you drag a file onto a folder icon in the toolbar, it will be placed inside the folder.

TIP Folder icons in the toolbar support OS X's spring-loaded folder feature; drag an item over a folder's icon in the toolbar and hold it there—a new window for that folder will appear, allowing you to place the file inside any sub-folder! (I'll talk more about spring-loaded folders later in this chapter in "File and Folder Finesse.") They also honor the Finder functionality whereby holding the command key when opening a folder will open it in a new window. (In other words, if you have a folder in the toolbar, command+clicking on the folder will open it in a *new* window, instead of in the existing window.)

Here are a few examples of custom toolbar items that you may find especially useful.

Documents folder By placing your Documents folder in the toolbar, you can quickly access your personal files; in addition, by taking advantage of the spring-loaded feature of toolbar folders, you can easily file documents into any sub-folders.

StuffIt Expander If you frequently download files from the Internet, you're bound to use StuffIt Expander quite often to "unstuff" compressed files. By placing Expander in the toolbar, it's always there when you need it.

AppleScripts If you have any AppleScripts that you use frequently, placing them in the toolbar gives you quick access, as well as the ability to drag and drop files onto them no matter where you're browsing. (Apple has provided a good number of toolbar-oriented AppleScripts at `http://www.apple.com/applescript/toolbar/`.)

Open Terminal in the current directory If you frequently use Terminal, you know that one of the most common inconveniences is changing the active directory to the one you want to use, especially if it's one you're already using in the Finder. By placing one of two excellent utilities, Open Terminal (`http://homepage.mac.com/thomasw/OpenTerminal/`) or Open Terminal Here (`http://www.entropy.ch/software/applescript/`), in your toolbar, you simply navigate to the desired directory in the Finder, and then click the icon in the toolbar. A new Terminal window is opened with the active path of the current Finder window. You can also drag a file or folder onto the icon to open a Terminal window with that file/folder as the working directory.

Trash Even though the Trash is always available from the Dock, some people prefer to have it close at hand in Finder window toolbars. Under Mac OS X 10.1.x, you could simply drag the Trash icon from the title bar of an open Trash window to the toolbar of any Finder window. Unfortunately, Apple removed that capability in OS X 10.2. However, it's still fairly easy to get your Trash in the toolbar.

1. Open the file `~/Library/Preferences/com.apple.finder.plist` in a text editor. (You may remember from earlier chapters that this is the Finder preferences file.)
2. Find the line that says `<key>toolbar-items</key>`, followed by a line that says `<array>`.
3. Create a new line below `<array>` (by pressing return) and insert the following text:

```
<dict>
<key>item-id</key>
<string>TCAN</string>
</dict>
```

4. Save your changes, then log out and then log in again. Your toolbar will now include the Trash. To move or remove the Trash from the toolbar, you should treat it like a standard toolbar item: command-drag it, or use the Customize Toolbar window.

Window Views and View Options

User Level: any
Affects: individual user
Terminal: no

As I mentioned earlier in the chapter, you can view the files and folders in a Finder window three different ways: icon view, list view, and column view. The first two are old hat to Mac OS users; the third is brand new in OS X. You can switch between views using the View toolbar item (which has buttons for icon view, list view, and column view, respectively) or by choosing the appropriate view (as Icons, as List, or as Columns) from the Finder's View menu.

TIP You can also switch between views using the keyboard: command+1 for icon view, command+2 for list view, or command+3 for column view.

You can choose different view options for different folders, which allows you to select the best view option for each window. For example, if you're looking at a folder of pictures, icon view lets you view extremely large icons, so as to take advantage of icon previews of graphics files. However, for folders of word processing documents, you may prefer list or column view because you can browse a large number of files in a list. Once you select a view, and view options, for a particular folder, the Finder remembers that view and its options, and will use them the next time you browse that folder.

Each view has different advantages and disadvantages, and different options; I've included a brief discussion of each.

Icon View

Icon view has been around as long as the Mac. Its main advantages are simplicity and the fact that you can clearly discern the type of file by its icon. In fact, if you have icon previews enabled in View Options, graphics files that have icon previews will be shown using those previews instead of their default file icon.

Navigating in icon view is fairly simple. Besides mouse actions, you can select a file or folder by typing the first few letters of its name. You can also move between items, in alphabetical order, using the keyboard by pressing the tab key (shift+tab moves between items in reverse alphabetical order). To open a file or folder, you double-click it (or select it and choose File ➢ Open, command+O, or command+down arrow). To move up the folder hierarchy, press command+up arrow, or command-click the folder name in the window's title bar. (You can also use the Path item in the toolbar, if enabled.)

These navigation tips may be obvious to you, but I mention them to contrast them with the methods of navigation used in column view, which I'll discuss shortly.

View Options for Icon View

If you view a folder as Icons, the View Options window changes to reflect this (Figure 5.10). The first option, unique to window View Options (it's not present in Desktop View Options), is to select whether the options you set apply to the current window only, or to all windows. However, it's not quite what it appears to be. What this *actually* means is "Apply to this window only" or "Apply to all windows of this view type." In other words, if you're changing settings for a window in icon view, and select "All windows," your settings will apply to all windows using icon view. The exceptions to the "all" setting are windows for which you have specifically set up *different* settings using the "This window only" setting. Is that confusing? A little bit, but it gives you the flexibility to set system-wide View Options for each type of window view, while still allowing you to have different settings for individual windows (one of the most requested features under older version of the Mac OS).

The next few settings ("Icon size" through "Keep arranged by") function identically to the corresponding settings in Desktop View Options, as discussed earlier in the chapter. The combination of a large icon size and "Show icon preview" can be quite useful when viewing a folder of photos if those photos have icon previews (Figure 5.11).

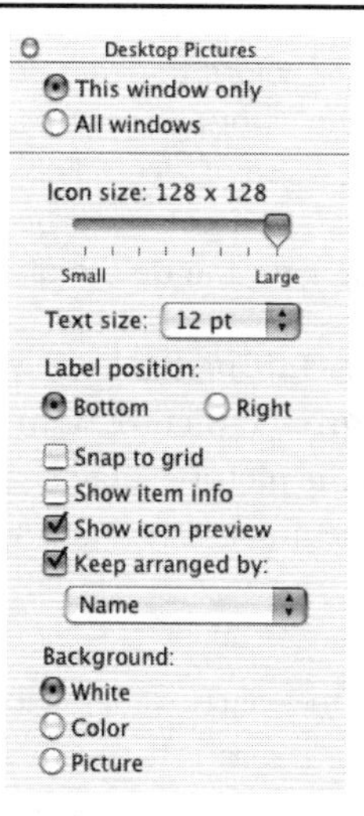

FIGURE 5.10:

View Options for icon view

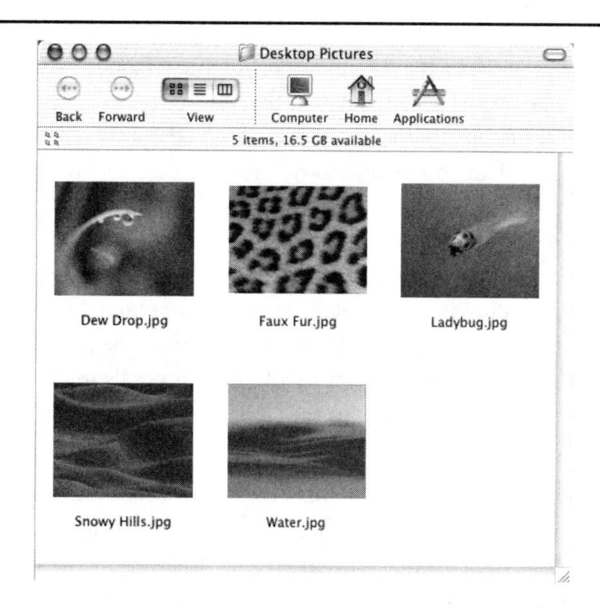

FIGURE 5.11:

A folder of pictures viewed using large icon previews

The final option is unique to icon view. Although window backgrounds are white by default, you can customize the appearance of the window background in icon view (again, for all windows using icon view or just the current one). If you select Color, and click on the color swatch that appears, you'll be presented with the standard Mac OS X Colors dialog, where you can choose a color using one of several selection panels (you can switch between them by clicking the icons at the top of the Colors window). From any of the panels you can click the magnifying glass icon to choose a color anywhere on your screen.

TIP You can save favorite colors that you use frequently in the Colors dialog. First, select the color using one of the color panels. Click anywhere inside the large rectangle at the top of the window that shows the selected color, and drag that color to the grid at the bottom of the window. The selected color will be added to the grid and available from within any application that supports the Colors dialog.

If you select Picture for the Background option, click the Select… button to navigate to your preferred background picture. Unfortunately, OS X won't automatically resize images to fit windows, so some pictures may be more or less appropriate for use as window backgrounds (some will be much too small, some much too large).

List View

List view has also been a part of the Mac OS for a long time; however, OS X has added a few twists (for the better). It's still the best view to use for seeing detailed information about a large number of files, and for easily selecting multiple files for use. It's also the view mode with the most options for sorting and organizing files and folders.

You navigate in list view much like you do in icon view. In addition to using the mouse, you can select a file or folder by typing the first few letters of its name, or move between items by pressing tab and shift+tab. To open a file or folder, you double-click it, or select it and choose File ➢ Open, command+O, or command+down arrow. Just as in icon view, you move up the folder hierarchy by pressing command+up arrow, or by command-clicking the folder name in the window's title bar. (You can also use the Back, Forward, and Path items in the toolbar, if enabled.) However, list view also provides the option to view the contents of a folder without leaving the current directory. By clicking the disclosure triangle next to a folder name, the contents of that folder will be shown in a hierarchical list (Figure 5.12). You can even view the contents of any sub-folders in the same way. You can also expand or collapse a folder's content listing by selecting the folder and pressing the right arrow key (to expand) or the left arrow key (to collapse).

By clicking a column heading, you can sort by that column (Name, Date Created or Modified, Size, Kind, etc.). Clicking a heading a second time causes it to sort by that column, but in reverse order (reverse alphabetical, older first rather than newer first, etc.). In addition, under OS X you can actually rearrange the order of columns by simply dragging them left or right to the desired location. The only restriction is that the Name column cannot be moved. Finally, you can resize a column by placing the cursor on the right edge of the column heading (until you see the left/right arrow symbol appear); then click and drag the cursor to make the column narrower or wider.

TIP You can change the selected sort column using the keyboard by pressing control+tab or control+I (that's an i, not an L) to move across columns left to right, or control+shift+tab or control+shift+I to move right to left.

View Options for List View

Like the View Options panel for icon view, the View Options panel for list view (Figure 5.13) lets you apply settings to a particular window or all windows, and you can select the font size for text labels. However, the rest of the settings are unique to the list layout. You have a choice of two icon sizes, both much smaller than most sizes available in icon view. You can also choose which informational columns (and thus how much information) to show in file/folder listings. However, in order to view all of the information on most screens, you'll need to spend a lot of time scrolling left and right, so it's generally useful to include only those fields of information you use frequently. (I usually show only date modified and size.)

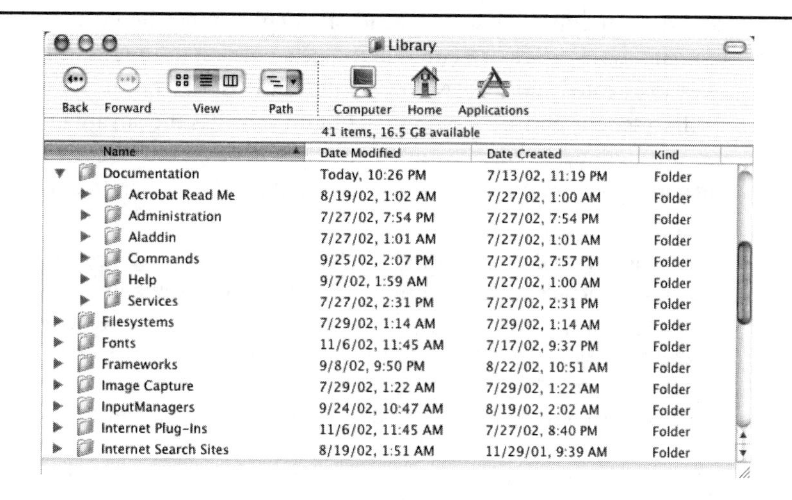

FIGURE 5.12: Viewing a folder's contents in list view

Applications
This window only
All windows
Icon size:
Text size: 12 pt
Show columns:
Date Modified
Date Created
Size
Kind
Version
Comments
Use relative dates
Calculate all sizes

FIGURE 5.13: View options for list view

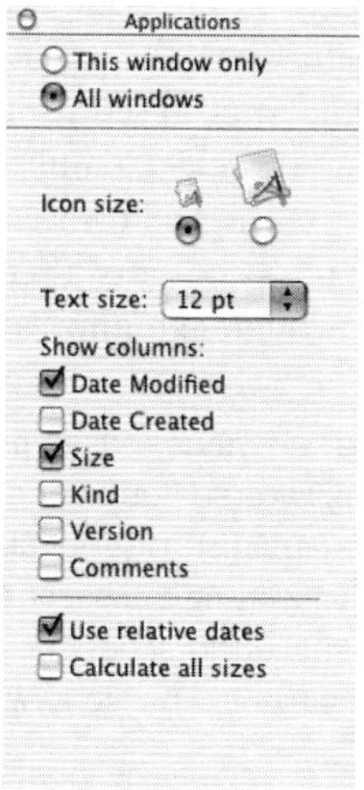

The "Use relative dates" setting applies only to Date Modified and Date Created columns. If a date is today or yesterday, instead of showing the calendar date, the information will be displayed as "Today" or "Yesterday." The "Calculate all sizes" option is only available if you have chosen to show the Size column; if checked, the Finder will calculate the size of folders (it normally only shows file sizes). Although this can be useful information, it slows down the Finder significantly. I only use this option when I really need it, and even then I only apply it to the current window.

Column View

Column view, modeled after the file browser in the NeXT operating system, is new to the Mac in OS X, and many users seem to have a love/hate relationship with it. Windows in column view have multiple columns instead of a single pane; when you select a file or folder in a column, its contents are presented in the next column to the right. If you run out of columns, new ones are created and the window scrolls to the right (thus it is often necessary to scroll back and forth to see the entire hierarchy). Column view has the advantages of letting you quickly navigate through nested directories, instantly see the path to the file or folder you're viewing (folders in the path are highlighted in gray), and quickly switch to another directory along that path.

TIP You can resize column width by selecting the column resize tab at the bottom of any column divider; all columns are resized identically. You can resize an individual column by holding the option key as you move the resize tab to the right of the column. If you simply want to resize a column to fit the longest item name in that column, double-click on the resize tab to the right of that column; all columns will be resized to that width. (Holding the option key down as you double-click on a resize tab will only resize that particular column.)

One of the biggest advantages of column view is the preview column. When enabled in View Options, the preview column—which is basically identical to the Preview panel of Get Info windows—allows you to preview many types of files without opening them. If a text file is selected in column view, the preview column will show a bit of the text of the file. If a graphics file is selected, you can see a smaller version of the graphic. But even more impressive is what happens if you select a multimedia file (a sound file or movie file, for example). The preview column presents you with a small QuickTime player that allows you to actually listen to or watch the file's contents! (See Figure 5.14.) In addition to the preview itself, the preview column also provides an impressive amount of information about the selected file.

TIP If you have a multi-button mouse, when previewing a movie file in column view, click and hold on one of the forward/reverse buttons on the right side of the preview player. Then (while still holding the mouse button), right-click. The forward/reverse buttons will turn into a speed/direction slider. Moving the slider to the left of the midpoint plays the movie in reverse (the further left you move the slider, the faster it plays in reverse); moving the slider to the right of the midpoint plays the movie forwards (the further right, the faster the playback).

Navigating in column view is quite a bit different than navigating icon or list view. Many of the keyboard combinations and menu commands that apply to other views do not work in column view, because an item is "opened" simply by selecting it. In addition to selecting files and folders with the mouse, you can also use the arrow keys to navigate. The up and down arrows move you up and down the list of items in a column, and you can move between columns using the left/right arrows. Unlike the other views, you cannot move between items using the tab key; however, you can still select an item by typing in the first few letters of the item name. The only caveat is that in column view, in order to select an item by typing, you have to make sure that the column that contains that item is active. You can tell which column is active because it's the one with an item highlighted in color, as opposed to items highlighted in gray (which indicates the current file path).

TIP If you want a folder to open in a new window instead of in the next column, command+double-click on the folder. It will open in a new window, using the view mode you most recently used to view that folder. (If you've never viewed the folder before, the new window will appear in icon view.)

Column View: Be Careful What You're Moving

When you click and drag an unselected file in icon or list view, that item always becomes the active (highlighted) icon. However, when you click and drag an unselected file in column view, this is not the case—if another file or folder was previously highlighted, it will remain so. In other words, a *different* file or folder may be highlighted than the one you're dragging. This inconsistent behavior in column view can lead you to move or delete an item that you didn't intend to—you generally assume that you're moving the highlighted item. For this reason, when I use column view, I find myself quickly clicking an item first to select it, just to make sure I'm dragging the correct file.

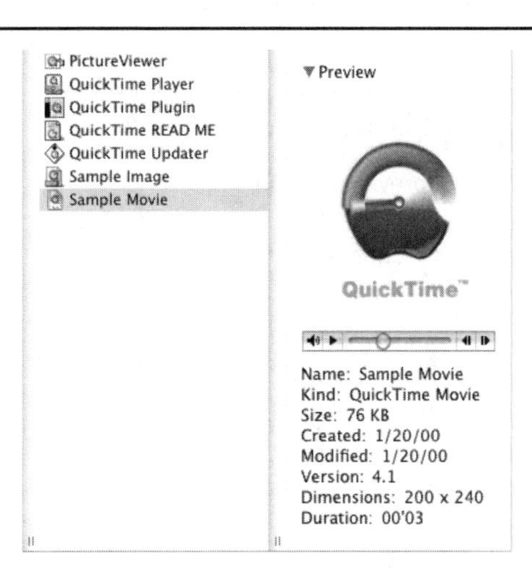

FIGURE 5.14: The preview column for a QuickTime movie file

FIGURE 5.15:
View options for column view

View Options for Column View

If you select View Options for a window in column view (or click in a window in column view if View Options is already open), you'll see the panel for column view options (Figure 5.15). You'll notice immediately how sparse it is compared to the options for other types of windows. You can select the text size for item names; to show or hide icons (items will be listed only by name; you will only be able to differentiate between folders and files by the arrow next to a folder that indicates selecting it will produce a new column for its contents); and to show or hide the preview column. Because of the way column view functions, there is no need (nor any room) for the kinds of options included in the other views.

TIP The setting for text size in Column View Options actually changes the icon size as well. This is the only view where this is the case, and it means that changing the text size affects the number of items that can fit in each window.

Getting Window Settings to Stick

Although OS X provides a number of options for viewing file directories, and allows you to easily change the size and width of windows, anyone who has used Mac OS X for a while can tell you from experience that figuring out when such settings are going to stick and when they aren't is often an exercise in frustration—or at least it seems to be.

The logic behind getting folder settings to stick is fairly straightforward, but not what you might expect. To put it simply, if a folder or volume has never been opened directly (in a new window), it will open in icon view, using any icon View Options settings you applied to "All windows." If a folder or volume has previously been opened, a window for that directory will

Continued on next page

open with the settings that were active the last time it was closed. The key part of that sentence is "the last time it was closed." If you open a new window for your startup drive, navigate to your personal Documents folder, change the view mode, resize the window, and then close the window, the settings you just changed will *not* apply to a new window for your startup drive—they'll apply to a new Documents window.

So to create default settings for a particular folder, what you need to do is open that folder, change your view options, resize the window to the appropriate size, and then close the window. The next time you open that folder, the window will remember your preferred settings.

That is, unless you change anything and then close the window while still viewing that directory....

Useful Window Tidbits

User Level:	any
Affects:	individual user
Terminal:	no

I've covered most of the major aspects of using windows and browsing directories in the Finder. However, I have a few tips that don't fit neatly into the above discussion. I've listed them here under the clever title of "Useful Window Tidbits." The tip table above applies to all of these tidbits.

Manipulate Windows in the Background

When you click inside, on the toolbar, or on the title bar of any visible window, that window becomes the *active* (frontmost) window. However, sometimes you don't really want to work with a window—you simply want to move it out of the way, resize it, or close it, without making it active. You can actually do this quite easily in OS X. First, you can use any of a window's title bar buttons—the close, minimize, and resize buttons, and toolbar widget—without making the window active. Second, if you want to physically move a window (perhaps to view something behind it), simply command-click the window's title bar and you can move it, still in the background, anywhere you like. When you release the mouse button, it will still be inactive.

View/Hide the Status Bar

Every Finder window, regardless of the view mode, has a status bar that lists how many items are in the currently viewed directory, how many of those items are currently selected (if any), and how much space is available on the current volume. However, many users aren't even aware that this helpful feature exists because it's hidden on their computer. If the status bar is hidden for your Finder windows, choose View ➢ Show Status Bar to reveal it. (If it is currently visible, you can hide it by choosing View ➢ Hide Status Bar.) This setting applies to all Finder windows; you can't show the status bar for some windows and not others.

View Long Filenames

Unlike earlier versions of the Mac OS, OS X supports long filenames—up to 255 characters! One drawback of these long filenames is that it's difficult to view them, especially in list and column window views, because column widths are seldom wide enough.

You may have discovered that if you have a file or folder name that is too long for the current column (in column view) or name column (in list view), hovering the cursor over the file or folder name for a couple seconds brings up a floating text box with the full text of the name. What you may not know is that if you press the option key and move the mouse cursor over such a lengthy name, the text box will appear immediately.

Scroll with a Hand (Drag Those Windows)

You know that if a Finder window isn't big enough to show all items at once, you can use the scroll bars to move up, down, left, and right within the window. Here's a better way for list and icon views: if you hold down command+option and click in an empty area of the window, the cursor turns into a hand that "grabs" the window background. You can then drag the window's contents up, down, left, and right. If you need to do a lot of window scrolling, this method is often much easier (and easier on your own hand) than using the scroll arrows.

Take Advantage of the Title Bar Icon

At the top of every Finder window (and every document window in any application, for that matter) you can see the name of the window or document. In addition, just to the left of the window name is a small icon. Although it might appear that this icon exists mainly as a visual aid to help you discern the window type—and that's quite a useful feature, especially when you have a number of windows open in different applications and the Finder—it also has another use, and that is as a proxy for the Finder icon.

What I mean by "proxy" is that anything you can do with a document icon or folder icon in the Finder, you can do with the title bar icon. To select it, click on it and hold the mouse button for a second (if you don't hold for a second, you won't be able to select it). You can then drag the icon to the desktop, to a folder, or to another volume. Wherever you place it, it will be moved or copied, or an alias to the file will be created. Unfortunately, exactly what happens isn't consistent, as different developers have decided to do different things by default. However, you can discern what will happen by the visual cues OS X provides: a standard cursor arrow means the file will be moved; an arrow with a green plus sign (+) means the file will be copied; and a curved arrow cursor means an alias will be created. In addition, just like in the Finder, you can modify the default behavior by pressing option or command+option while dragging the icon. I use the "make alias" option frequently to create an alias on the Desktop of a document I'm working on. (You can also take advantage of spring-loaded folders, which I talk about shortly, to place the file or an alias to it several levels deep in a folder hierarchy).

In addition to moving or aliasing to a file, if you drag the title bar icon to another application, it will be opened in that application, if possible (although this isn't recommended, as working on a document in two different applications is asking for trouble). If a document has unsaved changes, you won't be able to select the title bar icon—you wouldn't want to move a document with unsaved changes, or open it in another application. In order to take advantage of the title bar icon functionality, save any changes first.

Finally, in the case of Finder windows, you can use the title bar icon in reverse. You can drag files and folders *onto* the icon to place them in the current window's directory. This is especially useful when you can only see the title bar of a window (because the rest is obscured behind other windows), or when you want to make sure you're moving an item into the top level of the folder hierarchy of that window.

Print a Folder Listing

In Mac OS 9 and earlier, you could print the contents of a window by simply selecting the window and choosing a menu item. Unfortunately, Mac OS X hasn't yet implemented such functionality. Not to worry—here are a few ways you can print out a listing of a folder's contents.

Using the Finder and a text editor If you open the folder in the Finder, you can select all (Edit ➢ Select All or command+A), and use the copy command (Edit ➢ Copy or command+C) to copy the items to the clipboard. You can then open any text editor or word processor and paste the filenames into a text document. You can then print the resulting document. The only caveat to this method is that for some reason Mac OS X doesn't keep file and folder names sorted when it copies them to the clipboard from list or icon views. In order to get a properly sorted list, first switch to column view, then select all and copy.

Using Print Center If you drag a folder onto the Print Center utility (located in `/Applications/Utilities`), or the Print Center icon in the Dock (if applicable), Print Center will print a complete list of the folder's contents, including the filename, file size, and modification date of each size. This listing will even include invisible files.

Using Terminal If you open Terminal and navigate to the folder in question (or use Open Terminal Here, which I mentioned when talking about customizing Finder window toolbars), you can use the `ls` command to list the items in the folder, then copy the resulting output from Terminal into a text editor. (You could also output the listing directly to a file; I'll talk about that in Chapter 15.) The main drawback here is that the `ls` command has so many options that it may take you a bit of time to figure out exactly which options you want to use.

Using BBEdit The excellent text editor BBEdit has a built-in disk browser that allows you to view and print file directories. Simply select File ➢ New ➢ Disk Browser, and then navigate to the desired directory. You can print the listing directly from BBEdit.

FIGURE 5.16:
The Print Window print dialog

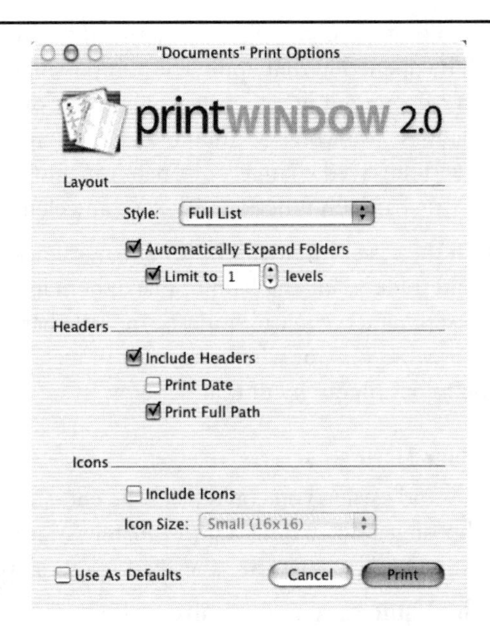

Using a Web browser If you drag a folder into most Web browser windows, they will present a listing of all the files in that folder, along with information about each file.

Using Print Window The excellent donationware Print Window (`http://www.swssoftware.com/products/printwindow.html`) allows you to print directory listings just as you did under Mac OS 9. When you launch Print Window, it runs invisibly in the background. To print a window or folder, you can open the window and (depending on how you've set up the Print Window preferences) press command+P or choose Finder ➢ Services ➢ Print File Listing. You can also switch to Print Window and select a folder listing you want printed. Finally, you can simply drag a folder onto the Print Window icon to print it. Before it prints, you're presented with a dialog (Figure 5.16) where you can choose whether you want to print all information or just filenames; whether you want just the topmost files and folders, or if you want a hierarchical listing of sub-folders and files as well; whether you want to print icons (and if so, what size); and what headers you want included, if at all.

Scroll Vertically

More and more Mac users are using mice and trackballs with scroll wheels. Although these devices are great for scrolling through web pages or word processing documents, they're also very useful for scrolling up and down in Finder windows. However, here's a tip you may not know about: if you hold the shift key down as you use the scroll wheel, Finder windows will scroll left/right instead of up/down—a great feature for column view or list view windows that are too narrow to display all information. This nifty feature also works in some third-party applications.

Useless Tip #2697: Slow Motion Windows

When you open or close a window in Mac OS X, the effect is fast, but smooth, thanks to the Quartz technology behind the Aqua interface. If you want to see this action in all its glory, press shift as you close a window (by clicking the red close button in the upper-left corner). You'll see the window close in smooth, slow motion. If you want to see it open the same way, press shift as you open it (assuming you have "Always open folders in a new window" selected in Finder Preferences; if not, you'll need to use shift+command).

File and Folder Finesse

As someone who's been using Mac OS X—or even Mac OS 9 or Windows—you're familiar with the basics of working with files and folders. Dragging files between folders or volumes, double-clicking to launch applications or open files and folders...these are the first things you learn about using a computer. However, in Mac OS X there are many other ways to do these things, and many other things you can do with files and folders. Here are some of the best tips. We'll start with contextual menus because they will be mentioned several times in the following pages.

Contextual Menus

One of the most useful ways to interact with files and folders in the Mac OS is using contextual menus. It is also the most infrequently used tool for almost every user I have ever worked with; in fact, many users don't even realize that contextual menus exist.

Contextual menus are accessed by holding down the control key as you click on a file or folder (also known as control-clicking) or, if you have a multi-button mouse, by right-clicking on a file or folder. The resulting menu is called "contextual" because the contents of the menu vary depending on the context (i.e., what you are clicking on). You can see an example of a few different contexts in Figure 5.17; the menu is different for a file, a folder, a volume, an application, the Desktop, and inside a folder.

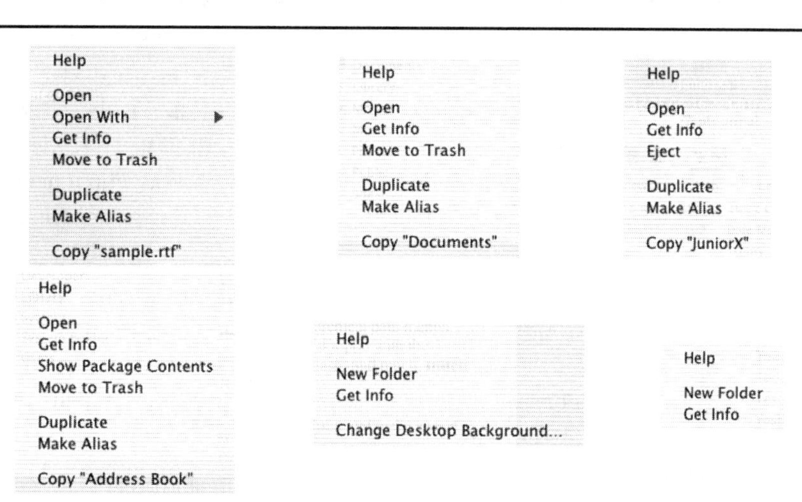

FIGURE 5.17: Contextual menus for a file, a folder, a volume, an application, the Desktop, and inside a folder

Although most Finder contextual menus contain the Help, Open, Get Info, Duplicate, Make Alias, and Copy commands, the rest of the menu is different for each file. You can move a file, folder, or application to the Trash using the contextual menu, or you can eject/unmount a volume. The menu for a file lets you open the file with a particular application (Open With…). The menu for an application lets you view the contents of the application package. Instead of confusing you with options that may not apply, the menu changes to accommodate the particular file that is selected. In addition, if you click on the Desktop or inside an open folder, you can create a new folder or get info on the existing folder (the Desktop is a folder), and the Desktop's contextual menu lets you open the Desktop pane of System Preferences. These differences illustrate what is meant by the term "contextual."

TIP Many applications also support contextual menus; however, instead of acting on files and folders in the Finder, these menus will allow you to perform actions on the documents or files being used in the application. Experiment a bit by control/right-clicking in various places and in various contexts within your favorite applications; you may be surprised at the additional power and flexibility that exists.

Now let's briefly revisit how to add your own contextual menu plug-ins.

Add Contextual Menu Items

User Level: normal or admin
Affects: individual user or computer
Terminal: no

The Finder's contextual menus provide many useful functions for working with files and folders; however, it's possible to add a good deal of functionality to these menus by installing what are called contextual menu plug-ins. These plug-ins provide additional functionality to the Finder's contextual menus such as the ability to view folder contents by simply control-clicking on a folder; or the ability to move file(s) to a specific location without having to drag them anywhere.

You can get new contextual menu plug-ins from the usual Mac software websites such as Version Tracker and MacUpdate. To install a plug-in, simply drag it to `/Library/Contextual Menu Items` (for use by all users) or `~/Library/Contextual Menu Items` (for use only by your own account). In order to take advantage of the new plug-in, you'll need to relaunch the Finder. You can do this by forcing the Finder to quit (it will relaunch) or by logging out and then back in.

A few of my favorite contextual menu plug-ins are the freeware CopyPath (`http://www.bergenstreetsoftware.com/`) and Open Subfolder X (`http://bubblepop.com/opensub/`), and the shareware Ittec (`http://www.balancesoftware.com/ittec/`). CopyPath lets you control/right-click on any Finder item and choose the CopyPath item to copy the item's complete file path to the clipboard (in either Unix or Mac format). Both Open Subfolder X and Ittec allow you to control/right-click on a folder or volume and get a contextual menu that includes a hierarchical menu of the folder or volume contents—moving the mouse over a sub-folder will present the contents of that folder, and so on. They're great ways to quickly navigate to a particular file or folder. For the extra shareware payment, Ittec provides a host of other features, including the ability to drag a file *out* of the aforementioned menu to another location, to list the contents of StuffIt archives, to move files to the Trash from within folder listings, and much more.

TIP Ittec and the shareware FruitMenu (`http://www.unsanity.com/`) both provide the ability to access contextual menus by clicking and holding the mouse button down. If you have a single-button mouse, this saves you from having to use both hands to access contextual menus.

Copying and Moving Files

User Level: any
Affects: individual user
Terminal: no

You know that you can move files between folders, and copy files between volumes, by dragging them. You probably also know that you can select multiple contiguous files in the same directory by shift-clicking them, or multiple noncontiguous files in the same directory by command-clicking them. Here are a few other tips for copying and moving files. (The tip table applies to all tips in this section.)

Copy Files/Folders without Dragging

If you view the contextual menu for a file or folder, one of the menu commands is Copy. If you select this menu item, the file or folder (and folder contents) aren't really copied—they're simply marked as being *able* to be copied. If you then control/right-click in an open area inside another folder or volume, the resulting contextual menu will include a new option: Paste (followed by the name of the item you had previously "copied"). If you select Paste in the menu, the Finder will copy the file or folder (and folder contents) to the current directory. (It will leave the original where it was.) This is a *great* way to copy a file to a different location; you don't have to actually drag it around, or worry about having two windows open next to each other. Copy, navigate, paste. Done. Although this feature has been around in Windows for quite a while, it's new to the Mac in OS X, and it's a welcome addition.

Move, Don't Copy

If you drag a file or folder from one location to another on the same volume, it is moved to the new location. If you drag the file or folder to another volume, it's copied to the new volume, and the original file or folder remains in its original location. That's fine, and makes sense, but how many times have you wanted to *move* a file to a different volume rather than copying it? Under OS 9 and earlier, you had to make a copy and then delete the original; that's no longer the case in OS X. Simply command-drag the file or folder from one volume to another, and the file is moved instead of copied. (Holding down option as you drag a file or folder still forces a copy—even on the same volume—just as it always has.)

Use Spring-Loaded Folders (and Toolbars!)

One OS 9 feature that was sorely missed OS X 10.1.x was spring-loaded folders. Apple restored this functionality in 10.2, and even added a bonus. To take advantage of spring-loaded folders, drag a file or folder onto a folder or volume; after a short delay (the duration of which is set in Finder Preferences), the folder or volume pops open in a new window, allowing you to drop the item into any sub-folder. If you then hold the item over one of those folders, the folder will open in a new window (and the previous folder will close). Using this procedure it is possible to quickly place a file inside any directory on your hard drive.

Spring-loaded folders work on the Desktop or in any window. In fact, if a folder opens (or is already open) partly off the screen, dragging a file or folder into the folder window and holding it will cause the window to actually *move* so that it is completely visible! Note that if a window is currently using column view, instead of "springing" open a new window, the columns will change to reflect the folder that is chosen for use—so you navigate columns just as you would normally, except that you drag the item over each sub-folder as it appears, rather than clicking each.

TIP Regardless of the delay you've chosen for spring-loaded folders, you can force them to pop up immediately by pressing the space bar as you drag an item over a folder or volume. In fact, you can actually disable spring-loaded folders in Finder Preferences, and the space bar will still force a folder or volume to spring open. This is a great way to avoid accidental pop-ups.

The bonus I mentioned that Apple has provided in OS X is that spring-loaded folders also work for Finder window toolbar items. If you have a volume or folder in your Finder toolbars (including the standard Home, Applications, etc., items), you can drag an item over it, and spring-loaded folders will take over.

TIP If you choose to hide mounted volumes on the Desktop, putting your hard drive in the toolbar is a great way to still take advantage of spring-loaded folders. If you have multiple hard drives, create a new folder in an out-of-the-way location and place aliases to each of your hard drives inside of it. Then drag this folder to the Finder's Finder toolbars You now have a spring-loaded toolbar item that lets you drag a file or folder to any location on any drive.

"Hold" a File or Folder Temporarily

Although Finder toolbars and spring-loaded folders are extremely helpful, there are still times when you wish you could stick a file or folder somewhere for a moment. Maybe you need to figure out where you want to put the item, or you need to dig through a bunch of folders to get to that place. Or maybe you want to put something aside for later use. A great little utility for just such a purpose is XShelf (`http://homepage.mac.com/khsu/XShelf/XShelf.html`). It provides a shelf

FIGURE 5.18: XShelf provides a shelf for temporary storage

where you can drag files and folders, or even text, graphics, or URLs from within applications (Figure 5.18). Items remain on the shelf until you remove them. Although XShelf doesn't seem like a big deal, it's one of those things that makes you wonder how you ever worked without it.

Opening (Files) With...

User Level: any
Affects: individual user
Terminal: no

Although you can open files by double-clicking them, or by dragging them onto an application's Finder or Dock icon, Mac OS X provides the ability to open a file, using any application, from the file's contextual menu. If you control/right-click on a file, one of the options is "Open With"; if you move the cursor over this item, a list of applications that can open the file will appear, along with the item "Other...." Selecting an application will open the file in that application. If the application you want to use to open the file isn't listed, choose Other... and you'll be able to browse to your preferred application. (This option gets used more often than you might think, as OS X isn't very good about listing all the applications that might be able to open a file.)

TIP If you control/right-click on a document, and then press the option key after the contextual menu pops up, the Open With option changes to Always Open With.... This feature permanently changes the application association for this particular file.

Open With... Using Zingg!

User Level: normal or admin
Affects: individual user or computer
Terminal: no

Although Mac OS X's "Open With" functionality is very useful, you can improve on it using the freeware contextual menu plug-in Zingg! (`http://www.brockerhoff.net/zingg/`). Zingg! adds its own Open With contextual menu item, but allows you to customize it. Instead of letting OS X guess which items might be able to open a file, you can choose which applications appear (and don't appear) in the sub-menu. You can also choose to only show Classic applications when the Classic Environment is running. I hope Apple will add this functionality in future versions of Mac OS X; for now, Zingg! is a great addition.

Go Directly to a Folder

User Level: any
Affects: individual user
Terminal: no

It's fairly easy to get to specific directories and files in Mac OS X; as mentioned earlier in the chapter, column view is especially quick for such purposes. In addition, using aliases, the Dock, or other launching utilities discussed in the Online Bonus Chapter, you can keep frequently used files and folders at your fingertips. However, there may be situations where you know exactly where a file or folder is, and want to get to it as quickly as possible. Mac OS X has great feature for these situations, called "Go To Folder." You can access it from the Finder by choosing Go ➢ Go To Folder… or by pressing shift+command+G. You'll be presented with a dialog (in the frontmost Finder window, or in a separate dialog window if no Finder windows are open) in which you can type the exact path to the Folder you wish to access.

TIP To speed things up, or just in case you don't know the exact name or spelling of a directory, the Go To Folder dialog box features auto-completion. Type in the first few letters of a folder, then press tab; if there is only one folder in that directory that starts with those letters, the rest of the directory name will be filled in automatically. For example, to get to the main Utilities folder, you could type **`/Ap <TAB> Ut <TAB>`**—the first tab would complete `/Applications` and insert the trailing `/`, and the second tab would complete `Utilities` and insert the trailing `/`. Hitting return would then go directly to the Utilities folder.

This feature is also an excellent way to get to hidden directories. For example, if you wanted to get to the `/etc/httpd/users` directory, which is normally hidden in Finder windows, you would simply access the Go To Folder… dialog, then type in `/etc/httpd/users`; you would be taken directly to that folder.

Alias Action

User Level: any
Affects: individual user
Terminal: no

Most Mac users have encountered aliases—shortcuts or placeholders that point to another file or folder. Many Mac users take advantage of aliases frequently. If you're working on a file, you can create an alias of the file on your Desktop for easy access (while the file itself remains in its original location). You can create a folder full of aliases to frequently accessed files and folders—in fact, that's exactly what the Favorites folder in OS X is. You can even create aliases to connected servers while they are mounted; the next time you want to access the server, you can just double-click the alias instead of going through the Connect to Server… dialog.

If you've never created your own aliases, you simply select a file or folder and choose File ➢ Make Alias (or press command+L). You can also control/right-click and select Make Alias from the contextual menu. An alias to the file is created, which you can move anywhere you like. Double-clicking the alias is exactly the same as double-clicking the original file. You can also drag and drop aliases, and onto aliases, just as you would the original file.

TIP If you hold command+option as you drag a file to another location, when you release the mouse button an alias to the file will be created there, leaving the original untouched. This is a great shortcut for placing an alias in a location different from the original file.

If you have an alias and you want to find out where the original item is located, click on the alias and choose File ➢ Show Original (or press command+R), or choose Show Original from the alias's contextual menu. A new folder will be opened in the original file's location, with the file highlighted. (If the file is on the Desktop, it will simply be highlighted.) Deleting an alias does not affect the original file in any way.

Although aliases provide a good deal of functionality on their own, here are a few other alias tricks you might find useful.

Use the Desktop as Your Home Folder

User Level: admin
Affects: individual user
Terminal: no

Although I've always been the type to keep documents and personal files inside the Documents folder (even under OS 9), I've met many Mac users who use the Desktop as their primary workspace—they keep their files, folders, everything out on the Desktop. In fact, I've talked to quite a few users who are now using Mac OS X who don't like the fact that their account is centered around their home folder. If you're one of these people, this tip is for you—you can actually change your home folder from `~/username` to the Desktop.

1. Navigate to `/Users` and select your home folder.
2. Create an alias to your home folder on the Desktop (hold command+option as you drag it to the Desktop).
3. Move anything currently on the Desktop into your current home folder by dragging it onto the alias you just created.
4. Drag the alias *into* your home folder.
5. Open Terminal and type **`sudo mv Desktop Desktop.Backup <RETURN>`**. Enter your admin password when requested. This renames your original Desktop folder (and keeps it handy if you change your mind about this later).
6. Again in Terminal, type **`sudo mv`** ***`aliasname`*** **`Desktop <RETURN>`**. This renames the alias that you previously created to "Desktop." As you know by now, the Desktop is simply a folder called Desktop in your home folder, so what you've just done is make an alias to your home folder the Desktop—thereby making the Desktop your home directory.
7. Log out and then back in to take advantage of the changes you just made. When you do, all of the items previously on your Desktop will be there again, along with all of the folders in your home directory.

TIP If you previously had set your web browser or any other application to save files to the Desktop, after using this tip you should update those settings to save to your home folder.

How Do I Go Back?

If you decide you want to go back to the standard home/Desktop setup, it's pretty quick and painless:

1. Open Terminal and type `sudo rm Desktop<RETURN>`. Enter your admin password when prompted. This command deletes the alias to your home folder that you previously named "Desktop."
2. Again in Terminal, type `sudo mv Desktop.Backup Desktop`. This renames the backup of your Desktop folder back to "Desktop."
3. Log out and back in. Your Desktop will be back to normal. You can now move any Desktop files you had previously moved to your home folder back to the Desktop. (Remember to reset your download settings in your browser and any other applications, if you had previously changed them for this tip.)

Open Groups of File, Folders, and Applications at Once

User Level: any
Affects: individual user
Terminal: no

This is just a quick tip that expands on the idea of aliases. If you want to quickly open a group of files, folders, or applications (or a combination of the three), you can create aliases to them and put them in a folder or on your Desktop. When you want to open them, you can select all of the aliases at once and double-click them (or select File ➢ Open or Open from the contextual menu).

That works fine, but it's kind of messy. And if you have several groups of aliases, you're looking at an even bigger mess. It turns out that several developers have created convenient solutions for such scenarios. The freeware utility HotAlias (`http://www.trufsoft.com/`), and the shareware apps AliasMultiplier X (`http://www.ziksw.com/`) and Multiple Launcher X (`http://www.naratt.com/MultipleLauncher.html`) all allow you to create single documents that, when launched, open a group or combination of files, folders, URLs, and/or applications. Although these applications are each a bit different, they all use a similar interface: you drag a combination of files, folders, applications, URLs—any type of Finder item—into a document window, arrange them in the order you want them to launch, and then save the document. Opening that document in the Finder launches/opens all the files inside.

These utilities are great for opening groups of files for a project—they work especially well at login. For example, in writing this book I needed Word, OmniOutliner, DEVONthink, TextEdit, a web browser, and various Finder folders open. I created a launch document that opened everything at once, and placed it in my Login Items in System Preferences. When I logged into my account, everything was ready and waiting for me.

Favorite Files and Folders

User Level: any
Affects: individual user
Terminal: no

I mentioned in the previous section that you can create a folder of aliases to frequently accessed files and folders in order to provide quick access to these items. Mac OS X actually provides a standard folder for such a purpose, and gives you easy access to it. This feature is called *Favorites*, and is one that many users don't take advantage of.

The Favorites folder is located at `~/Library/Favorites` (meaning each user has their own). You can access it from the Finder by choosing Go ➢ Favorites (or pressing shift+command+F). You can place aliases to files, folders, or applications in this folder (or the actual items, if you prefer), and when you want to access one of these items, you simply open Favorites using the same method. Even better, you can access individual items within the folder instantly by choosing Go ➢ Favorites ➢ *item name* (a sub-menu appears with the contents of the Favorites folder). Finally, if you customize Finder toolbars as discussed earlier in the chapter, one of the toolbar items is Favorites. If this item is in your toolbar, you can click it to instantly go to the Favorites folder; better yet, you can drag items onto the Favorites toolbar item to place them in the Favorites folder (hold down command+option to instead place an alias to the item instead of the original).

This is a great feature for accessing files and folders in the Finder. However, you can also access your Favorites in the Open/Save dialogs of Mac OS X-native applications (Figure 5.19). When you click on the navigation pop-up menu, you'll see a section called Favorite Places that lists the folders inside your Favorites folder. So if you place aliases to the folders where you most frequently save files to and open files from, you can go directly to them from within Open/Save dialogs. (You can also add folders to your Favorites from within these dialogs by clicking the Add to Favorites button.)

TIP In addition to accessing favorite folders, you can access the most recent folders you've opened via the Go ➢ Recent Folders submenu in the Finder.

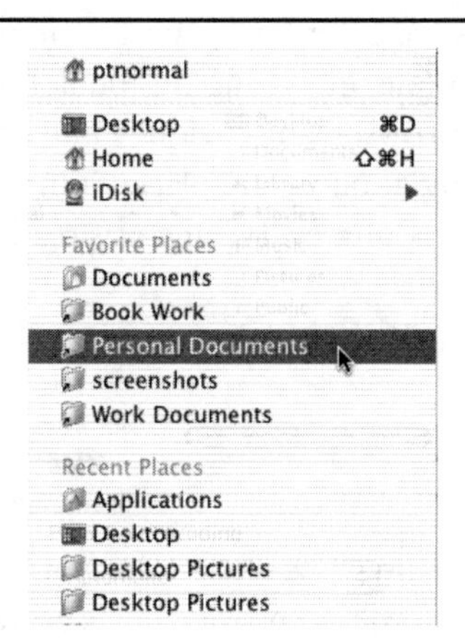

FIGURE 5.19:
Accessing Favorites from an Open dialog

Finding Files, Folders, and Information

It's easy to get to files and folders in Mac OS X—assuming you know where they are. But what about those times when you know a file's name, or part of its name, but you're not sure where you put it? What if you can't remember a file's name, but you remember some of the text you included in it? Or what if you need to find all of the files on your hard drive that mention a specific report you're working on? Fortunately, Mac OS X provides solutions to all of these dilemmas.

Find Files Faster

Mac OS X provides three ways to find files: Search, Find, and Locate. You're probably thinking, "Don't those mean exactly the same thing?!" Well, in English, almost, but in OS X, no. Here's how they differ, and when you'd want to use one over the other.

Search

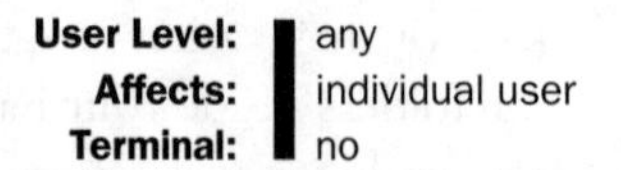

The Search function is only accessible if you've added the Search item to your Finder window toolbars (via the Customize Toolbar window). The reason for this is that the Search function only searches the contents of a window and any folders and sub-folders in that window. (Or, if you've selected a folder *within* the window, it searches just the contents of that folder.) In other words, if you know a file resides somewhere inside your Documents folder, you can navigate to your Documents folder, type in the name of the file (or part of the name) in the Search field, and press return to start the search. Once the search is complete, you'll see what looks like a standard Finder window in list view, except that it's divided into two panes. The top pane lists the results of your search—all files within the selected folder that match your search criteria. If you select a file, the bottom pane shows you the path to it (where it is located).

TIP The path pane (the lower pane of the results window that shows the path to a selected file) is resizable. If you make it larger, the path will be presented as a hierarchical folder path. If you make it smaller, the path will be reduced to a horizontal representation of the path. Double-click the resize bar and it will automatically resize to fit the horizontal presentation.

You can use any file in the top (results) pane just as if it was a file in a standard Finder window: you can open, move, copy, delete, Get Info, etc. You can also open the enclosing folder for the item by choosing File ➢ Open Enclosing Folder (or pressing command+R). The actions you can perform in the lower (path) pane are much more limited; you can double-click the item to open it, or on any folder in the path to open that folder. You can also use the File menu to perform certain tasks such as Get Info, Move to Trash, and Add to Favorites.

TIP Once you get a list of search results, you can use the Search function again to search *within* those results. For example, if your first Search returned too many results, you can enter a more specific search term to narrow down the matches without starting over.

Once you're done with your search, simply click the Back toolbar item to return to the previous (pre-search) window.

NOTE The toolbar Search item has two bugs as of OS X 10.2. The first is that it cannot search the Trash; if you open the Trash and try to use the Trash window's Search tool, you will always get no results. The second is that if you navigate to a folder using an alias to that folder, any toolbar Search you conduct will yield no results. Apple's solution is to reveal the original folder first (using the Finder's Reveal Original command), and then open the folder directly; you can then perform the Search.

Find

User Level: any
Affects: individual user
Terminal: no

The Finder's Find function is what most users probably think of when they think about finding files. You access this feature in the Finder by choosing File ➢ Find… (or pressing command+F); you're presented with a new Find window. Find is much more powerful than Search in that you can search specific places, or a combination of specific places, for files using a variety of criteria.

The "Search in" pop-up menu lets you choose to find files anywhere on all mounted volumes (Everywhere), on Local disks (meaning it will not search connected servers), in just your Home folder, or in Specific places. Selecting the last option adds a new window where you can add and remove volumes or specific folders on volumes. In addition to the Add button, you can also drag volumes or folders into the window to add them. Select a volume or folder and click the Remove button to remove it (or just uncheck it to omit it from the search without permanently removing it).

The standard search criteria are "file name contains" and "kind is *kind*." However, the options here can be changed to find ever-more specific combinations of criteria (Figure 5.20). You can add additional criteria using the Add Criteria… pop-up, and add additional iterations of existing criteria using the + buttons to the right. To remove a condition, click the – button next to it. The various pop-up menus allow you to customize how files should match the listed criteria. (Most of the criteria are self-explanatory; I'll talk about "content" in the next item.)

Once a Find search is completed, the results will appear in a window that looks exactly like the results window from the Search function, and you can work with items in the window in exactly the same manner. In fact, you can still use the Search toolbar item to search *within* the results of your Find!

TIP If you click on the word "Search" in a Finder window toolbar (just below the Search field), the Find window opens. Most users wouldn't give this a second thought, but since you now know the difference between Search and Find, it should seem a bit odd. Regardless, it's a convenient quirk in that placing the Search item in the toolbar gives you quick access to both features.

FIGURE 5.20:
A complex Find

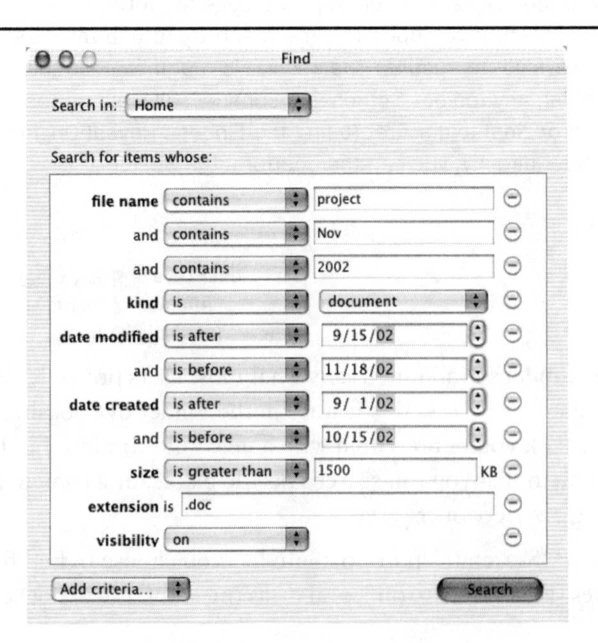

FIGURE 5.21: Locator provides a nice interface to the `locate` command

Unfortunately, despite the fact that files can still have file types and creator codes in Mac OS X, at the time of this writing, Apple had removed the ability to find files based on those criteria (it was possible in previous versions of the Mac OS, including OS X 10.1.x). If you need to find files by file type or creator code, and Apple hasn't included that ability in the Find function by the time you read this, your best bet is a utility I mentioned earlier in the chapter, File Buddy.

Locate

User Level: any (admin to update)
Affects: individual user (update affects computer)
Terminal: no

As a Unix-based system, Mac OS X includes the standard `locate` command. A file called the locate database keeps track of every file on every mounted volume. On a periodic basis, OS X updates this database to keep it current. You can access this database in Terminal using the `locate` command; you can narrow your searches using the Unix tool `grep`. (I'll talk more about `grep` in Chapter 15.)

You're probably wondering why you would ever use `locate`, or need to worry about `grep`, when the Find function works so well. One reason is that the Find command actually searches your drive(s) each time it runs, so it can takes a while (sometimes a *long* while). However, since the locate database already exists, the `locate` command is almost instantaneous. Another reason is that there are some excellent tools out there that allow you to take advantage of the locate database without dealing with Terminal. My favorite is the freeware Locator (`http://www.sebastian-krauss.de/software/`).

Locator provides a graphical interface to the `locate` command (Figure 5.21); you simply type in a word or string of words and press the Start button, and it searches the locate database for matching files. You can tell Locator to search specific volumes or folders by typing in a path in the In field, or by choosing it from the menu next to the field (check Recursive to search within sub-folders). Note that the locate database is case-sensitive; if you want Locator to ignore the case of your search terms, check the Case Insensitive box. (What is actually happening is that Locator is searching the locate database for all possible combinations of case; this means that case-insensitive searches will take more time than case-sensitive ones.)

TIP If you're a `grep` expert, but prefer the interface of Locator, you can have your cake and eat it too. Select Grep from the Locate pop-up menu, and then type your `grep` expression in the search field. You can also check the Regular Expression box to use regular expressions.

I mentioned previously that the locate database is updated periodically; the one disadvantage this has is that it's not "up-to-the-minute" up to date. If you want to make sure that your search will catch even the newest files, choose Database ➢ Rebuild Locate Database... This forces OS X to update the database. (You can see when the last update occurred by choosing Database ➢ Check last Locate Database Update.)

Locator has many other features that I simply don't have the space to cover here. A few quick examples: it can search for contents of packages; it can create special locate databases of removable volumes and media (so you can search for files on CDs or Zip disks even if they're in a closet); and it can index and search the ID3 tags of MP3 files.

Find Files by Their Content

User Level: any
Affects: individual user
Terminal: no

What if you need to find a file, and you don't know its name but you know a few words of its contents? Or what if you're trying to gather information for a report, and want to find every document on your computer that mentions a certain topic? The Find function of OS X has an additional criterion called "content" that lets you find files based on their contents. To take advantage of this feature, open a Find window in the Finder, and choose "content" from the Add criteria... pop-up menu. You can choose to search *only* by content by removing any other criteria, or you can further limit the search by adding more criteria.

The one caveat to finding files by content is that for it to work, you first need to *index* files. You can index entire volumes, or you can choose to index individual folders. Select a volume or folder, choose File ➢ Get Info (or press command+I), and then click the disclosure triangle for the "Content index" panel (Figure 5.22). You'll see whether or not the folder or volume has ever been indexed, and, if it has, when the index was last updated (in this case, never). Click the Index Now button to index the volume (or update the existing index, if it exists), or the Delete Index button to delete the existing index.

FIGURE 5.22: The Content index panel for a folder

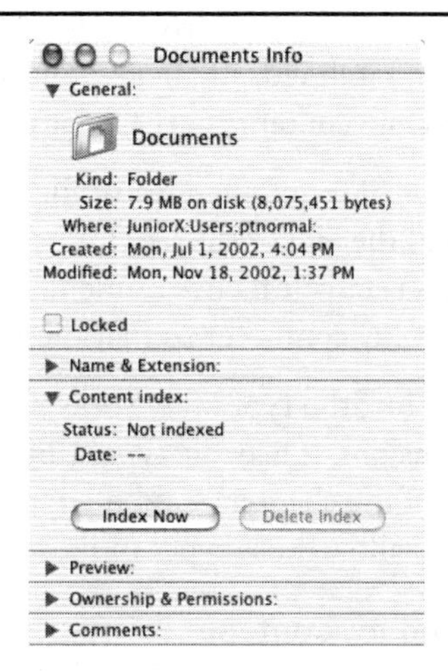

NOTE Because of permissions and security issues, it's not possible to index the boot volume. You must index individual folders.

The Finder doesn't actually index every word in a file; rather, it indexes what it considers to be important or identifying words—words that you would be likely to use when trying to locate each file. When I discussed the Finder Preferences, I mentioned that you can choose what language(s) the Finder uses when indexing volumes or folders. This affects content searches because the Finder indexes what it considers to be known words, and if you don't tell it to use Spanish, for example, it won't index Spanish words, and, therefore, you won't be able to find by Spanish content.

NOTE Each user has their own content index(es). These indexes are located at the root level of each indexed folder, in an invisible file called `.FBCIndex`.

Prevent Files from Being Indexed

User Level: admin
Affects: computer
Terminal: no

There are times when you may want to prevent certain folders from being indexed. There are also certain types of files you may not want indexed. (Indexing files takes quite a bit of time, and the indexes themselves grow in size the more files are indexed, so it's preferable to index just those files you may want to search.) Inside `/System/Library/Find` are text files that tell the Finder what gets indexed and what doesn't. By launching a text editor as root, you can edit these files to allow more files and folders to be indexed, or to further restrict indexing.

SkipFolders This file contains a list of folders that should not be indexed. By default, it contains only root-level directories. However, you can add directories to the end of the list, one per line, to prevent them from being indexed. For example, to prevent the Shared user folder from being indexed, add `Users/Shared`. (If you add a line with just `/`, it will prevent any indexing of any contents of the boot volume.)

StopExts This file contains a list of file extensions that should not be indexed. You can add your own to the end of the list; for example, I do a lot of statistical work, and the data files for the Stata statistical environment end in `.dta`. I've added `.dta` to the end of the StopExts file on my computer so that these data files don't get indexed.

StopTypes The StopTypes file works just like the StopExts file, except that instead of listing file extensions, it lists file types (the four-letter file type identifier I talked about at the beginning of the chapter). Add file types to prevent them from being indexed, or remove them to allow those types of files to be indexed.

Third-Party Find by Content

User Level: any
Affects: individual user
Terminal: no

One of the advantages of indexing is that content searches occur quickly. However, a disadvantage is that you have a content index in each indexed folder; for some folders these indexes become quite large. You can search for files by content (and by filename, for that matter) without indexing using the freeware EasyFind (`http://home.arcor-online.de/grunenberg/easyfind.html`). EasyFind works much like Locator, but with a simpler interface. You can choose to search for files, files and folders, or file contents. You can type a few words to search and then choose various Boolean options (and, or, phrase, or wildcard). Finally, you can choose case sensitivity, whether or not to search inside packages, and whether or not to include invisible items in your searches.

Since EasyFind doesn't use content indexes, it's quite a bit slower when searching for content within many files and folders. However, I've found that it's still quite fast, and it's a nice utility to have around.

Undo

This tip is one of the shortest in the book, but it's such a major feature, and one that so few people really know about or remember, that it deserves its own section.

Short and sweet: the Finder in Mac OS X has an *undo* function. If you accidentally move something somewhere, delete a file you didn't want to, or pretty much do any Finder action you wish you hadn't, choose Edit ➢ Undo (or press command+Z), and it will be undone. Write this tip down somewhere in plain sight, because it's difficult to remember simple things when you're panicking :-)

WARNING You can't un-empty the Trash using undo. That's why it asks you if you're sure you want to do it.

Super Saving (and Opening)

You've surely used OS X's Open and Save dialogs many times; they're one of those things you can't get away from. However, chances are you're not taking advantage of all the features they provide. Here are some tips for getting the most out of them, and how to add the features you've always wanted.

NOTE Most of the tips in this section apply to Mac OS X-native applications. They won't apply to Classic applications or to some Carbon applications that do not take full advantage of the OS X interface. (I'll talk more about application types in Chapter 7.)

Navigating Open and Save Dialogs

User Level: any
Affects: individual user
Terminal: no

Using Open/Save dialogs is one of those skills that no one ever really teaches you to do; you just figure it out as you go along. You probably realize you can create a new folder from within a Save dialog and then save your document inside it. But here are a few other tricks, some basic, some more advanced, that I hope will help you open and save better. The tip table applies to all of them.

Browse Save Dialogs

This is a basic one, but one that some users don't even realize exists. Many OS X Save dialogs default to the most basic of options (Figure 5.23a); by clicking the down arrow, you can expand it to the full OS X file dialog (Figure 5.23b). Once you make this change, it will stick for that application.

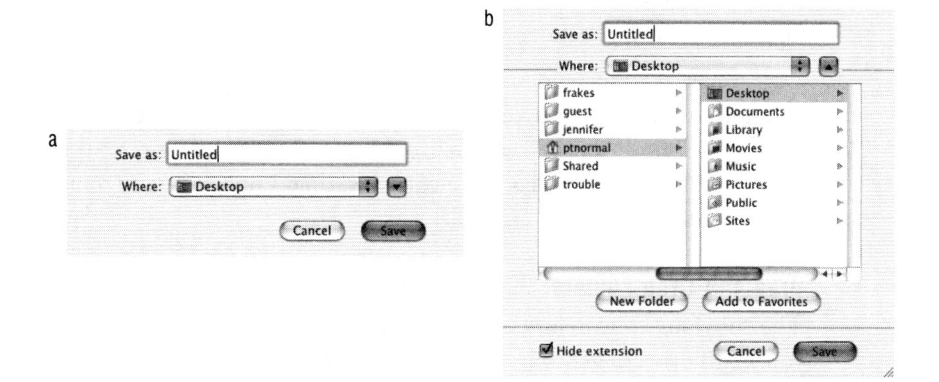

FIGURE 5.23: The simple (a) and expanded (b) Save dialogs

Quickly Access the Desktop, Home, and Documents Folders

If you want to open a file that's on the Desktop, or save something to the Desktop, pressing command+D in any Open/Save dialog will immediately switch the browser to your Desktop folder. Likewise, pressing shift+command+H in Open/Save dialogs will switch the browser to your home directory.

If you frequently open files from, and save files to, your Documents folder, you'll find that in most applications, the From and Where pop-up menus in Open and Save dialogs (respectively) include your Documents folder, and it may in fact be selected by default. However, if not, and if you want to get there quickly, press command+D in any Open/Save dialog to go to your Desktop folder. Then just press the down arrow (assuming the file browser is active; if not, press the tab key to activate it first); this will quickly change the focus of the dialog from Desktop to Documents. (If you've created additional folders in your home directory that fall between Desktop and Documents, you may need to press the down arrow more than once.) This procedure isn't perfect, but until Apple provides a keyboard shortcut for Documents, it's a decent workaround.

Open Multiple Files at Once

Many OS X Open dialogs will allow you to open multiple files from a single directory at once. Simply shift-click to select contiguous files, or command-click to select noncontiguous files, and then click the Open button.

Resize Dialogs

This is another basic one, but one that users seem to be shocked by when I point it out (plus, it has a neat hidden option). The default Open/Save dialog shows two columns of files, each with eight to ten files listed. But if, like me, you have a *lot* more than ten items in your Documents folder, or you tend to open or save files from and to directories that are several levels down, you find yourself scrolling up/down/left/right in the dialog. Simply grab the lower-right corner of the dialog and stretch it as wide and long as you want; your preferred size will be set as the default for that application. As you make the dialog box wider, more columns will be added.

However, if you would just like to make the *existing* column wider instead of adding more columns, hold the option key down as you resize the dialog box; the number of columns will remain the same, but they will change in size. (I personally prefer three wide columns, so I resize the dialog until it has three columns, then I option-resize to make those columns as wide as possible.)

Drag and Drop Folders

The "obvious" way to access a file or folder in an Open or Save dialog is to browse through your hard drive to get to it. However, if the folder you're trying to browse to is viewable in the Finder, drag it to the dialog; the browser will immediately switch to that folder, and you can save your file to that folder, or open a file that resides inside the folder. (If the folder is open in the Finder, you can also drag any file or folder within that folder to the Open/Save dialog to switch to it.)

In fact, if you always prefer to use the Finder or another quick-access method to navigate, you can hide or minimize the document or application that is displaying the Open/Save dialog, open the destination folder in the Finder, show the document or application again, and then use this tip to access that folder.

View Long Filenames

If a file or folder name is too long to fit in the current column width, you can resize columns using the tip I just mentioned. However, just as with Finder windows, you can hold the cursor over the file or folder; its full name will appear in a small text box that floats above the window. (Holding the option key down will often make the text appear immediately.)

Navigate Using the Keyboard

Although the feature is a bit quirky in its current implementation, you can use the keyboard to navigate Open/Save dialogs. Use the left/right arrow keys to highlight a file in a column, then type the first few letters of a file or folder in that column to select it; if it's a folder, you can press the right arrow key to move to the next column. Once you've selected a file to open, or a folder to save to, press return to open or save the file. (If you browse the wrong folder, you can use the left arrow key to move to the previous folder.)

TIP Sometimes you need to press tab in order to switch the active part of the dialog from the "Save as" field (in Save dialogs) or the "Go to" field (in Open dialogs) to the file browser.

Navigate Using File Paths

Most OS X Open dialogs feature a "Go to" field; if you know the full path to the file you're trying to open (or at least the path to an enclosing folder), this field allows you to type it in. If you've typed in the full path to the document, clicking the Open button or pressing return will open the document. If you've entered the path to a folder, the same action will switch the browser to that window.

TIP Although I don't use this feature often, I do use it when I want to access hidden folders (those that are usually invisible in Open/Save dialogs). For example, from TextEdit's Open dialog, if you type `/etc` in the "Go to" field and press return, you'll be able to access and open any file in the `etc` directory (which is usually inaccessible).

Open/Save Dialog Delight: Default Folder

User Level: normal or admin
Affects: individual user or computer
Terminal: no

Although the previous tips make browsing Open/Save dialogs much more pleasant, these dialogs still have a long way to go before they work the way they should, in my opinion. If you spend a lot of time opening or saving files, take a look at Default Folder X (`http://www.stclairsoft.com/`). Default Folder X adds a bunch of very cool features to all Open/Save dialogs; here are some of my favorites:

- Provides a menu listing all open Finder windows—you can select one from the window and the Open/Save dialog switches to that folder.
- When in an Open/Save dialog, you can click on any open Finder window to immediately switch to that window in the dialog.
- The last document/folder you accessed in each application is remembered.
- You can get information on a file or folder (using the Finder or your favorite file utility) from within Open/Save dialogs. You can also rename and delete files directly, without having to leave the dialog.
- Provides menus for recently accessed folders and Favorites.
- Provides a volumes menu that lets you quickly switch to any mounted volume; the menu also shows the available space on each volume *before* you try to save to it (Figure 5.24).
- Provides keyboard navigation that actually works in all applications.
- You can view invisible files in Open dialogs by holding down the option key as you access the dialog.
- Can open any folder visible in the dialog…in the Finder.

Default Folder is a utility that I consider to be a required part of any Mac that I use.

FIGURE 5.24:
Default Folder's volume menu

Moving On...

The Finder is and always has been the center of action on any Mac; however, in Mac OS X the Dock is its partner in crime. In the next chapter I'll cover the Dock, getting the most out of it, and using enhancements (and alternatives) to it.

P.S. If after reading this chapter, you're thinking "Wow, that was a lot of great info about the Finder!" check out the Online Bonus Chapter, "Furthering Finder Functionality." I'll show you how to get even more out of the Finder by adding menus, working with filenames, automating the things you do the most, and changing the overall appearance of Mac OS X. I'll also tell you how to fix a few of the most common Finder foibles.

CHAPTER 6

Developing a Dynamite Dock

(Or: Using the Dock, Dock accessories, and Dock alternatives.)

The Dock is probably the most recognizable—and controversial, if the discussion of it around the Internet is any indication—element of Mac OS X. If the Finder is, as I proposed in Chapter 5, the center of Mac OS X activity in general, the Dock is the center of application-related activity. It provides a straightforward way to launch applications, access application options, monitor application status, switch between running applications, and switch between windows within each application.

However, the Dock's functionality goes beyond just working with applications. It also lets you "store" Finder and application windows that you aren't currently using and, set up properly, lets you quickly access files and folders. It provides all this functionality in an interface that is intended to be easily accessible and easy to understand.

That said, because it tries to remain simple to use, and it appears to be a fixture that can't easily be replaced, the Dock has also taken its fair share of criticism. Users want additional features, better organization, easier customization, and quite a bit more. If the sheer number of Dock add-ons, alternatives, and outright replacements available around the Internet is any indication, a lot of users just aren't happy with their Dock. In this chapter, I'm going to cover how to take advantage of what the Dock can do and provide you with some solutions for the things it can't.

Dock Settings and Customization

Despite the fact that every promotional picture you see of the Dock looks exactly the same, it's actually quite flexible. OS X lets you change a few Dock settings via the Dock preferences pane, and third-party utilities provide a way to access a number of settings that aren't officially available yet.

NOTE Like the Finder, the Dock is simply an application that is set up by OS X to always be running. If you quit it, or it crashes, it will automatically relaunch.

The Dock Preferences Pane

User Level: any
Affects: individual user
Terminal: no

Like most other OS-related settings, you choose your Dock options from the System Preferences application (Figure 6.1). The first option, Dock Size, lets you choose the default size for the Dock. However, what it really sets is the *maximum* size of Dock *icons*. At the smallest setting, Dock icons will be 16 × 16 pixels, regardless of how few or many items you have in the Dock; at the largest setting, Dock icons will be a maximum of 128 × 128 pixels. The reason I emphasize "maximum" is because the Dock will never extend past the edges of the screen; if you have more items in the Dock than will fit on the screen at the chosen icon size, the Dock will automatically resize itself (and therefore the size of icons of Dock items) to fit the screen.

The Magnification setting allows you to see Dock items at larger sizes, even if you choose a small Dock Size, or if you have so many items in the Dock that it scales Dock items down to smaller sizes. If Magnification is enabled, when you move the mouse cursor over the Dock, the items directly beneath the cursor will be magnified (to the size determined by the Magnification setting). The quality of these magnified Dock icons is impressive; even more impressive is that windows that are minimized to the Dock remain "live"—whatever was going on inside the window at full size continues when the window is minimized (Figure 6.2). (I'll talk more about minimizing windows in a bit.)

FIGURE 6.1: The Dock preference pane

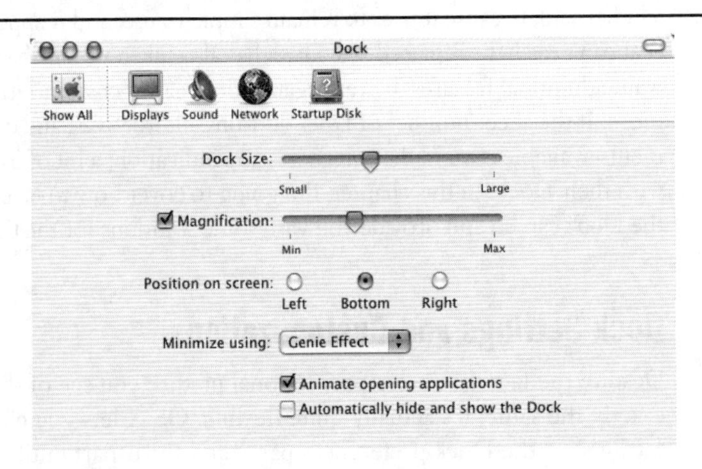

FIGURE 6.2:
A QuickTime movie playing in the Dock

TIP Want to make Dock magnification *really* big? Turn magnification on in Dock preferences. Open the Dock preference file (`~/Library/Preferences/com.apple.dock.plist`) in a text editor and find the line that says `<key>largesize</key>`. The next line is the maximum magnification size (enclosed by `<real>` and `</real>`). Change the value to something much bigger, like 384, save your changes, and then quit the Dock (it will relaunch). Don't be alarmed by the result. And don't worry—you can use the magnification slider to change it back to a normal size.

The "Position on screen" setting simply places the Dock on the left, right, or bottom edge of the main display. (Unfortunately, if you have multiple monitors, there's no way to move the Dock to a different screen.) The "Minimize using" setting changes the effect you see when a window is minimized to the Dock. To see the chosen effect, click the yellow minimize button in any window's title bar. The Genie Effect is a slower, genie-in-the-bottle action, whereas the Scale Effect is more of an immediate action that simply shrinks the window. The Genie Effect is very cool, but if you're like me, after the first few times you just want to get the window out of the way so you can get to work. There is also a third effect, the Suck In Effect, that's only available using a third-party utility like TinkerTool. I'll talk about that in the next section.

TIP Set the Minimize option to Genie Effect, and then minimize a window while holding down the shift key...very cool, eh?

"Animate opening applications" bounces applications in the Dock as they're opening. Although some people find this feedback useful, I personally prefer to disable it; the pulsing of the arrow beneath the application icon is good enough feedback for me.

TIP Disabling animated opening of applications will stop the icon bouncing that occurs when an application is launched; however, it will not prevent the "alert" bounce that occurs when an application is trying to get your attention. If, like me, you find the alert bounce annoying, check out the freeware Dock Detox (`http://www.unsanity.com/haxies/dockdetox/`).

Finally, if "Automatically hide and show the Dock" is checked, the Dock hides itself off the edge of the screen (bottom, left, or right) until you move the mouse up against that edge, at which point it pops up. If you're desperate for screen real estate, this can be a helpful option.

Note that you can also access most of the Dock's settings from the Dock item in the Apple Menu, and from the Dock itself. If you hold the mouse button down on the divider line in the

Dock (the line that divides application icons from icons for files, folders, and the Trash), you'll see a set of double arrows. Drag the mouse away from the edge of the screen to increase the size of the Dock (and therefore the Dock's icons); drag the mouse towards the edge of the screen to make the Dock smaller. (Holding down the option key as you do this forces the Dock to resize in specific intervals based on icon size: 16 × 16, 32 × 32, 64 × 64, 128 × 128.) If you control/right-click on the divider line, you'll get a Dock menu that contains many of the other Dock settings. Finally, you can move the Dock between the three screen positions by shift-clicking on the divider line and then dragging it around the screen.

Hidden and Special Dock Preferences

In addition to the settings in the Dock preferences pane, there are a few other settings that actually exist in OS X but haven't been officially implemented, as well as a few ways in which you can alter the Dock application itself to get it to behave differently. You can access some of the hidden settings via Terminal, but the easiest way is to using the freeware TinkerTool. More advanced options are available via the shareware TransparentDock, and you can give the Dock a complete makeover with the shareware Skin a Dock.

Hidden Dock Preferences via TinkerTool

User Level: any
Affects: individual user
Terminal: no

I've already talked about TinkerTool (`http://www.bresink.de/osx/TinkerTool2.html`) a few times; its Dock tab provides access to a few hidden settings. My favorite TinkerTool option, "Use transparent icons for hidden applications," changes the appearance of an application's Dock icon when the application is hidden (by using the Hide command in the application menu, or by pressing command+H). When transparent icons are enabled, a quick glance at the Dock tells you what applications are running but hidden. The second option, "Enable Dock shadow," simply enables a shadow around the Dock, much like the shadows around windows and menus.

The Position, Placement, and Minimizer Effect settings are similar to those in the Dock preference pane; however, each adds a few options not available normally. You can position the Dock at the top of the screen, have it start at the corner of the screen instead of the middle (so it expands at one end, rather than expanding in two directions), and select a new effect, Suck In. The Suck In Effect is a nice compromise between the boring Scale and the slow Genie.

Customizing the Dock Using TransparentDock

User Level: admin
Affects: computer
Terminal: no

TransparentDock (`http://www.freerangemac.com/`) provides access to the same hidden settings as TinkerTool, plus it lets you alter additional built-in settings that are not normally available. Although some of these settings—those that simply edit the Dock's preference file—do not require admin access, some actually alter the Dock application, and require you to authenticate. In addition, when you first attempt to make certain changes, Transparent-Dock will ask you if you want to back up your current Dock—by all means, do. If your customized Dock ever presents you with problems, you can use the "Reset from Backup…" option in the Reset Dock tab to restore the original Dock.

The number of appearance options available from TransparentDock's Custom Dock tab is impressive. You can change.

- the translucency and color of the Dock background (hence the name of the application)

(If you skip ahead to Figure 6.4, you'll see an example of a Dock that is transparent.)

- the color of Dock borders and the application triangle (the triangle that shows up below an application that is currently running)
- the"poof" action that occurs when you remove an item from the Dock
- the size of text used to show an item's name when you move the cursor over it.

TIP Get custom "poofs" from `http://www.resexcellence.com/user_poofs.shtml`. You can also create your own using any graphics application that supports the PNG format.

In addition, TransparentDock provides a number of options for Dock functionality in the Dock Setup tab (Figure 6.3). Some are self-explanatory, but a few aren't. In Single Application Mode, only the active application is visible (all other applications will be hidden). If Show Background Only Applications is enabled, any application that usually runs invisibly in the background will show up in the Dock. (Be careful with this option; since you can quit applications from the Dock,

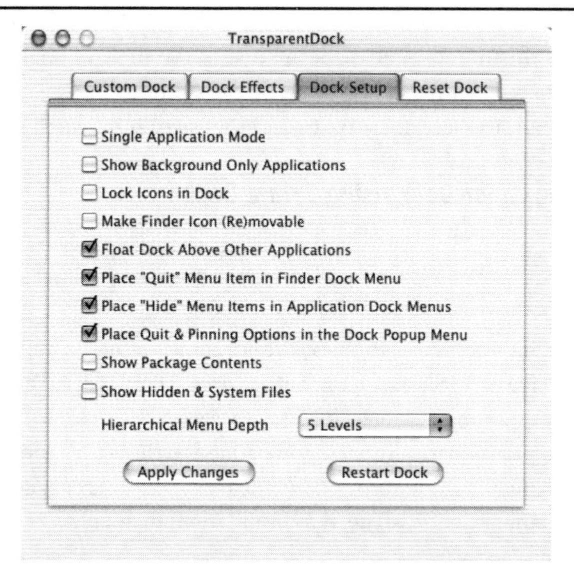

FIGURE 6.3: Dock Setup options in TransparentDock

this option gives you the opportunity to easily quit background applications. However, one reason some applications run in the background is because they aren't supposed to be quit. Plus, if you enable this option, your Dock can end up getting very cluttered.) If you disable Float Dock Above Other Applications, the Dock will act like a normal window, which means that it won't "float" on top of other windows—no more windows obscured by the Dock!

Two of my favorite options are to put the Quit menu in the Finder's Dock menu and the Hide menu in application Dock menus. There are times when you want to quit the Finder (for example, as discussed in the previous chapter, when you change the visibility of a file). This option lets you simply control/right-click on the Finder's Dock icon and select Quit from the resulting menu. Likewise, there are many times when you may want to hide an application so that its windows aren't in your way. You can do this normally from the application's application menu, or by pressing command+H from within the application. The problem is that to use either of these commands you need to first switch to the application you wish to hide. The Hide menu option puts a Hide command in every application's Dock menu, so you can hide any running application by control/right-clicking on its Dock icon and selecting Hide from the resulting menu. Holding down the option key as you access any application's Dock menu changes Hide to Hide Others, letting you quickly hide all other applications! (I'll talk a bit more about Dock menus shortly.)

TIP If you want the Hide item in application Dock menus, but don't care for the other options provided by TransparentDock, you can use the freeware Hide From Dock (`http://www.gwenhiver.net/applications/hidefromdock/`).

The final three options on the Dock Setup tab of TransparentDock apply only to folders and volumes placed in the Dock—they determine how many levels down you can see in a folder or volume's Dock menu, and what will or won't appear in those menus.

If all this functionality doesn't justify the meager shareware payment for TransparentDock, once you pay you can also save Dock configurations as "themes." Instead of manually changing individual settings, you can simply switch between saved themes.

Skinning Your Dock Using Skin a Dock

User Level: any
Affects: individual user
Terminal: no

Finally, if customizing the Dock's appearance using its built-in options isn't enough for you, the preference pane Skin a Dock (`http://www.ittpoi.com/sad.html`) lets you completely change the Dock's appearance using skins. It comes with a few skins of its own, and allows you to download new skins automatically as they are added to the Skin a Dock website. (You can also download new skins manually from `http://www.iheartny.com/xicons/dockskins.php`; however, if you download skins manually you also need to install them manually.)

FIGURE 6.4:
Dock-o-rama: the stock Dock; a transparent Dock created using Transparent-Dock; and a Dock skinned using Skin a Dock (top to bottom)

To install a skin, go to the Skin tab of the Skin a Dock preference pane, select a skin from the pop-up menu (Skin a Dock will give you a preview of the skin's appearance), and then click the Apply button. The Dock will quit, then relaunch wearing the new skin. A few additional options are available from the Options screen, such as which types of Dock icons should be skinned, and whether or not you want the Finder and Trash icons to be skinned, as well. (You can see a "skinned" Dock, as well as a transparent one, in Figure 6.4.) To remove all skins and return your Dock to its original state, uncheck the Dock Modifications Active box at the top of the preference pane, and click Apply.

TIP In addition to customizing your Dock using the tools discussed here, you can also change the stock Dock icons. For a good tutorial, visit `http://www.xicons.com/articles/dock.php`.

Using and Abusing the Dock

If you've spent any time at all working with Mac OS X, you already know the Dock basics: any application that is running shows up in the Dock (with a triangle beneath it), as well as any applications or files you add yourself (or, if you haven't modified the Dock in any way, any applications that were already in the Dock when you first booted into Mac OS X). You can click on any application icon in the Dock to switch to that application. Simple, right? Yes, it is, and that's part of the beauty of the Dock, especially for new users. However, if your Dock expertise doesn't go much beyond these basics, you're not taking advantage of all the features and power that the Dock provides. In this section I'll show you these features and how to get more out of them.

Accessing and Using Dock Items

User Level: any
Affects: individual user
Terminal: no

I'll talk about customizing the Dock's contents shortly, but first I want to make sure you're aware of everything you can actually *do* with an item once it's in the Dock. As you're surely already aware, clicking on an item in the Dock is just like double-clicking on it in the Finder: an application in the Dock will launch (or, if it's already running, will be made active); a file in the Dock will be opened using whatever application is associated with it; and a folder or volume in the Dock will open in a new Finder window.

In addition, all Dock items support drag-and-drop. If you drag a file onto an application's Dock icon, the application will attempt to open that file—this is one of the easiest ways to open a file in an application other than the one it is associated with (to open an Acrobat PDF file in Preview, for example). If you drag any kind of item onto a folder or volume in the Dock, it works just as if you dragged the item onto that folder or volume in the Finder (only without the spring-loaded folders).

Dock Menus

One of the least-used features of the Dock is Dock menus. Every item in the Dock has its own Dock menu, accessed by control/right-clicking on the item's Dock icon. This menu, by default, contains a Show In Finder command that will open a new Finder window to the actual location of the item (the Dock icon is simply a representation of the item, kind of like an alias). If the Dock item is an application that is currently running, its Dock menu also includes a Quit command and a list of currently open windows within that application. This is a great way to switch directly to a specific window in a specific application, even if you can't see it on your screen, without having to first switch to the application and then find the window from the application's Window menu. Finally, if the Dock item is a folder or volume, its Dock menu includes a hierarchical listing of everything inside that folder or volume.

TIP Since the Finder is an application, it follows that the Finder's Dock menu will always include a list of open Finder windows; select one to bring it to the front immediately.

In addition, many applications take advantage of the Dock's menu capabilities to add their own menu items. For example, Figure 6.5 shows the Dock menu for iTunes; you can see what track is currently playing, rate it for future reference, or control iTunes directly from the Dock menu. This is very handy when iTunes is hidden behind whatever application you're currently working in. Try control/right-clicking on other applications when they're running—you'll find that quite a few have their own customized Dock menus.

FIGURE 6.5:
iTunes' Dock menu

TIP If you hold down the option key when accessing an application's Dock menu, the Quit command changes to Force Quit; this is a convenient alternative to the Apple Menu's Force Quit command, since you can force quit the offending application directly.

Customizing the Dock's Contents

User Level: any
Affects: individual user
Terminal: no

One of the great things about the Dock is that although it comes preconfigured out of the box with the applications most people will use, *you* ultimately decide exactly what it will look like. Here are a few tips for customizing its content.

NOTE As I showed you in Chapter 1, you can limit a user's capabilities in the Accounts pane of System Preferences. If you've disabled "Remove items from the Dock" for a user, that user won't be able to modify the Dock's contents.

Left Side versus Right Side

You've probably noticed that the Dock is split into two sections by a thin vertical line. Apple's official names for these two parts are…the left side of the Dock and the right side of the Dock. (You'd think they would have come up with something a bit more clever, no?) If you've ever wondered what the difference is, it's actually rather simple: the left side of the Dock is for applications, and the right side of the Dock is for files, folders, volumes, and minimized windows (and the Trash, of course).

Adding Items to the Dock

Adding items to the Dock is as easy and intuitive as could be: just drag an item from the Finder to the Dock (applications to the left side; files, folders, and volumes to the right), and existing Dock items will politely move out of the way to make room for the new item. If an application is already running and you want to *keep* it in the Dock, control/right-click on the application's Dock icon, and select "Keep in Dock" from the resulting Dock menu. (You can also drag the application's Dock icon to any other position in the Dock; the application will remain in the Dock at that position after you quit it.)

TIP Often when you attempt to drag an item *onto* a Dock icon, the Dock thinks you're trying to add the item *to* the Dock, and the existing Dock icon will move out of the way. As you drag the item back and forth, the Dock icon keeps moving out from under the mouse. (It's kind of like that hallway "I'm trying to get past you but we look like we're dancing" routine.) You can prevent this—and make sure you're dragging *onto* a Dock item—by holding down the command key as you drag. This effectively locks Dock icons in their place as long as you hold the command key down.

Removing Items from the Dock

Removing an item from the Dock is even easier than adding it: drag the item's Dock icon anywhere outside of the Dock and release the mouse. The item will disappear in a puff of smoke. (This is the "poof" I mentioned earlier that you can customize using Transparent-Dock.) Note that if you drag a running application out of the Dock, its Dock icon will snap right back—since the Dock shows all running applications, you can't completely remove it while it is running. However, after you quit the application, it will no longer be in the Dock.

Question Mark in the Dock?

At some point you'll most likely see a question mark in the Dock where there was previously an application, file, or folder. This is the Dock's way of telling you that it can no longer find that item. Perhaps you deleted the item, or maybe you moved it to a different volume. On rare occasions it can even happen for seemingly no reason at all (although the cause is generally a bad Dock preference or mild disk corruption). To update the item, drag the question mark off of the Dock to get rid of it, then navigate to the item in the Finder and drag the actual item back onto the Dock. (If you're not sure what the item was, place the cursor over the question mark; even though the Dock item no longer works, it still presents the name of the item that was there before.) If you no longer want the item in the Dock, you can just drag the question mark off to delete it.

Accessing Files Quickly

You can drag any file into the right side of the Dock for quick access. However, chances are you want to do this with more than just a single document or file, and, well, the Dock only has so much room. A better approach is to drag folders to the Dock. In Chapter 5, I showed you how to add your Desktop to the Dock; you can use the same procedure to add any other folder as well. For example, you can place your Documents folder or your Home folder in the Dock; a control/right-click on the folder icon gives you a hierarchical menu of the folder's contents (and any subfolder's contents, and so on). Another approach that I use is to create a folder called "In Progress," into which I place aliases of all the documents or folders for projects on which I'm currently working. I can then access any of my work in progress quickly and easily.

Finally, you may remember from the last chapter that the Favorites folder (`~/Library/Favorites`) stores aliases to any files or folders you've designated as a Favorite from the Finder or any Open/Save dialog. If you put your Favorites folder in the Dock, you can add any file or folder to your Favorites folder (and, thus, to its Dock menu), by selecting it in the Finder and pressing command+T (or selecting File ➢ Add to Favorites).

Showing Mounted Volumes in the Dock

To take the "folder in the Dock" approach one step further, you can also drag any mounted volume to the Dock and get an instant, hierarchical menu of its contents. It can also be quite helpful if you like to have your Dock on the right side of your display—you can place your hard drive in the Dock, and then choose to hide mounted volumes in Finder Preferences.

The only drawback to this approach is that you have to manually place mounted volumes in the Dock when they mount, and manually remove them if they're unmounted or ejected. If this is a hassle for you, the freeware preference pane DockDisks (`http://www.charlessoft.com/`) will do the work for you.

Keeping Troubleshooting Utilities in the Dock

This is more of a tip than anything else, but it deserves separate mention. Every once in a while you may find that the Finder crashes or freezes and you can't get it to quit or restart on its own. Generally you could use the Force Quit option in the Apple Menu to quit the problem application, but that may not be possible if the Finder is the application having the problem. However, the Dock often still functions in these situations. If you keep the Process Viewer utility and/or Terminal in the Dock, you may be able to use one of them to force the Finder to quit, and it will relaunch on its own. (I'll talk more about force quitting applications in Chapter 7.)

Dock Storage: Minimizing Windows

You can hide any application using the Hide command in the application menu (or by pressing command+H). The problem with this feature is that often you don't want to hide the entire application and all its windows; you may just want to get one or two windows out of the way. In the classic Mac OS, you could simply double-click on a window title bar and the window would roll up like a window shade (in fact, the feature was actually called Window Shade); Mac OS X no longer provides this feature. What it *does* provide is a way to shrink windows down and place them in the Dock (called *minimizing*). You can minimize any window by clicking the yellow minimize button in the upper-left corner (or by pressing command+M). It will shrink into the Dock using the effect you selected in Dock preferences.

TIP To minimize all windows in a single application at once, hold down the option key as you click the minimize button. This even works for windows in the Finder.

When a window is minimized to the Dock, it looks just like a miniature version of itself (Figure 6.6); in fact, if you have magnification turned on, you can move the mouse over it and see a larger view (I showed you this earlier in the chapter when I talked about Dock preferences). Most minimized windows will also have a small badge icon that indicates the application to which they belong; applications with Apple's "brushed metal" look will simply show a small version of the window. Figure 6.6 shows minimized windows for the Finder, Preview, and QuickTime Player.

FIGURE 6.6: Windows minimized to the Dock

To get your window back to full size again, just click its minimized Dock icon; it will grow back to its original size and position. (If the minimized window is the only one open in an application, clicking the application's Dock icon will also restore the window.)

TIP If you have minimized windows for an application, and you then *hide* that application, the minimized windows will appear to vanish from the Dock. Don't worry, they're still there; as soon as you unhide the application, its minimized windows will reappear, still in the Dock. In fact, if you find that minimized windows are starting to take up a lot of Dock space (this happens to me with minimized Finder windows), you can hide the offending application (including the Finder) to temporarily hide the Dock icons for that application's windows.

Bringing Back the Window Shades

If you decide that you're really not a fan of this whole minimize-to-Dock thing, and you really, really liked the way Mac OS 9's WindowShades worked, you can get that functionality in OS X by installing the shareware preference pane WindowShade X (`http://www.unsanity.com/haxies/wsx/`). With WindowShade X installed, you actually get your choice of "get the window out of the way" behavior: windowshade the window, hide the entire application, minimize the window to the Dock, or make the window transparent (great for just peeking behind a window for a moment). In fact, you can invoke any of these four behaviors for any window. (It even gives you the cute WindowShade sound from OS 9.)

Dock/Keyboard Shortcuts and Commands

I've already mentioned a few of the things you can do using combinations of modifier keys and the mouse; a number of other Dock actions are also invoked using modifier keys; I discuss them all here, as well as the Dock's own keyboard-based application switcher.

Keyboard-Enhanced Actions

- Control/right-clicking a Dock item (or clicking and holding the mouse button down) brings up its Dock menu.
- Option+control/right-clicking a Dock item often reveals additional Dock menu options (including Force Quit in place of Quit).
- Control/right-clicking on the Dock's divider brings up the Dock's preferences menu.
- Option-dragging the Dock's divider line resizes the Dock in incremental steps. (You can resize it freely by simply dragging the divider line.)
- Shift-dragging the Dock's divider line allows you to quickly change the Dock's position on the screen.

- Command-clicking a Dock item reveals the item in the Finder.
- Option-clicking an application in the Dock launches the application (or switches to it, if it's already running) and hides the frontmost application. (Remember that "application" includes the Finder.) This also works when you option-click in a window in an application; you can quickly hide the frontmost application by option-clicking anywhere on the Desktop.
- Command+option-clicking an application in the Dock launches or switches to the application and hides *all* other applications.
- Holding down command+option as you drag a document onto an application in the Dock forces that application to open the document (even if it's not the application the document is normally associated with).
- Shift-clicking on a minimized window in the Dock restores the window in slow motion (useless, but cool to watch nonetheless).
- Pressing command+option+D toggles Dock auto-hiding on/off. This command can be useful if you normally show the Dock and an application's windows overlap the top of it (Internet Explorer is guilty of doing this quite often); if you press this key combination twice, it will quickly hide and show the Dock, and Mac OS X will automatically resize the offending application's windows so that they don't overlap. Note that if an application has its own shortcut that uses command+option+D, this won't work; you'll need to switch to another application, or the Finder, first.

The Dock's Application Switcher

In addition to the keyboard-mouse actions I just listed, the Dock also has a built-in keyboard-based application switcher, loosely based on Windows' Alt-Tab functionality. If you hold down the command key and then press the tab key repeatedly, each active application's Dock icon will be highlighted in succession, left to right, one application per tab. When you release the command key, the currently highlighted application will be activated. Using this procedure, you can quickly switch to any running application without taking your hands off of the keyboard. (You can cycle through running applications right to left by pressing shift+command+tab.)

Although this feature of the Dock has been around for a while, the release of OS X 10.2 provided a small but significant improvement in the way it works. Instead of starting this cycling randomly, or from the left side of the Dock, under 10.2 and later it starts with the most recently used application. In other words, if you're using Mail to check your e-mail, and then switch to your web browser, when you press command+tab the first highlighted application will be Mail, and then the sequence will continue left to right from the Mail icon. What this means is that you can quickly change to the last application by pressing command+tab once, and switch back and forth between two applications in this manner without using the mouse or looking at the Dock.

In addition to switching between applications, you can also perform other actions using the Dock's keyboard switcher. As a particular application's icon is highlighted, you can press the H key to hide that application, or press the Q key to quit it. As long as you hold down the command key, you can cycle through all running applications, hiding or quitting them, until you settle on an application and release the command key to switch to it.

TIP

One of the very cool things about drag-and-drop in OS X is that it works with the Dock's application switcher—you can actually switch applications *while* you're dragging a file or some data. For example, you can highlight and drag some text from an e-mail and, while still holding the mouse button down, press command+tab to switch to TextEdit. TextEdit will come forward, and you can then drop the dragged text into a TextEdit document window. (If a document isn't open, you can even press command+N to open a new one *while* you've got your text floating around with your cursor.) This is a great way to drag data to an application that's hidden behind other windows. (This feature also works with third-party keyboard application switchers, like those mentioned below.)

Since I'm on the topic of controlling the Dock with the keyboard, I should point out that you can also access the Dock, including *all* Dock items and Dock menus, by enabling Full Keyboard Access in the Keyboard pane of System Preferences. When activated, control+F3 activates the Dock; you can then use the left/right arrow keys to move between Dock items, and the up/down arrow keys to scroll through Dock menus. Hit the return key to select any item.

Third-Party Keyboard Application Switchers

The Dock's built-in keyboard application switcher is very nice, but it does have its faults. If you have a lot of items in your Dock, it can be difficult to see which application is highlighted. Plus, the order in which it switches between applications is rather simple: last application used, then left to right (or right to left). Finally, if you have the Dock set to auto-hide, when you press command+tab you have to wait for it to pop up.

There are several application switchers available for Mac OS X; my two favorites are LiteSwitch X (`http://www.proteron.com/liteswitchx/`) and Keyboard Maestro (`http://www.keyboardmaestro.com/`). I talk about Keyboard Maestro in the online Finder supplement when I discuss automation utilities. It includes a great application switcher as part of its feature set. LiteSwitch X, on the other hand, is a bit less expensive and it only does one thing (but it does it very well): keyboard application switching. After installing LiteSwitch X, you can choose the keyboard combination used to switch applications (either tab or return, combined with a modifier key such as command, option, or control), as well as whether you want all windows or just the frontmost window in an application to be brought forward when you switch to it.

Using LiteSwitch X works much like the Dock's application switcher; however, instead of forcing you to look at the Dock, LiteSwitch X put up a nice, clear display in the middle of the screen (Figure 6.7). The name of the selected application is displayed so you know exactly what application will be activated when you release the keys. In addition, you can click on any application icon *in* the display to switch to it immediately, or control/right-click on an icon to perform any of a number of actions on it, such as Get Info, Hide/Show, Relaunch, or Quit. You can also access any of these functions by pressing an appropriate key while the icon is selected in the window.

Finally, LiteSwitch X's switching algorithm (and Keyboard Maestro's, for that matter) is much better than the Dock's. Instead of a simple left to right order, LiteSwitch X places application icons in reverse order of recent use. The most recently used application is on the left, followed by the one you used just before that, and so on. An application you haven't touched in hours will sit all the way to the right. Most of the time this sort of arrangement works much better because you're switching between recently used applications.

Accessorizing Your Dock

It's clear from our discussion so far that the Dock provides much more functionality that it appears to at first glance. But another great thing about the Dock is that third-party developers have taken advantage of the Dock's own features—Dock menus and "live" icons, for example—to provide much more functionality. Here are a few choice examples of ways to accessorize your Dock.

Not-So-Ugly Docklings

In early versions of Mac OS X, Apple provided small Dock-based applications called Docklings. These applications didn't have any menus in the menu bar, and you couldn't even switch to them—they existed only in the Dock, and all their functionality was provided via their Dock icon and menu. A few third-party developers figured out how Apple made Docklings work, and the concept of Docklings caught on. However, despite their popularity, Apple eventually decided to get rid of Docklings. Not only that, but they changed the way the Dock worked, so some older Docklings refused to work properly.

The good news is that starting with Mac OS X 10.1, many of the features that made Docklings so popular—such as custom Dock menus—were available to normal applications. So the same sorts of functionality that made Docklings so popular could be provided via standard applications. Today scores of Dockling-like applications are available for download.

TIP Although most "real" Docklings no longer work properly, a few do. To try one out, simply drag it to the Dock. Click or control/right-click on the Dockling to see if it works. Or, better yet, use the freeware DocklingWrapper (`http://homepage.mac.com/bwebster/docklings.html`) to convert the Dockling into a standard application—after the conversion, launch it like any other application and access its Dock menu. Some older Docklings are available at `http://www.eskimo.com/~pristine/dockling.html`.

FIGURE 6.7: LiteSwitch's application switching display

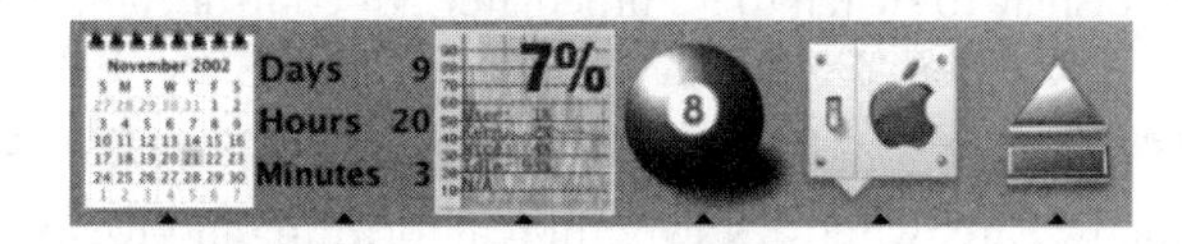

FIGURE 6.8:
Some Dock-based applications

Since there's not a lot of functionality to these Dock-based applications besides what they do in the Dock, the best way to give you an idea of what they can do is to show you. Figure 6.8 shows six different Dock-based applications. Left to right, they are:

- Calindock (`http://www.criticalmatter.com/calindock/`): a live calendar.
- Vanity Dockling (`http://www.ens-lyon.fr/~vbernard/MacOSX.html`): a running tab of how long your Mac has been running continuously.
- System Manager X (search at Version Tracker): a system monitoring utility; you can view any of its graphs in the Dock—this display is CPU usage.
- EightBall (`http://www.inferiis.com/products/eightball/`): ask it a question, click the icon, and it gives you the answer.
- Prefling (`http://homepage.mac.com/asagoo/prefling/index.html`): provides a menu for direct access to any preference pane.
- DocJector (`http://www.monkeyfood.com/software/docJector/`): provides a menu of all mounted volumes. Select one from the menu and it is unmounted and ejected. Great for unmounting discs that are hidden behind windows.

You'll notice that the Dock icons are fairly large in this picture; some of these apps—those that actually try to display something like a calendar or a graph—almost require you to use Dock magnification.

TIP Mac OS X's Clock application is another good example of a Dock application—in the Clock preferences, select "Display in the Dock" and you'll get a miniature clock icon that works in real time.

(Dock) Menus to the Max

I showed you earlier how a standard application (iTunes) could add custom items to its Dock menu to access features or add functionality. Taken to the extreme, it follows that an application could conceivably provide *all* of its functionality through its Dock menu. In fact, a number of utilities do just that. A few popular examples are the shareware Snard (`http://www.gideonsoftworks.com/snard.html`), the commercial DockExtender (`http://www.codetek.com/php/dockext.php`), and the freeware Yadal (`http://orane.org.free.fr/`).

Although all these utilities are excellent, and all behave very similarly, my favorite is Snard. Snard lets you construct a custom Dock menu, via drag-and-drop, that includes applications, files, folders—anything you could access in the Finder—and lets you group them in sub-menus if desired (Figure 6.9). I keep my most frequently accessed folders and utilities in my Snard

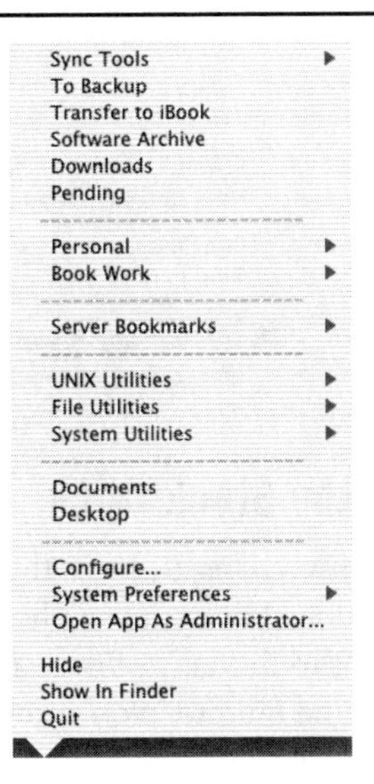

FIGURE 6.9: A custom Snard Dock menu

Dock menu so that I have quick access to them without littering the Dock. Snard also provides a feature called "worksets" that will open a list of files all at once so you can get to work quickly. Finally, you can actually open an application as root by holding down the option key as you select it from the Snard menu, or by using the "Open App As Root…" menu item.

Double (and Triple) Docks

Some people like having *lots* of items in easy reach; I've seen Docks with 50 or 60 items in them! There are of course options besides the Dock (I'll talk about a few in a moment), but some people just like the Dock, and dangnabbit, they want to use the Dock.

If you're one of these people, one solution you might consider is multiple Docks. You're probably thinking "Huh? How do I do that?" It's actually not as big of a deal as you might think. When you customize your Dock, your preferences are stored in a file. You could save a copy of that file, then change the Dock around, then save another copy, then change the Dock around, and so on, until you have several different copies of Dock settings. You could then quit the Dock and swap the preference files as it relaunches.

That's the idea, at least, and luckily there are some very handy utilities that do all the dirty work for you. DockFun! (`http://www.dockfun.com/`) and DockSwap (`http://pidog.com/OSX/`) both allow you to customize the Dock and then save it as a custom configuration. You can create numerous Dock configurations (one with all of your Internet apps, one for graphics programs, one with games, etc.), and easily switch between them. These two utilities are so similar that the biggest difference is the switching method (Figure 6.10). DockSwap uses its Dock menu, whereas DockFun! offers both a Dock menu and a floating palette.

The DockFun! website provides a unique video showing the use of multiple Docks; if you're interested in giving multiple Docks a try, it's a great place to start.

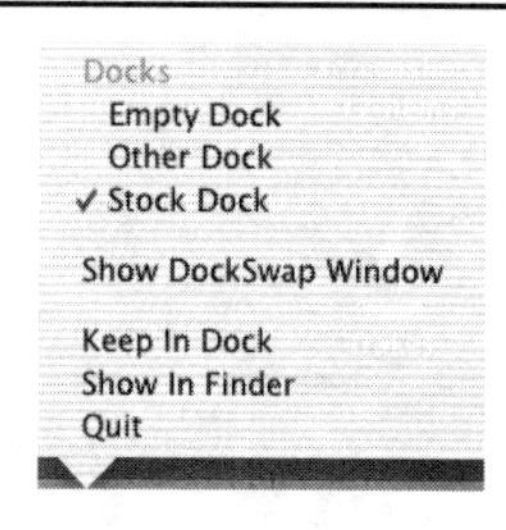

FIGURE 6.10: Switching Docks using DockSwap (left) and DockFun! (right)

Alternatives to the Stock Dock

Despite its functionality and ease of use, there are some common complaints heard about the Dock. I already mentioned one—it can't hold a lot of items without becoming overcrowded—but there are others as well. Many of these complaints revolve around its inflexibility: you can't move it to a second monitor, you're locked into a single view, and so on—everyone has a complaint or two about the Dock.

Part of the problem is that it's really a jack-of-all-trades. It launches, it switches, it stores, it controls, it slices, it dices. Putting such diverse functionality in one place, and keeping it easy to use, means that it isn't going to be as comprehensive at anything as some people would like. With that in mind, let's look at some "alternatives" to the Dock. I use the word in quotes because nothing is going to do everything the Dock can do; and chances are you aren't unhappy with everything about it. So instead I'm going to talk about third-party software that do Dock-type things exceptionally well.

I've divided this discussion into two groups of utilities: file access and launching utilities that are very different from the Dock, and utilities that are Dock-like in their solutions.

Un-Dock-Like Alternatives

It seems hard to believe, but people managed to access files and applications just fine before the Dock came around, even when they didn't want to browse through folders manually. Windows users have had the Start menu for years, and Mac users had the Apple Menu and utilities like ACTION Menus and Now Menus, as well as keyboard launchers.

Some of these same types of solutions have become popular in OS X, as menus and keyboard-based utilities are some of the most common methods for users to get to their files, folders, and applications.

Menus

If you're the type who likes to access things through menus, there are plenty of menu-based utilities to access files, folders, and applications. I've already mentioned a few of the best, Snard (earlier in this chapter) and MaxMenus (in Chapter 5). Snard also comes in a menu bar version; everything you can do using Snard in the Dock, as I described earlier, you can do from the menu bar.

However, MaxMenus is especially impressive in this capacity because of the ability to drag files onto application icons *in* menus, and the ability to create menus that contain both frequently used applications and currently running applications. For example, I've created a menu that contains my favorite drag-and-drop applications and all currently running applications, and assigned a keyboard combination to that menu. Whenever I have a file that I want to open in a certain application, I simply press the keys to activate the menu, and it pops up directly under the cursor. I then drop the file onto one of the application icons (Figure 6.11). In addition, you can also *act* on menu items—if you have a menu that includes running applications, you can quit, relaunch, force quit, or switch to any of them using the mouse or keyboard. You can even grab an item in any MaxMenus menu, and then drag it to the Finder, to the Dock, or to any other MaxMenus menu. Finally, you can assign a keyboard shortcut to any item in any MaxMenus menu by selecting the item and then pressing the key combination you want to assign to that item. The more I use MaxMenus, the more things I figure out to use it for.

Another great menu-oriented utility is piPop (`http://www.pidog.com/pipop/`). piPop works much like MaxMenus in that you can drag items onto menus. You can set your piPop menus to pop out from the side of the screen (like a hidden Dock), or to pop up anywhere on the screen using a key combination. In addition, you can "tear off" menus that then float above application and Finder windows (Figure 6.12).

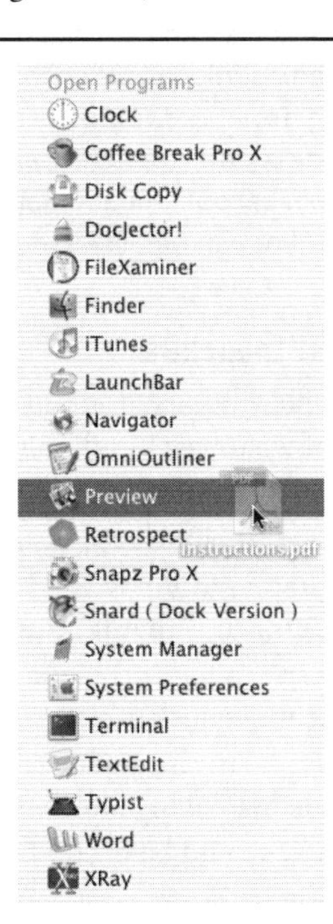

FIGURE 6.11: Using MaxMenus to open an Acrobat document using Preview

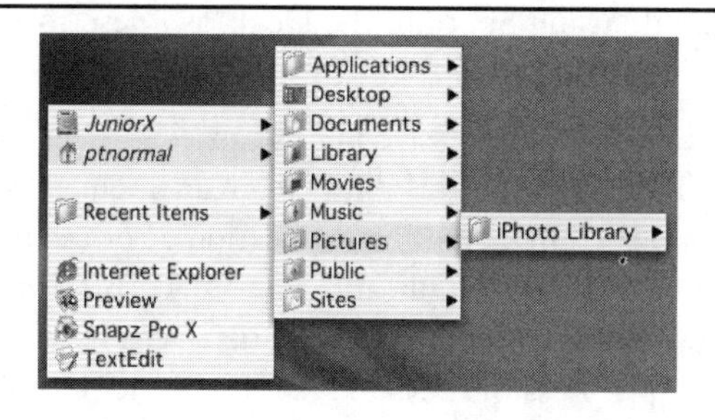

FIGURE 6.12: piPop's pop-up (left) and tear-off (right) menus

Finally, one of the easiest menu utilities to use is the shareware AliasMenu (`http://www.widemann.net/aliasmenu/index.html`). Any folder or folder alias that you place into the Alias-Menu Folder (`~/Library/AliasMenu`) will automatically become a new, hierarchical menu in the menu bar. For example, an alias of your Documents folder becomes a new Documents menu. By editing the names of items in the AliasMenu Folder (as explained on the Help screen), you can create keyboard shortcuts for items, reorder items, and create groups of items that are opened all at once. If you place text clippings in an AliasMenu menu, selecting that clipping will actually paste it into the frontmost application. (Creating a clipping named "Date" will automatically paste the current date!) AliasMenu allows you to choose the number of hierarchical levels in your menus, icon size, and spacing, and even designate keyboard commands to get info about a menu item or reveal it in the finder instead of opening it.

NOTE If you prefer to access files and applications from contextual menus, or would like to have such a feature as an additional option, a number of utilities provide application launching and file browsing from contextual menus, such as FruitMenu, Launch Items X (`http://www.naratt.com/LaunchItems.html`), and QuickAccessCM (`http://free.abracode.com/cmworkshop/`). In addition, as described above, MaxMenus and piPop provide pop-up menus that can be accessed anytime much like contextual menus.

Keyboard Launchers: LaunchBar

I'm one of those people who just don't like taking their hands off the keyboard—it generally interrupts the flow of whatever I'm doing. In fact, the first thing I do when I start playing around with a new piece of software is to check out the keyboard shortcuts listed in the menus. I set up hotkeys to launch applications, and, using a utility like Keyboard Maestro, QuicKeys, or Key Xing, I automate some of the things that I do most frequently. The only problem with this approach is that it requires me to remember an insane number of cryptic keyboard combinations—and every once in a while I press the wrong one and very bad things happen. If you're like me—heck, if you're even *remotely* like me—being able to launch applications and access files from the keyboard without having to remember myriad different key combination would be like taking another step up the evolutionary ladder. OK, maybe not that big of a deal, but it would be pretty cool, nonetheless.

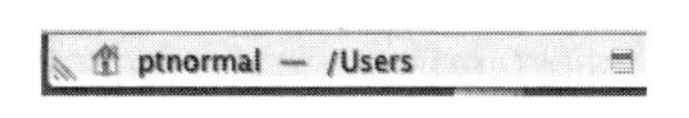

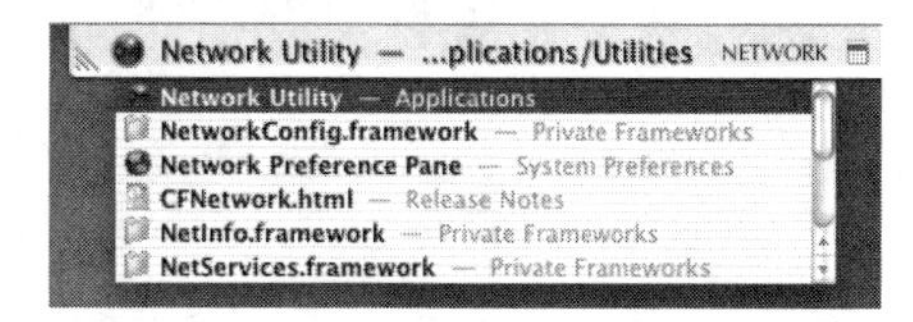

FIGURE 6.13: LaunchBar (top) and LaunchBar's results listing after typing *n-e-t* on my computer

So when I discovered LaunchBar (`http://www.obdev.at/products/launchbar/`), I was floored. Here was the utility I'd been waiting for; I paid for it five minutes after I downloaded. It was that good. The problem is that it's one of those things you can't explain very well—you have to use it to "get" it.

Put simply, you press a key combination (the default is command+space) and LaunchBar's small, well, "bar" appears (Figure 6.13). Type in the first few letters of the object you're trying to access—an application, a document, an e-mail address, a URL—or even the item's "initials," and LaunchBar makes its best guess as to what you're looking for, and presents a menu with its guesses. The more letters you type, the better guess it makes, the shorter the menu. When you've found the right item, press return to launch/open it (or command+return to show it in the Finder).

But what makes LaunchBar so incredible is that it *learns*. If you want it to select Photoshop whenever you type *PS*, you just type *PS* and manually select Photoshop from the list of possible matches. The *next* time you type in *PS*, it will give you a list of possible matches, but Photoshop will be selected by default. And so it goes, with every use, until after a short while it gets *exactly* what you want with only a couple of letters, no matter what those letters are. For example, my LaunchBar knows that "IE" means Internet Explorer, and that "XL" stands for Microsoft Excel. You can even access System Preference panes directly.

In addition, if you use the arrow keys instead of typing letters, LaunchBar lets you browse mounted volumes; when you get to the item you want, you can open it, show it in the Finder, copy its file path, or any of a number of other actions. You can even grab an item from LaunchBar and drag it to the Finder, the Dock or anywhere else, or drag an item from the Finder onto LaunchBar, type a few letters to get the appropriate application, and then drop the item onto it. As an added bonus, when you activate LaunchBar (via command+space), if you hit the space bar again or press command+R, LaunchBar becomes an application switcher.

The beauty of LaunchBar is in its simplicity; however, it's also quite powerful and configurable, far beyond what I have space to go into here. All I can say is that LaunchBar is, in my opinion, a utility everyone should at least try. I'm the first to admit that I'm at the extreme end of the keyboard-loving spectrum, and I realize that most users like a little mouse action now and then. But the truth is that sometimes using the keyboard is just faster and more convenient, and every person I've shown LaunchBar to has become a convert. In fact, the only applications I keep in my Dock nowadays are those that I tend to launch by drag-and-drop with documents. Everything else I launch via LaunchBar.

Dock-Like Alternatives

What if you *really* dislike the Dock? To some extent you're out of luck, because the Dock is *there* and you can't really do much about that (see the accompanying note). However, you can certainly hide the Dock and use one of several popular Dock-like alternatives.

The most popular Dock replacement is surely DragThing (`http://www.dragthing.com/`), which was around as a Classic Mac OS utility years before Mac OS X was even released. Another long-standing favorite is DragStrip (`http://www.aladdinsys.com/dragstrip/macindex.html`). However, some impressive challengers have been released over the past couple years, including WorkStrip X (`http://www.softchaos.com/`) and PocketDock (`http://www.pocketsw.com/PocketSoftware/pocket_dock.php`). Each takes a different approach, and just describing the visual (Figure 6.14) and interactive differences between them would take up a chapter in and of itself. Suffice it to say that they each provide multiple "Docks" or workspaces, each takes advantage of drag-and-drop, and each does things the Dock can't touch. Overall, I would say that DragThing is the most extendable and has the most options, PocketDock is the easiest to use (and can take advantage of many customizable skins), and WorkStrip X has the advantage of keeping track of recent projects and documents to make switching between them and accessing them easy.

FIGURE 6.14:

Some Dock alternatives (top to bottom): PocketDock, DragThing, and WorkStrip X

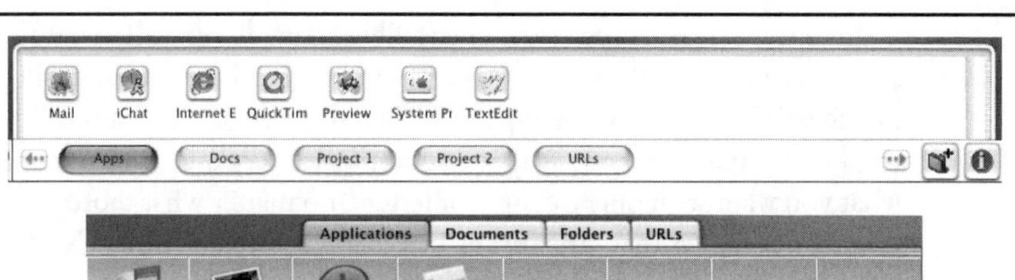

NOTE Under older versions of Mac OS X, if you really didn't like the Dock you could disable it, or even replace it with a third-party utility. However, under OS X 10.2 and later, Apple made some changes that make disabling it much less appealing. It's still doable, but generally not worth the effort. If you really don't like the Dock, remove everything from it, reduce it to its smallest size in the Dock preferences, place it on the side of the screen you frequent the least, and enable hiding. It shouldn't bother you much that way, and you can feel free to use whatever alternative you like.

The truth is it's really not possible to completely replace the Dock, especially not with a single utility. Just the fact that the Dock allows you to minimize windows (and other utilities can't) gives it at least one advantage. Plus, the Dock lets you instantly access any window in any application (including the Finder), which at the time of this writing isn't possible via any other software. Finally, all those cool features like Dock menus and "live" Dock icons that we've talked about in this chapter are only available through the Dock. Lose the Dock and you lose all that functionality.

That said, there are a lot of good reasons to use one of the above utilities. Being comfortable and happy with your computer is as much about personal preference as anything else, so if you're in the market for a Dock-like alternative (or even just a supplement), don't let my (too) brief comments on each make up your mind. I encourage you to download the demo versions of each and give them a try. If something other than the Dock makes your computer life better, more power to it, and to you.

Moving On...

By now we've covered pretty much everything you need to know to get your computer up and running (the way *you* want it), and you're well on your way to becoming a master at working with files, folders, and the Dock. Now we can finally move on to what you bought a computer for in the first place—running applications.

Chapter 7

Apple-ication Aptitude

(Or: Using Apple's applications, and applications in general.)

Mac OS X comes with the applications you need to do many things—e-mail, word processing, DVD watching, listening to music—right out of the box. I proposed in the previous chapters that the Finder and Dock are the centers of activity on your Mac, but you probably spend most of your *time* actually using applications. (After all, you didn't buy a Mac to move files back and forth all day, right?)

In this chapter, I'm going to give you some quick tips about using applications in general, but I'm going to spend most of my time covering the myriad applications and utilities that are included with Mac OS X—you may not even be aware that some of them exist! I'll also include some tips for working with text in OS X.

NOTE In most chapters I include the *user level/affects* box for every tip; however, since most application preferences are user-level preferences, unless otherwise noted, tips in this chapter can be performed by any user, and affect only that user.

Applications 101

Regardless of whether an application is a word processor or disk utility, whether it came with Mac OS X or you installed it yourself, chances are it behaves in certain ways common to all Mac OS X applications. You can launch it by double-clicking on its icon in the Finder or by clicking on its icon in the Dock; it has an application menu on the left side of the menu bar; you quit it by choosing *Application Name* ➢ Quit (or pressing command+Q). There are lots of other ways in which OS X applications behave similarly. Here are a few tips to help you better use applications in general.

Hiding and Minimizing Applications and Windows

This is a bit of a rehash of information I mentioned in the previous chapters, but I repeat it here in the interest of thoroughness. You can hide the frontmost application completely by choosing *Application name* ➢ Hide *application* (or by pressing command+H). If you've used a third-party utility to add the Hide command to application Dock menus, you can also use that method.

You can minimize any window to the Dock by clicking the yellow minimize button in the upper-left corner (or by pressing command+M, assuming the developer follows Apple's application guidelines). You can minimize *all* windows in a particular application by holding the option button down as you minimize any window belonging to that application.

Windowing Wiles

In older versions of the Mac OS, clicking on or in any application window brought *every* window in that application forward. However, in Mac OS X, clicking on or in an application window (including Finder windows) brings only that particular window to the front. If you want to bring all windows of a particular application to the front, just click on the application's icon in the Dock.

If you prefer the "classic" window behavior, where clicking on any application window brings *all* windows in that application to the front, check out Appendix A, "A Tale of Two Systems," for a few ways to bring that behavior to Mac OS X.

Customizing the Toolbar

I've covered customizing the toolbar in my discussions of several applications, including System Preferences and the Finder. However, most Cocoa applications, and some Carbon software, include this functionality (see "The Three C's of OS X Applications" sidebar). You can usually access this feature by choosing View ➢ Customize Toolbar…. In addition, you can change the toolbar view by clicking or command-clicking on the toolbar widget/button in the upper-right corner of any application window.

The Three C's of OS X Applications

When reading about Mac OS X, you may come across references to "Cocoa," "Carbon," and "Classic" applications. These are names for three different kinds of applications that work in Mac OS X:

Cocoa Cocoa applications are written entirely using Mac OS X–native programming tools (the *Cocoa Environment* for you techies out there). They run only in Mac OS X, and are able to take advantage of all the cool Mac OS X tricks such as Services, font panels, toolbars, and spell-checking. (I'll talk more about spell-checking, fonts, and Services later in this chapter.) TextEdit, Mail, and Stickies are examples of Cocoa applications.

Continued on next page

Carbon Carbon applications are written for OS X's Carbon Environment, and comprise the majority of Mac OS X applications at the time of this writing. The Carbon programming environment has actually been around for quite a while—Mac OS 8 and 9 could run many Carbon applications. In fact, this is one of the main reasons Carbon applications are so popular: many longtime developers who were familiar with writing Carbon applications for the Classic Mac OS could develop software for Mac OS X without much retraining. In addition, it is relatively easy for developers to Carbonize applications written for Mac OS 9—that is, to adapt them so that they work in Mac OS X. Thus many applications that existed for Mac OS 9 have been Carbonized and now work in both operating systems.

When writing applications in Carbon, or Carbonizing existing apps, developers can choose how much of the Mac OS X (Aqua) interface to include; for this reason, some Carbon applications look very much like Mac OS 9 applications, while others are, visually and functionally, almost indistinguishable from Cocoa apps. The exceptions are Cocoa-only features such as the Fonts panel.

Classic Classic applications are those applications written for Mac OS 9 or earlier that have not been Carbonized for use in Mac OS X. In order to run these applications, Mac OS X includes what is called the Classic Environment, which is basically a Mac OS X application that loads a copy of Mac OS 9, inside which the Classic application is launched. I talk about the Classic Environment and using Classic applications in Chapter 8, "Clobbering Classic."

Mac OS X also supports Java applications, and in fact Apple has provided the ability for developers to use the Mac OS X (Aqua) interface when writing Java applications. The advantage of Java applications is that they can theoretically be run on any platform that supports Java (Windows, Mac OS X, Unix, etc.). However, at the time of this writing Java applications are extremely rare.

Getting and Using Help

One of the most under-appreciated and under-utilized features of Mac OS X is its built-in help system. Available via the Help Viewer, which can be launched from the Help menu in any application, this system provides lots of info on OS X itself, and, if the application developer has provided it, information and assistance for individual applications.

There are three ways to use Help. The first is to search all installed Help modules. Simply enter a word or words relating to the topic for which you need assistance in the search field, press return, and Help Viewer returns a list of topics, ranked by relevance (how well each item matches your search). By clicking on the column headings in the results window, you can also sort the search results alphabetically or (perhaps most usefully) by the Help module each came from. The latter is helpful for finding which results pertain to the specific application you're using.

TIP

Advanced Help Viewer search techniques: when performing a search in Help Viewer, typing a + between words will only find Help pages that contain *all* those words ("and"). Inserting a | between words will find pages that contain any of those words ("or"). Typing ! before a word excludes any pages that include that word from the search results ("not"). If you want to group words, use parentheses. For example: *(window|menu) + application ! Finder* will find any page that includes "application" along with "window" *or* "menu," but does *not* contain "Finder."

The second way to use Help Viewer is to search within a particular module. Click the Help Center button in the toolbar to view the drawer of installed Help Center modules. Click on the relevant Help module (Mac Help for OS-related help, or individual application or topical modules), and use the search field in the toolbar to search within that module. (Note that for some reason, some modules don't seem to support module-specific searches—you get the same result as if you hadn't selected any module.)

The third way to use Help Viewer is to follow along with any built-in guides or tutorials the developers of an application (or the OS) has provided in their Help modules. Using Help Center, select the appropriate Help module, but instead of performing a search, use the links presented on the module's main Help page. Help Viewer will walk you through the help system for that particular module. This is an *excellent* way to learn tips and tricks for an application; for example, both iTunes and iPhoto have extensive Help modules with lots of tips and tricks.

At any time, using any of these techniques, you can use the Back button to go back to the previous screen(s); if you customize the toolbar with the Forward button, you can also go forward and retrace your steps. The Go menu also provides a list of recently accessed modules, as well as the results of the most recent search you performed.

TIP

If you find that the Help Viewer text is often too small, you'll appreciate the "Bigger" toolbar item, accessible by customizing the toolbar.

Exploring Menus and Preferences

This is a short tip, but an important one. One of the best ways to learn what an application can do, but one that many users never take full advantage of, is to explore the functions available from its menus and preference dialog(s). You'll often find features you didn't know existed, or realize that features you've been wanting are right there under your mouse.

Getting the Most from Mac OS X Applications and Utilities

As I mentioned earlier, Mac OS X comes with an impressive number of applications and utilities. Some of them you probably know well and may even use on a regular basis; others may be sitting on your hard drive unbeknownst to you. I'm going to talk about many of these programs, especially the gems that most people don't use but should.

NOTE Some of the OS X applications you're probably most familiar with are the "iApps" (iTunes, iPhoto, etc.), Mail, and Address Book. These are probably the most well-known and widely used OS X applications, and as such have entire books, websites, and mailing lists dedicated to them. Meanwhile, your Mac is full of other useful applications and utilities that rarely get mentioned. It's the latter group of applications I'm going to spend time on here. However, even though I don't talk about the iApps, Mail, and Address Book here in these pages, I still have some good tips for them. If you're interested, you can access these tips from the book's website: `http://www.macosxpowertools.com/`.

To give this discussion some semblance of organization, I'm going to split the built-in applications into two groups: "applications" (non-iApps that aren't utilities) and utilities (loosely defined as any Apple-provided application that resides in `/Applications/Utilities`). Unfortunately, the sheer number of applications (and the fact that some of them are quite simple in what they do or how they work) means that I'll gloss over a few; rest assured that if I don't give a particular application its fair shake, it's probably because you can easily figure it out on your own, or because I talk about it elsewhere in the book.

Mac OS X Applications

The "applications" are those applications that are located in `/Applications` (in other words, not in the Utilities folder). In a few cases, an application will have its own sub-folder; I've noted where that is the case.

Backup

The Backup application actually isn't installed by Mac OS X; it's only available to subscribers to Apple's .Mac service. (If you're a member, you can download Backup by browsing to `http://www.mac.com/` and going to the .Mac Downloads area.) Backup allows you to back up files, folders, or volumes to your iDisk or removable media such as CD-R or DVD-R. I talk more about using Backup (and other backup utilities) in Chapter 14.

Calculator

The Mac OS has always included a basic calculator application, but Mac OS X provides a much improved, and much more capable version. Besides the normal functions you find on your average calculator, it provides three new features:

Advanced Functions By clicking the Advanced button, the Calculator application expands to a full-featured scientific calculator, replete with trigonometric functions, exponentials, memory registers, and log functions. (If only it provided an option for RPN entry....)

"Paper" Tape Click the Paper Tape button and a drawer expands with a record of any calculations you've performed using Calculator. You can copy any part of the tape for pasting in another application, or you can save the entire tape to a text file by choosing File ➢ Save Tape As….

Conversions Probably the coolest feature of Mac OS X's Calculator is its conversion functionality. Type in an amount (area, length, weight, temperature, power, etc.), then choose the type of conversion you wish to perform from the Convert menu. Calculator gives you a window to choose the unit of measurement you're converting from and the measure you're converting to, and then does the conversion for you. It will even convert currency using the latest currency exchange rate (choose Convert ➢ Update Currency Exchange Rates to make sure you have the most recent rates).

TIP By clicking the zoom button (the green one in the upper left), you can reduce the Calculator to just the display; you can still control it using the keyboard, but you won't see the body of the calculator on the screen. In fact, if you're an awesome touch-typist, you can have Calculator read any total to you by choosing Speech ➢ Speak Total—you'll never even have to look at the Calculator application.

Chess

The Chess game lets you play against the computer, play against another person, or just watch the computer play itself (good for learning the game). If you play against the computer, you can choose (from the preferences dialog) how difficult the computer is to beat. You can view the board as a two-dimensional board, but using the three-dimensional setting shows off your Mac's graphics a lot better.

Chess also offers some nice extras. You can save your game in progress to finish it later. You can use Speech Recognition to play the game hands-free (e.g., "Knight b1 to c3"). Finally, if you're stuck, you can choose Move ➢ Hint to get a hint.

TIP If you want to disable the speech feedback window, choose Chess ➢ Preferences, and then uncheck the Use Speech Recognition check box.

Clock

The Clock application is one of those applications that doesn't get used much because of Mac OS X's built-in menu bar clock. Many users figure that since they've already got a clock in the menu bar, why waste screen space with a floating clock? Here's a tip—with the proliferation of application menus and menu bar items, most of us could use a little bit of extra menu bar space. Turn off the menu bar clock (in Date & Time preferences), and set the Clock application (via its preferences dialog) to display in the Dock. You can choose analog or digital display, but the digital display has the advantage of also showing the date.

DVD Player

If you've ever watched a movie on your DVD-capable Mac, you've used DVD Player. Although most of the controls and preferences are fairly straightforward, there are a few functions and commands that most people haven't discovered.

At any time you can view information about the current movie (time elapsed/remaining, chapter/track number, audio information) by choosing Window ➢ Show Info. When the info window is visible, Show Info changes to Hide Info. You can control the color and size of the info window via the DVD Player preferences dialog.

Advanced Controls

One of the most common questions about DVD Player is how to take advantage of special controls such as scan, slow motion, and frame-by-frame advance. At first glance, it actually doesn't appear to provide such functionality, yet it really is there. To scan, simply hold down the forward/reverse track buttons; the speed of the scan is determined by the setting in the Controls ➢ Scan Rate menu.

To access other advanced controls (Figure 7.1), click on the three small dots at the edge of the controller (on the right side for a horizontal controller, at the bottom for a vertical controller). A drawer will slide out with six additional controls: Slow, Step, Return, Subtitle, Audio, and Angle (hold the mouse over a button to see a tooltip that tells you what the button does).

If you don't like showing and hiding the controller manually via the Window menu, check the Hide Controller If Inactive For box in the Player tab of the preferences dialog. Enter a time, such as 10 seconds, and the controller will disappear whenever the mouse hasn't moved for 10 seconds; to get it to reappear, simply move the mouse or press the escape key.

Playing DVDs Automatically

If you want a DVD to start playing automatically when you insert it into your Mac, the procedure isn't entirely clear. First, you need to open the CDs & DVDs pane of System Preferences, and select Open DVD Player in the "When you insert a video DVD" pop-up menu. Second, in DVD Player preferences, you need to go to the Player tab and check the box next to Start Playing Disc in the "On Startup" section. When you have *both* these settings selected, inserting a DVD video will cause DVD Player to launch and automatically start playing the disc.

TIP If you tend to watch movies on your Mac at night, you may find the shareware iSleep (`http://isleep.free.fr/`) useful. It works with DVD Player and allows you to choose any of a number of actions to be performed when the movie has finished, or after a certain amount of time: pause, stop, quit, put the computer to sleep, or shut down the computer.

FIGURE 7.1:
DVD Player's advanced controls

Taking Advantage of DVD Player Scripts

Like iTunes and a few other Mac OS applications, DVD Player has its own script menu and includes several AppleScripts. From the script menu you can go directly to a specific chapter or a specific time on the DVD. Even cooler, if you have a favorite spot in a movie, you can use the Preferred Playback script to bookmark it—selecting Preferred Playback again will start the DVD at that spot. There are also a few other scripts for you to play around with, as well as a couple of AppleScript applets—scripts saved as standalone applications—available from the Applets sub-menu. The Preview Movie applet, for example, lets you view the first few seconds of each chapter of a DVD in sequence.

TIP If you like the idea of bookmarking DVDs, check out DVD Navigator (`http://www.blankreb.com/`). It allows you to create your *own* chapter catalogs for a DVD, and then lets you use those catalogs to navigate the disc. (You can still use the DVD's own chapter/scene selections, as well.)

Taking Screenshots of DVDs

Unfortunately, you can't take a screenshot of a DVD using the standard Mac OS X screenshot functionality. However, you can do so using the freeware DVD Capture (`http://www.blankreb.com/`). When launched, DVD Capture provides its own controller that allows you to play and pause the DVD (you should pause the DVD before taking a picture of it). You can choose to take a screenshot of the entire screen or of just the DVD Player window, and choose to save it to the clipboard or to a file. You can also choose to delay the capture for a few seconds, in case you want to include any menus or the controller in your picture.

Image Capture

Image Capture is used by iPhoto to automatically download pictures from your digital camera; however, most users aren't aware that you can also use Image Capture by itself—in fact, for some uses it's much faster and more convenient than iPhoto, and offers features not available anywhere else.

From the Image Capture preferences dialog, you can decide on the action you want Mac OS X to take when you connect your digital camera: nothing, open iPhoto, open Image Capture, or open another application. (You can make a similar decision if you have a supported scanner; you can choose what application to open when a button is pressed on the scanner.)

Once you've connected your camera, Image Capture provides you with several options. First, you can choose where you want images to be downloaded (from the Download To pop-up menu). Second, from the Automatic Task pop-up, you can decide what you want Image Capture to do with the photos once they're downloaded. The default is to do nothing, but you can have it create a slide show or web page, automatically resize the pictures to various dimensions, or Preview the images (using the Preview application). Click the Download button to download all the photos on your camera using the settings you've selected.

FIGURE 7.2:

The Download Some screen of Image Capture

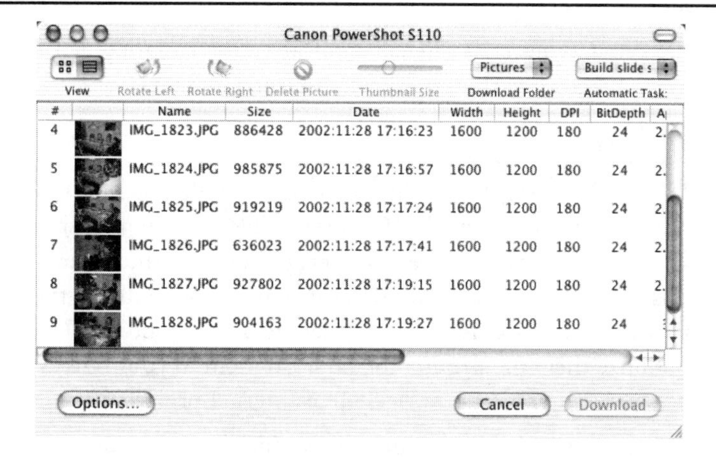

Where the more advanced features of Image Capture come into play are under the Options and Download Some screens. Click the Options… button and you'll see several tabs. The Download Options tab lets you delete photos from the camera after downloading, as well as adding custom data (custom icons, Get Info comments, and ColorSync profiles) to photos as they're downloaded. You can also choose to have photos downloaded automatically upon connect, and to set your camera's date and time. The Device Options tab provides information about the camera or scanner that is currently connected.

The View Options tab provides some interesting settings (icon size, list view columns, etc.), but you may be wondering where this mysterious "view" is located? That's where the Download Some screen comes in. If, instead of clicking Download to download all the pictures on your camera, you click Download Some…, you're presented with an advanced screen that shows (by icon or list view) previews of all the photos currently on your camera. If you choose list view (from the View toolbar item or the View menu), you're also provided with all of the columns you checked in the View Options dialog (Figure 7.2). Some of this information is incredibly useful, and not easily viewed anywhere else in Mac OS X (aperture, exposure, shutter, f-number, etc.).

In the Download Some window, you can also rotate photos left (counterclockwise) and right (clockwise) *before* downloading them. You have the same options available in the main Image Capture window (download locations and automatic tasks), as well as quick access to the Options dialog. To choose photos for downloading, command-click on them, or drag the mouse across multiple photos. Once you're ready, click the Download button to download the selected photos.

TIP

In the Download Some window, you can customize the toolbar to add a Thumbnail Size slider that allows you to dynamically resize the photo previews shown in icon view. You can also change the order of columns in list view by dragging the column header left or right, or sort by a column by clicking on the column header.

Internet Connect

Internet Connect is a catchall application for initiating dial-up, AirPort, and VPN connections. I'll cover each of these functions in Chapters 9 and 11.

Mac Slides Publisher

Like Backup, Mac Slides Publisher isn't installed by Mac OS X; it's only available to .Mac subscribers. I mentioned in Chapter 2 that you can publish photos on your iDisk to be used as a slide show by the Screen Effects preference pane. Mac Slides Publisher allows you to do this quickly and easily. Simply select a group of photos in the Finder or in iPhoto (make sure they're all in JPEG format) and then drag them onto the Mac Slides Publisher icon. It will optimize them for size and then upload them to your iDisk (using the member name and password entered in the .Mac tab of Internet preferences).

To subscribe to another member's slide show (or your own, for that matter), open the Screen Effects tab of System Preferences. Select the .Mac screensaver, and then click the Configure button. Enter the .Mac member name, choose your preferred Display Options, and then press OK. Since you'll be downloading the pictures from an iDisk, you must be connected to the Internet for this to work, but if so, you'll now have a slide show screen saver using the pictures the .Mac member has provided.

Preview

Preview is Mac OS X's universal graphics viewer and converter. It can view all of the following image/graphics formats: BMP, GIF, JPEG, JP2 (JPEG2000), MacPaint, PDF, Photoshop, PICT, PNG, QuickTime Image Format, SGI, TGA, and TIFF. In addition, using File ➢ Export…, it can export to all of these formats except GIF. While viewing an image file in Preview, you can also zoom in and out, rotate it left or right, or flip it on either axis (making Preview a nice tool for quickly performing basic image editing functions).

If you open a multipage PDF file, or a multipage fax document, in Preview, a drawer will slide out of the Preview window, presenting you with thumbnail previews of each page of the document. You can choose to hide the thumbnail drawer by clicking the Thumbnail item in the toolbar. The thumbnail drawer is also helpful if you want to open multiple files. If you drag them onto the Preview icon one at a time, or use the Open menu item and select them individually, each file will open in a new Preview window. However, if you drag multiple files onto the Preview icon in the Finder or the Dock, a single Preview window will open, and you can switch between images using the thumbnails in the drawer.

One of my biggest complaints about the thumbnail drawer is that it *really* slows Preview down. Luckily, you can choose whether the thumbnail drawer provides an image of each page (and the size of the image), the page/graphic name, or both, from Preview preferences. I set mine to show only the page/graphic name, and Preview is *much* faster.

TIP You can actually view animated image files (such as animated GIFs that are common on the Web) in Preview. Choose View ➢ Customize Toolbar, and add the Play button to the toolbar. Open the animated file in Preview and then click the Play toolbar item to view the animation. (When you view such a file in Preview, the thumbnail drawer will also show each frame as a separate thumbnail.)

Always Use Preview Instead of Acrobat Reader

Any PDF file created by Mac OS X or Preview will be opened by Preview. However, most PDF files you download from the Web or receive via e-mail will, by default, open using Acrobat Reader. Although Reader offers some features that Preview doesn't (text copying and form editing, to name a couple), many users prefer Preview for most PDFs. You can force Mac OS X to open *all* PDF files in Preview using a trick I mentioned in Chapter 5:

1. In the Finder, select any PDF file that has an Adobe Acrobat icon.
2. Choose File ➢ Get Info (or press command+I).
3. Expand the "Open with" panel.
4. Select Preview from the pop-up menu.
5. Click the Change All… button.

If you have a particular PDF file you want to open using Acrobat Reader, you can still drag it onto the Acrobat Reader icon, or choose File ➢ Open… from within Adobe Acrobat.

Using Preview to Save Edited Adobe Acrobat Forms

Acrobat Reader includes the ability to fill in PDF forms for printing. However, it does not allow you to *save* the form, meaning that if you close the PDF file, the next time you open it you have to fill in the form all over again. If this sounds familiar to you, here's a time-saving tip. Fill out the form in Acrobat Reader, and then choose File ➢ Print…, but don't click the Print button. Instead, at the bottom of the window, click the Save As PDF… button. Choose where to save the file and click Save. The resulting PDF file will look exactly like the original form, but with your information saved. You won't be able to further edit the form using Acrobat Reader, but you still have the original for that.

NOTE Mac OS X's printing dialogs actually use the Preview application to save files to PDF format. I'll talk more about this feature in Chapter 12.

This ability, and the ability to re-save PDF files from within Preview, is not always a good thing from the point of view of a PDF creator. PDF files created by Adobe Acrobat can implement certain security features that prevent things like printing and copying text. Re-saving a PDF file from within Preview, or (if printing is enabled) "printing" to a PDF file, effectively defeats many of these protections. Preview was actually a worse offender in Mac OS X 10.1 and earlier—it didn't honor any of these protections at all (you didn't have to re-save a file to defeat its security).

QuickTime Player

QuickTime Player allows you to play multimedia files, including such common audio and video formats as MP3, MPEG-4, WAV, AIFF, AAC, and AVI (and QuickTime, of course). You can view or listen to multimedia files stored on your own computer, or you can play back streaming multimedia content over the Internet.

TIP If you get annoyed by the promotional video for some new movie or game that always pops up when you launch QuickTime Player, open the QuickTime Player ➢ Preferences ➢ Player Preferences... dialog and uncheck the "Show Hot Picks movie automatically" box.

If you click on a link for a supported streaming media format in your Web browser, QuickTime Player will open automatically and begin to play it. If you have the URL of a streaming media file, choose File ➢ Open URL in New Player… and type (or paste) the URL into the dialog box. You can control playback options such as the size of the playback screen using the Movie menu, and you can save your favorite movies and streaming URLs as favorites using the Favorites menu.

NOTE Some AVI movies don't play properly on the Mac. You *may* be able to convert these problematic AVIs to QuickTime's .mov format using DivX Doctor II (`http://doctor.3ivx.com/`).

Each QuickTime Player window has its own volume and playback controls, but there are a couple hidden controls, as well. If you click the mouse in the progress bar in a Player window, you can jump directly to any part of the file. (If the file is located on your computer, playback will resume immediately at the chosen location; if it's a streaming file, it will take a few seconds to re-buffer the content at the new point of playback). If you have a mouse with a scroll wheel, rotating the scroll wheel during playback will enter frame-by-frame mode; you can use the scroll wheel to advance or rewind one frame at a time (click the play button or press the space bar to resume normal playback).

If you're playing a file with audio content, you'll see a graphical audio display on the right side of the progress bar. If you click on this display, the progress bar will switch to an audio control panel with balance, bass, and treble controls (click the display again to switch back).

Finally, if you find that you just can't get QuickTime Player to play loud enough, hold down the shift key as you press the up arrow key (volume up). When the volume slider is all the way to the right, keep pressing the up key and you'll find that the volume continues to get louder!

NOTE If you upgrade to QuickTime Pro, QuickTime Player provides additional editing and import/export options, video effects and codecs, and the ability to create your own QuickTime files from scratch.

Script Editor

The Script Editor application is actually located inside the AppleScript folder (inside the Applications folder). It allows you to write, record, and run scripts, as well as to view the AppleScript Dictionary for any application that supports AppleScript. I talk about AppleScript in the Online Bonus Chapter. If you end up learning how to write your own scripts, chances are you'll start out using Script Editor.

Sherlock

Depending on what version of the Mac OS you're using, Sherlock is one of any number of different applications or utilities—Apple seems to change their mind about what they want it to be with each system release. As of Mac OS X 10.2, it's Apple's Internet information search tool, which, when connected to the Internet, allows you to search for information via *channels*. Although it has an Internet search channel that scours a number of the major Web search engines, as well as a Picture channel that uses those search engines to search for images, most of the channels are, in fact, very topic specific (Figure 7.3).

FIGURE 7.3: Sherlock's channels

Some examples of information you can gather using Sherlock's channels are movie times and locations in your area (and even view movie trailers); the latest stock updates and news; business information using the local yellow pages, word definitions and translations; and items for sale on the eBay auction site. You can even get the latest flight status information from major airlines.

Sherlock doesn't do any of this searching itself; rather, it queries available search engines and then returns the results to you from within its own window. You won't get "better" results than if you used these engines yourself, but you get a nice, neat, all-in-one interface to many different search engines and data sources on your Desktop.

Sherlock sounds like a great utility, and it is; however, I really don't use it much. Overall, I prefer the shareware Watson.

My Dear Watson: A Better Sherlock

The shareware Watson (`http://www.karelia.com/watson/`) is a utility that looks and works similarly to Sherlock; in fact, with their toolbars configured similarly, as in Figure 7.4, it's a bit difficult to tell them apart. Whereas Sherlock offers "channels," Watson provides "tools"—both being content-specific modules that allow you to gather information via the Internet. However, Watson offers most of the features of Sherlock, plus many more.

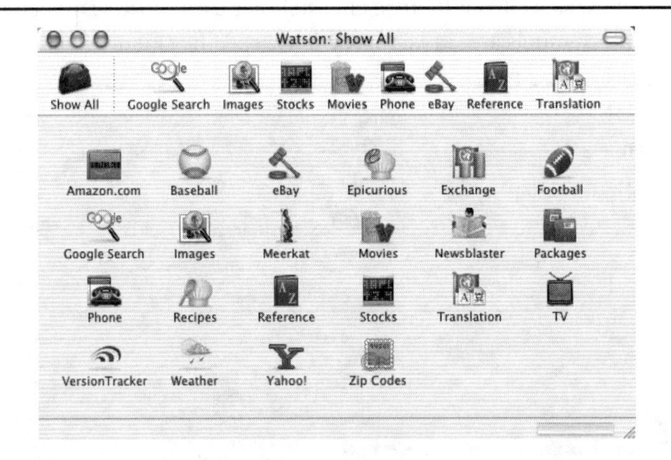

FIGURE 7.4: Watson, Sherlock's more capable twin

As Table 7.1 shows, Watson's tool list is quite extensive, and provides access to many additional types of information, from news to recipes to weather. Watson is also extensible via a plug-in architecture (some of the currently available modules were provided by third parties), so new tools are available regularly.

NOTE Both Watson and Sherlock accept plug-ins to add additional search tools, so the feature comparison in Table 7.1 is by no means exhaustive.

TABLE 7.1: A Sherlock and Watson Comparison

Sherlock "Channels"	Watson "Tools"
Internet	Google, Yahoo
Pictures	Image Search
Stocks	Stock Tracker
Movies	Movies
Yellow Pages	Phone Book (white, yellow, toll-free)
eBay	eBay Watcher
Flights	–
Dictionary/Thesaurus	Reference
Translation	Translation
AppleCare	–
–	Amazon.com
–	Baseball Scores
–	Epicurious (recipes)
–	Exchange Rates
–	Football Scores
–	Meerkat (tech news/information)
–	Newsblaster
–	Packages (tracking for Airborne, FedEx, UPS, USPS)
–	PriceGrabber (shopping price comparisons)
–	Recipes
–	TV Listings
–	VersionTracker
–	Weather
–	What's Better? (`whatsbetter.com` interface)
–	Zip Codes

The channel in which Sherlock has a clear advantage over Watson's tools is AppleCare. You can search and view the entire AppleCare Knowledge Base of articles, making Sherlock a quicker way to access this content than even Apple's own website (although if you click on a link within a document, it will open in your web browser). Sherlock's Yellow Pages channel also has a few nice touches. Once you locate a business, Sherlock downloads a local map showing you the location of the business, and (if you've entered your address in the preferences dialog), can provide you with specific driving directions. Finally, whereas Watson used to have its own airline flight status tool, it was removed in a recent version.

However, apart from these channels, I find Watson's tools to be either comparable or preferable. For example, Watson's Phone tool searches white pages, yellow pages, and toll-free directories; its

Reference tool searches many more databases, and many more types of databases, than Sherlock's Dictionary channel; and its Translation tool lets you choose between multiple online translation engines, compared to Sherlock's one. Sherlock is free with Mac OS X, but if you do a lot of online searching and information gathering, Watson is well worth the price.

NOTE There's actually a bit of controversy surrounding Sherlock and Watson. When Watson was first released, Sherlock looked and worked much differently (truth be told, it wasn't very popular). Watson got rave reviews, and even won Apple's own "Most Innovative Mac OS X Product" award. Come OS X 10.2, Sherlock got a major makeover that left it looking (and working) suspiciously like Watson. The two utilities aren't *exactly* the same, but they're close enough to raise some eyebrows.

Using Sherlock Location Files

If you find yourself doing frequent searches using a particular Sherlock channel, you can actually create Sherlock location files that, when opened in the Finder, launch Sherlock to the appropriate channel and initiate your search. Unfortunately, I don't have the space to show you how to do this here; however, you can visit the book's website at `http://www.macosxpowertools.com/` for the juicy details.

Stickies

The Stickies application is the Mac OS X adaptation of the old Mac "Post-It Note" standby. You can quickly create notes and "stick" them on the screen. Although many users consider Stickies to be something of a novelty with limited functionality, those who haven't yet used OS X's version may be surprised by what it can do.

As with Classic Stickies, you can create as many notes as you like, each with styled text and the "paper" color you choose. You can also import text from a text file or export the contents of a note to a text file (although in OS X's Stickies you can also export to RTF and RTFD, which is an RTF file with graphics).

However, the similarities stop there. Stickies now supports text colors, character-level formatting (the old version would only allow one format and font for an entire note), inserted graphics (drag any picture or graphic into a note), and unlimited note size (the old version limited notes to 8,000 characters). It also provides Find and Replace functionality that works within a single note or across all notes.

In addition, Stickies also sports some OS X touches. From the Note menu, you can make individual notes translucent, and you can also choose to make certain notes "float," meaning that they float above other application windows (making them behave like real notes stuck to your screen). Stickies also take advantage of OS X's Cocoa spell checker, available from the Edit menu. Finally, in any Cocoa or Services-compatible Carbon application, you can select text and then choose *Application Name* ➢ Services ➢ Make New Sticky Note to create a new note with the selected text as its contents. (I'll talk more about Services later in this chapter when I talk about working with text.)

TIP If you upgraded to OS X from Mac OS 9, and used Stickies under OS 9, you can choose File ➢ Import Classic Stickies... to import your old notes into the OS X Stickies database (the old database is located at `MacOS9 System Folder/Preferences/Stickies file`).

TextEdit

If you ever used SimpleText in Mac OS 9 or earlier, you know that it was (1) the built-in text editor; and (2) not very powerful or functional. TextEdit is similar to SimpleText in that it's Mac OS X's built-in text editor, but that's where the similarities end. TextEdit is an extremely powerful text editor with enough functionality to actually be called a word processor. It supports files of unlimited size, complex formatting (such as colors, kerning, ligatures, and super/subscripts), paragraph-level justification, find/replace, and graphics. It can open, edit, and save RTF formatted documents, supports Unicode text, text-to-speech, and can even render HTML and PDF files (drop an HTML document on TextEdit and watch it render the page, including linked graphics). Like Stickies, it supports Services and Mac OS X's spell-checking features, but unlike Stickies, you can enable on-the-fly spell-checking (via the preferences dialog), just like Microsoft Word. Finally, when working in rich text format, you can view and use a formatting bar and a ruler with tab stops and margin settings. You probably didn't even know about half of these features, right? Here are a few more tips.

Using Graphics in TextEdit Documents

To include a graphic in a TextEdit document, drag it to the desired position in the document. A bit counterintuitively, to apply justification to a graphic, select it in the document and then choose Format ➢ Text ➢ *justificationtype*. When you save the resulting document, the file extension will be `.rtfd` rather than `.rtf`. This signifies that the document includes graphics; in fact, it also signifies that the document is actually a package rather than a single file. You can control/right-click on the document and choose Show Package Contents from the contextual menu; you'll see that the package contains a standard RTF document along with any graphics included in the document.

Setting Up Default Document Attributes

Because TextEdit is so versatile, you need to decide what *new* documents will look like; you do this from the preferences dialog. You can choose between rich text (`.rtf`) and plain text (`.txt`). (Note that many complex formatting features are not available in plain text documents; if you are working with a document in one document type and want to change to the other, you can quickly do so by choosing Format ➢ Make Plain Text or Make Rich Text.) You can choose the default window size, word wrap, and fonts for new documents (including a different default font for rich text and plain text files), and you can choose what type of text encoding to use when you open and save documents (I generally recommend "Automatic" unless you have a specific reason otherwise). Finally, you can choose to enable or disable the toolbar ruler and OS X's built-in spell checker, and set your preferences for saving documents, which I talk about in the next section.

Options for Saving in TextEdit

The preference dialog gives you several options for saving files. By default, whenever you open and edit a file in TextEdit, it creates a backup of the original; when you save your changes, the backup file is deleted. By unchecking "Delete backup file," you can keep the backup as well as your newly edited version. You can also choose to overwrite files that have been marked as read-only (via Format ➢ Prevent Editing), and to save such files in writeable format.

WARNING If you use TextEdit to create or edit preference and/or configuration files (as discussed in various places in this book), make sure that before you save any changes to a document that TextEdit is treating the document as a plain text file. To be sure, check the Format menu—if it says "Make Rich Text," you know that the document is currently plain text. If it says "Make Plain Text," you should select that command to convert it to plain text. The reason for this is that rich text (`.rtf`) files contain formatting characters that will prevent your preference/configuration files from working properly.

Zooming in TextEdit

You can actually zoom in on and out of a document in TextEdit; this can be useful for examining small details or for seeing the big picture of how a document looks as a whole. (By zooming in, you can also see how beautiful text rendering is in Mac OS X—no matter how much you magnify text, is still looks sharp and smooth.)

To use this feature, choose Format ➢ Wrap to Page. The document view will change to a page layout orientation, and a zoom menu will appear in the lower-right corner. Select a zoom amount (from 10% to 1600%) and the page will be reduce or enlarged accordingly (Figure 7.5). To get back to window view, select the same menu item (which now reads Wrap to Window).

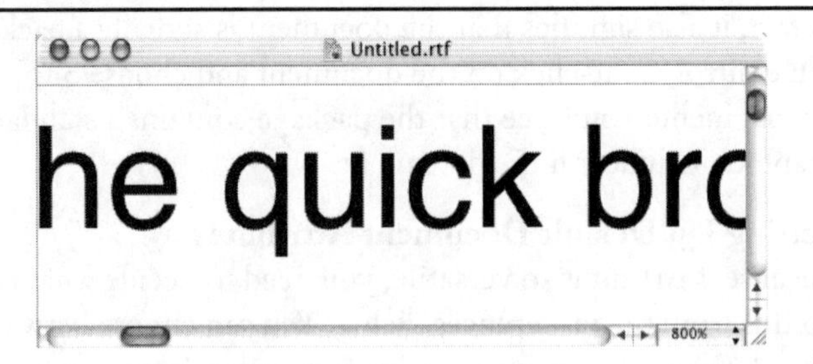

FIGURE 7.5: Using TextEdit's zoom function

The Utilities

I usually describe "utilities" as applications that let you change or monitor your Mac's behavior, or that help you better take advantage of your Mac's built-in capabilities. Although that's a good catchall description, for the purpose of this section we're going to use Apple's practical categorization of what a utility is: any application found in `/Application/Utilities`.

AirPort Admin Utility and Setup Assistant

These two utilities allow you to set up and manage AirPort networks. If you have a Mac with an AirPort card installed, the AirPort Setup Assistant walks you through the steps needed to join an existing AirPort network or to set up an AirPort Base Station from your computer.

The AirPort Admin Utility allows you to manage an AirPort Base Station. Using the Admin Utility you can restart your Base Station, upload firmware, upload a saved Base Station configuration file, set up an AirPort network password (Equivalent Network Password), and configure various other AirPort Base Station settings (e.g., DHCP, NAT).

NOTE The AirPort Setup Assistant requires you to have your AirPort settings set to DHCP; if you do not want to use DHCP you need to use the AirPort Admin Utility.

Apple System Profiler

Apple System Profiler provides comprehensive information about your Mac. The information available via Apple System Profiler is divided into six general areas:

System Profile Provides information on the version of the Mac OS your computer is running; the current user; general information about the computer itself; the amount of installed RAM and the RAM configuration; and the current network.

Devices and Volumes Provides information about the various buses on your computer (IDE, PCI, USB, FireWire, etc.) and the devices connected to each bus (including hard drive/volume information).

Frameworks Provides information on installed frameworks (function-specific portions of the OS), including version numbers and modification dates.

Extensions Provides information on installed kernel extensions, including version numbers and modification dates. The Get Info String column can sometimes be used to identify which kernel extensions were provided by Apple and which were not.

NOTE Under OS X 10.1, the Extensions tab provided very specific information about which kernel extensions were provided by Apple and which were not. Strangely, under OS X 10.2, Apple removed this functionality.

Applications Provides details on every non-Classic application installed on your computer, including version numbers. This tab can be an extremely useful quick reference guide when you need to check on application versions.

Logs Provides quick access to system and application crash logs generated by the Console utility (see "Console," later in this section, for more details).

You may find that a developer requests an Apple System Profiler report if you request technical support for their products. You can save such a report (in several formats) via Apple System Profiler's File menu; you can also open and view saved reports.

TIP You can actually access Apple System Profiler from the Apple Menu's "About This Mac" window. Just click the "More Info..." button and Apple System Profiler will launch. (If you just need to get the serial number of your Mac, click the OS X version number in the "About This Mac" window.)

Running Apple System Profiler from Terminal

In addition to using Apple System Profiler via the application's own interface, you can also use it in a more limited manner directly from Terminal. Type **`AppleSystemProfiler > `*`PathToFile`*** **<RETURN>**, where *PathToFile* is the path to, and name of, the file you want the Apple System Profiler report saved to (e.g., `~/Desktop/Report.txt`).

Bluetooth File Exchange

If you have a Bluetooth wireless adapter and another Bluetooth-equipped device (such as another Mac with a Bluetooth adapter), you can send files to the other device using the Bluetooth File Exchange utility:

1. Make sure both devices are set as "discoverable" (in Mac OS X, from the Settings tab of Bluetooth System Preferences).
2. Drag the file onto the Bluetooth File Exchange icon in the Finder or the Dock.
3. Click the Search button to locate any Bluetooth devices that are in range.
4. When the other device is found, click the Send button. (If the device is password-protected, you'll need to enter the device password to proceed.)

ColorSync Utility

The main function of the ColorSync Utility is to verify and repair any ColorSync/ICC device profiles on your Mac. These profiles, for displays, printers, scanners, cameras, and other ColorSync-compatible devices, ensure color accuracy across devices. You can verify or repair profiles via the Profile First Aid panel.

You can also view any installed profiles from the Profiles panel. Click on the disclosure triangle next to any group to view the contents of that group of profiles; clicking the small triangle in the upper-right corner of the Profile window allows you to group profiles by location, class, or space.

Finally, you can view information about connected devices from the Devices panel. Click on a device (a display, scanner, camera, printer, etc.) and you'll be presented with information about the device to the right. From the info area you can also select a different ColorSync profile for the device.

Console

While your Mac is running, OS X is quietly keeping track of low-level system errors and messages. When you launch Console, the `console.log` file shows these errors and messages. (Don't worry—even though it looks like there are a lot of problems, it's normal for the log file to be filled with incomprehensible messages.) More importantly for most users, Console lets you track application crashes and view the logs of those crashes. This functionality is disabled by default, but I recommend enabling it, as it can often provide you with clues as to the cause of an application crash (useful if you're trying to track down a persistent problem), and many developers will request a *crash log* if you request tech support. To enable crash reporting, choose Console ➢ Preferences, click on the Crashes tab, and check the box next to "Enable crash reporting." You can also choose to have crash logs displayed automatically; I personally find this option annoying, because each time an application crashes, Console will launch and pop up a window with the resulting crash log.

After an application crash, you can manually view the crash log from within Console (choose File ➢ Open Log…), from any text editor, or via Apple System Profiler. The log files themselves are located in `~/Library/Logs/CrashReporter`, identifiable by the name of the offending application. (If a developer ever asks you to send a crash log, this is where you get it.) The log file will tell you what the "Exception" was (what caused the crash), and will tell you which of the application's threads actually crashed ("Thread # Crashed"). Most of the time this info won't make much sense to the average user; however, a couple times I've been able to make educated guesses about what the problem was (a corrupt font is one example).

NOTE Multiple crashes for the same application will be appended to the same log file (`Mail.log` for Mail, for example). You can identify details for a specific crash via the Date/Time tag.

CPU Monitor

CPU Monitor provides several graphical representations of the load on your Mac's CPU(s), which can be enabled from the Processes menu (Figure 7.6). The Standard window provides a single meter (0–100%) that rises and falls with CPU usage. The Expanded window provides a moving representation of CPU use over time, and separates processes (via color) into system, user, niced, and background processes. The Floating window provides the same data as the Standard window, but presents it in a thin, translucent meter that can be arranged horizontally or vertically. Since CPU Monitor is something you would probably have running all the time if you used it, you can also choose to hide its icon from the Dock via its preferences dialog.

TIP You can orient the Floating window horizontally (via CPU Monitor Preferences), and drag it to the menu bar to get a menu bar CPU monitor. When I have it active, I have it set up vertically and place it at the very right edge of my screen.

FIGURE 7.6:
CPU Monitor displays (left to right): Standard, Expanded, Floating

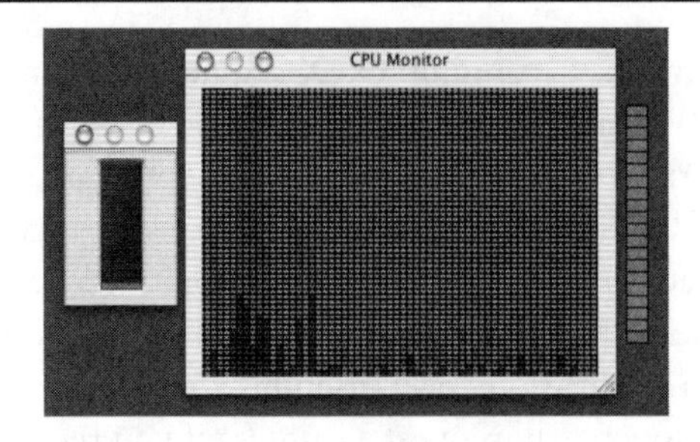

DigitalColor Meter

Used mainly by those in the graphic arts and design fields, DigitalColor Meter allows you to translate colors anywhere on your screen into color values in RGB, CIE, or Tristimulus format. From the pop-up menu in the DigitalColor Meter window, choose the color value format, and then move the mouse over any item or pixel on the screen to see its color value. You can control the aperture size of the selector using the Aperture Size setting, and the degree of magnification of the DigitalColor Meter inspector window from the preferences dialog.

Once you've found a color you want to use, press shift+command+H to "hold" it—you can then copy the color using the Color menu, or drag it from the color swatch to the storage area in Apple's Color Picker window. You can also save the contents of the inspector window for later use. If you're a graphics professional, DigitalColor Meter has a number of other useful features (and you're quite likely to already know exactly what they are and how to use them).

Directory Access

The Directory Access utility is used to configure access to directory services such as AppleTalk, LDAP, SLP, NetInfo, and Rendezvous. If you're using your Mac at home and these terms mean nothing to you, don't worry. Directory access is pre-configured for use in small networks such as a home or small office, and you can safely ignore it. If you're connected to a larger network that takes advantage of such services, chances are your network administrator will tell you how to set up Directory Access, or will do it for you.

"Disc Burner"

If you're looking for this utility, you won't find it, because it's not *really* an application. "Disc Burner" is what Apple used to call the Finder's ability to burn CDs and DVDs directly from the Finder. It's really a function of the Disk Copy utility. However, since it works a bit differently (and more simply) than Disk Copy, I'm going to talk about this functionality separately.

If you have a Mac or Mac laptop with a CD-R or DVD-R drive, inserting a blank CD (CD-R or CD-RW) or DVD brings up a dialog box asking you what you want to do with it. If you choose Open Finder, the blank disc will appear in the Finder. You can drag items onto it (up to the point where you fill it to capacity), and they will be "copied" to the disc (they actually aren't being copied to the disc; they're being copied to an invisible image of the disc which will later be burned). When you're ready to burn the disc, select it in the Finder, and then choose File ➢ Burn Disc… (Or, even easier, drag the disc to the Dock's Trash icon, which will turn into a "burn" symbol; dropping the disc on the symbol will burn it and then eject the finished product). You'll be asked what speed you want to burn the disc at (choose one equal to or less than the blank disc's speed rating, usually printed on the face of the disc), and then you can burn it.

NOTE CDs burned in the Finder are automatically created as *hybrid* CDs, meaning they are compatible with both Macs and Windows computers. DVD-Rs burned in the Finder are only compatible with Macs.

If you instead choose to open the blank CD or DVD in iTunes or (if you have a SuperDrive Mac) iDVD, the appropriate application will appear from which you can burn an audio or MP3 CD, or a DVD. Finally, you can choose to open the disc in Disk Copy, which provides additional options as explained next. (You actually have the additional options of opening the disc in another application, such as another CD/DVD-burning utility, or running a script, if you've set up an AppleScript to work with blank discs.)

NOTE In Mac OS X 10.1.*x* and earlier, inserting a blank CD instead brings up a dialog to create a Standard (HFS Plus/ISO 9660), iTunes (Audio CD), or MP3 (ISO 9660) disc. The first is a hybrid data CD, the second an audio CD that can be read by any audio CD player, and the third a CD of MP3s that can only be played using an MP3 player such as iTunes or an audio CD player that supports MP3 discs.

Disk Copy

If you've ever downloaded a disk image, you've seen Disk Copy in action; it's the utility that mounts disk images in the Finder. However, it can also create disk images—of folders, volumes, hard drives, CDs, or from scratch—and burn disk images to CD/DVD. You may wonder why you'd ever create a disk image, but they can actually be quite useful. For one thing, if you're sending a bunch of files to another OS X user, creating a disk image of the files means you can send just one file (and if you choose to create a compressed disk image, that file will be much smaller than the sum of all the files' sizes). For another, you can encrypt disk images as described below; no one but you, or anyone you give the image's password to, will be able to mount it or view its contents.

Creating/Converting Disk Images

You can create three kinds of disk images using Disk Copy. You can create a new, empty image by choosing File ➢ New ➢ Blank Image. You're presented with a dialog that lets you choose the size of the new image (the Size pop-up menu provides a few standard sizes, or you can choose your own), the format of the disk image (Mac OS, MS-DOS, or Unix), and, if desired, to use encryption. (By default, new disk images are created in read/write format, since the only reason you'd create a blank image is to add things to it.) Once you've chosen a location to save the new image and a name for the image, the Create button creates it; if you chose an encrypted image, you'll be asked for a password.

You can create a new image that is an exact copy of a hard drive, CD, DVD, or other removable media by choosing File ➢ New ➢ Image from Device. After selecting a device or mounted image, you'll be presented with a similar Save dialog; however, instead of disk format (which will automatically be copied from the device's disk format), you can choose the image format: read/write, read/only, compressed, or DVD/CD master. You can perform an identical action for a folder or volume by choosing File ➢ New ➢ Image from Folder or Volume. Finally, you can convert an existing image from one image format/encryption combination to another by choosing File ➢ Convert Image....

TIP You can also create an image from a folder, device, or volume by dragging the item onto the Disk Copy icon in the Finder or Dock. You can mount any image using the same action.

If you create a new disk image with either the read/write or CD/DVD master format (or convert an existing image to one of these formats), the resulting image will be editable, meaning you can delete files from the image or add files to it. If it turns out that your existing image is too small to hold the files you want to add to it, select File ➢ Resize Image... and select the image in the Open dialog. Using the pop-up menu at the bottom of the Resize Image window (Figure 7.7), you can choose to resize by measures of kilobytes, megabytes, or actual volume sectors.

NOTE Most of the Disk Copy functions are also available from its Dock menu; control/right-click on the Disk Copy icon in the Dock to access them. This allows you to access Disk Copy functions without having to switch to the application itself.

If you're interested, you can actually view a log of all Disk Copy activity by choosing Utilities ➢ Show Log; you can also clear the log from this menu—mine was over 200 pages long!

FIGURE 7.7: Using Disk Copy to resize a disk image

Burning Disk Images to CD/DVD

If you have a disk image that you want to burn to CD or DVD, choose File ➢ Burn Image.... Select the image and press the Burn button and you'll see the Burn Disc dialog. For more options, click the expand triangle in the upper-right corner; you'll be able to choose the burn speed and a few post-burn options. If you want to be able to burn additional sessions to the same disc (in other words, to create a multi-session disc), check the "Allow additional burns" box; you'll be able to burn additional content to the disc (provided you've placed it on a disk image and use the Burn Image command) in the future.

Creating Multi-Session CDs

It *is* possible to burn multiple sessions to CDs in Mac OS X. However, to do so, you *must* burn your data to CD using images and Disk Copy; you cannot use the Finder (Disc Burner). I hinted at this procedure in the previous tip:

1. Create a new disk image (new blank, from folder, etc.) with the first session of data.
2. Use the Burn Image command to burn the data to CD; in the Burn Disc dialog, expand the options and check the "Allow additional burns" box. This will burn the first session.
3. The next time you want to burn data to the CD, create a *new* image with that data (again, a new blank image, or an image from a folder). Select the Burn Image command again; this time the Burn Disc dialog will say "Append" instead of "Burn." Click the Append button to burn another session (again making sure that the "Allow additional burns" box is checked).
4. Repeat this process until the disc is full or you no longer want to burn further sessions to it (if the latter is the case, uncheck the "Allow additional burns" box).

NOTE If this procedure is too much of a hassle, the shareware CD Session Burner (`http://www.sentman.com/burner/`) provides a nice, neat interface for session burning.

Erasing Rewriteable Discs

If you have a Mac with a drive that supports CD-RW or DVD-RW discs (rewriteable), you can erase them completely for reuse by inserting a disc, and then choosing File ➢ Erase CD/DVD-RW Disc... and selecting the disc in the resulting dialog.

Advanced Disk Image Creation Using DropDMG

When you create a disk image using Disk Copy, you have the option of choosing a compressed image *or* an encrypted image—there's no way to have both. Using the shareware DropDMG (`http://www.c-command.com/dropdmg/`) you can create images that are both compressed and encrypted, using the same drag-and-drop or menu-driven process as Disk Copy. In addition, DropDMG offers additional image formats unavailable in Disk Copy (including images that will mount under Mac OS 9 and earlier), the ability to post-process disk images (further compress them, for example, for posting online), and can automatically limit images to a user-definable size (e.g., if the limit is set to 1MB, a 4MB folder will be split over four 1MB images). As a nice touch, you can also make your disk images auto-open when mounted (by default, disk images mount on the Desktop, and the user has to open them manually). If you use disk images a lot, DropDMG is well worth the small shareware fee.

Creating a Bootable Mac OS X CD Using BootCD

One thing you can't do using Disk Copy (nor most other CD or disk image utilities) is create a bootable CD that boots into Mac OS X. Such a disc, filled with your favorite utilities, would be an excellent "emergency CD" that you could use to boot up your computer in case of major problems. The good news is that the freeware utility BootCD (`http://www.charlessoft.com/`) can actually create a bootable disc image—using the copy of Mac OS X you have installed on your computer—which you can then burn to CD using Disk Copy. If you're in the market for such a bootable CD, the BootCD documentation provides excellent step-by-step instructions. (Be sure to read the section about how to boot your computer using the new CD!)

Alternatives to Disk Copy for Burning CDs and DVDs

If you burn a lot of CDs, and/or have specialized CD/DVD-burning needs, you might want to consider a dedicated CD/DVD-burning utility such as Discribe (`http://www.charismac.com/Products/Discribe/`) or Toast (`http://www.roxio.com/en/products/toast/`). Both utilities do everything that Mac OS X can do via Disc Burner and Disk Copy, but in a single package (in OS X, you can do some things in the Finder, but other things require Disk Copy). Plus both Toast and Discribe offer additional CD formats (such as VideoCD, XA, UDF, mixed mode, and CD Extra); simpler multi-session burning; Disc-At-Once and Track-At-Once burning (for creating professional audio CDs); CD copying; digital audio extraction; support for BURN-Proof drives; and disk image creation. Finally, both Toast and Discribe support far more CD and DVD drives than Mac OS X/Disk Copy/Disc Burner.

Toast costs a bit more than Discribe, but it also includes additional applications for creating photo albums, working with MP3 files, and recording audio from your Mac's audio inputs to CD. Both Toast and Discribe have interfaces that, though different from each other, are extremely easy to use. I highly recommend either of them if you do a lot of CD or DVD burning, and especially if you need to burn in a format other than MP3, audio CD, or simple hybrid data.

Disk Utility

I've already mentioned the Repair Disk Permissions feature of Disk Utility; however, it has a good deal of additional functionality, divided into five main areas:

Information Select a disk or volume in the disk/volume panel and you'll be provided with detailed information about that disk/volume, including the format, capacity, space available, number of files and folders, and (if a disk) the bus type, connection type, and whether the drive is designated as master, slave, or cable select.

First Aid Select a volume (a non-partitioned disk, or a volume of a partitioned disk) from the disk/volume panel to verify or repair permissions, or to verify or repair the volume itself. Note that you can only repair permissions on the *boot* volume, but you can only repair a *non-boot* volume. I talk more about this tab in Chapter 14.

Erase Select a disk or volume to erase it; you can choose the volume format (Mac OS Extended is recommended), the name of the volume post-erase, and whether or not you want the volume to be usable when booted into Mac OS 9. In OS X 10.2.3 and later, if you select an entire disk, you can click Options... to access the "Zero all data" feature. This feature not only erases the disk directory, but also overwrites every single sector of the disk with zeros, making recovery of the disk's contents much more difficult. This is a good idea if you're getting rid of your hard drive or computer. Note that whatever options you choose, you cannot erase the boot volume.

NOTE If you're interested in *securely* erasing your hard drive so that it's virtually impossible to recover its contents, I show you how in Chapter 13.

Partition If you want to divide a disk into two or more volumes (*partitions*), select the disk and then use the Volume Scheme panel to choose the number and size of the partitions. Note that you cannot partition the disk that contains the boot volume without first booting up off of a different disk. I talk more about partitioning drives in Appendix B.

RAID You can use the RAID tab of Disk Utility to set up a RAID (redundant array of independent disks) across multiple drives. Disk Utility offers a rather simple version of RAID, with only two options: striped (splits data across multiple disks for faster read/write access) and mirrored (duplicates data across multiple discs for reliability or for access by multiple users simultaneously). If you've set up a mirrored RAID, Disk Utility will also allow you to rebuild it in the case of a drive failure. To set up a RAID, drag multiple volumes to the Disk window and then select the scheme, name, and format. Note that RAID drives must be the same size, and that you cannot set up a RAID using the startup disk.

WARNING Using the Erase, Partition, or RAID features of Disk Utility will *erase* the affected volumes/disks. Be *sure* this is what you want to do!

NOTE I talk more about disk maintenance, and third-party disk utilities, in Chapter 14.

Display Calibrator

Display Calibrator is more accurately known as the Display Calibrator Assistant, as it allows you to calibrate your display and then walks you through a procedure to create a custom ColorSync profile for that display (which can then be chosen in the ColorSync pane of System Preferences). The procedure is largely self-explanatory; however, by checking the Expert Mode box on the Introduction (first) screen, you'll be presented with a few more options for calibration.

If you're not a graphics professional or someone for whom color accuracy is important, ColorSync and Display Calibrator won't be much use to you. However, Display Calibrator does allow you to change the gamma and white point settings of your display, so if you find your display to be too bright or dark, or the color to be "off," you can always experiment with the gamma and white point values to create a more pleasing display profile.

Grab (and Screenshots in General)

If you're a longtime Mac user, you're familiar with the keyboard combination shift+command+3 to take a picture of the screen (a *screenshot*). This still works in Mac OS X, as well as a plethora of other keyboard combinations.

TIP You can combine Mac OS X's zoom feature (in the Seeing tab of Universal Access preferences) together with any of the procedures listed below to take close-up pictures of any on-screen item.

Screenshots via the Keyboard

The following keyboard combinations can be used to take various types of screenshots in Mac OS X. The resulting screenshot will be saved in PDF format on the Desktop.

- command+shift+3: screenshot of the entire screen.
- command+shift+4: screenshot of part of the screen. The cursor will change to a crosshair/marquee, which you can use to select the area of the screen you wish to capture. When you release the mouse button, the screenshot will be taken. If you want to cancel the screenshot, press the escape key before releasing the mouse.
- command+shift+4, followed by the space bar: screenshot of any *item* on the screen. The cursor will change to a camera icon; as you move the camera around the screen, whatever item is directly under it will become highlighted. When you click the mouse button, the screenshot will consist of the highlighted area. This is a great way to take a shot of a particular window, the menu bar, the Dock, the Desktop (even behind windows), or any Dock or Finder icon.

TIP Pressing the control key simultaneously with any of these combinations will cause the screenshot to be saved to the clipboard instead of to a file. You can then paste it into any graphics-capable application. Note that if you have multiple monitors/screens, only the main screen—the one with the menu bar—will be copied to the clipboard.

Screenshots in a Format Other than PDF

By default, screenshots in Mac OS X are saved as a PDF file. In earlier versions of Mac OS X you could use a utility like TinkerTool to change this format; unfortunately that's no longer possible as of OS X 10.2. You can get around this limitation using a third-party utility, as I discuss later in this section, but there's a two-step way to do it using Preview.

1. Take a screenshot in Mac OS X, but save it to the clipboard instead of to a file (by holding down the control key as you press the appropriate keyboard combination).
2. Switch to Preview and choose File ➢ New From Pasteboard. Preview will show the screenshot in a new Preview document.
3. Choose File ➢ Export... to save the screenshot in any format you like. (You can also choose to print the screenshot or save it as a PDF.)

You could also open the standard PDF screenshot file in Preview and then export it to a different format, but the above procedure saves you a couple of steps and an extra file.

Screenshots Using Terminal

You can take screenshots using the **screencapture** command, which works identically to the various keyboard combinations. Type **screencapture** <RETURN> to see a list of options and the correct syntax for the command. (By selecting *interactive* mode, the space bar and escape keys function exactly as they do when calling a screenshot from the keyboard.) One advantage of this command is that it can be called from any script that can be run from Terminal.

Screenshots Using Grab

The Grab utility is a bit more limited than the various keyboard screenshot commands in that you can't take a picture of individual items. However, you can still use the marquee to select an area for a screenshot in Grab, and it has a couple of advantages of its own. First and foremost, it allows you to take timed screenshots—when you click the Start Timer button you have 10 seconds to prepare the screen for the screenshot. This is the only way to take a screenshot of a menu without using third-party software. Second, when you take a screenshot using Grab, it isn't automatically saved to the Desktop or the clipboard. Instead, a new window is opened in Grab with the contents of the screenshot. You can choose to copy the screenshot to the clipboard, save it to a file (wherever you like), or close the window and discard it. In other words, you get to inspect the screenshot and decide what to do with it immediately.

Via the Grab preferences, you can also choose to make the cursor visible (it's invisible in screenshots taken using the keyboard), as well as choose which of the Mac OS X cursors is used. Finally, if you choose Edit ➢ Inspector, an Image Inspector window opens that tells you the size and bit depth of each screenshot you take using Grab.

Third-Party Screenshots: Snapz Pro X

Although OS X's built-in keyboard commands and Grab utility provide a good deal of screenshot functionality, if you take a lot of screenshots you'll want an industrial-strength utility. Snapz Pro X (`http://www.ambrosiasw.com/utilities/snapzprox/`) is the OS X version of the longtime king of Mac OS screenshot utilities. Using Snapz Pro X you can take a picture of the screen, any object on the screen (including menus), or any selected part of the screen. When choosing a selected part of the screen, you can resize and move the selection to fine-tune it before the screenshot is taken. Using the Extra version of Snapz Pro X, you can also record movies of the screen.

In addition to the standard screenshot ability, Snapz Pro X also offers many more options than the standard Mac OS X functionality (Figure 7.8). You can assign your own keyboard command for screenshots, and you can choose what graphics format screenshots are saved in and where they're saved (they can also be copied to the clipboard or printed immediately). Other options include borders, scaling, watermarks, and color depth. If it's any indication of how versatile Snapz Pro X is, all of the screenshots in this book were taken using it.

FIGURE 7.8:
Screenshot options in Snapz Pro X

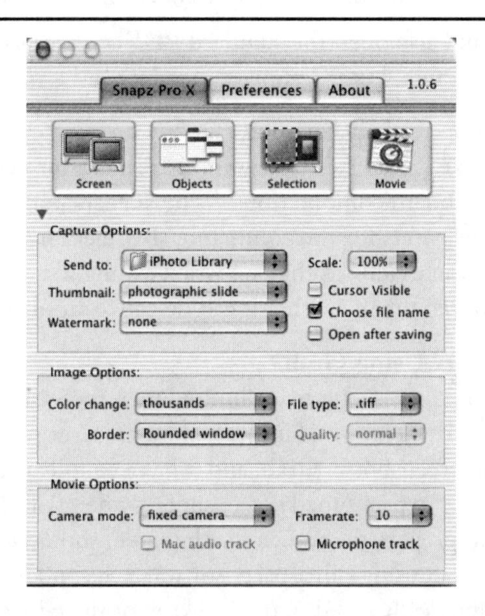

iDisk Utility

The little-known but extremely useful iDisk Utility is not installed by Mac OS X; like the Mac Slides Publisher application, it is only available to subscribers to Apple's .Mac service. (If you're a .Mac subscriber, login to your account at `http://www.mac.com/` and go to the .Mac Downloads area.) iDisk Utility provides four tools for working with iDisks:

Open Public Folder Allows you to quickly access another user's iDisk Public folder by typing in the user's member name (if the Public folder is password-protected, you'll be asked for the appropriate password).

Open iDisk Allows you to access your own iDisk (by default it uses the member name and password entered into the .Mac tab of Internet System Preferences) or another member's iDisk (provided you have the correct member name and password). Although you can always access the iDisk listed in Internet preferences via the Go menu in the Finder, this feature of iDisk Utility is useful if you have more than one .Mac account. (I'll talk about other ways to access multiple iDisks in Chapter 12.)

Public Folder Access Allows you to change the privileges other users have when accessing your own Public folder (Read-Only vs. Read-Write), and allows you to password-protect your Public folder. These options are exactly the same as the Public Folder Access options available from the iDisk tab of Internet preferences.

iDisk Storage Shows the current capacity of your iDisk as well as how much of that capacity is currently being used. (It also provides you with a button to quickly go to Apple's website to buy more space.) These are the same data available from the iDisk Storage section of the iDisk tab of Internet preferences.

Installer

The Installer utility, as discussed in Chapter 4, provides a common interface for developers (including Apple) to use for installing software packages. If an application or OS update is provided in `.pkg` format, it will be installed using the Installer utility.

Key Caps

Have you ever wanted to type a nonstandard character, such as the trademark symbol (™), the copyright symbol (©), or the ¿ used when writing questions in Spanish? The Key Caps utility lets you figure out such mysteries. When you launch Key Caps, it provides you with a graphical keyboard that mirrors the current keyboard attached to your Mac (or your PowerBook or iBook keyboard). If you press a key on your keyboard, the corresponding key will be highlighted on the Key Caps keyboard. But press any of the text modifier keys (shift, option, or shift+option), and the Key Caps keyboard will change to reflect the characters that are possible via those modifier keys (Figure 7.9). You can see that in the current font, ™ is typed by pressing option+2, © is accessed via option+G, and you can get ¿ by pressing shift+option+? What's more, to save you the trouble of retyping characters in another application, you can type them in Key Caps, copy them from the Key Caps text field, and then paste them in any other application.

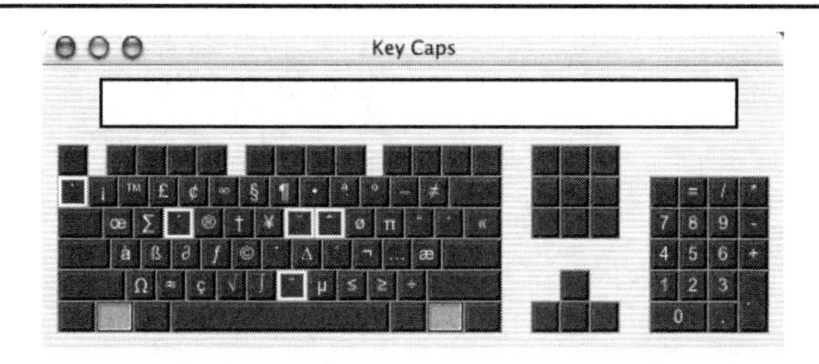

FIGURE 7.9: Using Key Caps to view characters in the current font that are accessible via the option key

Keep in mind that the current layout and key combinations are only applicable for the currently selected font. In other words, if you're using Times New Roman in your word processor, make sure you select the Times New Roman font from Key Caps' font menu before using it to find a particular character.

Alternatives to Key Caps: CharView and PopChar X

Although Key Caps is extremely helpful, it still requires you to figure out which key combination produces the desired character, and then either type that combination or copy and paste the character into another application. The excellent shareware utilities CharView (`http://www.alxsoft.com/mac/charview.html`) and PopChar X (`http://www.macility.com/products/popcharx/index.html`) both provide pop-up windows, accessible from the menu bar, that show all the possible characters in a chosen font (Figure 7.10). You can click on a character to have it copied to the clipboard, or even have it typed in the active application.

NOTE Mac OS X also includes its own character palette that lets you choose a character from any font. I talked about this palette in Chapter 2, when I discussed the Input Menu tab of International preferences.

FIGURE 7.10: CharView lets you quickly pick and type any character in any font

Keychain Access

Keychain Access lets you edit, manage, and control your Mac OS X Keychain and any passwords or notes stored in the Keychain. If you have no idea what your Keychain is, you're not alone—this is another one of those underused and even less understood parts of OS X. I'll tell you all about it in Chapter 13.

NetInfo Manager

NetInfo Manager lets you edit and manage NetInfo databases. I covered NetInfo databases and NetInfo Manager in depth in Chapter 1, and we'll actually work more with both of them in the chapters to come.

Network Utility

Network Utility is a fairly comprehensive application that allows you to monitor many facets of network traffic and Internet connectivity. The Ping tab is useful for verifying network connections: Enter a known site or server and click Ping; if you get a response, you can communicate with that computer.

Print Center

Print Center is, well, the center of printing in Mac OS X—where you manage printers and print jobs. I'll talk more about Print Center in Chapter 13, "Printing Practicalities."

Process Viewer

Process Viewer is a utility that shows currently running processes, provides information about each, and (using the Processes menu) allows you to quit or force quit them. (I'll talk about force quitting applications later in the chapter when I talk about frozen applications.) By default, it shows you every running process, along with the user that started each process (the current user's username for user-level processes, root for system-level processes); the status (running or idle) of each process; the current percentage of CPU time being used by each process; and the amount of memory being used by each process. You can sort the process listing by any of these values by clicking on the appropriate column head (the triangle symbol to the right of the column heads reverses the sort order). This can be quite useful for monitoring which applications are bogging down your CPU or hogging lots of memory. You can also choose to view only user-level or only root-level processes using the Show pop-up menu.

You can use the Find field to quickly find a particular process. If you click on the disclosure triangle next to More Info (at the bottom of the window), you can get detailed info on a selected process, such as the process ID and the parent process ID (if the process was launched by another process). For example, the parent process ID for the service *syslogd* (ID 1) tells you that it was launched by Mac OX's boot initialization routine.

Finally, you can change the refresh rate (how often Process Viewer refreshes the information on each process) using the "Sample every *x* seconds" box.

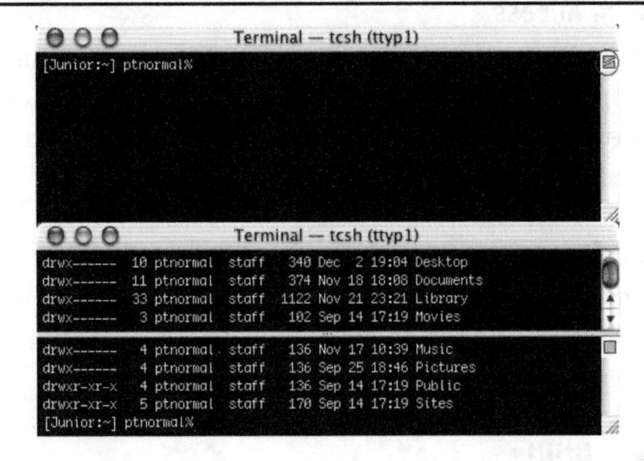

FIGURE 7.11: Split-screen mode in Terminal: the split-screen button (top) and split-screen mode (bottom)

NOTE Classic applications will not be listed in Process Viewer; only the Classic Environment itself will be visible (as "TruBlueEnvironme"). To see a listing of Classic processes, open the Classic pane of System Preferences and select the Memory/Versions tab.

Terminal

Terminal provides an interface for Mac OS X's command-line interface. We've already talked about Terminal many times in the book, and you've probably used it several times as you followed along with the examples I've provided. I'll talk more about Terminal and its various settings and functionality in Chapter 15; however, here are a couple tips you may find useful if you end up using Terminal regularly.

Splitting the Difference: Split Windows in Terminal

If you ever find yourself scrolling up and down in Terminal because you want to see something a few pages back in the buffer, while at the same time trying to type in a command, you'll love Terminal's split-screen mode. In the upper-right corner of any open Terminal window, just above the vertical scroll column, you'll see an icon that looks like a square that's been torn in two (circled in the upper-right corner in Figure 7.11). Click it and the window will be split in two. The bottom section will always show the command prompt, while you can scroll through the buffer in the top section. You can click on the divider and drag it up or down to change the relative sizes of the two sections.

Saving Custom Window Settings and Commands

In the Window Settings… dialog, also known as the Terminal Inspector (accessible via the Terminal application menu), you can set your preferred window settings, including colors, dimensions, display font and styles, buffer size, and window processes for the frontmost window. At the bottom of the window is a "Use Settings as Defaults" button that you can use to set the current preferences as the defaults for all new windows. However, if you tend to use different groups of settings, you can save each group individually. To do this, open a window, resize it to your preferred size, then select your settings from the Window Settings… dialog, and then close the Terminal Inspector. Then choose File ➢ Save As…, choose Main Window from the "What to save" pop-up menu, and save the Terminal window in a convenient location (it will automatically be saved with a `.term` file extension). You can even choose to have your saved Terminal window open automatically when Terminal starts up by checking the box in the Save dialog.

TIP One of my favorite Terminal window preferences is transparency, accessible by choosing Color from the Terminal Inspector window's pop-up menu. By increasing the transparency, you can view windows and files hidden behind the Terminal window. This can be extremely helpful when you're trying to view the spelling of a file or directory, or when you're trying to follow a tutorial from a website.

When you want to use these saved window settings, double-click on the saved Terminal file, or choose File ➢ Open… from within Terminal and select the saved Terminal file. You can use this procedure to save as many different groups of Terminal window settings as you like.

Note that if you want this saved Terminal file to automatically execute a specific command when opened, you can edit the file using a text editor such as TextEdit or BBEdit. Scroll to the end of the file, and insert the following text before the final `</dict>`:

```
<key>ExecutionString</key>
<string>command</string>
```

For example, you could type **`sudo -s`** to give yourself root access whenever this Terminal window is opened (you'd still need to provide your admin password), or **`ssh`** ***`username@serveraddress`*** to automatically connect to a remote server via SSH.

Basic Application Troubleshooting

There are many things that can go wrong with applications; although I generally shy away from troubleshooting information in the book, I'm going to briefly talk about the two most common application problems: freezes and corrupt preference files.

Dealing with Application Freezes

If an application crashes, it will usually quit automatically; you can generally just relaunch it and get back to work. However, sometimes the offending application won't quit—it will just sit there, unresponsive. In this scenario, the only way to get the application to quit is using a *force quit*. Whereas a standard quit (one you, as the user, initiate) allows you to save documents and allows the OS to elegantly stop the application, a force quit simply kills the application on the spot. You don't get to save any open documents, and any preferences you may have set during that session may not get written to the preference file. A force quit isn't graceful, but if it's the only way to quit a misbehaving app, it's quite useful.

You can force quit an application using three methods:

Force Quit from the Apple Menu If you select Force Quit… from the Apple Menu (or press command+option+escape), you're presented with the Force Quit window (Figure 7.12). By selecting an application and then clicking Force Quit, the application will be quit immediately (you'll get a dialog asking if you're sure). If an application is frozen (crashed but won't respond), it will generally be listed in red type in the Force Quit window.

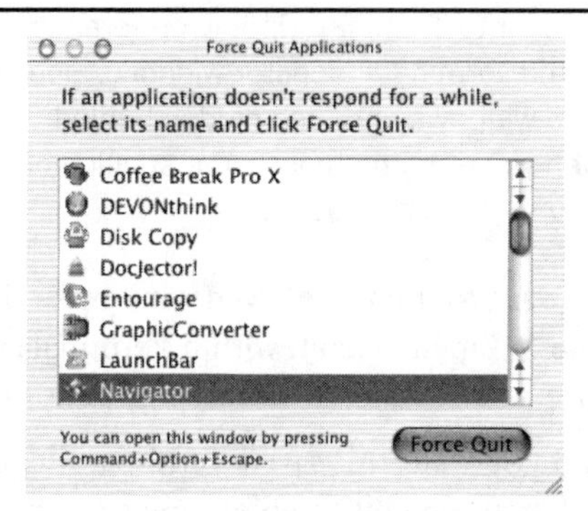

FIGURE 7.12: The Force Quit window

TIP You can quickly exit the Force Quit window by pressing the escape key, regardless of whether or not you have actually force quit an application.

Force Quit from the Dock I mentioned in the previous chapter that you can quit an application from its Dock menu (control/right-click on the application's Dock icon to access its Dock menu). If you press the option key while accessing the app's Dock menu, "Quit" changes to "Force Quit." Selecting this option is identical to using the Force Quit window. Note that if an application is frozen, sometimes you won't even need to hold down the option key; Force Quit may appear in the application's Dock menu automatically.

NOTE Because of the way memory protection does and doesn't work inside the Classic Environment, force quitting a Classic application will usually quit the entire Classic Environment and all other Classic applications.

Force Quit Using Process Viewer If you launch the Process Viewer utility (`/Applications/Utilities/Process Viewer`), you get a listing of all running processes (Figure 7.13). To quit an application, select it from the list of running processes (you can use the Find field to find it quickly if you know its name), and then choose Processes ➢ Quit Process. You'll be presented with a dialog asking if you want to Quit or Force Quit the application; in our scenario, you'd want to force quit. You'll notice that Process Viewer lists many more processes than the Force Quit window; the latter only lists standard applications that are visible in the Dock, whereas

Process Viewer lists all running processes, including background applications and system processes.

NOTE You can also force an application or process to quit using Terminal; I'll talk about that in Chapter 15.

Dealing with Bad Preference Files

A corrupt preference file can cause its corresponding application to misbehave; this is one of the most common causes of application problems in OS X. Why a preference file goes bad—a previous application crash, hard drive problems, etc.—isn't as important as what to do when it happens.

As I mentioned in Chapter 2, preference files are stored in `/Library/Preferences` (for system-wide preferences) and `~/Library/Preferences` (for user-level preferences), and generally have the name of the application in the filename. For example, `com.apple.TextEdit.plist` is the preference file for TextEdit. If you're having continual problems with a particular application, its preference file should be the primary suspect. Locate its preference file in the Preferences folder (you can use the Search field from a Finder window toolbar as described in Chapter 5 to find it quickly), and then drag it to the Desktop. Launch the application; if the problems are gone, you know the preference file you moved to the Desktop was the culprit, so you can delete it permanently (a new one was created when you launched the application). If the problems still exist, the preference file wasn't the cause (you can quit the application and replace the original preference file).

NOTE Note that preference files in the main `/Library` folder can only be deleted by an admin user.

FIGURE 7.13: Selecting a process to quit using Process Viewer

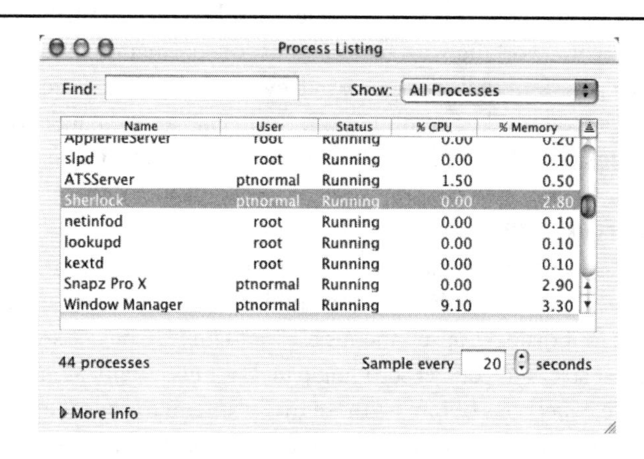

Text Testimonials: Working with Text in OS X

OK, so this section isn't really about applications, per se. However, much of what you do on your computer (e-mail, word processing, text editing, etc.) is text-related, and Mac OS X offers some helpful and unique ways to deal with text, so I decided that the topic deserved some mention of its own. I'm going to start by talking about tips that work only in Cocoa and some Carbon applications, and then move on to solutions that work in all applications.

Cocoa/Carbon Text Tips

Earlier in the chapter, when I talked about the various types of applications in Mac OS X, I mentioned that Cocoa applications could take advantage of all of the special application goodies in Mac OS X. I also mentioned that *some* Carbon applications, if the developer chose to do so, can also take advantage of these features. Here are some of the features I was talking about; Cocoa applications, such as iChat, Mail, TextEdit, and Stickies, as well as third-party Cocoa applications, can take full advantage of them; Carbon applications can use them as well, as long as their developers have included the necessary support.

Copy and Paste Formatting

If you've used Microsoft Word for word processing, you're probably familiar with its ability to copy and paste formatting, which can be very useful when you want one block of text to look like another. Cocoa applications *all* have this ability built in, and you can even copy text formatting from one Cocoa application and paste that formatting onto text in another. In most Cocoa applications, this feature is located at Format ➢ Font ➢ Copy/Paste Font.

Cocoa Keyboard Shortcuts

Applications generally have their own keyboard shortcuts for menu items and other frequently used commands; however, all Cocoa applications share a set of keyboard shortcuts that are used when working with text. The list of commands is much too long to include here, but if you open Terminal and type **`bindkey`** <RETURN> you'll see the entire list. Ignore the quotation marks around a key combination; the `^ character` stands for the control key. For example, typing control+T will transpose the characters to the left and right of the cursor.

The Fonts Panel

Accessible from any Cocoa application (and some Carbon apps) via Format ➢ Fonts ➢ Show Fonts, OS X's Fonts Panel is incredibly useful. If you resize it to its smallest size, you get the most basic font dialog: pop-up menus for font family, typeface style, size, and extras. Resize it to its largest size, and you get scrolling panels for each item, along with a Collections panel (you can create collections of fonts—those that you tend to use together—for quick access). In addition, if you select Show Preview from the Extras… pop-up, you get a small preview area that shows you the font, font style, and font size you've selected, along with a preview of your selection.

TIP You can change the preview text by double-clicking in the preview panel and typing your own text. If the preview text is too big to fit in the current preview area, click and hold on the area just below the preview area; you can drag downwards (or upwards) to resize it.

What makes the Fonts Panel especially useful is that it's a floating window, meaning you can keep it open all the time; when you want to use a different font, you just select it from the panel. (If you want to apply a font to a certain section of text, highlight the text and choose the font and style.)

You can also customize other parts of the Fonts Panel. By selecting Edit Sizes… from the Extras… pop-up, you can add or remove font sizes, and choose to view font sizes as a list, a slider, or both. To create your own collections of fonts, select Edit Collections… from the Extras… menu. Click the + button to add a new collection, or select an existing collection to rename or remove it using the - or Rename buttons. You can add or remove fonts to or from collections using the arrow buttons. You can also take advantage of the Favorites collection: add a favorite font style by choosing Add to Favorites from the Extras… pop-up; remove it by selecting it in the Favorites view and choosing Remove from Favorites.

TIP You can also access Mac OS X's Character and Color palettes from the Extras… pop-up menu.

Spell-Check

All Cocoa applications can use Mac OS X's built-in spell checker, available from the Edit menu. Some, such as TextEdit, even allow you to enable on-the-fly spell-checking—if a word is misspelled, it will be underlined in red within the document. You can control/right-click on a misspelled word to choose the correct spelling from a list of suggestions, or choose to ignore the word or add it to Mac OS X's dictionary so that it won't be flagged in the future.

Find and Replace

The Find dialog in Cocoa applications also allows you to replace found text with other text. This kind of functionality is most likely old hat to most users, as it has been around in Word and other word processors for years. However, one stumbling block in Find/Replace dialogs has always been how to find (or use in replacement text) characters such as returns and tabs (since the return key usually starts the find, and the tab key usually moves between fields in the find dialog box). To insert a return into a text field, press option+return; to insert a tab, press option+tab.

Services

Services, available from *Application Name* ➢ Services, provide some of the coolest features of Cocoa applications, but (seeing a pattern here?) most people don't even realize they exist. Or, because the Services menu item always exists, but only works in Cocoa or certain Carbon applications, many people think that Services are "broken" or don't work properly.

What are Services? They're one of those things that are harder to explain than they are to use. (That's my disclaimer, by the way, if the next few sentences are a bit hard to grasp.) Basically, Mac OS X allows applications and the system to provide services to *other* applications from *within* those applications. For example, you can select text in one application, and then send it to another application to work with it. In some cases you can even use the functionality of another application without leaving the one you're currently working in.

Perhaps an example will make this a bit clearer. In writing this book, I used a database program called DEVONthink to keep track of notes and tidbits of information that I might include in the book. I also spent a good deal of time reading the ReadMe files that come with shareware, freeware, and commercial software. In doing so, I often found useful information about an application that I wanted to remember for later. I could have selected the text from within TextEdit, copied it, switched to DEVONthink, created a new note, and then pasted the text into the note. However, with Services, I could simply highlight the text in TextEdit and then, from within TextEdit, use the DEVONthink service to automatically transfer the text to a new DEVONthink note (Figure 7.14—my Services menu will probably look different than yours, depending on what applications you have installed). What took five steps without Services took two steps with them. I also used this technique quite frequently when browsing Apple's online documentation; many web browsers also support Services, so you can select text in a browser window and then use Services to send the text to TextEdit or any other application that provides a Service.

FIGURE 7.14: Using Services to transfer text from TextEdit to a new note in DEVONthink

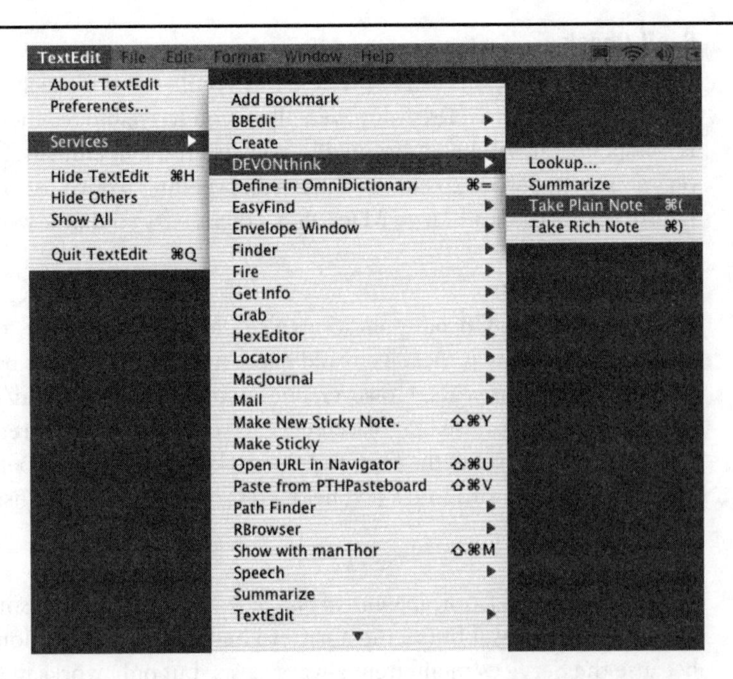

NOTE Services aren't limited to text, by any means; in fact, they're also supported by the Finder for working with files and folders. However, the vast majority of services are used for working with text, so I've included the discussion of them here.

Summarizing Text

One of the most interesting Services provided by Mac OS X is the Summarize Service. Select a block of text in a supported application, and then choose *Application Name* ➢ Services ➢ Summarize. A new window will open in the Summary Service that will automatically summarize the selected text (Figure 7.15). Using the Summary Size slider, you can choose how compact you want the summary to be (100% gives you the original text, 1%—which is only really 1% if you have a *lot* of text—gives you the smallest summary the Summary Service thinks can be used and still be meaningful.

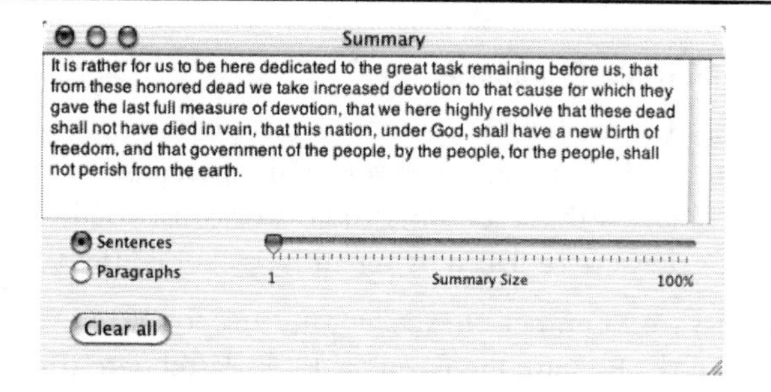

FIGURE 7.15: Using the Summarize Service, it's possible to make the Gettysburg Address even shorter

TIP If the Summarize Service sounds useful to you, but you spend most of your time working in applications that don't take advantage of Services, the contextual menu plug-in Abstracter (`http://www.mercury-soft.com/`) provides similar functionality to all applications.

Installing New Services

Many applications install their own Services the first time they run (or when they are themselves installed). However, some excellent third-party Services aren't provided by an application—they work on their own, and their only interface is the Services sub-menu. (You can find some by doing a search for "service" at `http://www.versiontracker.com/macosx/` or `http://macupdate.com/`.) These Services are installed much like many other system add-ons: place them in `~/Library/Services` (for use by the current user only) or `/Library/Services` (for use by all users). After installing a new Service, you need to log out and then back in to be able to use it.

Some examples of useful third-party standalone Services are WordService (`http://home.arcor-online.de/grunenberg/`), which provides a number of text formatting, conversion, and statistical functions; CalcService (from the same developer), which allows you to type a numerical expression and have it be replaced by the result of that expression; Terminal Services (http://homepage.mac.com/stas/terminalservices.html), which allows you to select text and have it executed as a command in Terminal; and NetService (http://www.dekorte.com/Software/OSX/NetService/), which allows you to perform a number of Internet-based searches on highlighted text—Web, map, Usenet, dictionary, Yellow Pages, and even the eBay auction site.

TIP Many Services (standard and third-party) are also accessible using keyboard shortcuts. These shortcuts are generally listed next to the Service name in the Services sub-menu.

Other Text Tips

If your favorite text-oriented application isn't a Cocoa app, or a compatible Carbon app, don't worry; there are still a number of great utilities out there to help you work faster and more efficiently. (All of these tips work in Cocoa applications, as well.)

Using Multiple Clipboards

The Mac OS has long had a universal clipboard—copy or cut text (or graphics) from one application or document, and you could then paste it into any other application or document. The problem is that each time you cut or copy, you lose the previous contents of the clipboard as they are replaced by the most recent content.

There are a number of excellent utilities for Mac OS X that provide *multiple* clipboards. Three of the best are the freeware PTHPasteboard (http://www.pth.com/PTHPasteboard/), and the shareware CopyPaste-X (http://www.copypaste-x.com/) and Keyboard Maestro (http://www.keyboardmaestro.com/). You can't go wrong with any of these utilities; however, they each take a different approach. PTHPasteboard is the one I use most frequently, mainly because I find it to be the simplest to use (although it has some great advanced features if you want to go beyond the basics). It keeps track of a user-defined number of recently used clipboard contents (it refers to them as "buffers") in a *pasteboard* window. You can paste the most recent ten clipboards at any time via keystrokes, with all clipboards available by revealing the pasteboard window. (If you use the pasteboard window often, you can even choose to have it always shown.) To paste a clipboard buffer into the frontmost application—including any styles and formatting—you simply press the number of the buffer you want to use, or click the buffer with your mouse (Figure 7.16).

In addition to the clipboard history pasteboard, PTHPasteboard also lets you create multiple *custom* pasteboards, each with multiple buffers, that store frequently used text or graphics. For example, I have one custom pasteboard that holds HTML tags, another that stores personal information such my home and work addresses, phone numbers, e-mail addresses, etc., and another one that stores e-mail signatures. I can access these pasteboards at any time with a keystroke, and then press a buffer number or click on a buffer to paste its contents. Finally, PTHPasteboard also operates as a Service, making it accessible via the Services sub-menu.

FIGURE 7.16:

PTHPasteboard's multiple clipboards

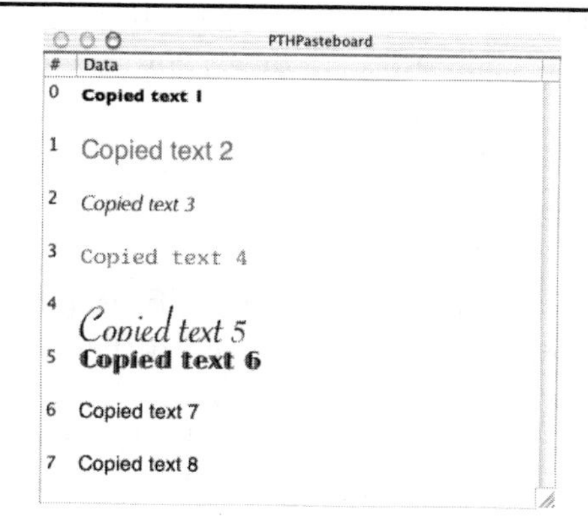

Having Your Computer Type for You

If you're like me, there are lots of things you type over and over again, such as the date, your name and address, your phone number, an e-mail signature (or several), and—for those of us who answer a lot of computer questions—even "stock" responses to common questions. Here are a few ways you can automate such typing.

Text Completion/Shortcuts

If you're the type of person who can remember key combinations and abbreviations, you'll love the shareware TypeIt4Me (`http://www.typeit4me.com/`). Once installed, you can set up shortcuts to frequently typed text that can be invoked from within any text field or document, and are triggered by your choice of keyboard commands. For example, the default TypeIt4Me trigger is the space bar; you can set up a shortcut whereby the letters *addy* stand for your home address. As you're typing in a document, type *addy* followed by a space, and TypeIt4Me automatically replaces *addy* with your full address as you keep merrily typing along. TypeIt4Me also includes several date and time shortcuts to quickly enter the date, the time, or both. The advantage of TypeIt4Me over other utilities is that if you can remember all of your shortcuts, it's amazingly fast and you never have to take your hands off the keyboard. The disadvantage is that you have to remember which combination(s) of characters are shortcuts for what text. If, like me, you tend to forget such things, you'll appreciate what I call "text typers."

"Type" Frequently Used Text

There are several utilities out there that I call "text typers"; these utilities will store various bits of text—words, sentences, or even multiple paragraphs—and type or paste them into a text field or document on your command. This may sound like exactly what TypeIt4Me does, but the difference is that for these utilities you don't have to remember any shortcuts; you press a key or click on a Dock icon, and you get a list of your stored text blurbs to choose from. The process takes a couple more steps, but you don't have to worry about remembering (or forgetting) the shortcuts.

I just mentioned PTHPasteboard, Keyboard Maestro, and CopyPaste-X (when I talked about multiple clipboards). All three allow you to save clipboards permanently, providing you with a quick and easy way to access frequently used text. You simply copy the text to PTH-PasteBoard, Keyboard Maestro, or CopyPaste-X, then when you want to paste it into a document, you use a keyboard shortcut to bring the utility to the front and then select which clipboard you want to paste.

But the text typer I use most often is Typist (`http://www.selznick.com/products/typist/index.htm`). Typist resides in the Dock and lets me create any number of text entries (including date/time templates). When I want to type one of those bits of text into a document I simply control/right-click on the Typist icon in the Dock, and a menu of my text bits appears (Figure 7.17). Selecting one of these items types it into the document. (If you're a keyboard lover, you can also assign a hotkey to Typist that brings up a list of shortcuts; use the cursor to select one and hit return to type it.)

FIGURE 7.17:

Typist's Dock menu lists the available text bits it can type

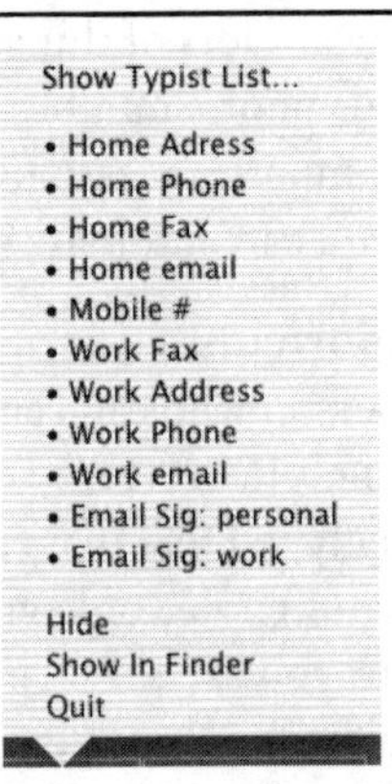

Write in Ink

In Mac OS X 10.2, Apple added a new feature to the OS called *Ink*. Using a supported graphics tablet, you can print text on the tablet and OS X will convert it and insert it into the current application. If you draw a picture or sketch using the stylus, Ink will convert it to a graphic and allow you to open it or paste it into any graphics application. You can also select menu items and "press" keyboard shortcuts using the stylus and graphics tablet. You can enable/disable Ink via the Ink pane of System Preferences (which only appears if a compatible graphics tablet is connected).

At the time of this writing, Ink only supports a few tablets from a single manufacturer (Wacom), and has a few glitches when interacting with applications. As a result, it is not yet widely used. I expect this will change as more and more tablets are supported and more and more users take advantage of the possibilities Ink provides.

Voice Recognition Software

In addition to the kinds of utilities I just described that you use via the mouse and keyboard, a couple of utilities allow you to dictate via a microphone and have your voice transcribed into text that can be entered into any application. ViaVoice (`http://www-3.ibm.com/software/speech/mac/index.shtml`) and iListen (`http://www.macspeech.com/products/iListen.html`) are the Mac OS X options available at the time of this writing. I haven't used either product, but both have received good reviews.

Taking Advantage of Clippings

The Mac OS has had text *clipping* files for years, and Mac OS X maintains this functionality. Highlight a block of text in almost any application, and you can then click and drag that text into a text field or document (in the same or another application). You can also drag the text to the Desktop or any Finder window to create a text clipping; the clipping's name will include the first few words of its contents. Double-clicking on a clipping file opens it in a window showing its contents; dragging the clipping to a text field or document pastes its contents at the location where you drop it.

Clippings are actually another way you can access frequently typed text. You can create clipping files of such text and then store those clippings in a folder or on the Desktop; you can then drag them into a document whenever you need a certain snippet of text. I personally use XShelf, mentioned in Chapter 5, to store a few frequently used clippings in a floating shelf that is accessible from within any application.

TIP There are two drawbacks to clipping files. The first is that unlike clippings in OS 9, you cannot copy their contents without first dragging them into another document. Second, you cannot edit their contents. If you tend to use clippings often and want to be able to edit them and copy them, the shareware application clipEdit (`http://www.everydaysoftware.net/clipedit/index.html`) allows you to do both, as well as to create new clippings without any dragging.

Cleaning Up Messy Text

You've surely been in this situation before: someone sends you an e-mail with text that you need to use, but it's full of e-mail quote marks (the > symbol), carriage returns, and unnecessary spaces. Or perhaps you've copied text from a web page or PDF file, and it's simply a mess. Chances are you either spend a good deal of time cleaning up the text, or you just say "forget it" and use it as is. If so, you should definitely give textSOAP (`http://www.unmarked.com/`) or TextSpresso (`http://www.taylor-design.com/`) a try.

Both utilities allow you to paste text into their "cleaning" window (or open a text file from within the application) and apply one of any number of text cleaning operations (textSOAP calls them "cleaners," TextSpresso calls them "filters"), from removing quote marks and extra spaces and carriage returns, to finding/replacing text strings, to stripping extraneous HTML tags that may have found their way into your text. In addition to cleaning up messy text, both utilities allow you to customize text in myriad ways automatically, using many different preconfigured cleaners/filters. You can also create your own cleaners/filters based on your own needs.

TextSpresso has a unique feature that allows you to batch clean a number of text files at once, and includes an amazing number of filters (over 200!) that perform specific combinations of tasks. For example, a set of HTML-specific filters provide the kinds of cleaning tasks you would be most likely to use on HTML files. It is also much more customizable. However, I still find myself using textSOAP more often, mainly because of the fact that it can operate as a Service. This means that if I have text in TextEdit, Mail, or any other Services-aware application, I can select that text and then choose *Application Name* ➢ Services ➢ textSOAP ➢ *cleaner name* and textSOAP will "clean" my text right there in the application.

Moving On...

I hope by now you're a more proficient user of OS X applications (especially the ones you didn't know much about before). But if you still have some older OS 9 applications that you need or want to use, you're also going to spend a good amount of time using OS X's Classic Environment. In the next chapter I'll show you how to make the best of that time (and of your Classic apps).

CHAPTER 8

Clobbering Classic

(Or: If you have to use the Classic Environment, how to make the best of it.)

If OS X is your first experience with a Mac, most, if not all, of your software was made for, or adapted to, Mac OS X. However, if you previously used OS 9 or earlier, you most likely have a good amount of software that isn't OS X – native. Luckily, Apple has provided a way for you to use such software under OS X, called the *Classic Environment*. In this chapter, I'm going to talk about using the Classic Environment and Classic applications, as well as some tips on how to make using both as painless as possible.

In addition to the information included in this chapter, if you're just now making the transition to OS X from OS 9 or earlier, or if you use both frequently, I've included a comparative discussion of OS X versus OS 9, and tips for working with the two, in Appendix A, "A Tale of Two Systems." If you long for some of the features of OS 9 that aren't a part of OS X, I'll show you how to get them; if you boot your Mac in both OS 9 *and* OS X, I'll show you how to make switching back and forth as smooth as possible.

NOTE All of the tips and procedures in this chapter are for any user level, affect only that individual user, and do not require Terminal. Because of this, you won't see the familiar tip table.

A Quick Primer on the Classic Environment

Mac OS X is a Unix-based operating system that offers advanced features such as protected memory, preemptive multitasking, dynamic RAM allocation, full multithreading, symmetrical multiprocessing, and a microkernel architecture. These are features not found in Mac OS 9 (which is why OS X is the "new and improved" Mac OS). If these terms don't make a lot of sense to you, that's OK;

what's important is to understand that because of its Unix base, Mac OS X is a completely different operating system than the "Classic" Mac OS.

Although these features are all dramatic steps forward in terms of performance and stability, one consequence is that applications written specifically for Mac OS 9 and earlier (Classic applications) are not compatible with Mac OS X, and those written specifically for OS X (Cocoa applications) do not run in OS 9.

NOTE I talked about the various types of Mac OS applications—Classic, Carbon, and Cocoa—in Chapter 7, "Apple-ication Aptitude."

This incompatibility presented a problem for Apple: When Mac OS X was first released, existing Mac users had a lot of Classic software that wouldn't run under OS X. Realizing that that people would be extremely reluctant to switch to Mac OS X if it meant having to dump all their existing software and start over (not to mention that such a dramatic change wouldn't have been much different than switching to Windows!), Apple came up with two solutions. The first was Carbon applications; as I explained in Chapter 7, Classic applications can be *Carbonized*, which means they can be partially rewritten to work in both OS X and OS 9. The major drawbacks to Carbonizing applications are that (1) they tend to be quite inconsistent in the extent to which they take advantage of Mac OS X features; and (2) for an application to be Carbonized, the developer has to undertake the effort (or hand the code over to a third party). For many (if not *most*) Classic software packages, developers are unwilling to do so, will not do so immediately, or are no longer even around.

The second solution is the Classic Environment. What the Classic Environment *is* is a bit difficult to explain (but I'll give it a try in a moment). What the Classic Environment *does*, quite simply, is allow you to run Classic applications from within Mac OS X. When the Classic Environment is running, you can launch most Classic applications and they'll run just as if they were launched in Mac OS 9. In addition, these applications will appear in the Dock just as Mac OS X applications do. If you're interested in the nitty-gritty behind Classic, the next section will give you a better idea of what's going on.

NOTE I'll be using a few terms in this chapter that can get confusing, so I want to lay them out here. When I talk about the *Classic Mac OS*, I'm referring to versions of the Mac OS prior to OS X (usually, OS 9). *Classic Environment* and *Classic* refer to the Classic Environment in OS X. *Classic applications* are those applications that are/were written specifically for OS 9 or earlier. Finally, if I mention the *Classic System Folder*, I'm talking about the copy of Mac OS 9 that is currently being used by the Classic Environment.

Classic Technical Details

From Mac OS X's point of view, Classic is simply an application (located at `/System/Library/CoreServices/Classic Startup`), just like Mail, Internet Explorer, and iPhoto. However, instead of being a visible application that shows up in the Dock and has its own menus, Classic runs in the background and provides a *hardware abstraction layer*, on top of which a full copy of Mac OS 9, located in a Mac OS 9 System Folder on your hard drive, is loaded. Classic applications then run *within* this copy of Mac OS 9, just as if the computer had booted into OS 9. Almost any application that is compatible with Mac OS 9.1 or later is compatible with Classic (Classic requires a System Folder with Mac OS 9.1 or later in OS X 10.1, and OS 9.2 or later in OS X 10.2).

NOTE A *hardware abstraction layer* is software that provides, and controls, access to a hardware device or system. Since you can't boot into two operating systems at the same time, the Classic application in Mac OS X provides a hardware abstraction layer, on top of which Mac OS 9 can run. As an example of how this works, when a Classic application accesses the Ethernet port on your Mac, what's really happening is that the Classic application is accessing the "Ethernet port" of Classic, which is then tunneled through Mac OS X to the actual Ethernet port.

Of course, this means that in order for Classic to function, a copy of Mac OS 9 must be installed on your Mac. If you install Mac OS X on a Mac that was previously running OS 9, that copy of OS 9 can be used for Classic; if your Mac came with Mac OS X pre-installed, you also have a copy of OS 9 pre-installed for use by Classic. (You can actually have more than one copy of OS 9 installed and decide yourself which one to use; I'll talk a bit about that when I discuss Classic preferences.)

Classic Support and Limitations

Because the Classic Environment loads a full version of Mac OS 9, it supports most of the same hardware, protocols, and input/output devices that would be supported if you actually booted into OS 9 on the same computer. However, since all communication between Classic and your computer's hardware has to go through Mac OS X, there are some limitations. For example, if Mac OS X does not support a port or a type of hardware, neither will Classic, and thus Classic applications running in Classic will not be able to access that port or hardware. In addition, some types of hardware that are supported by OS X are not available to Classic applications at all (e.g., internal modems). Below is a list of things that Classic does and does not support.

Supported

- USB
- FireWire
- Ethernet
- IDE
- SCSI
- PCI or PC expansion cards supported by Mac OS X
- Built-in audio/sound
- Built-in video

- Disk images
- Built-in ADB ports, but *only* for the primary keyboard and mouse—and an application crash may require you to restart Classic to regain the use of ADB.

NOTE Interestingly enough, the Classic Environment can sometimes support hardware that isn't officially supported by Mac OS X. For example, if a printer has drivers for OS 9, but not for OS X, you can often print to it from within Classic. I talk about how to use this capability to your advantage in Chapter 12.

Unsupported

- Built-in serial ports
- Infrared ports
- LocalTalk
- Internal floppy drives (however, external USB floppy are supported)
- PCI or PC expansion cards that are not supported by Mac OS X
- Modem-based applications (AOL, Z-term, and most fax software) cannot access your Mac's internal modem from within Classic. All network connections, including PPP connections, must be initiated under OS X and then funneled to Classic applications.

Pros and Cons of the Classic Environment

Overall the Classic Environment is fairly seamless; you simply launch your Classic applications and use them like any OS X application. You'll notice a few cosmetic differences in things like menus and Open/Save dialogs—which I'll talk about shortly—but other than that a Classic application runs just as it would under OS 9.

However, there are a few caveats to using Classic applications. First, Classic applications will run more slowly in Classic than if they were running on a computer booted into Mac OS 9. The reason for this should be clear: in OS X, a Classic application runs on top of OS 9, which runs inside Classic, which in turn runs on top OS X. These extra layers inevitably slow down the application's performance. The degree of this performance degradation varies, and seems to be reduced with each new update to Mac OS X, but it's there. Second, the fact that these extra layers exist means more chances for things to go wrong. You'll probably find that Classic applications are a bit less stable in Classic than they are when booted into Mac OS 9.

Finally, the advanced features provided by Mac OS X—the ones I mentioned at the beginning of this chapter—aren't available to Classic applications. The Classic Environment, as a Mac OS X application, benefits from protected memory and preemptive multitasking, but Classic applications running *within* the Classic Environment do not. They behave just like applications running in Mac OS 9. For example, if a Mac OS X application crashes, you can generally go right on working in other applications; however, if a Classic application crashes, it will often crash the entire Classic Environment (just as a Mac OS 9 application crash would often force you to restart your Mac).

Updating Classic System Software

Just as Apple releases updates to Mac OS X, updates to Mac OS 9 are periodically available. In Mac OS X 10.1, you could use the OS 9 Software Update control panel from *within* Classic to download an install the latest OS 9 updates. However, as of OS X 10.2, Apple has removed this functionality—running the Software Update control panel in Classic tells you that your OS 9 software is up to date regardless of whether it actually is or is not.

Under OS X 10.2 and later, at the time of this writing, you have to reboot into Mac OS 9 and use the OS 9 Software Update control panel to download and install any updates to OS 9. The problem with this approach is that Apple has recently begun releasing Macs that can no longer boot into OS 9. As a result, I suspect that you'll soon be able to update the copy of OS 9 used by the Classic Environment via OS X's Software Update.

The Classic System Preferences

User Level: any
Affects: individual user
Terminal: no

Using the Classic Environment is generally pretty simple, and doesn't require a lot of tweaking and twiddling. However, the Classic Environment does have a few of its own settings, as well as a few tools for monitoring it. These are found in the Classic pane of System Preferences.

The Start/Stop Tab (and How to Start Classic)

The general preferences for the Classic Environment are located in the Start/Stop tab; for most uses, this is the only tab you'll need to worry about. As I explained earlier, when you launch Classic, it loads an entire iteration of Mac OS 9. (In fact, when the Classic launch screen appears, if you click the triangle next to "Show Mac OS 9 desktop window," you'll see what looks like a Mac OS 9 startup screen, complete with the icons of OS 9 extensions as they load.) However, first you need to tell it *which* Mac OS 9 System Folder you want it to use. You do this in the box under "Select a system folder for Classic" (Figure 8.1). Each mounted volume is listed; if a particular volume has a valid Mac OS 9 System Folder installed, it is selectable. If a volume has more than one OS 9 System Folder installed, click the disclosure triangle to the left of the volume name to view them all. Select the desired volume or, if the volume has multiple System Folders, the desired System Folder, and the appropriate System Folder will be used by Classic the next time it is launched.

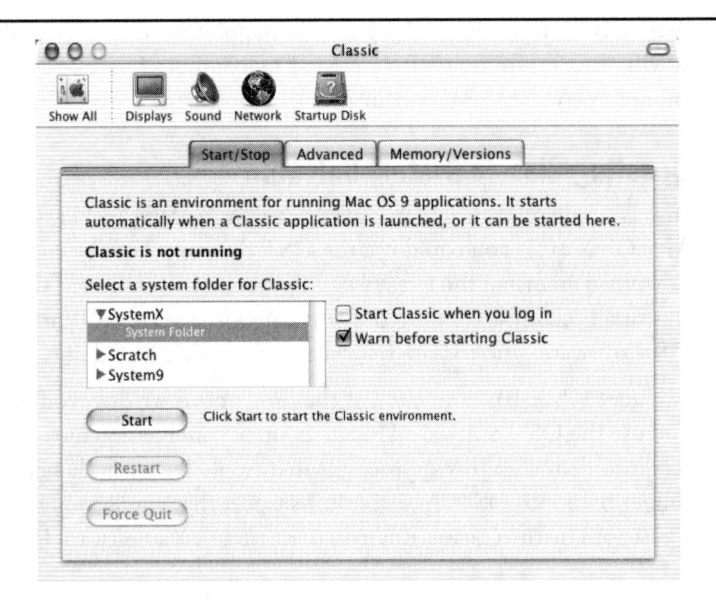

FIGURE 8.1: The Start/Stop pane of Classic preferences

NOTE If for some reason you boot between Mac OS X versions (for example, 10.1 and 10.2), note that once you've used a Mac OS 9 System Folder in Classic under OS X 10.2, it will no longer work under OS X 10.1's Classic Environment. (In general, it's safe to assume that this will apply to newer versions of Classic in Mac OS X, as well—once you use an OS 9 System Folder in a newer version of Classic/Mac OS X, it won't work with older versions.) Thus if you need to switch between versions of Mac OS X, I recommend having a different OS 9 System Folder for each Classic Environment.

TIP If you're having trouble selecting a System Folder or volume for Classic, I've included a few solutions later in the chapter under "Classic Trouble."

In general, there are three ways to launch Classic. The first, and easiest, is to simply launch any Classic application; the Classic Environment will automatically launch and load OS 9, then the application will be launched from within Classic. The second method is to check the "Start Classic when you log in" box in Classic preferences, which automatically launches Classic at login. The third way is to manually click the Start button in Classic preferences, which launches Classic immediately; after it's done loading, you can launch your Classic application(s). Although the first two methods are convenient, at the time of this writing they both seem to generate a fair amount of complaints and reports of problems. Therefore, I recommend that you just launch Classic manually when you need to use it. (A bit later in the chapter, in "Using Classic," I show how to do this from the Dock or using third-party apps so that you don't have to open System Preferences every time you want to use Classic.)

FIGURE 8.2:
The "Warn before starting Classic" dialog

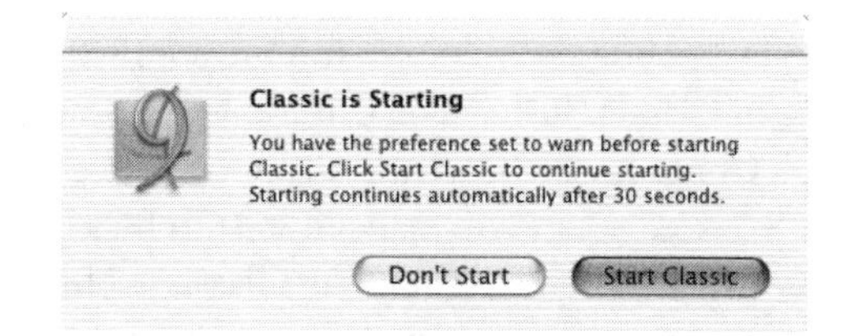

If Classic is running, the Start button changes to Stop. Clicking this button is identical to choosing the Shutdown command in Mac OS 9; all Classic applications will quit (you'll be able to save changes first), and then the Classic Environment will shut down. Likewise, the Restart button functions just like the Restart command in OS 9 (a shutdown followed by an immediate startup). Note that this Shutdown command affects only the Classic Environment, not Mac OS X. The third button, Force Quit, works exactly like the various force quit commands I discussed in Chapter 7, except that it immediately, and ungracefully, quits the Classic Environment and all Classic applications. You would use this command only when the Classic Environment crashes or freezes and you can't use any of your Classic applications. (Keep in mind that you'll lose any unsaved changes in Classic applications.)

The last option in the Start/Stop tab is "Warn before starting Classic." This option, new as of OS X 10.2, will warn you if you launch a Classic application and the Classic Environment isn't already running. If you used earlier versions of Mac OS X, you've probably experienced the frustration of accidentally launching the Classic Environment via inadvertently launching a Classic application (for example, by double-clicking on a document associated with a Classic application). You could click the Stop button in the Classic startup window, but Apple recommended against this. When this option is checked, before Classic is launched, you'll get a dialog asking if you really want it to (Figure 8.2).

The Advanced Tab

The Advanced tab of Classic preferences has a few additional options associated with the Classic environment. These are mainly "set and forget" preferences and options that you would use when troubleshooting.

Startup Options

When booting up your computer under OS 9, you could select several options, such as booting with extensions disabled, opening Extensions Manager, or holding various keys down to invoke other options or third-party utilities. Under Startup Options, you can access the same options when starting up the Classic Environment; just select the corresponding action from the pop-up menu and then click the Start Classic button (or Restart Classic if Classic is currently running). If you choose Use Keyboard Combination, a box will appear allowing you to designate the keys you want to be "pressed" as Classic is launched.

Why would you want to use these options? Remember that Classic loads a full version of Mac OS 9; just as you can have startup file conflicts in OS 9, so too can those kinds of conflicts occur in Classic. Just as you can use Extensions Manager (or similar utilities like Casady & Greene's Conflict Catcher, `http://www.casadyg.com/`) to manage startup files when booting into OS 9, so too can you manage startup files in Classic. (I'll talk more about this later in the chapter when I discuss optimizing Classic.) This option is a one-shot deal—it only affects the single startup or restart initiated by clicking the Start/Restart button in this tab.

The "Use preferences from home folder" option allows each user to have their own preferences for Classic applications. Under pre-10.2 versions of OS X, Classic applications each had a single preference file, shared by all users, located in the Preferences folder of the System Folder used by Classic. Under OS X 10.2 and later, if this option is checked Classic applications store their preferences in each user's `/Library/Classic/Preferences` folder.

NOTE If you have "Use preferences from home folder" enabled, the first time each user launches Classic the following folders will be created in their home directory (under `~/Library/Classic`): Apple Menu Items, Internet Search Sites, Launcher Items, Preferences, Shutdown Items, Startup Items. In addition, if they exist in the Classic System Folder, these folders will also be created in the home directory: Desktop Pictures, Favorites, Keychains, Locations, Shutdown Items (Disabled), Startup Items (Disabled), Volumes. The user will be asked if they want the contents of the corresponding folders in the Classic System Folder to be copied to their home directory. (One consequence of not allowing this copy is that the Chooser will not appear in the Apple Menu, meaning the user won't be able to print from within Classic.)

"Put Classic to sleep when it is inactive for"

When Classic is running, it takes up a good deal of system resources (RAM, CPU time, etc.). You can set the Classic environment to "sleep" after the amount of time you set in this section (provided no Classic applications are running); when Classic is sleeping, it uses virtually no system resources. However, many users have reported problems with Classic when using this option; when waking from sleep, the computer can freeze, or certain hardware functionality (e.g., the USB port) may no longer be accessible from Classic. I recommend setting this option to Never—if you can't spare the RAM, you're probably better off quitting Classic when you aren't using it.

Other Classic Utilities

The Rebuild Desktop button allows you to manually rebuild the Desktop database files used by Classic and Classic applications to associate documents with applications. This database is *only* used by Classic; it will have no affect on Mac OS X.

NOTE The Rebuild Desktop command only rebuilds the Desktop database files for the volume that contains the Classic System Folder. In order to rebuild the Classic Desktop databases for *all* mounted volumes, you need to use a procedure similar to that used in OS 9: use the "Use Keyboard Combination" options, and select command+option as the desired keyboard combination. When Classic has almost finished loading, this will bring up the standard OS 9 dialogs asking you if you want to rebuild the Desktop for each volume. (As a bonus, Classic can rebuild them simultaneously, rather than one at a time as OS 9 generally does it.)

The Memory/Versions Tab

The Memory/Versions tab of Classic preferences doesn't really contain any preferences; it is instead a way to monitor Classic and any running Classic applications. The bottom of the window provides information on the version of Mac OS 9 being used by Classic, the versions of the Classic support files installed in the Mac OS 9 System Folder (discussed below), and the version of the actual Classic Environment application.

The Active Processes box shows any Classic applications currently running, along with their memory usage (Figure 8.3). This is similar to what you would see in the "About this Computer" box in the OS 9 Finder. If you check the "Show background processes" box, you'll also be able to view any background applications running in Classic.

FIGURE 8.3: The Memory/Versions tab of Classic preferences

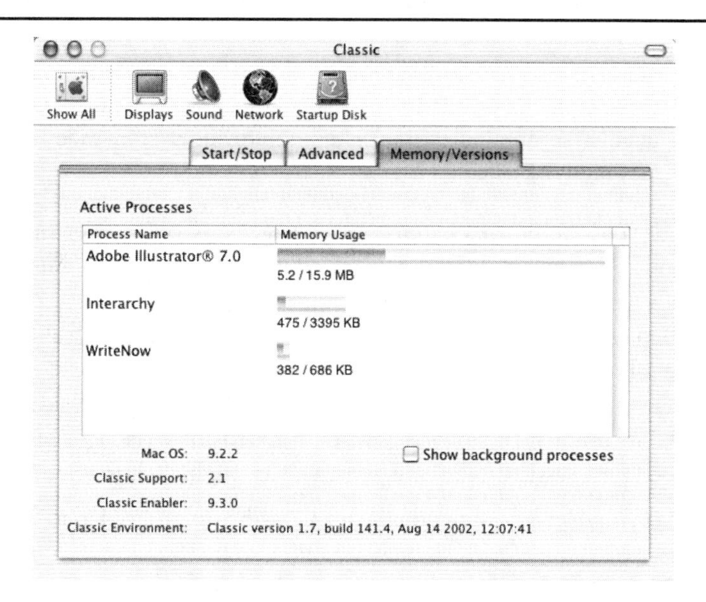

Optimizing Classic

Before I get into using Classic, I want to briefly talk about a few ways in which you can make it work better, faster, and with more stability.

Customize Your System Folder for Classic

As I mentioned when discussing Classic preferences, when Classic loads Mac OS 9, it goes through much of the same startup process that would occur when booting directly into OS 9, including the loading of extensions and control panels. This is great news if some of your Classic applications require specific startup files to function. However, in practice, you probably don't *want* all of the startup files that load when booting into OS 9 to load when starting Classic, for three reasons. First, many extensions and control panels simply don't work in Classic—they don't cause any problems, but they don't provide any functionality, either (for example, control panels that would provide system-wide functionality that is already provided by Mac OS X, such as the Appearance or File Sharing control panels). Second, just as in OS 9, many startup files use RAM, so the more that are loaded at startup, the more RAM Classic will require to run.

Finally, and most importantly, many extensions and control panels either work inconsistently in Classic, or actually cause problems when loaded by OS 9 in Classic. Yes, you read right—startup/extension conflicts are alive and well inside the Classic Environment. So it follows that removing all but the essential startup files from your Classic System Folder will improve stability and possibly even performance.

NOTE Some of the third-party extensions and control panels that cause the most problems with Classic are those that alter the appearance of OS 9 (such as many file-launching or menu utilities), or that patch the system to provide system-wide functionality (such as utilities that affect virtual memory).

If you've ever used Extensions Manager or Conflict Catcher in OS 9 to manage startup files, you know the drill—you're provided with a list of startup files, and you check or uncheck the box next to each to enable or disable it, respectively (Figure 8.4). You can open Extensions Manager or, if installed, Conflict Catcher, from the Control Panels folder in the Classic System Folder (or access it from Apple Menu ➢ Control Panels when a Classic application is active). If you'll be using the same System Folder for Classic and when booting into Mac OS 9, I recommend creating a new set in Extensions Manager or Conflict Catcher that is only used for Classic (I call mine, creatively enough, "Classic Set").

If you decide to slim down your Classic System Folder, first use the list of files I've provided here to figure out which ones are required by Classic itself ("OS 9 Startup Files Required by Classic"). Then install or enable any third-party startup files needed by applications and/or hardware you'll be using in Classic (for example, Microsoft Office 2001 requires certain startup files to function properly).

TIP If you need to install third-party startup files into the Classic System Folder, and those files require an installer, it's often easier to do this when booted into OS 9. Boot into the copy of OS 9 used by Classic (by choosing that System Folder in Startup Disk preferences and restarting), install all of your third-party Classic applications and startup files, and then boot back into Mac OS X. If you're wondering what all the third-party startup files do, so you can make a decision about enabling/disabling them, check out my own guide to the Classic System Folder, InformINIT (`http://www.InformINIT.com/`), or use the file descriptions provided by Casady & Green's Conflict Catcher (`http://www.casadyg.com/`).

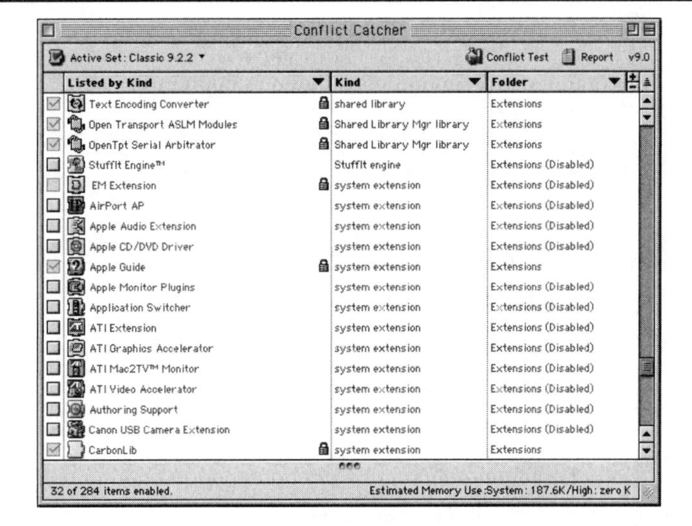

FIGURE 8.4: Using Conflict Catcher to manage Classic startup files

OS 9 Startup Files Required by Classic

Although you can optimize the Classic System Folder by removing startup files (extensions, control panels, etc.), there are a few files that are required for Classic to function; the list below will help you figure out what *not* to remove. If any of these files are missing when Classic starts up—including the first time you ever launch Classic—you'll get a dialog box telling you that needed files are missing, and that Classic needs to install them (you should let it).

If you're running Mac OS X 10.2 or later, the files required by Classic are as follows:

Root level of System Folder:

- Classic*
- Classic Support*
- Classic Support UI*

Continued on next page

Control Panels folder:

- General Controls*
- Keyboard*
- Startup Disk*
- USB Printer Sharing

Extensions folder:

- Apple Guide*
- AppleScript*
- AppleShare
- CarbonLib*
- Classic RAVE*
- File Sharing Extension
- Global Guide Files
- InputSprocketClassic*
- LaserWriter 8
- Network Setup Extension*
- Open Transport*
- Open Transport ASLM Modules*
- OpenGLLibrary
- OpenTpt Remote Access
- PrintingLib
- PrintMonitor
- QuickDraw™ 3D RAVE
- USB Printer Sharing Extension

If you're running Mac OS X 10.1.5 or earlier, the list is slightly different:

Root level of System Folder:

- ProxyApp (pre-OS X 10.1.5 only)
- Classic*
- Classic Support*
- Classic Support UI*

Continued on next page

Control Panels folder:

- General Controls*
- Startup Disk*
- USB Printer Sharing

Extensions folder:

- Apple Guide*
- AppleScript*
- AppleShare
- CarbonLib*
- Classic RAVE*
- File Sharing Extension
- Global Guide Files
- LaserWriter 8
- Open Transport*
- Open Transport ASLM Modules*
- OpenGLLibrary
- OpenTpt Remote Access
- PrintingLib
- PrintMonitor
- QuickDraw™ 3D RAVE
- USB Printer Sharing Extension

Items with an asterisk (*) are the minimum files you need under Mac OS 9.2.2 (the most recent version of OS 9 at the time of this writing) to start the Classic Environment at all—in other words, the minimum needed to start up Classic without being asked if it can install "needed files." However, with only these files, you may not get full functionality. In addition, you may want to enable the `Shared Library Manager` and `Shared Library Manager PPC` extensions, since many third-party applications, such as Microsoft Office 2001, require them.

Customize the Classic System Folder: ClassicBooster

If you don't want to customize or create your own Classic set in Extensions Manager, you can use the shareware ClassicBooster (`http://www.cogco.co.uk/ClassicBooster/`) to do the dirty work for you. When you launch ClassicBooster, it creates a new Extensions Manager set that includes only the essential startup files required by Classic; you can then manually add any other files you want included in the set. ClassicBooster also claims to accelerate future startups of Classic by caching extensions.

Partitions and Multiple System Folders

If you frequently switch between booting into Mac OS X and booting into Mac OS 9, I recommend that you have two System Folders, one optimized for Classic, the other fully loaded with all of your standard OS 9 goodies that you can use when booting into OS 9. I also recommend that you do this using multiple hard drives, or (if you only have a single drive) by partitioning your drive. Rather than discussing such a setup here, I'm going to refer you to the detailed discussion I've provided in Appendix A, "A Tale of Two Systems."

Buy More RAM

OK, this isn't really a way to "optimize" Classic. In fact, one could argue that it's just the opposite—a way to get around optimizing it. Either way, if you use Classic a lot, you should really consider buying and installing extra RAM. The reason for this is that the Classic Environment isn't a text editor that takes up a tiny amount of memory; it's loading an entire copy of OS 9 and running applications on top of that, so its memory demands can get quite large. Even though Mac OS X's virtual memory system is quite good, the truth is that if you don't have enough RAM, performance can be affected (both the performance of Classic and the performance of OS X as a whole). I personally feel that OS X by itself requires at least 256 MB of RAM, and starts to really shine with twice that—the increase in speed and stability is significant. If you use Classic frequently, add another 128MB or even 256MB. (To give you some perspective, our iBook has 640MB, and the PowerMac has 1.12GB.) RAM is cheap nowadays; take advantage of it.

Using Classic

As I wrote earlier in the chapter, using Classic is for the most part straightforward—when Classic is running you simply launch and use Classic applications as you would any other applications. You can even copy and paste data between Classic and OS X applications, or use drag-and-drop to move data between them. However, there are a few areas, such as printing, where you'll need to set things up, a few areas in which Classic might not behave the way you expect, and a few ways you can make using Classic a bit easier.

Other Ways of Starting and Stopping Classic

I recommended earlier that you start and stop Classic manually, due to potential problems with having Classic start at login or when launching a Classic application. Unfortunately, launching Classic manually is a bit of a hassle, since you have to open System Preferences to do so. Here are a few other ways you can start and stop Classic that are quite a bit more convenient.

Start/Stop Classic from the Dock

The easiest way to start up Classic without any third-party software is to place the Classic Startup application in the Dock (by dragging it to the Dock from its location at `/System/Library/Core Services/Classic Startup`). When you want to start up Classic, just click the Classic Startup icon in the Dock. The only drawback to this method is that you still have to *quit* Classic by opening the Classic pane of System Preferences—you can't quit it by control/right-clicking on the Classic Startup icon in the Dock and choosing the Quit command. (In fact, the Classic Startup application only runs until Classic finishes loading, so you can't tell if Classic is running by looking at the Classic Startup icon in the Dock; however, if you click the icon while Classic is already running, a message will pop up to let you know.)

Two third-party utilities that offer a bit more functionality are the shareware Classic Toggler (`http://www.northernsoftworks.com/classictoggler.html`) and Classic? (`http://xgadgets.com/classic.php`). Classic Toggler is a standard OS X application; when you launch it, its Dock menu includes Startup and Shutdown commands for the Classic Environment. In addition, by switching to Classic Toggler, you can use the Classic menu to instantly launch the OS 9 Chooser or Extensions Manager, launch frequently used Classic applications, and access Classic items such as the OS 9 Desktop, Apple Menu, Control Panels, and the System Folder (and you can install items in these folders by dropping them on the Classic Toggler icon in the Dock). As an added bonus, by choosing Classic ➢ Preferences Manager... or Classic ➢ Desktop Manager... you can quickly synchronize items between your OS 9 and OS X Preferences folders or Desktop folders, respectively.

Classic? provides options similar to Classic Toggler, but since it is a Dock Extra rather than a dedicated application, all of its functions are contained in its Dock menu (Figure 8.5). You can start or stop Classic, force quit Classic, rebuild the Classic Desktop, and quickly access Classic control panels as well as Quick Classic Items (basically any applications or aliases you place in `~/Library/Application Support/Classic?`). You can also quickly view the Classic Environment's memory and CPU usage right from the menu.

FIGURE 8.5: Classic? provides a helpful Dock menu for working with Classic

Both Classic Toggler and Classic? also provide excellent visual feedback about whether Classic is currently running (see "How Can I Tell If Classic Is Running?").

Start/Stop Classic from the Menu Bar

If you're partial to the menu bar, or if your Dock is just too cluttered, there are a couple of great Menu Extras that let you control the Classic Environment. The freeware Classic Spy (`http://www.anoshkin.net/`) provides a simple menu that allows you to start or stop Classic (including a force quit of Classic, if necessary) or to open Classic preferences. The shareware Classic? that I just talked about also comes in a Menu Extra version that offers the same features as the Dock Extra version.

NOTE Both of these Menu Extras require the freeware Menu Extra Enabler (`http://download.unsanity.com/`) to function properly under OS X 10.2.

Classic Peculiarities

Although you can switch to and between Classic applications using the Dock just as you can with OS X applications, there are a few ways in which Classic doesn't work quite as seamlessly

How Can I Tell If Classic Is Running?

One complaint that many users have about the Classic Environment is that it's sometimes difficult to tell if it's currently running. If you're the type who wants the ability to quickly see if Classic is running, here are a few solutions:

- Open Classic System Preferences; if Classic is running, you'll see the bold text "Classic is running" in the Start/Stop tab (and the Start button will have changed to Stop).
- If a Classic application is running, you'll see its icon in the Dock, which means Classic is running. (This may seem obvious, but I know users who keep a tiny Classic app, such as Note Pad, running just so they can tell that Classic is running.)
- Mac OS X's Force Quit window will list the Classic Environment in the list of running applications when it is active. Likewise, the Process Viewer utility will include "TruBlueEnvironme" in the list of running processes, and the top command in Terminal will include "TruBlueEnv" in the list of processes when Classic is running.
- The third-party utilities I recommended for starting and stopping Classic (Classic Toggler, Classic?, and Classic Spy) all provide visual feedback as to whether or not Classic is running, either via their menu bar or Dock icons. In addition, the freeware system monitoring utility System Manager (`http://www3.nb.sympatico.ca/gamson/SystemManager/`), also has great Dock and menu bar displays; I personally use it as my own Classic indicator.

as Apple would have you believe. Most of these inconsistencies relate to appearance—application windows, menus, Open/Save dialogs, and the Apple Menu—but there are also issues that arise in terms of preferences and application launching.

Appearance

When you switch back and forth between OS X and Classic applications, you'll notice immediately that Classic applications don't take advantage of OS X's Aqua interface. Windows have the Mac OS 9 *Platinum* appearance (including the WindowShade button, which works as expected), as do menus and dialog boxes. The menu bar itself changes to an OS 9-style menu bar, including the OS 9 application menu and the traditional Apple Menu (Figure 8.6). Classic windows also don't take advantage of such Aqua features as transparency and live resizing.

Another area where you'll see significant differences between Classic and OS X application is Open/Save dialogs. Again, because Classic applications cannot take advantage of the Aqua interface, they use the older dialog boxes found in OS 9—either the standard modal dialogs that are not movable and force you to address them before doing anything else, or the newer Navigation Services dialogs that are only modal for the current application. Contrast these dialogs with OS X's dialogs, which are document specific (you can switch to any other application, or even other documents in the same application, when an Open/Save dialog is open).

NOTE Some applications that have been Carbonized for OS X will use OS 9–style dialogs if the developer did not choose to take advantage of Mac OS X's Aqua dialogs.

Application Launching

Although the process of launching Classic applications is nearly identical to the process of launching OS X applications, there are a couple of situations where the existence of the Classic Environment can throw a wrench in the process. The first is related to Carbon applications; the second has to do with having both a Classic and OS X version of the same application on your hard drive.

Launching Classic and Cocoa applications is simple; Classic applications launch in Classic and Cocoa applications launch in OS X. However, some Carbon applications—those that are not OS X–only—will actually launch in both OS X and OS 9. This presents an interesting challenge for your Mac. When you double-click on such an application, how does it know whether to launch in OS X or Classic? The answer is a simple setting in the application's Get Info window (Figure 8.7). By checking "Open in the Classic environment," the application will always open in Classic; unchecking the box will cause the app to open in OS X.

Tex-Edit Plus File Edit Special Font Size Style Sound Scripts Window Help Mon 5:45 PM
File Edit Special Font Size Style Sound Windows Help 5 45 Tex-Edit Plus

FIGURE 8.6: The menu bar for Tex-Edit Plus in OS X (top) and Classic (bottom)

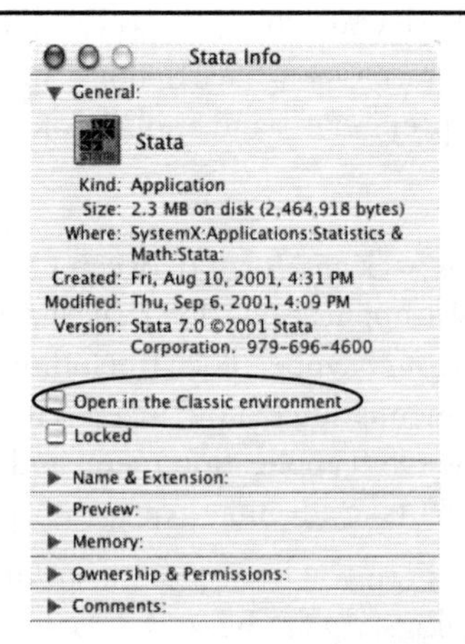

FIGURE 8.7: The Stata statistical package can be launched in either OS X or Classic.

The other anomaly can occur when you have both a Classic and OS X version of the same application on your Mac (for example, the e-mail client Microsoft Entourage). Assume for the moment that you've chosen Entourage as your preferred e-mail client in both Classic and OS X. If you click on a mail link in a Classic application, and the OS X version of Entourage is running, the URL will be opened (via a new e-mail message) in that version; however, if the OS X version isn't running, the mail link will be opened in the Classic version. This bug is due to the way in which Classic views OS X's application packages. As discussed in Chapter 7, an application package is actually a folder disguised as a single file. OS X understands this organizational trick, but Classic doesn't; it sees an application package as a folder. Thus when Classic needs to open a file in an application, if the application is already running, it works fine; however, if the application isn't running, sometimes Classic cannot "find" the OS X version. When this happens, Classic then looks for a Classic version of the application. The good news is that this is a fairly obscure bug—you need to have separate versions of an application on your hard drive with the OS X one *not* running, and then open a file or URL that is opened using that application. Mail clients and web browsers are the most common culprits.

Preferences

Classic applications use their *own* preference files, located in either `/Classic System Folder/Preferences` or `~/Library/Classic/Preferences` (depending on the setting you've chosen in Classic preferences). Although this method of organization generally works well, there are two areas in which it can become confusing: when you have two versions of an application, one that runs in Classic and one that runs in OS X (or a Carbon application that can open in either one); and when you're dealing with networking and Internet preferences.

Many applications have both OS X and Classic versions. If for some reason you use both of these versions (for example, certain web pages seem to work better with the Classic version of Internet Explorer than the OS X version), keep in mind that the two use *different* preference files, so unless you set them up identically, they may behave differently (in fact, you may *want* them to behave differently, so this isn't necessarily a bad thing). Likewise, as mentioned above, some Carbon applications can run in either OS X or Mac OS 9, and will use a different preference file depending on the environment in which they're launched.

In terms of Internet and networking preferences, you'll remember that all Classic networking is tunneled through Mac OS X. This means that the settings you choose in the Network pane of OS X's System Preferences also apply to Classic. However, the Internet settings and behavior of Classic applications are *not* controlled by the settings in OS X's Internet preferences. Rather, Classic uses the settings in the Classic Internet control panel or InternetConfig utility. For example, both OS X's Internet preferences and the Classic Internet control panel have settings for your preferred web browser or e-mail client. If these settings are different, clicking on a URL or e-mail link in an application may produce different results depending on whether that application is a Classic or OS X application.

Classic Applications and Memory

In addition to the application launching topics already discussed, there are a couple memory-related issues you should be aware of if you use Classic often.

The first is that virtual memory appears to applications to be disabled within the Classic Environment. Any Classic application that requires that virtual memory be enabled will not run in Classic. (In reality, virtual memory is active across OS X and the Classic Environment; however, since virtual memory is managed by OS X, the Classic Environment disables OS 9's own virtual memory system.)

The second issue relates to memory allocation and Classic applications. OS X manages the memory allocated to OS X applications, and to the Classic Environment itself. However, since Classic is running an actual copy of Mac OS 9, applications running *within* Classic use OS 9's memory management system. This means that whereas OS X applications will be given as much memory as they need, when they need it, Classic applications still use the memory settings in their Get Info windows. When you use the Finder's Get Info command on a Classic application, a Memory panel is provided to allow you to manually set the memory allocation requested by the application when it is launched. This means that, just as in OS 9, if a Classic application can't open a file because it doesn't have enough memory, you'll need to quit the application, increase its memory allocation, and then try again.

One bonus of the Classic Environment over a Mac running OS 9 is that OS X gives the Classic Environment a full *2GB* of memory space. This means you can give Classic applications much more memory than you would have given them had you actually booted into OS 9. Although you don't want to abuse this feature—the more memory you allocate to Classic applications, the more OS X will need to rely on virtual memory, so the more your Mac will have to swap memory to and from the hard drive—it's safe and often very convenient.

Using the Classic Apple Menu

When a Classic application is active (and the menu bar takes on the Classic Mac OS appearance), you can actually use the Classic Apple Menu just as you did in Mac OS 9. You can even customize it, just as you may have done under OS 9, by customizing the contents of `/Classic System Folder/Apple Menu Items` (if you don't have "User preferences from home folder" checked in Classic preferences) or `~/Library/Classic/Apple Menu Items` (if you do). In fact, many people who are fond of the Classic Apple Menu keep a Classic application running at all times just so they can switch to it to access the Classic Apple Menu.

If you want a similar Apple Menu in OS X, or you'd prefer the ability to access it without switching to a Classic app, check out Appendix A for some solutions.

Printing in Classic

I discuss printing in OS X a bit later in the book (Chapter 12). However, printing is one of the few ways in which Classic has its own, independent, settings. As long as your printer is *visible* to the Classic Environment (meaning it's connected to a supported port or available via OS X's network connections), you use the Classic Chooser (located in the Apple Menu Items folder described above) to choose the printer, just as you would have done if you had booted into Mac OS 9. Unfortunately, OS 9's Desktop Printers are not supported by Classic, so you have to use the Classic PrintMonitor application (located at `/Classic System Folder/Extensions/PrintMonitor`) to monitor print jobs.

NOTE The fact that the OS 9 Chooser controls printing in Classic means that to print from Classic you need to install the appropriate OS 9 printer drivers.

Classic Trouble

I mentioned earlier in the chapter that because using Classic involves so many layers, there are more places where things can go wrong. In addition, because Classic boots up a full version of Mac OS 9, most things that could go wrong in OS 9 can also go wrong in Classic. Although I can't spend too much time talking about troubleshooting the Classic Environment, here are some of the most common problems people have with using Classic. In addition to the issues discussed here, Appendix A includes a discussion of some of the problems you may encounter when switching between booting into OS X and OS 9.

Startup File Conflicts

As I previously explained, just as OS 9 was sometimes plagued by startup file conflicts, the Classic Environment can suffer the same fate. If you find that Classic is freezing during startup, or that Classic applications are behaving oddly (but OS X applications are working fine), the problem could be caused by startup files that don't play well together.

As under OS 9, the first step towards determining if a startup file is at fault is to start Classic with extensions and other startup files disabled. In the Advanced tab of Classic preferences, under Startup Options, choose Turn Off Extensions from the pop-up menu, and then click the Start Classic button. If Classic loads properly and your problems are gone, a startup file conflict is probably the culprit. (If not, then some more advanced troubleshooting methods are in order.)

How to manually discern which startup file(s) are the source(s) of your problems is both too deep (in terms of length of the discussion) and too basic (this kind of troubleshooting has been around the Mac platform for 15 years or so) a topic to get into here. Instead of explaining the procedure, I again recommend that you download Casady & Greene's Conflict Catcher if you don't already have a copy. Besides its excellent startup file management abilities, which I talked about earlier in the chapter, it also has an automated conflict test feature to help you find the cause of startup file conflicts. Even though Conflict Catcher was written for Mac OS 9, it has been updated to run within the Classic Environment. Best of all, whereas the testing procedure in OS 9 required multiple restarts of your computer, when Conflict Catcher runs in Classic, you can do other things on your computer; Conflict Catcher will automatically restart Classic in the background as it tests.

Classic and Classic Application Crashes

It's bound to happen sooner or later—one of the applications you're running in Classic crashes. Unfortunately, Classic isn't as stable as Mac OS X, so chances are the application won't exit gracefully. If it crashes and quits, chances are it will cause the entire Classic Environment to crash and quit as well. However, it may be frozen, or it may freeze the entire Classic Environment. If so, here are some ways to get out of it.

If one of your Classic applications freezes, you should generally treat it just like any other application, and use one of the methods discussed on Chapter 7 to force quit it. However, be aware that force quitting a Classic application will almost always force the entire Classic Environment to quit; you should first try to save any changes in open documents in other Classic apps.

In addition to Classic application freezes, sometimes the Classic Environment itself will crash or freeze. If it crashes, it will usually quit entirely (taking any running Classic applications with it). However, if it freezes, you'll need to quit it yourself. The easiest way to escape a frozen Classic Environment is to click the Force Quit button in the Start/Stop pane of Classic System Preferences. This will quit Classic immediately, along with all Classic applications, without giving you a chance to save your work. (Although that's probably not an issue if you've resorted to force quitting Classic.) If this doesn't work, remember that Classic is simply an OS X application; you can use any of the procedures I listed in Chapter 7 when I discussed how to force a misbehaving application to quit.

Inability to Select a System Folder in Classic Preferences

Sometimes a Mac OS 9 System Folder that you know exists isn't listed in the Classic pane of System Preferences. You can often remedy this by switching to the Startup Disk pane of System Preferences, selecting that System Folder as the startup OS, then switching back to Classic preferences (you may need to quit System Preferences and relaunch it in between). Generally the System Folder will now appear as a valid selection for use in Classic. After you've selected it, be sure to go back to Startup Disk preferences and re-select your normal startup volume as the startup OS.

Another solution, if this one doesn't work, is to open Terminal and type **`sudo bless -folder9 "/System Folder" -setOF`** **<RETURN>** (if the System Folder you're trying to use for Classic is located on the boot volume) or **`sudo bless -folder9 "/Volumes/`*`volumename`*`/System Folder" -setOF`** **<RETURN>** (if the System Folder resides on a different volume; *volumename* is the name of the volume). This command tells Mac OS X that the referenced System Folder is indeed a bootable (and thus selectable) System Folder; you should then be able to select it in Classic preferences.

Moving On...

Now that we've covered the specifics of files and applications, as well as the Finder and the Dock, it's time to move on to the realm of connectivity. Networks and the Internet; sharing files and connecting to remote computers; and printing…these are the topics of the next part of the book. By the time we're done, you should be your own network administrator.

Part III

The Internet, Networking, Sharing, and Printing

CHAPTER 9

Networking Notables and Internet Illuminations

(Or: Connect and surf faster, easier, friendlier.)

If you're a typical Mac user, you spend a good amount of time each day using the Internet: sending and receiving e-mail, surfing the Web, downloading files, and/or chatting with friends. In addition, you may be connected to a local network, through which you access printers and other computers.

Although networking and the Internet are incredibly broad topics that could each fill volumes, in this chapter I'm going to touch on some of the things you're most likely to do on your Mac. For example, I'll cover some tips for Internet and Network preferences, as well as some ways to get more out of the Web. I'll also mention some great sources of information on setting up your own Internet services on your Mac. (If you're interested, I talk about Mail, Apple's e-mail app; some other e-mail solutions; the Address Book applications; and Internet chat applications in the online supplement covering the iApps and Mail.)

I'll also talk about how to *share* files and information with other people over a network or the Internet in Chapter 10.

NOTE Because this isn't a introductory-level book, one of the assumptions I make is that you're already connected to the Internet, and you've already got your Internet/network settings from your ISP (or your network administrator if you're on a LAN). If you've got an Internet router, including an AirPort Base Station or other wireless router, I'm also assuming that you've already got it set up and working.

Network Basics

Before I get into some tips for network and Internet setup (using the Network and Internet panes of System Preferences), I want to briefly discuss *networks* and *network ports* in Mac OS X, because many users confuse the two.

A *network* is a group of devices connected in a way that allows them to exchange data with each other. A network can be as simple as a laptop, desktop, and printer in your home, or as complex as millions of computers located all over the world (which is what the Internet really is). Some networks are public (the Internet), whereas others are private (a LAN at your office). Generally speaking, if two or more computing devices are communicating, they are doing so over some kind of a network.

A *network port* in Mac OS X refers to the type of connection your computer uses to connect to a network: Ethernet, modem, AirPort/802.11 (wireless), Bluetooth, etc. Even FireWire can be used for networking, although at the time of this writing such networks are rare.

It's important to know the difference between these terms, and to understand that there is no inherent link between them. For example, you could use Ethernet to connect to the Internet, but use AirPort to connect to other computers in your office or home. Or you could use AirPort to connect to other computers (and even printers connected to those computers), but use your Mac's built-in modem for dial-up Internet access. In our home, our iBook uses AirPort to connect to the Internet and our desktop Mac, but Bluetooth to send files to a friend's laptop and our wireless phone.

Now that I've got that out of the way, let's talk about the various network- and Internet-related settings.

Internet and Networking Setup Subtleties

Even though I said at the beginning of the chapter that I was going to assume you've already got your Mac on the Internet, and maybe even set up your own home network, I'm going to quickly talk about the settings used for these connections, as there are some neat features with which many users aren't entirely familiar. These features and settings are contained in a few different System Preferences panes, and in the Internet Connect Application.

The Network System Preferences

User Level: admin
Affects: computer
Terminal: no

As I mentioned at the beginning of the chapter, I'm assuming that you've already entered your network/ISP settings and are connected to the Internet (and possibly even to other computers or networked printers on a local network). So let's skip to two of OS X's very cool network-related features: port priority and Locations.

OS X has the ability to mix and match network types and network ports, making it extremely flexible. However, it also has the ability to automatically adapt to various network situations, and to quickly switch between sets of network port configurations that you've defined, making it the most adaptable OS on the market.

Enabling/Disabling Network Port Configurations

When you open the Network pane of System Preferences, the Show pop-up menu lists the currently active network port configurations. (In OS X 10.1.x, these were called Active Network Ports, which is an easier name to say and remember, but I'm going to stick with "network port configurations" or "active network interfaces" since these are the hip terms now, it appears.) By selecting a network interface from the Show pop-up, you're presented with various tabs that allow you to input various settings that are *specific to* that particular network port configuration. I stress the phrase *specific to* because this is where all that flexibility I talked about comes in. The TCP/IP settings for Ethernet can differ from the TCP/IP settings for AirPort, which can differ from the TCP/IP settings for modem connections.

In addition, *which* tabs show up differs for each type of port configuration. If you have an AirPort card, the AirPort configuration shows TCP/IP, AppleTalk, Proxies, and AirPort. The tabs for a modem are TCP/IP, PPP, Proxies, and Modem. Ethernet gets TCP/IP, PPPoE, AppleTalk, and Proxies. So each type of network port configuration has its own group of settings.

NOTE Although Mac OS X allows you to enable TCP/IP on multiple network ports simultaneously, it does *not* allow you to enable AppleTalk on multiple ports at the same time. Well, it will let you, but it won't work, and you'll probably get an error message telling you that AppleTalk can only be active on a single port.

In addition to providing the ability to select each network port configuration, the Show pop-up menu also includes an item called, curiously enough, Network Port Configurations. Selecting this item provides a list of all the active network interfaces that you could select from the Show menu. What's more, you can actually turn particular configurations on and off. For example, if you only connect to the Internet using an AirPort card, you can disable all the other port configurations (Figure 9.1). Disabling a network interface not only prevents it from being active; it also removes it from the Show pop-up menu. You can also create a new port configuration, or duplicate or delete an existing one, using the buttons on the right. Finally, you can rename a port configuration by double-clicking on its name.

Although you can probably think of a situation where you might need to create a new network interface (you installed new networking hardware would be a good example), you may be wondering why you'd ever want to disable, delete, or duplicate a port. The reason relates to the feature I mentioned at the beginning of this section, port priorities.

FIGURE 9.1:

Using the Network Port Configurations dialog to disable unused network interfaces

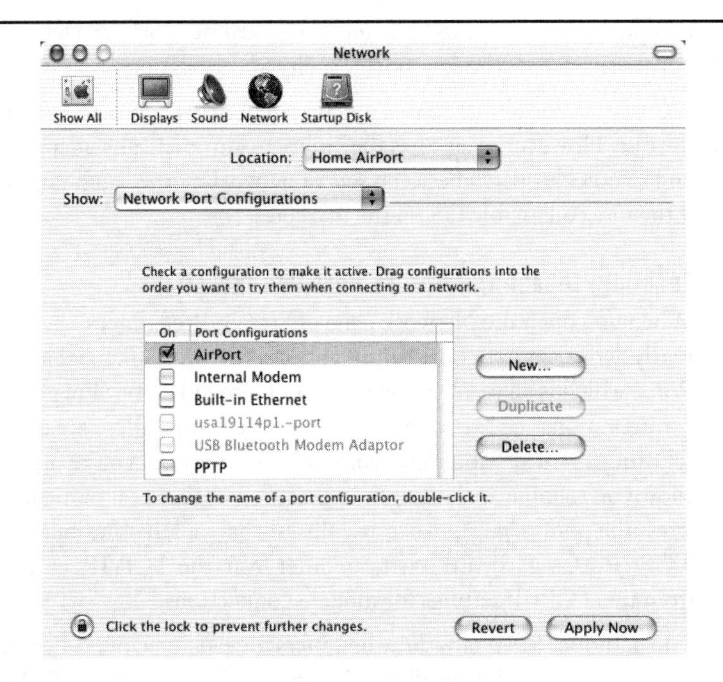

TIP If you have multiple ISP accounts, you can create a new Modem configuration for each one. For example, I have two modem configurations on my iBook, one called Mindspring Modem and another called PacBell Modem. I can quickly connect to either of these accounts using the modem status menu or the Internet Connect application.

Understanding and Using Network Port Priorities

As should be clear by now from the discussion, you can create multiple network port configurations and have them all active at the same time; in network geek-speak this is called *multihoming*. However, in addition to being able to *use* multiple network configurations simultaneously, Mac OS X also has the impressive (and impressively useful) ability to *prioritize* them. In other words, not only can you enable TCP/IP on your Ethernet port, internal modem, and AirPort card at the same time, you can also tell Mac OS X which one you want to use as your primary connection, your secondary, etc. In fact, you can have as many network port configurations active as you have available network ports. When you do something that requires a TCP/IP connection (check your e-mail, access a web page, connect to a remote server), OS X will try your first TCP/IP-enabled network interface. If that fails, it will try the second, and so on, until it either makes a successful TCP/IP connection or gives up after trying them all.

The way you prioritize network port configurations is so obvious and simple that it's...well, not really obvious. In Network preferences, you go to the Network Port Configurations dialog (from the Show pop-up). Then you just drag each port configuration up or down. The port you move to the top of the configurations listing is the first to be used, and so on down the list. Yes, it's really that simple.

As an example, my desktop Mac normally uses DSL (via Ethernet) to connect to the Internet. However, sometimes my DSL provider is, shall we say, less than reliable. So my backup is a dial-up connection. I have two network port configurations active, Ethernet and Internal Modem, and Ethernet is first in the priority listing. Whenever I try to access the Internet, my Mac first checks the DSL connection; if it's working, it uses it. If not, it then automatically dials up my ISP via the phone line.

NOTE Although the idea behind port priorities is very cool, and most of the time it works great, sometimes it doesn't. Sometimes OS X will try your first port configuration, and if it doesn't work, it just sits there—it doesn't even bother to try the next configuration. In situations like this, you can try to rearrange port configuration order, or enable/disable various configurations. However, an easier solution is to use Locations, discussed in the next section.

Using Network Locations

If your Mac never leaves home, you may never need to change your network settings. However, for many users (especially iBook and PowerBook users) this isn't the case. You may use different network settings at home than you do at work; or you may travel between a number of places—work, home, friend's homes, relative's—each of which has its own network setup. You could manually enable/disable network port configurations, or change settings, whenever you move, but that would be a hassle (and the more places you use your Mac with different network settings, the bigger the hassle it would be). A better solution is built into Mac OS X: network Locations.

A network Location is a group of network port configurations and their settings. You can have as many Locations as you want, and easily switch between them as you need. In fact, you already have at least one network Location, as OS X created the very first one when you first set up you Mac for Internet access. It was called Automatic, and you can see it at the top of the Network pane of System Preferences, in the Location pop-up menu.

Setting up Locations is fairly easy, and switching *between* Locations is even easier. To create a new Location:

1. In the Location pop-up menu, choose New Location…
2. Name your new Location and click OK.
3. Make sure the new Location is selected from the Location pop-up menu, and then configure your network preferences for the new Location. Add/remove/enable/disable network interfaces, enter the settings for each interface, and prioritize them as needed.

Repeat the above process for each new Location you want to create.

If you want to create a new Location that is based on or similar to an existing Location, select "Edit Location…" from the Location pop-up menu, select the Location you want to use as a model, then click the Duplicate button and give the copy a new name. You can then select the new Location from the pop-up menu and edit it as needed. The Edit menu item can also be used to delete or rename existing Locations.

To switch to a different Location, you simply select it from the Location pop-up menu, and then click the Apply Now button at the bottom of the Network preferences window. But there's an even easier way. Instead of opening System Preferences every time you want to change Locations, Mac OS X's Apple Menu has a convenient Location sub-menu. Choose Location ➢ *Location Name* and OS X will make the change for you. Your new settings take effect immediately.

TIP If your iBook or PowerBook has an AirPort card, having the card active uses a good amount of battery power when you aren't plugged into an AC outlet. In fact, even the modem card uses some juice when you're not using it. So it follows that disabling the AirPort card and/or the modem when you don't need them will extend your battery life. An easy way to do this is to create a new network Location that has the AirPort and/or Internal Modem network interface(s) disabled (or even deleted). When you're about to unplug, switch to this Location. Another alternative is to enable/disable the AirPort card using the Internet Connect application or the AirPort menu item. However, I personally have a Location called No Network that has no active ports; I use this whenever I'm in transit or don't need any network access. This method also prevents your modem from trying to dial up when OS X doesn't find a network.

To give you an idea of the flexibility that the combination of port priorities and network Locations provide, I have the following Locations defined on our iBook:

All Off All network port configurations are disabled.

Home AirPort AirPort is the only active connection, and AppleTalk is enabled. I get both Internet and local network access via AirPort. I use this when I'm not near my desk.

Home AirPort/Modem AirPort and the Internal Modem are active. I use this when I use the iBook at my desk. If the DSL is acting flaky, the iBook dials up my ISP for Internet access, but uses the AirPort card for local network access.

Travel AirPort The only active port is the AirPort card and AppleTalk is disabled. I use this Location when I'm accessing the Internet via a wireless access point—in a coffee shop, at a conference, etc.

Travel Ethernet DHCP The only active port is Ethernet, AppleTalk is disabled, and the Ethernet port is set to use DHCP for Internet access. This is the Location I use when connecting to broadband networks in hotels or other locations when I travel or do consulting work.

Travel Modem I've enabled a separate modem configuration for each of my ISPs. I've also edited the phone number list in Internet Connect (explained later in the chapter when I talk about the Internet Connect application) with phone numbers for the place(s) I'll be visiting for each ISP. I use this Location most often when I'm traveling and my only Internet access is via dial-up.

Granted, my setup isn't typical, as most people don't have the need for so many varied network setups. But isn't it great to know you could do it if you wanted to?

Using Mac OS 9–like Locations in Mac OS X

User Level: admin
Affects: computer
Terminal: no

If you used Mac OS 9 or earlier, especially on a PowerBook, you're probably thinking that OS X's Locations are similar to "locations" using OS 9's Location Manager. However, OS X's Locations only apply to network settings, whereas OS 9's Location Manager also controlled things like default printers, time zones, startup files, and more.

If you miss OS 9's ability to control these other settings when you change locations, you'll appreciate the shareware Location X (`http://homepage.mac.com/locationmanager/`). Location X works with OS X's Locations functionality, but adds the ability to also change settings for QuickTime, the time zone, the default printer, and sound volume. It also lets you run AppleScripts and shell scripts when you change Locations, and you can use it to change your preferences for Apple's Mail or Microsoft's Entourage e-mail clients, as well.

Location X runs as an application; the first time you launch it, it creates its own locations based on the Locations you've set up in Network preferences. By selecting a location and then clicking the Edit button (or choosing Location ➢ Edit…), you'll see a dialog with all of the possible settings Location X can change for you (Figure 9.2). First choose which settings you

FIGURE 9.2: Location X changes various settings when you switch "locations"

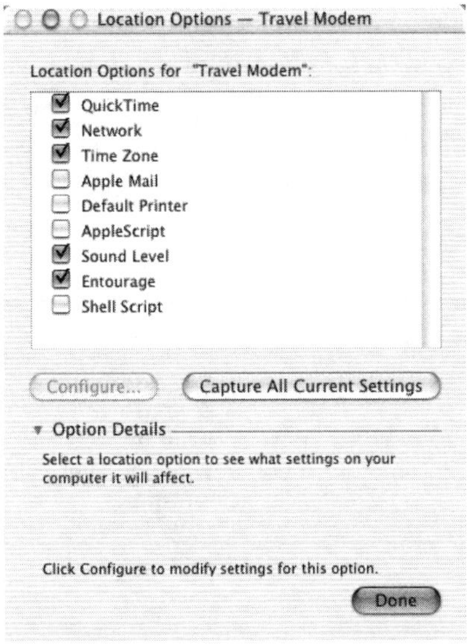

want it to change when switching to that location (Network is selected by default), then configure those settings.

You can configure each setting two different ways. (Before you make any changes, you should click the padlock icon to authenticate, since some of the changes you'll be making will require admin access; provide your admin password when prompted.) The first method is to select a setting and then click the Configure… button. For those settings set in System Preferences (QuickTime and Time Zone), Location X will open System Preferences for you; make the appropriate changes and then switch back to Location X—the current settings will be restored when you're through. For those settings that require changing your preferences in an application (Apple Mail and Entourage), Location X will launch the application; make the changes to the application's preferences and then switch back to Location X (again, your original settings will be preserved). For those settings that require a simple menu selection or slider (Network, Default Printer, and Sound Level), Location X will present a pop-up menu. Finally, for AppleScript or Shell Script, Location X will present you with a dialog window; you can either drag the scripts to the window, or use the Add… button to navigate to them.

The second way to configure settings—for all but the AppleScript and Shell Script options—is to manually change them using Network preferences, Sound preferences, QuickTime preferences, etc., and then to click the Capture All Current Settings button. All the current settings will be saved to this location.

You can also add new locations in Location X by clicking the Add button or choosing Location ➢ Add. However, whereas the first time you run Location X it creates its own location for every Network Location, on subsequent launches simply uses its own group of locations. In other words, if you create a new network Location in Network preferences, Location X will not automatically create a corresponding location of its own; you'll have to create one yourself.

You can switch between Location X's locations by selecting a location and then clicking the Make Active button (or choosing Location ➢ Make Active). If you've enabled the Location X Menu in the preferences dialog, you can also switch locations even when Location X isn't running. If any changes require admin access, you'll be asked for your admin password; after that all your settings will change to reflect the new location (including the network Location, if applicable). This is a great way to quickly change your Mac's settings.

IP over FireWire

I mentioned earlier that at the time of this writing, networking over FireWire was quite rare. However, by the time you read this, it will probably be more common, so I'm going to talk about it a bit. IP (Internet Protocol) networking over FireWire is exciting and cool because FireWire is

Continued on next page

much faster than most of the other connection methods used for networking. In fact, FireWire's theoretical data transfer speed is about 40 times faster than standard 10BaseT Ethernet and AirPort, and about 4 times faster than 100BaseT Ethernet. So if you network your Macs together using FireWire, your network will scream.

Using FireWire networking is actually quite easy. First, you need to make sure your Macs have IP over FireWire support—chances are that a recent OS X update added it, but if not you may need to go to the Apple Software Update web page to download the drivers: `http://www.info.apple.com/support/downloads.html`. Once you've installed the drivers (or you go right to this step if you didn't need to install them), open Network preferences on both computers and make sure FireWire is listed as a Network Port Configuration. If not, add a new interface using the instructions I provide in the main text ("The Network System Preferences"); choose FireWire as the port. Then in the Network Port Configurations window, drag the FireWire configuration to the top of the list. (As explained in the main text, this ensures that your Mac will try to use FireWire networking first, and if it can't use it for a particular task, it will use the second configuration, and so on.)

Next, connect two Macs together using a FireWire cable (you can also use two FireWire cables and a FireWire hub, if that's your setup). You can now connect from one computer to the other for File Sharing or any other type of networking. (If you're not sure how to use File Sharing, I'll talk about it in the next chapter.) In fact, if you have just a small home network, this is probably the ideal network setup, because the data transfer speeds are so much faster than Ethernet or AirPort.

(You can even share your Internet connection with another Mac over FireWire; however, at the time of this writing the procedure is fairly complicated, as it's still in the testing process. I hope that by the time you read this, Apple will have instructions on their website, or even in your Mac's Help.)

Copying and/or Backing Up Network Preferences

If you want to make a backup copy of your network preferences (a good idea, although you should be backing up much more than just your network preferences—see Chapter 14), the preferences file is located in the hidden directory `/var/db/SystemConfiguration`. The easiest way to access this directory is to open a new Finder window, choose Go ➢ Go to Folder…, type the path I just showed you, and click the Go button. The file that contains your network preferences is called `preferences.xml`. Copy it to a safe location.

In addition, if you're setting up a new Mac that will use many of the same network settings, you can copy this file to the same location on the new Mac (you'll need root access, or a utility such as File Buddy that you can open as root using Pseudo or Snard, as discussed in Chapter 1). The new Mac will then have the same network preferences as the original Mac.

The Internet System Preferences

User Level: any
Affects: individual user
Terminal: no

The Internet pane of System Preferences is where each user sets up their default settings for Internet-related services. If you have a .Mac account, it's also where you can enter your account information and configure and monitor your iDisk. The preference pane is divided into four tabs: .Mac, iDisk, Email, and Web.

.Mac

If you have a .Mac account (`http://www.mac.com/`), the .Mac tab is where you enter your member name and password. Your Mac uses these settings in a few different ways. First, if your main e-mail account is your .Mac account, the Email tab of Internet preferences (discussed in a moment) can use this information to configure your e-mail account settings. Second, the iDisk tab of Internet preferences (also discussed in a moment) uses these settings to access your iDisk. Finally, if you use the Finder's Go ➢ iDisk command to access your iDisk, these settings are used to indicate the name of the iDisk and its password.

NOTE You can access other iDisks (other members' iDisks, or your own if you have multiple .Mac accounts) using Apple's iDisk Utility. In the next chapter, I'll also show you how to keep "bookmarks" for multiple iDisks.

iDisk

In Chapter 7, I covered the iDisk Utility. The iDisk tab of Internet preferences contains two groups of options (iDisk Storage and Public Folder Access) that are identical to those in the similarly named tools of iDisk Utility. iDisk Storage shows you the current usage and capacity of your iDisk, using the member name and password entered in the .Mac tab, and allows you to "Buy More" if you need it (connecting you to Apple's .Mac website to do so). The Public Folder Access section lets you change the permissions for the Public folder on your iDisk—these permissions (Read-Only or Read-Write) apply to *other* users, not you (you always have full read/write access to your iDisk). In addition, if you want to further secure your Public folder, you can enable a password; when enabled, other users will be required to enter this password to access your iDisk's Public directory. If you've made any changes in the Public Folder Access section, click the Apply Now button to enable them.

Email

The Email tab of Internet preferences has two sections, one for choosing your e-mail client, the other for providing a default e-mail account. If you've never done so before, choose your preferred e-mail client; Apple's Mail is the default choice, but you can choose the Select… option and navigate to any other e-mail client (Entourage, Eudora, Netscape, etc.). You can even choose a Classic e-mail client if you still haven't imported your OS 9 e-mail to OS X. Keep in mind that this setting is used only when Mac OS X receives a request to send an e-mail. For example, if you click on an e-mail address on a web page, OS X will open the e-mail application selected here, and open a new message to that e-mail address.

The e-mail account information in the lower part of the window is used by Mail (and most other e-mail clients) to automatically configure an e-mail account. When you first started up in OS X, you were prompted to enter this information by the Setup Assistant. You can also change it manually if you change e-mail accounts. However, note that although Apple's Mail will automatically update its e-mail account information to reflect these changes, not all third-party e-mail clients will—if you're using another client, double-check its settings. In addition, if you have multiple e-mail accounts, you'll need to set them up separately in your e-mail client, including Mail.

NOTE If your e-mail account is a .Mac account, and you check the "Use .Mac Email account" box, the information entered in the .Mac tab of Internet preferences is automatically used for the Email Address, User Account ID, and Password fields, and OS X also fills in the remaining fields with the correct info.

Web

The Web tab lets you select your default web browser behavior. The Default Web Browser is the browser Mac OS X will launch (or open a new page in, if it's already running) when you click on a URL in an e-mail message, text document, or any other application. It's also the application that will be used if you double-click on a Web Location file. (I talk more about Web Location files later in this chapter.)

The other two settings in this tab, Home Page and Download Files To, are only used if your browser supports Apple's Internet preferences system. Most do; however, a few don't, and use their own preferences instead. Home Page tells your browser what page to go to when you click the browser's Home button or choose Home from its menus. The Download Files To setting tells your browser where files should go when you click a link on a web page to download a file.

TIP In addition to your home page, there is also a preference for the default search engine; unfortunately, as of OS X 10.2 you can't access this setting from the Internet pane of System Preferences. However, if you launch Classic, and then open the *Classic* Internet control panel (located in *`Classic System Folder`*`/Control Panels/Internet`, or *`Classic System Folder`*`/Control Panels (Disabled)/Internet` if you've disabled it using Extensions Manager), you can actually change the setting from there.

Adding Other Browsers Using Browser Wars

You may have noticed that by default, the Default Web Browser includes only a single web browser to, um, "choose" from. If you want to use another browser as your default, you have to manually navigate and select it. This isn't a big deal if you only make this change once. But if you're like me and you like to try out different browsers, it gets to be a pain. Enter the freeware Browser Wars (`http://www.tepidcola.com/`), which does a very simple thing: it edits the settings file that Internet preferences uses for this menu. Double-click the Browser Wars "install" package and Terminal launches. Enter your admin password, confirm the installation, and the script backs up the original settings file and installs a new one that includes pretty much every web browser on the market. The next time you open the Internet pane of System Preferences, the Default Web Browser pop-up will contain a veritable cornucopia of browsers to choose from.

Using a Local File (or Your Bookmarks/Favorites) as Your Home Page

Since my laptop isn't always connected to the Internet, I prefer not to use the URL of a remote website as my home page—mainly because it isn't always accessible, but also because if I have "Connect automatically when needed" selected in the Modem configuration of Network preferences, every time I open my browser, my laptop tries to dial up my ISP. To solve this, I've created my own "home page" that is simply an HTML file of my favorite links, as well as some text info that I tend to forget (such as my home computer's IP address). I then enter the local address of this file in the Home Page field of Internet preferences. (Another solution is to simply leave the Home Page field blank, which doesn't load *any* page until you specifically enter a URL it the browser's address field, or click a URL in another application. This can be helpful if you want to use your browser without being connected to the Internet.)

If you'd like to use a local file as your home page, the easiest way to get its address is to use your favorite browser. Select File ➢ Open… (or File ➢ Open File…, depending on the browser), and navigate to the local file. When you click the Open button, the file will open in your browser. More importantly, the file's address will appear in the browser's address bar. Simply copy it and then paste it into the Home Page field in Internet preferences. As an example, the location of my personal home page document is `file://localhost/Users/frakes/Documents/homepage.html`.

If you like this tip, but don't want to (or don't know how to) create your own "home page," you might consider using your browser's bookmarks/favorites file. Your bookmarks/favorites are actually contained in a single file, created by your browser. You use the procedure I just described for getting the address of a local file to get the address of your bookmarks file, and then paste it into Internet preferences. This is actually a nice option for many people, since they tend to access many of their bookmarks frequently. If you don't know where your browser's bookmarks file is at, here are some hints:

iCab `~/Library/Preferences/iCab Preferences/Hotlist.html`

Internet Explorer `~/Library/Preferences/Explorer/Favorites.html`

Mozilla `~/Library/Mozilla/Profiles/default/bookmarks.html`

OmniWeb `~/Library/Application Support/OmniWeb/Bookmarks.html`

If you use the Camino or Opera browsers, or Apple's own Safari, their bookmark files can't be used as your home page because they aren't in HTML format. However, you *can* export your bookmarks to HTML format from within Camino and Opera, and then use the resulting file as your home page. For Safari, until Apple adds an Export command, you'll have to use a third-party bookmark utility (like those I discuss later in the chapter) to convert your bookmarks to a standard HTML file.

Accessing Hidden Internet Preferences

Most web browsers have a section in their preferences dialog for "helper" applications—applications used to deal with files and protocols that the browser doesn't handle. For example, Internet Explorer has a setting that tells it what to do with downloaded files that end in `.sit` (StuffIt archive files) and what to do when the user clicks on an FTP link on a web page. Users of Mac OS 9 will remember that the Internet control panel actually allowed you to customize the settings for helper applications, and those settings were used not only by many web browsers, but also by the OS itself—when you opened an Internet location file, or when you clicked on an Internet address in a text document or e-mail message.

It turns out that Mac OS X has the same settings, but they've been hidden. It's a safe bet that Apple will allow you to access them via the Internet preferences pane at some point in the future, but at the time of this writing the only way to get to them is to edit a fairly obscure XML file using a text editor... or install a neat freeware preference pane called More Internet (`http://www.monkeyfood.com/software/`).

Once you install More Internet, you can access it via System Preferences. In the More Internet window, you'll see a list of protocols/file types on the left, and the application that will be used for the selected protocol or file type on the right (Figure 9.3). To change the chosen application, just drag your preferred application to the window; it will be assigned to the selected protocol or file type. You can also add new protocols or file types to the list, or remove existing items, using the Add… and Remove buttons.

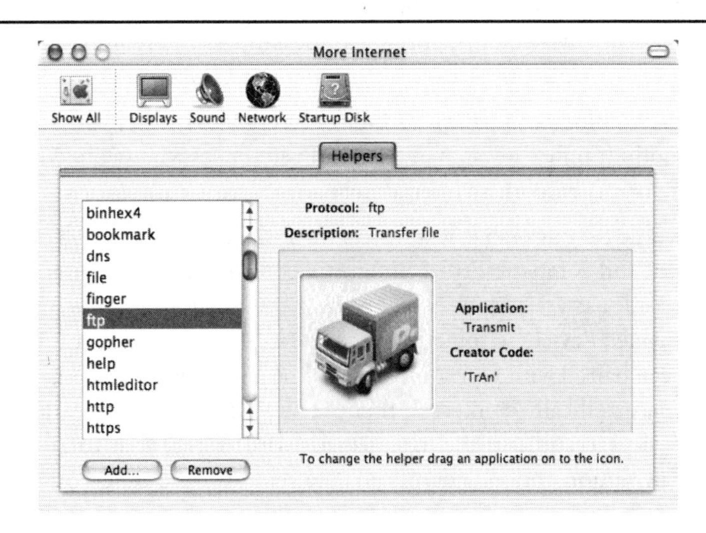

FIGURE 9.3: Using More Internet to assign applications to Internet protocols and file types

More Internet is also available as a standalone application called Vince; however, its interface isn't as nice, and I personally prefer the preference pane approach since that's where such settings belong (in my opinion).

The Bluetooth System Preferences

Bluetooth is a relatively new wireless networking protocol that allows Bluetooth-enabled devices within range of each other (up to 30 feet, or 100 feet, depending on the device) to communicate. Bluetooth is similar to the 802.11 (AirPort) wireless networking standards, but with two significant exceptions. The first is that Bluetooth is a low-bandwidth protocol; it can't transfer nearly as much data as AirPort can. (In terms of data throughput, you can think of it this way: if AirPort is the wireless equivalent to Ethernet, Bluetooth is the wireless equivalent to a USB or serial cable.) The second difference is that whereas AirPort is multi-device network protocol—you can connect your AirPort-enabled Mac to a large network of computers, printers, etc., and even to the Internet—Bluetooth is a *paired* or *direct* technology. Rather than connecting a computer to a network, with Bluetooth you create a private network of two devices by connecting those devices directly with each other—you *pair* them. Apple introduced support for Bluetooth in Mac OS X 10.1, but you had to install the software drivers separately. Beginning with 10.2, Bluetooth support was integrated into the OS.

Some examples of Bluetooth pairings are a mobile phone and a hands-free headset; a mobile phone and a computer; two computers; a computer and a printer; a computer and a keyboard; and a mobile phone and a PDA. Using these pairings, you can send data back and forth. For example, you can use your wireless phone as a modem, or, using Apple's iSync utility, you can synchronize your Mac's Address Book with your contacts on your Bluetooth-enabled wireless phone or PDA. The only requirement is that both devices be Bluetooth enabled. In the case of phones, printers, and PDAs, Bluetooth capability will generally be built in. In the case of your computer, at the time of this writing Apple has made Bluetooth either built-in or available on every new Mac model, portable or desktop. If you're using an older Mac without built-in Bluetooth, you can buy a relatively inexpensive USB adapter that's about the size of a piece of candy.

The Bluetooth pane of System Preferences is where you control how your Mac uses Bluetooth. It only shows up in System Preferences when your Mac has Bluetooth support built-in, or a Bluetooth adapter attached.

The Settings tab is where you turn Bluetooth on and off, and control the access level, security, and compatibility of Bluetooth connections. The Discoverable option, when checked, broadcasts your Mac's presence over the Bluetooth frequencies so that other Bluetooth-enabled devices within range can see it. If you uncheck this box, devices that have previously been paired with your Mac will still be able to connect to it, but others will not "see" it unless you specifically connect to them. The Require Authentication setting forces other Bluetooth devices to authenticate (using a password) before they can connect to your computer. The Encryption option encrypts all data sent over the Bluetooth connection so that anyone else in the area who might intercept it (using their own Bluetooth device) cannot use that data without your password. The Support Non-Conforming Phones option uses a less efficient connection that is more compatible with older Bluetooth-enabled phones. Finally, the "Show Bluetooth status in the menu bar" option provides a new Bluetooth menu that lets you monitor Bluetooth connections as well as enable/disable discoverable mode and Bluetooth itself.

The File Exchange tab (called Receiving Files under some versions of OS X) lets you decide on the default behavior when another Bluetooth device attempts to send a file or data to your Mac, and the location where accepted items will be placed. Under OS X 10.2.4 and later, it also includes a Bluetooth File Transfer section that lets you allow other Bluetooth-enabled devices to browse a particular folder on your computer.

In OS X 10.2.4 and later, the Devices tab lets you view paired and connected Bluetooth devices, as well as disconnect devices or pair with a new device (by choosing Paired Devices from the Show pop-up menu and then clicking Pair New Device). In addition, by clicking the Setup New Device button, the Bluetooth Setup Assistant launches and walks you through the procedure of configuring a Bluetooth phone or PDA for use with your Mac.

Under OS X 10.2.3 and earlier, setting up Bluetooth devices is a bit more complicated. The Bluetooth preference pane doesn't include the Devices tab, but instead includes Serial Ports and Paired Devices tabs. The Serial Ports tab allows you to create emulated serial ports to which you can "connect" Bluetooth devices. This is necessary for some software to be able to connect to these devices. For example, the Palm synchronization software requires you to choose a port in the HotSync preferences. To create a new port, click the New… button, provide a name for the new port, choose whether it's an incoming or outgoing port (for printers, choose outgoing, for PDAs, choose incoming), and then click the Select Device… button to scan for the Bluetooth device this port will be associated with. You can also choose to require authentication and/or encryption.

The Paired Devices tab lets you pair your computer with another device. Click the New… button, and a window will pop up that allows you to select "discoverable" devices; wait for a few seconds as your Mac scans for nearby Bluetooth devices. Once the scan has competed, select the desired device and then click the Pair button. Once a device is paired with your Mac, you no longer need to keep it or your Mac discoverable, as they will always be able to communicate. (You can also delete a pairing to prevent the device from communicating with your Mac; you can always re-pair them again later.)

Using Bluetooth Devices

Once you've paired your Mac and another Bluetooth device, you can send data between them using various methods. If you're using a Bluetooth printer, simply setting up the printer in Print Center lets you use it whenever needed. In the case of a Palm PDA, the HotSync software takes care of most data exchanges.

If the device supports file transfers, you can also use Apple's Bluetooth File Exchange (located in `/Applications/Utilities/`) to send files—just drag a file onto the Bluetooth File Exchange icon, and you'll get a list of Bluetooth devices in range (if the desired device isn't listed, click the Search button to force your Mac to re-scan for devices). Select the desired device and then click the Send button to send the file.

If your Mac or PowerBook has Bluetooth capability (either built-in, or using a USB Bluetooth adapter), and you have a Bluetooth-enabled cellular/wireless phone, you can actually use your phone as a modem. This is a very cool thing, since it means you can connect to the Internet and download mail or surf the Web even if you're far away from your home network or a telephone line. (Note that some cellular phones and service plans have both "voice" and "data" rates. You may even be able to set your Mac up to use your standard *voice* connection and airtime.) Although I don't have space here to show you how, if you're using OS X 10.2.4 or later, the Bluetooth Setup Assistant makes it fairly easy to set up.

NOTE If you have a Bluetooth-enabled Sony/Ericsson mobile phone, you really have to try out the preference pane Sony Ericsson Clicker (`http://www.salling.com/`). It turns your phone into a remote control that you can use to control iTunes, iDVD, PowerPoint, or Keynote whenever you're in range—fun at home and quite useful when giving presentations. In addition, it includes a "proximity sensor" that detects when your phone is in range of your Mac; it can run any AppleScript when your phone leaves the proximity of your computer, and another when it returns. For example, you can have a password-protected screen saver launch when you leave your office and then disappear when you come back!

The Internet Connect Application

The Internet Connect application serves four purposes: to initiate dial-up ISP connections, to initiate "Point-to-Point Protocol over Ethernet" (PPPoE) ISP connections, to connect to AirPort networks, and to initiate Virtual Private Network (VPN) connections. If your connection to the Internet is via DSL, cable modem, or another type of Ethernet connection, and your ISP doesn't use PPPoE you may have never even opened the Internet Connect application (unless you use its VPN feature to connect to an office network over your broadband connection). In fact, even if you use a dial-up or AirPort connection, you may have never used Internet Connect if you have the AirPort and/or Modem menus enabled in Network preferences—since you can initiate your connections using those menus. Nonetheless, Internet Connect has a few useful features you may want to know about.

Internet Connect assumes that you've already entered all of your settings and configured all of your network ports in Network preferences; if not, you can click the Edit… button near the bottom of the Internet Connect window to open Network preferences.

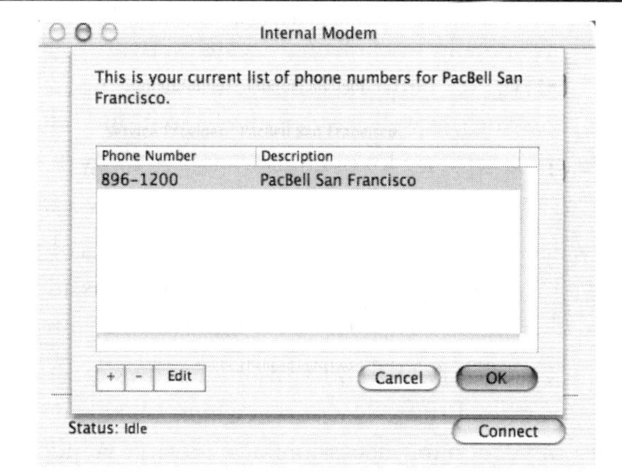

FIGURE 9.4: Editing the dial-up numbers used by Internet Connect

Using Internet Connect

If you only have a single network port configuration that requires a connection (modem, PPPoE, AirPort, etc.), the Internet Connect window will simply provide you with the appropriate settings and controls for that type of connection. However, if you have multiple port configurations that require connections, you'll see a Configuration pop-up that lets you choose *which* network configuration you'd like to use to connect. The window's options will change to reflect the type of port configuration you choose.

For example, if you choose any type of modem configuration, you'll see the information you previously entered in the PPP tab of the modem settings in Network preferences. However, one nice bonus is that the Telephone Number pop-up provides a list of all numbers you've used with that port configuration. This can be very handy if you tend to travel a lot and use different dial-up numbers with the same ISP, as you can select any number you've ever dialed for that ISP quickly. You can also add (or remove) numbers from the list by selecting Edit… from the pop-up menu (Figure 9.4). (In Mac OS X 10.1 and earlier, the only way to do this was to edit a preference file!) If you chose not to save your dial-up password in the modem settings of Network preferences, you can enter it manually here. Clicking the Connect button will dial your ISP and connect you to the Internet. Once you're connected, the Status area of the window provides your IP address, connection speed, time connected, and visible indicators of data being sent and received.

The PPPoE window looks almost identical to the modem version except for the fact that there's no phone number pop-up menu. The AirPort configuration, on the other hand, looks significantly different. You can turn your AirPort card on or off using the AirPort Power setting—turning it off is a good practice when you're traveling with a laptop, as the AirPort card uses battery power—and the Signal Level meter lets you see how strong a signal your AirPort card is receiving. You can choose between multiple AirPort networks using the Network pop-up;

if you choose a network that requires a password, you'll be presented with a dialog asking for that password. Finally, by choosing Create Network… from the Network pop-up, you can create your own AirPort network, using your own computer as the base. You give your network a name and password, as well as a default channel, and other users will be able to connect to it. (If your network is getting a lot of interference, you can change to another channel to see if the signal improves.)

Finally, each of the various configuration screens of Internet Connect allows you to turn its respective menu item on and off; these menu items allow you to quickly connect and disconnect, and also provide a visible status indicator of your connection.

Internet Connect has two other useful features most users don't know about: the ability to connect to Virtual Private Networks (which I'll talk about in Chapter 11), and the connection log. The connection log, accessible by choosing Window ➢ Connection Log, shows a complete record of all modem and PPPoE connection activity. By enabling "verbose logging" in Network preferences (from the modem or PPPoE Options dialog), you can get even more detailed logging. If you're having trouble connecting, or sustaining a connection, the connection log should be your first place to look for clues as to the cause.

Midnight (or Any Other) Rendezvous

In Mac OS X 10.2, Apple introduced a new technology called Rendezvous. Based on the Zero Configuration Networking (zeroconf) standard (`http://www.zeroconf.org/`), Rendezvous provides a way for you, the user, to set up a local network of devices—computers, printers, servers—without having to deal with IP addresses, complicated network setups, or obscure networking protocols. In effect, you connect two computers and they'll immediately be able to take advantage of each other's services.

The beauty of Rendezvous is that it works over your existing network. Once you've got your network set up, you go to the Sharing pane of System Preferences and enter your preferred Rendezvous name in the Rendezvous Name field—this is the name other users will see when they connect to your computer via Rendezvous. Plug your Mac into a local area network, and without any further ado, you can see other Rendezvous-enabled devices and they can see you. In fact, even if you don't set up any other networking preferences, Rendezvous works great; you can simply connect two Macs using an Ethernet cable and they will communicate perfectly, allowing you to chat, share files, share printers, etc.

Although most of the services that you'll take advantage of using Rendezvous are *sharing* services—file sharing, Windows sharing, printer sharing—that I'll be talking about in the next few chapters, I mention Rendezvous here because it also works for things like iChat (which has its own Rendezvous buddy list) and iTunes (a version that allows you to share/access iTunes music libraries should be available by the time you read this).

Continued on next page

How Does Rendezvous Work?

If you're curious, what's really happening behind the scenes is the following. When you connect to a local network, you computer picks an IP address for itself, chosen from a subnet that has been allocated for zeroconf networking by the Internet Assigned Numbers Authority (IANA). This IP address is in *addition* to any IP address your computer may already have been assigned for Internet access, and is an *internal* address (meaning that it is only used on the local network, and cannot be accessed by computers not on that local network). Your computer then sends out a query using the Address Resolution Protocol (ARP) standard to see if any other device on the subnet is already using that address. If so, your Mac chooses another address and sends another query; once it's found an unused IP address, it grabs that address as its own.

After staking a claim on a local IP address, your computer then assigns its Rendezvous name (the one in Sharing preferences) to that local IP address. It does this using the Domain Name System (DNS) protocol that is used to assign domain names to IP addresses (e.g., why you can type `cnn.com` instead of the `cnn.com` server's IP address). In fact, you'll notice in the Sharing pane of System Preferences that Rendezvous Name field is followed by the text `.local`. The `.local` domain has been assigned to Rendezvous, so any Rendezvous-enabled devices are given domain names based on the `.local` domain—your computer is simply *Rendezvous-Name.local*. You'll see in Chapter 12 ("Printing Practicalities") that when you share a printer, it's Rendezvous name will be an extension of your computer's name: *PrinterName@Rendezvous-Name.local*. The main difference between Rendezvous names and "true" Domain Name System names are that, again, Rendezvous names are only used on your local network, so your Mac doesn't have to query one of the Internet's DNS servers to resolve the name into an IP address.

Rendezvous Connection Caveats

A couple of caveats about Rendezvous: First, as I mentioned, Rendezvous is only used for devices located on a *local* network; for another user to see your computer using Rendezvous, they have to be connected to the same local network as you. In fact, they have to be connected to the same *subnet* of your local network. (A subnet is a subsection of a local area network, designated/delineated by a network administrator; if you're using a network in your home or small office, this restriction won't affect you at all. If you're connected to a large LAN with multiple subnets, it just means that Rendezvous will only work for other devices connected to the same subnet.)

Second, Rendezvous has some built-in security measures that are intended to prevent network security breaches; these measures may prevent certain Rendezvous devices from working (specifically, those devices that don't follow the Rendezvous guidelines precisely). If you find that certain Rendezvous-enabled devices don't appear when they should, open Terminal and type **`sudo sysctl -w net.inet.ip.linklocal.in.allowbadttl = 1`** **<RETURN>**; provide your admin password when prompted. If this fixes the problem, the cause is a not-fully-Rendezvous-compliant device. (You should contact the manufacturer to see if they have a more permanent fix; if they don't, you'll have to type this command each time you restart, since it only "fixes" the problem until shutdown.)

Sharing Your Surfing Signal

I talk about most of the features in the Sharing pane of System Preferences in Chapters 10 (sharing files), 12 (sharing printing), and 13 (using OS X's built-in firewall). However, one of these features, *Internet Sharing*, belongs here. Internet Sharing lets you share a single Internet connection (dial-up, broadband, etc.) between multiple local computers. It does this using *network address translation*.

Network Address Translation Translated

When you connect to the Internet via your ISP or your business or organization's network, your computer is usually assigned an IP address that uniquely identifies it to the rest of the Internet. This IP address is very much like a street address for postal mail—anything you send out has your return address so that the recipient knows exactly where to send replies. When you connect to a web server, for example, and request a web page, your IP address tells the server exactly where to send that page for viewing. Since most ISPs only provide you with a single IP address, you can't connect multiple computers to the Internet at the same time, since whenever one of them requested data from the Internet, all of them would receive that data (since they'd all have the same IP address).

The solution to this problem is to employ an Internet router that provides network address translation (NAT). The router takes on the actual IP address assigned by your ISP, and then provides *internal* IP addresses to each connected computer. (Internal addresses are a specific range of IP addresses that uniquely identify computers on a *local* network; they don't really mean anything on the Internet and can't communicate via the Internet without an Internet router in between.) The router then *translates* traffic from your computer to the Internet (so that the data appears to come from your ISP-assigned IP address), and from the Internet to your computer (so that requested data finds its way back to your computer, instead of one of the other computers being managed by the router).

To further the "street address" analogy, an Internet router is like the mailroom at a large company. To the post office, all mail is going to and coming from a single address; but the mailroom makes sure that outgoing mail gets out, and that incoming mail gets forwarded to the correct recipient. By using an Internet router, multiple computers can access the Internet over a single connection, but to your ISP and anyone else outside your network, it appears as though only a single computer is online.

OS X's Own Internet Router

User Level: admin
Affects: computer
Terminal: no

Most Internet routers are hardware devices that provide routing services for broadband connections such DSL and cable; a few, such as Apple's AirPort Base Station, also work with dial-up connections. Mac OS X actually includes a software router—based on the Unix program natd—that works with both broadband and dial-up connections. Called *Internet Sharing* in OS X, this router is set up from the Internet tab of System Preferences' Sharing pane. Just like with a hardware Internet router, other computers on your network can take advantage of your Mac's Internet Sharing via Ethernet or wireless (AirPort) connections, so a small home or office network of computers can easily share the same Internet connection. If you want to take advantage of Internet Sharing, here's how to set it up.

1. From the Mac that will act as the Internet router, connect to the Internet as you normally would, using your Mac's internal modem or a broadband modem.
2. Open the Sharing pane of System Preferences, click the Internet tab, and then click Start to start the natd (Internet Sharing) service.
3. To share your Internet connection over your Ethernet port (i.e., to other local computers connected to your computer via Ethernet), check the box next to "Share the connection with other computers on Built-in Ethernet." If you have an AirPort card installed and want to share your Internet connection with other AirPort-equipped computers, check the box next to the AirPort option (this option only appears if you actually have an AirPort card installed). If you're only sharing over Ethernet, you're done! If you're sharing over AirPort, you need to continue to Step 4.

NOTE You can't share an Internet connection via AirPort if *your* computer is actually getting its Internet connection via AirPort. To share your Internet connection over AirPort, "Allow this computer to create networks" must be enabled in the AirPort tab of the AirPort configuration in Network settings.

4. If you're sharing your Internet connection over AirPort, click the AirPort Options… button. In the resulting dialog, enter a name for the AirPort network you're about to create. Check the "Enable encryption (using WEP)" box (unless you want anyone within 100 feet or so to be able to hitchhike on your connection). Type in a password (twice to confirm it), and then select 128-bit from the "WEP key length" pop-up menu. Click OK to create the new network.

Internet Sharing is now enabled and running; to connect other local computers to your network, see the next section.

NOTE Unfortunately, at the time of this writing, Internet Sharing does not remain enabled after shutting down or restarting. If you want to share your Internet connection regularly, you have to manually enable Internet Sharing in Sharing preferences each time you start up.

Connecting to Internet Sharing on Another Mac

User Level: admin
Affects: computer
Terminal: no

If you've set up Internet Sharing and want set up other Macs to use your Internet connection, or if you need to set up your own computer to access Internet Sharing on another Mac, here's how. These instructions apply to the computer *accessing* the shared Internet connection, not the one sharing it.

1. Open the Network pane of System Preferences. (If the computer already has networking settings, create a new network location, as explained earlier in the chapter; you don't want to wipe out the existing settings.)

Via Ethernet

2. In the Network Port Configurations dialog, make sure Ethernet is listed at the top of the active port configurations. Then select the Ethernet port from the Show pop-up menu.
3. Click the TCP/IP tab, and then select Using DHCP from the Configure pop-up menu. Click Apply Now to activate the new settings.

Via AirPort

2. In the Network Port Configurations dialog, make sure AirPort is listed at the top of the active port configurations. Then select the AirPort port from the Show pop-up menu.
3. Click the TCP/IP tab, and then select Using DHCP from the Configure pop-up menu.
4. Click the AirPort tab, and make sure "Show AirPort status in menu bar" is enabled. Click Apply Now to activate the new settings.
5. From the AirPort menu in the menu bar, choose the network's name (this is the name given to the AirPort network when Internet Sharing was started); enter the network's password when prompted.

You should now be able to use the Internet via the computer providing Internet Sharing. Of course, this means that you can only access the Internet when that computer is on and connected.

Better Browsing Basics

I've spent most of this chapter helping you get the most out of your network/Internet settings and connections. I'd like to spend the rest of it talking about web browsing, since it's probably the most popular use of the Internet (followed closely by e-mail), yet one of the areas where users generally work the same way they did when they first starting surfing. These tips are fairly general and should work with any web browser.

Surfing with ICeCoffEE

User Level: normal or admin
Affects: individual user or computer
Terminal: no

You surely get a lot of your URLs right from web pages—you see a link and click on it. But how often do you find URLs in e-mail messages, text documents, application "About" boxes, or other sources *besides* web pages? Probably fairly often. If you're lucky, your e-mail client lets you click on a link to open it in your browser, but some don't. On top of that, what about all those URLs that are in text documents, dialog boxes, and the like?

Mac OS 9 and earlier had a clever third-party extension called ICeTEe that allowed you to command-click on a text URL to open it in your browser. Nicholas Riley has provided the same functionality in OS X via his freeware ICeCoffEE (`http://web.sabi.net/nriley/software/`). After installing ICeCoffEE and then logging out and back in, you'll be able to command-click on a URL in any Cocoa application to open it in your default web browser (the one selected in Internet preferences). I probably use this feature 20 to 30 times a day! The only drawback is that applications that haven't been updated to use OS X's text engine generally don't work with ICeCoffEE.

An added bonus of ICeCoffEE is that it adds a Services menu—that includes access to *all* Services, not just ICeCoffEE— to the text contextual menu (the one you get when you control/right-click on text in a Cocoa application). Although you could just as easily highlight some text and then go to the Services menu in the Apple Menu, having it in the contextual menu is a nice feature.

Simple (and Slick) Searching

One of the most frequent activities people do when surfing the Web is to search for things: information on Google, products on eBay, news, software updates... if it exists, someone's trying to find it. Yet the average search goes something like this: go to your web browser, type in the search engine URL (or, if you have the site bookmarked, select the bookmark), type in your search term(s), then wait for the results. It's not too big of a deal, but what if you could just press a key, type in a word or two, and everything else was automatic?

Just as it's true that if something exists, someone's trying to find it, it's also true that no matter how few steps it takes, someone wants fewer. The result is a plethora of "search assistance" utilities that make searching the Web easier. I used to think these utilities were, well, silly...until I found a couple that were both unobtrusive and powerful. These gems are the freeware utilities Searchling (`http://web.ics.purdue.edu/~mthole/searchling/`) and SearchBar (`http://www.pommsoft.com/searchbar/`). Both provide floating windows that allow you to search any of a number of search engines or websites. Both also provide a hotkey that automatically brings it to the front for quick searching. Although SearchBar's list of search engines and websites is much more extensive, and it provides quite a few more features than Searchling, I actually prefer Searchling because it's simple and elegant. Searchling exists only in the menu bar. You can either click on its icon, or press command+option+/, and a small text field drops down (Figure 9.5). You can choose the site to search from the pop-up menu to the left (many sites have options you can choose from the menu on the right), enter the text to be searched and hit return, and your web browser is opened to the results of the search.

Reading over what I just wrote, it may not seem like a lot of time or effort saved, but it really is. In writing this book I used Google several times each hour to find the URL for a piece of software. The procedure used by Searchling—command+option+/, type a few words, press return—is *much* faster than the typical search steps. Not to mention better on the hands and wrists.

FIGURE 9.5: Searchling lets you search many different sites and search engines quickly and easily.

TIP Speaking of search engines, a hidden gem is Google's Mac-specific search: `http://www.google.com/mac`.

Browsing the Browsers

At the time of this writing, Mac OS X comes with Microsoft's Internet Explorer pre-installed and selected as the default Web browser. Although Internet Explorer is an excellent browser (and provides the best compatibility with Web sites designed for the Windows version of Internet Explorer), along with the growing popularity of Mac OS X has emerged a growing number of excellent alternatives, including Apple's own Safari. I would be remiss if, in the midst of all the ways I encourage you to get more out of your Mac, I didn't also encourage you to explore alternative Web browsers. There are currently at least seven viable alternatives to Internet Explorer—browsers that you could feasibly switch to for all your browsing. None of them offer the same feature set as Internet Explorer, but they compensate by offering additional features such as tabbed browsing, pop-up ad blocking, and content filtering, to name a few. These browsers are:

- Camino (formerly Chimera Navigator): `http://www.mozilla.org/projects/camino/`, free.
- iCab: `http://www.icab.de/`, shareware.
- Mozilla: `http://www.mozilla.org/releases/`, free.
- Netscape: `http://channels.netscape.com/ns/browsers/`, free.
- OmniWeb: `http://www.omnigroup.com/applications/omniweb/download/`, commercial.
- Opera: `http://www.opera.com/products/desktop/`, commercial.
- Safari: `http://www.apple.com/safari/`, free.

My personal favorites are Camino and Safari. Camino is fast, looks great (it uses Mac OS X's Aqua interface and provides such Aqua features as customizable toolbars and transparency), and supports almost every website and plug-in I've come across. In addition, it has some really great features that I find it hard to do without after using them. The first is "tabbed" windows. I tend to open a lot of web pages at once. In Internet Explorer this means opening a lot of different windows; in Camino, each page opens within the *same* window. Each window gets its own "tab" at the top of the main browser window (Figure 9.6). I have my preferences set so that command-clicking on a link on a web page opens it in a new tab *behind* the tab I'm currently viewing. Another feature Camino provides is pop-up ad blocking. Since I started using Camino I haven't seen a single pop-up ad! Finally, Camino supports grouped bookmarks. Every morning I invariably visit the same six or seven websites for news and information. I've bookmarked these sites in a "group" bookmark; selecting this bookmark opens each page in its own tab, all at the same time.

You can customize Camino using some great freeware utilities like SpeedChimera (`http://homepage.mac.com/reedm/SpeedChimera.html`) and ChimerIcon (`http://homepage.mac.com/reinholdpenner`) and automatically download and install the latest development version using the excellent CaminoKnight (from the same developer as ChimerIcon). In addition, you can edit the Camino preference files—using SpeedChimera or a text editor—to enable features and tricks such as those found at `http://www.efritz.net/chimeratricks.html`.

Apple's own Safari is also excellent, and appears to be taking the crown of "browser of choice" for many Mac users. It's fast, stable, has a great—and familiar, if you've used any of Apple's iApps—interface, and by the time you read this should be pre-installed on all new Macs. It also has a few unique features, such as a built-in Google search system, the best bookmarks system of any browser, and built-in Rendezvous support—local Macs with Personal Web Sharing enabled (see Chapter 10 for more info on Personal Web Sharing) will show up in Safari's Rendezvous list as Rendezvous bookmarks. In addition, Apple has worked hard at making Safari as compatible as Internet Explorer so that we Mac users don't have to feel like second-class citizens when trying to access online banking and other Windows-oriented web services.

Like Camino, Safari is also quite customizable, with over 50 utilities for Safari available at the time of this writing, and more being released each week. Browse over to `http://www.versiontracker.com/macosx/` or `http://www.macupdate.com/` and do a search for "safari" and you'll get more results than you know what to do with. In addition, Apple has provided a number of Safari-enhancing AppleScripts at `http://www.apple.com/applescript/safari/`.

TIP

To see a list of Safari's keyboard shortcuts (there are lots of them), control/right-click on the Safari icon, and then select Show Package Contents from the resulting menu. Navigate to `/Contents/Resources/English.lproj/Shortcuts.html`. Drag this file onto the Safari icon in the Finder or the Dock to open it in Safari; to keep it handy, add it to your Safari bookmarks. (What you're actually doing is creating a link to one of the Safari Help files, but this bookmark is much faster than launching Help just to view keyboard shortcuts.)

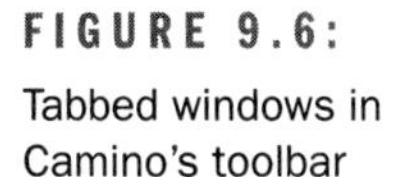

FIGURE 9.6: Tabbed windows in Camino's toolbar

But don't take my word for it; download a few of these browsers and give them a try; they're each unique in their own way, and all of them give Internet Explorer a run for its money. Even better, whereas Internet Explorer is lucky to get an update every six months, most of these alternative browsers are updated quite regularly—some weekly or even nightly!

Location Files, Part I

If you've ever downloaded software (freeware, shareware, etc.), chances are you've seen a file that says "Visit the website!" or something like that. Double-clicking that file opens the company's website in your Web browser. This is a nice trick for the software developer, but these kinds of files, called *Internet Location* files, are easy to create and use yourself. (Although the names are similar, don't confuse location files with network Locations, discussed earlier in the chapter.)

You can create a Location file several ways. The first is to drag a link/URL from a page in your web browser to the Finder (the Desktop, a folder, etc.). A Location file will be created that, when opened, will point your browser to that URL. This is a simple way to create a Location file for a site you haven't yet visited. The second method is to select the URL of the current page in your browser's address bar, and then drag it to the Finder. This is the easiest way to create a Location file for a page you are currently viewing.

NOTE Unfortunately, when you drag a link from a web page in Microsoft's Internet Explorer, Explorer downloads the text of the link's web page, rather than creating a location file. To create a location file, you need to control/right-click on the link, select Copy Link to Clipboard, and paste the URL into an application like TextEdit; you can then drag the URL to the Finder to create a Location file, as described below.

The third way is to highlight a URL in almost any text field—a text editor, an e-mail client, a word processor, a text field in a browser window—then drag that highlighted text to the Finder. OS X will automatically create a Location file for you. This is a great way to create a Location file when you find a URL in a ReadMe file or an e-mail message that you want to look at later. (Sadly, this won't work in Microsoft Word, since Word uses its own text engine that doesn't fully support OS X's drag-and-drop functionality.)

TIP If you frequently visit a website that requires a username and password to access—not sites that have "account logins" on the web page itself, but rather those that present a password dialog before you can even get to the website—you can actually include your username and password in a Location file. Open TextEdit and type the URL in the following format: `http://`*`username`*`:`*`password`*`@`*`domain`*, where *username* and *password* are the login name and password for the site, and *domain* is the URL you would normally use to access the site (minus the *http://*, which is already included). Highlight the entire URL and drag it to the Finder to create a new Location file that automatically provides your password information to the Web server.

I use Location files all the time when I see a web site or page that I want to come back to later, but I don't want to add to my browser's "permanent" bookmarks (e.g., a news article, an interesting site), or when someone sends me a URL to check out. I simply create a Location file on the Desktop, and it serves as both a temporary bookmark and as a reminder to go back and look at the website. However, you can also use Location files as an alternative to your browser's bookmarks/favorites. I'll talk about why you might want to do that in the next section. In case you're wondering, Location Files, Part II is located in Chapter 11—you can quickly access file servers and remove volumes using them.

Better Bookmarks (a.k.a. Finer Favorites)

You probably use your web browser's bookmarks or favorites feature to bookmark sites that you visit often, or to keep track of sites that you want to come back to later. However, you may not know that there are other ways to manage URLs besides the functionality built into your web browser. Why *wouldn't* you want to use your browser's built-in abilities? One reason is that third-party bookmark utilities provide a lot more functionality. The other is that you may want to be able to access your bookmarks no matter what browser you use—if you can use your bookmarks from within any browser, you're no longer tied to using a single one for fear of "losing" all those sites you've collected over the years.

Favorites from the Finder (and Dock)

The simplest way to have a universal set of bookmarks is to use Internet Location files as described in the previous section. Create a folder in the Finder and call it Bookmarks or Favorites, and create and/or place Location files inside. If you drag this folder to the Dock, as I showed you in Chapter 5, you can quickly access its contents—in this case, bookmarks to your favorite websites—by control/right-clicking on the folder in the Dock (Figure 9.7), and then selecting a Location file. You can even arrange your Location files into subfolders. (You can choose which browser will open Web Location files using the web tab of Internet preferences; in addition, most browsers also let you open Web Location files by dragging the files onto their icon in the Dock or into any open browser window.)

FIGURE 9.7: A homemade menu of bookmarks/favorites in the Dock

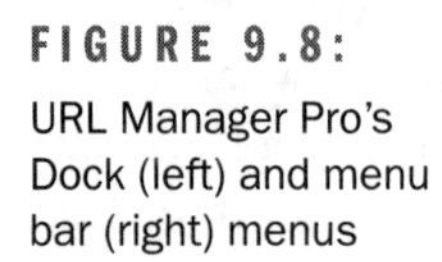

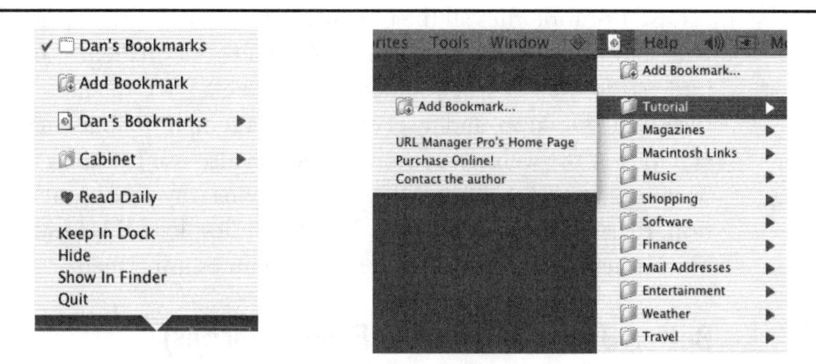

FIGURE 9.8: URL Manager Pro's Dock (left) and menu bar (right) menus

Managing Bookmarks Using URL Manager Pro

Although using location files in the Dock is quick and convenient, it doesn't offer a lot of functionality. If you're a heavy user of bookmarks/favorites, and especially if you tend to use several different browsers, your new best (browsing) friend is going to be URL Manager Pro (`http://www.url-manager.com/`)—UMP for short. UMP lets you use any number of bookmark files, and lets you access those bookmarks from within any application using its Dock menu (Figure 9.8). Selecting a URL from a bookmark file opens it in the web browser you've selected in Internet preferences. (If you have multiple bookmark files, you can also open them from the Cabinet submenu.) Even better, you can *add* a bookmark from within any browser via the Dock menu; you can even add a note to the bookmark when you save it—I use this on URLs that aren't very descriptive to help me remember what the site is. (A nice touch is that you can place the bookmark directly into a sub-folder of your bookmarks file by selecting the Add Bookmark item inside the sub-folder—a feature not available in most browsers.) You can even keep e-mail addresses in your UMP bookmark file; selecting an e-mail bookmark opens a new outgoing e-mail message, addressed to the chosen e-mail address, in your e-mail client.

In addition to its Dock menu, UMP supports what it calls *shared menus* in Internet Explorer, Netscape, Camino, OmniWeb, Opera, and iCab, as well as in most e-mail clients. These shared menus appear in the menu bar when a browser is active (or when any Internet-related application is active, if you prefer), and provide quick access to UMP's features, as well as to any of your UMP bookmark files (Figure 9.8). The great thing about these shared menus is that selecting a Web bookmark from within a browser using UMP's shared menus will open that Web page in the current browser, regardless of which browser is your preferred selection in Internet preferences.

If being able to use the same bookmarks in all your browsers isn't enough, UMP also offers some great bookmark management tools. You can import bookmarks from your existing browser's bookmarks/favorites, and you can export your UMP bookmarks to text, HTML, or location files. You can upload your bookmarks file(s) to an FTP site so that you can access it from multiple computers. You can sort bookmarks in a number of different ways, eliminate duplicate bookmarks, search bookmark URLs, titles, and notes...the list goes on and on. If you're a web addict, URL Manager Pro is one of the most useful utilities you can find.

Synchronizing (Bookmarks) Succinctly

So what if you're not as bonkers for bookmarks as I am, and you don't need something like URL Manager Pro? What if you just wish you could consolidate or synchronize your bookmarks/favorites between browsers? The shareware Bookit (`http://www.everydaysoftware.net/bookit/`) is the answer for you. When you run Bookit, it asks you which browsers' bookmarks you want to synchronize (it supports Camino/Chimera, iCab, Internet Explorer, Mozilla, Netscape, OmniWeb, Opera, and Safari), and which is your default/preferred browser. It then opens a window with your default browser's bookmarks in the main window—this will become your "universal" bookmarks file—and a list to the right of any bookmarks found in your other browsers that don't exist in your default browser's bookmarks (Figure 9.9). Clicking on a bookmark on the right shows you the full URL, as well as which bookmarks/favorites file it comes from; drag it to the main window to add it to your main bookmarks file. (You can also create new folders, rearrange bookmarks and folders, and perform other organizational tasks on your main bookmarks file.)

Once you're done consolidating and organizing all your browsers' bookmarks, click the Write... button; you'll be asked which browser(s) you want to use this new master bookmarks file. Bookit will then create a new, updated bookmarks/favorites file for each of the browsers you select. You can also choose to write a Bookit file to be used by the Bookit Dockling or menu; the Dockling and menu let you access your master bookmarks file at any time from the Dock or the menu bar, respectively.

The only downside to Bookit is that it doesn't automatically consolidate all your bookmarks/favorites; you have to run it periodically and repeat the process described above. However, it allows you to use your browsers' bookmarks/favorites, instead of a third-party bookmark utility, which some users find more convenient. If you don't care about the extra features of something like URL Manager Pro, Bookit may serve your needs just fine.

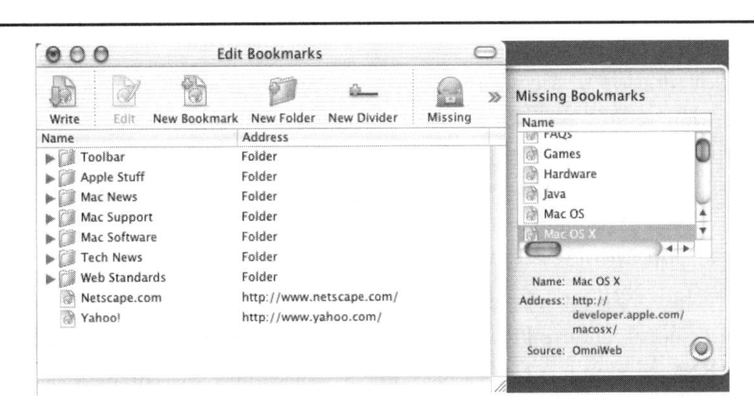

FIGURE 9.9: Bookit lets you synchronize the bookmarks of all your browsers.

Preventing Pop-Ups (Pop-Up Ads, That Is)

User Level: any
Affects: individual user
Terminal: no

I mentioned earlier that many of the web browsers available for Mac OS X have pop-up advertisement blocking built in. However, the browser used by more Mac users than any other (at least at the time of this writing), Internet Explorer, does not. When using Internet Explorer, you're at the mercy of web advertising. To make matters worse, both advertisers and legitimate website content take advantage of pop-up windows, so the solution isn't as simple as being able to "turn off" pop-ups.

Fortunately, there are a couple of good utilities on the market designed specifically for blocking pop-up ads in Internet Explorer. Unpopular (`http://www.rampellsoft.com/`) and Pop-Up Zapper (`http://www.batista.org/`) both prevent pop-up ads from, well, popping up. In addition, they both offer varying levels of anti-pop-up protection, since some sites may use pop-up windows that you *want* to see. You can also customize both by choosing particular sites to block or allow pop-up windows. Finally, both utilities allow you to turn them off temporarily in case you want to allow all pop-ups.

The main difference between the two utilities is in how they decide what *not* to block. Pop-Up Zapper tries to block every pop-up window unless you specifically tell it to allow them from certain domains or sites. Unpopular, on the other hand, uses a database of known sites, updated regularly by the developers, to decide what to allow and prevent. Using feedback from users, the developers have created a list of "desired" pop-up sites (such as polls on the CNN website) and "undesired" sites, and Unpopular periodically updates its preferences by accessing this database. As a user, you can contribute to the database yourself using Unpopular's reporting feature.

Getting Your Internet Explorer Windows Back to Size

User Level: any
Affects: individual user
Terminal: no

In addition to the annoyance of pop-up ads themselves, another problem with ads (and even some legitimate sites) is that they resize your browser windows, and, at least in the case of Internet Explorer, the new (undesired) window size sticks. You end up having to manually resize your browser back to your preferred size. (The reason I single out Internet Explorer here is that many other web browsers remember your preferred window size when a website or pop-up ad resizes the browser window.)

If you find this as annoying as I do, here's a trick that will save you some mousing about. In Explorer, choose Favorites ➢ Organize Favorites ➢ New Favorite. Name it something like Restore Window Size, and in the Address field, type **`javascript:window.resizeTo(880,600)`**.

(The first number is the width of your preferred window size in pixels; the second is the height. Adjust the numbers to your preference.) Click OK and the new Favorite is created. Whenever your Explorer window gets resized, select this new Favorite from Explorer's Favorites menu, and the window will be restored to your preferred size.

Setting Up Servers

User Level: admin
Affects: computer
Terminal: possibly

Before we move on, I want to squeeze in a few quick notes about setting up more advanced Internet services on your Mac. In the next chapter I'll talk about setting up web and file servers; however, you should be aware that in addition to being a great desktop operating system, Mac OS X is also an industrial-strength server platform. It comes with built-in web, mail, FTP, file, Telnet, SSH, and print servers. By activating these, or installing alternatives, you can turn your Mac into a real Internet powerhouse. Here are just a few articles and web resources that can get you started:

- Email Servers and Mac OS X (`http://www.stepwise.com/Articles/Workbench/eart.index.html`): an excellent site with information on replacing OS X's built-in sendmail server with the more secure—and generally more well-respected—postfix mail server.
- Homemade Dot-Mac with OS X (`http://www.macdevcenter.com/pub/a/mac/2002/08/09/homemade_dotmac.html`): a tutorial for setting your Mac up to provide many of the same services available through Apple's .Mac service.
- Serving iCal Calendars Using WebDAV (`http://www.macdevcenter.com/pub/a/mac/2002/09/20/ical_webdav.html`): a tutorial on how to set up a WebDAV server using OS X's built-in Apache web server. You can find out more about WebDAV from `http://www.webdav.org/`, but the quick "Why would I want it?" explanation is that with WebDAV enabled on your Mac, you can host your own iCal calendar without having to sign up for Apple's .Mac service.

Moving On...

Now that you've gotten some good tips on making network connections, it's time to take advantage of them. The most common uses for network connections are Internet use, file sharing/access, remote access and control, and printing. I covered Internet use a bit in this chapter, and in the online supplement to the book on the iApps and Mail. In the next few chapters I'll show you how to share files with others and access files on other computers; how to control your Mac remotely and how to take advantage of Mac OS X's impressive printing features.

Chapter 10

Stellar Sharing Strategies

(Or: All the ways you can share your files with others.)

It used to be that sharing files with other people meant copying those files to a floppy (or, if you were lucky, to a CD-ROM) and then handing (or mailing) the floppy or CD to the recipient. The advent of high-speed Internet connections has changed all that, as most people can now use e-mail to send files back and forth. However, sometimes e-mail isn't the best solution—very large files and shared files that multiple users need to work on are a couple of good examples—and not everyone likes filling up their e-mail inbox with files.

Luckily, Mac OS X is the most flexible OS on the planet in terms of its varied offerings for sharing files and data (generally called *sharing*; shared volumes or directories are often called *shares*). You can share files with other users of your computer, over a local network, and even over the Internet. What's more, you often have multiple ways to share files with each group of people. In this chapter, I'm going to cover all of the ways in which you can share files, starting with local sharing and then moving on to network and Internet sharing. For each method of sharing, I'll make it clear what can be shared, who can and can't access files, how to configure sharing, and how other users can access shared files. I'll also show you how to go beyond the standard options provided by Mac OS X to make your Mac a supercharged sharing machine.

TIP

In this chapter I explain how *other* users can access *your* shared files; in the next chapter I cover how *you* can connect to shares on your own computer or *other* computers.

As you read this chapter, keep in mind that unless otherwise noted, "sharing" includes the ability to both read and write files. If you provide someone with access to a directory, they can not only read files within that directory, but they can usually copy files *to* that directory, as well. So sharing is not only a good way to provide access to files; it's also a good way for others to give files to you.

NOTE Most of the techniques in this chapter for sharing files require an Internet connection. I'm going to assume that you have Internet access and that you know how to connect to the Internet.

WARNING If you're sharing files remotely (over a network or over the Internet), you're opening up your computer to other users that you can't see and whose identity you can't verify. This means that if you enable any type of remote sharing, you should be sure that the users of your Mac have good passwords, and change them periodically; it also means you should consider some type of network/firewall security. I talk about these topics in Chapter 13.

Sharing Locally: The Public and Shared Folders

User Level: any
Affects: individual user
Terminal: no

The simplest form of sharing in OS X is to make files available for other people who actually sit at your computer. Mac OS X has two ways of doing this.

What Does It Share?

Mac OS X has two special types of folders specifically designed to share files with other users of your computer. The first is a special folder called `Shared`, located in the main `/Users` directory. The Shared folder is different from other user folders in two significant ways. First, it does not correspond to any particular user; rather, it exists regardless of how many (or few) user accounts exist on your Mac. Second, all users can view the contents of the Shared directory, can move files to it, and can create files inside of it. In other words, as the name implies, it is a folder that is *shared* by all users.

The second way to share files with other local users is to use your personal Public folder, located at `/Users/`*`username`*`/Public`. Whereas most user-level folders prevent other users from even viewing their contents, the Public folder allows other users to view its contents and access files inside of it. You can make files available to other users by placing them in your own Public folder, and other users can share files with you by placing them in their own Public folder.

TIP The Public folder has a special folder inside of it called `Drop Box`. If you Get Info on this folder, you'll see that, for everyone but the owner, its permissions are set to "Write only (Drop Box)." Think of this folder as your own personal mailbox—other users can drop files inside, but no one except you can get them out, or even verify that they exist. This folder is OS X's way for users to exchange files securely.

There are two caveats I should mention when it comes to the Shared and Public directories. The first is that file permissions still apply. Documents created in these folders are set, by default, to allow other users Read Only access, and documents copied or moved to them retain their original permissions. In other words, if you want others to be able to edit a file that you place in one of these directories, you may need to manually change its permissions as discussed in Chapter 1. This includes the Drop Box—if you give someone a file you want them to be able to edit, be sure to give them Write access before putting it in their Drop Box.

The second caveat is that by default, placing files in the Public or Shared folders provides the same level of access to *all* other users. If you have a sensitive document to which you want to limit access to a single individual, a better approach is to use their Drop Box. However, what if you want to provide access to a file to a *group* of users, but not *all* users? The answer is to use groups, as discussed in Chapter 1. You can create a group that includes only those users to which you want to give access to a file. Using the Finder's Get Info command or a utility like XRay or FileXaminer, you would give the members of that group Read Only or Read & Write access, while restricting Others to No Access. You can then place the file in the Shared folder or your Public directory—even though the file will be in plain sight, only members of the group will be able to access it.

Finally, you may be wondering what the difference is between the Public and Shared folders. Besides the existence of the Drop Box in Public folders, there are two main differences. First, Public folders are set to allow Read & Write access to the owner, but Read Only access to other users, whereas the Shared folder allows Read & Write access for all users. Second, Public folders are accessible remotely via Personal File Sharing (which I'll talk about in a bit) by default, whereas the Shared folder is not.

Who Can Access Files?

Any user who has an account on your Mac has access to the main Shared folder and to every user's Public folder.

How Do I Configure It?

Other than being careful with the permissions of files you place in the Public or Shared directories, no configuration is necessary.

How Do Others Access Files?

Other users can access files in these folders by simply navigating to them in the Finder.

Sharing Files Locally Using Multiple Volumes/Drives

Although I cover the topic of multiple volumes and drives in more detail in Appendix B, I want to mention it here as it relates to sharing files and file security. If you have multiple hard drives or volumes (including multiple partitions of a single hard disk), you should be aware that the default permissions for files created on any non-boot volume are Read & Write for the owner, and Read Only for everyone else. Thus, saving a file to a non-boot volume is identical to saving it to a Public folder. This may be exactly what you want—many people use such a secondary volume as a place to share files. However, if it's not, you can change permissions for individual folders or documents on the volume (or for the entire volume) using the Finder's Get Info command. Another solution is to create files in a "private" area of your own user folder first, and then copy them to the non-boot volume (since files copied to a shared area retain their original permissions).

At the other extreme, perhaps you have an extra hard drive that you want to use for shared projects—what if you *want* all users to be able to read and write to all files? Simply select the drive on the Desktop or in a Finder window and select File ➢ Get Info. In the Ownership & Permissions panel, check the box next to "Ignore ownership on this volume." Now OS X will ignore any and all permissions and restrictions on files on that volume. (Note that this change requires admin access.)

Sharing Files Locally: Bluetooth

User Level: any
Affects: individual user
Terminal: no

In Chapter 9, I mentioned that OS X supports the Bluetooth wireless protocol, and supports Bluetooth as a way to exchange data between two computers within range of each other. You can use Bluetooth to your advantage as a way of quickly sharing small files between two Bluetooth-equipped computers.

NOTE Because of its relatively slow speed, Bluetooth isn't the best way to share large files; however, for anything under a few hundred kilobytes, it should be fine.

What Does It Share?

Via "browsing" (explained below), you can share files in the Shared user folder (or any other single folder you designate) over a Bluetooth connection. In addition, you can send individual files directly to another Bluetooth-equipped Mac on a case-by-case basis.

Who Can Access Files?

Any Mac or Windows computer that has been paired with yours (as described in Chapter 9) can send files to and receive files from your Mac (or browse your Shared folder, provided that option is enabled). Because other users need to provide a Bluetooth authentication password to pair their computer with yours, standard OS X user accounts are unnecessary. (This makes

Bluetooth a convenient option for one-time file exchanges, since you don't need to set up a special account on your Mac.)

How Do I Configure It?

There is really very little configuration necessary for basic Bluetooth sharing; if you've paired with another Bluetooth-enabled computer, you're already set up and can exchange files as described below.

However, under Mac OS X 10.2.4 and later, you can take advantage of Bluetooth *browsing*—the ability for a paired computer to actually browse a directory of files and access the files much like it would using Personal File Sharing or FTP. To enable Bluetooth browsing, go to the File Exchange tab of Bluetooth preferences. Under the Bluetooth File Transfer section, check the box next to "Allow other devices to browse files on this computer." By default, they can browse the Shared user folder; however, you can choose any folder on your computer by clicking Choose Folder....

WARNING Because permissions do not apply when using Bluetooth browsing, be sure to choose a folder that doesn't contain sensitive data (or contain any sub-folders that may contain sensitive data). Unless the only computer that will pair with your Mac is another computer of your own, I recommend sticking with the Shared user folder.

How Do Others Access Files?

As I mentioned earlier, there are two ways to share files via Bluetooth: direct Bluetooth transfers and Bluetooth browsing.

Exchanging Files via Bluetooth File Exchange (Individual File Transfers)

If another computer is paired with yours, you can send individual files to it using the Bluetooth File Exchange utility (located in `/Applications/Utilities`). To do so, drop a file onto the Bluetooth File Exchange utility icon in the Finder (or choose File ➢ Send File... from within Bluetooth File Exchange, and then navigate to the file); a dialog will appear asking you to select the Bluetooth device to which you want to send the file. If you have multiple Bluetooth pairings, as I do, you can view just paired computers by selecting Computers from the Device Type pop-up menu (Figure 10.1). Click Send to initiate the file exchange. If the user of the selected computer has chosen to accept files automatically, the file will be transferred immediately; if not, the transfer will not commence until the user has manually accepted the file.

TIP If you need to send multiple files or documents via Bluetooth File Exchange, it's often easier to combine them into a single StuffIt or Zip archive so that you only have to send one file. (See "When to Compress Files for Sharing.")

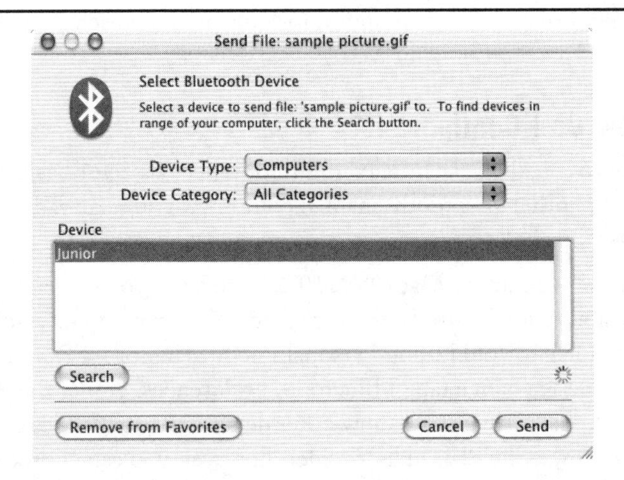

FIGURE 10.1: Selecting a device to send a file via Bluetooth

The process works in reverse if another user wants to send a file to your Mac. They initiate a transfer, and if you've selected "Accept files without warning" in the File Exchange tab of Bluetooth preferences, the file will be saved to the directory you've chosen under "Folder for accepted items." If you've instead selected "Prompt for each file," a dialog will appear that tells you the name of the file and which paired device is sending it, and asks you if you want to accept the file.

Exchanging Files via Bluetooth File Transfer (Browsing)

If you prefer to allow other users to browse a folder on your hard drive and send files to, or retrieve files from, that folder, you need to enable the Bluetooth File Transfer option as described earlier. They will then be able to connect to, and browse, that particular folder at any time.

For Mac users, this is done by launching Bluetooth File Exchange and choosing File ➢ Browse Device.... In the resulting dialog (which looks almost identical to the Send File... dialog), they should select your Mac, and then click Browse. A navigation dialog will appear (similar to an OS X Open/Save dialog) that includes Get... and Put... buttons. To download a file from your Mac, they should select it in the dialog and click Get...; conversely, to copy a file to your Mac, they should click Put... and then select the file from their own hard drive.

If you've enabled the Bluetooth status menu in Bluetooth preferences, you can access both the Send File and Browse Device commands from the menu bar at any time.

NOTE Keep in mind that the settings for Bluetooth File Exchange (sending/receiving individual files) and Bluetooth File Transfer (browsing) are independent. (Yes, it's confusing that Apple has named the former using the same name as the application you use to do both.) The ability to accept or reject each file sent to your Mac does not apply via Bluetooth browsing, and the folders used by each are different, as reflected in the File Exchange tab of Bluetooth preferences.

Root and Admin Access and Sharing

For each type of sharing that I discuss in this chapter, I provide a summary of which files users can access. However, be aware that if you have enabled the root account, anyone logging in to your Mac (remotely or locally) *as* the root user will generally be able to access any file on your computer, regardless of the standard restrictions that are in place. (The lone exception to this would be Web Sharing; unless you've manually configured your Mac to provide access outside of the standard Web Sharing folders, user level doesn't apply when connecting.) This is a good argument for not enabling the root account if you have any remote sharing services enabled.

What's more, if you've enabled Remote Login (which I talk about in the next chapter), any admin user will be able to remotely enable the root account, and then log in using that account. This is a good argument for not giving out admin-level accounts to other users (or for not enabling Remote Login, depending on how you look at it).

Sharing Remotely: iDisk

User Level: any
Affects: individual user/.Mac account
Terminal: no

If you're a subscriber to Apple's .Mac Internet services, one of the benefits is your own personal iDisk. I've talked about iDisks a couple times already in the book, but I want to discuss it here as a way to share files. Although an iDisk technically isn't part of OS X, I include it here for two reasons. First, many Mac users *are* .Mac subscribers. Second, and more importantly, since iDisks are hosted on Apple's servers rather than on your own computer, placing files that you want to share on your iDisk means that you don't have to enable any sharing services—which in turn means that you don't have to worry as much about the potential for security issues that enabling such services brings.

What Does It Share?

Your iDisk shares any files that you place in its Public folder. (The Public folder on your iDisk is independent of your `~/Public` directory; however, the two are similar in that they are the only personal folders to which other users have access.)

TIP If you give someone your .Mac username and password, they can view *all* files in *all* folders of your iDisk. If you want to securely share files with a group of people in different locations, buying a .Mac account and sharing the username and password is quite convenient.

Who Can Access Files?

Any user with an Internet connection, including both Mac and Windows users, can access your iDisk.

How Do I Configure It?

If you have only a single .Mac account, enter your .Mac username and password in the .Mac tab of Internet preferences. Then select Go ➢ iDisk (or press shift+command+I, or click on the iDisk toolbar item if you've added it to Finder window toolbars) to mount your iDisk in the Finder. Place any files you want to share in the Public folder at the root level.

If you have multiple .Mac accounts, an easier way to mount them is to use the iDisk Utility mentioned in Chapter 7, available from Apple's .Mac website (`http://www.mac.com/`). In the Open iDisk pane, enter a member name and password and click the Open button.

TIP If you have multiple .Mac accounts, or if you frequently access multiple iDisks, a much more convenient way to access them is using Location files. I discuss these Location files in the next chapter when I talk about how to connect to shares.

Finally, using either the iDisk tab of Internet preferences, or the Public Folder Access pane of iDisk Utility (Figure 10.2), you can control access to your iDisk's Public folder. You can decide whether other users have Read-Only access (which prevents them from editing or placing files on your iDisk) or Read-Write access (which lets them both access files on and copy files to your iDisk). You can also decide whether users will have to provide a password to access your iDisk's Public folder.

FIGURE 10.2: Using iDisk Utility to control access to your Public folder

How Do Others Access Files?

Users of Mac OS X can access your iDisk in two ways. Using the Open Public Folder pane of iDisk Utility, they can simply enter your member name and click the Open button (if you've set your iDisk to require a password, they'll be asked to enter it; they should use "public" as the username).

OS X users can also access your iDisk by selecting Go ➢ Connect to Server… (or pressing command+K) in the Finder, and then entering `http://idisk.mac.com/membername/Public` in the Address field. If your iDisk is password-protected, a dialog will appear; they should enter "public" as the username and your iDisk's Public folder password in the password field.

Users of other operating systems can access your iDisk's Public folder using the following techniques:

Mac OS 9 Choose Apple Menu ➢ Chooser, and then click the AppleShare icon on the left. Click the Server IP Address… button on the right, enter **`idisk.mac.com`** in the Server Address field, and then click Connect. In the resulting dialog, enter your .Mac member name (and, if applicable, your Public folder password) and then click Connect. Unfortunately, according to Apple, users connecting from OS 9's Chooser, which connects via AFP (Apple File Protocol, discussed later in the chapter) rather than WebDAV (an extension of the HTTP protocol used for web pages), will not be able to copy files to your iDisk Public folder or save changes to documents that reside in your iDisk Public folder.

Windows XP Open My Computer and then choose Tools ➢ Map Network Drive. Enter `http://idisk.mac.com/membername` (where *membername* is your .Mac member name). For authentication, use your .Mac member name and, if necessary, your Public folder password.

Windows 2000 Open My Computer and then choose Tools ➢ Map Network Drive. Click "Web folder or FTP site," and then enter the address provided above.

Windows 98 Open My Computer, open the Web Folders icon, and then double-click on Add Web Folder. Enter the address provided above.

Sharing iDisk Files Using a Web Page

In addition to providing direct access to your Public folder, you can also set up a web page that allows other users to view or download files located in that folder. Go to the main .Mac web page (`http://www.mac.com/`) and click on the Home Page graphic. Log in to your .Mac account, and on the main Home Page page, click the File Sharing tab. Click a color for your File Sharing web page, and you'll be presented with the configuration screen. You can edit the text on the page by clicking the Edit button, and update the web page (if you've recently added files) by pressing the Update button. Once your File Sharing page is ready, press the Publish button to make your Public folder files available via the Web. (Once you do this, you'll be presented with the URL of your File Sharing page—make sure you keep a record of it.)

When to Compress Files for Sharing

When sharing files, especially over a network or Internet connection, there are a couple of things to keep in mind. The first is that even though most Internet connections today are much faster than those of a few years ago, many people are still using dial-up connections, and even broadband connections have their limits. If you're sharing files over the Internet, or over a slower local connection such as Bluetooth, I highly recommend using a file compression utility to make your shared files as small a possible. This will shorten the time it takes others to download or access files, and it will save bandwidth for you.

Luckily, OS X ships with a good compression utility. Aladdin's DropStuff (inside the `StuffIt Lite` folder in `/Applications/Utilities`) is a shareware version of the commercial StuffIt package. If you drop individual files or entire folders of files onto its icon, they will be compressed using the StuffIt compression format; the end result is a single file that is significantly smaller than the original. If you'll be sharing your files with Windows users, a better choice would be Aladdin's DropZip utility (located in the same folder), which instead compresses your files using the `.zip` format, more common on the Windows side of things. (Another option, if you're sharing files with only Mac users, is to create compressed disk images; I discuss how to do this in Chapter 7.)

Compression won't be convenient for files that will be used often, such as documents that are in progress or project files that multiple users will be accessing frequently, but for files that you are simply making available for a single download (or for download by a number of people), compression is a very good idea.

The second thing to be aware of when sharing files is that the file structures of some files on the Mac platform can present problems for Internet transfers. As discussed in Chapter 5, many Mac files—especially those from Mac OS 9 and earlier, but also many created in Mac OS X—are comprised of two parts: a data fork and a resource fork. Simply put, the data fork contains the file's data, and the resource fork contains information about the file. Unfortunately, although Apple's Personal File Sharing protocol keeps both forks intact, some other Internet protocols, such as FTP (discussed shortly), can strip the resource forks in transit. In addition, copying a file to a Windows or Unix computer and then back to the Mac may also strip the resource fork. (This generally isn't a problem for common document formats such as HTML, text, Word, and Excel files; it becomes an issue with more complex files such as applications.)

For this reason I also recommend using a program such as DropZip to compress files for sharing over FTP or with Windows or UNIX computers—such compression will preserve the resource fork.

WARNING If you've given your iDisk's Public folder a password, be aware that iDisk's File Sharing web page does *not* honor that password. Thus, if you make files available using .Mac's Home Page feature, *any* user who knows your .Mac member name will have access to the files in your iDisk's Public folder. To prevent this, Home Page provides a way to protect your site with its own password—just click the "Protect this site" button on the main Home Page web page. Also, if you take advantage of the Home Page password protection option, be aware that *both* your username and password are case sensitive, so when you provide another user with the URL to your website, be sure the username portion of it is capitalized correctly.

Sharing Remotely: Personal File Sharing

User Level: admin to enable and configure; any user can share files
Affects: computer
Terminal: no

If you'd rather not have to upload files to an iDisk to share them, you can use one of OS X's built-in file sharing services. These services allow others to access files that actually reside on your computer, over a network or the Internet. Like Mac OS 9 before it, Mac OS X provides—via Personal File Sharing—Apple's own File Sharing protocol (also called *Apple File Protocol* or AFP), which is the best way to share files with other Macs over a local network. However, unlike OS 9, it is also a fast and reliable way to share files over the Internet.

What Does It Share?

By default, Personal File Sharing provides non-admin users with remote access to the files in their own user folder, and to files in other users' Public folders. This means that if you want other users to be able to access files using Personal File Sharing, be sure to put those files in your Public Folder. However, it's possible to further restrict access, or to provide access to additional directories; I'll talk about how to do both under "How Do I Configure It?"

NOTE When admin-level users connect over Personal File Sharing, they have the same access to files as they would if they were sitting at the computer. In other words, they can access any file except for those inside other users' private directories.

Who Can Access Files?

By default, individuals with a user account on your computer can access their own user folder, and other users' Public folders, via Personal File Sharing. In addition, users *without* an account can connect as Guest (more on that in a bit), but their access is restricted to just Public folders. The only caveat is that to connect, remote users must have a Mac that supports Apple File Protocol over TCP/IP (which is basically Mac OS 9 or OS X).

WARNING By default, an admin-level user can also remotely connect *as any other user* via Personal File Sharing by using the user's username and their *own* admin-level password (more on connecting below). This is a true administration feature, as it allows the administrator to test normal user accounts and their Personal File Sharing access. However, because this feature can be misused in the wrong hands, it's yet another reason not to provide admin access to anyone who doesn't absolutely need it.

How Do You Configure It?

Once you've got a network or Internet connection, Personal File Sharing requires little configuration for basic operation. First, you give your computer a Computer Name and a Rendezvous Name in the Sharing pane of System Preferences. The first is your computer's "official" name—this shows up in Finder windows and in Terminal—whereas the Rendezvous Name is your computer's name as it appears to Rendezvous-enabled devices. (I discussed Rendezvous in the previous chapter.) Then you simply check the box next to Personal File Sharing in the Services tab (Figure 10.3). To stop sharing files this way, either uncheck the box, or select Personal File Sharing and click the Stop button on the right. Once you've enabled Personal File Sharing, you'll see a helpful message at the bottom of the window: "Other Macintosh users can access your computer at `afp://yourIPaddress/`".

FIGURE 10.3: Enabling Personal File Sharing in Sharing preferences

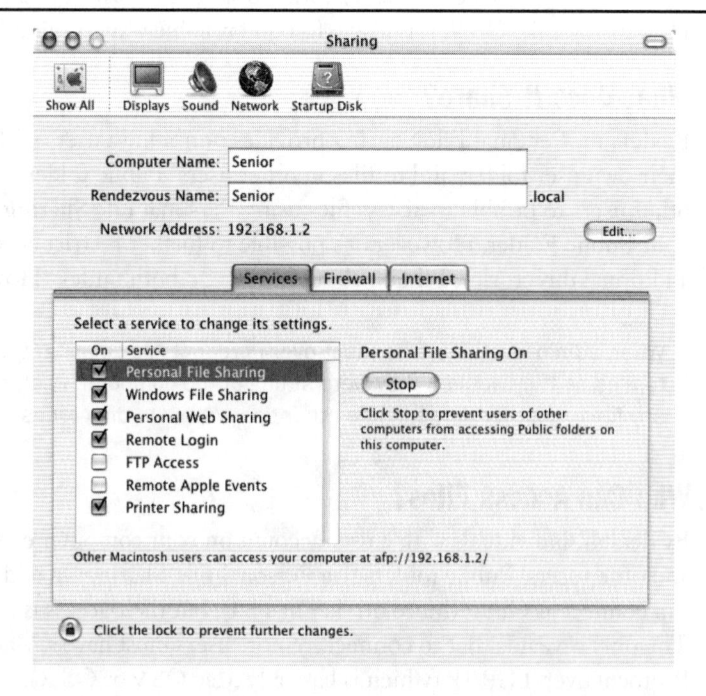

NOTE If you're behind an Internet router, the IP address provided by the Sharing preference pane will only be valid for other users on your local network; in addition, if you have a dynamic IP address, it will only be valid until your ISP provides you with a different one. See the sidebar "Your IP Address: Internet Routers, Port Caveats, and Dynamic IPs" for information on working around these limitations.

Although enabling Personal File Sharing for basic operation is quite simple, there are a number of options available to you via third-party utilities. You can disable Guest Access, create sharing-only user accounts, disable the sharing of some or all Public folders, enable the sharing of additional directories, and much more. Here are some of the most convenient and useful options and how to enable them.

Disabling Guest Access to Personal File Sharing

By default OS X's Personal File Sharing allows Guest users—users who don't have their own account on your computer but can still connect and access a limited group of files (those in Public folders). Although this feature is quite useful for providing access to certain files for remote users without having to create local accounts for them, it also means that anyone who knows your IP address can potentially connect as a Guest user and access Public files. Although this is not a major security issue—the only "damage" a Guest user can do is to download copies of files in Public folders—you may not want to completely open up your Public files to the… um, public.

If Guest Access concerns you, you can disable it (and re-enable it at any time) using the donationware SharePoints (`http://www.hornware.com/sharepoints/`). A few other, simpler, utilities out there allow you to toggle Guest Access, but SharePoints does so much more, and I'll use it for so many of the examples in this section, that I consider it to be the Swiss Army Knife of Personal File Sharing utilities. (It also has other capabilities; you may have used it in Chapter 1 to set up a new group.) It's available as both a preference pane and an application. I personally prefer the preference pane version (it seems more intuitive to me to work with Personal File Sharing settings in System Preferences), but I'm going to use the application version for this discussion because the screenshots are clearer. Both versions function identically. To disable Guest Access, launch SharePoints and then follow these steps:

1. Click on the AFS Properties tab (AppleFileServer Properties in older versions of SharePoints).
2. In the Miscellaneous Properties section, uncheck the box next to Allow Guess Access.
3. Click the Update AppleFileServer Properties button. You'll be asked for your admin-level username and password.
4. Click the Restart AppleFileServer button to restart Personal File Sharing. (If it is currently disabled, this will start it up for you.)

Other users will no longer be able to log in as Guest and access user Public folders. (See "How Do Others Access Files?") To re-enable Guest Access (or if for some reason your Mac never had it enabled), use the same procedure but *check* the box next to Allow Guest Access instead.

TIP Most of the Personal File Sharing custom settings I discuss in this chapter are accessible via Terminal and/or NetInfo Manager. However, using a utility like SharePoints is so much easier and—because there's no chance for mistyping—safer that there's really no reason not to use it.

Creating File Sharing Only Users

If you've disabled Guest Access, you may be wondering how you *allow* remote access to Personal File Sharing to individuals who don't have a local account. You could create a single, extra user account and then provide that username and password to everyone you want to be able to access files over Personal File Sharing. However, that would be a rather inconvenient and messy solution. A better solution is to create "File Sharing Only" users. Again, SharePoints is the easiest way to do this.

File Sharing Only users can connect to Personal File Sharing, but can't log in locally, don't have their own user directory, and cannot log in using the Remote Login feature (discussed later in this chapter when I cover SFTP sharing, and in the next chapter when I talk about Remote Access). These types of user accounts are ideal for users who will never actually sit down at your computer and log in, but with whom you want to share files. To create a File Sharing Only account using SharePoints:

1. Click on the Users & "Public" Shares tab.
2. Under Individual Users, fill in the user's full and short name (just as if you were setting up a new account in Accounts preferences).
3. In the Group pop-up menu, select "staff." (If you've set up any groups of your own, and you want the new user to be a member of one of those groups, you could select that group name instead.)
4. Click the Get Next UID button; SharePoints will automatically assign the new user the next available user ID (Figure 10.4).
5. Ignore the Public Directory Shared? pop-up menu; users created within SharePoints do not have Public folders. (This option exists to allow you to edit existing user accounts, as described in the next section.)
6. Click Add New User (provide your admin username and password if prompted), then click Restart AppleFileServer to restart Personal File Sharing.

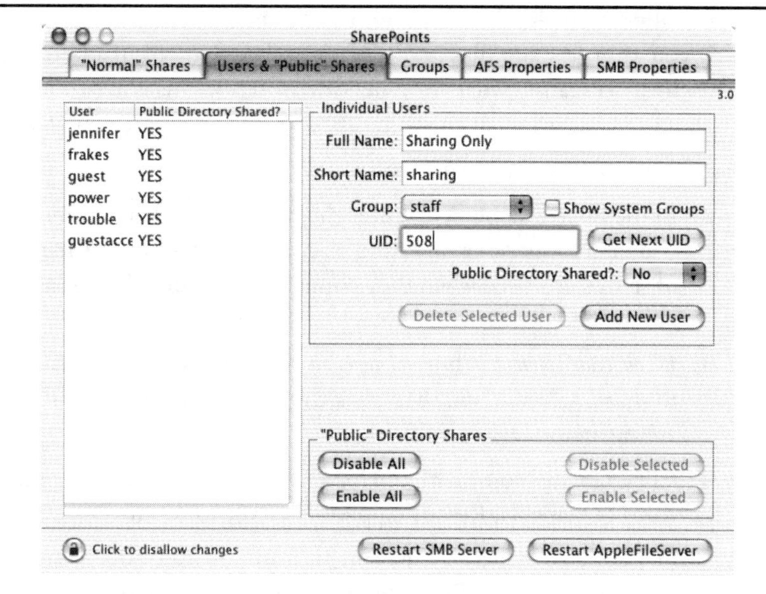

FIGURE 10.4: Setting up a File Sharing Only user in SharePoints

The new user you just created will be able to log in via Personal File Sharing and view Public folders, but will have no other system privileges.

Disabling/Enabling Sharing of Public Directories

What if you *don't* want remote users to be able to access certain, or all, user Public folders? You can use SharePoints to disable the sharing of individual Public folders, or you can choose to disable *all* Public folder sharing and then manually enable the sharing of other folders (using the next tip). For example, you could choose to disable all Public folder sharing, and then provide access to the Shared folder instead. To edit the sharing of *Public* folders:

1. Click on the Users & "Public" Shares tab.
2. In the User column on the left, select the user whose Public folder you want to prevent from being shared.
3. In the "Public" Directory Shares section, click Disable Selected. (Or click Enable Selected if you had previously disabled sharing for that user and want to re-enable it.) If asked, enter your admin-level username and password.
4. Repeat Steps 1–3 to disable/enable sharing for additional users' Public directories.
5. Click Restart AppleFileServer to restart Personal File Sharing.

TIP You can quickly disable or enable the sharing of *all* Public directories using the Disable All and Enable All buttons.

Enabling Sharing of Additional Directories

If you want to share files in directories other than, or in addition to, Public folders, you can do this by creating what are called *sharepoints*. (This is actually where SharePoints got its name—it was originally just a utility to help you create new sharepoints.)

1. Click on the "Normal" Shares tab.
2. In the Share Name field, enter the name of the share. This can be the name of the folder you plan to share, or anything else. However, since this name will be included in the list of shares users see when they connect to Personal File Sharing, it should be something unique and descriptive.
3. Click the Browse… button next to the Directory field. Navigate to the folder you want to share, select it, and then click the Open button. The path to your chosen folder will appear in the Directory field.
4. Click Create New Share to create the share; if prompted, enter your username and password. Then click Restart AppleFileServer to restart Personal File Sharing.

You can delete a share by selecting it from the list of shares and then clicking Delete Selected Share. You can also use SharePoints to quickly change the permissions of the shared directory by selecting a share and then clicking then Show File System Properties button. A drawer will slide out that shows the current owner, group, and permissions for the selected share. You can change them via the pop-up menus. However, SharePoints can only change the permissions for the top level of the shared directory. To provide more or less access to the files within the directory, you should use the Finder's Get Info command or a third-party file utility.

TIP To disable a custom share without deleting it, select the share in the list of Normal shares, select "Disabled (-)" from the AppleFileServer (AFS) Sharing pop-up menu, click Update Share, and then click Restart AppleFileServer.

Enabling Personal File Sharing over AppleTalk

Although Mac OS X shies away from AppleTalk (it will only use it for local networking if you specifically enable it), AppleTalk is still the predominant networking protocol for many older Macs. In fact, some older versions of the Mac OS—still in use on older Macs and in many schools—don't even support Apple's IP-based file sharing protocol. This can present a problem if you're trying to share files with these computers. However, although Apple doesn't advertise it, Mac OS X does support File Sharing via AppleTalk. To enable it, launch SharePoints, and in the AFS Properties tab, check the box next to Use AppleTalk in the Miscellaneous Properties area. You'll need to click the Restart AppleFileServer button to restart Personal File Sharing; once it starts up again, your Mac will be visible on an AppleTalk network.

Activating the Personal File Sharing Log

Users of Mac OS 9 may remember the File Sharing Monitor, which provided you with a list of connected File Sharing users. Mac OS X doesn't include such a feature (it's reserved for OS X Server); however it does include the ability to keep a detailed log of all Personal File Sharing activity. Fire up SharePoints again, and in the AFS Properties tab, look at the Logging Properties section. If you check the Enable Logging box, OS X will begin to log any or all of the types of activities checked in the boxes to the right (Logins, Logouts, etc.). By default, the log is located at `/Library/Logs/AppleFileService/AppleFileServiceAccess.log`. Remember that you have to click the Update AppleFileServer Properties button, and then the Restart AppleFileServer button, for your changes to be applied.

You can view the log in text editor like TextEdit at any time; however, you won't be able to automatically view updates. If you want to watch the log in real time, you can use one of the log-viewing utilities I mention in Chapter 14. In addition, a quick and easy way to view real-time updates is to open a new Terminal window and type **`tail -f /Library/Logs/ApplefileService/AppleFileServiceAccess.log <RETURN>`**. This will show the log in the Terminal window, including additions to the log (i.e., activity) as they are written.

Other Options in SharePoints

In addition to the options I've discussed here, SharePoints also provides a number of other features you'll have to explore for yourself. I mentioned the ability to create groups in Chapter 1, but you can also create a welcome message that other users will see when they connect, change the ports used by Personal File Sharing, and even set up idle timers so that users are automatically disconnected if they are idle for too long. You can also configure and customize OS X's Windows File Sharing (which I'll talk about later in the chapter).

How Do Others Access Files?

How other users access Personal File Sharing on your Mac depends on whether they're connecting over a local network or over the Internet, and whether they're connecting from Mac OS X or Mac OS 9 and earlier. To make things easier, I'm going to talk about each separately. Once connected, regardless of the method, the user will get a dialog to enter their username or password (unless they're using Guest Access, in which case they'll skip that step). They'll then get a dialog box where they can choose which sharepoints (for guest, normal, and File Sharing Only users) or which volumes (for admin users) they want to mount on their own Desktop. From there they can access files just as they would on any other mounted volume.

Local network: Mac OS X From another Mac running OS X on a local network, the user simply has to choose Go ➢ Connect to Server… (or press command+K) in the Finder, and then click the triangle to expand the Connect to Server window (to show the server browser). Due to the magic of Rendezvous, your Mac will show up in the browser by its

Rendezvous name; they should select it and click Connect. If the browser is taking a long time to locate your Mac, they can also enter `afp://rendezvousname.local` in the Address field (where *rendezvousname* is your computer's Rendezvous name), and then click Connect.

Local network: Mac OS 9 Users of Mac OS 9 should choose Apple Menu ➢ Chooser. On the left side of the Chooser window, select the AppleShare icon. Then on the right, click the Server IP Address… button. In the resulting dialog, they should enter your *local* IP address (if both computers are behind an Internet router, or have been given their own static IP addresses, this will be the IP address provided in Sharing preferences), and then click Connect. Note that if you enabled AppleTalk File Sharing, when they click the AppleShare icon, your Mac should show up on the right side of the Chooser; they should simply select it and click Connect.

Local network: Mac OS 8.*x* and earlier If you've enabled AppleTalk File Sharing, users of pre–OS 9 systems should choose Apple Menu ➢ Chooser, and then click the AppleShare icon on the left side of the Chooser. They should then select the icon for your Mac on the right side (it should show up automatically) and then click Connect.

Via the Internet: Mac OS X Mac OS X users accessing your Mac over the Internet should choose Go ➢ Connect to Server… (or press command+K) in the Finder to bring up the Connect to Server dialog. In the Address field, they should enter `afp://yourIPaddress` (or replace *yourIPaddress* with your domain name, if you have one assigned to your Mac), and then click Connect.

Via the Internet: Mac OS 9 Mac OS 9 users accessing your computer over the Internet should follow the same procedure they do when accessing over a local network; the only difference is that they should enter your *Internet* IP address (or domain name) rather than your local one. If you have a static IP address and are not behind an Internet router, the two will probably be the same.

If you don't have a static IP address, or you're behind an Internet router, this adds a few wrinkles when other users try to access your Mac over the Internet. See "Your IP Address: Internet Routers, Port Caveats, and Dynamic IPs."

Your IP Address: Internet Routers, Port Caveats, and Dynamic IPs

In many of the methods for file sharing that I discuss in this chapter—specifically, Personal File Sharing, Windows File Sharing, Personal Web Sharing, FTP, and SFTP—users trying to access your files will need to provide your computer's IP address. If the other users are on your local network, they can simply use the IP address listed in the Services tab of Sharing preferences (the one that appears when you enable a Sharing service). However, users accessing your Mac *over the Internet* may need to use a different IP address.

Continued on next page

If your ISP or network administrator provides your computer with a static IP address, and your computer is not behind some sort of Internet router, you don't need to worry; the address listed in Sharing preferences is the same for locally networked and Internet users. However, if your computer is behind an Internet router, you'll need to do some work of your own to allow others to connect. (I discussed Internet routers in the previous chapter; they're basically devices that allow multiple computers to share a single Internet connection; many are hardware devices, but if you're connected to another Mac that's sharing its Internet connection with you—using OS X's Internet Sharing—that Mac is acting as an Internet router.) In addition, if your ISP or network administrator doesn't provide you with a static IP address—one that remains the same at all times—you'll need to do some additional legwork to make it easy for others to connect.

Internet routers and IP addresses

If you connect to the Internet through an Internet router, your ISP-assigned IP address identifies the router, not any individual computer connected to the router. This presents a problem when sharing files over the Internet, as a user who connects to your IP address actually connects to the router instead of your computer. The end result is that the user will receive an error.

Luckily, there's a solution to this problem. As I'll discuss in more detail in Chapter 11, every computer connects to the Internet over a multitude of *ports*, each dedicated to certain types of data. These ports are different from OS X's *network ports*; in terms of Internet service and protocols, a port is specific service on a computer or server that deals with a certain type of data. For example, Apple's File Sharing Protocol uses port 548 by default—when your computer receives data intended for port 548, it directs that data to the Personal File Sharing service. Using specific ports in this manner allows data to be transferred more efficiently and effectively.

By taking advantage of these service-specific ports, you can enable what is called *port mapping* or *port forwarding* on your Internet router. Basically, port mapping is a way to tell your Internet router that data intended for certain port should *always* be directed to a specific computer behind the router. For example, you can elect to have all attempts to connect to Personal File Sharing (which uses port 548) on a specific computer forwarded—or *mapped*, in tech-speak—to that computer.

To set up port forwarding, you should consult your Internet router's manual or help files. On most models, it's as easy as entering the port number you wish to forward, followed by the name or internal IP address of the computer to which you want data for that port to be forwarded. To help you out, here are the port numbers for most of OS X's sharing services:

FTP (FTP Access): 20, 21

SSH (Remote Login and SFTP): 22

HTTP (Web Sharing): 80, 427

SMB (Windows File Sharing): 139

AFP (Personal File Sharing): 427, 548

Continued on next page

(You can see a complete list of ports used by Mac OS services at `http://docs.info.apple.com/article.html?artnum=106439`.)

One downside to port mapping when it comes to sharing files over the Internet is that only a *single* computer behind your router can provide each type of sharing service. For example, if your computer is mapped for Personal File Sharing, *all* requests on port 548 will be directed to your computer, even if another Mac behind your router also has Personal File Sharing enabled.

Port Caveats

While I'm on the topic of ports, I should mention another potential drawback of the port system: the ability of ISPs to prevent certain ports from transferring data. Some ISPs prohibit their users from setting up "servers"—their term for any service used to distribute files over the Internet. To prevent such services while still allowing standard Internet access, they generally block only known "server ports"—ports used by well-known file sharing services. Some of the most commonly blocked ports are those used by HTTP (Web) servers and FTP servers. In addition, ports used by file sharing systems such as Kazaa and Napster may also be blocked. If you're having trouble sharing files with others, or accessing files on your own computer from another computer, you may be the victim of port blocking. (Although I understand the motivation behind port blocking, I personally think that there's a difference between sharing pirated music and software and sharing personal files. In my opinion, ISPs should concentrate on monitoring excessive data transfers, rather than preventing all file sharing, legitimate or not.)

Fortunately, because Mac users usually constitute a minority of an ISP's customers, many ISPs aren't familiar with all of the sharing services available in OS X. As a result, the ports used by many Mac-only services (e.g., Personal File Sharing) are rarely blocked. So if one sharing method doesn't work for you, consider using a different method.

That being said, if you're set on using a particular service but your ISP blocks the port used by it, you can change its port by editing the `/etc/services` file (which must be done as root). Each service in this file has an entry, or several entries, that looks like this:

```
ftp       21/tcp      #File Transfer [Control]
ftp       21/udp      #File Transfer [Control]
```

where *21* (in this FTP example) is the port number. You would simply change the port number to one that isn't blocked by your ISP (either by asking them which ports they do and do not block, or by trial and error). Just make sure that you aren't changing to a port used by *another* service—the services file is organized by port number, so you can generally just read down the list until you find a port that isn't used by anything else. After making a change, you'll need to save the file and then restart, since services and services information are loaded at startup, prior to login.

Continued on next page

Note that for other users to access a service on a non-standard port, they'll need to explicitly include the port number after your IP address, separated by a colon (e.g., *serveraddress:port*).

Dynamic IP addresses and sharing

If your connection to the Internet is via PPP or PPPoE, or if your office network provides you with an IP address via DHCP, your IP address may change periodically—this is called a *dynamic* address. Unfortunately, dynamic IP addresses are a major pain if you're trying to share files over the Internet; if you give someone your IP address, they have to connect to your computer before your IP address changes, and there's no guarantee that your IP address will be the same the *next* time they attempt to connect.

There are really only two ways to deal with dynamic IP addresses and sharing files. The first is to simply provide your current IP address to others *each* time they want to access your computer. The excellent freeware DockIP (`http://www.kainjow.com/dockip.html`) is a great little app with a Dock menu that provides your current IP address—if you're behind an Internet router, it even provides your external IP address instead of just your local (router-assigned) IP.

If you'd rather not have to give others your IP-address-of-the-moment each time you want to share files, you'll have to use one of the *dynamic DNS* services out there. These services provide you with either your own domain name, or a sub-domain of their main domain (e.g., *`yourname.theirdomain`*`.com`). Using a small client application that you run on your own computer, these services keep track of your IP address each time you connect to the Internet and then forward any requests intended for your domain to your actual *current* IP address. Thus instead of giving other people your IP address, you simply give them your domain name.

Although I've never used any of these services, the most popular seem to be `http://www.DynDNS.org`, `http://EasyDNS.com`, and `http://ZoneEdit.com`. At the time of this writing, the dynamic DNS client of choice (which provides your current IP address to the dynamic DNS hosting service) for OS X seems to be DNSUpdate (`http://www.dnsupdate.org/`).

Sharing Remotely: FTP

User Level: admin
Affects: computer
Terminal: no

Personal File Sharing is probably the most feature-rich and flexible OS X method of sharing files over the Internet or a network. However, it has the distinct disadvantage of only allowing sharing between Macs (unless you install special software on a Windows computer, but that's beyond the scope of this book). Because of this, Mac OS X also provides a number of ways to share files between Macs and non-Macs. FTP, which stands for *File Transfer Protocol*, is one of these: OS X has an FTP server built in. FTP has been a staple of Unix servers since well before the Mac OS and Windows even existed, and is largely platform agnostic (it allows connections between Macs, Windows, Unix, Linux, and many other operating systems).

WARNING FTP has one *major* drawback: it is one of the least secure methods of communicating between two computers. All usernames, passwords, commands, and file data are sent in plain text, meaning that anyone who might be able to intercept that data would be able to easily figure out the username and password of anyone who connects (and may be able to then use that data to log into other services). For this reason, I recommend *not* enabling FTP Access. I'm going to talk about it briefly, but if you need FTP-like sharing capability, you're far better off using Secure FTP (SFTP) which I talk about later in the chapter.

What Does It Share?

With FTP Access enabled, users will have the same level of access to files that they would have if they were sitting at the computer. In other words, normal users will have full Read & Write access to their home directory, Read Only access to other users' Public folders and the Shared user folder, and Read Only access to most other files on your computer. (An admin user will have much more leeway.)

Although this type of access should be fine if you know and trust your users, it does post some added security risk, especially if you're providing access to unknown or untrustworthy people. With FTP, Read & Write access means the ability to download, upload, rename, and delete files, and Read Only access means the ability to download files. Thus, any admin-level user who connects via FTP will be able to perform some pretty serious file operations, and even non-admin users will be able to download (and thus view the contents of) many non-private files (i.e., files not located inside private user directories). For example, in the stock configuration of OS X's FTP Access, a normal user could connect and then download all of the files in `/Library/Preferences`—some of which may contain software licenses—or a file like `/var/db/SystemConfiguration/preferences.xml`, which contains all of your network settings.

Who Can Access Files?

If FTP Access is enabled, anyone with a user account on your computer can connect to it via an FTP client (from any platform: Windows, Mac, or Unix). However, it's possible to restrict the list of users who can connect over FTP; I've explained how to do this under "How Do I Configure It?"

WARNING Most FTP servers have a way to provide anonymous access—users can log in with the username *anonymous* and no required password. The way many Unix FTP servers, including the one in OS X, enable this feature is to check for a user account called "ftp." If that account exists on the computer, anonymous access is turned on automatically. So unless you want to enable anonymous access to your Mac, don't create a user account called "ftp."

How Do I Configure It?

To enable FTP Access, check the box next to FTP Access in the Services tab of Sharing preferences. If you want to configure some of the more advanced options that the FTP server offers, you need to manually edit configuration files or use a third-party utility as described below.

Disallowing FTP Access to Certain Users

If you're going to enable FTP Access, I recommend disallowing access to everyone but the specific users you want to use it. To do this, you need to edit the file `/private/etc/ftpusers` (you'll need to launch a text editor as root to edit the file). At the bottom of the list of usernames, type the short username of any user to whom you *don't* want to provide FTP access. Save the file, disable FTP Access, and then enable it again.

Confining User Access to Certain Folders

It's actually possible to configure Mac OS X's FTP server to restrict access to certain directories; unfortunately, space constraints prevent me from covering that topic (especially since I don't recommend FTP in general). In addition, Mac OS X 10.2 "broke" the common method of restricting access on FTP servers; I hope by the time you're reading this, Apple has fixed the FTP server to honor these methods. If you're interested in how you would do this, and more, check out the Unix configuration utility The Moose's Apprentice (`http://www.wundermoosen.com/wmTMA.htm`), which is not only an excellent utility for configuring FTP options, but also provides a great deal of information about many Unix configuration files in its documentation (which is available online at `http://www.wundermoosen.com/TMAHelp/TMA_Help.htm`).

Compressing/Encoding Files

Another drawback of FTP is that sometimes Mac files transferred over FTP lose their resource forks (those that *have* resource forks, that is). For this reason it's often a good idea to use a utility like DropStuff to not only "stuff" files that will be transferred via FTP, but to also encode them in BinHex format (available from the DropStuff preferences dialog). See "When to Compress Files for Sharing" for more info.

How Do Others Access Files?

Users will be able to access files via FTP from any platform using any standard FTP client. In their FTP client, they should enter your IP address (or your domain name, if applicable) as the server address, and should use their username and password on your computer as their login name and password. (Again, keep in mind the caveats about IP addresses I've mentioned throughout this chapter.)

Alternatively, many web browsers also understand FTP; users can generally enter `ftp://`*`youripaddress/`* as the URL, and their browser will then ask them for their username and password.

Finally, since FTP is technically a command-line application (it's been in use since long before graphical computing interfaces made their debut—graphical FTP clients are simply providing you with a pretty face to hide the command line), anyone with a terminal or console application and Internet access can connect using the command **`ftp`** ***`youripaddress`***. They'll be prompted for their username and password; once they're logged in, they can use standard `ftp` commands to access files.

NOTE Mac OS X keeps a log of all FTP activity when FTP Access is enabled; it's located at `/private/var/log/ftp.log`. You can view this log in any text editor, or by using one of the log file utilities I mention in Chapter 14. In fact, if you have a broadband connection, you'll probably see lots of attempts to log in—your friendly neighborhood (or other-side-of-the-world) hacker is testing to see if you've enabled anonymous FTP access. Note that if you allow OS X's weekly maintenance scripts to run (as described in Chapter 14), your FTP log will only include FTP events from the past week, beginning Saturday.

Sharing Remotely: Secure FTP (SFTP)

User Level: admin
Affects: computer
Terminal: no

As I mentioned in the previous section, FTP is convenient but extremely unsecure. I just don't recommend it unless you have no other choice for sharing files, and even then I recommend creating a single, non-admin user account for sharing files via FTP. If you'd like to gain the cross-platform advantages of FTP without the security issues, you should instead consider Secure FTP (SFTP).

Like FTP, SFTP is actually a command-line method for connecting to servers and working with files. However, whereas FTP uses a clear-text connection, SFTP uses the secure shell (SSH) protocol to connect, meaning all communication between the client and server, including passwords and data, are encrypted to prevent anyone who might intercept the data from being able to use it.

The *downside* to using SFTP is that it requires you to enable Remote Login (SSH) on your Mac. I'll talk more about Remote Login in the next chapter, but for now you simply need to understand that it provides remote users with a console connection, and basically allows them to do anything they could do using Terminal while seated at your Mac. For non-admin users this isn't too much of a concern, but an admin-level user could wreak havoc (for example, by enabling the root account and then logging in as root, where they would have unfettered access to your system). I'll show you a way around this risk under "How Do I Configure It?"

What Does It Share?

SFTP provides the same level of access to the same directories as the default configuration of FTP Access. However, note that if you've edited the various FTP configuration files to provide more or less access over FTP, SFTP does *not* honor those changes.

Who Can Access Files?

Just like FTP, anyone with an account on your computer can connect via SFTP when it is enabled. They will be able to access files from any platform (Windows, Mac, or Unix).

How Do I Configure It?

Contrary to what you might think, to enable SFTP you do not have to enable FTP Access. Rather, you enable Remote Login in the Services tab of Sharing preferences. However, as I mentioned above, this also enables SSH, which allows any user on your computer to issue Terminal commands remotely. Here's how you prevent this for certain users.

Disabling SSH Access (While Still Allowing SFTP)

I'll talk more about Remote Login in the next chapter, and about *default shells* in Chapter 15, but for now suffice it to say that when a user logs in remotely using SSH (secure shell), their default shell is loaded. The shell is how they work with the Terminal's command line, and using it they can access almost any command-line application (including the `sftp` utility). In addition, each user has a configuration file that determines what their default shell is (there are several different popular shells that can be used). Using these two facts, we can edit a user's account settings so that instead of a shell, only the SFTP application itself is loaded—thus allowing them to use SFTP remotely, but disallowing any other remote activity. Here's how:

1. If Remote Login is enabled, disable it in Sharing preferences.
2. Open NetInfo Manager and authenticate by clicking the padlock icon.
3. Using the directory browser, navigate to `/users/`*`username`*, where *`username`* is the user for whom you want to restrict access to just SFTP. Select that username.
4. In the Property/Value(s) window, scroll down to the "shell" property. Double-click on the corresponding entry in the Value(s) column (which will most likely be `/bin/tcsh`) to make it editable.
5. Delete the existing value, and type `/usr/libexec/sftp-server` in its place (Figure 10.5).
6. Choose Domain ➢ Save Changes to save your changes, and then quit NetInfo Manager.
7. Re-enable Remote Login in Sharing preferences.

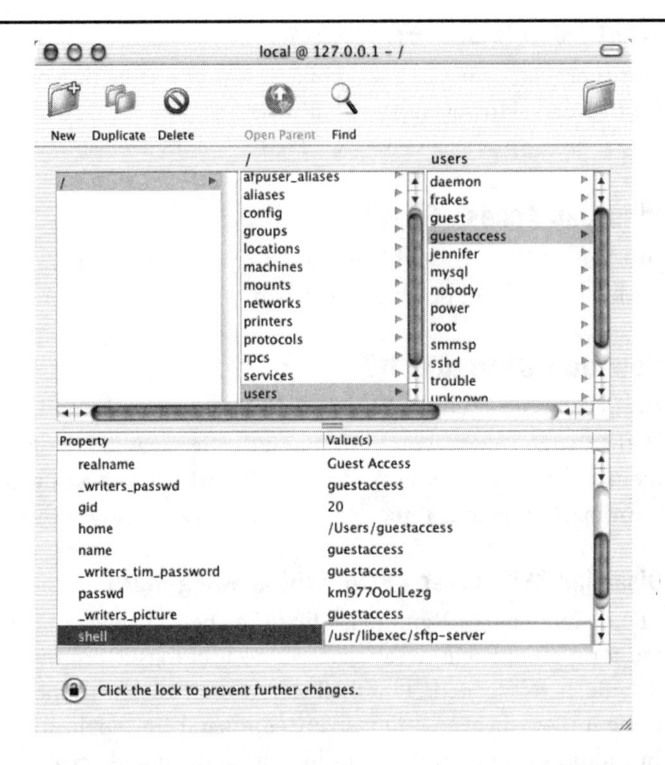

FIGURE 10.5: Using NetInfo Manager to limit a user's Remote Login capability to SFTP

What you just did was tell OS X that when the user logs in, the default shell it should load is `sftp-server`, which isn't really a shell. Since the `sftp-server` application is the command-line utility used to access files via SFTP, the user will still be able to access files (either using the command-line or a graphical SFTP client, as described in "How Do Others Access Files?"), but they won't be able to do anything else.

NOTE The downside to this procedure is that as long as the user's default shell is set to `sftp-server`, they won't be able to use Terminal or perform any type of command-line activity, even if they're sitting at your computer. However, you can easily edit their account in NetInfo Manager to restore their default shell when needed. This tip is useful mainly for remote users who have no use for full shell access.

How Do Others Access Files?

Just as with FTP, users will be able to access files via SFTP using any SFTP client. (In fact, many FTP clients also support SFTP; however, you need to specifically tell them to use SFTP instead of FTP when connecting.) In their SFTP client, they should enter your IP address or domain name as the server address, and use their username and password on your computer as their login name and password.

Alternatively, since SFTP uses the command-line application `sftp`, just like FTP uses `ftp`, users can connect through a terminal or console application by using the command `sftp` *`youripaddress`*, at which time they'll be prompted for their username and password. Once they're logged in, they can use `sftp` commands to access files.

Sharing Remotely: Windows File Sharing (SMB)

User Level: admin
Affects: computer
Terminal: no

Sharing files on your Mac with Windows computers has always been a bit of a hassle, especially for your Windows friends. Without installing third-party software, their computers don't understand the Apple File Protocol (AFP) used by Personal File Sharing, and FTP requires them to use a special FTP application or the command line—it's just not as convenient for them as accessing files on other Windows computers. Wouldn't it be great if they could mount your shared folders like any other Windows share?

Starting with OS X 10.2, Apple included a version of the open-source Samba server (`http://www.samba.org/`), which shares files using the SMB/CIFS (Server Message Block/Common Internet File System) protocol—the same protocol used by Windows for sharing files. Using Samba (known in OS X as *Windows File Sharing*) you can make your files available to Windows users (and Unix computers that understand SMB/CIFS), and your shares will appear on their computers as any other Windows volume or share.

What Does It Share?

By default, users can only access their *own* home directory (`/Users/`*`username`*) via Windows File Sharing. In fact, when they connect, their home directory will be mounted as a shared volume. So in order to share a file with someone who is logging into your Mac through Windows File Sharing, you'll need to place the file in their Public folder (via the Drop Box), not yours. Likewise, for them to share a file with you, they'll need to place it in their own Public folder, since that's the only location they can access that you also have access to.

That being said, it's possible to share other directories, and to share them with more than a single user. I'll show you how under "How Do I Configure It?"

Who Can Access Files?

In order to connect to Windows File Sharing and access files, users must have an account on your Mac. In addition, you (or another administrator) must manually *enable* their account to allow Windows File Sharing access (as explained in the next section).

TIP Obviously, users can connect to Windows File Sharing from a Windows computer. However, they can also connect from another computer running OS X 10.2 or later (I'll show you how in the next chapter when I talk about connecting to Windows shares). Thus if you're sharing files with both Windows and Mac OS X users, you can use Windows File Sharing for both—you don't have to turn on Personal File Sharing just for the Mac folks unless you want to take advantage of Personal File Sharing features.

How Do I Configure It?

Unlike most of the other types of sharing in OS X, basic Windows File Sharing requires two steps. First, you have to enable the service itself: in the Services tab of Sharing preferences, check the box next to Windows File Sharing. Second—and this is a step that many people forget, but that is required for access—you must enable/disable the ability to connect to Windows File Sharing for each user *individually*. Open the Accounts pane of System Preferences and select a user. Click the Edit User… button, and in the resulting window check the box next to "Allow user to log in from Windows" (Figure 10.6). Unfortunately, this requires you to enter a new password for the user. If you know the user's password (or if it's your own account) you can simply re-enter the current password. If you don't, just enter something easy to remember, give the new password to the user, and then let them change it back.

Although this is a bit of a pain as compared to enabling other types of sharing, it has the advantage of letting you easily decide which users can and cannot connect remotely without having to mess with configuration files.

FIGURE 10.6: Enabling a user to be able to connect via Windows File Sharing

NOTE Although the setting is called "Allow user to log in from Windows," it should actually be called "Allow user to log into Windows File Sharing." Because Windows File Sharing is simply a way to share files using the SMB/CIFS protocol, it's possible to access Windows File Sharing from any computer that understands SMB, including other Mac OS X computers and many Unix computers. This box must be checked to access files using SMB, regardless of the type of computer or OS.

In addition to the standard Windows File Sharing setup, you can customize Samba to provide access to other files and folders, and to allow guess access. Here are a few easy ways to do so.

TIP If after reading the tips I include here for configuring Windows File Sharing, you decide that you *really* want to become a Samba pro, an entire copy of the book *Using Samba* is actually included with Mac OS X. You can view it by opening the file `/usr/share/swat/using_samba/index.html` in your web browser. A newer version of *Using Samba* is available as an actual book, but the information in this free, older version is still extremely useful for understanding the nitty-gritty behind Samba.

Using Samba Server Package

Although you could manually configure the Samba settings file (`/etc/smb.conf`), the easiest way to customize Windows File Sharing is to use the free Samba Sharing Package (`http://xamba.sourceforge.net/ssp/index.shtml`). Once you download Samba Sharing Package (SSP), you should place the `SambaSharing.prefPane` in `/Library/PreferencePanes`, and move the Samba Server Config Tool and Popup applications into `/Applications`. Then launch System Preferences and select the Samba Sharing pane; you'll be asked to provide your admin username and password.

Using SSP to enable additional shares is similar to using SharePoints to enable shares for Personal File Sharing. The difference is that SSP creates complete configuration files for the Samba server; you select a configuration file to be used for Windows File Sharing options whenever you start the service. In a way, this is a bit like OS X's network Locations—you can save "sets" of settings and easily switch between them.

In the Global tab of Samba Sharing preferences, you can start and stop Samba Sharing; this is identical to enabling and disabling Windows File Sharing in Sharing preferences. However, you can also switch between your various Samba configurations from the pop-up menu (switching configurations automatically restarts the Samba server). This means that if you want, you can enable standard Windows Sharing (the "default" configuration) most of the time, and, when needed, switch to a more specialized configuration that provides different levels of access. If you click the Edit button, the currently loaded configuration will be opened for editing (unless the "default" configuration is active—it can't be edited). The Help button at the bottom of the window opens the Samba Sharing documentation in your preferred web browser. A few ways to use configurations to your advantage follow.

NOTE Be sure to read the Samba Sharing Package documentation for information on limitations of Samba and Windows File Sharing connections.

Creating Additional or Other Shares Using Samba Sharing Package

To create a new Samba configuration file with custom shares, click on the Configurations tab, and then click the New button (you could also select the default configuration and click Duplicate). Give it an easily recognizable name; for example, I've created a configuration called Shared Folder that I've set up to allow users to access the Shared user folder via Windows File Sharing. I have another one called Consulting that allows clients to access files in a particular folder of project files. The Samba Server Config Tool will launch to allow you to customize the configuration. (You can also select a non-default configuration and click the Edit button to edit any existing configuration). Any configurations you create here will be accessible from the pop-up menu on the Global tab of Samba Sharing preferences. To configure your new configuration file using Samba Server Config Tool, including customizing shares, follow these steps:

1. Click the Server tab and enter a server name in the Servername field. This is how your computer will appear in Windows' Network Neighborhood (on a local network). It can be whatever you want, but it must be unique and shouldn't include any special characters (i.e., limit it to numbers and letters). You can also customize the Comment field, although it won't affect how your computer shares files.
2. If you're on a local network with Windows machines, choose the same Workgroup name as the other computers. This will allow Windows computers to see your computer in Network Neighborhood. If you choose a different Workgroup name, they'll have to browse Entire Network, find your Workgroup, and then access that Workgroup. (If you're on a Windows NT network, this field *must* be the NT Workgroup name.)
3. If you're on a local Windows network, and the network administrator tells you that you need a WINS address, enter it here. If not, or if you're not on a local Windows network, leave this blank.
4. Switch to the Global tab and select the account you want to use for "guest" access from the Guest Account pop-up. For most cases, you should just accept the default of "unknown." (See "Creating 'Guest' Users for Windows File Sharing" for more details.) Most of the other details on this tab can be left at their default values. You would only uncheck Filter Files if you want remote users to be able to see invisible/hidden files. If you want to restrict access *only* to certain IP addresses or domains, enter them in the Allow Hosts field, separated by commas. (If this field is left blank, all IP addresses are allowed.) Conversely, you can deny access to certain IP addresses or domains by entering them in the Deny Hosts field. Finally, checking the Messages option allows you to send messages to connected users using the Popup application.

FIGURE 10.7: Using Samba Sharing Package to enable the sharing of the Shared user folder via Windows File Sharing

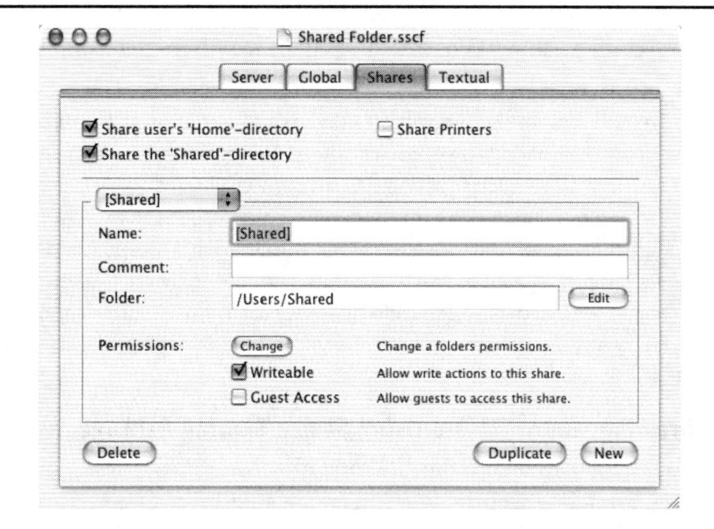

5. Switch to the Shares tab to configure which directories are to be shared. You can enable or disable the sharing of each user's home directory (Figure 10.7), and the Shared directory, by checking/unchecking the respective box.
6. At this point, if all you wanted to do was change the home and Shared folder access, you can choose File ➢ Save to save changes you've made to the configuration. To create new shares, continue to Step 7.
7. Click the New button at the bottom of the window to create a new share. Give the share a name (enclose the name in brackets and don't use spaces or special characters); this name will show up when a Windows user accesses your server in Network Neighborhood. You can also choose a comment, which will be shown next to your share in Network Neighborhood. Enter the path to the folder you wish to share, or click the Edit button to navigate to it. If you want to change the permissions of the folder you're sharing, click the Change button to be presented with a dialog that allows you to set the owner, group, and privileges. Finally, decide if you want other users to have Write access, and whether or not you want people to be able to access the new share without entering a login name or password (guest access).
8. If you want to edit an existing share, choose it from the pop-up menu and edit any fields as needed. You can also delete a share by selecting it from the pop-up menu and clicking the Delete button, or duplicate an existing share by selecting it and clicking the Duplicate button (you can then edit the copy as needed).
9. Choose File ➢ Save to save your new configuration.

TIP When creating new shares, it is much safer to create several shares of individual folders than to share an entire drive or a folder that contains sub-folders you don't want to share.

You can now go back to the Global pane of Samba Sharing preferences to switch to your new configuration. Windows File Sharing will restart using the new configuration file.

NOTE The utility SharePoints, which I discussed earlier in the chapter as a way to configure Personal File Sharing, also allows you to customize Windows File Sharing. Although it doesn't offer quite as much functionality as Samba Sharing Package, you may find its interface easier to use (it has similar interfaces for both Personal File Sharing and Windows File Sharing). In fact, if you already have Personal File Sharing sharepoints defined (as described earlier in the chapter), you can simply enable them for use with Windows File Sharing, as well. SharePoints also allows you to hide specific files from remote Windows File Sharing users, and to change your workgroup name. Check out the SharePoints documentation for more info.

Creating "Guest" Users Using Samba Sharing Package

You can generally use the "unknown" account for "guest" (non-user account) access. However, for added security you can create additional user accounts on your computer for use as guest Windows File Sharing accounts, and then use the Samba Sharing preference pane to customize the files those users will be able to access. Unfortunately I can't explain the entire process here due to space restrictions; however, the Samba Sharing Package Help files have a very detailed description of how to configure these user accounts using NetInfo Manager so that they will only be able to access your computer through Windows File Sharing. Click the Help button on the Global tab, then click the "Using SSCT" link. Scroll down to the "Guest account" section for details.

Monitoring Windows File Sharing Using Samba Sharing Package

The Connections tab of Samba Sharing preferences provides a list of all currently connected users. It also provides information on the computer from which they're connecting (name and IP address), and the share they are accessing. (If you see a user called "unknown," it's usually a guest user.) You can immediately disconnect a user by selecting their name and pressing the Disconnect button. The window is refreshed each time you access the Connections tab; you can use the Refresh button to manually refresh it.

You can also browse the Samba log files; switch to the Extras tab and click on either of the buttons in the Logfiles section to view them using OS X's Console utility.

Changing Just Your Workgroup Name Using Directory Access

If the default Windows File Sharing settings and access are fine with you, but you just want to change your computer's Windows Workgroup name so that it's easier for Windows users on your local network to locate you, you can do so using Apple's Directory Access application (located in `/Appliations/Utilities`). Launch Directory Access and then follow these steps:

1. Authenticate by clicking the padlock icon.
2. In the Services tab, select SMB and then click Configure....

3. Type the new Workgroup name (or select it from the drop-down menu if applicable), and then click OK.
4. Click the Apply button, and then quit Directory Access.
5. In Sharing preferences, stop Windows File Sharing, and then start it again.

TIP You can also change your workgroup name using SharePoints (via the SMB Properties tab).

Alternatives to Windows File Sharing

If your Mac is on a Windows network, or you find yourself a heavy user of Windows File Sharing, you might want to consider the commercial software DAVE (`http://www.thursby.com/`). DAVE is a full-featured Mac/Windows file and print sharing package that provides a good deal of additional functionality in terms of sharing files with and connecting to Windows computers. For example, DAVE provides additional levels of access security, a simpler procedure for setting up additional shares, allows you to share your printers with Windows computers, and works with the NTFS file format used by Windows servers. It also provides additional features with respect to connecting to Windows shares, which I'll mention in the next chapter when I talk about how to connect to Windows shares from OS X.

How Do Others Access Files?

How Windows users will access your Mac depends on whether they're on the same local network as you or they'll be connecting over the Internet.

Local network If you're on the same local network as your Windows users, they should simply open Network Neighborhood (My Network Places on Windows XP); if you've set up your Workgroup to be the same as theirs, your computer will show up. (If not, they'll need to open Entire Network and find your Workgroup name first.) When they open your computer, they'll see the shares they can access. To open a share, they'll need to provide their username and password.

Internet If Windows users are trying to access your Mac over the Internet, they'll have to use a technique similar to accessing your iDisk:

Windows XP Open My Computer and then choose Tools ➢ Map Network Drive. Enter `\\yourIPaddress\sharename` (where *sharename* is the name of the share on your Mac that they are trying to access). When prompted, they should provide their username and password for *your* computer, not their own.

Windows 2000 Open My Computer and then choose Tools ➢ Map Network Drive. Click "Web folder or FTP site," and then enter the address provided above.

Windows 98 Open My Computer, open the Web Folders icon, and then double-click Add Web Folder. Enter the address provided above.

Network File System (NFS) Sharing (and Connecting)

As a Unix-based operating system, OS X also supports the Network File System (NFS) protocol, a common method for sharing files between Unix systems. Unfortunately, NFS sharing isn't enabled by default in OS X. (A major reason is that nowadays most Unix computers support SMB/CIFS, so they should be able to access Windows File Sharing.) In addition, enabling NFS sharing is a fairly complex procedure. However, if you have a need for sharing files with non–OS X Unix computers, and those computers can't access SMB/CIFS shares, NFS may be your only option.

Although I don't have the space to discuss NFS sharing and connecting here, I want to direct you to a couple of resources that can help you out. The shareware NFS Manager (`http://www.bresink.de/osx/NFSManager.html`) takes the pain out of the process by providing an Aqua (graphical) interface for setting up NFS sharing, and for connecting to NFS shares on other Unix computers. In addition, the NFS Manager website contains an excellent guide to using NFS Manager (`http://www.bresink.de/osx/DocsNFSManager/index.html`) that also provides detailed background information on NFS.

Sharing Remotely: Personal Web Sharing

User Level: admin
Affects: computer
Terminal: no

The final way that OS X shares files is via the Web. OS X provides a complete install of the industrial-strength Apache web server (`http://www.apache.org/`)—the same one used by many of the biggest websites on the Internet. While it may sound a bit strange to include a web server as a way to "share" files, that's exactly what you're doing: allowing other users to access files on your computer. And since Apple includes Personal Web Sharing in the Sharing pane of System Preferences, I'm going to treat it like a sharing service.

What Does It Share?

Personal Web Sharing actually shares at both the user level and at the computer level. More specifically, it can share the contents of each user's `/User/`*`username`*`/Sites` folder, as well as the contents of `/Library/WebServer/Documents`. I say *can* share because OS X is configured, like most web servers, to *not* show the contents of directories; rather, you can only access a file if you have its complete file name or if it's linked from another web page that you can view. By default, unless someone accessing a website on your Mac knows the URL of a specific file, all they'll be able to see is the file `index.html` or `home.html`—which is the default page for any website—at the root level of your Sites or Web Server Documents folders.

FIGURE 10.8:

A default user website in OS X

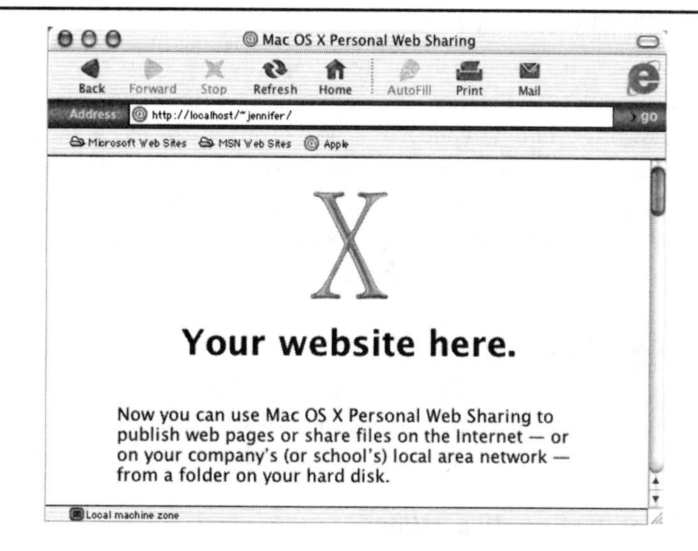

NOTE Since Personal Web Sharing is intended to be a way to share a website over the Internet, each user's Sites folder and the main web server Documents folder have basic websites pre-installed. You can view these default websites in your browser if you enter `http://localhost/` (for the main Documents folder) or `http://localhost/~`*`username`* (for any user on your Mac) (Figure 10.8). (*localhost* tells your browser to access the *local* web server.) If you replace these default website files with your own website, people around the world can view that site by pointing their web browser to your Mac.

However, even though the main purpose of Personal Web Sharing is to share websites, you can also use it as a way of sharing other files, as well. Any file that you place in your personal Sites folder will be available to anyone who has the full address of that file. For example, if you put a document called `report.doc` in your Sites folder, you can tell your coworker to enter `http://`*`yourIPaddress`*`/~`*`yourusername`*`/report.doc` in their web browser and it will be downloaded to their computer. At the same time, no one else will know that file even exists. The disadvantage (or advantage, depending on how you look at it) of Personal Web Sharing is that unless you're a web server guru who knows how to trick out your Apache installation, users can only *download* files from you; they can't upload files. However, Personal Web Sharing can be a very quick and convenient way to provide someone with access to a file without having to give them a user account or configure any other services.

TIP Unless you've purchased your own Internet domain and have it assigned to your personal Mac, I recommend using your personal Sites folder for sharing files and websites. The `/Library/Web Server/Documents` folder can be used, but it is generally intended for computers that are used as dedicated web servers, and placing files there requires admin access.

Who Can Access Files?

Although it's possible to configure Apache to require usernames and passwords to access files, by default Personal Web Sharing does not limit access to particular users or require any passwords. Thus anyone with a web browser can access the files in your Sites folder or the main Web Server Documents directory. However, as I mentioned above, unless you purposely *link* to files (by editing the `index.html` file, or creating your own, and including URL links to other files and web pages in it), only those users who know the exact links to specific files will be able to access them.

How Do I Configure It?

To enable Personal Web Sharing, you just need to check the box next to Personal Web Sharing in Sharing preferences. Apache will start up, and you've got a web server every bit as powerful as many of the major sites on the Internet.

Other Configuration Options

Because Personal File Sharing is actually a complete installation of the Apache web server, it's incredibly configurable and extendable. It's possible to configure Apache so that specific files and folders inside the various web document folders require usernames and passwords. You can install PHP or use CGI scripts. Pretty much anything that can be done with a web server can actually be done on your Mac. Unfortunately, I don't have the space to show you all the cool things you can do with Apache, but I encourage you to browse the full Apache manual installed on your computer; you can access it by pointing your web browser to `http://localhost/manual/`.

WARNING Most of the tweaks and changes you make to Apache are done within the file `/etc/httpd/httpd.conf`. Sometimes Mac OS X system updates install a new version of this file that provides additional or different Apache functionality. Unfortunately, this means you lose all of your customizations. Apple's installer will often back up the existing file (the 10.2.4 update renamed the existing file as `httpd.conf.applesaved`), but to be safe you should be sure to back up this file before installing any system updates (assuming you aren't backing it up as part of your normal backup strategy). If a system update removes your edited version, you can use the backup copy to add your customizations to Apple's newly installed version. (In fact, it's a good idea to *always* make backups of any `.conf` file that you manually edit, just in case something like this happens.)

How Do Others Access Files?

If you're simply using Personal Web Sharing to share individual files with remote users, you'll need to give them the precise URL of each file: `http://`*`yourIPaddress`*`/~`*`yourusername`*`/`*`filename`*. If you've created sub-folders inside of your Sites folder, the address to files inside those folders would be `http://`*`yourIPaddress`*`/~`*`yourusername`*`/`*`foldername`*`/`*`filename`*. By entering the URL to a file in their web browser, the file will be downloaded to their computer.

FIGURE 10.9:

SharingMenu gives you quick access to Sharing services.

If you're actually using Personal Web Sharing as a web server, you should give other people the URL of `http://yourIPaddress/~yourusername/` to allow them to view your website (assuming you've followed the standard of using `index.html` or `home.html` as your website's home page). You could also give them the specific address of any other web page in your Sites directory.

TIP If you're new to HTML and web pages, check out the default `index.html` web page inside your personal Sites folder (type `http://yourIPaddress/~yourusername/` in your web browser). It gives you a quick primer on using your Sites folder for a website.

Quick Access to Sharing Services

User Level: admin
Affects: computer
Terminal: no

If you're really getting into this whole sharing thing, and you find yourself frequently opening System Preferences just to enable or disable one or another Sharing service, you'll appreciate the freeware SharingMenu (`http://www.mani.de/sharingmenu/`). When launched, it provides a small menu in the menu bar that allows you to toggle each Sharing service on or off (Figure 10.9). It also lets you quickly enable and disable Guest Access to Personal File Sharing, which can be a real convenience if, like me, you normally keep Guest Access turned off, but occasionally turn it on for a few minutes to share a file with someone. (Remember: if you drag SharingMenu to your Login Items preferences, it will launch automatically at login.)

Moving On...

Now that you're an expert at sharing files with other users, you may be wondering exactly how to connect to other computer or servers (or even to your own from another location). In the next chapter I'll cover Mac OS X's various methods for connecting to shares and servers. I'll also talk about ways in which you can connect to and control your Mac from afar.

Chapter 11

Connection Convenience and Remote Control

(Or: Access files on other computers and control your home computer from the beach house.)

In addition to being the most flexible OS around for sharing files and data, Mac OS X is also the most compatible when it comes to connecting to servers and shared files. Plus, as both a Unix OS and a Mac OS, it provides several options for remote access and control.

In this chapter I'm going to show you how to connect to virtually any type of remote server and share you'll encounter. If you find yourself connecting to the same computers or shares often, I'll also show you how to streamline the connection process. Finally, I'll show you some of the options available for connecting to your own computer, and controlling it, from afar.

NOTE As with the previous chapter, I'm going to assume that you have Internet access and that you know how to configure and connect.

IP Addresses, URLs, and Ports

Before I get started with connection strategies, I want to cover a topic that will make the rest of the chapter much easier to read and use, and that's the issue of the address you use to connect to another computer. Most of the sections in this chapter have one thing in common: you're connecting to another computer over a network (LAN, WAN, or the Internet). To make such connections, you need to know the *IP (Internet Protocol) address* or *domain name* of the target computer. You also need understand how to provide that address. Here are some issues to be aware of when dealing with IP addresses, URLs, and ports.

What's the Address?

Every computer on the Internet has its own IP address that uniquely identifies it (much like a street address for a residence). These IP addresses are formatted as *x.x.x.x*, where each x is a number between 0 and 255, and connecting to another computer involves providing its address to your own computer, so that it knows the exact destination it's attempting to reach. This means that if you're trying to connect to another computer or server over the Internet, you need to make sure you have the correct IP address.

NOTE In many cases (especially on the Web), you don't have to remember the actual numerical address; you only have to provide a *domain name* (e.g., cnn.com, apple.com, white-house.gov), and your computer and the Internet's DNS (Domain Name System) servers work together to figure out the actual IP address for you.

Unfortunately, there are a few wrinkles when it comes to IP addresses, such as issues with Internet routers and dynamic IP addresses; I covered these issues in the previous chapter. As the person *connecting* to another computer, these issues don't affect you as much—it's the responsibility of the server's owner/administrator to figure them out, and to simply provide you with an IP address that works. However, I mention the issue here because if for some reason you can't connect to a remote computer, keep in mind that the reason might actually be a problem with the IP address you've been given (i.e., it might not be your fault).

Finally, if you're connecting to another computer on a local network and both computers are behind an Internet router, there's a good chance the other computer will have what is known as an *internal* or *local* IP address. These addresses—in the format of 10.x.x.x, 172.16.x.x, or 192.168.x.x—are not used for Internet communication; they are reserved for traffic inside a local network.

NOTE If you're lucky enough to be on a local network with other Rendezvous-capable computers, you won't have to worry about IP addresses or domain names. In most cases connecting is as simple as clicking on a computer's name in dialog box.

URLs: Not Just HTTP

Anyone who's surfed the Web has seen plenty of URLs—the addresses of web pages. However, most users are unaware of what that URL actually signifies, and that URLs are not at all specific to the Web.

A URL (Uniform Resource Locator) is a string of characters in a specific format that provides a standardized way of locating a resource (such as a file). Although URLs are most commonly used for websites and web pages, they were designed to be extremely versatile, and as such are used for many different types of computer-to-computer connections (and sometimes even for accessing files on your own computer). In fact, as I show you how to connect to various types of sharing services, you'll find that in many cases Mac OS X *expects* you to use URLs. What's more, as you'll discover later in the chapter, once you get the hang of URLs you'll find that you can use their standardized nature to your advantage by creating Internet Location files as shortcuts.

The official format of a URL is `protocol://server:port/directory/file`. Here's what each part means:

Protocol The protocol can be HTTP (hypertext transfer protocol, for websites), FTP (file transfer protocol, for FTP servers), SMB (server message block, for Samba file servers), AFP (Apple File Protocol, for servers using Apple's File Sharing), FILE (for local files), or one of a number of other methods in which data is transferred over the Internet.

Server The IP address or domain name of the computer hosting the resource you're attempting to access.

Port The specific port on the server that handles the service you're accessing. As I mentioned in the previous chapter, because a single computer can provide multiple services (web serving, e-mail, file sharing, etc.), each service is assigned a specific port number(s). These ports aren't physical ports (like Ethernet, modem, and USB ports); rather, they're a way to divide network traffic and route it to the appropriate service on a computer. For example, a connection to port 80 on most computers tells the host computer that the connecting computer is attempting to access a web page. To make things easier for users, almost every type of Internet service has a default port (`http://www.iana.org/assignments/port-numbers`); if a port is not included in a URL, the default port is assumed. For example if you enter a web URL into your browser, but do not include port 80, your browser automatically includes :80 in the URL when it sends a request to the web server. (See "Servers and Alternate Ports," for what to do when a server uses a nonstandard port.)

Directory and file Much like the path to a specific file on your computer, the `/directory/file` portion of a URL tells the server exactly which directory and/or file you wish to access on the remote computer/server. If no path is included, the server automatically directs you to a specific directory or file (depending on how the server is set up).

TIP It's possible, when connecting to some servers, to include your name and password in the URL. For example, if you're connecting to a website for which you have a user account, you can often include your name and password in the URL like this: `http://username:password@server/path/`. However, this is generally risky since URLs are almost always sent over the Internet in plain text. It's better to connect and *then* provide your name/password, as many servers have the ability to communicate securely after the initial connection.

NOTE For more information about URLs, check out `http://www.w3.org/Addressing/rfc1738.txt`.

Servers and Alternate Ports

I mentioned earlier that most Internet protocols communicate over default port numbers. This ensures that computers are able to communicate easily. For example, FTP generally uses ports 20 and 21, HTTP uses port 80, and Apple's File Sharing uses ports 427 and 548. However, there are times when a server may use a different port than expected. For example, as mentioned in the previous chapter, some Internet service providers block standard file sharing/FTP ports to prevent users from sharing files over the Internet. As another example, some network administrators use firewalls to block all but the essential ports (web and e-mail, for example) to increase network security. To get around such restrictions, the owner of a server can manually configure it to use a different port for a particular service(s). If this is the case, they will most likely provide you with the correct port to use, and you should include the port number in the URL as described above.

Servers Simplified

Now that you understand what kind of address or domain name you need in order to connect to another computer, to make the rest of this chapter easier to read I'm going to refer to that address or domain name simply as the *server address*. For example, if I say that to connect to Personal File Sharing on another Mac, you need to type **afp://*serveraddress*/**, you should replace *serveraddress* with the appropriate IP address or domain name of the computer to which you're trying to connect (including the port number, if the service is using a nonstandard port on the target computer). This will save me a lot of repetitive explaining, and you a lot of confusion, later in the chapter.

Connecting to Shares on Other Computers/Servers

User Level: any
Affects: individual user
Terminal: no

In the previous chapter, I showed you how to configure your Mac to share files with other users, and how those other users can connect to your computer. In this section, I'm going to explain how *you* can connect to *other* shares and servers using Mac OS X. In some situations the procedures are identical; however, in other instances the procedures are much different.

NOTE In all of the examples I include here, I assume that you have an account that provides you with access to the share or server to which you're connecting (or that the server allows guest access), and that you have the IP address or domain name of the share or server. When I refer to your *username* and *password*, I'm talking about your username and password for the share or server, not your Mac OS X username and password (unless, of course, you're connecting to your own Mac from another location).

The Connect to Server Dialog

In many of the connection procedures I discuss in this chapter, you'll need to use OS X's Connect to Server dialog (Go ➢ Connect to Server… in the Finder), which provides a way for you to connect to other computers, both locally and over the Internet. (Keep in mind that "Server" is really just Mac OS X's way of referring to a computer that is sharing files for other computers to access. A server could be a high-end file server, or it could be someone's PC in their home, set up to share files.)

When you select Connect to Server… you're presented with the basic version of the Connect to Server dialog (shown in the graphic below). To connect to another computer or server, you enter its URL in the Address field (using the format described earlier in this chapter, including the protocol—AFP, FTP, SMB, etc.). The At: pop-up menu lists Recent Servers (those to which you've recently attempted to connect), as well as Favorite Servers (those you have manually added to your Favorites list using the Add to Favorites button); select one from the menu to have it automatically entered into the Address field.

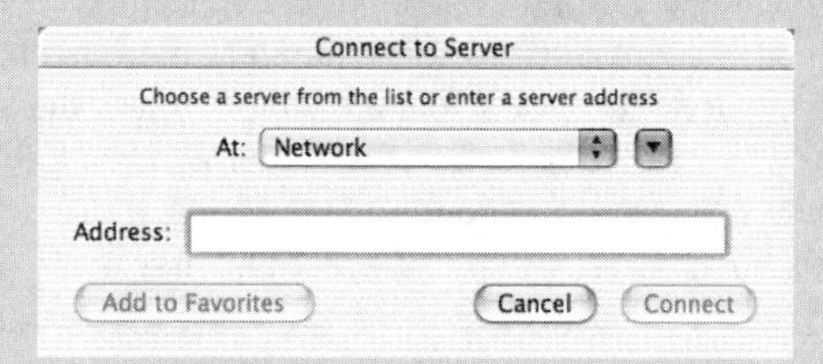

In addition, you can click the disclosure triangle (to the right of the At: pop-up menu) to use the expanded dialog view (shown below). Using this view, you can browse servers on your local network, including those in local AppleTalk zones (if AppleTalk is enabled) and Windows workgroups, as well as other Rendezvous-enabled computers (in the Local group). Click the workgroup, zone, or Local group on the left to see available servers on the right.

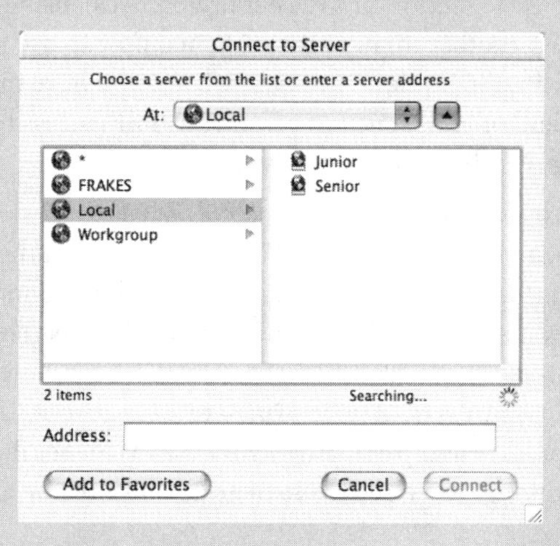

Continued on next page

Once you've typed in a server address, selected a Favorite or Recent server, or selected a local server in the server browser, click Connect to initiate a connection. What happens after you click Connect depends on the type of server to which you're connecting; I'll talk more about the process used for each in other parts of the chapter.

Favorite and Recent Servers

If you want to add a server as a Favorite, type in its address or choose it in the browser, and then click Add to Favorites *before* you press the Connect button. If you want to remove a server from the Favorites list, select Remove from Favorites... from the pop-up menu. You'll be presented with a dialog listing all of your Favorites; select one or more and click Remove to remove it from the list. Alternatively, you can use the Finder to go to `~/Library/Favorites`. You'll notice that each Favorite is simply a Mac OS X Internet Location file located inside this folder; if you drag it to the Trash, it will no longer show up in the list. (I'll show you how to use this design to your advantage later in the chapter.)

As I already mentioned, once you attempt to connect to a server, that server is listed in the At: pop-up under Recent Servers. Unfortunately, there is no "remove" item as there is for Favorites. Fortunately, Recent Servers are stored exactly the same way that Favorites are; go to `~/Library/Recent Servers` in the Finder and you'll find an Internet Location file for each server. Drag unwanted Location files to the Trash, and their corresponding server addresses will no longer show up as Recent Servers.

Connecting to iDisks

I mentioned earlier in the book that you can connect to your own iDisk using the Finder's Go ➢ iDisk command (which accesses the iDisk corresponding to the member name and password in the .Mac section of Internet preferences), using Apple's iDisk Utility, or using the Finder's iDisk toolbar item. I also explained how to use iDisk Utility to open another member's iDisk Public Folder. However, what if you have more than one iDisk of your own? Or what if a friend or colleague has given you "full" access to their iDisk (which requires you to provide their member name and password)?

Although most servers use only one protocol, .Mac's iDisks actually support two: Apple File Protocol (AFP) and the World Wide Web Distributed Authoring and Versioning (WebDAV) protocol. Using the Finder's Go ➢ iDisk command, or connecting via iDisk Utility, uses WebDAV, but you can use AFP URLs in Connect to Server. This means that by using Connect to Server, you can quickly connect to any iDisk for which you have a member name and password. In the Address field, type **`afp://idisk.mac.com/`** and click Connect. You'll be asked to provide a username and password—enter the .Mac member name and password for the iDisk. After verifying, you'll see a File Sharing—like dialog asking you which volume you wish to mount (the iDisk will be the only choice available). Click OK and the iDisk will be mounted in the Finder (on the Desktop if you have chosen to show connected servers on the Desktop in Finder preferences; otherwise visible in any Finder window via the Computer view). Once an iDisk is mounted, you can copy files to and from it, and edit files on it (since you've logged in as the "owner").

AFP versus WebDAV

You may be curious about the differences between AFP and WebDAV when it comes to iDisks. You know about AFP from the previous chapter, but I only mentioned WebDAV briefly. It's basically a way to provide read/write capabilities via a Web (HTTP) connection. Because HTTP is platform-independent, the fact that iDisks use WebDAV means that they're accessible from computers running Mac OS, Windows, and various versions of Unix/Linux. However, there are a couple of differences between AFP and WebDAV. The first is that using AFP is time-limited; if you don't use a mounted iDisk for a certain amount of time, you'll be automatically disconnected. An iDisk mounted using WebDAV/HTTP, on the other hand, stays mounted until you manually disconnect. The second difference is that you can only connect to another .Mac member's iDisk Public folder (described below) using WebDAV/HTTP; AFP is not an option.

NOTE For more info on WebDAV, check out `http://www.webdav.org/`. If you find yourself connecting to other WebDAV servers, you'll find the freeware WebDAV client Goliath (`http://www.webdav.org/goliath/`) to be a great tool.

Connecting to iDisk Public Folders

Even though iDisk Utility provides an easy way to access the Public folder of any iDisk, you still have to launch iDisk Utility. Personally, I would rather just press command+K in the Finder and use the Connect to Server dialog; to me, this is much quicker and more convenient. To do this, type **`http://idisk.mac.com/`*`membername`*`-Public`** or **`http://idisk.mac.com/`*`membername`*`/Public`** (where *membername* is the user's .Mac member name) and click Connect. If the iDisk's owner has set up a password for their Public folder, you'll see a password dialog; enter *`public`* for the name, and then the password. The iDisk's Public folder will be mounted in the Finder or in the Computer view of any Finder window, depending on your Finder preferences. (If you're wondering what the difference is between the two URL formats, the main one is that *`membername`*`-Public` causes the Public folder to be mounted with the owner's name visible; this is helpful if you access more than one Public folder, as you can quickly see whose Public folder is mounted.)

TIP If you frequently access multiple iDisks or iDisk Public folders, I'll show you how to make connecting more convenient later in the chapter, under "Connecting to Frequently Accessed Servers and Shares."

Connecting to Personal File Sharing

There are two ways to connect to a Mac OS X computer that is sharing files using Personal File Sharing. If the other Mac is running OS X 10.2 or later, and is on a local network with your Mac, you can open Connect to Server and click on the Local or * groups in the left column; other Macs on your local network will show up in the right column (as shown in "The Connect to Server Dialog" sidebar earlier in the chapter). If you've enabled AppleTalk on one of your network ports, the Connect to Server browser will also show you any AppleTalk zones on your network, and any computers with File Sharing enabled in those zones. Select the Mac to which you want to connect and click Connect.

TIP If a locally networked Mac that should appear doesn't, try entering **`afp://rendezvousname.local`** in the Address field, where *`rendezvousname`* is the other computer's Rendezvous name, as shown in the other computer's Sharing preferences.

If the other Mac isn't on the same local network, or if it doesn't support Rendezvous, you'll need to enter its IP address instead. This is most often the case for using Personal File Sharing over the Internet. Enter the target computer's IP address (or domain name, if applicable) in the format `afp://serveraddress`, and then click Connect.

Once the connection is successfully initiated, you'll be asked for your username and password—remember that these will be your username and password on the Mac to which you're connecting, not on your own computer. Assuming you provide the correct info, you'll be presented with a list of available sharepoints on the server (the other Mac). If you're a non-admin user on the Mac to which you're connecting, the list will include your own home directory, the Public folders of other users, and any custom sharepoints, if applicable, to which you have access. If you're an admin user on that Mac, it will include your home folder and all mounted volumes (Figure 11.1).

If you're connecting over the Internet to a Mac running File Sharing under OS 9, that Mac must have "Enable File Sharing clients to connect over TCP/IP" checked in the File Sharing control panel.

FIGURE 11.1: Connecting to Personal File Sharing as a normal (left) and admin (right) user

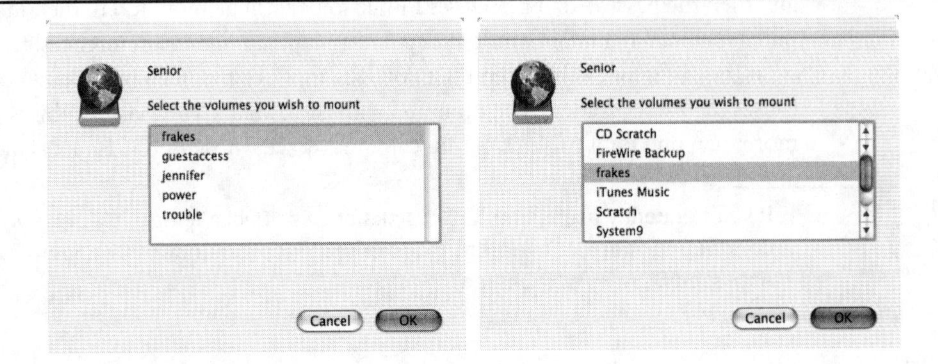

NOTE By default, admin-level users can access all mounted volumes when they connect via Personal File Sharing; as a result, they don't see any custom sharepoints (since they already have the ability to view the entire volume that contains the sharepoint). If you have an admin account on a computer and need to verify that a custom sharepoint is functioning properly—for example, after setting one up as described in Chapter 10—you can connect as any non-admin user (such as one that *can* view sharepoints) by using their username and your *own* admin password. (As I mentioned in the last chapter, the downside to this functionality is that it allows any admin user to gain access to any other users' files.)

File Sharing Login Options

When you connect to another Mac using Personal File Sharing, you have a few options when it comes to logging in. In the name/password, dialog, click Options… to get a list of connection preferences. The first, Add Password to Keychain, creates a new Keychain entry for that server (see Chapter 13 for more info about the Keychain in OS X). The next time you connect to that particular server, the password field will automatically be filled in for you. The second option lets you choose to send your password in "clear text." If this option is enabled, your password will not be encrypted or otherwise protected, so anyone who might be able to intercept communication between your Mac and the target Mac will be able to figure out your password. Because this is an obvious safety risk, I recommend keeping this option disabled. (In fact, because this option is unsafe, the third option tells your Mac to warn you whenever you send a password in clear text.)

If the computer to which you're connecting has Remote Login—which I'll talk more about later in the chapter—enabled in Sharing preferences, that means that your computer can communicate with it using a secure shell (SSH) protocol; all communication over that SSH connection will be encrypted. By checking "Allow Secure Connections using SSH," you can tunnel your File Sharing connection over this encrypted connection. If the target computer has Remote Login enabled, I highly recommend enabling this option.

Connecting to Windows Shares

With Mac OS X, the Mac is finally a functioning member of Windows networks right out of the box. As explained in the previous chapter, SMB/CIFS is the standard sharing protocol on computers running Microsoft Windows, and OS X includes significant SMB support, allowing you to connect to Windows shares as easily as you connect to Personal File Sharing on other Macs. In addition, if another Mac has Windows File Sharing enabled, you can even connect to it using SMB, just as if it was a Windows computer.

To connect to a local Windows share (one on your local network), open Connect to Server, make sure it's expanded to show the connection browser, and select the Windows workgroup (on the left) in which the target computer is located (Figure 11.2). Select the computer to which you want to connect (on the right), and then click Connect. You'll be asked which share on the computer you want to access; select one from the pop-up menu and click OK. In the subsequent authentication dialog, the workgroup name of the Windows computer will already be entered; just enter your username and your password and then click OK. (If you want OS X to remember your password the next time you connect to this particular Windows share, check the "Add to Keychain" box.) The Windows share will be mounted and you can use it like any other mounted volume. (You may find the above procedure to be reversed—you may be asked to provide your name and password first, and then select the share that you want to access.)

NOTE One limitation of Mac OS X's Connect to Server browser is that it will only show computers on the same subnet as your computer. This isn't a problem for most small office or home users, but if your Mac is on a large network that has been split into multiple subnets by your network administrator, you won't be able to see Windows computers in other subnets. To connect to one of these Windows computers, you'll need to use the procedure for connecting to remote computers, discussed in the next paragraph.

To connect to a remote Windows share, open Connect to Server and type ***smb://serveraddress/share/*** in the Address field, where *serveraddress* is the IP address or domain name of the Windows computer, and *share* is the name of the share (a drive, volume, or directory that has been shared by the computer's owner/administrator). Unlike the procedure for connecting to a Windows computer on the same subnet, which will prompt you for the share you wish to access if you don't specify one, Windows computers require you to provide the specific share you're trying to access when connecting remotely. (If the share name contains spaces, type **%20** in place of each space.) Click Connect to initiate the connection. If you have trouble connecting to a Windows share using a domain name, see if using the actual IP address works; I've found that IP addresses seem to work better when connecting via SMB URLs.

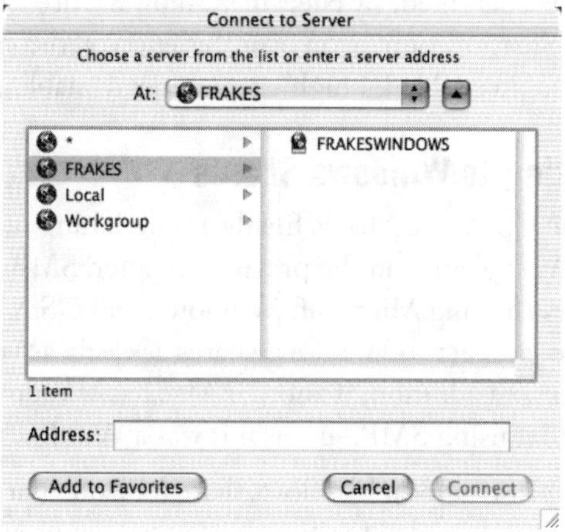

FIGURE 11.2: Using the Connect to Server dialog to browse Windows workgroups

You'll then be asked to provide the workgroup in which the remote computer resides, your username, and your password. After entering the correct values and clicking OK, the Windows share will be mounted. Note that you can also include the workgroup name in the original URL by typing **`smb://`*`workgroup;serveraddress/share/`***.

Once the Windows share is mounted, you can work with it as you would any other mounted volume (within the privileges you have for the share, of course.) However, you should be aware that Mac OS X allows you to use certain characters in the names of files that the Windows OS does not; specifically, these characters are ? [ ] / \ = + < > ; : " , | *. (That final period is the end of the sentence, not one of the "forbidden" characters.) If you try to copy a file from your Mac to a Windows share and the filename contains one of these characters, you'll get an error message "Error code = -43." You'll need to edit the name of the file and try the copy again.

Limitations to Mac OS X's Windows Share Access

Although OS X includes significant support for accessing Windows shares, at the time of this writing it does have a few limitations in addition to the one I mentioned above about only being able to view Windows computers located on the same subnet:

- OS X supports SMB over TCP/IP, but not over NetBEUI; thankfully, most newer versions of the Windows OS share files over TCP/IP.
- Administrative shares (those that end with a *$* character) are not accessible from a Mac without using a utility like DAVE (discussed below).
- At the time of this writing, you can only connect to a single SMB volume at one time. If you need to mount a different Windows share, be sure to drag the first to the Trash to unmount it first, then connect to the second. Mounting more than one SMB volume simultaneously can cause a kernel panic.
- Many users experience problems—such as system freezes—if they put their Mac to sleep or disconnect from their Internet or network connection with a Windows share mounted. You should be sure to unmount Windows shares before disconnecting or putting your Mac to sleep.

Alternatives to Mac OS X's Windows Access: DAVE

Although it's great that OS X provides the ability to connect with Windows shares right out of the box, this ability is somewhat limited in its functionality. For example, I already mentioned that OS X can only browse workgroups that are located in the same subnet as your computer. Another commonly encountered shortcoming is that OS X does not support Windows Shortcuts (they show up as generic files and do not link to their targets). If you only occasionally connect to Windows shares, you'll probably be perfectly happy with OS X's connection capabilities. However, if connecting to Windows shares is something you do frequently, or if your Mac sits on a large Windows network, you may want more functionality than OS X provides.

Thursby Software's DAVE (`http://www.thursby.com/`) is far and away the most comprehensive utility for interacting with Windows computers and networks from your Mac. I mentioned it in the last chapter as a way to extend your Mac's ability to share files with Windows computers, but it's a powerful tool for *connecting* to Windows computers, as well. Some of the advantages that DAVE provides over Mac OS X's built-in functionality include the ability to authenticate with a Windows network at login in order to mount shares on the network without entering your name and password; the ability to mount multiple shares quickly; the ability to browse workgroups and Windows computers throughout a network, not just on the local subnet; support for Windows Shortcuts; and the ability to change your Windows network password from your Mac. Another nice bonus is that by putting the DAVE installation CD in a Windows computer, you can quickly verify that it is properly set up to share files over a network. If you're having connection problems, this is a great feature that can help you isolate the cause (either with your Mac or with the Windows computer).

DAVE is a bit more expensive than much of the software mentioned in this book; however, if your Mac sits on a Windows network, DAVE is well worth the investment. Instead of just providing a way to interact with Windows computers, it makes your Mac a full citizen on Windows networks.

Connecting to FTP/SFTP Servers

A decade ago, FTP was the dominant way to share and access files over the Internet. Shareware and freeware, documents, software updates—all of these were commonly distributed using FTP servers. Nowadays FTP has been relegated to second-class citizenship, for a few reasons. The first is that other, more convenient, methods have been developed; whereas FTP generally required you to transfer files using a command-line prompt, or at best a dedicated FTP client, other methods (including a few discussed in this chapter) allow you to mount remote folders and volumes in the Finder and use them just like local volumes. Second, the increasing influence of the World Wide Web means that distributing files via web servers is much more reliable than using FTP servers—everyone has a web browser. Finally, as I discussed in the previous chapter, FTP itself is not a secure protocol, so using FTP for anything other than anonymous (guest) access is a security risk.

Nevertheless, because FTP servers are simple to set up and provide excellent data transfer speeds, they're still a popular way to share files such as software over the Internet. Developers often use them to provide evaluation versions of software or software updates, and end users use them to exchange files. In addition, most website management (the uploading and downloading of web pages) is still done via FTP. What's more, SFTP—the secure implementation of FTP that uses SSH (secure shell) access to encrypt all data—is becoming more and more popular as a substitute for FTP; since it's cross-platform, SFTP is a secure way to share files both within and between platforms. Here are a few of the ways you can connect to FTP and SFTP servers.

WARNING Because of the security issues inherent to FTP connections, I recommend using FTP only with servers that allow anonymous (guest) connections, and only for transferring non-sensitive data and files. If you need to send sensitive information and/or you want to make sure no one can discern your username and password, try to use SFTP instead.

NOTE As I mentioned in the previous chapter, FTP and SFTP are actually command-line applications; FTP and SFTP clients that feature graphical interfaces are actually issuing the appropriate commands to the FTP/SFTP server for you. If you like doing things the hard way, you can open Terminal and do everything manually. Use `man ftp` or `man sftp` in Terminal to get the complete manual for each application.

FTP via Your Web Browser

Because FTP is such a common method for distributing software, most web browsers include a limited degree of FTP support. I don't recommend using a web browser for interactive FTP use, but if you have the complete URL to a file that resides on an FTP server (e.g., `ftp://`*`server/directory/filename`*), and that FTP server allows guest access, the easiest thing to do is often to simply type or copy/paste the URL into your web browser; the file will be downloaded to your computer. Unfortunately, none of the web browsers available at the time of this writing support SFTP.

FTP/SFTP Using a Dedicated FTP/SFTP Client

If you actually need to interact with an FTP or SFTP server (upload files, rename files, etc.), the best way is to use a dedicated FTP/SFTP client. These applications provide you with the full range of FTP/SFTP functionality; under OS X, most also have excellent user interfaces that make working with servers easy and convenient.

The most popular FTP/SFTP clients for OS X are the commercial/shareware Interarchy (`http://www.interarchy.com/`), RBrowser (`http://www.rbrowser.com/`), Transmit (`http://www.panic.com/transmit/`), and Gideon (`http://www.gideonsoftworks.com/gideon.html`), and the freeware Fugu (`http://rsug.itd.umich.edu/software/fugu/`). Interarchy provides an extensive feature set unmatched by any other FTP/SFTP client, and has become the "power user" client of choice. However, the newest version of Transmit provides an excellent set of features (including some unique features like file previews and a built-in text editor) along with an interface that is head and shoulders above any other, in my opinion. For this reason, I'm going to use Transmit to show how to connect to an FTP or SFTP server. Keep in mind, however, that all FTP/SFTP clients operate similarly in terms of connecting and interacting.

FIGURE 11.3: Using Transmit to connect to another computer via SFTP

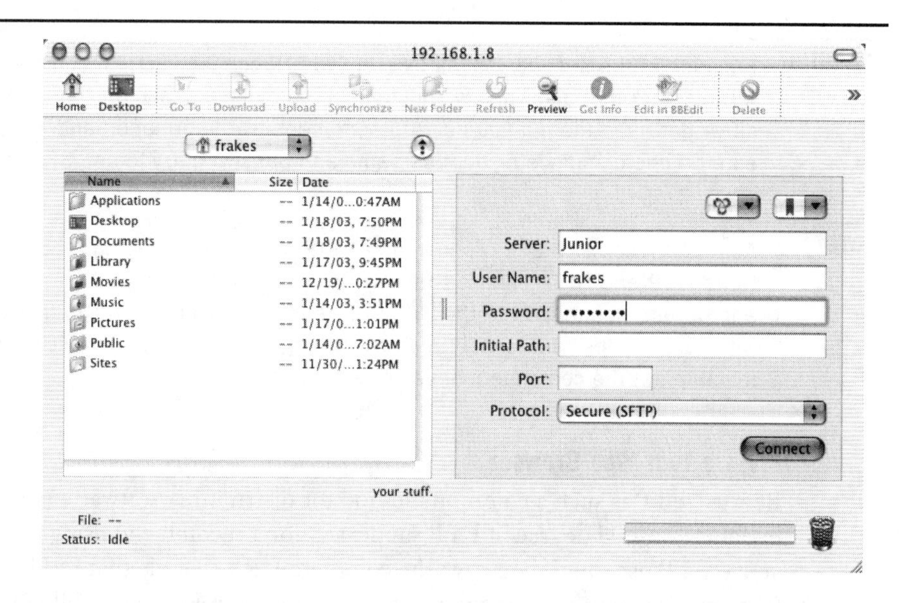

NOTE There are also a few very good FTP-only clients, including Captain FTP (`http://captain-ftp.xdsnet.de/`), Fetch (`http://www.fetchsoftworks.com/`), and RBrowser Lite (`http://www.rbrowser.com/`). Because they don't support SFTP, I rarely use them; however, if you use standard FTP frequently, they're worth considering.

Connecting

To connect to an FTP or SFTP server, most clients present you with a connection dialog that asks for the server address, username, password, and other information (Figure 11.3). In the case of Transmit, you're also asked which protocol to use, FTP or SFTP. (Some clients instead provide different connection dialogs for FTP and SFTP.) In the server field, enter the server's IP address or domain name (don't include `ftp://`; the client will do that for you when you connect). If you're connecting anonymously, enter anonymous in the username field and leave the password field blank (or enter your e-mail address; some anonymous servers require this). If you're connecting via SFTP (or to an FTP server that requires an account), enter your actual username and password.

TIP If your FTP/SFTP client supports Rendezvous (an example is Transmit), you can select local, Rendezvous-enabled FTP/SFTP servers from the client's Rendezvous menu instead of entering the server's IP address.

If you know specifically what path you want to connect to on the target computer, you can enter it in the Initial Path field (you'll also see this field as Directory in some clients). Finally, most FTP/SFTP clients give you the option of specifying a nonstandard port if the target computer isn't using standard FTP (20 and 21) or SFTP (22) ports.

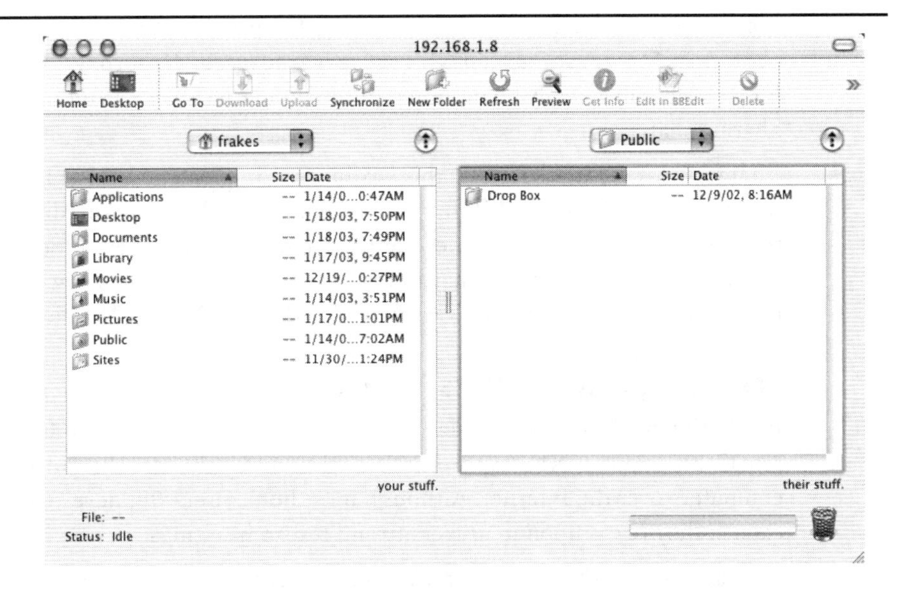

FIGURE 11.4: Transmit shows you "your stuff" and "their stuff" when connecting to a server.

Once you've entered the required information, click Connect (or OK in some clients) and the application will connect to the FTP/SFTP server. However, instead of the share/server mounting in the Finder as it does with Personal File Sharing or SMB access, all interactions with the server will take place from within the FTP/SFTP client. Depending on which client you're using, what you see can look like a Finder window, a file browser, or, in an application like Transmit, a dual-paned window that shows you the contents of a directory on the server and a directory on your own computer (Figure 11.4); the latter can be useful for moving files between your own computer and the FTP/SFTP server.

You can generally navigate within those directories to which your account has access. You can also upload, download, rename, and delete files as needed (again, provided you have the appropriate privileges). Most Mac OS X FTP/SFTP clients provide excellent ease of use: double-clicking a file in a server window, or dragging it to your Desktop or a Finder folder, downloads it; dragging a file from your computer to a server window uploads it. (In the dual-pane method used by Transmit, you can simply drag files between panes.) Most clients also have extensive additional options for working with files, accessible through the client's menus. For example, Interarchy and Transmit allow you to synchronize remote and local folders—if you manage a remote website, this is a great way to automatically upload any web pages or files you've recently edited or added.

A Step Forward: FTP in the Finder

As I mentioned above, one drawback of FTP has always been that you're forced to use either the command line or a dedicated FTP client to access shared files. However, with OS X 10.2 Apple began to integrate FTP browsing into the OS X Finder. To get a glimpse of how FTP in the Finder works, go to Connect to Server and enter the FTP server's address in the form

ftp://*serveraddress*/. You can even include a directory and/or a username and password in the format **ftp://*username*:*password*@*serveraddress*/*directory*/**. Click Connect and the FTP server will actually be mounted in the Finder just like a Windows SMB share or File Sharing sharepoint.

Unfortunately, at the time of this writing, the implementation of FTP in the Finder is not flawless. For example, SFTP isn't supported, you can't upload or edit files (you have only read-only access), and sometimes the Finder crashes. However, it looks like a promising avenue. I hope that by the time you read this, or soon after, this new approach will be improved to the point that we rarely need dedicated FTP/SFTP clients.

Connecting to NFS Servers/Shares

In addition to Windows and Mac shares, OS X can also connect to Unix Network File System (NFS) exports. NFS exports are a common way to share directories that reside on Unix computers over the Internet. Although most home users will never encounter an NFS export, they're common in university and research settings.

To access an NFS share, open Connect to Server and enter the URL of the share in the format **nfs://*serveraddress*/*exportpath***, where *exportpath* is the path to the particular Unix directory you wish to access. You'll be asked for your username and password, after which the export will be mounted in the Finder much like any other remote share.

TIP To automatically mount NFS shares, check out NFS Manager, which I mentioned in Chapter 10.

Connecting to Frequently Accessed Servers and Shares

Although there may be times when connecting to a particular server is a one-time deal, there's a good chance that if you're accessing files from a remote computer, you'll be doing so more than once. In this section I'm going to show you how to take advantage of functionality discussed previously to make repeated connections more convenient.

Using Aliases (iDisk/AFP/SMB/NFS)

I talked about aliases in Chapter 5 as a way to quickly access files and folders, but they're also extremely useful as a way to quickly access iDisks as well as Personal File Sharing, Windows SMB, and Unix NFS shares. Once a share is mounted on your computer (under "Computer" in a Finder window, and on the Desktop if you've chosen to show mounted volumes on the Desktop via Finder preferences), make an alias of the share itself. You can store this alias anywhere on your hard drive, and the next time you want to connect to the share, simply open the alias. You'll be presented with the name/password dialog; enter the appropriate information and the share will be mounted, without having to use the Connect to Server dialog.

FIGURE 11.5:

Adding your username and password for a remote server to the Keychain

If you tend to access the same sub-folder on a remote share, you can actually make an alias to that folder or directory, rather than to the share itself. Double-clicking such an alias will mount the share in the same way, but the sub-folder will automatically be opened for you.

To make things even more convenient, for many servers, you can avoid having to enter your name and password by saving your login information in your Keychain (see Figure 11.5). When you first connect to the share, click the Options… in the name/password dialog and check the "Add Password to Keychain" or "Add to Keychain" box. Your login info will be saved and automatically entered the next time you double-click the alias to the share. (I'll talk more about the Keychain in Chapter 13.)

TIP

You can make aliases to all of your frequently accessed shares and servers and then take advantage of one of the methods for quick file access described in Chapters 5 and the Online Bonus Chapter. For example, put all of these aliases in a single folder, and then drag that folder to the Dock. You'll get instant access to any of your remote shares by control/right-clicking on the folder in the Dock. You can also drag shares (or subdirectories of shares) directly to Finder window toolbars; the new toolbar item will remain even after you unmount it. This saves you the trouble of creating an alias, and a quick click on the toolbar item will mount the share (and, in the case of a subdirectory, open that directory).

Using Internet Location Files (i.e., Location Files, Part II)

I've mentioned Internet Location files in several places throughout the book. They're OS X's way of creating a "bookmark" for a particular URL. Double-clicking on an Internet Location file opens the enclosed URL appropriately; for example, HTTP Location files are opened in your default web browser. What you may not be aware of is that, like URLs themselves, Internet Location files support many different protocols: an AFP Location file will attempt to mount a File Sharing sharepoint, and an FTP Location file will attempt to connect to an FTP server. If you could create your own Internet Location files, you'd have a great tool for quickly accessing remote computers, right?

Fortunately, Internet Location files are extremely easy to create, but the way to do so isn't completely obvious.

1. Open a text editor such as TextEdit or BBEdit.
2. Type in the complete URL of the server/share you want to access; I've included examples of the most common types below.
3. Highlight the complete URL.
4. Drag the highlighted URL to the Finder (the Desktop or any other folder).

An Internet Location file will be created (Figure 11.6). You can double-click on the file to access the share or server just as if you had opened Connect to Server and typed the URL in manually. In fact, most URLs can also contain a username and password, saving you the trouble of having to enter them each time you connect. You can also rename Location files as you please; it won't affect their ability to connect.

FIGURE 11.6: Internet Location files for (left to right) an iDisk, an FTP server, and a local Mac running Personal File Sharing

The only downside to Internet Location files is that you can't edit them directly. If you need to change the address or any other information contained in an Internet Location file, you'll have to throw away the original and create a new one. Before you throw it away, drag it into an open text document (which will paste the URL into the document); edit the URL as needed, highlight it, and then drag it to the Finder to create a new Location file.

Location File Formats

Table 11.1 shows the formats for URLs supported by Internet Location files; Table 11.2 indicates how to include username and password info in the Location file. If you can put up with slightly less convenience (having to enter the password manually), for security reasons I generally recommend not including the password.

WARNING If you include your username and password in Location files, be sure to store these files somewhere secure—inside the private areas of your user folder—so that other users don't have access to them!

NOTE Note that in the case of FTP Location files, the default setting in OS X is to use the Finder to connect. If you'd rather use a dedicated FTP client, you'll need to edit the FTP Helper setting using the third-party utility More Internet, as described in Chapter 9.

TABLE 11.1: Common Location File (URL) Formats

Type of Connection	URLs Supported by Internet Location Files
iDisk	afp://idisk.mac.com/*membername*
iDisk Public Folder	http://idisk.mac.com/*membername*/Public
Personal File Sharing/AppleShare	afp://*serveraddress/*
Specific Volumes or Sharepoints via Personal File Sharing	afp://*serveraddress/volume or share name* (Use *%20* in place of spaces in volume or sharepoint names.)
Personal File Sharing via Rendezvous	afp://*rendezvousname*.local (Add */volume or share name* to the end to connect to specific volumes or sharepoints.)
FTP	ftp://*serveraddress*
FTP (anonymous access)	ftp://anonymous@*serveraddress*
NFS exports	nfs://*serveraddress/exportpath*

TABLE 11.2: Location File Formats, Including Passwords

Type of Connection	URLs Modified with Passwords
iDisk	afp://*membername*:*password*@idisk.mac.com/*membername*
iDisk Public Folder	http://public:*password*@idisk.mac.com/*membername*/Public
Personal File Sharing/AppleShare	afp://*username*:*password*@*serveraddress/*
Specific Volumes or Share Points via Personal File Sharing	afp://*username*:*password*@*serveraddress/volume or share name*
Personal File Sharing via Rendezvous	afp://*username*:*password*@*rendezvousname*.local (Add */volume or share name* to the end to connect to specific volumes or sharepoints.)
FTP	ftp://*username*:*password*@*serveraddress*
NFS exports	nfs://*username*:*password*@*serveraddress/exportpath*

Unfortunately, at the time of this writing it's not possible to create an Internet Location file for SMB shares or SFTP connections. However, I suspect that Apple will soon fix this, given how convenient Internet Locations can be. Assuming this bug does get fixed, here are the formats for SMB and SFTP Locations. Note that because SFTP connections first establish a connection, and then send the password securely, you can't include the password in the URL:

smb://*serveraddress/share*

smb://*workgroup;username*:*password*@*serveraddress/share*

sftp://*serveraddress*

sftp://*username*@*serveraddress*

Once you've created Internet Location files, you can put them in the Dock, in a folder in the Dock, in a menu, or any other place where you have quick access to them. Here are a couple ideas for how to take advantage of them.

Using Location Files with Dock and Custom Menus

In Chapters 5 and its Online Bonus Chapter, I talked about adding custom menus to OS X as a way of quickly accessing files and folders. If you have several remote servers or shares that you access frequently, Dock menus and custom menus can be extremely convenient. You can place all of your Internet Location files in a folder and drag that folder to the Dock, and you have an instant Dock menu that provides one-click access to any server (Figure 11.7). Likewise, if you use one of the many third-party menu utilities, you can add your Location files to their menus for quick access. I personally prefer the freeware iChoose (`http://www.luckysoftware.dk/ichoose.php`). You can drag Internet Location files into the iChoose preferences pane and they'll be added to your iChoose menu (Figure 11.7). In addition, iChoose lets you add URLs directly (in the formats listed above), without having to create Location files first.

TIP You can also drag Location files to Finder toolbars to provide quick access.

Using Location Files as Recent Servers and Favorites

If you don't want to clutter your Dock or use a third-party menu, you can use your Internet Location files with Mac OS X's built-in Favorites and Recent Servers features to gain quick access to remote shares.

I mentioned earlier in the chapter that when you access a server via Connect to Server, OS X creates a Location file in `~/Library/Recent Servers`, and when you add a server as a Favorite, a Location file is created in `~/Library/Favorites`. These files are simply standard Internet Location files. What this means is that by placing Internet Location files that you've created into one of those two directories, they'll show up in the At: pop-up menu in Connect to Server (under Recent Servers or Favorites, respectively). The Recent Servers list shows a maximum of five Locations/servers, but the Favorites listing shows as many servers as there are Location files in the Favorites folder.

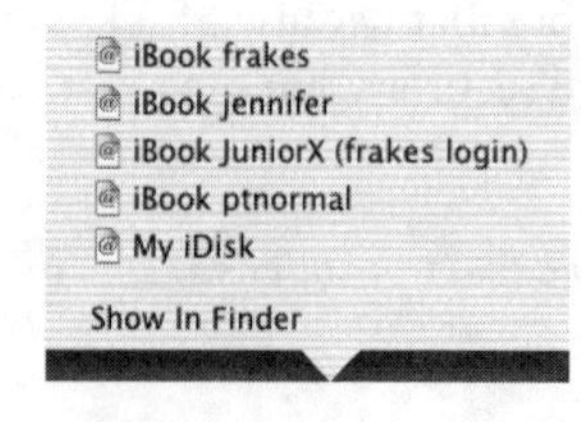

FIGURE 11.7: Accessing favorite servers via the Dock (left) and iChoose (right)

WARNING If you place an Internet Location file in `~/Library/Favorites` or `~/Library/Recent Servers`, it will show up in the At: menu in Connect to Server not by the name of the Location file, but by the URL contained in it—including any username and password. This isn't too bad when you're using Location files within your own account, but be aware that if someone else has access to your Location files, they could use this trick to view your name and password.

Automatically Connect to Shares/Servers at Login

If you use a particular remote share or server on a regular basis, you may find yourself connecting to it each time you log in. Under Mac OS 9, when you connected to an AppleShare volume you could choose to have the volume mounted at startup automatically. Although this option is gone in Mac OS X, you can combine Internet Location files with OS X's Login Items to gain similar functionality. Simply drag the Internet Location file for the server or share to which you want to connect into the Login Items pane of System Preferences (preferably at the bottom of the list of login items, so that it's opened last), and the next time you log in the server or share will be mounted automatically.

TIP Mac OS X also has the ability to use "auto mount points," which are basically a way to automatically mount shares at startup—meaning that these shares will be available to everyone rather than just an individual user. Unfortunately, Apple hasn't provided an easy interface to create auto mount points. The author of SharePoints, which I've mentioned in several places in the book, has created a useful utility called SharePoints AutoMounter (`http://www.hornware.com/sharepointsautomounter/`) that lets you do this. If you need to automatically mount shares/servers at startup so that they're available to all users, you should give SharePoints AutoMounter a try.

Connecting to Virtual Private Networks (VPN)

To ensure the privacy of data sent over the Internet, many businesses and universities use a technology called Virtual Private Networking (VPN). A Virtual Private Network lets a remote user communicate with another computer or a company LAN over a normal Internet connection, but creates a secure "tunnel" between the two. Data is encrypted at one end and then decrypted at the other end; data that isn't encrypted using the same key (password) used at the creation of the VPN can't enter the tunnel, and no one can access data in the tunnel without the correct key.

Until recently, most VPN client software was Windows-only, effectively keeping Macs out of many corporate networks. However, beginning with OS X 10.2, your Mac has a VPN client built in. This VPN client supports Microsoft's Point to Point Tunneling protocol (PPTP), meaning you can connect to many Windows networks that require VPN connections without any additional software. Unfortunately, unless you know exactly where to look, you'll probably never find it—Apple buried it deep in the menus of the Internet Connect application.

If you need to open a PPTP VPN connection, launch Internet Connect and select File ➢ New VPN Connection Window. If this is the first time you've tried to use OS X's VPN client, you'll get a message that "Your computer needs to be set up for VPN (PPTP) connections." Click Continue and OS X will set things up for you.

The VPN Connection window (Figure 11.8) asks for the VPN server's address (get this from your network administrator), as well as your network username and password. (Click the Add to Keychain box to have OS X remember your password for this connection.)

TIP If you're connecting to a Windows network, your username might actually be your network domain followed by your actual username, in the format `domain\username`—check with your network administrator to be sure.

Click Connect to initiate the connection. The status bar at the bottom of the window will tell you if your connection is successful, and will then show a timer of how long your VPN connection has been active. In addition, if you open the Network pane of System Preferences after connecting to a VPN, you'll find that a new Network Port Configuration called PPTP has been created, and that you've been given an IP address on the remote network.

Once you're connected to your company or organization's network via VPN, your Mac will think it's actually sitting on that network. You should be able to browse Mac and Windows shares in the Connect to Server dialog, and connect to shares just as you would if your Mac were on the local network.

NOTE Although PPTP is the current Windows VPN standard, a protocol called IPSec is the standard on many Unix systems, and is becoming increasingly popular even on Windows networks. At the time of this writing, OS X includes support for IPSec, but does not include a built-in IPSec client; however, the third-party VPN Tracker (`http://www.equinux.com/us/products/vpntracker/index.html`) and VaporSec (`http://www.afp548.com/Software/VaporSec/`) both provide one at a reasonable price. On a similar note, some Cisco VPN servers require a proprietary VPN client; if your network is using a Cisco VPN server, your network administrator should be able to provide you with the appropriate client.

FIGURE 11.8: Mac OS X's VPN Connection dialog box

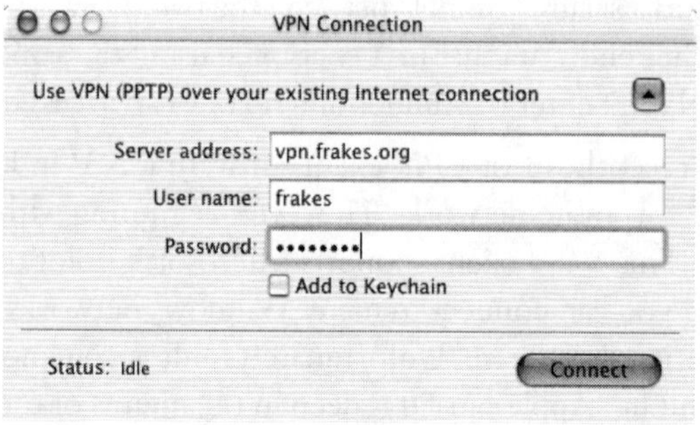

VPN Connection

Use VPN (PPTP) over your existing Internet connection

Server address: vpn.frakes.org

User name: frakes

Password: ••••••••

Add to Keychain

Status: Idle

Connect

Remote Access and Control

In addition to sharing files with other computers and accessing files on other computers, it's also possible to access and control a Mac running OS X remotely (from another computer). Maybe you want to move a file from your private Documents folder to your Public folder so that another user has access to it, but aren't sitting at the computer at the time. Perhaps you want to make sure Software Update runs on another computer in your home or office without having to sit down and log into that computer. Or maybe you're trying to troubleshoot a problem on another computer and seeing what the other user is seeing will help you better understand what's going wrong. Each of these tasks can be accomplished remotely using either OS X's built-in abilities or with the help of third-party software.

Remote Login

The simplest type of remote "control" of a Mac—in terms of both the interface and the tools needed—is called Remote Login, and is built into every Mac running OS X. To enable Remote Login, simply open the Sharing pane of System Preferences, and check the box next to Remote Login in the Services tab. To the right you'll see the message "Remote Login On." What this actually does is enable OS X's built-in SSH (Secure Shell) server. SSH allows a remote computer to connect via a command-line interface, authenticating and encrypting all communication between the server and the remote computer.

NOTE If you've ever used a Telnet connection, an SSH connection will look very familiar; it's basically a secure, encrypted form of Telnet.

Once Remote Login is enabled, any user with an account on your Mac can connect using a command-line application (such as OS X's Terminal or Window's Console), and then log in using their username and password. Once connected, the user can execute pretty much any command available to them when physically sitting at the computer, logged in, using Terminal. In the case of an admin user, this is an incredible amount of power, so be *very* careful who has admin access on your machine if Remote Login is enabled.

As a side note, despite the name, Remote Login doesn't have to be *remote*—you can actually log in to your own computer from another user account *on* your computer. For example, if another user is currently logged in and you want to move a file from your Documents folder to a publicly viewable directory so that the user can access it, you can launch Terminal from within *their* account, but log in to your computer via SSH using your *own* username and password. You can then move the file (as described in the example a bit later in the chapter) and disconnect. This is a lot more convenient than having the other user log out, logging in to your own account via the login window, moving the file, logging out, and then having the other user log in again. (That being said, although this is a neat trick, using the `su` , or *switch user*, command—**su *yourusername* <RETURN>** and then entering your password—does the same thing without requiring that Remote Login be enabled.)

Connecting via Remote Login

To connect to a Mac using Remote Login, open Terminal on another Mac (or Console on a Windows computer or any Unix command-line app), and type **ssh *username@serveraddress*** **<RETURN>**, where *username* is your short username (on the computer to which you're connecting) and *serveraddress* is the IP address (or, if applicable, the domain name) of the target computer. (If you're connecting from another Mac, and your short username is identical on both Macs, you can just type **ssh *serveraddress*** **<RETURN>**; OS X will automatically send your username for you.) After a few seconds you'll be asked for your password; after providing it you'll see a standard command-line interface, just as if you were using Terminal in person.

NOTE To log in to the local computer (the one you're actually using) to test that SSH is working properly, type **ssh *username*@localhost <RETURN>.**

Once you're connected to the remote computer, your command-line prompt will change to reflect that you're no longer working locally; for example, in most shells, the name of the remote computer will be included in your Terminal prompt. At any point, type **exit** **<RETURN>** and you'll be logged out and disconnected.

Internet Location Files and Remote Login

Earlier in the chapter I showed you how to create Internet Location files for frequently accessed servers and shares. You can actually create these Location files for SSH connections, as well. Use the same steps you would use to create any other type of Internet Location files, but for the URL type ssh://*username@serveraddress*. Opening the resulting Location file will launch Terminal and initiate an SSH connection with the server using the appropriate username. (You can't include your password in an SSH location file, since the remote computer won't ask for your password until *after* a secure connection is initiated.)

Using Remote Login

As I stated earlier, once logged in to a Mac remotely you can do anything that you could do if you were using Terminal while sitting at the computer. Because of the sheer number of commands and applications that can be run from Terminal, I can't provide you with a comprehensive list of possible tasks. However, I talk a good deal more about Terminal commands in Chapter 15. In addition, here are some of the most common commands.

man	Read the manual page for a command (e.g., man *commandname*)
ls	List the files in the current directory
pwd	List the path of the current directory (the *working* directory)
cd	Change directory (e.g., cd /Users/Shared to switch to the Shared user folder)
mkdir	Create (make) a new directory (e.g., mkdir 'New Files' to create a new directory named New Files)

`rmdir` Remove/delete a directory (e.g., `rmdir 'New Files'`)

`mv` Move file (e.g., `mv /Users/`*`username`*`/`*`document`* `/Users/Shared/`*`document`* to move a file from inside your user folder to the Shared user folder)

`cp` Copy file (e.g., `cp` *`document document2`* to make a copy of *document* named *document2*.)

These are just a few (very, very few) of the commands you can use when logged in remotely. To give you a better idea of the kinds of things you can do using Remote Login, here are a few short examples.

Moving a File from Your Documents Folder to Your Public Folder

User Level: any
Affects: user
Terminal: yes

Imagine that you have a document on your computer that you want another user to be able to access. However, that document is currently inside your Documents folder, and you're not at home to move it someplace where the users can get to it (such as your Public folder). You can use Remote Login to move it or copy it to your Public folder.

1. Log in remotely by typing **`ssh`** ***`username@serveraddress`*** **<RETURN>** in any command-line application. Enter your password and press return.
2. Your initial working directory (the directory you are "in" when you first log in) will be your user folder; type **`ls`** **<RETURN>** to view the names of all the folders in your home directory.
3. Change to the directory that contains your file. Do this by typing **`cd`** ***`foldername`*** **<RETURN>**, where *foldername* is the name of the folder you want to switch to. For example, switch to your Documents folder by typing **`cd Documents`** **<RETURN>**. ("Changing directories" in Unix is much like opening a folder in the Finder—you're opening a folder to work with files inside of it.) Type **`ls`** **<RETURN>** again to view the contents of the folder you just switched to.
4. Continue to use `cd` and `ls` until you find the document you want to move. (If you want to move up a level—say, from Documents to your main user folder—type **`cd ..`** **<RETURN>**. This is the Unix command for viewing the folder enclosing the current directory.
5. Once you find your document, type **`mv`** ***`documentname`*** **`/Users/`*****`username`*****`/Public/`*****`documentname`*** **<RETURN>** (where *documentname* is the exact name of the document and *username* is your short username) to move it from the current directory to your Public folder. If you'd rather keep the original document where it is and make a *copy* of it in your Public folder instead, type **`cp`** ***`documentname`*** **`/Users/`*****`username`*****`/Public/`*****`documentname`*** **<RETURN>**.

After following these steps, your fellow user(s) will be able to access the document in question by opening your Public folder (either while sitting at your computer, or via one of the remote sharing options discussed in the previous chapter).

TIP As I mentioned earlier, you can use this same procedure if you *are* near your computer, but you don't want to make the other user log out, then log in yourself, move the file, log out, then have the other user log in again. Simply launch Terminal from within the other user's account, type **ssh *yourusername*@localhost <RETURN>**, provide your password, and then move the file as described above. When you're done, type **exit <RETURN>**. (Although as I mentioned above, a better way to do it would be to just use the su command: **su *yourusername* <RETURN>**.) The ability to login to your own account via Terminal from within another user's account is a real time-saver and convenience that I use quite frequently.

Quitting an Application That's Taken over Your Mac

User Level: admin
Affects: user
Terminal: yes

Sometimes an application will "hang"—it will freeze and take up so much of the CPU that you can't even use the Force Quit window to quit it. In situations like these, if you have Remote Login enabled, you can sometimes quit the application remotely, giving you back your Mac.

1. From another computer, log into your Mac using SSH.
2. Type **`top -u`** **<RETURN>**. This will present you with a list of all running applications, sorted by CPU usage—chances are the problematic application will be listed first, since it's hogging the processor. Note the PID (process ID) number of that application on the left.
3. Press the Q key to quit the top utility and return to the Terminal prompt.
4. Type **`sudo kill -9 PID`**, where PID is the process ID number of the problematic application (which you got from the `top` display). Enter your password when prompted. This will unmercifully quit the application
5. Log out, walk back to your computer, and enjoy not having to restart.

Although this process isn't foolproof—some crashes are so severe they don't even let you log in remotely—when it works, it's often a real timesaver.

Using Software Update Remotely

User Level: admin
Affects: computer
Terminal: yes

I talked about the Software Update application in Chapter 4. However, there is also a command-line version of Software Update that is accessible via Terminal—and, thus, when logged in remotely. Although this feature is priceless for a network administrator who is supporting many Macs, it can be quite useful even for the home user. For example, my home office has a G4, but we also have an iBook on an AirPort network. Occasionally I'll run Software Update and find that a new update is available. In the past, this meant having to go find the iBook (wherever it might be in the house) and then running Software Update on it. But under OS X, I can simply launch Terminal on the G4, log in to the iBook remotely, and update the software right from my desk. (I'm not lazy; I'm just busy. Really.)

Here's how you do it (in this example, "target computer" is the computer you're updating, and "remote computer" is the computer from which you'll be accessing the target computer):

1. Log in to the target computer remotely using SSH.
2. Type **`sudo softwareupdate`** **<RETURN>** and provide the password for your admin-level account when prompted. Software Update will run on the target computer, and you'll be provided with a list of available updates by name, each with a corresponding number. For example, on a recent update, I was presented with the following output:

```
- 3283
  Internet Explorer 5.2 Security Update (5.2.2), 9330K
- 3359
  QuickTime (6.0.2), 19620K - restart required
- 3339
  StuffIt Expander Security Update (7.0), 4420K
```

   The updates are listed with version numbers, file sizes, and whether or not a restart of the remote computer is required. In addition, each update is preceded by an identifying number.

3. To install an update, type **`sudo softwareupdate`** ***`update#`*** **<RETURN>** where *update#* is the number listed next to the desired update. For example, to install the QuickTime update listed above, I typed `sudo softwareupdate 3359`. Enter the admin password when prompted.
4. When the installation is complete, you'll see a message in Terminal letting you know that the update has been installed. If the update does not require a restart, you can simply type **`exit`** to log out of the target computer. If the update requires a restart, you'll receive a message telling you to restart immediately. Luckily, you can do this remotely, too. Simply type **`sudo reboot`**, and enter the admin password at the prompt. You will be logged out of the target computer, and the target computer will restart. (Note that remote reboot is not the same as choosing Restart from the Apple Menu. Remote reboot does not save documents or close databases—it simply kills every running process and restarts. If you think someone might be using the remote machine, or there may be unsaved documents open, it's probably safer to ask the user to restart the machine, or restart it yourself later.)

TIP When using Software Update remotely, you can actually install more than one update at once. To do so, simply include the update numbers in the same command: `sudo software update` *`update# update# update#`* <RETURN>. The updates will be installed consecutively, and you will be notified when they are all completed.

Desktop Control: VNC

Remote Login is extremely powerful; however, it requires some knowledge of Unix commands and it has a horrible user interface (unless you really *like* using a command line to get things done). There are times when it would be nice to actually see the screen of another computer, and control it as if it were right in front of you. For example, helping someone troubleshoot a computer is much easier if you can see exactly what they're seeing. Another example is when you want to turn a Sharing service on or off in Sharing preferences—doing so is tricky in Terminal if you don't know what you're doing, but if you can control the mouse on your computer from another computer, you can actually open System Preferences, switch to the Sharing pane, and click the appropriate box yourself. Finally, many parents with very young children like to monitor their child's computer use.

One solution is what is known as *virtual network computing* (VNC). By running a VNC *server* on a computer, VNC *clients* can connect to that computer, view its screen, and even control it—all from another computer on a local network, or even from a computer halfway around the world.

Setting Up a VNC Server on OS X

There is currently an open-source project dedicated to producing a VNC server for Mac OS X, called OSXvnc (`http://sourceforge.net/projects/osxvnc/`). There are several implementations of OSXvnc that you can install on your Mac, the most elegant of which is the freeware Share My Desktop (`http://www.bombich.com/software/smd.html`). It allows you to set up either a user-level server (one that can be started and stopped by any user, and in fact requires a user to manually start and stop it) or a system-wide VNC server that is enabled at startup.

Starting a User-Level VNC Server

User Level: any
Affects: individual user
Terminal: no

If you only plan to use a VNC connection once in a while—for example, when a user needs help—it's probably better to simply have the user start the VNC server when needed. You can actually install a copy of Share My Desktop on each of your computers, in the `/Applications` folder so that any user can access it.

To start the VNC server, a user simply needs to launch Share My Desktop and click the large "Start sharing" button. The window will then show the connection information, including the IP address, port number, and password to connect, which Share My Desktop created for you automatically (Figure 11.9). (The connection info is also copied to the clipboard, so that the person starting the server can paste it into an e-mail and send it to the person trying to connect—a nice touch!) Keep in mind the caveats I mentioned in Chapter 10 about IP addresses when you're behind a router.

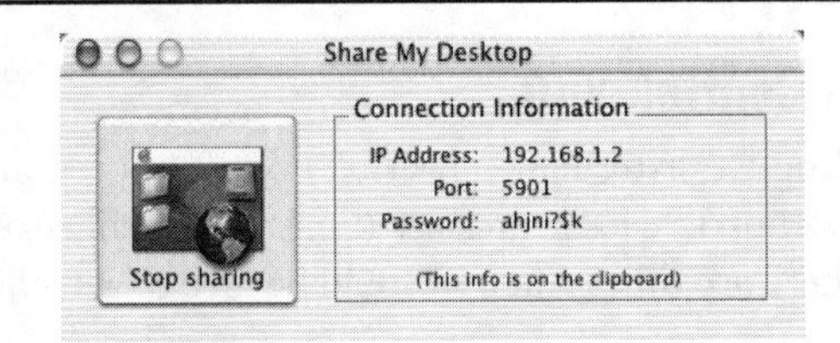

FIGURE 11.9: Share My Desktop shows you everything you need to know to connect to the local VNC server.

It's as simple as that; your VNC server is up and running. However, there are a few options you can take advantage of via the Share My Desktop preferences dialog. You can create your own password, change the port used by the server (don't use any port lower than 5900), hide the password (so that it doesn't show up in the Share My Desktop window), and set up Energy Saver settings (so that the computer doesn't go to sleep or dim the screen when someone else is accessing it).

When you're done with the VNC server, you can stop it by simply clicking the "Stop sharing" button.

Starting a System-Level VNC Server

User Level: admin
Affects: computer
Terminal: no

What if you want your VNC server to be running 24/7? For example, if you want to be sure that you can access your computer via VNC no matter the time or need, you'll want the VNC server to always be enabled. Share My Desktop allows you to install a version of the VNC server in OS X's Unix application directories, and installs a system-level startup item (remember those from Chapter 3?) so that your VNC server is always running. Tech support staff frequently use this type of setup so that they can access computers and provide support when needed. Personally, I have the VNC server running on my computers at home so that I can perform administrative tasks and provide tech support to family and friends, even when I'm not at home.

To install the system-level VNC server, launch Share My Desktop and select File ➢ Manage System VNC Server. Then follow these steps:

1. Authenticate by clicking the padlock button and providing your admin password.
2. Click Install System VNC to install the VNC software and startup item.
3. Choose your server settings in the Step 2 box: Provide a password for the server (VNC clients will need to enter this password to connect), a preferred port number (again, something higher than 5900), and the name you want your computer to appear as when others connect via VNC. Check the "Start VNC server on startup" box, and, finally, decide whether you want to allow your computer screen to dim and/or your computer to go to sleep. (Keep in mind that if you let your computer go to sleep, users—including you—can only connect via VNC when it is awake.) Click Apply Settings.
4. Click "Turn on System VNC" to start the VNC server.

NOTE Once you've set up a system-level VNC server, you can't control the server using the main Share My Desktop window; you have to use the Manage System VNC Server window.

Controlling Your Mac via a VNC Client

Once you've got the VNC server running on your Mac, you can connect to it using its IP address and the port number and password you provided (or that Share My Desktop provided for you). The only thing you need is a VNC client. There are VNC clients available for every platform, so you can actually connect to and control your Mac from any computer anywhere there's Internet access. In terms of VNC clients for OS X, I prefer VNC Thing (`http://www.webthing.net/vncthing/`), mainly because it allows you to resize the client window (it scales the display to fit) and because it allows you to "bookmark" VNC servers.

To connect to a VNC server using VNC Thing, select File ➢ New Session… The connection dialog is extremely simple: enter the IP address of the server, including the port number, and the password (not your personal password, but the VNC server's password). There are a few other options available to you by clicking the disclosure triangle at the bottom of the connection window; the most useful is "Shrink to fit," which automatically shrinks your view of the server's Desktop to fit the VNC Thing window. When you click OK, a window will appear showing you the server's Desktop; by default this window covers the entire screen, but you can resize it to whatever size you choose (Figure 11.10).

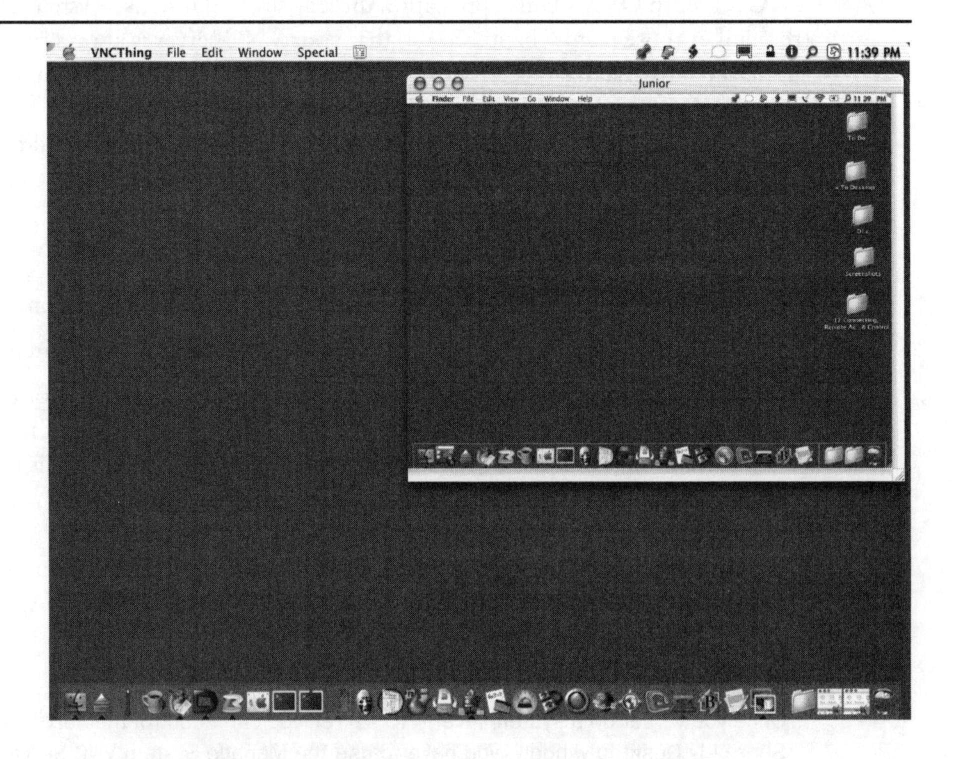

FIGURE 11.10: A VNC client/server connection lets you control one Mac from another.

When you move your cursor over the VNC Thing window, you'll notice that it changes to a smaller cursor; the means you're actually controlling the cursor on the remote computer. Anything you do with the mouse and keyboard here are actually also taking place on the remote computer.

Although VNC technology is very cool and quite useful, there are a few caveats to keep in mind:

- Because using VNC is so graphics-intensive, performance isn't great—you'll notice that when you move windows around on the remote computer, it takes a few seconds for the VNC Thing window to reflect the changes.
- Your Mac must be able to communicate via IP with the computer that is trying to connect. If you or another user is trying to connect to your Mac over the Internet, your Mac must currently be connected to the Internet. If you or another user is trying to connect from a computer on a local network, your Mac needs to be connected to the network and have a local IP address.
- Unlike Remote Login, which lets you log in as any user, VNC lets you see and control the computer as whichever user is currently logged in. Remember that you're not really logging in; you're simply seeing whatever is going on onscreen. If you have a system-level VNC server installed, this means that you can actually log in and out of accounts (as the VNC server will let you connect even when no other users are logged in, so you can see and use the login screen). However, if you rely on a user-level server, you can only connect when a user has started the server manually, and logging out of that user's account will shut down the VNC server.

NOTE OSXvnc and its clients are actually very good as far as free VNC servers and clients go. However, if you need more functionality, you may want to consider the commercial software Timbuktu Pro (`http://www.netopia.com/en-us/software/products/tb2/index.html`). Timbuktu provides all of the remote control functions of OSXvnc, plus more advanced features such as the ability to transfer files between the local and remote computers via drag and drop; the ability to talk to the user of the remote computer via your Mac's microphone and speaker; and the ability to automate actions using AppleScript. In addition, Apple has its own commercial offering, Remote Desktop (`http://www.apple.com/remotedesktop/`) that's aimed more at the education and organizational markets.

Moving On...

While we're on the topics of networks, sharing, and connecting, another related topic is printing—connecting to printers, sharing printers, and configuring printers. In the next chapter I'll cover printing in OS X, from the basics to more advanced features and functionality.

CHAPTER 12

Printing Practicalities

(Or: Supporting unsupported printers, enhancing printing, and other (print) pressing questions.)

If you've been using Mac OS X for a while, you may already have a printer hooked up and working. If so, in this chapter I'll show you how to take advantage of OS X's advanced printing technologies to manage printers and print jobs, share your printer with other computers, print remotely, and print in Classic. I'll also show you how to add a few needed or helpful features using third-party software.

However, if you're coming to OS X from OS 9 or Windows—or even if you've recently upgraded from an older version of OS X—you may have found that your old printer no longer works in OS X 10.2. In that case, I'll also show you how to take advantage of OS X's open-source roots to add support for "unsupported" printers and, I hope, get your old printer up and running.

Printing Basics

Before I talk about setting up and managing printers in OS X, you should know a bit about types of printers and printing connections, how to install additional supported printer drivers and PPDs, and a bit of background on OS X's actual printing system.

Printer Types

There are generally two kinds of printers on the market today: PostScript and non-PostScript. PostScript, a standard printing/programming language, was once only available on expensive laser printers but has recently become common even on lower-priced printers. OS X includes a universal PostScript driver that provides basic support for any PostScript Level 2 or Level 3 printer, and supports additional printer-specific features (multiple paper trays, varying print quality, etc.) via printer-specific PostScript Printer Description (PPD) files. Because of its built-in PostScript driver, OS X can print to any PostScript Level 2 or Level 3 printer right out of the box; however, you many not be able to access features specific to a printer until you install and/or select its correct PPD file. (Although as I'll explain in a moment, this is often done for you, automatically.)

Non-PostScript printers, such as many inkjet printers, use a technology known as Printer Control Language (PCL); PCL printers don't take advantage of a universal printing engine, so each printer requires its own driver (which also supplies information about printer-specific features). The downside to PCL is that unlike PostScript printers, if you don't have the proper driver your printer usually won't print at all.

Luckily, your Mac supports an impressive number of printers right out of the box, due to the fact that many PPD files and non-PostScript printer drivers are pre-installed with OS X.

NOTE You can see the official list of printers supported by OS X at `http://www.apple.com/macosx/upgrade/printers.html`. You can also see a list of provided PPD files at `http://docs.info.apple.com/article.html?artnum=107002`, and a list of pre-installed inkjet printer drivers at `http://docs.info.apple.com/article.html?artnum=107001`. Note that in many cases a driver will also work with closely related printers from the same printer manufacturer and model line.

Printer Connections

Whether a printer is usable with OS X depends not only on whether or not a printer driver or PPD file is available for it, but also on whether or not it can connect to your Mac. OS X supports non-AppleTalk printing via USB, Ethernet, FireWire, Bluetooth, and serial ports. It also supports many serial-to-USB and parallel-to-USB adapters, so it's often possible to use older serial and parallel printers even if your Mac doesn't have the right ports. Unfortunately, support for AppleTalk printers is much more limited; only those connected via Ethernet are (officially) supported. (If your LocalTalk printer is still worth a good deal of money, you can buy a third-party LocalTalk-to-Ethernet bridge; however, for inexpensive printers, the cost may not be worth it.) OS X can also print to any supported printer that can be seen on a network, whether that network is Ethernet, AirPort/wireless, or FireWire. Finally, OS X can print over the Internet to printers that have their own IP address.

NOTE After reading the previous two sections, you may have noticed that OS X does not officially support a good number printers—including many older printers from Apple. In addition, a number of newer printers (especially "multifunction" models) do not yet have official drivers available. I'll show you how to add support for many of these printers later in the chapter (see "Supporting Unsupported Printers").

Installing "Supported" Printer Drivers and PPDs

User Level: admin
Affects: computer
Terminal: no

In addition to OS X's built-in drivers and PPDs, many printer manufacturers release new printer drivers that either aren't part of OS X's library or are more recent versions of drivers that are. Some are automatically made available to you through OS X's Software Update system. However, because many aren't, you should always check the website of the manufacturer of your printer to make sure you have the latest version. If an updated or new driver is available, download it and follow the included installation instructions; in most cases this requires an administrator account. If the downloaded file is simply a PostScript Printer Description, you should manually place it in the appropriate Printers directory (see "Where Are the Printer Drivers?").

Reinstalling OS X's Printer Drivers

There are a couple situations where you may not have the full complement of stock OS X printer drivers and/or PPD files: (1) you installed OS X yourself, and in the "Customize" dialog you unchecked some or all printer drivers; or (2) you manually removed drivers and PPDs to free up space on your hard drive (see "Cleaning House: Removing Unnecessary Printer Drivers," later in this chapter). Whatever the reason, it's possible that you might need some of those drivers back later. Here's how to get them:

1. Insert Disc 2 of your Mac OS X Install CDs.
2. Locate the file `AdditionalPrinterDrivers.mpkg` (or `.pkg`—some versions of the package use a different file extension), and double-click it. This launches the OS X Installer application.
3. Provide your admin password.
4. Select your startup volume as the destination for installation, and then click Continue.

If you don't want to install *all* of the stock printer support files, you can instead open a manufacturer-specific package (e.g., `EpsonPrinterDrivers.pkg`) to install printer support for a specific brand of printer.

Understanding CUPS

Although most users never think twice about the guts of their computer's printing system, in the case of OS X it's actually a useful topic to broach. OS X has always had a fairly advanced printing system; however, beginning with OS X 10.2, Apple completely replaced the previous printing engine with the Common Unix Printing System (CUPS). CUPS, originally developed by Easy Software Products (`http://www.easysw.com/`), was created to provide an open-source, standard printing architecture that any version of Unix could use. Apple decided to take advantage of OS X's Unix roots by licensing CUPS and using it as the basis for printing.

CUPS provides many of the features you'd expect from an advanced printing system (many of which I'll talk about in this chapter): print queuing, spooling, and management; network browsing and directory services for printers; print logging and accounting; print filtering; and a large number of built-in drivers for popular printers. However, it also provides convenient command-line and web-based management, and its open-source nature makes it extensible not just by Apple, but also by developers and even users.

CUPS means three things for you as a user. First, it means that it's easier for printer manufacturers to write drivers that will work with OS X. Second, it means that it's easier for *others* to develop printer drivers when the manufacturer won't—this is a major benefit, as I'll explain a bit later in the chapter (see "Supporting Unsupported Printers"). Finally, because CUPS can be managed from both a web browser and Terminal commands, OS X's printing system has become one of the most flexible and adaptable of any OS on the market.

TIP If you're interested in learning more about CUPS, check out `http://www.cups.org/`or the documentation already installed on your computer at `http://localhost:631/documentation.html`.

Where Are the Printer Drivers?

In Mac OS X, printer drivers and support files are located in several places. The basic printing interfaces, as well as PPD files for Apple printers, are installed by Mac OS X in `/System/Library/Printers`. Third-party printer drivers and PPDs—both those installed by OS X and those installed manually by users—are located in `/Library/Printers`. It's also possible for users to install printer drivers and/or PPDs in `~/Library/Printers`, but those drivers and PPDs will only be available for the user who installs them.

Printer Prep: Setting Up and Managing Printers in OS X

Setting up a printer in OS X is remarkably easy, as most printers are genuinely "plug and play." Provided you have the appropriate driver or PPD file installed, when you connect a printer to your Mac, OS X will automatically detect it, recognize the manufacturer and model, select the appropriate driver or PPD file, and create a print queue for it. However, there are several ways you can access printer options, manage printers, and customize print queues in OS X, and there may be times when you need to set up a print queue/printer manually. The two most common and convenient ways to manage printing in OS X are the Print Center utility and the new CUPS web interface.

Note that when you add or set up a printer in OS X, what you are really doing is creating a print *queue*. OS X uses this queue to manage jobs for the printer. When you print "to" a printer, you're actually sending a document to its queue; when the printer is available, the next document in the queue is printed. As I talk about managing printers and print jobs, it's helpful to remember this distinction.

NOTE It's also possible to manage printers and print queues using Terminal and NetInfo Manager. However, Apple has provided Print Center and the CUPS web interface so that you can *avoid* having to use these tools, so I'm not going to spend time on them here.

Using Print Center

User Level: any
Affects: all users
Terminal: no

The hub, if you will, of printing in OS X is the Print Center utility (`/Applications/Utilities/Print Center`). Using Print Center, you can add and delete printers, configure printers, and start and stop print queues (Figure 12.1). It also launches automatically whenever you print to allow you to manage your print jobs—its Dock icon shows you the number of pages left to print—and quits automatically when printing is complete (unless you had manually launched it, in which case it remains open). Here's how to use Print Center, and how to take advantage of some features that aren't quite obvious.

FIGURE 12.1: The Print Center utility

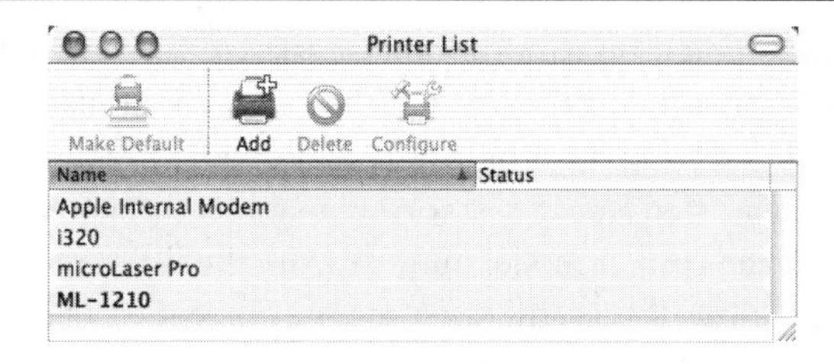

WARNING I mentioned in Chapter 7 that you shouldn't move Apple's applications from their default locations. This is especially true for Print Center; if you move it out of the Utilities folder, you may not be able to print.

Adding Printers

As I mentioned previously, in most cases OS X will automatically detect and configure your printer. However, in the even your printer isn't automatically set up in Print Center when you connect it, you'll need to set it up manually. This is also generally the case when you need to add a printer that is not connected directly to your Mac. How you manually add a printer depends largely on how it's connected.

Adding USB, Rendezvous, and AppleTalk Printers

If the printer you wish to use is connected to your Mac via USB, or is accessible over a local network:

1. Click the Add Printer toolbar item (or choose Printers ➢ Add Printer…).
2. In the resulting dialog, select the connection method—USB, Rendezvous, or AppleTalk—from the pop-up menu. A Rendezvous printer will generally be a printer that is shared by another Mac running OS X, or a network printer that supports Rendezvous. (For more on Rendezvous, see Chapter 9.) If you select AppleTalk and your network is divided into AppleTalk zones, select the zone in which the printer is located from the zone pop-up menu. Finally, you may see other options here that have been provided by third-party printer drivers (e.g., Epson AppleTalk, Epson USB); the applicability of these other options is generally fairly obvious. For example, Epson AppleTalk printers may not be visible via the AppleTalk item; you need to select Epson AppleTalk instead.

NOTE If you are trying to add a printer that is being shared by another Mac OS X computer (via Printer Sharing), you must first enable "Show printers connected to other computers" in Print Center preferences.

NOTE To connect to an AppleTalk printer, make sure AppleTalk is enabled for the appropriate connection type (Ethernet, AirPort, etc.) in Network preferences.

3. A list of printers available to you via the chosen connection method will appear. Select the printer you want to add. In most cases, OS X will automatically select the correct printer driver or PPD for the printer (assuming it is available on your Mac), and "Auto Select" will be shown at the bottom of the dialog box. If you see "Generic" or an incorrect model number listed, select the correct manufacturer from the Printer Model pop-up, and then select the correct model number from the list of printer models from that manufacturer that will appear. If you still don't see the correct PPD or driver for your printer, but you know it's installed, you can select Other… from the pop-up menu and navigate to it manually.
4. Click Add to add the printer.

Adding LPR Printers (Print via IP)

If you have access to a printer that has its own IP address (common in business environments), you can print to it over a local network or the Internet via Line Printing (LPR). However, setting up an LPR printer is slightly different than adding most other printers:

1. Click the Add toolbar item or select Printers ➢ Add Printer….
2. In the resulting dialog, select IP Printing from the pop-up menu.

3. Enter the IP address or domain name (if applicable) of the printer in the Printer's Address field. If you're printing to a print queue on a server, enter the IP address of the queue instead. For most IP printers, you should keep "Use Default Queue on Server" checked.
4. You can print using the "Generic" setting, but to take advantage of printer-specific features, select the printer manufacturer from the Printer Model pop-up. A list of models from that manufacturer will appear; choose the appropriate model.
5. Click Add to add the printer.

Adding a Printer Shared by a Windows Computer

Due to OS X's built-in Samba support, you can print over a local network, or even over the Internet, to a printer connected to—and being shared by—a Windows computer. However, at the time of this writing, there is a minor bug in OS X that requires you to enter a command in Terminal to get this feature working, so first launch Terminal and type **`sudo ln -s /usr/bin/smbspool /usr/libexec/cups/backend/smb`** **<RETURN>**. Then restart your Mac. (I hope by the time you read this Apple will have fixed this bug; if so, entering this command won't hurt anything.)

Once that step is out of the way, printing to printers shared by Windows computers should work fine forevermore. To add such a printer in Print Center, follow these steps:

1. Hold down the option key and click the Add Printer toolbar item—this enables some advanced features in the Add Printer dialog.
2. From the pop-up menu, select Advanced (it should appear at the bottom of the menu).
3. In the resulting Advanced dialog, select "Windows Printer via SAMBA" from the Device pop-up menu (Figure 12.2).
4. Enter the SMB URL of the printer in the Device URI field; use the format `smb://`*`username`*`:`*`password@workgroup`*`;`*`serveraddress/printer`*. *Serveraddress* is the name of the server or computer that is sharing the printer, and *printer* is the name of the printer share set up on the Windows computer. If a username, password, and/or workgroup are not required, you can leave them out (e.g., `smb://`*`serveraddress/printer`*).

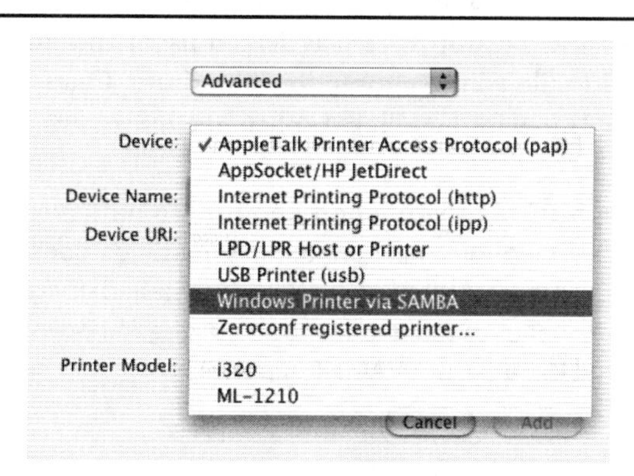

FIGURE 12.2: Setting up a printer being shared by a Windows computer

5. Choose the printer manufacturer from the Printer Model pop-up menu, and then choose the specific printer model from the list of models.
6. Click Add to add the printer.

NOTE Since many Windows printers don't have drivers or PPD files for OS X, you may need to install third-party drivers in order to print to a printer shared via Windows. See "Supporting Unsupported Printers," later in this chapter.

Adding a Printer via Directory Services

OS X also supports Directory Services, which are common in large network environments. To add a printer that is available via Directory Services, simply select Directory Services from the pop-up menu in the Add Printer dialog (instead of USB, IP Printing, etc.). You'll get a list of available printers; select one and click Add. All printer configuration has already been handled by your network administrator.

Configuring Printers/Print Queues

Once you've added a printer/print queue to Print Center, you have two ways to customize and configure it. The first, available for all printers, is to select the printer and choose Printers ➢ Show Info. The resulting Printer Info window has three panes, accessible from the pop-up window. The Name & Location pane allows you to rename the printer—this is the name that shows up in the Print Center window as well as in the Printer pop-up menu in print dialogs. The Location field is a description of the printer's location; you can change this to something more meaningful to you (e.g., Room 3027) if you like.

The second pane, Printer Model, is generally fixed for non-PostScript printers. However, for PostScript printers, you can use the manufacturer pop-up menu to change the PPD file associated with your printer. Choose the printer's manufacturer, and a list of installed PPDs for that manufacturer's printers will appear in the Model Name box; select the desired one. If your PPD isn't listed, you can choose Other… from the menu and navigate to it manually. Finally, the Installable Options pane provides a way to choose settings for printer-specific features—these features, such as default paper tray and memory settings, are actually provided by the PPD file you've chosen for the printer. Once you've made changes to a printer using the Show Info window, click Apply Changes to save them.

TIP Although OS X is very good about automatically selecting the appropriate printer driver/PPD file for a new printer, it sometimes doesn't configure the new print queue to take advantage of all of your printer's installed options. Be sure to check the "Installable Options" panel to make sure you're taking full advantage of features like multiple paper trays and extra printer RAM, if applicable.

The second way to configure a printer—and this option is available only for inkjet printers—is by using the third-party printer utility for your model of printer. These utilities are located in `/Library/Printers`, by manufacturer. For example, the utility for my Canon inkjet printer is located at `/Library/Printers/Canon/BJPrinter/Utilities/BJPrinterUtility`. Luckily, you don't have to dig through your hard drive to access these utilities; simply select your printer in Print Center and choose Printers ➢ Configure Printer (or press the Configure toolbar item). The printer utility for your printer will automatically be launched. These utilities vary in their functionality but most let you clean print heads, check ink tank levels, and set printer-specific options. (Note that third-party printer utilities do not work if your printer is connected to an AirPort Base Station's USB printer port.)

In addition to printer-specific options, you can also set the default paper size for *all* printers in Print Center preferences.

TIP If you have multiple printers configured, you can choose which is the default printer—the one your Mac will print to unless you specifically tell it otherwise—by selecting it in Print Center and choosing Printers ➢ Make Default (or pressing command+D).

Deleting Printers

To delete a printer (which deletes the printer's queue, as well), select the printer in Print Center and click the Delete toolbar item (or choose Printers ➢ Delete Printer). If there are print jobs queued for that printer, you'll be asked if you want to wait for them to finish or delete the printer immediately (which cancels pending print jobs).

Managing Print Queues

As I previously mentioned, every printer you add to Print Center is actually a representation of a print *queue* that is used by OS X to manage jobs for the respective printer. This is an important distinction because it means that up until the very last moment, when the print job is actually spooled to your printer for printing, it is actually queued on your computer (or, if printing to a printer hosted by another Mac, on their computer). Print Center provides you with a way to manage these queues.

Stopping/Starting Print Queues

If you want to put all print jobs for a particular printer on hold, select the printer in Print Center and then choose Printers ➢ Stop Jobs; the queue for the printer will be stopped. You can still "print" to the printer queue, but your documents will not actually be sent to the printer until you restart the print queue (Printers ➢ Start Jobs). You can also double-click a printer name in Print Center, or select it and choose Printers ➢ Show Jobs to view its queue, then click the Stop Jobs toolbar item to put the printer queue on hold; the toolbar items changes to Start Jobs to indicate that the queue is currently stopped (Figure 12.3). Click Start Jobs to resume the queue.

FIGURE 12.3:

Stopping a printer queue via the Show Jobs window

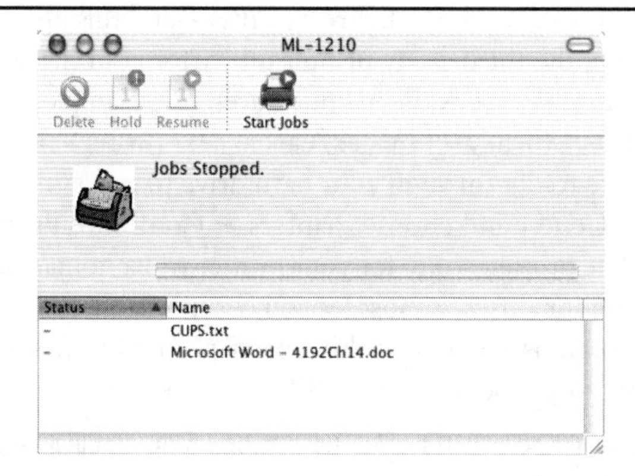

If you or any other user tries to print to a stopped queue, you'll receive a dialog asking you if you want to restart the queue or simply add your document to the queue. If you choose the latter, your document will be printed whenever the queue is started again. In fact, under OS X 10.2 and later, when you click on the Printer pop-up menu in any print dialog, you'll see an exclamation point next to those printers that are currently on hold.

TIP Use print queues to your advantage: if you're on the road with your PowerBook or iBook (or if you're at home but for some reason your printer is unavailable), stop the print queue for your printer. You can print as many jobs as you like, and they'll all be queued. Once you're connected to your printer again, start the queue and all of your print jobs will be printed.

Holding Individual Print Jobs

There are times when you want to hold a *particular* print job, but not *all* print jobs. As an example, sometimes I print documents at a friend's home office; he doesn't mind a few pages here and there, but he'd be a bit less understanding if I tried to print a 150-page software manual using his inkjet printer. You can actually put an individual job on hold but still but allow other jobs to proceed. (This can also be quite helpful if you have a small print job stuck behind a large one; you can put the large one on hold until the small one prints.)

To do this, select the appropriate printer/print queue in Print Center, and then choose Printers ➢ Show Jobs (or double-click on the printer). You'll see the list of currently queued jobs at the bottom of the window. Select the job you want to hold, and then click the Hold toolbar item (or choose Jobs ➢ Hold Job). The Status column changes to "Hold" and the document will not print until you select it and click the Resume toolbar item (or choose Jobs ➢ Resume Job). Other jobs in the queue, however, will print normally.

Deleting Print Jobs

If you ever change your mind about printing—perhaps you realize that you need to make a few changes to a document—you can delete individual jobs or all jobs at once. Open the Show Jobs window for the affected printer queue, and then select the job you want to delete (command-click to select multiple jobs). Click the Delete toolbar item and the print job(s) will be permanently deleted. Note that if the job has already started printing, any pages that have already been spooled to your printer will still print.

Moving Jobs between Printers/Print Queues

If you've printed a document to one printer, and decide that you would rather print it to another, it's actually easy to do so (assuming, of course, that the job is still in the queue and hasn't yet printed). Open the print queue the document was originally printed to (by double-clicking on the printer or selecting the printer and choosing Printers ➢ Show Jobs), and then drag the job (or multiple jobs) from the queue window onto the desired printer in the main Print Center window (or into the desired printer's own Show Jobs window); the print jobs will be moved to the new printer's queue.

TIP In addition to dragging print jobs between printers, you can actually drag documents themselves onto printers in Print Center (or into a printer's Show Jobs window) to print them. I'll talk more about this feature later in the chapter (see "Printing Pointers").

Customizing Print Center

User Level: any
Affects: individual user
Terminal: no

In addition to the features I've already mentioned, Print Center has a few options of its own that make it a bit more convenient to use. Like most Cocoa applications, you can customize the Print Center toolbar. In addition to the standard toolbar items—Make Default, Add, Delete, and Configure—you can also include buttons to show pending jobs or show info for a particular print queue, as well as to stop and start a print queue.

In addition—and this is one of the hidden gems of Print Center—you can add several columns to the Print Center window that provide very useful information. The View ➢ Columns submenu lists several columns that you can show or hide. By enabling these columns, the main Print Center window can show you a good deal of additional information about each printer, including whether it is stopped or printing; the actual driver or PPD used by the printer; whether it's a local or remote printer, and which computer or server is sharing it ("Host"); the printer's Location note (normally only visible in the Printer Info window); and the number of jobs currently in its queue.

TIP If you have a lot of printers set up (this can happen if you've used several different printers, or if there are a lot of networked and/or shared printers accessible by your Mac that have been automatically set up by OS X), enable the Favorite column in Print Center, and then uncheck any printers that you don't use. All printers will still show up in Print Center, but only those selected as "Favorites" will show up in the Printer pop-up menu in printing dialogs.

Using the CUPS Web Interface

User Level: any
Affects: all users
Terminal: no

Although some of the benefits provided by CUPS—such as the ability to write new drivers and to manage printing via the Terminal—are tasks that most users will never undertake, CUPS' web interface is handy for even the novice user. You can access this interface from any web browser by entering the address `http://127.0.0.1:631/`. (You may need to enable Printer Sharing in Sharing preferences before this URL will work; you can then disable Printer Sharing if you're not using it.) I'll show you how to use some of its features over the next few pages.

NOTE You can theoretically access any OS X Mac's CUPS web interface via `http://`*`server-address`*`:631/`. However, by default only someone accessing the CUPS web interface from the same computer can make changes. If you want to prevent others from viewing the web interface on your computer at all, you should block port 631 using a firewall, as described in the next chapter.

As you'll see in some of the examples I present, for *most* printer/print queue management, Print Center is much easier to use. However, some features are only available via the web interface. If you'd like to learn more about CUPS or the CUPS web interface than what I include here, the CUPS Software Administration Manual is available at any time (it's actually installed on your computer) at `http://127.0.0.1:631/sam.html`.

NOTE The address `http://127.0.0.1` is a URL that tells your Mac to connect to itself rather than to another computer. Your Mac may also be able to connect to itself by using its own Rendezvous name: `http://`*`RendezvousName`*`.local`. In fact, sometimes Mac OS X—in the interest of "ease of use"—will tell your web browser to substitute the latter URL for the former. Unfortunately, the CUPS web interface will not allow you to make any changes to printers or print queues unless you specifically use `http://127.0.0.1`. If you can't connect to the CUPS web interface, or if you *can* connect, but get an error that "You don't have permission to access the resource on this server" when you try to make changes, check the URL and make sure you're accessing `127.0.0.1:631`, and not *`RendezvousName`*`.local:631`.

Adding Printers

For USB printers, you're generally better off using Print Center; however, if you're connecting to a networked printer and you have the printer's address, it's fairly simple to use the web interface.

1. Go to `http://127.0.0.1:631` in any web browser.
2. Click the "Do Administration Tasks" link.
3. Under Printers, click Add Printer (Figure 12.4).
4. Give your printer a name, location, and description (e.g., *Office_Printer*, *Room 3027*, *Laser Printer on 3rd Floor*). Note that the printer's name is actually the queue name, and can only contain letters, numbers, and the underscore symbol. The "description" field will show up later in Print Center as the "name" field. Click Continue. These fields are mainly used for identification purposes, which can be quite helpful if you have a number of printers.
5. On the Device screen, select the appropriate connection method from the Device pop-up menu—this is the connection or protocol used to communicate with the printer. For LPD printing, select "LPD/LPR Host or Printer"; for a printer being shared by a Windows computer, select "Windows Printer via SAMBA"; and so on. Note that in some cases, you'll actually see your printer listed in this menu; that means OS X automatically recognized it. Click Continue.

FIGURE 12.4:
CUPS' printer administration web page

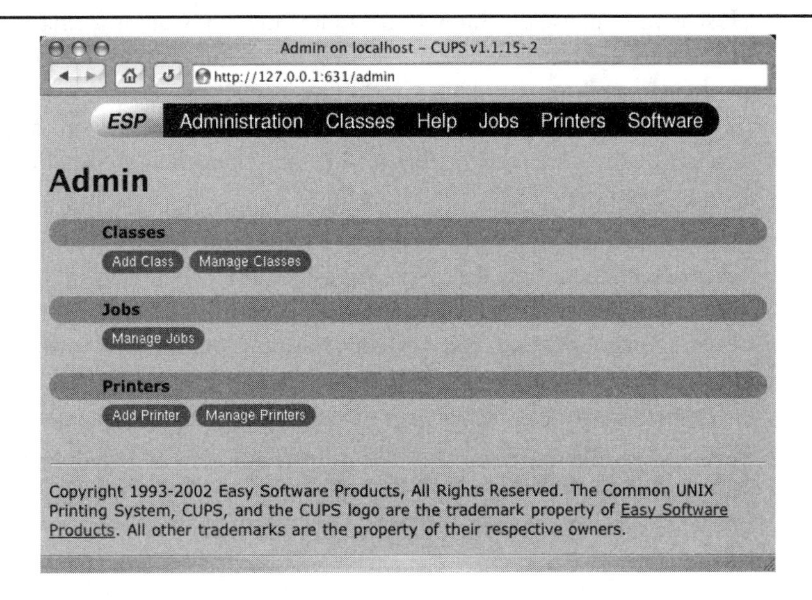

6. On the Device URI screen, enter the URI (Uniform Resource Identifier, similar to a URL) for the printer. For networked printers, this will be in the format `http://`, `ipp://`, or `smb://`, as described earlier when I talked about setting up printers using Print Center. Generally the person who set up the printer will be able to provide you with the correct URI (or your printer's manual will tell you how to get it). If your printer is connected via USB, open Terminal and type **`lpinfo -v <RETURN>`** to get a list of connected devices and their URIs; for example, my laser printer has a URI of `usb://Samsung/ML-1210?serial=0`. (Although if you have a USB printer, I highly recommend using Print Center rather than the web interface.) Click Continue.
7. On the Model/Driver screen, select your printer's manufacturer and click Continue. On the second Model/Driver screen, select the correct PPD file or driver for your printer. Click Continue.

You should get a message that your printer has been added successfully. You can open Print Center and see the printer just as if you'd added it from within Print Center.

TIP If the CUPS web interface didn't provide the correct PPD file as one of the choices in Step 7, you can choose any PPD file, and then later change to the correct one using Print Center's Show Info window.

Configuring/Modifying Printers

Just as you can use the Show Info window in Print Center to change the name, location, and PPD for a printer, you can use the CUPS web interface to change these settings from your web browser. From the main CUPS screen, click Manage Printers. Scroll to the printer you want to modify, and click Modify Printer (you can also click on the printer name or icon to go to a dedicated screen for that printer, and then click Modify Printer).

The Modify Printer procedure walks you through the same steps you would go through to add a printer; however, the existing values for your printer are already entered. On each screen, make any desired changes and then click Continue. (Simply click Continue if no changes are needed on a particular screen.) This feature basically lets you alter an existing printer's name, location, address, and/or PPD file without having to delete it and start over.

Unlike the Printers ➢ Configure Printer command in Print Center, which launches a printer-specific utility for those printers that have one installed, the "Configure Printer" button in the CUPS web interface doesn't do anything. Perhaps in a future update it will provide some functionality, but for now you'll have to access printer utilities through Print Center.

TIP One other nice feature of the CUPS web interface, when it works, is the "Print Test Page" button, available for any printer on the Manage Printers page and on each printer's own configuration page (accessible by clicking on the printer icon or printer name). The test page features a gradient sample and color wheel and is helpful for checking color accuracy and toner levels. It's also a useful troubleshooting tool if you're having trouble printing from within a particular application: if the test page prints, you know your printer is connected and working, and the problem is most likely with the application. (Unfortunately, the test page doesn't work at all for some people; so if it *doesn't* print, that doesn't necessarily mean your printer is broken.)

Deleting Printers

To delete a printer/print queue from the web interface, access the Manage Printers screen (click Manage Printers from the main page or from the Administration Tasks page). Find the printer you want to delete and click the Delete Printer button. (You can also click on the printer's name or icon to go to the printer's own page, then delete it from there.) You'll be asked if you're sure; click Continue.

WARNING Unlike deleting a printer in Print Center, the CUPS web interface will not warn you if there are pending print jobs in the printer queue. The printer will be deleted immediately, along with any and all queued jobs.

Creating Printer Classes

One feature available via the CUPS web interface that isn't available in Print Center is the ability to create and manage *printer classes*. Printer classes are collections of printers, grouped together. Instead of printing to a particular printer, users can print to a *class*; the print job is queued in a class queue rather than a printer queue. Jobs in the queue are forwarded to the first available printer in the class. Although printer classes are probably overkill for most home users, in large network environments printer classes help distribute printing among several printers, spreading the workload and generally ensuring that print jobs are processed as quickly as possible. Unfortunately, when you print to a class, you don't get any feedback letting you know *which* printer actually handled the job, so this feature is most useful when the printers in the class are located physically near each other.

To create a print class, first you need to set up the printers that will be included in the class and add them via Print Center or the CUPS web interface. Then follow these steps:

1. From the main CUPS web interface click Manage Printer Classes.
2. On the Printer Class page, click Add Class.

3. Just as you would a new printer/print queue, provide a name, location, and description of the new class (which is really just a new queue). The name of the queue can only contain letters, numbers, and the underscore character.
4. On the next page, "Members for *ClassName*," select the members you would like to include in the printer class. Hold down the command key as you click to select multiple printers (Figure 12.5). Click Continue. Note that if you have previously created other printer classes, they'll also be listed—you can actually include classes *within* other classes.

The new printer class queue has been created. In fact, if you open Print Center, you'll see it listed as an available printer. It will also show up as an available "printer" in all print dialogs.

TIP If you enable Printer Sharing (discussed later in this chapter), any printer classes you have defined will also be shared. You've created, in effect, your own multiple-printer print server!

NOTE To delete a printer class, you need to select it in Print Center and click the Delete toolbar item (or choose Printers ➢ Delete Printer). There isn't any easy way to delete a printer class via the web interface.

Managing Print Queues

The CUPS web interface gives you similar control over print queues as Print Center; however, it also provides one extra feature: the ability to reject new print jobs without affecting jobs already queued.

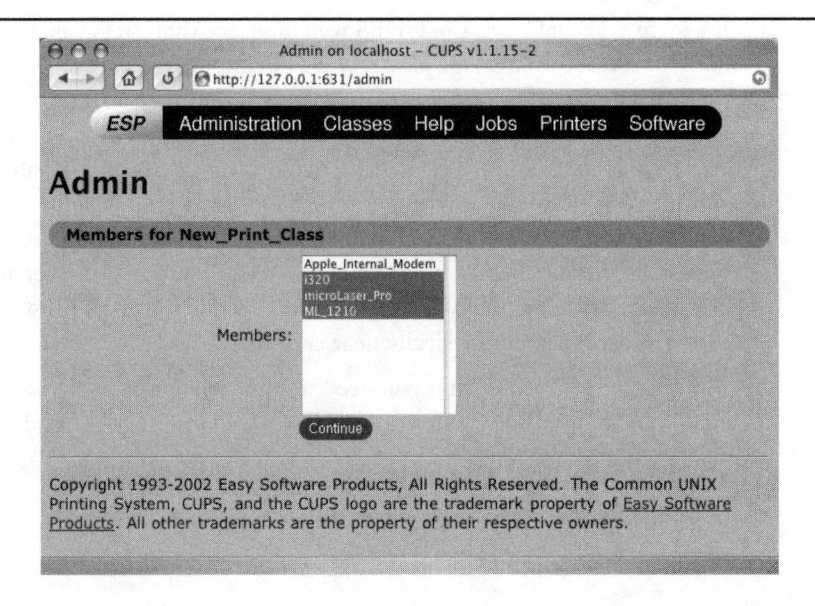

FIGURE 12.5: Selecting printers to be added to a printer class

Stopping/Starting Print Queues

By clicking Manage Printers on the main CUPS web page, you're taken to a list of all printer queues. Clicking the Stop Printer button for any printer will stop the corresponding print queue, and all pending jobs will be held. The Stop Printer button will change to read Start Printer, and the icon for the printer will change so that the printer is not currently active (Figure 12.6). You can of course start the printer again by clicking Start Printer. (You can also access the Start/Stop Printer buttons from the printer's own page, which I talk about below.)

Rejecting/Accepting New Print Jobs

Immediately to the right of the Stop/Start Printer button is the Reject Jobs button. This feature, unique to the web interface, allows print jobs that are *already* in that printer's queue to print, but prevents any new jobs from being printed to it. Users will see the "stopped" symbol (the grey exclamation point) next to the printer in print dialogs as if the printer has been stopped, but existing jobs will still be allowed to proceed.

Managing Pending Print Jobs

There are two ways to manage jobs via the web interface. To view just the jobs for a particular printer, go to the Manage Printers screen, and then click on the name or icon for a particular printer. You'll see a list of all pending jobs for that printer. If you want to view *all* jobs pending for *all* printers, click Manage Jobs on the main web interface page. You'll see a similar list of pending jobs, but this one includes all printers (on both screens, you can tell which printer a job will be printed to by looking at the ID column).

FIGURE 12.6: Active (top) and stopped (bottom) printers in the CUPS web interface

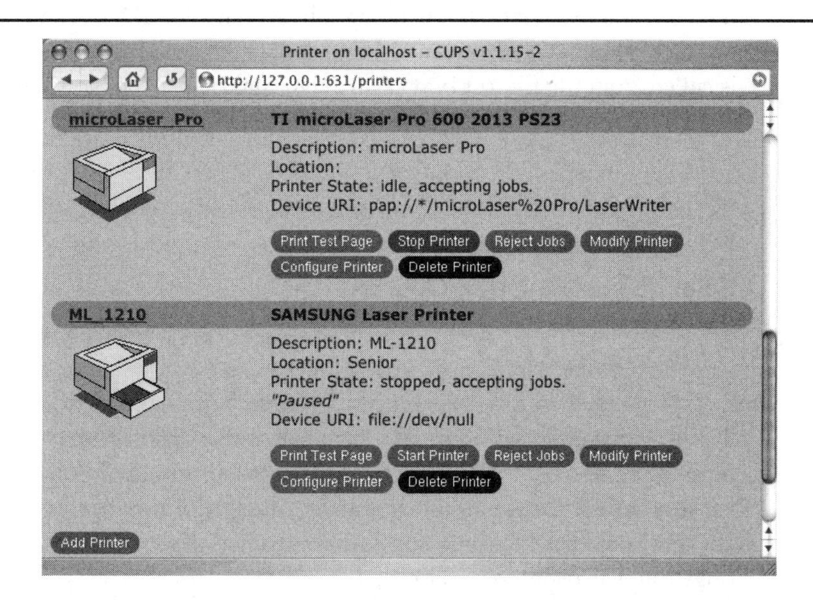

NOTE Keep in mind that you'll only *see* jobs if there are currently jobs waiting to be printed; if you don't print many documents at once, you'll rarely see a long queue of print jobs. If you're really curious, stop a printer queue and then print several documents to that printer; you'll then be able to "Manage Jobs." (When you're done you can just delete the jobs without printing them.)

The information presented for each job is the same, whether you're looking at all jobs or just those for a specific printer. The Name column tells you the name of the document. The User column tells you the username of the person who printed the document. The State column tells you the current status of the job; if it's been waiting, the column will tell you when it was initially "printed" by the user.

The Control column provides you with the same controls as the Show Jobs window of Print Center. The Cancel Job button deletes a print job from the queue. The Hold Job button keeps the job in the queue, but allows other jobs to print ahead of it; it won't be printed until you resume it.

Viewing Logs of Completed Print Jobs

Another feature unique to the web interface is the completed jobs log. The Show Completed Jobs button is located on both the printer-specific and master Manage Jobs screens. Clicking it shows you a history of jobs printed via your computer. (If you click Show Completed Jobs from a particular printer's job screen, you'll see a history of jobs printed by that printer; if you click it from the overall jobs screen, the list will include jobs printed by all printers.) The info is similar to that on the pending jobs screen—job ID, document name, user, and state—but includes a Size column that shows the size of each printed document. This information is culled from the file `/private/var/log/cups/page_log`; you can actually edit the CUPS configuration file to control how many jobs are logged (see below).

The Completed Jobs screen also includes a Restart Job button next to each job; however, unless you manually enable the "Preserve Job Files" setting in the CUPS configuration file this button will give you an error.

Editing/Enabling CUPS Options

User Level: admin
Affects: computer
Terminal: no

The CUPS configuration file is located at `/private/etc/cups/cupsd.conf`, and contains most of the settings for the CUPS web interface and server. Although any user can open the `cupsd.conf` file to view it, it can only be edited with root access (which means that to make changes you'll have to run a text editor as root as described in Chapter 1). Here are a few settings you may be interested in.

NOTE Some OS X system updates replace your CUPS configuration file with an updated version, so if you make changes to it, you may have to re-add those changes to the new `cupsd.conf` file after the update.

#PreserveJobHistory Yes Whether or not the Completed Jobs log is enabled; default is Yes.

#PreserveJobFiles No Whether or not actual print jobs are saved; default is No. If you set this to Yes, the Restart Job button on Completed Job screens will actually allow you to reprint an old print job. However, if you enable this feature, you *definitely* want to reduce the number of jobs logged (see the next setting), because CUPS will store a complete copy of every print job—that can eat up quite a bit of hard drive space.

#MaxJobs 500 The maximum number of recent print jobs logged by CUPS; default is 500. If you change it to "0" there will be *no* limit. To disable logging, instead use the PreserveJobHistory setting (above).

To change any of these settings, open the `cupsd.conf` file (as root) in a text editor. Find the line that contains the setting you want to change, and remove the # symbol from the beginning of the line. (The # symbol tells CUPS to ignore that setting and use the default; removing the # tells CUPS to pay attention to the line.) Enter the new value (**Yes**, **No**, or the appropriate number), and then save the file. You'll need to restart your Mac for the settings to be applied, as CUPS loads its configuration file at startup.

There are actually many, many more settings in the `cupsd.conf` file that can be edited. Many are easy to figure out (especially using the instructions that are included right in the file), but others are intended mainly for IT types. I encourage you to skim through the file to see what a server configuration file looks like. You can even experiment with various settings.

WARNING As with any important system file, be sure to make a backup copy of the `cupsd.conf` file before making any changes. If something goes wrong, you can always replace the edited version with the original.

Setting Up Printers in Classic

User Level: any
Affects: depends on Classic preferences
Terminal: no

I discussed the Classic Environment in Chapter 9; however, I didn't talk about *printing* in Classic. For good or bad, Classic doesn't use OS X's printing technologies, and thus doesn't use the printer(s) you've set up in Print Center or the CUPS interface. In fact, printing is one of the areas where Classic behaves just like a Mac running OS 9. In order to print from Classic applications, you need to set up your printers *within* Classic; in fact, once you do so, you can print from within Classic even if you've never set up a printer in OS X itself.

To print in Classic, you need to first make sure your printer has drivers available for OS 9—if it doesn't you're pretty much out of luck. If it does, you need to install them in the Classic System Folder. For drivers that can be manually installed via drag-and-drop, you can actually do this when booted from OS X. In addition, some Classic printer driver installers will run in the Classic Environment. However, some Classic printer driver installers will only run from OS 9, so you may need to reboot into OS 9 to install.

If you find yourself in the rare situation where (1) your printer's drivers can only be installed using an installer; (2) the installer will only run when booted into OS 9; and (3) your Mac is one of the newer models that won't boot into OS 9, then things are a bit trickier. You'll need to find a Mac that *will* boot into OS 9, install the drivers there, keep track of exactly what is installed and where, and then manually copy those files over to your Classic System Folder.

NOTE In addition to installing Classic drivers for your printer, printing in Classic requires that the Print Monitor application be installed in the Classic System Folder's Extensions folder. This shouldn't be a problem, since it is installed there by default by OS 9; however, if you have moved it elsewhere manually, you won't be able to print in Classic.

Once you've installed the OS 9 drivers for your printer, start the Classic Environment, then open the Chooser utility (either by navigating to `/Classic System Folder/Apple Menu Items/Chooser`, or by switching to a Classic application then selecting Apple Menu ➢ Chooser). Choose your printer using the instructions provided with your printer, and then close the Chooser.

TIP If you've enabled "Use preferences from home folder" in Classic preferences, each user will have to set up the printer in Classic on their own (although you'll only have to install the Classic printer drivers once). If you *don't* have this checked, you'll only have to select a Classic printer in the Chooser once, as all users will share the same printer preferences.

Once you've up your printer in Classic, you can print from within any Classic application.

Using Classic to Print to Unsupported Printers

User Level: any
Affects: individual user
Terminal: no

If you have a printer that is supported in Classic, but is *not* supported in OS X (even using open-source printer drivers, as discussed in "Supporting Unsupported Printers"), you can take advantage of Classic to print. As I'll show you a bit later in the chapter, OS X allows you to "print" to a PDF file from within any application. You can then open the resulting PDF file in the Classic version of Acrobat Reader (usually installed with OS 9—if not, you can download it from the Adobe website at `http://www.adobe.com/products/acrobat/readstep.html`), and print from there. I actually know users who never use Classic to run Classic applications but keep it running all the time to print this way because their older printers aren't supported in OS X.

Cleaning House: Removing Unnecessary Printer Drivers

User Level: admin
Affects: computer
Terminal: no

Although OS X includes drivers and PPD files for hundreds of printers, if you're like most users you only use one or two printers. You can actually delete the support files for other printers and save quite a bit of hard drive space—400MB or more! To delete extra drivers, navigate to `/Library/Printers` and follow these steps:

1. Manually delete the folders for printer manufacturers (Canon, Epson, HP, Lexmark, etc.) other than the one for your printer. Do not delete the `PPD Plugins` or `PPDs` folders. Note that if you have a `SmithMicro` folder, you shouldn't delete it, as it actually contains the fax software (FaxSTF) that came with your Mac, and you should also not delete the `DAVE` folder, if present, as it contains support files for the DAVE Windows file sharing, networking, and printing package.
2. Open the PPDs folder and navigate to `PPDs/Contents/Resources`. If you're only using U.S. English support in OS X, you can delete all but the `en.lproj` folder. If you're using other language support, you should keep the `en.lproj` folder plus the folder that corresponds to the language you use (`fr.lproj` for French, `it.lproj` for Italian, etc.).

NOTE Although deleting extra printer drivers will free up some disk space, if you've got a big hard drive with lots of free space there's really no reason to do so—having extra drivers won't hurt anything, and if you ever get a new printer (or, in the case of a PowerBook or iBook, need to connect to a different printer while you're on the road), you'll probably end up having to reinstall the correct drivers.

Supporting Unsupported Printers

I mentioned at the beginning of this chapter that OS X provides built-in support for a large number of printers. However, the truth is that there are a lot of other printers out there—some old, some new, some that were extremely popular, and even some that were touted as being "Mac-compatible"—that aren't officially supported under OS X 10.2 and later. If your printer is one of them, don't give up and buy a new printer just yet: you may be able to add support for it on your own.

One of the advantages of Apple's decision to use CUPS as its core printing technology is that as an open-source system, CUPS is easily extensible. In addition, because of the popularity of Unix among techies, there is a talented pool of programmers who spend their time (often without compensation) working on open-source projects. The end result is that there are developers all over the world who are writing printer drivers for Unix computers that use CUPS. By installing these drivers, you can instantly gain support for hundreds of additional printers: older inkjet printers, LocalTalk printers, QuickDraw printers, PostScript Level 1 printers, large-format printers, dot-matrix printers, and even new, "Windows-only" printers. In addition, even some printers that *are* officially supported in OS X are *better* supported through open-source drivers. For example, many Epson printers support borderless printing, but some of the official Epson drivers don't allow it; the open-source drivers do.

The two main sources for CUPS-compatible printer drivers are the Gimp-Print Project (`http://gimp-print.sourceforge.net/MacOSX.php3`) and LinuxPrinting.org (`http://www.linuxprinting.org/macosx/`). Gimp-Print drivers are supplied as a single installer package that provides support for over 300 printers (mostly inkjet but also many laser printers), whereas the LinuxPrinting.org drivers are provided in smaller packages based on printer brand/type: Brother, Hewlett-Packard, Apple ImageWriter, PostScript Level 1, and Samsung. You can see the complete lists of supported printers at `http://gimp-print.sourceforge.net/p_Supported_Printers.php3` and `http://www.linuxprinting.org/database.html`. The Gimp-Print page even shows the degree of current support for each printer: fully operational, operational, needs testing, or untested. What's more, since many printers work well with drivers for closely related models, even if your printer isn't listed, it's worth a try before you go out and buy a new one. (If a particular printer model isn't listed, you can even submit a request for a driver; there's no guarantee, but there's a good chance someone will try to help you out.)

TIP

You'll notice that the lists of printers supported by Gimp-Print and the LinuxPrinting.org drivers include many "Windows-only" printers. In case you're wondering, the answer is yes: by using these open-source drivers, many Windows-only printers are instantly usable on your Mac!

In the section that follows, I'm going to show you how to install and use the Gimp-Print driver package. Although I'm prevented by space constraints from doing the same for the various LinuxPrinting.org packages, rest assured that they work in much the same way, and include detailed documentation to guide you through the process.

Installing and Using Gimp-Print Drivers

User Level: admin
Affects: computer
Terminal: no

If your printer is listed as being supported by the Gimp-Print package, you're a free download away from being able to print again. Although installing and using the Gimp-Print drivers is fairly straightforward, there are a couple places where it's easy to get tripped up.

NOTE In case you're wondering where the Gimp-Print project got its name, it's because it began as a printer plug-in for the Unix graphics application The GIMP.

Installing the Gimp-Print Package

Installing the Gimp-Print package actually involves two steps. The first is installing the drivers themselves. The second is installing a package called ESP Ghostscript. Some applications, such as Adobe Illustrator and Photoshop, and Apple's own AppleWorks, generate their own PostScript code. This causes problems for the Gimp-Print drivers, so a third-party PostScript interpreter is needed as a go-between. ESP Ghostscript, another free, open-source product, fills this need. In fact, once you install it, it operates invisibly and you never even know it's there. Here's how to install both:

1. Download the Gimp-Print package from `http://gimp-print.sourceforge.net/MacOSX.php3`. You'll see several download options; I recommend the one that says "newest final release" (as opposed to the one that says "newest pre-release," which means it's still in testing). From the same page, download the ESP Ghostscript package. Both downloads will be in the format of OS X disk images.
2. Mount both disk images in the Finder (by double-clicking them or dragging them onto the Disk Copy utility).
3. If your printer connects to your Mac via a USB cable, make sure it's connected and turned on.
4. Open the Gimp-Print image and double-click the Gimp-Print installer package (it should be called something like `Gimp-Print 4.x.x.pkg`). Provide your admin username and password, and then follow the on-screen instructions. Exit the installer when finished.
5. Open the ESP Ghostscript image and double-click the `ESP Ghostscript.mpkg` package. Follow the same procedure as in Step 4.
6. Restart your Mac.

You've just added support for a few hundred additional printers. The next step is to set up your printer.

Setting Up Printers Using Gimp-Print Drivers

Because the Gimp-Print drivers are fully CUPS-compatible, you could use the CUPS web interface to set up your printer. However, I find that Print Center is much easier for such simple tasks. The only tricky part is that you have to access Print Center's "Advanced" options screen.

Setting Up a Locally Connected (USB) Printer

1. Launch Print Center (in `/Applications/Utilities`).
2. Hold down the option key and click the Add button in the Print Center toolbar. (The option key enables access to the Advanced setup options.)
3. Click the pop-up menu at the top of the window and select Advanced.
4. Click the Device pop-up menu; your printer should appear at the bottom of the menu. (If it doesn't, double-check to make sure your printer is connected and turned on.) Select it from the menu.
5. If desired, change the Device Name to something more exiting or meaningful. (But don't change the Device URI—that's how your Mac keeps track of the printer.)
6. Click the Printer Model pop-up menu, and select the printer name or model number. If your printer is not listed, but you have a PPD file for it, select the Other… option and navigate to it in the resulting file browser (the PPD file must be located on your hard drive).
7. Click Add to add the printer.

TIP Some AppleTalk printers—and LocalTalk printers connected via a LocalTalk-to-Ethernet adapter—are also supported by Gimp-Print. Simply follow the instructions provided for setting up a USB printer; your printer should show up in the Device pop-up menu (Step 4) just like a USB printer would.

Setting Up a Printer Connected via TCP/IP

If your printer (or, in the case of many business environments, print server) is not connected directly to your Mac but is available via TCP/IP (a network connection), you need to set up an IP printing queue rather than a local printing queue. You should get the IP address and queue name of the printer or print server from your network administrator, then follow these steps:

1. Click Add in the Print Center toolbar.
2. Click the pop-up menu in the resulting window and select IP Printing.
3. In the Printer's Address field, enter the IP address of the printer or print server (or the domain name if it has one), and enter the name of the print queue in the Queue Name field.

4. Click the Printer Model pop-up menu, and select the name or model number of the printer (or, as above, if you have a specific PPD file for the printer, select Other… and navigate to it).
5. Click Add to add the printer.
6. If you want to change the name of your newly added printer, select it in the Print Center window and then select Printers ➢ Show Info. From the pop-up menu, select Name & Location, and enter your preferred name in the Printer Name field. You can also add a more meaningful location in the Location field.

TIP To add a printer being shared by a Windows computer, follow the same steps listed under "Using Print Center" earlier in the chapter; the difference is that now you'll have a whole lot more printer drivers to choose from.

Using Gimp-Print-Supported Printers

As I mentioned earlier, once you've set up a printer using the Gimp-Print drivers, it functions much like any other printer. You can set it as your default printer in Print Center or the CUPS web interface, or you can select it for any individual print job using the OS X Print dialog. The one area where Gimp-Print drivers differ is in accessing special printer features. Many manufacturer-provided printer drivers alter the main print dialog itself to provide additional printer features. However, because the Gimp-Print drivers all use a standard interface, when you print to a Gimp-Print-supported printer, the options pop-up menu includes a new Printer Features panel. This panel will show all of the additional options specific to your printer.

The only caveat to using Gimp-Print (and other open-source) drivers is to remember that they don't come from the printer manufacturer. In most cases they work like a charm; however, sometimes they don't, and the printer manufacturer—which evidently doesn't support the printer fully to begin with—probably won't help you with any problems you might have. Be sure to check out the driver rating to see if all of your printer's features are supported. However, it's important to keep some perspective: for many printers, open-source drivers are the only solution. In addition, the open-source community is generally responsive to requests for help and bug reports. Be sure to check out the forum and feedback links on the Gimp-Print and LinuxPrinting.org websites.

Sharing Your Printer

I covered most of the items in the Sharing pane of System Preferences in Chapter 10. However, one that I didn't cover was Printer Sharing. If you have several Macs on a local network, Printer Sharing—which works seamlessly with OS X's Rendezvous technology—is actually quite amazing.

When Printer Sharing is enabled on your Mac, any print queue that has been set up for a printer connected to your Mac (either via Print Center or using the CUPS web interface) will be shared with other Macs running OS X. Other Macs will be able to see and print to those printers as if they were actually connected to those Macs. Even better, Printer Sharing doesn't just work with those printers that are officially supported by OS X; if you've installed the Gimp-Print package, for example, to add support for a printer, that printer will also be available to other Macs on your network. And unlike Mac OS 9's similar functionality, USB Printer Sharing, Printer Sharing in OS X works for any printer connected via USB, Ethernet, wireless (AirPort), and even FireWire.

Enabling Printer Sharing is as simple as opening Sharing preferences and checking the box next to Printer Sharing. Other Macs on your network simply need to check "Show printers connected to other computers" in Print Center preferences. Printers shared by your Mac will automatically be set up in Print Center for them. After that they can print to your shared printer as if it was connected to their own computer.

NOTE Some OS X system updates replace your CUPS configuration file (`/etc/cups/cupsd.conf`) with an updated version. The newer version usually has Printer Sharing disabled. This means that if you use Printer Sharing, you'll often have to re-enable it after updating OS X.

Your Mac's Rendezvous Name and Printer Sharing

Printer Sharing works with Rendezvous to provide printing services to other local computers. This means that other local Macs set up a queue for a printer that you're sharing using your Mac's Rendezvous name (set up in Sharing preferences) as the printer's address. If you change your Rendezvous name while Printer Sharing is enabled, Macs connected to your printer can get confused (since the printer is no longer "where" it was before). In fact, in some situations changing your Rendezvous name will actually corrupt the following preference files on those computers:

- `com.apple.print.custompresets.plist`
- `com.apple.print.defaultpapersize.plist`
- `com.apple.print.PrintCenter.plist`

If this happens, they may need to delete these preference files before they can print again.

If you want to change your Rendezvous name, you should first disable Printer Sharing, change the name, and then enable Printer Sharing again. Other Macs may have to re-select the shared printer(s) in Print Center.

Sharing Printers with a Mac Running OS 9 Normally, Macs booted into OS 9 will not be able to access a printer shared by a Mac running OS X. However, you can enable USB Printer Sharing in the Classic Environment, which will allow OS 9 computers to print to a USB printer connected to an OS X computer.

The problem is that, according to Apple, you shouldn't have Printer Sharing in OS X and USB Printer Sharing in the Classic Environment enabled at the same time. For more details, see `http://docs.info.apple.com/article.html?artnum=107060`.

TIP You *may* be able to access a shared printer from OS 9 via LPD (an IP-based printing protocol). For details see `http://www.macosxhints.com/article.php?story=20020901005320524`.

Sharing Printers with Windows Computers If you enable Printer Sharing *and* Windows File Sharing in Sharing preferences, Windows computers on your local network will also be able to access your shared printers. However, instead of using Windows' Add Printer Wizard, Windows users should go to Network Neighborhood and locate your computer. If they open your computer's icon, any printers being shared by your Mac should be visible. They can right-click on one of them and select Install to print to it (although they will have to have the appropriate driver installed on their Windows computer).

Sharing Printers over the Internet If you'd like to—or would like someone else to—be able to print to a shared printer from elsewhere on the Internet (or from a different subnet of the same network), you can do so using IPP (Internet Protocol Printing). Here's how you do this from another Mac running OS X.

1. From *your* Mac (the one sharing the printer), open the CUPS web interface in your browser. Go to Manage Printers, and then click on the printer you wish to access. Note the URL in your web browser's address field. (For example, for my Samsung laser printer, the address is `http://127.0.0.1:631/printers/ML_1210`.)
2. From the *other* Mac (the one you want to use to print to your shared printer), launch Print Center and access the Advanced Add Printer dialog (hold down the option key and click the Add toolbar item, then select Advanced from the pop-up menu).
3. In the Advanced dialog select "Internet Printing Protocol (http)" from the Device pop-up menu. Enter a name for the printer in the Device Name field, and then enter the address of the printer in the Device URI field. *However*, in the address you noted above, replace `127.0.0.1` with the actual IP address of the computer sharing the printer. Then, select the correct printer brand and model in the Printer Model section. Click Add to add the printer.

Assuming that both computers are connected to the Internet, you should be able to print over the Internet by simply selecting the new printer in print dialogs.

NOTE If the computer sharing the printer is behind a firewall and/or router, remember the caveats I explained in Chapter 10 about IP addresses.

Printing Pointers

If you've ever printed a document on a Mac, you know that the process is pretty straightforward. Once you've got a printer set up, you choose File ➢ Print (or press command+P) from within any application, and you're presented with the standard print dialog. If you have more than one printer, you can choose the printer to which you want the document to print from the Printer pop-up menu. If you have any saved printing presets (I'll talk about how in a bit), you can choose one from the Presets pop-up. Finally, you can customize the settings for each particular print job by clicking on the printing options pop-up menu and browsing the options panels. (The options pop-up menu is the one that isn't labeled, but its default is "Copies & Pages.") When you're ready to print you click Print.

TIP When you click the Printer pop-up menu in any print dialog, if you hold the mouse over a printer name for a few seconds, a tooltip box will appear that shows you the Location and Host information for that printer.

However, there are a number of other options available to you, both from within the print dialog and via third-party software. Here are a few of the best tips for printing in OS X.

NOTE A tip not included here is how to print the contents of Finder windows; I covered that back in Chapter 5.

Saving Custom Print Job Settings

User Level: any
Affects: individual user
Terminal: no

In any print dialog, you can use the Options pop-up menu to choose settings such as the number of copies, the pages to print, page layout, output options, paper trays/feeding, and any application specific printing settings that may appear. If you find yourself using the same custom options frequently, you can save that set of options as a printing *preset.*

First, choose your settings in each of the Options panels (accessible via the Options pop-up menu). When you're satisfied, click on the Presets pop-up menu and select Save As… Give the preset a name and click OK. The next time you print, you can select the preset from the Preset menu and the document will be printed using that set of custom options.

TIP You can see a summary of the settings in a custom preset by selecting the preset and then choosing Summary from the Options pop-up menu.

You can also delete and rename presets by selecting the preset you want to delete or rename, and then choosing the appropriate command from the Presets menu. Finally, if you want to alter an existing preset, select that preset, make your changes from the various Options panels, and then select Save (instead of Save As…) from the Presets pop-up menu.

"Printing" to a PDF File

User Level: any
Affects: individual user
Terminal: no

Because PDF (Portable Document Format) files preserve a document's fonts, graphics, and layout, and can be viewed on any platform using a free viewer such as Acrobat Reader (or, in the case of OS X, using the Preview or TextEdit applications), PDF has become a universal standard for document publishing and sharing. You've surely downloaded PDF files, or had them sent to you via e-mail.

In Mac OS 9, Windows, and other operating systems, creating a PDF file requires purchasing commercial software such as Adobe's Acrobat. However, PDF is actually a native file format in OS X, which means that if you can print a file, you can create a PDF version of it.

To create a PDF of a document, open the document as if you were going to print it (using whatever application you would normally use to open and print the file). Select File ➢ Print… (or press command+P) to access the print dialog. However, instead of clicking the Print button, click the Save As PDF… button. Choose a location to save the file and click Save. Your document will be converted to a standard PDF file that you can then distribute (or save for posterity).

TIP If you've added PDF workflow items to your print dialog (see "Working with PDFs: PDF Workflows"), the Save As PDF… button will instead be a button that looks like a PDF document; clicking this button gives you a pop-up menu of choices, one of which is Save As PDF…

It's also possible to create a PDF by clicking the Preview button in any print dialog, which opens the Preview application with a replica of the document as it will look when printed out. If you then choose File ➢ Save As… you can save the preview as a PDF. Finally, you can create a PDF of an existing graphic file by opening it in Preview and then using the File ➢ Export… command to convert it to PDF.

TIP You can use the Save As PDF feature in your web browser to save copies of online receipts and documents.

The main difference between OS X's PDF files and those created by the commercial Acrobat software is that Acrobat allows you to include bookmarks, clickable URLs, and other interactive features inside the PDF files it creates. However, for most documents, OS X's simple PDF format is an excellent substitute.

NOTE Preview v1.1, which shipped with OS X 10.1.5, is lacking a few of the features of later versions. However, it also had a bug that doesn't honor some of the security features of many PDF files, most notably the "no printing" setting. Although this was clearly not intended to be a feature, many people find it to be just that—they keep a copy of v1.1 around even after upgrading to a later version of OS X—since it allows you to print copies of PDF documents that can't be printed from Acrobat Reader or newer versions of Preview.

Working with PDFs: PDF Workflows

User Level: normal or admin
Affects: individual user or computer
Terminal: no

In addition to the ability to save a document as a PDF file, OS X (version 10.2.4 and later) also allows you to *process* the resulting PDF file using an application, an AppleScript, a Unix application or script, or the Finder. Apple calls this functionality *PDF workflow*, and it adds enormous potential for working with PDFs.

Oddly enough, at the time of this writing, PDF workflow is actually hidden by default. In order to enable it, you need to manually create one of the following folders:

- `/Library/PDF Services`
- `~/Library/PDF Services`

Once you've done this, the Save As PDF... button in all Print dialogs will be replaced by a button that looks like an actual PDF document. Clicking this button presents you with a pop-up menu of PDF workflow options (Figure 12.7).

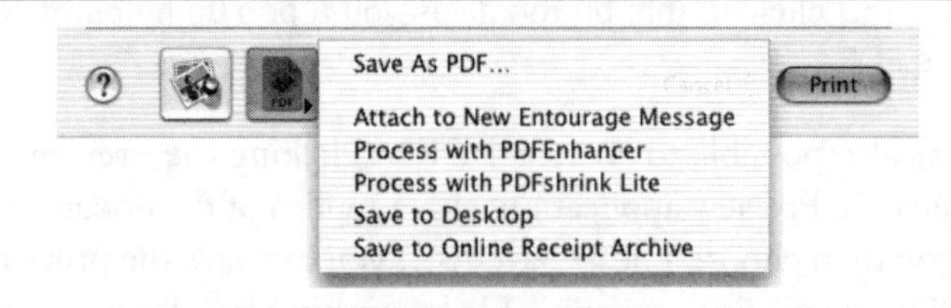

FIGURE 12.7: The PDF workflow pop-up menu includes whatever items you've placed inside the PDF Services folder(s).

If you haven't placed anything inside your PDF Services folders, unlike Figure 12.7 your only option will be Save As PDF... However, if you place items in your PDF Services folders—`/Library` for all users, `~/Library` for your own account—they will appear as options for creating and processing a PDF file from the current document. (You can actually place items inside `/Network/Library/PDF Services`, as well, and they will appear in your PDF workflow menu; however, you still need a PDF Services folder inside `/Library` or `~/Library` in order for the menu to be activated.) Here are the kinds of items you can add to your PDF Services folder(s), and what they do when selected from the PDF workflow pop-up menu:

Folder (or alias to a folder) Creates a PDF file and save it in the chosen folder. The PDF file is named using the document title. For example, if you use PDFs to save copies of online receipts or documents, place an alias of the folder you use to store those PDFs in your PDF Services folder. Whenever you want to save a PDF of an online document, simply select the folder name from the PDF workflow pop-up menu. The PDF will be created and automatically moved to the folder for you. (If you want to save PDFs to your Desktop, place an alias to ~/Desktop inside ~/Library/PDF Services.)

Application (or alias to application) Creates a PDF file and then opens/processes it using the chosen application. For example, if you want to create a PDF and then immediately open that PDF in Adobe Acrobat or another PDF-processing utility, you would simply place an alias of the application in one of the PDF Services folders—select it from the PDF workflow pop-up menu to create the PDF and open it in Acrobat or the selected utility.

TIP If you place an alias of your e-mail client (Mail, Entourage, Eudora, etc.) inside your personal PDF Services folder, selecting it from the PDF workflow pop-up menu will create a PDF file of the current document, and then attach it to a new outgoing e-mail message. The only drawback is that at the time of this writing, the name of the PDF attachment will simply be "Print job." If you want a more descriptive name, you'll need to use AppleScript.

AppleScript (or alias to an AppleScript) Processes the PDF file using the chosen AppleScript. Many publishing and graphics companies have complex AppleScript-based document processing systems. Instead of saving a PDF and then manually dropping it onto an AppleScript, you can simply select the AppleScript from the PDF workflow menu.

Unix tool (command-line application or shell script) Processes the resulting PDF file using the Unix application or shell script. Selecting a Unix tool from the PDF workflow menu creates the PDF file and then provides the Unix tool with the PDF title, the CUPS options for the print job, and the path to the spooled PDF.

NOTE When selecting an application, AppleScript, or Unix tool from the PDF workflow menu, unless the application or script actually moves or saves the PDF file somewhere, it will be located in `/tmp`, the default location for temporary PDF files.

Once you've added items or aliases to the PDF Services folder(s), you can actually rename the items or aliases so that their names more clearly identify what they will do. For example, if you include an alias to a folder in which you want to store PDF files, you can rename the alias "Save to PDF Archive"; this name will appear in the PDF workflow menu instead of the actual folder name. You'll notice in Figure 12.7 that I've renamed the items in my own PDF Services folder in such a manner.

NOTE For more information about the PDF workflow system, check out Apple's own documentation at `http://www.apple.com/applescript/print/` and `http://developer.apple.com/techpubs/macosx/CoreTechnologies/graphics/Printing/PDF_Workflow/pdfwf_intro/index.html`.

Creating a "Virtual" PostScript Printer (aka Printing to a PostScript File)

User Level: any
Affects: individual user
Terminal: no

If you work in the graphics industry (or if you have ever interacted with those who do), you've probably encountered the concept of "virtual printers"—printers that don't actually print, but instead save a document as a PostScript file. If the virtual printer is set up to be the same printer model as the one that will eventually print the document, it can actually be sent directly to the printer without any formatting or previewing. Doing this in OS X requires two actions: setting up the virtual printer, and "printing" to that printer.

To set up your virtual printer:

1. In Print Center, click the Add Printer toolbar item, and then select IP Printing from the pop-up menu.
2. Enter **`localhost`** in the Printer's Address field.
3. Uncheck "Use default queue on server" and give the queue a descriptive name (e.g., "Virtual Printer").
4. Select the printer manufacturer and model from the Printer Model pop-up and resulting list of printers. (If the file will eventually be printed on a specific printer, be sure to select that printer here.)
5. Click Add to create the virtual printer.

To "print" to the printer and create a PostScript file of a document:

1. Open the document as if you were going to print it; choose File ➢ Print… (or press command+P).
2. Select your virtual printer from the Printers pop-up menu.

3. From the options pop-up menu, select Output Options. Check the "Save as File" box, and choose PostScript from the Format pop-up menu.
4. Click Save... and choose a name and location for the saved file, and click Save.

NOTE If you don't set up a virtual printer, you can still create a PostScript file; simply follow the steps for creating a PostScript file, but choose one of your existing printers from the Printers pop-up menu. However, you must choose a PostScript printer or PostScript won't show up as an Output Option.

Bringing Back OS 9's Desktop Printers

User Level: any
Affects: individual user
Terminal: no

One of the features found in OS 9 that is missed the most in OS X is Desktop Printing. In OS 9 and earlier, setting up a printer also set up a Desktop Printer. If you dragged a file onto the Desktop Printer, it would be printed; if you double-clicked on the Desktop Printer, you could view and manage its print queue.

Opening a printer in Print Center provides virtually identical functionality to Desktop Printing in terms of printing queues, but many people miss the drag-and-drop printing functionality of OS 9. Here are two ways to get it back.

Printing Directly to Print Center

When you open a document in an application and then print it, you're basically sending it to a print queue. One of the little-known secrets of OS X is that you can skip the "opening" phase altogether. If you open Print Center, you can actually drag any document *onto* a printer/print queue in the Print Center window; it will be added to the queue and printed, using that printer's default settings. (This does require that the application that would normally print the document be open; it will be launched if it isn't. However, you still avoid having to open the document and walk through the printing process.) Alternatively, if you're viewing an individual print queue via its Show Jobs window, you can drag a document directly into the window to add it to the queue. Finally, you can even drag a document onto the Print Center icon (including its Dock icon) and it will automatically be printed using your default printer.

When using these techniques, a few applications that don't support "direct printing" (printing without user input) will still display the printing dialog before printing; unfortunately, there's no way around this.

TIP If you control/right-click on a document to get the Finder's contextual menu, and select Print Center from the Open With submenu, it will be printed immediately.

Printing Using DropPrint

If you'd like something that works as closely as possible as OS 9's Desktop Printing, consider the shareware DropPrint (`http://home.attbi.com/~dreamless/dropprint.html`). If you drag a file onto the DropPrint icon (in the Finder or the Dock), it will be printed immediately; in this respect it works much like Desktop Printing. However, DropPrint also provides a number of other nice features. My favorite is you can print OS X text clippings without having to first drag the clippings into another application. DropPrint can also send PostScript files (such as those created using the procedure explained earlier in the chapter) directly to PostScript printers via TCP/IP or AppleTalk without having to set up any printers on your Mac. You simply enter the printer's IP address or AppleTalk name/zone in DropPrint preferences, and DropPrint will send the files directly to the printer. DropPrint also has its own Quick Print Text window into which you can drag clippings or paste the contents of the clipboard and print without using any other application. Finally, in applications that support Services, you can select text and then choose *ApplicationName* ➢ Services ➢ Print This Text to print *only* the selected text, instead of the entire document.

Printing Selectively

User Level: any
Affects: individual user
Terminal: no

Do you ever find yourself printing an entire web page, when all you really want is some portion of the text on that page? Or printing an entire e-mail message or Microsoft Word document, only to find that you throw most of the printout away? I'd guess that this is a pretty common occurrence for most people. One solution is to copy text from the web page or document and then paste it into a new document, but this can get quite tedious. If this is an issue for you, the shareware utilities iPrint, PrintMagic, and WebPrint Plus (all from MacEase, `http://www.macease.com/`) provide a novel solution.

All three of these utilities offer the ability to select *just* the content you want to print—including the ability to filter out web graphics and ads from web pages—and then print it using a key combination similar to OS X's own (control+option+P). So instead of printing out a messy four-page website, you can select just the few paragraphs you want to print. This "selective printing" not only saves you the trouble of having to scour through long printouts; it also saves toner/ink, and if you choose to filter out graphics and ads, it makes printing web pages significantly faster.

PrintMagic and WebPrint Plus also add the ability to print text clippings and highlighted text via drag-and-drop: drop them onto the application's icon and you can print it immediately, or after editing and/or annotating the text. Both also allow you to add date/time stamps, URL stamps, and your own notes to printouts. Finally, both can also be used as "Desktop Printers" (much like DropPrint, discussed earlier).

WebPrint Plus, the most feature-rich of the three, adds the ability to print text out using various spacings (to leave room for handwritten comments). But it also lets you edit the content of your printout on the fly via a built-in text editor, and then lets you take that content and either print it, save it to your hard drive, or transfer it to the clipboard or another application via drag-and-drop or copy/paste. These features make WebPrint Plus an excellent note-taking and data-mining utility in addition to its printing abilities.

Problematic Printing

Although printing generally works smoothly in OS X, sometimes things go wrong. I can't get into every possible problem, or every possible solution, but there are two solutions that generally fix the most common printing problems.

Running Repair Disk Permissions

Many printing-related problems are due to one or more files that are used by the printing system having incorrect permissions. This can happen due to corruption, a misbehaving printer driver installer, or any number of other causes, but when it happens, the only thing you can do is get the permissions set correctly. Running Disk Utility's Repair Disk Permissions function, as described earlier in the book, is the best solution and will fix many printing problems.

Using Print Center Repair

The shareware Print Center Repair (`http://www.fixamac.net/software/pcr/`) offers a variety of printing-related "fixes." Like Disk Utility, it can reset file permissions (although it confines its permission-fixing to printing-related files, whereas Repair Disk Permissions affects *all* non-user files on your startup volume). However, Print Center Repair can also repair problems with printing spools and the CUPS directory itself, delete troublesome temp and preference files, and even delete printer drivers (by manufacturer). It also keeps a log of all of its functions. Unfortunately, I don't have the space to cover all of its functions in detail, but the ReadMe file that accompanies Print Center Repair provides a good deal of information about each function, including appropriate warnings about those functions that warrant them.

Moving On...

In the previous two chapters, I showed you all the ways in which you could share files with others and access shares on other computers. In this chapter I also showed you how others can access your printers and printing queues. One of the consequences of having so many ways to communicate with other computers is that there are many ways for malevolent hackers to get into your computer—many more so than with the classic Mac OS. In the next chapter, I'll talk about how to keep your data and personal information private from other users of your computer, other users on your local network, and from nasty people "out there" on the Internet.

Mastering Your Mac—Security, Maintenance, and Unix

CHAPTER 13

Strengthening System Security and Fine-tuning Firewalls

(Or: You don't have to unplug your computer to keep it—and yourself—safe.)

One of the biggest computer-related topics nowadays is security: keeping your computer safe from hackers on the Internet, keeping your data safe from prying eyes, and keeping your e-mail and files safe from viruses. Thankfully, OS X is pretty secure out of the box, but you can reduce or increase that level of security depending on how you use your computer.

In this chapter, I'm going cover a range of topics relating to system security. I'll show you how to use OS X's built-in firewall to keep your computer private, and how to use OS X's multi-user capabilities to keep your data private. I'll show you how to prevent others from booting up your computer without your permission, and how to encrypt and delete your data to keep it super-safe. I'll also cover OS X's Keychain and how to take advantage of it. Finally, I'll talk a bit about viruses and what you can do to keep them off of your Mac.

TIP There's no way I can over everything security-related in one chapter. If you're interested in learning more about Mac OS security, be sure to surf over to `http://www.securemac.com/`.

Security Basics

When people talk about "computer security" they're really talking about three different topics: (1) keeping your computer safe, meaning preventing other people from gaining access to it (either over a network or in person); (2) keeping your data safe, meaning preventing others from accessing or using your data and personal information; and (3) keeping your computer virus-free. These three topics can actually be mutually exclusive. For example, you can allow someone to access your computer, but still keep them from accessing your private data. You can also do a great job of preventing others from accessing your computer and your data, but still be vulnerable to viruses. Because of this I'm going to divide this chapter into sections based on these three aspects of system security.

However, before I do that I want to talk about some more general pointers for keeping your computer safe and sound. Below are some guidelines that will increase the security of your system significantly. If you read nothing else in this chapter, read these.

Remember that accounts are your friend. User accounts are the backbone of OS X's system security. Having a single account that anyone can access—many people use such a setup because they find accounts to be confusing, intimidating, or just a hassle—means that everyone has access to everyone else's data. If nothing else, set up an admin-level account of your own, and create another non-admin account for your family or coworkers.

Limit administrator access to those who truly need it. Administrative access is a dangerous tool in the wrong hands, even if those hands aren't purposely malicious. Limit admin-level accounts to *only* those people who need it regularly. For example, my computer has two admin-level accounts: my own, and the emergency/troubleshooting account I recommended in Chapter 1. Every other account is a normal user. If someone needs to do something that requires an administrator, they can let me know. (In addition to limiting admin access, this also means that I'm aware of all admin access and actions.)

View the login window as "Name and password," hide the restart and shut down buttons, and disable password hints. If your Mac(s) are in a public location, these three options from Accounts preferences are vital. It's better to use the "Name and password" option rather than "List of users" for the login window because listing all users makes it much easier for someone to hack into a computer—they only have to guess one piece of information (a password) instead of two (both the name of a user and that user's password). The "Hide the Restart and Shut Down buttons" option prevents people from restarting your Mac and possibly using one of the startup options (single-user mode, boot off of CD, etc.) to gain access. Finally, although password hints are helpful for legitimate users, they also make it easier for malicious users to gain access to your Mac or other users' accounts.

Use good passwords. Your account password is the key to your computer. Just as some keys can be copied and some can't, some passwords are easy to figure out and some aren't. If you don't want someone to access your account, don't use a password that's easy to figure out (e.g., your birthday, your significant other's name, your pet's name, your anniversary, your child's name, your favorite sports team, etc.). The best passwords are random combinations of numerals and lower- and uppercase letters. Unfortunately, the best passwords are also the hardest to remember. One trick is to think of a book or song title; take the first letter of each word, add a few numerals, change the case of a few letters, and you have a password that's not too hard to remember, but is still difficult for someone else to figure out. For example, take the song "(I Can't Get No) Satisfaction," add in the year the Chicago Bears won the Super Bowl, alter the case, and you get iC19gN86s. It looks pretty random, but you can reconstruct it quite easily if you forget it. (This advice goes for online passwords, as well—don't use a weak password to access your bank account via your bank's website!). Another good suggestion is to use different levels of passwords for different types of accounts. For "throwaway" accounts—registrations on web sites that don't have any real security concerns—use something easy to remember. For things that are important, such as your email account or online banking sites, use more secure passwords, like those described here. (In addition, especially for sensitive accounts such as online banking sites, be sure to read the next item on changing your password frequently.)

Change your password periodically. Even the best password can be compromised. Someone might see you type your password, or you might connect to your computer or a website over a non-secured connection (meaning someone could "eavesdrop" on your network connection and get your password). To ensure security, you should change your password on a regular basis. In fact, many network administrators force users to change their password on a monthly basis.

Only enable services that you regularly use. In Chapter 10, I explained how to enable various Sharing services and Remote Login. Although these are great features, the more of them you have enabled, the less protected your computer is from a network or Internet hacker. You should only enable those services that you actually need and use. In fact, if you only use a service infrequently (for example, to allow someone to access files on your computer), it's safer to just enable that Sharing service when it is needed, and then disable it after you're through.

TIP I didn't cover the Remote Apple Events setting of Sharing preferences in this book. Apple Events are a way for applications to communicate with each other, and are used extensively between applications on your own computer. However, it's also possible for networked computers to use Apple Events to control applications on other computers. This can be quite helpful in some situations, but it also poses a significant risk if an application or person uses Apple Events maliciously. Suffice it to say if you need Remote Apple Events enabled, you'll generally know it; if not, keep it disabled.

Keep the root account disabled. As discussed in Chapter 1, there is little reason to have the root account enabled; you can generally do anything you need to do via the `sudo` command in Terminal or by launching specific applications as root using a utility like Pseudo or Snard. But apart from the "don't need" argument, there is a compelling "should not" argument: since the root account is so powerful, if someone should figure out a way to log in to your computer as root, your entire system, and any data anywhere on your hard drive, is compromised.

WARNING If you really want to enable the root account, make *sure* you use a good password for that account!

If you connect remotely using an admin account, make sure you connect securely. When you connect to your computer remotely over a secure connection, all traffic between you and your computer is *encrypted*, meaning it's encoded so that the data is useless to anyone who intercepts it. If you use a non-secure connection, it's possible for your account name and password to be compromised, and for someone else to later log in to your computer using them. Although any such breach is a bad thing, it's much worse if the compromised account is admin-level. As I explained in Chapters 10 and 11, connection methods like SSH, SFTP, SMB, and File Sharing are encrypted; FTP and Personal Web Sharing are not.

Secure your physical location. This one may sound obvious, but you'd be surprised how many people do everything they can to secure their computer from remote access, yet they walk away from it—logged into their account—in an environment where anyone can sit down and have full access. Although this isn't as much of an issue in a single-user home environment, it can be a major issue in an office setting, or even in a home where parents and kids are using the same computer. (I'll talk more about local security later in the chapter.)

Encrypt your wireless connections If you have an AirPort Base Station or other wireless router, be sure to use WEP encryption (an option in the setup dialog or screen). This will encrypt the signal between the router/Base Station and your computer so that anyone who might intercept it can't easily see the data being transmitted.

Don't open files, launch applications, or even mount disk images unless you know where they came from (and are expecting them). Unfortunately, most computer viruses are spread via files or applications, opened by the user because they look innocuous. Fortunately, viruses are rare on the Mac platform, and most Windows viruses can't do anything to your Mac. Still, it's better to be safe than sorry. In addition, Mac disk images can be configured to run an application or script when mounted, so a malicious user could distribute harmful code this way. So be careful when mounting disk images if you aren't sure where they came from.

Keeping Your Mac Safe: Networks and the Internet

The vast majority of today's Mac users are on the Internet, many of them using broadband connections. Although this is great for web browsing, sharing files, playing games, and many other Internet-related activities, it also means that network security is much more important today than it was when most users were connected to the Internet via slow dial-up connections (if they were connected at all). Remember that when you connect to the Internet, you're actually connecting to one huge network of computers, all of which can theoretically connect to, or at least contact, your computer. Some are used by people you *want* to be able to connect (Personal File Sharing users, for example), but most aren't. If one of the more unsavory characters can find a way into your Mac, they may be able to erase files, steal personal information, or use your Mac as a relay for unsolicited e-mail or Internet attacks on other computers. Needless to say, these are officially Bad Things.

I already mentioned, both in the previous section and in Chapter 10, that three of the best things you can do to prevent unauthorized network access are to turn off unnecessary services (Personal File Sharing, FTP Access, Remote Login, etc.); make sure that users have effective passwords; and restrict access to secure methods such as Personal File Sharing, SFTP, and SSH. These steps are easy to take and provide a significant increase in system security, since hackers generally try to take advantage of enabled services and use them as "doors" into a system. However, the truth is that operating systems have vulnerabilities. Even when you think you have all the windows of opportunity closed tight, it's possible that the operating system itself has a security flaw. This is where firewalls come in.

What Is a Firewall?

At the most general level, a *firewall* is software that acts as a gateway between a network or single computer and other networks. In the case of a single computer, a firewall is usually an application that watches all network traffic as it enters the computer. In the case of a network, the firewall typically operates on a router or gateway server through which all external traffic must pass. In either case, the firewall intercepts all incoming network traffic at the packet level (packets are small pieces of network data) and decides which packets of data should be forwarded to the network or computer and which should be rejected.

Firewalls operate based on *rules*, set up by the firewall's administrator; every packet of incoming data is compared to these rules and either forwarded to its intended destination or refused. Some rules are based on packet origin: did the data come from a domain or IP address designated as "safe?" (The downside to these types of rules is that domains and IP addresses can be faked, or "spoofed" in network parlance.) Others are based on ports: is the firewall supposed to allow network traffic on the port the packets are destined for? (You'll remember our discussion of ports in Chapter 10.) Finally, rules can also be based on protocols: is the protocol used by the data (TCP or UDP, types of transmission protocols) allowed, especially for the particular destination port? As a packet of data is compared to each rule, it is either *allowed* or *denied*. If it is specifically allowed by a particular rule, or makes it past all rules without being denied, it gets passed through the firewall to the network or computer. If it's denied by *any* rule, it doesn't get through. Although each rule is surprisingly simple, the complete system of rules can be very complex.

NOTE Most firewalls also include logging features that allow you to see a record of denied network traffic.

The benefit of a firewall is that unlike *disabling* specific services on your computer—which may still leave vulnerable ports open—a firewall *enables* access for only those ports you know you (or others on your network) need to use. Think of a firewall as the security guard for a gated community. Even if you happen to leave a window open in your house, the security guard should keep out anyone who might sneak in that window.

NOTE In addition to keeping bad traffic out, firewalls are also used to restrict access to external content for computers behind the firewall. For example, a network administrator can restrict traffic from certain websites, or close the ports used by streaming video or audio. This is especially true on larger networks, like those in business and academic settings.

The most effective firewalls are dedicated computers that are separate from the rest of the network and do nothing else but act as firewalls; in this scenario the firewall computer can't accidentally provide access to the network via its own security flaws. Many hardware routers provide effective firewall services for the same reason (see "Hardware Routers as Firewalls"). However, even software firewalls that run on your own computer can be extremely effective if set up properly. These firewalls monitor all the traffic that passes through your network ports (modem, Ethernet, AirPort). Mac OS X actually has a software firewall built in. (I'll talk about it later in the chapter.)

The biggest problem end users generally have with firewalls is that if they're too restrictive, you can't access content you want to access (streaming media files, or even web pages), and other users can't connect to your computer to access Personal File Sharing and other services. Whether you're using an Internet router or OS X's built-in firewall (or both), in the next couple of sections I'll tell you how to set up and use your firewall, including opening up access when you need to.

Hardware Routers as Firewalls

As I mentioned, most hardware routers provide firewall services. This is true even of the Internet routers many home users use to share an Internet connection between multiple computers. As I discussed in Chapter 9, Internet routers use network address translation (NAT)—the process of translating the destination address of incoming Internet traffic to the internal IP address of the destination computer—to allow multiple computers to use a single Internet connection. If you request a web page from a web server, your Internet router knows to forward that data to your computer when it arrives. However, the flip side of NAT is that if a web server sends a page that you didn't request, it won't be forwarded. Since the outside world cannot connect to a computer behind the router unless that computer specifically requested such contact, any unrequested traffic dies at the router. This system provides an effective firewall for computers behind the router.

But what if your computer is behind an Internet router and you *want* certain people or computers to be able to initiate communications? For example, if you have Personal File Sharing enabled, users trying to connect to your computer to access files will have their attempts rebuffed out of hand by your router. In this situation, you need to set up *port mapping* on your router. If you remember from Chapter 10, every service on a computer is assigned specific ports. Personal File Sharing, for example, uses port 548. Port mapping (also called *port forwarding*) allows you to specify that all traffic to a certain port or ports be forwarded to a certain computer behind the router. In the example of Personal File Sharing, you would tell your router that any incoming traffic for port 548 should be forwarded, requested or not, to the *internal* IP address of the computer with Personal File Sharing enabled.

How you do this varies from router to router, but most have a pretty straightforward interface, accessible from a web browser on a connected computer. For example, our home has a Macsense XRouter (which is very similar to the popular Linksys routers); it has a settings page called Virtual Server that lets you map particular ports to internal IP addresses (Figure 13.1). (See "Port Portals: Common Ports Used by OS X Services" for a list of ports used by OS X for providing services.)

FIGURE 13.1:

The port mapping settings for a Macsense Internet router

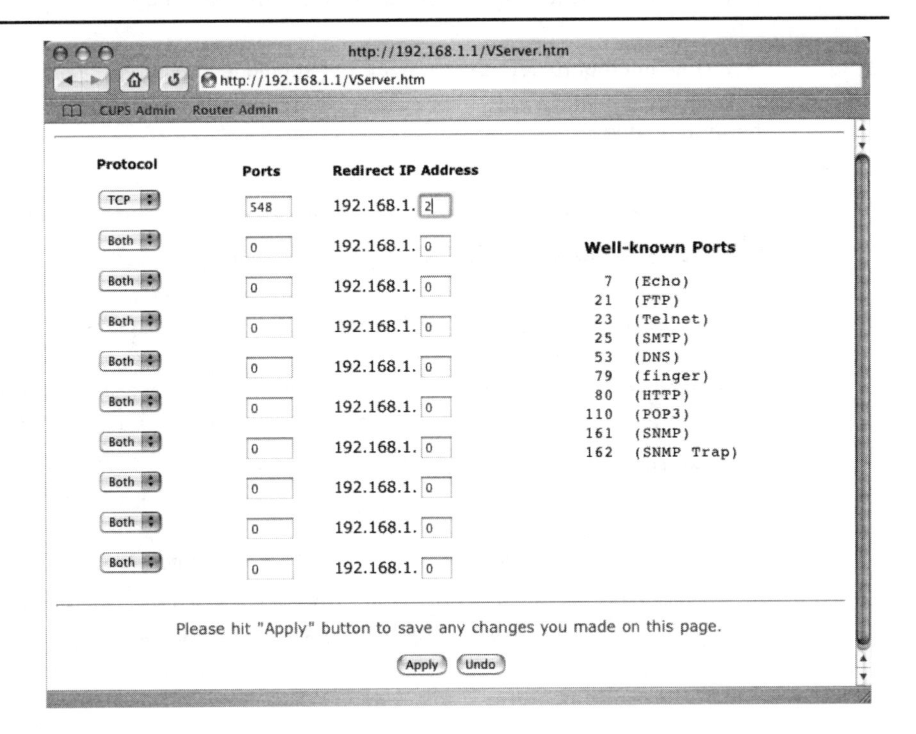

NOTE As a rule, you don't want to open too many ports using port mapping, since that port is then open for anyone, not just those who have legitimate reason to connect to your computer.

The downside to port mapping is that you can only map a port to *one* computer. In other words, if you have three computers behind an Internet router, all sharing a single external IP address, only one of the three computers can share files over the Internet via Personal File Sharing. All three will be able to share files with each other, but only the one that is designated as the target computer for incoming traffic for port 548 will receive Internet File Sharing requests. If you want another one of the computers to share files over the Internet, you'll need to use a *different* service (Windows File Sharing, SFTP, NFS, etc.) on that computer and have the corresponding port traffic mapped to it.

Finally, some routers also have a feature that opens up NAT for *all* ports for one computer. This feature is designed for use with computers running so many services that setting up port mapping would be too much of a hassle (or sometimes just because the router doesn't provide enough port mapping setting fields). I don't recommend using this feature unless you absolutely have to, since it defeats the purpose of having a firewall at all.

NOTE Having an Internet router doesn't mean you should ignore OS X's built-in firewall, especially if your Mac is connected to the Internet over broadband. Two layers of security are always better than one.

Port Portals: Common Ports Used by OS X Services

If your Mac is behind an Internet router and you need to use port mapping to allow others to access services on your Mac, here are the ports used by the most common OS X services. Keep in mind that you don't need to map ports for services *you* access on *other* computers over the Internet (e.g., retrieving e-mail from your ISP); you only need to worry about ports for services your Mac is actually serving/providing to other computers over the Internet.

Port(s)	Protocol	Service
20 and 21	TCP	FTP
22	TCP	SSH (secure shell) and SFTP
80	TCP	Web Sharing (HTTP), WebDAV, and iDisk
123	TCP and UDP	Network Time Protocol (NTP) (used if you've enabled a network time server in Date & Time preferences)

Continued on next page

Port(s)	Protocol	Service
137 and 138	UDP	Windows Name Service (WINS) and Network Neighborhood (used by Windows File Sharing)
139	TCP	Windows File Sharing (SMB)
427	TCP and UDP	Personal File Sharing (AFP) and Web Sharing (HTTP)
445	TCP	SMB (without netbios)
515	TCP	LPR (Internet printing)
548	TCP	Personal File Sharing (AFP)
554	TCP and UDP	QuickTime Streaming (RTSP/QTSS)
631	TCP	CUPS web administration
2049	UDP	Network File System (NFS)
3031	TCP and UDP	Program Linking
3283	UDP	Apple Network Assistant, Apple Remote Desktop
5190	TCP	iChat file transfers
5298	TCP and UDP	iChat via Rendezvous
6970–6999	TCP and UDP	QuickTime Streaming (RTSP/QTSS)
7070	TCP and UDP	QuickTime Streaming alternate (RTSP/QTSS)

For the full list of OS X ports, check out `http://docs.info.apple.com/article.html?artnum=106439`. You can also visit `http://docs.info.apple.com/article.html?artnum=24514` for more information from Apple about ports in general. Also, if you've installed third-party networking software (such as Timbuktu, discussed in Chapter 11), be sure to check its documentation to see if it uses a non-standard port.

OS X's Built-in Firewall

Although firewalls used to be the purview of well-paid network administrators, nowadays many home computers take advantage of firewalls, either by installing third-party software or by taking advantage of security built into their operating systems. Mac OS X can do both. I'm going to talk about third-party firewalls—briefly—a bit later in the chapter, but the truth is that the firewall that comes with OS X, the Unix program `ipfw`, is actually quite capable, and Apple has provided a very simple interface for basic setup and configuration. In addition, with a little knowledge and/or some help from third-party utilities, you can customize it to be as comprehensive as you need.

Enabling and Configuring the OS X Firewall: Basics

User Level: admin
Affects: computer
Terminal: no

To enable OS X's built-in firewall, go to the Sharing pane of System Preferences, and then click the Firewall tab. Click the Start button, and the firewall is enabled. It's really as simple as that. OS X's firewall comes preconfigured with several general rules that allow the Internet/network traffic most users would want, while blocking traffic most users wouldn't want. (See "OS X's Default Firewall Rules" for a list of these default rules.)

What's more, OS X comes with preconfigured rules that open traffic for particular Sharing services. If you enable any services in Sharing preferences (Personal File Sharing, Remote Login, FTP Access, etc.), OS X automatically enables the particular firewall rule that opens traffic for the port(s) used by that service. You can see these predefined rules in the Allow box in the Firewall tab (Figure 13.2). To really appreciate how easy OS X makes this, switch to the Services tab in Sharing preferences, and enable one of the services. If you switch back to the Firewall tab, you'll see that OS X has automatically enabled the rule to allow access. If you disable the service, OS X will disable the corresponding rule.

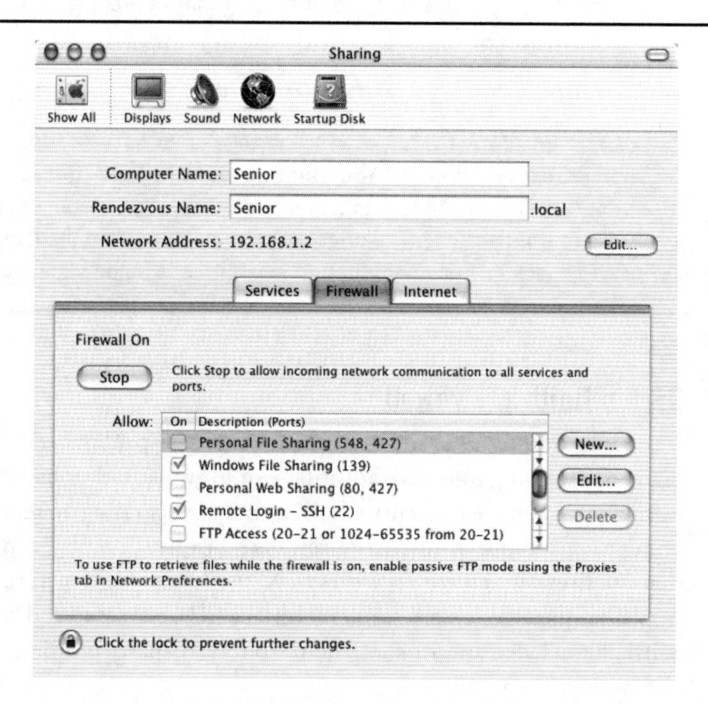

FIGURE 13.2: Mac OS X's firewall preferences

NOTE As noted at the bottom of the Firewall tab, if you want to download files via FTP when the firewall is enabled, you need to open Network preferences, switch to the network port used for Internet access, and then switch to the Proxies tab. Check the box next to "Use Passive FTP Mode (PASV)." This enables *passive* FTP transfers. The reason this is necessary has to do with the difference between *active* and *passive* FTP modes; many firewalls block all active FTP traffic. This procedure is not needed for other people to connect to your Mac via FTP Access.

You can also "open" ports in your firewall for many popular services by clicking the Edit… button. In the resulting sheet, the Port Name pop-up menu lists some of the more common services (AOL Instant Messenger, ICQ, IRC, Retrospect, and Timbuktu are a few examples). Select a service and the "Port Number, Range or Series" field lists the ports that will be opened; click OK and the change takes effect, and is then listed in the Allow box. What you've actually done is add a new rule to your firewall's configuration file. To remove the rule, either uncheck it in the Allow box, or select it and click Delete.

If you're using a service that isn't listed in the Port Name pop-up menu (in the Edit… sheet)—for example, many MP3-swapping applications and file sharing systems like Kazaa use specific ports—select Other from the Port Name pop-up menu; the "Port Number, Range or Series" box will become editable. Enter the ports you need to open, enter a name for the firewall rule in the Description field, and then click OK to create the new rule. It will appear in the Allow box just like OS X's predefined rules.

Firewall Rules Explained

As a Unix program, OS X's firewall, `ipfw`, uses a simple text file for its settings. Each firewall rule is simply a line of text in that file. The basic rules for `ipfw` firewall have a particular format:

```
RuleNumber allow/deny ip/tcp/udp from ip/any to port/any in/out/via
```

`RuleNumber` is a number assigned to the rule; incoming data is checked against rules in numerical order, so a lower number rule will be encountered earlier than a higher number. This number is important because once a packet of data is allowed or denied (i.e., matches a rule), it does not get checked against any other rule.

`allow/deny` is the action taken by a rule. An `allow` rule allows packets that match the rule to pass the firewall; a deny rule prevents matching packets from passing.

`ip/tcp/udp` designates which type of packets the rule should check: `tcp`, `udp`, or both (`ip`).

`from ip/any` designates which source the rule should check for; an IP address means the rule will only apply to data packets from that IP address, whereas any will check all data.

Continued on next page

`to port/any` designates which destination port the rule should check for; including a port number means the rule will only apply to data packets destined for that port, whereas `any` means the rule applies to all destination ports.

`in/out/via` tells the rule to check *in*coming packets, *out*going packets, or packets passing through a particular interface (`via`). For example, the first rule of OS X's firewall is `allow ip from any to any via lo*`. This rule tells the firewall to allow any traffic via the interface `lo*`. Its purpose is to allow traffic from any local service (* is a wildcard, meaning it matches any number of any characters). Another example of an `ipfw` firewall rule is `allow tcp from any to 22 in`. This rule tells the firewall that if it encounters incoming TCP traffic from any source to port 22 on your Mac, to allow that traffic to pass.

As a packet of data enters your network port, it encounters the firewall, which checks it against the rules, in numerical order. If the data packet doesn't match the first rule, the firewall attempts to match the second rule, and so on. As soon as the data packet matches a rule, and is allowed or denied, the process stops. There are actually many more options available in `ipfw` rules. If you're really interested, type **`man ipfw` <RETURN>** in Terminal to see the `ipfw` man page.

Configuring the OS X Firewall: BrickHouse

User Level: admin
Affects: computer
Terminal: no

In addition to the basic firewall configuration options offered in the Firewall tab of Sharing preferences, it's possible to use Terminal or several third-party utilities to customize OS X's built-in firewall. In fact, because of third-party utilities such as BrickHouse (`http://personalpages.tds.net/~brian_hill/brickhouse.html`), sunShield (`http://homepage.mac.com/opalliere/shield_us.html`), and Xupport (`http://www.computer-support.ch/Xupport/info.html`), there's little reason for most users to even venture into Terminal to configure their firewall. (Although to be honest, I do use Terminal every once in a while to see a list of currently active firewall rules; type **`sudo ipfw list` <RETURN>** to see yours.)

BrickHouse is my pick as the most user-friendly utility for enhancing and extending the OS X firewall. Its setup assistant walks you through the process of customizing your firewall. When you first launch the application, it asks you what type of connection you have to the Internet (modem, DSL, cable, etc.), as well as whether you have a dynamic or static IP address. It then asks you what Public Services you want others to be able to access (Figure 13.3). All of OS X's Sharing services are listed, but BrickHouse also includes many others, such as

Quake 3 Arena (a network-based game), mail services (if you run your own e-mail server), and even high-end database services like 4D and Oracle. If you click on a service, BrickHouse will provide you with details about the service itself and the ports used by that service. Select any service you use regularly, and then click Continue. (Remember, you don't need to enable things like POP3 Mail to use e-mail; these are for services *you* are providing on *your* computer. Also, don't worry about things you might someday use; you can always add rules later.)

The next screen, Blocked Services, is a bit confusing, mainly because of the way `ipfw` works. The window lists many common server hacks and attacks. By default, *all* of these hacks are already blocked by the firewall as general "denied" traffic; however, BrickHouse allows you to view denied traffic in its Monitor window. By creating rules that specifically deny each of these hacks and attacks, the Monitor window will provide much more detail. (Like the Public Services screen, clicking on a hack or attack provides information about it.) Think of the Blocked Services screen as a list of items that you want to be able to identify in your firewall's logs.

Finally, the Firewall Setup Complete screen lets you apply the rules you just set up to the current firewall configuration by clicking Apply Configuration. If you want this configuration to be used every time your Mac boots up, click the Install Startup Script. This installs a configuration script that applies your settings each time your Mac starts up. (Remember our discussion of the StartupItems folder in Chapter 3? This is an example of a script that resides inside that folder.)

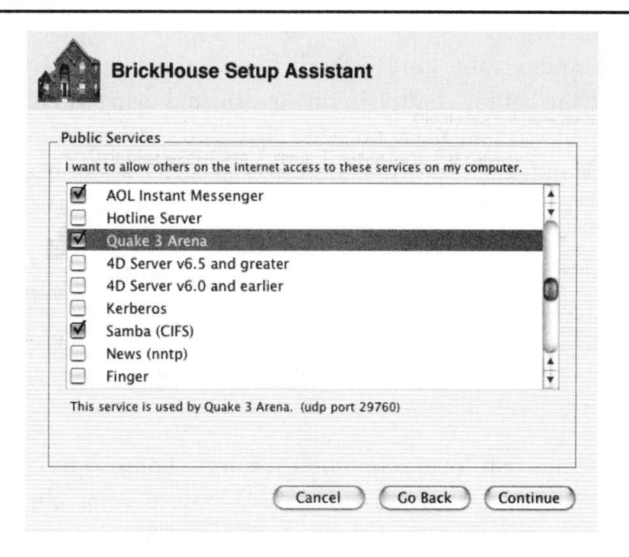

FIGURE 13.3: BrickHouse's Setup Assistant lets you add less common services to your firewall rules.

WARNING The Setup IP Sharing button allows you to modify the settings for the `natd` program used by OS X for Internet Sharing. Unless you are using Internet Sharing *and* know exactly what you're doing in terms of `natd` configuration, I'd leave it alone.

You can re-run the BrickHouse Setup Assistant at any time to reconfigure your settings (and install an updated startup script) by clicking the Assistant button in the main window. However, you can also view and edit firewall rules manually. In the main BrickHouse window (which defaults to the Quick view), click the tab for the network interface you use for Internet access (Ethernet, Modem, PPP, PPPoE, or AirPort). You'll see a list of rules (called *Filters* by BrickHouse) with their conditions—action, type of service, from, and to—clearly identified. To edit any Filter, select it and click Edit Filter (or click Delete Filter to remove it completely). You can also add a rule by clicking Add Filter; BrickHouse provides a helpful interface for setting up the new rule. You can also edit the order that rules are applied; rules are listed in order from top to bottom; to make a rule apply earlier, drag it towards the top of the list, to make it apply later, drag it towards the bottom.

If you prefer to edit your firewall rules and settings manually, click the Expert button in the toolbar. You'll be presented with a commented script that you can edit to your preference. However, like the IP Sharing settings, if you're not 100 percent sure about what to do here, leave the Expert screen to the experts.

Regardless of *how* you made changes (using Quick or Expert view), click the Apply button in the toolbar to apply those changes to the current firewall settings. If you want those changes to be permanent, click the Install button in the toolbar to install an updated startup script.

Another great feature of BrickHouse is that you can create different sets of firewall rules using the Settings button in the toolbar, and then switch between them as needed (remember to Apply changes after you switch between settings). Finally, BrickHouse also provides Log and Monitor windows that allow you to keep track of firewall activity (e.g., denied requests). You can even filter the log by rule number to see if a particular rule has been applied.

TIP Using BrickHouse, you can actually enable the firewall for multiple network ports, and can in fact set up *different* firewall rules for each port. For example, if you connect to the Internet via Ethernet, but connect to other computers in your home or office via AirPort, you can set up different firewall settings for each. Simply check the Enable Firewall box for the appropriate network port(s), and then configure each the way you want.

To remove BrickHouse's configuration, choose Options ➢ Clear All Rules and the click the Apply button. (If you've installed a startup script, also choose Options ➢ Remove Startup File.) You can then go to the Firewall tab of Sharing preferences and set up the firewall as you normally would.

OS X's Default Firewall Rules

If you enable OS X's built-in firewall and have no Sharing services enabled, the firewall uses a fairly simple set of rules:

```
02000 allow ip from any to any via lo*
02010 deny ip from 127.0.0.0/8 to any in
02020 deny ip from any to 127.0.0.0/8 in
02030 deny ip from 224.0.0.0/3 to any in
02040 deny tcp from any to 224.0.0.0/3 in
02050 allow tcp from any to any out
02060 allow tcp from any to any established
12180 reset tcp from any to any setup
12190 deny tcp from any to any
```

If you enable any Sharing services, OS X automatically adds the appropriate rule(s) to allow that service to function properly:

```
02070 allow tcp from any to any 80 in (Personal Web Sharing)
02080 allow tcp from any to any 427 in (Personal Web Sharing)
02090 allow tcp from any to any 548 in (Personal File Sharing)
02100 allow tcp from any to any 427 in (Personal File Sharing)
02110 allow tcp from any to any 20-21 in (FTP Access)
02120 allow tcp from any 20,21 to any 1024-65535 in (FTP Access)
02130 allow tcp from any to any 3031 in (Remote Apple Events)
02140 allow tcp from any to any 22 in (Remote Login)
02150 allow tcp from any to any 139 in (Windows File Sharing)
02160 allow tcp from any to any 631 in (Printer Sharing)
```

Third-Party Firewalls for OS X

In addition to OS X's built-in firewall, there are also several third-party firewalls on the market, including the shareware Firewalk X (`http://www.pliris-soft.com/products/firewalkx/index.html`) and the commercial Norton Personal Firewall (which is part of the Norton Internet Security package, `http://www.symantec.com/sabu/nis/nis_mac/index.html`) and Intego NetBarrier (`http://www.intego.com/netbarrier/home.html`). Third-party firewalls work in much the same way your built-in firewall does. However, they also tend to add a better interface (much like BrickHouse), as well as more "convenience" features. For example, FireWalk X and Personal Firewall allow you to specify which applications can (or cannot) access the Internet, which can protect you from *Trojan horses*, which are applications that try to covertly send data from your computer. All three also offer firewall logging and monitoring, and instant alerts (via sounds, pop-up messages, and/or e-mails) to let you know when unauthorized attempts to access your Mac are made.

In addition, Intego NetBarrier and Norton Privacy Control (which comes bundled with Personal Firewall in the Norton Internet Security package) provide an innovative approach to protecting your personal data. They allow you to enter confidential data, such as credit card numbers, social security numbers, unlisted phone numbers, passwords—any kind of info you want to make sure doesn't get surreptitiously obtained—into a database. They then watch all outgoing Internet and network traffic; if one of your private bits of data is being sent out, they stop it, let you know what the data is and where it's being sent, and ask for your approval. (If you want to regularly allow a certain piece of data to be sent to a specific website or computer, you can also specify such an exception.)

Keeping Your Mac Safe: Local Access

As I mentioned earlier in the chapter, an effective firewall can't stop someone from walking up to your Mac and trying to access it. In order to truly have a secure computer, you also need to secure it from local access. You can take several approaches to local security, including preventing startup, enabling auto-logout, and locking the screen when you step away from the computer. I'll talk about each of these approaches here.

NOTE Although home computers aren't as susceptible to local "hacking" as those used in office environments, you may still find some of these techniques useful, especially if you keep sensitive data on your home computer, or if you have children that you don't want using the computer unsupervised.

Securing Startup: Open Firmware Password Protection

You may recall that I talked about Open Firmware in Chapter 3. As part of your Mac's BootROM, it loads at the beginning of the startup process, which means that Open Firmware controls all access to your Mac. By enabling Open Firmware Password Protection, your Mac can only be booted (this includes a startup after a restart) by someone who knows the Open Firmware password, or can be restricted to only boot using the startup volume selected by an admin user the last time it was booted (i.e., someone can't reboot your Mac and change startup volumes to circumvent security). In addition, all other startup options listed in Chapter 3 (single-user mode, booting from a CD, safe boot, target disk mode, etc.) are disabled to prevent a malicious user from using them to gain access to your computer.

WARNING Before enabling Open Firmware Password Protection, make *sure* your Mac is compatible with this feature and has the latest version of Open Firmware installed. You can find a list of compatible Macs and firmware updates at `http://docs.info.apple.com/article.html?artnum=106482`. In addition, *DO NOT* update your Mac's firmware with Open Firmware Password Protection enabled, or you risk not being able to boot your computer! If you need to update firmware, disable Password Protection first.

Enabling Open Firmware Password Protection

User Level: admin
Affects: computer
Terminal: no

There are actually two ways to enable Open Firmware Password Protection. The easiest way is to download Apple's Open Firmware Password utility, available at `http://docs.info.apple.com/article.html?artnum=120095`. After you launch the utility, click Change. Check the box next to "Require password to change Open Firmware settings", and click OK. You'll be asked to authenticate using an admin username and password, and then you'll be told that your settings were successfully saved. Enabling Password Protection this way provides the "command" level of Open Firmware protection, which means it only disallows startup commands. It still allows users to restart the computer and boot up again.

For an additional level of security not provided via Apple's utility, you can enable "full" Open Firmware protection, which not only disallows startup commands, but also disallows startup itself unless you provide the correct Open Firmware password. However, to enable full protection, you need to restart your Mac and invoke Open Firmware at startup:

1. Restart or start your Mac, holding down command+option+O+F. This will bring up the Open Firmware prompt.
2. At the prompt, type **password <RETURN>**.
3. When prompted, enter the password you wish to use and then press return. Enter it again for verification, and press return again.
4. At the next prompt, type **setenv security-mode full <RETURN>**. This enables "full" Open Firmware protection.
5. Type **reset-all <RETURN>** to restart your Mac. As your computer restarts, you'll of course be required to provide your Open Firmware password.

TIP If Open Firmware Password Protection is active and you need to temporarily use a different startup disk at startup, hold down the option key as if you were invoking the Startup Manager. Enter your Open Firmware password, and the Startup Manager will appear.

Disabling Open Firmware Password Protection

User Level: admin
Affects: computer
Terminal: no

If you want to disable Open Firmware Password Protection permanently, or if you just need to disable it temporarily in order to reset your Mac's PRAM, use single-user mode, or access other startup options, you have two options. The first is to launch the Open Firmware Password utility, uncheck the "Require password" box, and then click OK. Once you provide an admin username and password, the Open Firmware password will be removed.

You can also disable protection by booting into Open Firmware:

1. Restart your Mac and hold down command+option+O+F until you see the Open Firmware prompt.
2. Type `setenv security-mode none <RETURN>.`
3. Type the existing password and press return.
4. Type `reset-all <RETURN>` to restart.

Password protection will now be disabled. To enable it again, use the procedure described in the previous section.

Recovering from a Forgotten Open Firmware Password

User Level: anyone with hardware access
Affects: computer
Terminal: no

Open Firmware Password Protection is the most secure method of local protection you can use on your Mac without buying third-party security software (and it's even better than some of those). The downside to this is that if you lose your Open Firmware password, you could be in trouble! However, in the event this ever happens, there is a "back door" to gain access to your Mac.

1. Open your computer's case to expose the RAM slots.
2. Add or remove some of your RAM—you basically need to change the total amount of RAM in your computer—and then close your computer up again. (If you only have one DIMM (RAM module), you'll need to add RAM, since you won't be able to remove any.)
3. Boot your computer holding down command+option+P+R until you hear three (3) chimes. This resets your computer's PRAM three times.
4. Release the keys and allow your computer to startup normally.

The Open Firmware password is now disabled. You can shutdown your computer and restore its RAM to the previous amount. Of course, you'll notice that the above procedure does not require any password or admin account. Anyone with access to your Mac's RAM slots can do it, which is why if you have a desktop Mac, you should use the lock slot to keep others from opening it up (especially if your Mac is in a public location). If you have a PowerBook or iBook, you're especially susceptible to this trick, since you can't lock the RAM slots.

NOTE There was also a Classic application called FWSucker (`http://www.securemac.com/openfirmwarepasswordprotection.php#fwsucker`) that could extract your Open Firmware password from NVRAM (a bit of low-level memory where the Open Firmware password is stored). However, this utility does not appear to work in the Classic Environment.

Auto-Logout: Log Users Out Automatically

User Level: admin or normal
Affects: computer or individual user
Terminal: no

If your biggest security problem is that you (or others) forget to log out after using the computer, you can take advantage of one of OS X's built-in features—the screen saver—to automatically log users out. The freeware screen saver module LogOut (`http://homepage.mac.com/swannman/FileSharing1.html`) works just like any other screen saver module, but instead of dimming the display or filling the screen with interesting graphics after a period of inactivity, it (ungracefully) logs the current user out and returns the Mac to the login screen. This may not be the best solution for a computer used by only one or two people (see the next section for another approach), but in a lab setting, LogOut can be extremely valuable.

To install LogOut, drop the `LogOut.saver` screen saver module into `/Library/Screen Savers` (for all users) or `~/Library/Screen Savers` (for a specific user). Open the Screen Effects pane of System Preferences, choose LogOut as your screen effect, and then in the Activation tab choose the amount of inactivity until the screen effect starts. For example, if you set the Screen Effects preferences to start effects after 20 minutes, LogOut will automatically log the current user out after 20 minutes of inactivity. (Be sure you make it long enough to allow for normal pauses in work, otherwise you or other users will probably be extremely frustrated by premature logouts!) I recommend against assigning any Hot Corners when using this module, as a stray mouse movement might log users out accidentally.

WARNING Be aware that LogOut performs an ungraceful logout, meaning that applications are quit immediately without prompting the user to save open documents. However, if your main concern is security, this is probably less of an issue than leaving an account logged in.

Locking the Screen Temporarily

If you want to prevent access to your account, but don't want to log out (e.g., if you're just stepping away from your computer), your best bet is to lock the screen. OS X includes a screen lock, accessible via Screen Effects and the Keychain menu extra.

Locking the Screen via Screen Effects

User Level: any
Affects: individual user
Terminal: no

I covered Screen Effects' password feature in Chapter 2, but here's a recap. In the Activation tab of Screen Effects preferences, if you select "Use my user account password," you'll be required to provide your account password when exiting the screen saver. This is a good feature for keeping your computer somewhat secure when you step away—after a set amount of inactivity (also set in the Activation tab), the screen saver will kick in, providing password protection with it.

To make this feature a bit more effective, you should choose a Hot Corner (in the corresponding tab of Screen Effects preferences). With a Hot Corner active, when you are about to step away from your computer, just drag the cursor into that corner and the screen saver/ password protection will immediately activate.

Locking the Screen via the Keychain Menu Extra

User Level: any
Affects: individual user
Terminal: no

The problem with using Screen Effects to lock your screen is that if you don't set a Hot Corner, there is a delay (set by you in Screen Effect preferences) between when you stop working and when the screen saver starts; on the other hand, if you enable a Hot Corner, it's easy to hit that corner with the mouse unintentionally, locking your screen. A better solution, in my opinion, is to use the Keychain menu extra. The Keychain menu extra's main purpose is to allow you to access your Keychain, but it also allows you to lock the screen immediately. (I'll talk about OS X's Keychain, and the Keychain Access application, in a bit.)

You can enable the Keychain menu extra by launching the Keychain Access application, located in `/Applications/Utilities`. Choose View ➢ Show Status in Menu Bar and the menu extra will be added to the menu bar (it will look like a small padlock); it will remain there even after you quit Keychain Access. To lock your screen, simply choose Lock Screen from the new menu; whatever screen effect you've chosen in Screen Effects preferences will be started, but to stop the screen effect and get back to work you need to enter your account password—even if your Screen Effects settings do not have a password enabled.

TIP Although locking the screen via the Keychain menu extra functions just like enabling a Screen Effects password, the two are actually independent; you can use Screen Effects as a screen saver without the lock, but can still gain the benefit of the lock when you want it.

Keeping Sensitive Data Safe

For the most part, securing your Mac (physically and over a network) means that your data is safe, as well—if no one else can get to your data, no one else can use it. However, if you're *really* concerned about security, it's good to have an additional layer of protection. After all, there's always the chance that someone can gain access to private files and folders. For example, if your computer is ever stolen, all bets are off. Likewise, if someone, somehow, gains admin access to your Mac, they can use the root account and/or sudo in Terminal to access any user's files, even those in your private user folder. Finally, remember that OS X's permissions are not enforced when booted into OS 9. Thus if you have data that is particularly sensitive—confidential documents, passwords for online accounts, etc.—you may want to consider additional security.

Mac OS X provides a few solutions for securing sensitive data and personal information, including the Keychain and file encryption. In addition, third-party software provides other options such as secure file deletion and network monitoring. I'll talk about all of these in this section. In addition, if you have multiple volumes and/or partitions, be sure to check out the section on permissions and security in Appendix B, as non-boot volumes handle permissions differently than your main OS X volume.

NOTE Many people use invisibility as a mild form of security (e.g., making files invisible so that other users can't see them). This is only a passable tactic for *hiding* files, and it's definitely not a legitimate method for *securing* data. Any semi-experienced user will be able to easily find such files using the Finder's Find command or Terminal.

The Mac OS X Keychain

The Mac OS X Keychain is another one of those features that is incredibly powerful but rarely understood. What is it? The short answer is that—like its namesake, a ring that holds all your keys—the Keychain is a database that holds all your passwords. The long answer is that the Keychain is a secure database that not only stores passwords for everything from websites to servers to encrypted files and images, but also provides a mechanism whereby applications can access those passwords automatically (with your permission, of course). It also allows you to securely store other information as needed.

The idea of the Keychain is fairly revolutionary: when you log in to your account, your Keychain is unlocked. Whenever you encounter a password dialog—on a website, in a "Connect to Server" dialog, when mounting a protected disk image—the Keychain asks if you want to store that password. If you say yes, a new password entry is entered into your Keychain. The *next* time that same password dialog appears, the application requesting your password connects to the Keychain and says "Hey, can I have the password for this?" Assuming you've given that application permission, the Keychain responds with "Sure, here it is." You don't have to remember each and every password, nor do you have to manually type passwords every time you want to access a password-protected site, server, disk, or file.

There are two caveats to realizing the potential of the Keychain. First, applications must be written to be Keychain-aware. In other words, if an application doesn't explicitly work with the Keychain, your passwords cannot be automatically stored and, more importantly, can't be automatically retrieved. The second is actually a built-in security measure: to add a password to the Keychain, you must specifically tell Keychain to add it, and for an application to access that password you must specifically allow it. (I'll talk more about how to do both in the next section.)

In addition to its ability to work with applications to make your password-laden life easier, the Keychain also has two other convenient uses. You can use it to store *any* password you want by manually adding it, and you can store larger batches of text using secure notes. I'll talk about both in a bit.

NOTE Your original Keychain was created when your user account was created, and by default has the same password as your user account. This allows your Keychain to be unlocked automatically when you log in. However, you can lock and unlock your Keychain manually at any time, and you can change your Keychain password so that it isn't automatically unlocked at login. I'll talk about these options in "Working with Your Keychain: Keychain Access."

Using the Keychain with Keychain-Aware Applications

Using the Keychain with applications that are Keychain-aware is actually quite easy. The first time you provide a password (e.g., when connecting to a server, mounting an encrypted disk image, checking e-mail), you'll see a check box that says something to the effect of "add password to Keychain" (different applications phrase it differently). If you agree, your password is saved. (What you've actually done is create a new Keychain entry; I'll talk more about these entries in the next section.)

The *next* time you access that same server, image, e-mail account, etc., the application (or the Finder) will access your Keychain and attempt to automatically retrieve the correct password. You'll receive a dialog asking if you want to allow access (Figure 13.4). Clicking Deny prevents the application from grabbing the password this particular time (in which case you'll need to enter it yourself). Allow Once allows access this particular time, but you'll be asked again the next time this password is requested by the application. Always Allow will allow the application to access the password this time and any time in the future (although you can manually reverse this decision as described in the next section).

The key here is that applications must be Keychain-aware. For example, e-mail clients like OS X's Mail and Microsoft's Entourage support the Keychain, as do web browsers like Safari and Camino. The Finder is also Keychain-aware, which means that you can save passwords for any server you access via "Connect to Server…" Unfortunately, Microsoft's Internet Explorer, one of the most popular Mac web browsers, does not support the Keychain at the time of this writing.

NOTE If an application changes in any way—for example, if you update it or install a new version—its access to the Keychain is reset, even if you previously chose to Always Allow access to a particular password. The next time it requires that password, you'll be asked to Deny or Approve access again.

FIGURE 13.4:

You can deny or allow an application access to your Keychain.

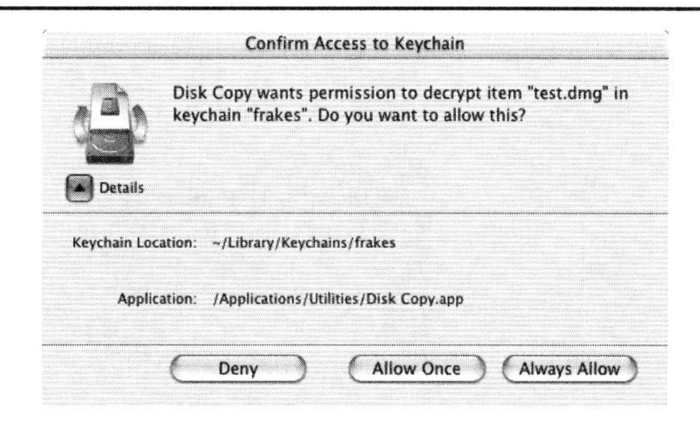

Working with Your Keychain: Keychain Access

User Level: any
Affects: individual user
Terminal: no

Your Keychain generally operates in the background, working with applications when needed. However, there are a number of reasons why you would need direct access to it. OS X provides this access via the Keychain Access utility, located in `/Applications/Utilities`. When you launch this application, you're presented with a list of all the items in your Keychain (Figure 13.5), including information about the item's name, kind, creation date, and modification date. You can sort the listing by any of these attributes by clicking on a column header (or by choosing View ➢ Sort). You'll notice that your Keychain can actually contain both passwords (Internet passwords, application passwords, disk image passwords) and *secure notes*. I'll talk about secure notes in a bit under "Adding Keychain Items: Secure Notes."

Viewing and Editing Keychain Items

Clicking on any Keychain item provides information about that item at the bottom of the window. The Attributes tab provides information about the contents of the item. In the case of passwords, it lists the name of the item (often the domain of the website or server, or the name of the application it applies to); the kind of item; the account name, if applicable; the specific URL, application name, or disk image name the password is used for; and any comments you may have added about the item. In addition, if you check the "Show passphrase" box, you can view the password stored in that item (you'll be required to enter your Keychain password to do so). The "Copy Passphrase to Clipboard" button will copy the password to the clipboard so that you can paste it in another application (again, after providing your Keychain password).

In the case of secure notes, the Attributes tab shows the name of the note, the creation and modification dates, and a "Show note" box instead of a "Show passphrase" box (although it works the same way).

FIGURE 13.5:

A list of Keychain items in Keychain Access

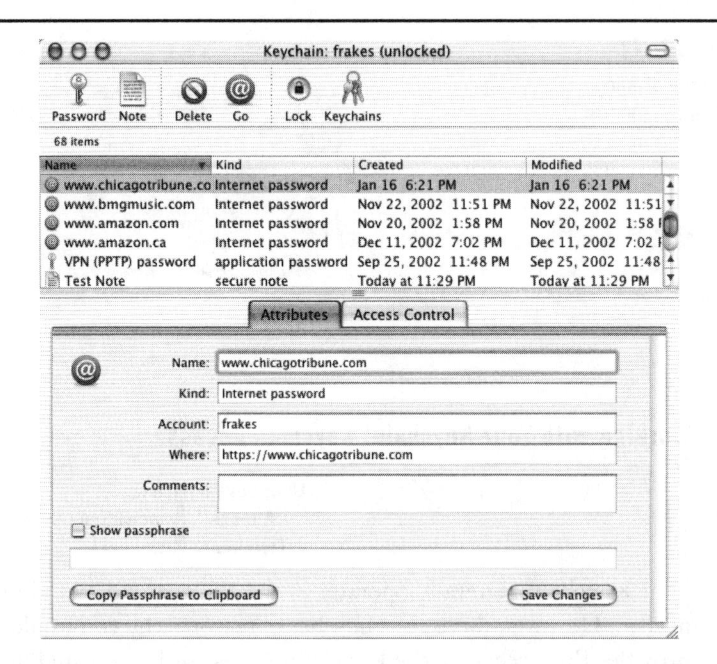

You can edit any of these fields by simply clicking in the field; however, the only ones you should generally change are the Comments field and the passphrase field (which, oddly enough, isn't labeled, but is just below the "Show passphrase" checkbox), and even then, only if your password has actually changed. When you're done editing, make sure you click the Save Changes button at the bottom of the window.

The Access Control tab is where you control access to the Keychain item. By selecting "Always allow access to this item," any application that requests the password or note can access it without any interaction from you. If you select "Confirm before allowing access," a dialog will appear each time an application requests access—this is the dialog I mentioned earlier that gives you the choice to Deny, Allow Once, or Always Allow. In addition, if you enable the "Ask for Keychain password" option, this dialog will also require your Keychain password for an extra layer of security. The "Always allow access by these applications" box lists any applications you've given permission to access this item. If you want to add applications (for example, if you change e-mail clients or web browsers, and want the new one to be able to access your e-mail or website passwords), click Add and navigate to the application. Again, after making any changes here, click Save Changes to apply them.

TIP If you want to compare two or more Keychain items simultaneously, you can create multiple Keychain Access windows by choosing Window ➢ New Viewer Window.

Adding Keychain Items: Passwords

In addition to allowing applications to add new Keychain passwords, you can manually add them yourself. To create a new Keychain password, click the Password item in the toolbar, or choose File ➢ New ➢ New Password Item.… A dialog will appear asking you for the name of the new item (e.g., *Mac.com e-mail account*), the account or username associated with the password (e.g., *frakes*), and the password/passphrase you want stored in the Keychain. If you check the Show Typing box, you'll be able to see the password as you type it. Click Add to create the new item. If you want to associate the new password item with a particular application, select the item and then add an application in the Access Control tab as described above.

TIP You don't have to restrict your Keychain to just passwords used by applications. It's also a great place to store any other passwords or numbers you need to remember: bank "phone-tellers," PIN numbers, ATM card passwords, even software serial/registration numbers. In fact, using your Keychain is a lot more secure than writing them down on paper!

Adding Keychain Items: Secure Notes

In addition to storing passwords in your Keychain, you can also create secure notes. Secure notes are just standard text notes, but because they're part of your Keychain, they're safe from prying eyes—no one can view them unless they have your Keychain password. They're a *great* way to store sensitive data—anything you need to keep private. Secure notes are one of those "hidden" features that Apple should make more obvious.

To create a secure note, click the Note item in the toolbar, or choose File ➢ New ➢ New Secure Note.… In the New Secure Note Item dialog, enter a name for the new note, and the contents of the note. Click Add and the note is created.

Deleting Keychain Items

If you ever need to delete a Keychain item (you cancel an account, you no longer need a secure note), just select the item and click the Delete item in the toolbar (or choose Edit ➢ Delete). You can also control/right-click on the item and select Delete from the contextual menu.

"Going" to Keychain Items

The Keychain Access toolbar has an item called Go that looks like the @ character (visible in Figure 13.5). What this button does depends on what kind of Keychain item is selected when you click it. If a secure note is selected, Keychain Access simply switches the Attributes display to that note. However, for password items, the item is actually "opened." Internet passwords open your preferred web browser to the URL listed in the Where field of Attributes. Disk image passwords attempt to mount the password-protected disk image. iTools/iDisk passwords attempt to mount your iDisk in the Finder. Application passwords launch the application listed in the Access Control tab. Although I personally don't use this feature much, I can see how it might be a nice shortcut.

Locking and Unlocking Your Keychain

Even if your Keychain is unlocked, passwords and notes contained in your Keychain are inaccessible by default. However, chances are you've enabled Always Allow access to many passwords for convenience, so some applications have free reign over their passwords, so to speak. If you want to temporarily prevent any applications from accessing passwords in the Keychain, or if you're stepping away from your computer and want to make sure no one can access the information in your Keychain, you can *lock* it. A locked Keychain is inaccessible by applications, and can only be opened/enabled/unlocked by using your Keychain password (by default, your account password).

There are several ways to lock you Keychain. The first is to launch Keychain Access and click the Lock item in the toolbar (which then changes to Unlock). You can also choose File ➢ Lock *keychain name* or File ➢ Lock All Keychains (if you have multiple Keychains—see "Creating and Deleting Additional Keychains"). To unlock the Keychain again, click the Unlock item (or choose File ➢ Unlock *keychain name*) and provide your Keychain password.

Another way to lock and unlock your Keychain is to use the Keychain menu extra, enabled by choosing View ➢ Show Status in Menu Bar from within Keychain Access. Once enabled, you can lock and unlock your Keychain (or Keychains, if you have more than one) by simply clicking on the Keychain menu extra. You'll be asked for your Keychain password, of course, to unlock a Keychain. (You'll remember the Keychain menu extra from earlier in the chapter when I showed you how to lock your screen.)

Finally, you can have your Keychain automatically locked after a period of inactivity, as described in the next item.

Keychain Settings (Including Changing the Keychain Password)

The Keychain Access application doesn't have its own preferences; however, each Keychain has settings that control the behavior of the Keychain itself. To access these settings, launch Keychain Access and choose Edit ➢ *keychain name* Settings.

NOTE If you have multiple Keychains, each has its own settings. Click the Keychains item in the toolbar (or choose View ➢ Show Keychains) to see a list of Keychains; select a Keychain and then access the Settings dialog.

The first setting, "Lock after *x* minutes of inactivity," will automatically lock the Keychain after the number of minutes of inactivity you choose here. *Activity* is defined as your accessing the Keychain, including viewing or editing any Keychain item, or any application accessing the

Keychain. Note that if your e-mail client stores your e-mail account passwords in the Keychain, and checks for new mail frequently, it's possible that your Keychain may never lock using this feature.

The second option, "Lock when sleeping," automatically locks your Keychain when your computer goes to sleep. When you wake it up, you'll be required to enter your password before you or any application can access your Keychain.

Finally, you can change the password for your Keychain by clicking Change Passphrase.... Enter the new password twice, and then click OK. However, if you want your Keychain to be automatically unlocked at login, it must use the same password as your user account. Thus, if you change your Keychain password, you might want to also change your account password so that they match.

NOTE If you change your *own* account password in My Account or Accounts preferences, your Keychain password will automatically be changed to match. However, if you use your admin power to change another user's account password, their Keychain password *won't* be automatically updated, and thus won't automatically be unlocked when they log in. They'll need to change their Keychain password, in Keychain Settings, to match their new account password.

Creating and Deleting Additional Keychains

Although every user has a single Keychain by default, it's actually possible to have more than one. For example, perhaps you want to keep your personal Keychain data separate from your business/professional Keychain data. To create a new Keychain, choose File ➢ New ➢ New Keychain.... You'll be asked to name the new Keychain, and then provide and verify a Keychain password; this password can be the same as or different from your existing Keychain password.

There are a few things to be aware of when working with multiple Keychains. First, by default Keychain Access shows the contents of your original Keychain. To view others, click the Keychains item in the toolbar, or choose View ➢ Show Keychains, and a Keychain Files drawer will slide out of the side of the main Keychain Access window. If you select one of your Keychains from the list, Keychain Access will show its contents.

TIP You can view multiple Keychains simultaneously by opening multiple Keychain Access viewer windows and choosing a different Keychain in each.

The second thing to consider is that one of your Keychains is automatically designated as your *default* Keychain. You can change this setting by selecting another Keychain in the Keychain Files drawer and then choosing File ➢ Make *keychain name* Default. Which Keychain you select doesn't affect the ability of applications to access Keychain information; however, when you choose to *add* a password to the Keychain, it is always added to the default. Thus if you're using one Keychain for personal info, and one for business info, you need to switch the default back and forth each time you want to add a password to one or the other.

Finally, only your default Keychain will be unlocked at login, even if all of your Keychains use the same password as your user account.

To delete a Keychain, select it from the Keychain File drawer and then choose File ➢ Delete *keychain name*. You'll be asked if you want to delete just the references to the file (meaning the Keychain file will still exist, but it won't show up in Keychain Access unless you add it again—see "Transferring a Keychain to a Different Account or Different Mac"), or if you want to delete references and the Keychain file itself.

You can also delete Keychains manually in the Finder—they're stored in `~/Library/Keychains`. If you quit Keychain Access and then drag a Keychain to the trash, then next time you launch Keychain Access the Keychain will be gone.

WARNING Once you delete a Keychain, it's gone for good, as is all the data contained in it. Be sure you really don't need it, or you've transferred its contents to another Keychain, before deleting it.

Transferring a Keychain to a Different Account or a Different Mac

User Level: any
Affects: individual user
Terminal: no

If you've built up a hefty Keychain—one with a lot of entries, notes, etc.—you can actually use that Keychain with a different user account or on a different Mac. Some examples are if your main Keychain is on your desktop Mac, and you want to use it on your PowerBook; if you've just created a new user account and want to transfer over all of your passwords; or if you're using a friend's Mac or a Mac in a lab. Here's how you do it. (If you have multiple Keychains, just follow the procedure here for each one.)

1. Make your Keychain (located at `~/Library/Keychains`) accessible by the other computer or account. You could burn it to a CD or copy it to a portable hard drive, or even copy it to an iDisk and then connect to the iDisk from that computer or account. If you're just moving the Keychain between accounts, you could put the file in the Shared folder and change permissions to allow access by everyone—don't worry, no one can open it without your password.
2. Log in to the account you'll be using.
3. Launch Keychain Access and choose File ➢ Add Keychain.

4. Navigate to your Keychain in the Open dialog, and click Open.
5. When prompted, provide the Keychain password. Your Keychain will be added.

After adding your Keychain, you'll probably actually have two or more Keychains, since the account you're using already had its original Keychain.

When Keychains Break: Keychain First Aid

User Level: any or admin
Affects: individual user's Keychain
Terminal: no

Because the Keychain manages so many different pieces of information—and the more information it manages, the more frequently it is accessed—it's possible for your Keychain file to eventually develop minor corruption. Keychain corruption is generally manifested in problems such as your e-mail client repeatedly asking you for your mail account password, even though it's saved in your Keychain; your .Mac password not being saved in Internet preferences; or OS X repeatedly asking you to unlock your Keychain. If you experience such odd behavior, there's a good chance your Keychain needs to be repaired.

Apple provides a utility called Keychain First Aid for download at `http://docs.info.apple.com/article.html?artnum=107234`. Once you download and launch it, enter your username and password, select Verify, and then click Start. Your Keychain will be checked for problems. If any are found, you'll see a description of each, and you'll be prompted to repair them (Figure 13.6). Select Repair, and then click Start. You can print, copy, or save the log of any verification or via the Edit and File menus.

An administrative user can also verify and repair other users' Keychains. Instead of entering your own username and password, enter the username and password of another user. (Unfortunately, you must know the user's password, or else change it first using Accounts preferences.) When you click Start, you'll be prompted for an admin username and password. One main difference is that when verifying or repairing another user's Keychain, you won't see the details of the verification or repair.

FIGURE 13.6: Keychain First Aid found problems with this Keychain.

NOTE By default, repairing a Keychain using Keychain First Aid resets the settings for that Keychain to unlock at login and remain unlocked until logout. You can change this behavior by editing the Keychain First Aid preferences.

Alternatives to the Keychain

Although the Keychain is incredibly useful, and does what it does very well, many people find its secure notes and general password/data storage functionality limiting. If you want a more flexible way to store sensitive text, the shareware LittleSecrets (`http://www.mani.de/`) allows you to create multiple note databases, each encrypted and requiring its own password. Each database can store as many separate notes as you want, using styled and colored text (the Keychain only supports plain text). In addition, each database of notes is searchable, which is a major plus if you're working with lots of text. Finally, LittleSecrets is Keychain-savvy, so you can store your database passwords in the Keychain.

If you're looking for a more convenient way to store passwords and other information for use in non-Keychain-savvy applications (or just information like PIN numbers, credit card numbers, and other private info), a search for "password" on the VersionTracker or MacUpdate websites will present you with a number of choices. My favorites are the shareware Web Confidential (`http://www.web-confidential.com/`) and Password Retriever (`http://www.koingosw.com/`). Web Confidential has the advantage of integrating nicely with many browsers (it's related to URL Manager Pro, which I recommended earlier in the book), and is Keychain-aware itself, so you can save your Web Confidential database password in your Keychain. On the other hand, Password Retriever has, in my opinion, a better interface—you can view multiple items at once, like Keychain Access, and there are more options for categorizing and viewing items. Both utilities will automatically generate random passwords for you, and both encrypt their databases using extremely secure algorithms.

Encrypting Data

User Level: any
Affects: individual user
Terminal: no

If you're careful with account passwords and file permissions, your data is pretty safe from other users—provided they can't access your user account. If that's a risk for some reason, or if you're just the careful type, you can add another layer of security by encrypting especially sensitive files and folders so that even if someone can get to them, they can't use them. Although there are a number of third-party utilities that provide the ability to encrypt files, OS X lets you do this using the Disk Copy utility, which I described in Chapter 7. Drag a folder of files onto the Disk Copy icon in the Finder or the Dock, and a Save dialog appears

(Figure 13.7). Select the desired Image Format (use read/write if you want to be able to edit or change the files you're encrypting), and select "AES-128 (recommended)" for Encryption (this uses 128-bit encryption, which is a very secure algorithm for encoding files), and then click Save. You'll be asked for a password, and whether or not to add that password to the Keychain; click OK and the image will be created.

FIGURE 13.7:

Encrypting a folder of files using Disk Copy

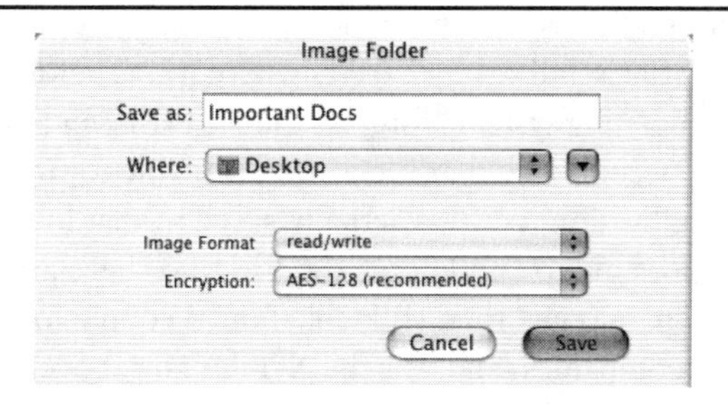

WARNING To quote Apple, "the encryption used by Disk Copy is 128-bit, equivalent to that used in the banking industry. If you forget the password to your encrypted disk image, your data will be irretrievably lost."

Instead of encrypting an existing folder, you can also create a blank encrypted image and then drag documents to it as needed. Regardless of which method you use, the resulting disk image can only be mounted and used by someone with the password you provided (or, if you added the password to the Keychain, access to your Keychain). Although I explained how to do this in Chapter 7, Apple's official instructions can be found at `http://docs.info.apple.com/article.html?artnum=107333`.

TIP If you create an encrypted image to store sensitive documents, be sure to delete the original documents afterwards—I've forgotten to do this myself. If you want to securely delete such files, check out the next section.

One other cool use of encrypted disk images is to send data securely over the Internet—if you encrypt a file or files and then send the encrypted image as an e-mail attachment, it's virtually impossible for anyone who might intercept that e-mail to gain access to the data (provided you didn't include the password in the body of the e-mail, of course).

If you'd like an even higher level of encryption, and/or if you'd prefer the ability to encrypt files and folders directly (instead of via disk images), you may want to consider a third-party utility like the commercial software Tresor (`http://www.warlord.li/english/products.html`). Tresor uses even better encryption technology than Disk Copy, and lets you drag and drop files and folders onto the Tresor icon to encrypt them immediately.

Secure Deletion

User Level: any
Affects: individual user's data
Terminal: no

One of the biggest myths of computer use is the idea that "deleting" a file really gets rid of it. Most people assume that when you empty the Trash, your file is gone forever. The truth is that the file is still sitting exactly where it was before you deleted it. What *actually* happens is that the operating system "forgets" the file exists, and makes a notation in the disk directory that the space occupied by that file is now available to store other data. But until other data—a file, an application, etc.—is actually saved to that location, the original file is still there. In fact, it's possible to "undelete" the file, and there are utilities available on every computer platform that do just that. (I'll talk about a couple for OS X in the next chapter.) In addition, there are companies (and, for the X-Files fans, government agencies) whose sole business is retrieving "deleted" data from hard drives.

This is normally not a problem, as you usually don't care if an item is technically still on your hard drive—you just don't want to see it and you want to make the space it occupied is available for other data. However, if you have especially sensitive data that you want to delete, and you want to make sure no one can retrieve it, you want to delete it *securely*. Secure deletion is the process by which a file is not only removed from the disk directory, but the area of the drive where it was stored is actually overwritten by new data—sometimes by a constant stream of zeros (since all data on a hard drive is actually a series of zeros and ones), sometimes with a random sequence of data. In addition, the more times you overwrite the space, the less likely it is that anyone would ever be able to retrieve the file. (The government's intelligence agencies actually have a standard number of overwrites that they classify as "secure.")

There are a number of secure deletion utilities for OS X; one of the best is also free: SafeShred (`http://codetek.com/php/safeshred.php`) offers security protection from "Home User" to "Secret Agent" (basically, how many times a file is overwritten with random data). To securely delete a file, you simply drag it onto the SafeShred icon.

WARNING When you drag an alias onto an application, the application will try to open the *original* file—that's how aliases are supposed to work. However, this also means that if you drag an alias onto SafeShred or any other secure deletion utility, the *original* file will be deleted, *not* the alias!

Finally, what if you've previously deleted files that you *wish* you'd securely deleted? Many utilities allow you to securely overwrite all "free" space on a drive to ensure that any files that have previously been deleted aren't retrievable. The shareware Shredder (`http://www.dekorte.com/Software/OSX/Shredder/`), for example, provides secure file deletion like SafeShred, but also has a Shred Free Disk Space feature that overwrites free disk space using a procedure "based on the standard outlined in U.S. Department of Defense Manual 5220.22 M." In other words, it should be adequate for you and me.

WARNING Before you use any utility that securely deletes files, or securely erases free disk space, be *sure* you don't want the file, or that there are no deleted files that you might ever want to try to unerase—these procedures will make that virtually impossible.

Before You Get Rid of Your Drive or Computer...

Along the lines of the previous paragraph, what if you're about to sell your computer, or get rid of a hard drive, and you want to make sure no one can retrieve any data from it? Your best bet is to use a utility like Shredder to securely erase free disk space. However, if you're using OS X 10.2.3 or later, another option is to use Disk Utility's "Zero all data" option (accessible via the Options... button on the Erase tab). This will write a value of 0 to every single block on the drive. For additional security, run this option multiple times—magnetic media can sometimes have a "memory" effect that make it possible to extract previous block values, and multiple "zeroing" reduces the chances of this.

NOTE The "Zero all data" option of Disk Utility is only available for entire hard drives, not individual partitions. In addition, it may not be available for some third-party hard drives. For more information about this feature, check out `http://docs.info.apple.com/article.html?artnum=107437`.

Protecting Yourself (and Your Friends) from Viruses

Viruses are the bane of a Windows user's existence. Between Outlook viruses, Outlook Express viruses, data-deleting viruses, Trojan horses, and any number of other nasty things transmitted from one computer to another, it's almost impossible (and certainly unwise) to use a Windows computer without an antivirus utility. Fortunately, the Mac OS (both OS 9 and OS X) is fairly virus-free. Windows viruses generally take advantages of technologies or security flaws in Windows to do their damage, so the Mac OS isn't susceptible. And although there *are* Mac viruses, they're very rare. This means that whereas antivirus software is a requirement on a Windows PC, on the Mac side the issue is more one of "Am I at risk?"

If you don't download a lot of new, strange software, don't really exchange data (CDs, Zip disks, floppy disks, etc.) with other Mac users, and don't receive lots of e-mail from Windows users, you're actually at a pretty low risk for viral infection. Most viruses are transmitted via e-mail attachments (which is why I told you at the beginning of the chapter never to open an attachment you didn't ask for), infected downloads, or files swapped with infected computers, so if you don't interact with any of these things, chances are you're pretty safe.

However, if you do tend to come in contact with these types of files, a good antivirus utility like Norton AntiVirus (http://www.symantec.com/nav/nav_mac/index.html) or Intego VirusBarrier (http://www.intego.com/virusbarrier/home.html) will ensure that you don't catch the latest computer flu. These utilities automatically scan downloaded files and removable media, monitor e-mail attachments that you receive before you open them, and even watch for suspicious activity on your hard drive. If they find a virus, they "disinfect" it, or else warn you not to open the infected file. Both also check for the latest virus definitions over the Internet to make sure your antivirus software can catch even the newest bugs.

TIP Mac users regularly receive Windows viruses as e-mail attachments. Although these viruses can't hurt your Mac, they can still hurt the Windows PCs used by your friends, family, or business associates! Good antivirus software like the two mentioned here also prevents you from passing on a Windows virus to your Windows friends.

In addition to traditional viruses, there are also viruses that infect Microsoft Office files. These files, called *macro viruses*—which are actually *much* more common for Mac users than traditional viruses—take advantage of the macro programming language available in Word and Excel to infect your computer. Word and Excel actually provide you with a warning when you open a document that contains macros—the one you probably always ignore (I know I do). Thankfully, most antivirus utilities also protect you against macro viruses.

Moving On...

Files, the Finder, applications, the Dock, networking, security.... We've covered most of the topics that deal with *using* your Mac and OS X, so we're coming down to the home stretch. In the next chapter I'll show you how to keep your Mac in tip-top shape through some old-fashioned Mac maintenance.

Chapter 14

Mac Maintenance and Administrative Actions

(Or: How to keep your Mac in tip-top shape.)

Thus far in the book I've showed you how to better use OS X and, I hope, how to better understand it. However, in this chapter I'm going to take a detour and spend some time showing you how to keep your Mac running smoothly, and how to perform some basic administrative tasks. I'll cover routine disk maintenance and repair; disk fragmentation and optimization; clearing cache files; and using Unix cleanup routines. I'll also talk about reading log files, adjusting application priorities, and automating and scheduling tasks. Finally—and possibly most importantly—I'll cover some basics about backups.

The contents of this chapter will help to ensure that you can actually *use* your Mac—in other words, you can spend your time enjoying OS X instead of worrying about disk problems, slowdowns, and lost files. In addition, you'll learn a few tricks that will let you run your Mac like a pro.

NOTE In the interest of readability, in this chapter I use the terms *drive*, *disk*, and *volume* interchangeably.

Disk Drive Diligence

Today's hard drives are marvels of technology. They store upwards of billions of bits of data on tiny magnetic sectors, and spin as much as 24 hours a day, and yet the vast majority of time they work problem-free and last for years. Unfortunately, things can and do go wrong, but even then there are things you can do to keep your drives running well, and to fix them when they don't.

NOTE There are a number of third-party hard drive repair and maintenance utilities available for OS X; the truth is that it can get pretty confusing which ones do what. In the discussion that follows, you'll get a good idea of the features and abilities of each. I don't have the space to give you a how-to or walk-through of each, but by giving you a taste of which utilities to consider for particular uses, you'll be better able to decide which you might want to purchase for yourself. Note that almost all disk utilities currently available for OS X are incompatible with the UFS volume format. (HFS Plus is the default for Macs, but UFS is an option if you manually reformat a volume.)

WARNING Before you perform any sort of repair or maintenance on your hard drive(s), you should make sure you've backed up any important data. It's rare that a repair will actually cause you to *lose* data, but it's possible. I hope you back up regularly and this isn't an issue...you do back up regularly, right? (This is just the first of many nagging lectures about backing up your important data that I'll be giving you in this chapter.)

Doctoring Disk Directories

When you stop to think about it, your hard drive is a pretty amazing thing; you have hundreds of thousands of files stored on it, yet you can access any of them at a moment's notice. This ability to store and access files quickly is provided by your drive's *directory*. The directory is like a card catalog or computer database at the library—the books are spread all over the building, but the catalog/database exists in a central location and lets you quickly figure out where each book is actually located. Your disk directory works similarly: it keeps track of where every file is located on your hard drive (specifically, the exact *blocks*—tiny storage spaces on the drive's magnetic platters—where all of the file's data are stored), so that your hard drive's read/write heads can access them on command. (I hope I didn't date myself too much by using the term "card catalog" there.)

Although the disk directory generally works well, it isn't foolproof. Just like the old card catalogs could sometimes fall victim to lost cards, or books wouldn't actually be where the catalog said they'd be, disk directories can develop errors and corruption so that files (or parts of files) aren't where the directory says they should be. (Or, even worse, files are listed in the directory that no longer exist, and vice versa.) The worst cases of directory problems can result in lost data or even a computer that refuses to boot. Lesser instances can manifest themselves in sluggish system performance or problems opening applications or documents.

If you're experiencing problems with your computer that can't be traced to a bad preference file or that affects all users, your first step should be to verify and/or repair your drive directory. However, minor directory corruption (which can eventually lead to bigger problems) often exhibits no symptoms at all, so you may never know you have it until you have it *bad*. So even if you aren't experiencing problems, I recommend periodically running the same procedures as routine maintenance—this will often catch minor problems before they can affect anything seriously. You can verify and repair your existing directory using tools provided with OS X, or you can rebuild your directory from scratch using third-party software.

NOTE *Each* hard drive, drive partition, or other volume has its *own* directory. If you have multiple volumes, you'll have to check and/or repair the directory on each separately.

Note that if you're experiencing problems due to corrupt *files or applications*, rebuilding the disk directory won't do you any good. The only solution is to reinstall the application, or restore the file from a backup. (You do have a backup, don't you?)

Apple's Disk Utility

User Level: admin or any (see note below)
Affects: computer
Terminal: no

Apple's officially supported method for verifying and repairing disk directories is to use Disk Utility's Verify Disk and Repair Disk functions. I talked about Disk Utility in Chapter 7, but as a refresher, launch Disk Utility, select the First Aid tab, select the desired volume on the left, and then click Verify Disk (to check the directory) or Repair Disk (to repair the directory). I generally just use the Repair Disk button, since it takes about the same amount of time as Verify, and if something's wrong I want it fixed. What the Verify/Repair function of Disk Utility does is examine your hard drive to see whether or not what's *on* the drive matches what the directory actually *says* is on the drive. If there are any discrepancies, it edits the directory accordingly.

The main drawback to using Disk Utility is that you can't use it to verify or repair the directory of the volume from which OS X is booted. (This is actually true of most disk repair utilities.) In other words, to repair the startup drive, you either need to boot from another OS X volume and then run Disk Utility, or you need to use the OS X Installer CD or DVD. To use the Installer CD or DVD, place the disc in your optical drive, restart your Mac, and hold the C key down as your computer reboots. You'll eventually see the OS X Installer screen. Select Disk Utility from the Installer menu, and then choose your normal startup volume to repair it.

NOTE You need admin access to use Disk Utility when booted into OS X. However, any user who can reboot your Mac can use Disk Utility from the OS X Installer CD/DVD.

It's possible to run the same diagnostic and repair routines used by Disk Utility using single-user mode and `fsck` at startup; I'll show you how next.

Disk Utility at Startup: *fsck*

User Level: any user who can restart
Affects: computer
Terminal: yes

If you don't have your OS X Install disc handy and need to verify or repair your boot volume (for routine maintenance or because you're having problems that actually prevent you from booting into OS X at all), you can boot into single-user mode and run OS X's `fsck` (*file system consistency check*) utility from the command line.

NOTE The `fsck` utility is automatically run after a system crash under OS X 10.2 and later (which is why there is a long delay after a system crash before you see the familiar boot panel).

As I discussed in Chapter 3, if you hold down command+S as your Mac boots, you'll eventually see a command-line interface; this is called single-user mode. If you then type **`/sbin/fsck -y`** **<RETURN>**, you'll invoke the `fsck` utility, which, according to Apple, runs the exact same diagnosis and repair routines Disk Utility uses. (The `-y` option tells `fsck` to automatically answer "yes" to any suggested repairs; you should always include this option.) You'll see some lines of text as the utility checks various aspects of your drive's directory.

When `fsck` is finished, you'll see one of two messages. If you're told that your volume "appears to be OK," your drive is in good shape. However, if you see the message "FILE SYSTEM WAS MODIFIED," that means that `fsck` found problems and attempted to repair them. In this case, you actually need to run `fsck` again, using the same command as above. The reason is that larger problems can sometimes conceal smaller problems, and vice versa. Once a problem is fixed, you want to check the disk again to make sure there aren't any other lingering issues. Repeat the procedure until you get the message that everything is OK. When you're done, type **`exit`** **<RETURN>** and your Mac will continue booting normally.

NOTE By default, `fsck` verifies and repairs only the boot volume (the one chosen in the Startup Disk preferences pane prior to the last restart or shutdown). This is by design, since you can easily verify and repair non-boot volumes using Disk Utility when booted into OS X.

TIP Because I keep my Mac running all the time (I put it to sleep when I'm not using it, instead of shutting it down—Apple's recommended approach), I rarely restart. When I do restart, I almost always run `fsck` at startup as routine maintenance. It only takes an extra minute or two, and it helps keep the directory on my boot volume healthy.

WARNING If after several runs, `fsck` reports the same exact error each time, the problem may be too severe for `fsck` to fix. You may need to use a third-party disk utility, such as one of those discussed in the next section, to repair or rebuild your directory.

Third-Party Directory Repair/Rebuilding

User Level: depends on the utility
Affects: computer
Terminal: no

Disk Utility and its command-line counterpart `fsck` are powerful utilities, and many users may never have a need for anything else; however, there are limits to what they can do. For example, there are times when a disk's directory is so badly damaged that it can no longer be repaired. (This is generally what happens when Disk Utility tells you it cannot repair a problem, or when `fsck` repeats the same error over and over.) In these situations, what you really need to do is discard your existing directory and build a new one from scratch. Although Apple's built-in tools can't do this, several commercial third-party utilities can.

Alsoft's DiskWarrior (`http://www.alsoft.com/DiskWarrior/index.html`), Micromat's Drive 10 and TechTool Pro 4 (`http://www.micromat.com/`), and Symantec's Norton Utilities (`http://www.symantec.com/nu/nu_mac/index.html`) all provide some way of replacing your existing (and assumed to be problematic) directory with a new one. Norton Utilities will rebuild *parts* of the directory, which is better than trying to repair it if there are significant problems, but Drive 10, TechTool Pro 4, and DiskWarrior will completely rebuild the directory from the ground up (or from the disk up, so to speak). (In practice, Drive 10 and TechTool Pro 4 will only create a completely new directory if absolutely necessary; otherwise they will repair or rebuild just those parts of the directory that need it. DiskWarrior, on the other hand, always builds a new directory—that's its forte.)

Which should you use? In this particular situation, I'm a big fan of DiskWarrior, mainly because it appears to do the most complete and comprehensive job at rebuilding disk directories—it even lets you compare the contents of the original directory with the new directory, including any file differences, *before* replacing the original directory. Alsoft also claims that DiskWarrior optimizes the directory so that it is more efficient than the directories repaired or created by other utilities. In my own experience, I've seen DiskWarrior save data on a drive that was given up for dead—it was able to recreate a usable directory where no other utility could. If there's a criticism of DiskWarrior, it's that it *only* rebuilds disk directories, whereas the other utilities mentioned in this section also have substantial additional functionality (which I'll talk about later in the chapter); however, DiskWarrior is so good at what it does that it's worth buying DiskWarrior *and* something else if you want those other features.

TIP Just to be on the safe side, I boot from the DiskWarrior CD (or from another bootable volume) about once a month and rebuild the directories on all of my mounted volumes, but especially my regular boot volume.

Journaling: Your Drive's Personal Diary

Beginning with OS X 10.2.2, Apple included support in OS X for a new hard drive filesystem feature called *journaling*. The purpose of journaling, to paraphrase Apple, is to protect the integrity of your disk's filesystem; it helps prevent your disk from getting into an inconsistent state, and expedites disk repairs if your system fails.

When journaling is enabled, any change made to your hard drive (a file saved, a file deleted, a file moved, etc.) is recorded in a...well, a journal. The information in this journal includes the time of each change and the actual changes made. (The journal doesn't keep track of each change forever. Once the journal reaches an upper size limit, new change records bump the oldest records out.)

The benefit of journaling is realized when your Mac crashes or, for whatever reason, you need to force a reboot. Normally, when your Mac shuts down, it cleans up after itself, including writing any cached data to disk and verifying disk directories. A crash or forced reboot often doesn't allow these cleanup tasks to occur, so OS X tediously checks your boot drive—the entire thing—at the next startup for file and directory inconsistencies and other problems. With journaling enabled, your Mac can use the journal to restore the drive to a state that was known to be healthy. In addition, because your computer uses the journal to see which particular parts of the hard drive were most vulnerable to problems (those most recently accessed), it can concentrate on those at startup, instead of wasting time on sectors that haven't been accessed in months; the obvious additional benefit is much faster reboot times. (You can read more about journaling at `http://docs.info.apple.com/article.html?artnum=107249`.)

If the benefits of journaling don't seem to be very enticing to you, keep in mind that journaling was developed mainly for servers—computers with very large hard drives where data integrity is paramount and which can't afford to be offline for long periods of time. In fact, at the time of this writing, journaling was only officially supported on Mac OS X Server, not the client version of OS X (the version that ships with most Macs). If you open Disk Utility on Mac OS X Server, there is a simple option to turn journaling on and off; this option doesn't appear when you launch Disk Utility on a non-Server version of OS X.

That being said, remember when I told you earlier in the book that OS X and OS X Server are basically identical under the hood? That holds true here, as well, and journaling is also part of the standard version of OS X. It's just that Apple hasn't given you an easy way to enable it. Yet. (I expect that by the time you read this, or shortly after, journaling will be a standard option available from Disk Utility.) If you're interested in enabling journaling on your non-Server version of OS X, I'm going to show you how. But first I'm going to try to warn you off.

Continued on next page

Journaling Caveats

Despite its obvious benefits, there are a few caveats with journaling. First, and most importantly from a data standpoint, with journaling enabled you shouldn't use `fsck` to repair your hard drive at startup; be sure to read the following Apple Knowledge Base article about disk repairs with journaling enabled: `http://docs.info.apple.com/article.html?artnum=107250`. Similarly, many disk utilities—at the time of this writing—haven't been updated to work with journaling. For example, running DiskWarrior on a journaled volume will disable journaling; you'll have to re-enable it afterwards. Second, OS X will set aside a chunk of hard drive space for journaling data; the bigger your hard drive, the bigger the chunk of space. This means that the amount of space you have available for other files will be reduced. (However, in all fairness, this should only be an issue if your hard drive is almost full.) The third thing to consider is that the space set aside for journaling must be contiguous; it can't be split up all over the drive. If your drive is highly fragmented, I suggest you defragment it first before enabling journaling. (I discuss defragmentation and optimization later in this chapter.) Fourth, recording every single change made to your hard drive doesn't happen in a vacuum; it will affect your system's performance. According to Apple, OS X Server includes some tweaks that reduce the degree to which journaling slows down the system, but (again, at the time of this writing) the standard version of OS X doesn't have these tweaks. My guess, however, is that when journaling is made available in the standard version of OS X, these optimizations will come with it. Fifth, journaling is only compatible with HFS Plus; if your drive is formatted as UFS, you can't enable journaling. Finally, since journaling isn't yet officially supported on the standard version of OS X, don't expect Apple's Tech Support to help you with it.

Enabling Journaling

Whew! Those caveats out of the way, if you're still interested in enabling journaling, there are two ways to do it: using Terminal or via a third-party utility. (Assuming, of course, that Apple hasn't yet made journaling available via Disk Utility by the time you read this.)

Enabling and Disabling Journaling via Terminal To enable journaling using Terminal, type **`sudo diskutil enableJournal '`*`mountpoint`*`'`** **<RETURN>**, where *mountpoint* is the path to the drive for which you want journaling enabled; provide your admin password when prompted. (For the boot volume, the mountpoint is /; for other volumes, use /`Volumes`/*`volumename`*.) It's that simple. To disable journaling, type **`sudo diskutil disableJournal '`*`mountpoint`*`'`** **<RETURN>**.

Enabling and Disabling Journaling via Third-Party Utilities Even easier than using Terminal is using a third-party utility like Xupport (`http://www.computer-support.ch/Xupport/`). Launch Xupport, and click the System… button. In the System panel, find the Journaling section. From the pop-up menu, choose the mounted volume for which you want to enable journaling, and then click the "on" button (you'll be asked for your password). To check the status of journaling on any volume, select the volume from the pop-up menu and then click the "check" button. To disable journaling for a volume, select the volume and then click the "off" button.

Recovering Files

User Level: depends on the utility
Affects: computer
Terminal: no

Repairing your disk directories is all fine and dandy, but what if you've actually lost data? For those situations you need a utility that can access your drive's data directly and recover files. If your hard drive ever develops problems serious enough to cause you to lose files and data, you're probably going to want to get them back, and it's best to have the tools you'll need for such a recovery beforehand. (Although, of course, a good backup strategy will help you avoid such situations entirely.)

The first thing to note is that unless your hard drive actually fails (breaks), data is rarely actually *lost*. It's often right there on your hard drive, but either your directory is damaged, or the file(s) have been deleted from the directory but not overwritten/erased (as explained in Chapter 13 when I discussed secure deletion of files). In the first case, fixing the directory as explained above may "find" the data, or you may need a utility that actually scours your drive to recover lost files. In the second case, a utility that recovers deleted files may be able to help; I discuss a few of those utilities in the next section.

Data Rescue X from Prosoft (`http://www.prosoftengineering.com/products/data_rescue.php`), TechTool Pro 4, and Norton Utilities all provide file recovery functionality. TechTool Pro and Norton Utilities use a method whereby they back up your disk directories at user-specified intervals. If you lose a file due to drive or directory problems, they can reference one of these past directories; if a file has not been overwritten, they can rescue the file for you. (This is similar to OS X's *journaling* feature; see the sidebar "Journaling: Your Drive's Personal Diary" for details.)

Data Rescue probably has the best reputation for rescuing files based on the OS 9 version of the utility, and all accounts seem to confirm that the OS X version is just as effective. Like DiskWarrior, Data Rescue does one thing, but does it well. Instead of relying on saved directories, it analyzes every single block of your drive and recreates both directory and file information. I've been lucky enough never to have needed such a powerful tool (knock on wood), but I've heard from a number of people that Data Rescue has been able to recover files when all other utilities have failed.

Undeleting Deleted Data

User Level: depends on the utility
Affects: computer
Terminal: no

Being meticulous about keeping your drives and files healthy helps prevent data loss due to drive problems, but it can't save you from yourself. If you've ever thrown away a file that you later realized you needed, only to find that you'd already emptied the Trash, you know exactly what I'm talking about. If you're a frequent "accidental deleter," there are a few utilities available that could save your bacon. Norton Utilities, Tech Tool Pro 4, and Prosoft's Data Recycler (`http://www.prosoftengineering.com/products/data_recycler.php`) all offer some degree of protection against accidental (or even purposeful) deletion. However, they take different approaches.

Norton Utilities' UnErase function relies on the fact that data isn't really erased when you empty the Trash, but is in fact still there, intact, until another file is written to the same space on your drive. It scours your drive for data, and if it finds the file(s) you want to undelete, it recovers them. The downside to UnErase is that although it works great if you realize you need to retrieve a file immediately after deleting it, its ability to recover data is reduced dramatically the more time that elapses. This is because the more time that goes by, the more files are written to your hard drive, and thus the greater the chance that data will be written to the same parts of the hard drive on which your deleted file(s) reside.

NOTE When you "undelete" data, you should *always* restore it to a drive *other* that the one from which you're recovering it. If you try to restore it to the same drive, the newly restored file could accidentally overwrite some of the file data you're trying to recover. Luckily, UnErase requires you to save the recovered file(s) to a different volume.

Data Recycler (and reportedly TechTool Pro 4, although it hasn't officially been released at the time of this writing, so I can't confirm) take a different approach than Norton Utilities. Rather than counting on data to still be on the drive, it creates a *cache* of deleted files. This cache resides in its own hard drive space, and keeps a copy of any files you've deleted. Files remain in the cache until enough new files are deleted (which adds them to the cache) to move older files out, causing them to be deleted permanently. (You can choose how big you want the cache of deleted files to be; how big of a cache you choose, combined with the size and number of files you delete, determine how much protection you have.) If you want to recover a deleted file, you simply open Data Recycler, select the file from the list of "deleted" files, and then tell Data Recycler to restore it.

TIP In addition to files that you've thrown away yourself, Data Recycler can also restore files deleted by the OS (e.g., temporary files deleted after a system procedure is completed), files deleted from within applications such as iPhoto, and even files deleted from within Terminal using the `rm` command!.

Keep in mind that the flip side of "Trash cache" utilities is that if you want to make sure a file is permanently deleted you'll need to manually tell the utility not to protect that file; TechTool Pro 4 and Data Recycler each do this a bit differently, but they both have the capacity. Or you can use one of the "secure deletion" utilities I mentioned in Chapter 13.

WARNING If you use a "secure delete" utility to delete files permanently, as described in Chapter 13, no utility will be able to recover these files. After all, that's why you used the utility in the first place, right?

Defragmenting Drives

User Level: depends on the utility
Affects: computer
Terminal: no

Even though you may keep your drives and directories error-free, that doesn't necessarily mean they're in tip-top shape. *Fragmentation* is a common issue that develops over time and can't be fixed by rebuilding directories or examining hardware.

In you're not familiar with the term "fragmentation," it simply means that files are stored in *fragments* about your hard drive, rather than in contiguous segments. Fragmentation actually isn't a problem for new (or newly formatted) drives, since most of the files on the drive—the operating system and stock files and applications—are generally concentrated in one part of the drive and the rest of the drive is free. New files can thus be written in contiguous chunks where the free space starts. However, as you delete files from your disk, small blocks of free space appear here and there. When you save a new file, or when a new file is created by the OS, instead of placing it in contiguous empty space away from existing files, in the interest of efficiency the OS tends to try to find space for it among existing files. If a block of contiguous free space isn't available, the file will be split up into smaller segments, each of which is saved to smaller free spaces across the drive.

Over time, as you save, copy, and delete files to and from your disk, files become increasingly fragmented (Figure 14.1). This has several consequences. First, since files are broken up into many pieces, it takes more time and more disk action to access them than if they were in contiguous blocks. Second, because the disk directory for a highly fragmented volume is much more complex than one for a volume with low levels of fragmentation, the chances of directory problems are higher. Finally, because virtual memory swap files are, at the most basic level, simply files on your hard drive, severe fragmentation causes swap files to be spread out across your drive, which can slow down system performance, and, conversely, swap files themselves can exacerbate fragmentation. (This final issue is one of the arguments for moving your virtual memory swap files to an alternate drive; I discuss that topic in Appendix B.)

Under Mac OS 9, fragmentation was a major issue that could severely impact your computer's performance. OS X deals with disk fragmentation much better, but fragmentation can still affect system performance and can contribute to directory corruption (although the

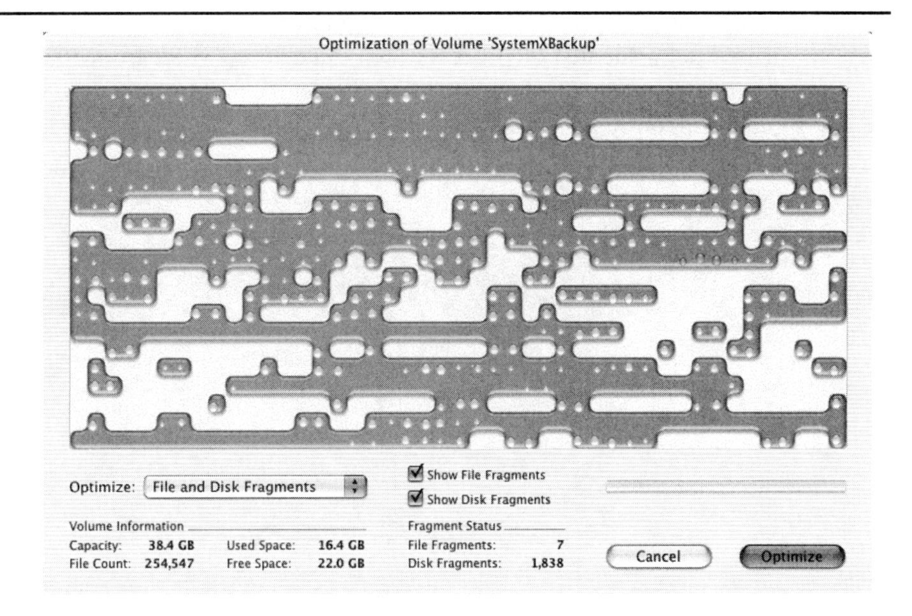

FIGURE 14.1: A graphical representation of disk fragmentation (courtesy of Drive 10)

topic is subject to some debate). Fortunately, many of the tools already discussed here can be used to defragment your drive(s). Drive 10, TechTool Pro 4, and Norton Utilities (via its Speed Disk feature) all have the ability to defragment drives, and all work fairly similarly. (DiskWarrior 2, for OS 9, comes with a utility called Plus Optimizer that will defragment OS X disks. Unfortunately, you can only use it on a Mac that will boot into OS 9. At the time of this writing, an OS X version of Plus Optimizer is not available, but is in the works.)

WARNING Before you use *any* utility to defragment a volume, be sure to verify and, if necessary, repair any problems on the volume *first*. Defragmenting a damaged volume can result in data loss. This is also another good argument for backing up—if the defragmentation procedure is interrupted for any reason, it's possible to lose data or, in extreme cases, the entire volume.

For example, in Drive 10 you choose Services ➢ Optimize Volume… and a window pops up with a list of volumes. Choose the volume to be optimized, and click Analyze. (As with all optimization utilities, the volume to be optimized can't be the boot volume, nor can it be the volume on which the utility is located—this is why most come with bootable CDs.) Drive 10 then presents a graphical representation of the volume's contents (this is what I showed you in Figure 14.1). You can choose to optimize the volume based on File Fragments (which reunites each file's pieces into a single contiguous block), or based on File and Disk Fragments (which additionally groups all files onto contiguous drive space, leaving as much contiguous free space as possible). The graph will actually be updated in real time as the drive is defragmented—a process which can take anywhere from 20 minutes to a few hours, depending on the size of the drive and the degree of fragmentation. When it's done, the graph will look like Figure 14.2—fragment-free.

FIGURE 14.2: The volume from Figure 14.1 after being defragmented

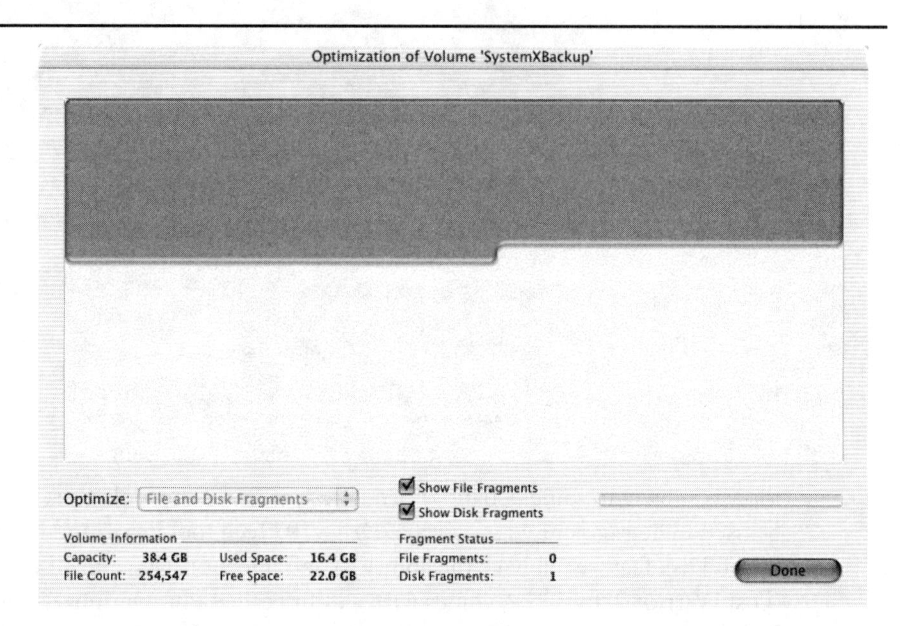

NOTE Some users avoid defragmenting utilities, and instead back up their entire volume, erase it, and then restore it from the backup, assuming this method will give them a drive that is no longer fragmented. However, this is only the case if the utility you use for backups copies files contiguously; many instead copy the drive back bit-for-bit. This procedure is safer from a data standpoint, but it means that your restored drive will be just as fragmented as it was before.

Organized Defragmenting: Optimizing

In addition to *defragmenting* your drive—making sure that each file resides on a contiguous section of the hard drive—several utilities allow you to *optimize* it. Optimization can take two forms. TechTool Pro, Drive 10 (via the File and Disk Fragments option), and DiskWarrior 2's Plus Optimizer take the basic approach of simply relocating all files in one large contiguous block, leaving as much contiguous free space as possible.

Norton Utilities' Speed Disk component, on the other hand, bases its defragmentation routines on *profiles*. You select the profile that most closely resembles what the chosen volume will be used for (some examples are General Use, CD-ROM Mastering, and Recently Used Files), and Speed Disk will defragment the volume, but will also move certain files to certain locations based on their use and type. For example, the Recently Used Files profile places those files that were most recently modified closest to free space, on the assumption that you (or the OS) are more likely to modify those files again—thus helping to slow future fragmentation. Most profiles also place system files in close proximity to each other, predicting that they're more likely to be accessed closely in time.

TIP Because of their slower speeds, CDs actually benefit from optimization much more than hard drives; Speed Disk's CD-ROM Mastering profile is useful for optimizing CD images before burning.

I mentioned earlier that the value of defragmenting is often debated; the idea of optimization is even more of a hot topic. However, some people swear by it—I've even seen custom Speed Disk profiles, designed specifically to optimize OS X boot volumes, floating around the Internet. I've defragmented my boot volume, and definitely noticed an increase in system performance. However, I haven't (yet) "optimized" it, so I can't tell you how much it helps as compared to defragmentation.

NOTE If you're curious about Apple's stance on defragmenting, you can read the following Knowledge Base article: `http://docs.info.apple.com/article.html?artnum=17933`.

Make Your Own Bootable Utility CD

Earlier in the chapter I mentioned that most disk utilities that modify the startup disk—to repair it, defragment it, or optimize it—require you to boot from another volume or from a special CD. Most of these utilities in fact come with their own bootable CD. Unfortunately, there are two problems with these CDs. The first is that as new Mac models are released, these "bootable" CDs are often outdated and no longer boot the newest hardware. The second is that each of these CDs generally includes only a single utility.

The solution to both problems is to create your own bootable OS X utility CD. In Chapter 7 I recommended the application BootCD (`http://www.charlessoft.com/`) as a way to do this. The steps to making such a CD are lengthy, so I can't include them here, but the BootCD documentation is excellent and easy to follow. You can include *all* of your favorite disk utilities on your custom CD, and they'll all be available to you at once when you boot from that CD.

Disk Drive Diagnosis

User Level: depends on the utility
Affects: computer
Terminal: no

Although it's certainly true that today's hard drives are more reliable than ever before, that doesn't mean they're foolproof. Hard drives are susceptible to both environmental factors and, occasionally, manufacturing defects. So, ideally, in addition to periodically checking your disk directories, you'll want to make sure your hard drive itself is working right.

There are three approaches to hard drive testing. The first, used by Norton Utilities' Disk Doctor, TechTool Pro 4, and Drive 10, is to scan every single block on your drive to make sure each is working properly. If the utility finds a bad block or sector, it disables that particular bit of the hard drive so that it will never again be used for storing data. This is actually a fairly common problem, but once a bad block or sector is deactivated, your drive should operate perfectly.

The second method, used by TechTool Pro 4 and Drive 10, is to perform a battery of hardware tests on the drive that checks everything from the correct power supply voltage to the ability of the drive to read and write to both the drive's disk platters and its RAM buffer. If a problem is found, you're notified of what that problem is and what can be done about it.

Finally, many recent EIDE hard drives—which includes all those used in today's Macs—include a system called Self-Monitoring Analysis & Reporting Technology (SMART). SMART is a system through which the hard drive communicates with the host computer and provides information about the operating state of the drive. The SMART system monitors several aspects of the drive's performance and compares them with expected values for that particular drive model to determine if the drive is operating as it should. If a problem or anomaly is detected, the SMART system can produce an alert. Since most hard drive problems develop gradually rather than suddenly, such an alert can give you advanced warning and a chance to save important data (and then have the drive repaired or replaced).

Unfortunately, the SMART system can't notify you of errors on its own; it requires software that communicates with the drive and reports any warnings to the user. Currently, only DiskWarrior, Drive 10, and TechTool Pro 4 support SMART. If you're using one of these utilities, you can check your manual for information on how a SMART warning would be reported to you.

In reality, hard drive failures are rare; however, when they happen, the aftermath can be fairly disastrous (in terms of data loss). Good backups are your best protection, but you can take advantage of tools like those discussed here to at least get some advance notice of an impending failure.

Data Despair?

I've talked about all the ways in which you can keep your disk directories, files, and drives healthy, but what about worst-case scenarios? What if you drop your PowerBook onto concrete and the hard drive no longer responds? What if your G4 tower is caught in an office fire (or drowned by the fire hoses trying to put out the fire)? What if a lightning storm fries your computer and your hard drive(s) with it? What if the hard drive just goes kaput on its own? These are pretty horrible things to think about, but the truth is that they can and do happen. If you find yourself in a situation where an important hard drive doesn't respond to the utilities mentioned here, and you don't have a proper backup, it's time to get out your checkbook—your only choice may be to spend some dough and have your data recovered professionally. I've never had to do this, but the most reputable name in the business is DriveSavers (`http://drivesavers.com/`). They actually take your drive apart and examine the data in a sterile lab, platter by platter. They're not cheap, but if you're using their services, your data must be worth something.

NOTE If you need to recover data after a disaster (manmade or otherwise), I'm going to assume that you have a proper backup, but that by some horrible twist of fate your backup was damaged or lost or stolen or that there's some other explanation as to why you don't have a good backup. If you don't have a recent backup, you *must* read the part of this chapter dedicated to the topic.

Maintenance Magic

Keeping your drive(s) healthy is an obvious form of Mac maintenance. However, OS X presents several other "opportunities" for maintenance that many Mac users have never encountered before. (How'd you like that use of euphemism?) Here are three you should know about.

Periodic Permissions Patching

User Level: admin
Affects: computer
Terminal: no

I talked about repairing permissions and privileges in Chapter 1 as a way to fix permissions-related problems. In Chapter 4, I also recommended repairing permissions before and after installing major system updates. However, in my experience, permissions get screwed up on their own fairly regularly. Most of the time the consequences are extremely minor; however, I find it useful to run Disk Utility's Repair Disk Permissions function on my startup drive on a regular basis. (I tend to run it once a week.) I can't guarantee any results, but I can tell you that I've seen fewer permissions-related problems, and fewer problems in general, since I've made this one of my regular routines.

TIP I showed you how to run Repair Disk Permissions in Chapter 1, but if you're interested, I'll show you how to make it run automatically in the background later in this chapter under "Automating Admin Actions."

Running Routines (Unix Routines, That Is)

User Level: admin
Affects: computer
Terminal: possibly

Because OS X is based on Unix, it still exhibits a few remnants of classic Unix behavior. One of these is its reliance on "cleanup" scripts. Unix operating systems maintain a number of activity logs (discussed later in the chapter), databases, and temporary files that need to be cleaned out and/or updated periodically. To take care of these tasks, Unix computers (including yours, running OS X) use three scripts, called *daily*, *weekly*, and *monthly*, to perform these actions. These scripts remove unnecessary temporary files, archive or delete old log files, and update databases (such as the `locate` database I talked about in Chapter 5). They run, as you might guess, daily, weekly, and monthly, respectively.

Unfortunately, on many Macs these scripts never get run. Because Unix computers have historically been used as servers or number-crunching workstations, system administrators didn't want to run these scripts—which can take a good deal of time and system resources—during the day when users were most likely to be using the computer. So, since most Unix computers were left running 24/7, they took advantage of Unix's `cron` automation utility to schedule the execution of these scripts at times when computers would least likely be in use. (I'll talk more about `cron` later in the chapter.) Over time, these execution times became standardized across entire distributions of Unix; in OS X, the *daily* script is scheduled to run every morning at 3:15 A.M., the *weekly* script is scheduled for 4:30 A.M. Saturday mornings, and the *monthly* script will be run at 5:30 A.M. on the first day of each month.

The problem is that most Mac users don't leave their computers on all night—if your computer isn't running (and awake), the scripts don't get run, so your temp files don't get deleted, your log files grow larger, and your databases aren't updated. Although this isn't a disaster, your log and temp files can grow very large over time, and if you actually use any of the databases in question (such as the `locate` database), they won't be updated versions. If your computer is shut down or asleep at night, here's how to get these scripts to run.

TIP If you *do* leave your computer on at night, you may as well skip to the next section right now, because you're set.

There are actually a few simple solutions to this predicament. The first is that you can occasionally leave your Mac running at night so that the scripts will run. For example, if you leave your Mac on every Friday night/Saturday morning, and the last day/first morning of every month, your monthly and weekly scripts will run as scheduled, and the daily script will at least be run once per week, which is sufficient for most users.

The second approach is to use utility like the freeware MacJanitor (`http://personalpages.tds.net/~brian_hill/macjanitor.html`) or the shareware Xupport (mentioned earlier in the chapter) to run any or all of the scripts at your leisure. When you launch MacJanitor and provide your admin password, you can execute any of the scripts by clicking on its button in the toolbar, or click the All Tasks button to run all three (Figure 14.3). The bottom of the window displays the scripts log output so you can see what is happening. Xupport's Optimize panel offers similar options.

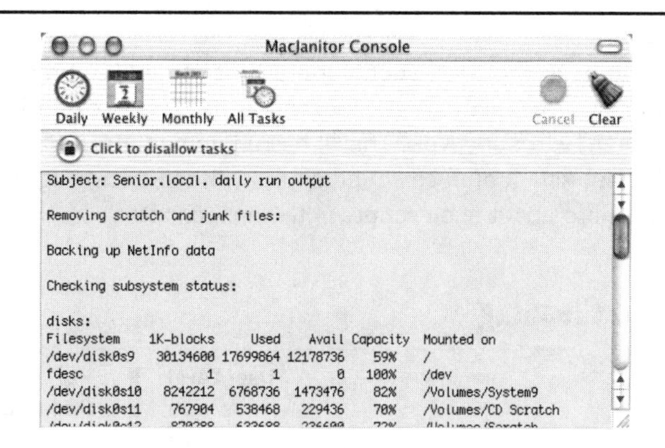

FIGURE 14.3: MacJanitor lets you manually execute OS X's periodic maintenance scripts.

TIP If you're feeling adventurous, you can do the same thing as MacJanitor and Xupport using Terminal. Simply type **`sudo periodic`** ***`script`*** **<RETURN>**, where *script* is **`daily`**, **`weekly`**, or **`monthly`**. After providing your admin password, the script will run, and you can feel good knowing that you used a Unix command line to run the script just like they did in the old days.

The only downside to using a tool like MacJanitor or Xupport (or Terminal) is that you have to *remember* to use them. If automating the process is worth a few bucks to you, check out the shareware Macaroni (`http://www.atomicbird.com/`). Macaroni runs as a preference pane and provides two helpful features. First, each time you start up, Macaroni checks each script's schedule, and then checks to see if the script was actually run on schedule. If a script *didn't* run when it was supposed to, Macaroni runs it. This way your maintenance scripts never get behind schedule. The second feature is that you can actually change the schedule (by day) on which the scripts are run. For example, you can choose to have the daily script run every other day instead of daily. Or you can change the day of the week or month on which the weekly or monthly script (respectively) should be run.

TIP As a bonus, Macaroni can even schedule other shell scripts to be run at certain intervals and can run OS X's Repair Permissions feature on the schedule you choose.

If you're curious as to exactly what the daily, weekly, and monthly scripts actually do, they're located at `/etc/periodic/daily/500.daily`, `/etc/periodic/weekly/500.weekly`, and `/etc/periodic/monthly/500.monthly`. You'll probably find the code to be little more than gobbledygook unless you're a Unix pro, but the comments (preceded by `#`) are often fairly descriptive. You can also download MacJanitor (mentioned above); it comes with a text file called "What Is It Doing?" that includes a brief summary of each script in plain English. Finally, each script produces its own log file (`daily.out`, `weekly.out`, and `monthly.out`), stored in `/var/log`.

TIP If you have your *own* shell scripts that you'd like run daily, weekly, or monthly, you can actually place them in `/etc/periodic/daily`, `/etc/periodic/weekly`, or `/etc/periodic/monthly`, respectively. They'll be run immediately after the standard cleanup scripts—the last action of each script is to check the enclosing folder for other scripts to run. (I'll talk more about shell scripts in the next chapter.)

Cache Cleaning

User Level: any or admin
Affects: individual user or computer
Terminal: no

Remember back in Chapter 2 when I told you that many problems with the System Preferences application (a freeze at launch, multiple instances of the same preference pane, etc.) can be fixed by throwing away its cache file? This issue of corrupt cache files isn't isolated to System Preferences. The truth is that cache files are used quite frequently in OS X as a way to store frequently accessed data and, as a result, can impact a lot of things.

For example, one of the most common cache-related issues under OS X 10.2 is a situation where you can no longer drag files or folders in the Finder. No matter how hard you try, they appear to be permanently glued in place. One solution is to delete certain cache files from your `~/Library/Caches` directory. A number of other problems in Jaguar can similarly be solved by discarding files in that folder, or in several other local- and system-level cache folders (e.g., /Library/Caches, /System/Library/Caches, and /System /Library/Extensions.kextcache).

In addition to occasionally contributing to problems, some cache files grow larger and larger over time, taking up more and more disk space. (I recently checked my Caches directory and found that it was over 200MB in size.) If you're a neat freak, you may enjoy throwing out unnecessary cache files that are just cluttering your hard drive.

Although you could clear out many of these files manually, there are two utilities that do an excellent job of automating the process: the donationware Dragster (http://ifthensoft .com/) and the shareware Jaguar Cache Cleaner (http://www.northernsoftworks.com/ jaguarcachecleaner.html). Dragster is specifically designed to fix the bug described above where you can't drag items in the Finder. It deletes a specific list of cache files (and a few preferences files, such as the Finder preferences) that have been directly linked to the glitch. I've personally experienced the "no drag" problem twice, and both times Dragster solved the problem. In addition, at your request it can also delete several other Finder- and Dock-related files that can contribute to Finder problems, such as *all* the invisible .DS_store files that exist in every folder on your hard drive. (These files contain your individual window preferences; when one or more is corrupt, you can experience odd window behavior.)

Jaguar Cache Cleaner (JCC), on the other hand, attempts to fix the aforementioned Finder bug, but it also deletes many other files that may be related to a broader range of system issues. However, because it deletes more files, some of which may include important information, JCC's developer recommends that you first try other troubleshooting options, such as running Disk First Aid to repair your disk and permissions. If you decide to use JCC, you can choose the Light Cleaning option first; if that doesn't work, a Deep Cleaning option deletes a more extensive list of files. You can also choose to have JCC clean (read: delete) files in just your user cache directory, the local cache, the System cache, and/or other users' cache directories.

NOTE Both Dragster and Jaguar Cache Cleaner require a restart after doing their job, so be sure to save any documents before running either utility. In addition, both also require an admin password if you want them to remove any system- or local-level files.

In addition to its "cleaning" functionality, Jaguar Cache Cleaner also has a few other features. Although they're unrelated, having them in easy reach can be convenient. For example, JCC lets you enable and disable journaling on any mounted volume (see the sidebar on journaling earlier in the chapter for details). JCC will also allow you to manually run OS X's three maintenance scripts, as discussed in the previous section, and run the Repair Disk Permissions routines without having to open Disk Utility. (I show you how to automate this in the next section.) Finally, JCC has two features that I don't really recommend using: first, you can manually delete virtual memory swap files—I don't like this feature because you generally shouldn't be deleting swap files; a simple restart will remove them all for you without the possibility of adversely affecting OS X's virtual memory system. Second, JCC lets you drop into single-user mode from the Finder. I don't recommend this because you still have to restart after using single-user mode via JCC, so you may as well just restart and access single-user mode normally.

TIP I tend to manually empty the three `/Caches` directories every few weeks, and turn to Dragster or JCC only when I experience strange Finder or application behavior that I can't fix by throwing away preference files.

If you're still running OS X 10.1.*x*, some of the problems described above can be attributed to a few other files in addition to cache files. These files are located in `~/Library/Preferences`, and all begin with `.LS`. Both utilities described above will also remove these files for you.

Admin Artistry

In addition to the maintenance-related tasks I've been talking about, there are a few other tips I'd like to point out that are administrator-related; specifically, how to schedule events and actions, how to adjust application priorities, and how to better work with OS X's log files.

Automating Admin Actions

User Level: normal or admin
Affects: user or computer
Terminal: possibly

I mentioned earlier in the chapter that OS X's cleanup scripts are run by the Unix utility `cron`. This utility runs in the background whenever your computer is running. Every minute, it checks schedules called *crontabs* (short for *cron tables*) to see if any command or script is supposed to be run at that time; if it finds one (or more), it runs them. Although most users don't even realize that `cron` exists, now that you do, you can use it to your advantage.

In theory, `cron` can only execute commands that you would type into Terminal; however, since you can run complex shell scripts from the command line, `cron` can launch them, too. In addition, OS X includes a special Terminal command, `open`, that allows you to open any file or document as if you'd double-clicked on it in the Finder. This adds a whole 'nother level of power to the `cron` utility—AppleScripts can be saved as stand-alone applications, and can themselves run shell scripts, so the `cron` utility in OS X can schedule and automate pretty much anything you want to do in the Finder, in scriptable applications, and in Terminal (the *shell*)—or any combination of the three.

I'm not going to get into super-complex shell/AppleScript automation here, but I do want to give you a few (simple) examples of how you might take advantage of `cron` on your own computer. Because `cron` is a command-line program, its syntax can get pretty messy; however, like many other command-line applications in OS X, someone has put a nice face on it and made it easy to use. CronniX (`http://www.koch-schmidt.de/cronnix/`) is a donationware utility that lets you edit the system-level crontab, as well as additional user-level crontabs.

NOTE In general, you only want to edit the system's crontab in CronniX if you need to execute a command that requires root access. For all other uses, you should edit your own user-level crontab. If you're curious, the system's crontab is actually located at `/etc/crontab`; Individual user crontabs are located in `/var/cron`.

By choosing File ➢ Open System Crontab, you can view and edit the main system-level crontab (you'll need to provide your admin password to edit it). In addition, by choosing File ➢ Open for User… and typing in a username, you can view and edit any user-level crontab (again, to edit another user's crontab, you'll need to provide your admin password).

Unless another utility has scheduled an event, your own user-level crontab is likely to be empty. To see what a crontab entry looks like, open your *own* crontab, and then choose File ➢ New Default Task. CronniX will create a new sample task that displays the text "Happy New Year!" (Figure 14.4).

What this entry says is that at the time 0:00 (`cron` uses 24-hour time, so 0:00 is midnight), on the first day of the first month, the text "Happy New Year!" should be "displayed." (I put *displayed* in quotes because what really happens is that an e-mail message is sent to the local `sendmail` spool, which on most Macs isn't going to do anything you'll ever see. But at least it's a good example for seeing the format of a crontab entry in CronniX.) You can double-click on any field and edit its value; when you're finished editing, click the Save button in the toolbar.

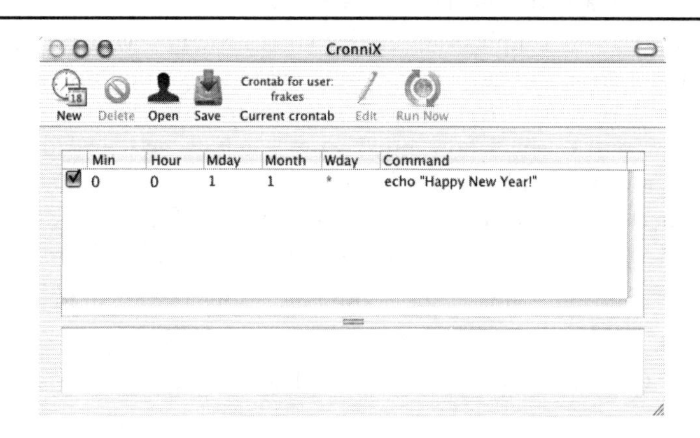

FIGURE 14.4: A sample crontab entry in CronniX

TIP CronniX has an excellent online manual that I highly recommend reading at http://www.koch-schmidt.de/cronnix/docs/index.html.

If you're curious what a system-level crontab looks like, open the file /etc/crontab in a text editor (or type **more /etc/crontab <RETURN>** in Terminal, which is a bit easier). At the very least, it will contain three scheduled events:

```
15  3  *  *  *  root  periodic daily
30  4  *  *  6  root  periodic weekly
30  5  1  *  *  root  periodic monthly
```

If the names of the commands look familiar, it's because each of these lines is the schedule for the cleaning scripts I talked about earlier in the chapter; the periodic command runs scripts located in the daily, weekly, and monthly folders I pointed out. In fact, if you look at the first five columns, you'll see that they correspond to the minute, hour, day of the month, month, and day of the week fields in CronniX, and, in the context of those fields, correspond to the days and times I told you that these scripts are scheduled to run.

Here are a couple of examples of ways to use CronniX and cron that you might find useful.

NOTE As I previously mentioned, if your computer is asleep (or off), cron does not run, nor does it check to see if it "missed" any scheduled events while your computer was asleep or shutdown. So in order for an event to be executed, your computer must be running and awake at its scheduled execution time. (With respect to OS X's cleanup scripts, which don't get run if you turn your Mac off at night, if you're feeling adventurous you can use CronniX to edit their cron entries—via the System Crontab—so that they run during the day instead.)

Getting a Daily Report of Free Space

This is very simple example that shows you how you can run a command-line program using cron, and have its output saved to a text file. It may not be useful to you, but it's good for demonstration purposes. Suppose that you do a lot of work with big files, and you want to check how much room you have on your hard drive each morning. You could manually get info on the drive in the Finder, but wouldn't it be nice if your computer checked for you and put the results in a text file on your Desktop? Let's say, just for the sake of argument, that you think this is a neat idea. Here's how you can do it.

1. Launch CronniX and choose File ➢ Open Crontab for User... and click Default. (You could also enter your own username and click Open).
2. Choose File ➢ New Task. You'll be presented with an event editing sheet (Figure 14.5).

FIGURE 14.5:
Creating a new `cron` task in CronniX

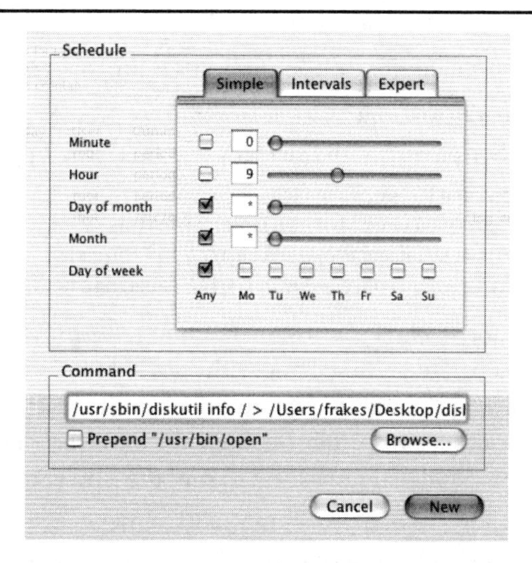

3. Choose the time you want the disk info to be gathered—if you want it to happen every day, check the boxes next to "Day of month" and "Month" (this tells `cron` you don't care what day of the month or month it is) and the Any box next to "Day of week." In my example in Figure 14.5, I told `cron` to execute the command every day at 9 A.M..
4. In the command field, type **`/usr/sbin/diskutil info / > /Users/`*`username`*`/Desktop/`*`filename`*`.txt`**, where *username* is your username, and *filename* is the name you want the output file saved as. The first part of this command, `/usr/sbin/diskutil`, is the path to the `diskutil` program (the same one you'd be using if you typed **`diskutil`** in Terminal). The `info` argument tells `diskutil` to get info on the drive specified (/ means the boot volume). Finally, the last part of the command specifies the name of the output file, and where it should be saved.
5. Click New to create the new task.
6. Click the Save button in the toolbar.

Now every morning at 9 A.M., a new text file will be created on your Desktop that contains information about the boot volume, including the amount of free space remaining. This is admittedly a very simple event, but it shows you the kind of things that you can do with `cron`.

Repairing Permissions Periodically

Earlier in the chapter I recommended periodically running OS X's Repair Disk Permissions functions to keep things running smoothly. You can actually use a simple AppleScript to run Repair Disk Permissions. However, since you can also run AppleScripts from the command line, you can actually *schedule* AppleScripts using `cron`. Here's how to have Repair Disk Permissions run automatically in the background, on a schedule you decide.

First, you need to create the AppleScript:

1. Launch the Script Editor application (in `/Applications/AppleScript`).
2. Create a new script by choosing File ➢ New Script, and then typing the following bit of AppleScript code into the *lower* text field (the upper field is for comments):

```
do shell script
'sudo diskutil repairPermissions / >
/Users/username/Desktop/repairpermissions.txt'
password yourpassword with administrator privileges
```

   where *username* is your username, and *yourpassword* is your admin password. (Those are three separate lines, starting with "do," "sudo," and "password.") This AppleScript executes a shell script (the text in quotes) that runs the Repair Disk Permissions utility and then saves the log of repairs to your Desktop in a file called "`repairpermissions.txt`." Since the utility requires administrator access to run, the AppleScript also provides your password.

3. Choose File ➢ Save As… In the Save dialog, select "Application" from the Format pop-up menu, and check the box next to Never Show Startup Screen. Give the AppleScript a name and save it to your ~/Applications folder.

NOTE I strongly recommend saving this script in your *own* Applications folder because it contains your admin password. Saving the script in a publicly accessible directory means that any other user could open the script and get your password.

The next thing to do is to create a new crontab entry for your script. Fortunately, using an AppleScript is much easier than entering a Terminal command:

4. Open the System Crontab in CronniX and then drag your newly created script into the System Crontab window. A new event will be created that runs your script.
5. Select the new event, and then click the Edit item in the toolbar to edit the event.
6. In the Schedule section, select the times and days you want the script to be run. I personally have this script set to run once per week, which may be overkill. You can instead choose to run it once a month by checking the box next to Month (which tells `cron` to run the script regardless of the month) and entering a date (1-31) in the field to the right. (I recommend using 1-28, since using a date of 29, 30, or 31 means that the script won't run in months with fewer days.) In the Hour and Minute fields, enter a time of day that your computer is likely to be running (hours are in 24-hour format).
7. Click Apply to apply your edits to the entry.
8. Click the Save toolbar item to save your changes to the System Crontab; provide your admin password when prompted.

Adjusting Application Priorities

User Level: normal or admin
Affects: user or computer
Terminal: no

One of the things that make OS X so much more powerful than OS 9 is that it doesn't allow a single application to monopolize your computer. The downside to this is that sometimes you *want* a single application to be able to monopolize your computer. For example, Connectix's Virtual PC (`http://www.connectix.com/`) emulates a complete Windows PC on your Mac, which takes a lot of processing power. To get the best performance possible, you want Virtual PC to be able to get as much of the processor as possible.

Unix allows an admin user to change application *priorities*—via the `renice` command—so that applications that are given higher priority can take more than their normal share of system resources, and those given lower priority have to wait in line, so to speak, until applications with higher priorities can spare some. Unfortunately, changing application priorities in Terminal is a bit messy; on the few occasions when I need to do it, I use a third-party utility like the freeware ProcessWizard (`http://www.lachoseinteractive.net/`) or the shareware Renicer (`http://www.northernsoftworks.com/`).

ProcessWizard is probably a better choice if you want to manually assign higher or lower priorities to specific applications. It sits in the menu bar, and when you click on its icon a sheet drops down listing all applications (or, via the pop-up menu, background apps, user-level system processes, or non-user system processes) (Figure 14.6). By dragging the slider next to a process to the right, you're increasing its priority; if you drag a slider to the left, that application's priority is reduced. (After changing a priority, you're asked for your admin password.)

NOTE Process/application priorities can range from –20 to 20, with zero being the default value for every process when it's first launched.

Renicer works a bit differently than ProcessWizard, and is what you should use if you want behavior similar to the way OS 9 used to work—that is, for the frontmost application to have the highest priority. When you launch Renicer and provide your admin password, it sits in the background and automatically increases the priority of the frontmost application, in order to increase its performance relative to other processes. When you switch to a different application, the prior application's priority is reset to zero, and the new frontmost application is "reniced" to a higher priority, and so on—the frontmost application will always have the highest priority. You can also specify particular applications so that they always get high priority, even when they're in the background (or so that they always get low priority, even when they're in the foreground). Finally, you can also choose the priority value given to the frontmost app, from 0 to 20, and the value given to "low priority" processes, from –20 to 0.

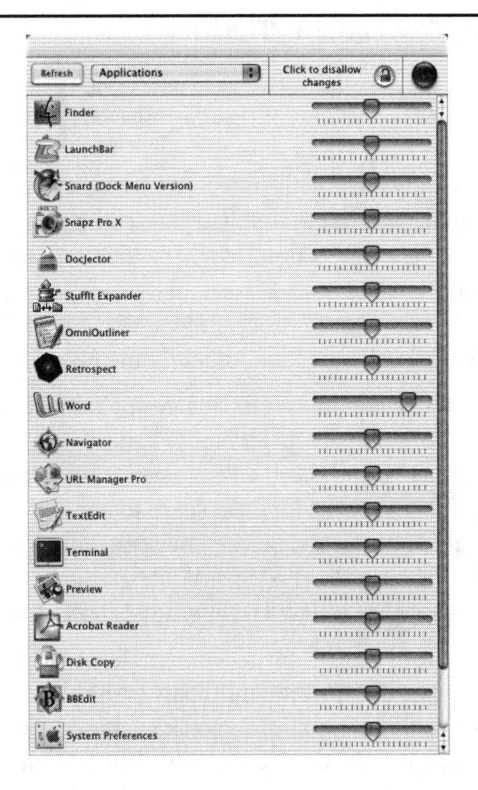

FIGURE 14.6: ProcessWizard lets you "renice" any running process.

Looking over Log Files

User Level: any
Affects: NA
Terminal: no

I mentioned in Chapter 7 that many applications, as well as OS X itself, generate logs of their activity. Although most of the time log files aren't too useful for the average user, if you're experiencing problems they sometimes provide information that can help you (or the developer of an application) track down the cause.

As I mentioned in Chapter 7, you can use OS X's Console application, as well as Apple System Profiler, to view log files. However, if you want a better interface (trust me, if you ever need to actually *read* these things, you want a better interface), the shareware LogMaster (`http://www.nucleus.com/~fenn/soft.html`) is a significant improvement over Console or Apple System Profiler (Figure 14.7). Logs are organized in groups, represented by icons (System, Apache, CUPS, Samba, CrashReporter, and User); within each group of logs, the pop-up menu on the right allows you to select a particular log to view.

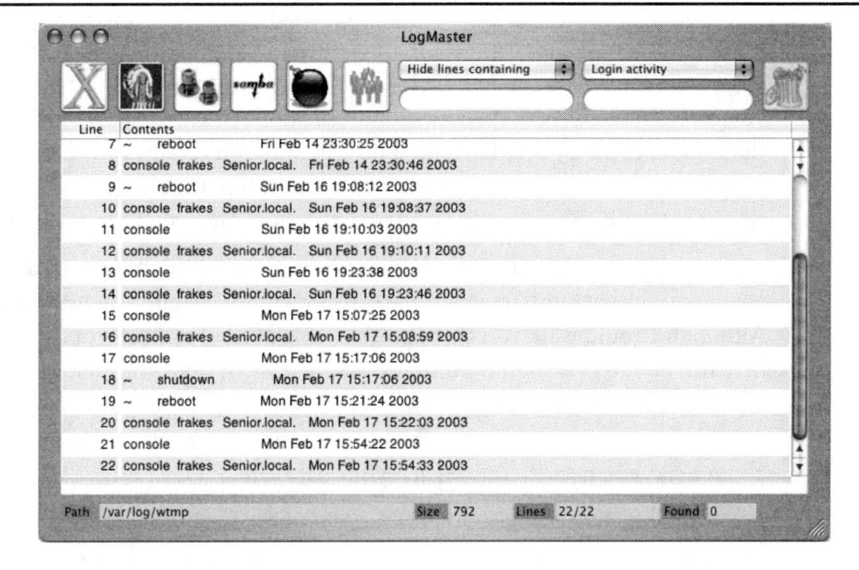

FIGURE 14.7: LogMaster provides advanced log viewing features.

Once you're viewing a log, you can choose to filter lines containing (or not containing) particular strings of text using the middle pop-up menu and text field. In addition, the text field on the right allows you to search for a text string; any lines in the log that contain that string will be highlighted. You can also select individual or multiple lines and then copy them for pasting into an e-mail or text document, or choose File ➢ Mail Log… or Mail Selection… to e-mail the entire log or just the highlighted portion. (You'll be asked for a recipient, title, and any comments, and then LogMaster will use the settings in the Email tab of Internet preferences to send the e-mail—you don't even need to have your e-mail client running.)

Finally, for advanced users LogMaster offers features like *listen daemons* that listen to a particular port and log incoming traffic, a web server that allows you to view logs in any web browser, and automated actions that are triggered when a specific string is detected in a new log entry.

Backup Basics

There are a lot of bad things that can happen to your computer: hard drive problems, system crashes, theft, power surges, and physical damage are just a few of the kinds of things that can change your computer from a useful tool to a pile of plastic and silicon (or, in the case of theft, an empty space on your desk) in a matter of seconds. However, as bad as such events are, for many (if not most) people, the bigger loss is the actual *data* that was on the computer. After all, computers may be expensive to replace, but no amount of money can replace your data or the time and effort you spent creating it.

There's an old (but appropriate) saying in computers that goes something like this: "There are two kinds of people—those who *have* lost data, and those who *will* lose data." If you use computers long enough, you'll fall victim to an event like those described above. Or you'll find yourself a victim of your own missteps. (I'll admit to accidentally deleting a folder of documents that shouldn't have been deleted.) The only way you can prevent such an event from being truly disastrous is to back up your data. In fact, I'll put it bluntly—you can master every topic in this book, but if you're not backing up important data, you're not a "power user."

The subject of data backups is a complex one, and there are scores of ways in which you can go about backing up. There are also many different utilities available to help you. Although I could walk you through the steps needed to perform a certain type of backup, it may not be the best method for you. Because my space is limited, I'm instead going to talk about some of the basics of backing up, including general strategies and tips. If you're not schooled in the art of backups, the ideas discussed here should at least get you thinking about what you need to do to keep your data safe.

Finally, I'm also going to mention some of the tools that are out there to help you make backing up less of a hassle, and a couple of utilities that will allow you to *synchronize* volumes or directories. (Synchronization is technically a form of backup, but it's also a matter of convenience if you just want to keep the same data on two computers or volumes.)

Backups 101

Everyone's heard about the concept of "backing up data," but few people really take a step back and think about the process methodically. Here are some things to consider when deciding on a backup strategy.

How Much/What to Back Up

How much of your data you should back up depends on two things: which files are *vital*, and how much time you're willing to spend getting your computer back up and running. The first criterion is simple—if you need a document and it would be difficult, impossible, or impractical to recreate, make sure it gets backed up. This is a good argument for making sure that you at *least* back up your `~/Documents` directory on a regular basis (and for making sure that you store your documents and personal files *in* that directory). If anything ever goes wrong, at the very least you'll still have your personal files, documents, e-mail, etc.

The second criterion, however, is one that many people never consider—in addition to losing documents, a computer disaster can result in the loss of applications, third-party system add-ons, preference files, browser bookmarks, and many other types of data that may not be "vital," but that nevertheless are important to your everyday work. If they don't get backed up and your hard drive dies, is stolen, or has to be rebuilt for any other reason, anything that wasn't backed up is going to have to be manually reinstalled (in the case of applications and system add-ons) and/or set up (application preferences, bookmarks, system settings, etc.). If you can't afford to spend the kind of time necessary to restore your computer to its "working" status from scratch, you should consider backing up more than just your Documents folder.

In my opinion, you should *always* make sure `~/Library` is backed up in addition to your Documents folder, since your Library folder contains all of your personal settings and support files. For example, your Address Book database, iCal calendars, personal system add-ons, OS X Favorites, Keychain file, browser bookmarks, application settings, and possibly even your e-mail are stored in your personal Library folder. Backing up this folder will save you a *lot* of work if you ever have to start over.

WARNING I mentioned in Chapter 5 that OS X uses invisible files quite frequently; unfortunately, these files do not get copied when your drag a folder between volumes, meaning that you can't simply back up your Library folder (or an entire OS X volume) using drag-and-drop in the Finder as you could in OS 9. You need to use a utility that is OS X–savvy (or Terminal's `ditto -rsrc` command).

Finally, if you want to be sure to get *all* of your personal data, including your iPhoto databases, iTunes music, the contents of your Desktop folder, your personal website files, etc., you need to back up your entire user folder. The only drawback is that photos and music take up a lot of space. But, again, it gets back to how much work you're willing to do to get back to your original state after a disaster. If you can't spare the hours it took you to rip your music from CD to MP3 for iTunes, you should back up your iTunes Music folder (inside `~/Music`); likewise for your iPhoto database of photos (inside `~/Pictures`).

TIP The discussion here makes a good argument for *always* storing important documents inside the folders you regularly back up. It also makes a good case for installing system add-ons at the user level, rather than the system level, since a good backup of user folders means you won't have to reinstall these add-ons in case you ever have to rebuild your hard drive.

If you're an admin user, you have a few additional things to consider. First, are you responsible for making sure *other* users' data is backed up? If so, you'll want to back up other user folders, as well. Second, do you have the time to manually reinstall every application? If not, consider backing up the Applications folder. Finally, do you have the time to manually reconfigure the entire system? In the worst case scenario, your computer will need to be set up from scratch, meaning you'll have to install OS X, create all user accounts, restore applications and user data, edit preferences and possibly configuration files, and so on. Personally, I don't have time for this, since my Mac is my livelihood, so I actually back up my entire system.

TIP Another benefit of having a complete system backup is that if your computer ever starts having serious problems, instead of spending time tracking down problems, you have the option of simply erasing the hard drive and restoring everything from the last "healthy" backup.

How Often to Back Up

The question of how much time you can afford to lose is also relevant when you're deciding how *often* to back up. To put it another way, in the event of a data disaster, you'll have to manually re-create any work you completed between the time of the disaster and the time of your last backup. If you only back up once a week, that means you could conceivably lose up to a week's worth of work. If you back up once a day, the most you could lose is a day's work. (If your work is especially important or time-sensitive, you can—and should—back up documents you're working on even more frequently.)

Local or Removable Backups?

How "safe" your backups are depends largely on where they reside. Here are a few examples, in increasing order of safety:

- If you just want to make sure you have an extra copy of a document or documents in case you change your mind about edits or modifications you're making, simply making copies on your hard drive is sufficient. However, this is more of a "convenience" backup than a true backup procedure, since it won't help you if your hard drive dies—you'll lose all of your copies with the originals.
- If you have a second internal hard drive, you can copy or (using a backup utility like those mentioned later in the chapter) archive files to the extra hard drive. This provides a convenient and fairly reliable backup, since the second drive should still work fine even if your primary hard drive dies. However, such a backup won't do you much good in the event of theft or disaster (such as a fire or severe power surge), since the second hard drive will fall victim to the same fate as the primary drive.

WARNING Disk partitions that reside on the same physical hard drive are not a good choice for backups, since a hard drive failure will generally render all partitions on that drive equally inoperable.

- If you have some sort of removable or portable media, such as an external hard drive, CD-R or CD-RW, DVD-R, magneto-optical disk, tape drive, etc., you can use it for backing up data. The advantage here is that not only is your data stored on a *different* storage device than your internal hard drive, but the backup is also removable/portable, so it can be stored separately from your computer. If your backups are kept at a different location than your computer, your data is still safe in case of theft or disaster.

TIP If your main reason for backing up files isn't necessarily safety from theft or disaster, but rather to have an immediately accessible copy of all data in case of drive failure, you can use two identically sized hard drives to create what is known as a *mirrored RAID*. When you have such a setup, all data is written to both drives at all times, so you always have two copies of every piece of data. I don't have the space to go into detail about RAIDs, but you can use Disk Utility to create them.

Businesses that rely on data often take these measures to the extreme. For example, many businesses use a system of on-site/off-site rotating backups. They continually back up data throughout the day, and at the end of each day they give their daily backup media to a data storage service that stores it in disaster-proof, secure data vaults. At the same time, the service returns a previous day's media to the company for use in the next round of backups. This setup ensures that the current day's data is immediately accessible, but data from previous days, weeks, or even years, is securely stored at a remote, secure location. This may sound extreme to the average home user, but if data is the heart of your business, such measures are standard practice.

What Kind of Media to Use for Backups

In addition to thinking about what to back up, and how often to do so, you should also consider what kind of media to use. There are a few things to think about when considering backup media: reliability, cost, performance, capacity, reusability, and portability. Here are some of the most common types of media, and their performance on these criteria:

CD-R Extremely reliable, provided you use reliable blank media (some of the bargain brands are reported to degrade over time). Blank CDs are extremely cheap (100 for around $30 for name-brand media), and hold 650–700MB each. Data must be written using a CD-R drive, but can be retrieved using any CD-ROM drive. Unfortunately, discs cannot be reused and are easily damaged.

CD-RW Almost identical to CD-R discs, but can be erased and reused (but for a price—CD-RW discs are significantly more expensive than CD-R media). Require a CD-RW drive to write data, but data can be read from most CD-ROM drives.

DVD-R Similar to CD-R discs, but with a much larger capacity (>4GB per disc) and more expensive ($5–$10 per disc). Require a DVD-ROM drive to write and retrieve data.

Zip disk Although Zip disks are very popular, I don't recommend using them for backup purposes. As a floppy disk-based medium, they are not reliable enough, in my experience, to be used for data backup.

Magneto-optical disk Considered to be the most reliable backup media on the market, and a good compromise between the reliability of optical media and the speed of magnetic (hard drive) media. They are the most expensive media in terms of cost/capacity. Disks are small, reusable, and almost indestructible.

Magnetic tape The mainstay of large-capacity commercial backups because of its combination of reliability, small physical size, and cost per GB (when purchased in bulk, less than $10 for 40GB of storage). Tapes can be reused many times. The downside to tape is that restoring files is very slow, and most tape drives do not allow random access (i.e., you can't mount a tape and copy files; you have to use a backup utility to restore files). Subject to data loss from strong magnetic fields.

Hard drive Overall, less reliable than other media, but considering that you're storing a copy of data, rather than the *only* copy, generally reliable enough. Second only to tape in terms of capacity for the price. Drives of 80GB can be had for under $100, and $300 can get you 300+GB. Backing up and retrieving data is very fast. Can be erased and reused easily. Larger than other media, but in a portable enclosure, still "tote-able." Like tape, subject to data loss from strong magnetic fields.

Online/Network In addition to local, physical media, it's also possible to use an online or networked backup service. For example, Apple's .Mac service allows you to use its Backup application to back up files to your personal iDisk over the Internet. Another popular Mac-focused online backup service is BackJack (`http://www.backjack.com/`). The clear advantage to an online backup is that it is located off-site. The disadvantages are than you must be connected to the Internet to back up or restore; copying files is usually slower than with local media; and the amount of data you can back up is often limited. (.Mac's iDisks only store 100MB of data unless you pay to upgrade your storage.)

Backup Strategies

Unfortunately, the subject of backup strategies is a complex one that requires far more space than I have here; entire books have been written on the topic. If you're interested in more information on specific backup strategies, I recommend Adam Engst's series of articles for the TidBITS electronic newsletter at `http://db.tidbits.com/getbits.acgi?tbser=1041`. In addition, Apple's Knowledge Base contains an article that includes a number of strategies for backing up, as well as a useful section that outlines the steps to take if you ever need to restore user folders; you can read that article at `http://docs.info.apple.com/article.html?artnum=106941`.

In case you're curious about my personal backup strategy, keep in mind that as a writer, *all* my work is on my computer, and losing a week's worth of data could be disastrous. For example, it could mean losing an entire chapter of this book! So I practice "backup overkill"—I can't afford to lose even a day's work. Here are the parts of my backup strategy:

- I have a second internal hard drive that I use to mirror my boot volume. Every morning at 2A.M., a shell script (created using Carbon Copy Cloner, which I'll talk about in the next section) runs that compares the contents of the backup drive with the boot volume; any new or modified files are copied to the backup drive, and any files deleted from the boot volume are also deleted from the backup. This means that the backup drive will always contain an *exact* copy of my *entire* boot volume as of 2 A.M.. If my boot volume has problems, I can quickly erase it and restore it from the backup (or, if I just need a copy of one or more files, I can simply copy them from the backup drive). If my boot volume fails completely, I can simply select the backup drive as my startup disk and keep working. The only thing I lose is any work I've done between the time of the problem and 2 A.M. earlier that day. (Which, I hope, is taken care of using the next item.)

- I also have a small, external FireWire hard drive that is used for periodic backups throughout the day. I use Retrospect (a backup utility mentioned in the next section) to automatically back up my Documents and Desktop folders at 10 A.M., 1 A.M., 5 P.M., 9 P.M., and 1 A.M. every day. If anything happens, I lose a few hours of work, at most. This backup drive also comes with me whenever I leave home for more than the day.
- I have a magneto-optical (MO) drive that I use for "permanent" off-site backups. Once every couple of weeks, I back up my Documents folder to MO disks, and then take those disks to a friend or relative's house for storage. (I sometimes also use CDs to burn copies of photos, older documents, and other files that I want to keep safe, and store those off-site.)

This strategy is both convenient and secure, as it lets me immediately get up and running in the event of a serious hard drive problem, but it also keeps a regular backup of the most important files that is stored off-site in case of a major disaster. It sounds like overkill, but keep in mind that for this book I tested literally hundreds of pieces of software—many of which altered the OS, and some of which were beta versions—so I was asking for trouble on a daily basis. On more than one occasion my Mac had serious problems due to my experimentation, yet I was never down for more than a couple of hours.

Backup Utilities

There are more backup-oriented utilities for OS X than you can shake a stick at—a search for "backup" on VersionTracker.com produces almost 60 results! In addition, you can use Terminal manually, or via a utility such as Carbon Copy Cloner, to copy or synchronize files from one volume to another.

I would love to walk you through some of my favorite backup and synchronization utilities—really, I would; there are so many cool backup utilities out there now that there's no excuse *not* to back up—but I'm running out of space in this chapter. Instead, I'm going to mention a few of the best; most have great documentation that, along with the general backup concepts I've covered, should get you up and running quickly. Most also offer additional features like *scheduled backups* (updating your backup with new and modified files according to a schedule), *cloning* (making an exact copy of a folder or volume that is usable in the Finder), and *synchronization* (a two-way procedure used to keep two folders or volumes up to date so that they each contain the newest version of every file).

NOTE Most backup utilities require administrator access, since they need to back up files regardless of the owner, and since they usually require a system-level startup item or access to the system's crontab to schedule automated backups.

In terms of traditional "backup" software—utilities that are intended to help you archive files for safekeeping, and restore them if needed at a later date—Dantz's Retrospect (`http://www.dantz.com/products/mac.html`, commercial) has long been the king, and for good reason. It's got more features and functionality than anything else on the market, making it the most powerful and flexible option available. Home users should consider the Express or Desktop versions, which offer more than enough features for most people. The main differences are that Desktop—which costs a bit more—adds the ability to back up to tape drives, to back up over a network, to watch for laptops and back them up when they connect to the network, and the ability to create custom file filters that control exactly what files are backed up (or not).

Although Retrospect is highly respected as a backup tool, the main criticism of it has been its user interface and learning curve. Because it has so many features and options, it can be a bit intimidating; in addition, the average user really doesn't need many of its more advanced features. As a result, a lot of alternatives to Retrospect have sprung up. Two of the best are Prosoft's Data Backup X (`http://www.prosoftengineering.com/products/`, commercial) and the shareware DéjàVu (`http://propagandaprod.com/`). Data Backup X actually has many (though not all) of the same features as Retrospect, but its interface is much more accessible for the average user. For example, you can execute an immediate backup, restore files from backup, copy/clone files or a volume, synchronize folders or volumes, or compress a folder or volume, all by simply clicking on a button in the main window (Figure 14.8). Data Backup X also has a convenient "compare folders" function that tells you the differences between the contents of any two folders. If you want to create a scheduled action, the various options are explained clearly so that you know exactly what your newly created schedule will do, and when. Data Backup X is fairly new to OS X, but it should give Retrospect a run for its money as one of the best full-featured backup utilities for home users.

DéjàVu is much more limited than Retrospect or Data Backup X, but it's also incredibly easy to set up. It runs as a preference pane, and provides a simple list of folders to be backed up (Figure 14.9). You click the + button to add a new schedule, select how often you want it backed up (daily, weekly, or monthly), and then choose the folder to be backed up and the destination for the backup. The Options screen lets you specify the times and days/dates the backup should occur, and you can also choose to mirror the folder instead of archive it (mirroring means that if you delete a file or folder from the original folder, it will also be deleted from the backup).

Finally, DéjàVu provides a convenient display of when the most recent daily, weekly, and monthly backups were executed, so you know exactly when your files were last backed up.

FIGURE 14.8: Data Backup X's main (left) and new scheduled action (right) windows

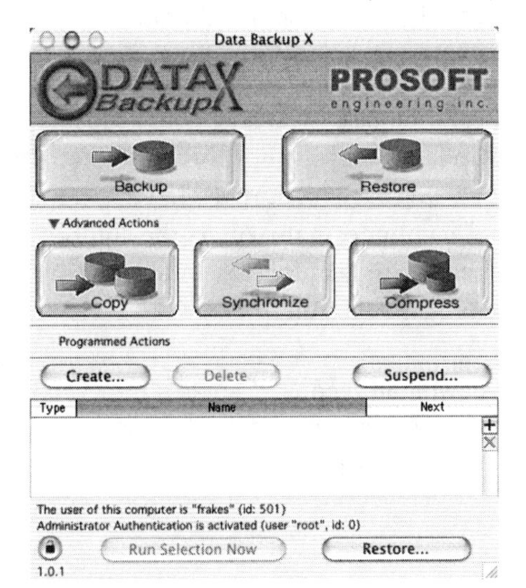

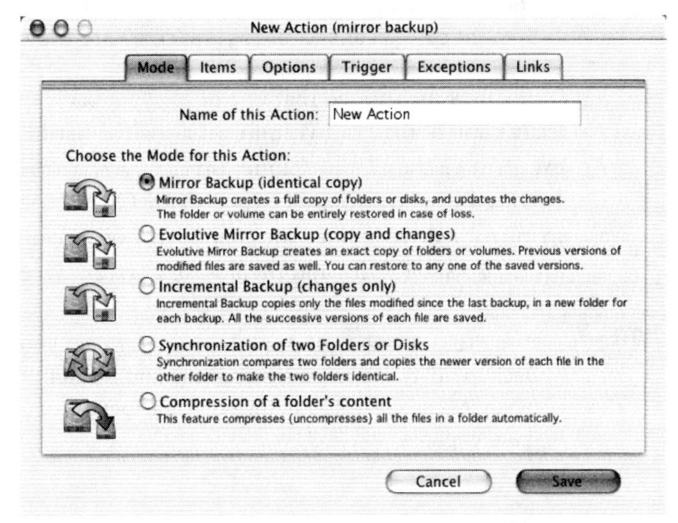

FIGURE 14.9: DéjàVu's backup scheduler is simple to set up.

TIP If your main goal is to synchronize two folders or volumes so that they each contain the newest version of every file—for example, to keep your Documents folder on your laptop and your desktop Mac in sync—you may want to consider a dedicated synchronization utility. The shareware ExecutiveSync (`http://www.executivesync.com/`) and Chrono-Sync (`http://econtechnologies.com/`) are two of the best.

Finally, I mentioned that one of my "get back up and running fast" strategies is to keep an exact copy of my boot volume on a second hard drive, updated nightly. For this I use the excellent Carbon Copy Cloner (`http://www.bombich.com/software/ccc.html`). In Chapter 4 I showed you how to use Carbon Copy Cloner to "clone" a volume; it also offers the ability to mirror a drive and update that mirror on a regular schedule. In fact, it actually does this by creating a shell script and then using a system-level crontab entry to run it!

NOTE If you're a member of Apple's .Mac service, you can download a copy of Apple's own Backup utility. However, I personally find Backup to be extremely limited and don't recommend it. There are too many other inexpensive backup solutions available that are much more capable.

Moving On...

Now that you've learned more about what it takes to keep your Mac running smoothly, it's time to move on to the ultimate "power user" topic: Unix. I've talked about OS X's Unix background many times over the past 14 chapters, and I've even had you work with it a number of times. But in the next chapter I'm going to talk about the Unix underneath OS X in depth, cover some more complex Unix exercises, and even show you how to take advantage of those Unix roots to install and use additional software titles.

CHAPTER 15

Utilizing Unix

(Or: Unix is not just a four-letter word.)

Although OS X is built on Unix, Apple has done an amazing job of shielding users from the command line; in fact, it's possible to completely ignore the Unix layers running "under the hood," if desired. Nevertheless, every time OS X boots up, it starts out as a command-line system, loading the familiar Aqua interface only after the Unix-based *Darwin* environment—which is always in the background, managing hardware and software—is ready. This means the command line is the ultimate power tool in OS X. It provides a "back door" to many advanced and hidden capabilities built into OS X.

In addition, OS X's Unix compatibility allows you to use a host of powerful (and often free) Unix programs. The best known is probably the Apache web server, but OS X also runs hundreds of other Unix-based programs such as the `vi` and `emacs` editors, the `ipfw` firewall, and the `perl` programming language (all built into the standard OS X installation; adding more programs can be surprisingly easy). Although OS X's Unix subsystem can be a bit intimidating to new users, Darwin brings a wealth of new capabilities to OS X. I'll spend this chapter talking about many of these features, and showing you ways to take advantage of them.

As I mentioned in the book's acknowledgments, the bulk of this chapter's content was contributed by Chris Pepper. You can find Chris online at `http://www.reppep.com/~pepper/`.

What Is Unix Doing in Mac OS X?

To leapfrog past limitations built into the Classic Mac OS (particularly in the areas of stability, memory management and multitasking), Apple went back to the drawing board for Mac OS X. The result was a hybrid operating system based on NeXTStep—a Unix-based OS developed by NeXT Computer, Steve Jobs' post-Apple company—but with an interface closer to Mac OS 9. The bulk (and benefits) of each system have been carried forward into OS X: the BSD Unix/Mach layer of NeXTStep is now called Darwin and manages booting, memory management, multitasking, and drivers; a few of the best aspects of the NeXTStep interface have been combined with Apple's Classic Mac OS appearance to create the Aqua interface; finally, the advanced programming environment developed at NeXT has become what we now know as Cocoa. (You'll remember Cocoa from Chapter 7 when I talked about Cocoa applications.)

As a result of its hybrid nature, OS X is extremely mature and stable in some areas, but less mature in others. Apple has changed many Application Programming Interfaces (APIs) with each revision, and continues to flesh out aspects of the system. In many cases, Apple has included useful features of NeXTStep, FreeBSD, and NetBSD without providing easy access to this functionality.

The good news, as you have seen in examples throughout the book, is that Terminal provides access to a great deal of this untapped power. In addition, many developers have created third-party tools that allow you to access features Apple hasn't (yet) exposed, without having to delve into Terminal. NFS Manager (mentioned in Chapter 10), which allows you to use the NFS client and server built into OS X, and BrickHouse (discussed in Chapter 12), which provides an interface for the built-in `ipfw` firewall, are good examples. Apple continues to expose more hidden functionality with each release, and Mac OS X Server distinguishes itself largely by providing better Aqua configuration tools for programs included in OS X. However, because most of the actual features of OS X Server exist in the standard version of OS X, power users with sufficient knowledge are able to take advantage of Mac OS X Server's functionality using the much less expensive non-Server version of OS X. What's more, knowledge of the appropriate command-line programs and third-party utilities can often provide access to "next year's" features before Apple makes them officially available.

NOTE For more information about Mac OS X's underlying architecture and Apple's open-source Darwin project, check out `http://developer.apple.com/darwin/projects/darwin/` and `http://developer.apple.com/macosx/architecture/`. You can learn more about OS X's Unix roots at `http://developer.apple.com/techpubs/macosx/Darwin/GettingStarted/PortingUNIX/background/index.html`.

Understanding Unix: Philosophy and Design Decisions

For many years, the Mac OS and Unix were at opposite ends of the computing spectrum. Apple has consistently worked to make the Mac easier to use and more consistent in its methods of operation than other computers, while Unix developers…haven't. This isn't because Apple was smart and Unix developers were dumb, but rather because they had very different priorities. A little understanding of the attitudes behind Unix can help you understand the different choices that Unix developers have made, and what they achieved. The goal of Mac OS X, after all, is to unite both efforts into a consistent whole, with advantages from both sides of its heritage.

The canonical book about Unix is *The UNIX Programming Environment* (`http://cm.bell-labs.com/cm/cs/upe/`), and its title illustrates the most significant difference between Unix and the

Classic Mac OS: Unix was originally intended to be a tool for programmers. This is in sharp contrast to Apple's portrayal of the Classic Mac OS as a friendly tool to bring computers to "the rest of us." Unix's designers hoped that its users would learn programming by using Unix, whereas Apple decided that users should be shielded from such "intimidating" details. Thus, while the Classic Mac OS has made a point of insulating users from the innards of the operating system, Unix has focused on providing full access to those details.

Now that Apple has officially killed off Mac OS 9 in favor of Mac OS X, Mac users have a few adjustments to make; understanding a bit about Unix can make those adjustments much more rewarding, and less frustrating.

Some Specifics of Unix Philosophy

Unix is not only different than the Classic Mac OS in the way it looks. Its very nature—the way it runs, the way it uses and manages files, and even the extent to which it trusts the user—is vastly different. I talked a bit about this in Chapter 1 when I discussed file organization and user accounts. Here are a few other things to keep in mind as you get to know the Unix side of OS X.

The Unix Approach to Getting Things Done

Unix systems are normally controlled through a *shell* program (discussed in more detail in the next section). Shells have two modes, *interactive* and *scripted*. In scripted mode, a shell reads a file of commands and executes them, normally without user interaction; in interactive mode, the shell accepts commands from the keyboard in real time. Both modes, however, use the same syntax and commands. This means that when you type a Unix command and press the return key to execute it, you have just written and run a one-line program. In this way, Unix breaks down the barrier between *programming* a computer and *using* a computer, and encourages normal users to become programmers.

In the Mac OS (including X), the Finder is the centerpiece. It's the fundamental program that you use to start other applications and to manage your files. In a Unix environment, including OS X's Darwin, the shell is the program launcher, but file management is delegated to other programs, including `cp` (copy), `mv` (move or rename), and `rm` (remove). In contrast to the Finder, the shell is deliberately kept small (300KB, versus 6MB for the Finder) to make the whole system more modular.

Carrying this further, Unix emphasizes small and flexible programs and facilitates linking them together to solve larger problems. (If you remember Apple's OpenDoc technology, now you know where Apple got the inspiration.) Unix links programs with files, pipes, redirection, and various other channels in order to accomplish more complex actions (see "Program Input and Output" later in the chapter for more on linking programs). In fact, even basic use of the command line often involves linking two or more programs.

To perform groups or series of actions, Unix systems use *scripts* of linked shell commands. In fact, many of the startup services I talked about in Chapter 3 are in fact sophisticated shell scripts. These shell scripts provide excellent examples for understanding and manipulating the way the system works—imagine being able to look inside a crashing extension in Mac OS 9, see the bug causing the crash, and fix it. Unix makes this feasible (although not necessarily easy).

Why Permissions Are Important

In an attempt to shield users from the consequences of mistakes, OS X's graphical interface provides warnings before performing dangerous actions (e.g., confirmation before emptying the Trash). Unix is much less protective—it will silently allow a user to delete essential files, rendering the system unusable, so long as the user has the appropriate privileges. This is why Unix books (and Chapter 1 in this book) routinely warn about the dangers of root access, and the useful but dangerous `rm -R` command, both of which can wreck a Unix system if used improperly. Permissions mitigate this risk by preventing casual users from tampering with system files, and help prevent 4-year-olds from trashing vital files. By encouraging users to work in non-privileged accounts, and requiring the entry of a password to perform dangerous actions, Unix actually goes further in safeguarding certain actions, while still giving users complete control over their systems.

Files and...Well...More Files

It may sound strange, but nearly *everything* is a file in Unix. What you would think of as "normal" files—a text document, spreadsheet, etc.—are very similar to files in the Classic Mac OS: sequences of bytes. However, a directory is really just a special file containing a list of files the "directory" contains. Disks and disk partitions are special files called *block devices*; terminals (representing user input and output) are character files, and various other useful objects, including monitors, keyboards, and running programs, are *character devices*. This enables the file security model (owners, groups, and permissions) I've discussed previously to manage other resources, such as shared memory and sending messages between users.

In addition, files have two separate parts: a name (also called a path), and data contained in the file. Most operating systems can have empty files that have a name but contain no data, but Unix also allows special files that contain usable data, but have no filenames, or that have more than one filename. Again, this extends the power of Unix by allowing standard file-handling code to communicate with other programs (using special files called standard input, standard output, and standard error), or the screen and keyboard. This also helps make programming easier, since powerful file management is provided "for free" by the OS, and it helps make shell programming more like interactive use, providing much of the power of AppleScript across command-line programs without requiring programmers to add special AppleEvent support.

Getting Started with Terminal and a Shell

You can think of Terminal's command-line interface as a way to look "under the hood" of Mac OS X. You can see what's going on, and even poke around a bit, if you like. However, it's important to realize that working at the command line isn't really working *in* Terminal so much as *through* it. Terminal is simply a tool that acts as an intermediary between you and the command-line environment; it doesn't *do* much of anything itself (somewhat like the steering wheel and pedals of a car, which don't actually move the car down the road, but enable you to direct the engine and wheels).

The most important program in a command-line interface is the *command shell*. The shell is your agent, relaying your commands to the kernel and other programs, showing you their responses, and providing a programming environment in which you can execute commands and scripts. Modern shells also provide a great deal of assistance in managing the command line—to help make using other command-line programs more efficient. The default shell in OS X is called `tcsh`, and is used whenever you launch Terminal (unless you've specifically told the system to use a different shell); we'll look at `tcsh` later in the chapter. More advanced `tcsh` programming, including looping and `if/else` processing, is beyond the scope of this book, but if you'd like to read further, the `tcsh` manual page (and the Internet) contain a wealth of further information on shell programming.

Command-Line Programs Included in Mac OS X

Hundreds of command-line programs are already installed on your Mac in several directories; the PATH variable lists these directories. I'll talk more about PATH later in the chapter (see "Variables"), but for now you might be interested in viewing a list of the available programs. Here are a few Terminal commands to try; since the `echo`, `ls`, and `du` commands only *report* data (i.e., they don't change anything), it's safe to experiment with them.

`echo $PATH <RETURN>`

Lists the directories on your computer where command-line programs are stored, separated by colons.

`ls /usr/bin <RETURN>`

Lists the programs residing in `/usr/bin`.

`du -ks /usr/bin/* | sort -n <RETURN>`

Lists the contents of `/usr/bin`, providing each file's size in kilobytes, sorted by size. The asterisk is what is called a *wildcard*; it means "any character or characters, including no characters," and tells the du command to list *all* files in `/usr/bin`.

A command line generally consists of a command program (the first word of the line) followed by *arguments* that tell the program exactly what to do. When you press the return key, the shell interprets the command line, passes it to the specified program, and then displays the program's output, if there is any.

Most commands are individual programs, each much smaller than a full Mac application and located in one of the directories you saw in your `PATH`. However, each shell contains a set of built-in commands as well. In `tcsh`, typing **`builtins`** **<RETURN>** (try it now) lists these internal commands, and you can see instructions for using them in the `tcsh` manual page (under "Builtin commands"; I'll talk more about manual pages in a bit). Builtins like `set` and `printenv` manage `tcsh` itself; builtins like `foreach` and `while` provide programming functionality, and builtins like `ls-F` and `time` provide frequently used capabilities without execution of external programs.

Command Structure: An Example

Let's try a few simple commands and analyze what they do. The meanings of each *argument* are determined by the command they follow, but most arguments specify either files to manipulate (read, write, search, move, etc.) or *options* that modify the program's behavior.

Options (also called flags) modify the behavior of a command; for example, the `grep` command's `-i` option makes `grep` (a text-searching utility) ignore case when searching (the default is to search case sensitively). To help distinguish options from other arguments, options are normally preceded by a dash (-). They can be combined in any order; however, they must precede other (non-option) arguments on the command line. In addition to on/off switches, more complicated options may be followed by additional text, as a sort of argument to the option itself.

WARNING Unix filesystems and Unix programs are case sensitive, whereas the Classic Mac OS, OS X's Finder, and Apple's HFS and HFS Plus file systems are case insensitive and case preserving. For example, using UFS (the Unix File System), you can save different files named *MyFile* and *myfile* in the same directory, but on HFS Plus volumes the names are equivalent, so the second file overwrites the first. This is also important because Unix programs tend to be case sensitive, and assume that the file system is as well. For example, if you search for *myfile* in Terminal (even on an HFS Plus volume) the program you're using (`locate`, `tcsh`, `ls`, `grep`, etc.) will ignore *MyFile*, as it is assumed to be a different file. (Although you can force `tcsh`'s command completion to be case insensitive with **`set complete=enhance`** **<RETURN>**. See the `tcsh` manual page under "Completion and listing" for full details.) For more information on the challenges of combining Unix and the Mac OS, check out `http://www.usenix.org/publications/library/proceedings/usenix2000/invitedtalks/sanchez_html/`.

Finally, although the order of options is unimportant, the order of *other* arguments is generally very important. For example, the command `grep/bin/sh/etc/rc` would search for the string /bin/sh in the file /etc/rc (and would find it); if you instead used grep/etc/rc/bin/sh, it would search for any occurrence of the string /etc/rc in the file /bin/sh (and wouldn't find it).

Table 15.1 lists a few commonly used commands, along with their basic functions, some possible options, and normal arguments for each (if applicable).

TABLE 15.1: Some Basic Commands

Command	Function	Options	Other Arguments
ls	List files	"-l": use long listing format "-F": show file-type suffixes	Which files to list, or which directories' contents to list (defaults to current directory)
pwd	Print Working Directory	N/A	N/A
cd	Change Directory	N/A	Which directory to change to (defaults to user's home directory)
grep	Search	"-i": search case insensitively "-v": search for non-matching lines "-l": list files that match, but don't show the actual matches	1: string for which to search 2: file(s) to search
curl	Download or Upload files	"-i": include http header in output "-o ***file***": save output in *file* (otherwise it is sent to standard output) "-O": use the remote filename (from the URL) as the local filename "-u ***user:password***": provide this username and password to the remote sever; if password isn't supplied, curl will prompt for it (this is more secure, as command-line arguments may show up in ps and command history)	URLs (HTTP, FTP, or various other formats) to get or put
open	Open in Finder	"-a": specify application for opening file	Which file/folder/application to open

Basic Commands: A Walk-through

It's time to see some of the commands I just talked about in action. Launch Terminal (or open a new Terminal window if it's already running) and follow along.

1. Type **`ls` <RETURN>**. The output of the command lists the contents of the default directory. But what directory is that?
2. Type **`pwd` <RETURN>** to see what the current *working* directory is. (The working directory is the one you are currently working in; it's a bit like the frontmost window in the Finder.) Chances are it will be `/Users/`*`YourUsername`*, your home directory—this is the default directory when you open a new shell session (Terminal window).
3. Type **`ls /` <RETURN>**. This command shows the contents of the top level of the startup disk (called the *`root`* directory—distinct from the `root` user). If you had typed just **`ls` <RETURN>**, you would have gotten a listing of the current working directory—in this case your home folder. However, by providing a directory path (in this case, /) as an argument, you instructed the `ls` command to give you a listing of that directory, instead.

WARNING In the Classic Mac OS (and from within applications in the Classic Environment), the top level of the file system is the Desktop, and each mounted volume appears there, along with any files in the Desktop Folder(s) of any mounted disks. In the OS X Finder, the top level of the file system is Computer, and all mounted disks and a Network item are there. In Unix (and therefore in Terminal in OS X), the top level of the file system is called "/" (the "root" of the file system) but is only the top-level directory of the startup volume; other disks and removable volumes are mounted inside `/Volumes`. (These are the most common layouts, although there are others that crop up in specific circumstances, such as Internet Explorer's Address field.) Because of these different—and confusing—approaches, it's important to realize that some items (particularly disks) are in different places depending on whether you're in a Classic, Cocoa, Carbon, or Unix application.

4. To move to the root directory type **`cd /` <RETURN>**. Note that after this command, the prompt shows a slash instead of a tilde, since you're no longer in your home directory.

TIP As I discussed in Chapter 1, ~/ is a way of referring to your home directory, and / is a way of referring to the root directory. In the shell (Terminal), you can use ~ or ~/ to refer to your home directory. For example, to change to your home directory, type **`cd ~` <RETURN>** or **`cd ~/` <RETURN>**. To refer to another user's home directory, use the username as well, as in ~*`username`* or ~*`username/`* (or `~root` or `~root/` for the home directory of the root user, `/var/root` by default).

5. Now that the root level of your startup disk is the working directory, using `ls` without any arguments lists the files there, instead of listing those in your home directory. You can add the `-l` option (the letter "l", not the number one) for a detailed ("long") listing and the `-F` option to view file-type suffixes. (Since options can be combined

and reordered, `ls -lF`, `ls -Fl`, `ls -l -F`, and `ls -F -l` are all equivalent.) In the detailed listing you'll see a few items with a dash in the first column and no suffix; these are standard files. Entries with a "d" in the first column and a slash suffix are directories. Files with an "l" in the first column and an @ symbol at the end are symbolic links (the Unix version of OS X's aliases); the long listing indicates the destination/target of the link using an arrow (e.g., `var@ -> private/var`).

6. Type **pwd <RETURN>** to confirm that you're actually at the root level of the startup disk.
7. Type **cd <RETURN>**. Note the prompt—it looks like you're back in your home directory, doesn't it? Type **pwd <RETURN>** to be sure. When you use the `cd` command without any arguments, it automatically (and conveniently) changes the active directory to your home directory.

TIP Files and directories in Unix normally have lowercase names and no spaces (spaces would complicate commands); for example, `etc` and `usr`. Apple has traditionally capitalized the first letter of each word in file and folder names and (in OS 9 and earlier) often used spaces (e.g., System Folder, Control Panels). In OS X, Apple avoids spaces in filenames, but does use capital letters on Apple-installed items (e.g., StartupItems). This makes it easy to figure out that `/etc/rc` is a traditional Unix file, while `/System/Library` is an Apple creation. However, in Terminal, spaces in file or path names can create problems, because they can be interpreted as spaces between command arguments. If you need to type a filename with a space or punctuation character, you should either put quotes around the whole filename or pathname (e.g., **ls '/System Folder' <RETURN>**), or use a backslash (\) just before the special character to *escape* it, so it's interpreted as a standard ASCII character, rather than its special meaning (e.g., **ls /System\ Folder <RETURN>**).

Learning New Programs: The *man* Command

When you need to use an unfamiliar command-line program, the `man` command is your friend. The `man` program takes one or more program names as arguments, and shows a descriptive manual page (often called the *man page*) for each listed program. As an example, typing **man ls <RETURN>** describes the `ls` program, including all 26 of its options. Most of these options are rarely needed, but you'll find several that can be very useful, as seen in Table 15.2.

TABLE 15.2: Some Useful Options for `ls`

option	function
-F	Include file-type suffixes
-R	List subdirectories recursively

Continued on next page

TABLE 15.2 CONTINUED: Some Useful Options for `ls`

option	function
-a	Show all files (normally, `ls` and other commands ignore files with names that start with a period, often called *dotfiles*; you'll remember from Chapter 5 that these files are normally invisible in the Finder)
-d	Show directories and symbolic links, instead of the files they contain or point to
-l	Use long format
-k	Show sizes in kilobytes instead of bytes
-t	Sort by modification date, recently modified items first

Most programs have fewer options than `ls`, and most options are never needed. However, as a new Unix user, you're likely to find yourself looking up many new and seldom-used commands for a while. Fortunately, `man` is powerful and easy to use. Unfortunately, manual pages are not always well written, and early versions of Mac OS X shipped with obsolete and incomplete `man` pages; Apple improved the state of `man` pages with OS X 10.1, and man pages in 10.2 are now generally correct and current.

The *man* Command in Action: Leveraging Other Programs

The `man` command is a good example of Unix philosophy—it combines multiple programs to perform its function. Because command descriptions are often more than one screen long, `man` uses a *pager* program to allow keyboard-based scrolling through the manual "page." The most popular pagers in OS X are `more` and `less`, each of which has its own `man` page. Fortunately, `less` is compatible with `more`'s commands, and both provide online help with the "h" key. Basic commands for both `more` and `less` are shown here.

Command	Function
h	Get help
q	Quit pager
<Space>	Scroll one page
/word	Search for *word* may actually be one or more characters, but punctuation marks may have special meanings, per `grep`).
/word/i	Search for word, case insensitively
.	Repeat last command

In addition to the pager, `man` uses `gzip` to read manual page source files (which are normally compressed to save space). Both the `more` and `less` pagers, in turn, incorporate regular expression syntax taken from the `grep` command.

TIP To learn more about the man command itself, try **man man**. To find help when you aren't sure what command you need, try **man -k *word***, where *word* is a word related to what you want to do; this will search the installed manual pages for occurrences of *word* in command names or descriptions. (You can also use **apropos *word***, which is equivalent to **man -k *word***.)

Finally, if reading long manual pages in Terminal is not your cup of tea, there are several utilities that present manual pages using a nice graphical interface; many even include clickable links to the manual pages of related commands. To view the current batch of these utilities, do a search for "man page" at on VersionTracker.com or MacUpdate.com.

Shells: *sh* versus *csh*

Steve Bourne was the creator of the first Unix shell, and with classic Unix terseness named it sh. The sh shell is extremely powerful, but, in a deliberate attempt to make interactive use as similar as possible to programming or "scripting," lacks many convenience features. Several alternative shells are included in OS X, notably csh (the incompatible C shell, with syntax closer to the C programming language), Bourne's own sh-compatible bash (the "Bourne Again Shell"—the default on Linux systems), and the csh-compatible tcsh—OS X's default.

As a rule, shells are fully compatible with either sh or csh, layering additional features on top of one or the other. For example, OS X uses a copy of bash as sh, and tcsh as csh (see Listing 15.1). This works because bash is backwards compatible with sh, and tcsh is compatible with csh (more details are available in their man pages). For maximum portability, system scripts are normally written in the basic sh syntax, and avoid advanced features of other shells that may be unavailable on some systems. In fact, the Unix boot process is based on sh scripts. This makes understanding and modifying the system startup process much easier, as the basic levels of the system consistently use the sh dialect.

NOTE While there are many differences between csh and sh syntax, they do not affect basic command invocation; rather, they show up in more advanced areas, such as variables, error redirection, conditional execution, and looping. Most examples in this chapter will work in any of the shells provided with OS X, but system scripts are written for sh, and user commands are normally written for tcsh. For more on variables in tcsh (which are handled differently than in sh-based shells), see the "Variables" section later in this chapter.

Listing 15.1 OS X includes several shells; here we see that sh and tcsh are located in /bin. If we look for other shells in /bin, we find that there are actually five. Finally, we see that sh is really bash, and that csh is actually the same as tcsh.

```
[g4:~] power% which sh tcsh
/bin/sh
/bin/tcsh
g4:~] power% ls -l /bin/*sh
```

```
-rwxr-xr-x  1 root  wheel  540884 Nov 22 19:47 /bin/bash
-r-xr-xr-x  1 root  wheel  315136 Nov 22 19:47 /bin/csh
-r-xr-xr-x  1 root  wheel  540884 Nov 22 19:47 /bin/sh
-r-xr-xr-x  1 root  wheel  315136 Nov 22 19:47 /bin/tcsh
-rwxr-xr-x  1 root  wheel  828780 Nov 22 19:47 /bin/zsh
[g4:~] power% diff --report-identical-files /bin/sh /bin/bash
Files /bin/sh and /bin/bash are identical
[g4:~] power% diff --report-identical-files /bin/tcsh /bin/csh
Files /bin/tcsh and /bin/csh are identical
```

As mentioned above, the default shell for OS X is `tcsh`. This is a good choice, as `tcsh` is sophisticated and has many convenient features that make using a command line easier and more efficient. Several other shells are provided with OS X, including `bash`, that provide many of the same conveniences.

Using Another Shell

To try another shell temporarily, just type its name within your current shell (e.g., **bash <RETURN>**). This will run the specified shell as a command (i.e., within your default shell), until you exit (by typing **exit <RETURN>** or **logout <RETURN>**, or pressing control+D), at which point you'll return to `tcsh`.

Command-Line Assistance

One of the areas in which `tcsh` excels is assisting you with interactive use. The `tcsh` shell can complete words automatically for you, offers good support for editing of command lines, and stores previous command lines for reuse. In addition, it has a spell checker that is surprisingly successful at DWIM (do what I mean). Table 15.3 includes some keyboard shortcuts for command-line editing in `tcsh` (most also apply to `bash`).

TABLE 15.3: Keyboard Shortcuts in the `tcsh` shell and `bash`

Keystroke	Effect
control+U	Clear line (this works in most Unix programs, and will either clear the whole line, or clear only the part of the line from the cursor to the beginning, leaving everything afterwards)
control+A	Move cursor to beginning of line
control+E	Move cursor to end of line
tab	Auto-complete current command/file/directory name (a beep here means there are ambiguous possibilities—type a bit more to remove the ambiguity, and then press tab again)
up arrow	Show previous command in history
down arrow	Show next command in history

Variables

Programming languages use *variables* to store working information, and shells are no exception. The tcsh shell uses both *local* and *environment* variables. Local variables are internal to a running copy of the shell, whereas environment variables are passed along to other programs the shell executes. Listing 15.2 shows an example of *local* variables in action.

Listing 15.2 Local variables in tcsh

```
[g4:~] power% set
PROXYFTP        ()
PROXYHTTP       ()
_       cd ..

addsuffix
argv    ()
cwd     /Users/power
dirstack        /Users/power
echo_style      bsd
edit
gid     20
group   staff
history 100
home    /Users/power
loginsh
owd     /Users/power/fink-0.5.0a-full
path    (/sw/bin /sw/sbin /bin /sbin /usr/bin /usr/sbin /usr/X11R6/bin)
prompt  [%m:%c3] %n%#
prompt2 %R?
prompt3 CORRECT>%R (y|n|e|a)?
promptchars     %#
shell   /bin/tcsh
shlvl   1
status  0
tcsh    6.10.00
term    vt100
tty     ttyp4
uid     504
user    power
version tcsh 6.10.00 (Astron) 2000-11-19 (powerpc-apple-darwin)
➥options 8b,nls,dl,al,sm,rh,color
```

If you look at what tcsh keeps in its local variables, you should recognize a lot of shell housekeeping information, such as the prompt string, working directory, username and user ID (uid), and various other bits. These variables are set automatically during tcsh's initialization process, but tcsh's behavior can be customized by setting a variety of additional special variables (explained under "Special shell variables" in the tcsh man page).

Shell Prompts

Unix shells normally present a *prompt* when they are ready to receive commands. You type in the desired command at the prompt and then press the return key to process it. When the system finishes executing the command, it presents another prompt. Prompts are generally controlled by a local `prompt` variable, and can provide useful information. Apple's default value for `prompt` is `[%m:%c3] %n%#`, which expands to [*<hostname>*:*<current directory>*] *<username><prompt character>*.

Each time `tcsh` presents a prompt, it scans through the value of the `prompt` variable, converting special tokens (sequences of characters starting with a percent sign) to the correct values, and then displays the prompt. The `%c3` token is *expanded* to the current directory, truncated to the last *three* (3) path elements so the prompt doesn't fill the whole line. The final prompt character indicates what type of shell is running. If the shell is running as root, the prompt will be #; if the user is not root, and the shell is `csh`-based, the prompt character is normally %, whereas `sh` shells use $ as the default non-root prompt. For example, on a system named g4, the initial prompt for the user *power* would be `[g4:~] power%`. To see other tokens you can put into your prompt, read the `prompt` entry under "Special shell variables" in the `tcsh` manual page.

To manage local variables, `tcsh` provides the `set` command. Without any arguments, `set` shows all local variables and their values (see Listing 15.2). To set a variable, use the command **`set myvariable=myvalue`** **<RETURN>**, which creates *myvariable* (if it wasn't already defined) and sets its value to *myvalue*. For example, the following command creates a new variable, *quantity* and sets its value to *10*:

```
[g4:~] power% set quantity=10
[g4:~] power%
```

The `echo` command prints the arguments it receives from the shell (which does variable expansion before passing them along to `echo`), so it is often used to show the values of variables. For example:

```
[g4:~] power% echo quantity
quantity
[g4:~] power%
```

Not what you expected? The above command told the shell to simply echo the word *quantity*. To use the *value* of a variable in a command line, precede its name with a dollar sign (`$`):

```
[g4:~] power% echo $quantity
10
[g4:~] power%
```

This usage tells the shell to send the *value* of the quantity variable to the `echo` program.

NOTE Unfortunately, sh and csh use different syntax to *set* variables, but use them similarly once set. More detail is available under "Variable substitution" in the tcsh manual page and under "Variables and Parameters" and the export command description in the sh manual page.

Environment variables are very similar to local variables, but as I mentioned previously, environment variables are passed along to other programs the shell executes. Environment variables are more important than local shell variables because they affect every program you run (local variables only affect the shell itself). To help you distinguish them from local variables, environment variables generally use capitalized names (local variables are usually lowercase). The tcsh shell complicates things a bit by using several local variables (such as path) that correspond to environment variables (such as PATH), but for the most part the distinction holds true. Listing 15.3 shows environment variables used by tcsh.

Listing 15.3 Environment variables in tcsh

```
[g4:~] power% setenv
TERM=vt100
USER=power
HOME=/Users/power
SHELL=/bin/tcsh
HOSTTYPE=macintosh
VENDOR=apple
OSTYPE=darwin
MACHTYPE=powerpc
SHLVL=1
PWD=/Users/power
LOGNAME=power
GROUP=staff
HOST=hostname.example.com
PATH=/sw/bin:/sw/sbin:/bin:/sbin:/usr/bin:/usr/sbin:/usr/X11R6/bin
MANPATH=/sw/share/man:/sw/man:/usr/local/share/man:
➥/usr/local/man:/usr/share/man:/usr/X11R6/man
INFOPATH=/sw/share/info:/sw/info:/usr/local/share/info:
➥/usr/local/lib/info:/usr/local/info:/usr/share/info
PERL5LIB=/sw/lib/perl5
[g4:~] power% setenv HOSTTYPE g4
[g4:~] power% echo $HOSTTYPE
g4
[g4:~] power%
```

The most important variable for everyday use is PATH, which controls where the shell (and other programs) looks for commands. Think how tiresome typing **/usr/bin/ls /Users/*username*** **<RETURN>** each time you wanted to use the ls command would become! With the PATH environment variable set to include the directory that contains the ls program (/usr/bin) and the PWD variable set to /Users/*username*, tcsh can expand ls to /usr/bin/ls for you, and ls knows to display /Users/*username* if you don't specify otherwise.

To define and assign environment variables, use the `setenv` command; its syntax is similar to that of `set`, but with a space instead of the equal sign.

Making Permanent Changes to *tcsh*

Changes made to `tcsh` during a shell session are normally lost after logout. To enable you to make changes that affect all future `tcsh` sessions, `tcsh` *sources* (executes the contents of) several files each time it starts (as described in the `tcsh` manual page under "Startup and shutdown"). First, each time `tcsh` starts, it executes any commands included in `/etc/csh.cshrc` and `/etc/csh.login`. (These are the *system-wide* initialization files, since every `tcsh` user on the system uses them.) In addition, if `~/.tcshrc` (a `.tcshrc` file in your personal home directory) exists, `tcsh` will source that; if not, it will source `~/.cshrc`, if available. Finally, `tcsh` sources the file `~/.login` if it exists.

This can all be confusing, but on a single-user system you can simply put `tcsh` commands in `~/.cshrc`, and they will be run every time you log in. If you have a `~/.tcshrc` file, it will be used *instead of* `~/.cshrc`. Since Apple doesn't provide either of these files for new users, you shouldn't have any trouble as long as you use one or the other consistently.

To create your own `.cshrc` or `.tcshrc` file that will be sourced every time `tcsh` runs, you can use any text editor that can read and save Unix-style line breaks (including Apple's TextEdit, if you choose Plain Text from the Format menu). You can include whatever `tcsh` commands you want, but `set`, `setenv`, and `alias` are the most common. Note that if you have BBEdit (`http://www.barebones.com/`) version 7.0 or later installed, you can actually type **`bbedit -u ~/.cshrc`** **<RETURN>** (or **`~/.tcshrc`**) in Terminal to edit the file in BBEdit.

In versions of OS X prior to Jaguar, Apple customized `tcsh` extensively, activating useful features that are generally disabled by default. With the release of Jaguar, Apple disabled most of this customization, making `tcsh` behave more like it does on other platforms. To see Apple's previous enhancements, check out the files in `/usr/share/tcsh/examples`.

Command Aliases

In addition to programs and builtins, a shell command might also be an *alias*. Not to be confused with Finder aliases, command aliases are user-defined commands that can be used to override existing commands (perhaps by making `rm` require confirmation before deleting files) or to create new shortcut commands with your favorite options, such as making `l` mean `ls -lF`. An alias command consists of a command word (the alias) and the command (and any options) you want executed when you use the alias (called the *expansion*).

To create a new alias, you need to use the `alias` command with two or more arguments: the first argument is the name of the new alias, and the rest of the line its expansion. For example, typing **alias shedit pico ~/.cshrc <RETURN>** creates a new alias, shedit, that, when typed in Terminal, is expanded by the shell to the command pico ~/.cshrc (which opens your shell configuration file in the pico text editor). I created this alias for myself because I could never remember the name ".cshrc"—I would always type ".schrc" or some other variation. Now whenever I want to edit my shell configuration, I simply type **shedit <RETURN>**.

When used without any arguments, the alias command lists any defined aliases (Apple doesn't provide any by default, so you probably won't see any if you try this and you haven't created any aliases of your own). If you use the alias command followed by a defined alias name, tcsh will show the expansion for that alias. If you decide you want to get rid of an alias, simply type **unalias *aliasname* <RETURN>** to remove it. These instructions for using aliases may sound complicated, but alias is actually quite simple and extremely useful. See Listing 15.4 for an example.

NOTE Note that if you use the alias command during a shell session, the alias you created is only valid until you log out. To make sure an alias is always available, you need to add it to your shell configuration file (see the sidebar "Making Permanent Changes to tcsh").

Listing 15.4 Using alias and unalias (the first line produces no response because no aliases exist yet)

```
[g4:~] power% alias
[g4:~] power% alias rm rm -i
[g4:~] power% alias l ls-F
[g4:~] power% alias sw ssh www
[g4:~] power% alias
l        ls-F
rm       (rm -i)
sw       (ssh www)
[g4:~] power% alias rm
rm -i
[g4:~] power% l
Desktop/   Library/   Music/     Public/
Documents/ Movies/    Pictures/  Sites/
[g4:~] power% unalias l
[g4:~] power% alias
rm       (rm -i)
sw       (ssh www)
```

Wildcards

Wildcard expansion is an extremely useful shell feature (handled similarly in both sh-based and csh-based shells, fortunately). Wildcards are characters with special meaning to the shell; the two most common wildcards are the question mark, ?, which stands for exactly one instance of any character (like a Joker, which can substitute for any other card), and the asterisk, *, which can represent anything, from nothing to a sequence of different characters. When you type a command containing wildcard characters and press the return key to execute it, `tcsh` examines each word containing wildcards and computes all the valid filenames that match the typed pattern; it then replaces the wildcard word with all the matches alphabetically. That sounds far more complicated than wildcards really are; here's an example that illustrates the concept more clearly:

```
[g4:~] power% ls /bin/*sh
/bin/bash /bin/csh  /bin/sh   /bin/tcsh /bin/zsh
[g4:~] power% ls /bin/?sh
/bin/csh /bin/zsh
[g4:~] power% ls /bin/??sh
/bin/bash /bin/tcsh
[g4:~] power% ls /bin/bash /bin/tcsh
/bin/bash /bin/tcsh
```

In this example, `*sh` means "any word of any length that ends in sh"; `?sh` means "any three-letter word that ends in sh"; and `??sh` means "any four-letter word that ends in sh."

Shell Scripts

If you type one or more valid commands into a text file and then save the file as *myscript* (just an example name), you can execute all of the commands contained in that file, one after another, by typing **sh */pathtofile/myscript* <RETURN>** or **tcsh */pathtofile/myscript* <RETURN>** (depending on what scripting syntax you used when writing the commands).

TIP To make a proper shell script that will garner the respect of Unix users everywhere, you should add comments describing what the script does and an initial line identifying which interpreter (shell) the script is written for, and give the script *execute* permission (using the command **chmod u+x *myscript* <RETURN>** in Terminal), so that it can be run as a normal program. To make sure your comments aren't interpreted by the shell as commands, begin each comment line with #. When the shell reads the script, it ignores everything after #, until the end of the line. In addition, the first line of a script is special; it should use the format `#!/path to interpreter` (i.e., `#!/bin/sh` for an `sh` script).

In fact, a significant proportion of the programs on a Unix system are just sophisticated scripts, as we can see by examining the programs in `/usr/bin` using the `ls` and `file` commands (Listing 15.5). In this example, we see that there are 552 programs (`wc -l` counts the number of lines in the listing), which includes over 50 `sh` scripts, over 400 compiled programs, and 40 `perl` scripts (`grep -c` counts the number of files that contain the designated text—which indicates each type of script—in the directory).

Listing 15.5 Types of Files in /usr/bin

```
[g4:~] power% ls /usr/bin | wc -l
552
[g4:~] power% file /usr/bin/* | grep -c Bourne
55
[g4:~] power% file /usr/bin/* | grep -c "C shell"
3
[g4:~] power% file /usr/bin/* | grep -c Mach-O
407
[g4:~] power% file /usr/bin/* | grep -c perl
40
```

In fact, if you think way back to Chapter 3, I pointed out that part of the OS X system initialization process is the execution of the script `/etc/rc`. Listing 15.6 shows the first 20 lines of `/etc/rc`, so you can see an example of an `sh` script.

Listing 15.6 How does OS X finish starting up? It runs an sh script!

```
[g4:~] power% file /etc/rc
/etc/rc: Bourne shell script text
[g4:~] power% head -20 /etc/rc

#!/bin/sh

##
# Multi-user startup script.
#
# Copyright 1997-2002 Apple Computer, Inc.
#
# Customize system startup by adding scripts to the startup
# directory, rather than editing this file.
##

##
# Set shell to ignore Control-C, etc.
# Prevent inadvertent problems caused by interrupting the shell during boot.
##

stty intr  undef
stty kill  undef
stty quit  undef
stty susp  undef
[g4:~] power%
```

Program Input and Output

One of the concepts that makes Unix so powerful and flexible is the premise that small, reusable programs can be combined to perform complex tasks. A program that takes input, processes it in some way, and produces output is called a *filter*, and extremely powerful processes can be created by combining simple filters. Among the most useful filters are `grep`, which searches for matching text, and `sort`, which can merge and/or sort files (sorting in forward or reverse order, alphabetically or numerically). Results may be saved to a file, fed to a pager like `more` or `less`, or passed on to another program, such as `head` or `tail` (to select the top or bottom lines from the summary of matches).

Pipes ("|")

Pipes accept the *output* of one program (called `stdout`, for standard output) and feed it to another program's *input* (called `stdin`, for standard input); pipelines may connect several different programs together, each with its own options. (I actually showed you a few examples of pipelines in Listing 15.6.) The pipeline **`ls -lt /usr/bin | more <RETURN>`**, for example, lists programs in `/usr/bin`, with details, sorted chronologically, one page at a time. In Listing 15.7, `| head -5` shows the first 5 lines of output and `| wc -l` counts lines.

Listing 15.7 Sample pipelines

```
[g4:~] power% ls -lt /var/log | head -5
total 888
-rw-r-----  1 root  admin   35493 Jan 15 21:27 system.log
-rw-r-----  1 root  admin   14140 Jan 15 18:58 lastlog
-rw-r-----  1 root  admin    3492 Jan 15 18:58 wtmp
-rw-r--r--  1 root  wheel  175874 Jan 15 03:15 daily.out
[g4:~] power% ls /usr/bin|wc -l
     552
```

File Redirection ("<" and ">")

The shell has built-in operators that allow you to use a file at the beginning of a pipeline (to read data from it) or at the end of a pipeline (to write data to it). To effectively use a file as the beginning of a pipeline, you use <, which tells the command to read from the file (technically, `tcsh` connects the command's standard input to the specified file). Similarly, > tells the shell to put output from the command *into* a file (>> tells the shell to *append* output to the end of an existing file, instead of replacing the contents of the file).

NOTE Many command-line programs support reading from and writing to files internally (i.e., the program itself reads and/or writes, instead of piping data in and out using the shell). The two techniques are normally equivalent, but some programs only support one or the other. For shell scripts, *standard input* and *output* tend to be much easier, since the script has its own `stdin` and `stdout` that can be redirected at runtime.

Errors and warnings are handled as a separate file that also goes to the terminal intermingled with standard output; these errors and warnings are not picked up automatically when redirecting standard output, since they might require different handling than non-error output. To redirect these errors, called *standard error*, use >& (or >>& to append).

WARNING Basic pipes and input/output redirection are very similar between sh and csh, but redirecting standard error is different in csh or tcsh than in sh or bash.

To illustrate file redirection, in Listing 15.8 I echo into a *file* (instead of Terminal), overwrite the file with a second use of echo, and then—using a third echo—append to the file instead of replacing it. The second half of the example confirms that using a file argument for grep is equivalent to using grep without arguments (so that it searches standard input) and then feeding the file into grep's stdin.

Listing 15.8 Using input/output redirection

```
[g4:~] power% echo 1 > testfile
[g4:~] power% cat testfile
1
[g4:~] power% echo 2 > testfile
[g4:~] power% cat testfile
2
[g4:~] power% echo 3 >> testfile
[g4:~] power% cat testfile
2
3
[g4:~] power% grep -i computer ~/Library/Preferences/com.apple.finder.plist
 <key>ComputerOptions</key>
  <key>ComputerBackgroundType</key>
  <key>ComputerIconViewArrangeBy</key>
  <key>ComputerIconViewIconSize</key>
  <key>ComputerScrollPosition</key>
  <key>ComputerToolbarVisible</key>
  <key>ComputerUseCustomIconViewOptions</key>
  <key>ComputerViewStyle</key>
[g4:~] power% grep -i computer < ~/Library/Preferences/com.apple.finder.plist
 <key>ComputerOptions</key>
  <key>ComputerBackgroundType</key>
  <key>ComputerIconViewArrangeBy</key>
  <key>ComputerIconViewIconSize</key>
  <key>ComputerScrollPosition</key>
  <key>ComputerToolbarVisible</key>
  <key>ComputerUseCustomIconViewOptions</key>
  <key>ComputerViewStyle</key>
[g4:~] power%
```

Inline Execution (` `)

Sometimes you need to use the output of one command as arguments to another command, instead of as standard input. Unix provides backticks (the ` character, generally the unshifted tilde key, above the tab key) to do this, as shown in Listing 15.9. In the first example, which produces a list of directories; in the second example, the output of the `which` command is used as arguments for the `ls` command, producing a listing of those directories.

Listing 15.9 Using backticks to feed filenames from the `which` command's standard output to another command as arguments

```
[g4:~/Library/Preferences] power% which bash sh tcsh csh
/bin/bash
/bin/sh
/bin/tcsh
/bin/csh
 [g4:~/Library/Preferences] power% ls -l `which bash sh tcsh csh`
-rwxr-xr-x  1 root  wheel  540884 Dec 19 22:19 /bin/bash
-r-xr-xr-x  1 root  wheel  315136 Dec 19 22:19 /bin/csh
-r-xr-xr-x  1 root  wheel  540884 Dec 19 22:19 /bin/sh
-r-xr-xr-x  1 root  wheel  315136 Dec 19 22:19 /bin/tcsh
```

NOTE Be careful connecting programs when working with filenames that contain spaces. If one program generates a line with a filename such as `System Folder`, and another program processes that line, it may incorrectly treat `System` and `Folder` as two different files. If you want to pass filenames with spaces, you can put *double* quotes around the backticks, as in `du -ks echo "`find ~ -type d`"`.

Installing Unix-Based Software

Because Unix is used on wildly different equipment, and because Unix users have traditionally customized their software much more than Mac users, Unix software is normally distributed in *source kits*. Source kits are basically raw programming code that users can then *compile* to run on their own system. (Compiling is a process by which source code is processed to run on a particular platform or operating system.) Increasingly, developers have been adding support for Darwin to their source kits, bringing a wealth of "new" software to OS X.

Under OS 9, software was normally compiled by the developer and packaged with an installer *before* distribution to the user for installation. Unix software installation is a bit more complicated; because of this, there are actually three methods of installing software on OS X:

OS 9 style Traditional pre-compiled software with an installer or script (like Apple's software), or as an application package that takes advantage of drag-and-drop installation.

Traditional Unix style Source code designed for manual compilation and installation by the user.

Newer Unix style Scripted porting.

In Chapter 7, I covered software distributed via the first method. Here's some information on the others.

Source code kits Source kits typically include the software's source code, documentation files, a configuration script, and a *Makefile*, which actually provides the procedure that should be used to compile and install the software. Each kit is different, but the most common procedure for installing software from source kits is the following (using a fictional software *program-1.2.3*):

1. Unpack the software: **`tar xzf`** ***`program-1.2.3.tar.gz`*** **<RETURN>**. Most source kits are distributed as `tar` archives that are then compressed with `gz`; such compressed archives are called *tarballs*, and may also use the `.tgz` suffix. You can also expand such archives using StuffIt Expander. Tarballs generally unpack to create a directory named with the program name (`program-1.2.3`) that contains all the files needed to build the program. The `tar` program normally creates this directory inside the current working directory.
2. Change to the newly created directory: **`cd`** ***`program-1.2.3`*** **<RETURN>** (or **`cd ~/Desktop/`** ***`program-1.2.3`*** **<RETURN>** if you used StuffIt Expander to unpack the tarball to your Desktop folder).
3. See what you've just unpacked: **`ls -F`** **<RETURN>**. Documentation filenames are often all caps.
4. Read the documentation for the software: **`more`** ***`README INSTALL`*** **<RETURN>** (or whatever the documentation files are named). Find the exact procedure to follow, along with any desired options to specify in the next step.
5. Configure the Makefile: **`./configure`** **<RETURN>**. This command runs a `configure` program included with most kits that inspects your system and creates or adjusts the Makefile as necessary. The `./` is necessary because the `configure` program is in the newly extracted directory, which is probably not listed in your `PATH`.
6. Compile the software using instructions in the Makefile by typing **`make`** **<RETURN>**. The `make` program follows a procedure in Makefile (capitalization may vary) in the current directory.
7. Install the compiled software: **`sudo make install`** **<RETURN>**. The `make` program runs again—this time following a different procedure within the Makefile—to copy the previously compiled files to their final locations.

NOTE Compilation can usually be done as a normal user, but the actual installation of the compiled software generally requires making changes to system directories like `/usr/local/bin`, which requires root-level access (`sudo`). This is the reason Apple's Installer often prompts for an administrative password.

8. Update the list of available commands: **`rehash`** **<RETURN>**. The `csh`-based shells keep an internal list of known commands so they don't have to scan all the directories in your `PATH` each time you execute a command; `rehash` updates that list.

NOTE In an attempt to avoid conflicts with core OS software installed in /usr/bin and /bin (for user-level programs) and /usr/sbin and /sbin (for root-level programs), most third-party programs are installed in /usr/local/bin. Unfortunately, /usr/local/bin is no longer in the default PATH Apple supplies. This means that if you install software from a source kit, you may need to add /usr/local/bin to your PATH. You can do this in one of two ways: (1) type **setenv PATH $PATH":/usr/local/bin" <RETURN>** in Terminal; or (2) add the line setenv PATH $PATH":/usr/local/bin" to your ~/.cshrc or ~/.tcshrc file.

Scripted porting If the procedure described above looks like a lot of trouble to you, scripted porting may be the answer. In this scenario, a group of people figures out how to compile and install several pieces of software on a given operating system, and then generates scripts for a porting program that allows that program to follow their procedures and build the software automatically. These people are called *porters*, because to *port* software is to alter it so it works on a different platform. On OS X, Fink (http://fink.sourceforge.net/) is by far the most advanced and popular porting system. At the time of this writing, Fink provides almost 2,000 ports, and installation of Fink packages is normally as simple as typing **fink install *packagename* <RETURN>**. The Fink User's Guide says it best: "Fink is a distribution of Unix Open Source software for Mac OS X and Darwin. It brings a wide range of free command-line and graphical software developed for Linux and similar operating systems to your Mac." Fink can download source files from the Internet, *patch* (modify) them to work on OS X if necessary, compile the patched software, and then install the compiled software inside the Fink directory (normally /sw).

Because it's so useful, I'll show you how to use Fink in the next section.

Apple's Developer Tools: Required

I mentioned in the Introduction that you should install Apple's Developer Tools on your Mac—either using the CD that came with OS X or your Mac, or by downloading it from Apple's Developer site. For advanced Unix work, the Developer Tools aren't just recommended—they're required. Apple's tools include a current compiler set that allows you to actually build the software we're looking at here.

In addition, once you've installed the Developer Tools, you'll have a host of new programs in /usr/bin. (If you already had Terminal windows open when you installed the Developer Tools, type **rehash <RETURN>** in each one to recognize these newly installed programs.) If you're curious, type **ls -lt /usr/bin <RETURN>**, to see a list of things installed along with Apple's compiler. Apple's tools are based on gcc, the GNU Compiler Collection. You can learn more about gcc at http://www.gnu.org/software/gcc/.

Installing Fink

The Fink system is available in two different versions. The Fink Binary Installer is a double-clickable `.pkg` file for Apple's Installer, and the Fink Source Release is a pure command-line installer. Both provide a basic set of command-line tools to get Fink running (including the `fink` program itself), and a set of package files that Fink can use to install other programs. In addition, the Fink Binary Installer includes a selection of pre-compiled packages (to save time) and is based around the `dselect` and `apt-get` programs, which provide a text-based menu system to control Fink. (Unfortunately, `dselect` and `apt-get` don't work well in Fink yet.) The Fink Source Release uses the `fink` command instead of `dselect` and `apt-get`, and is also able to download, patch, compile, and install software; list installed and available packages; and update itself from the master Internet site. As of this writing, the Source Release is much easier to use.

To install the Fink Source Release, follow this procedure (version numbers and URLs may be different by the time you read this):

1. Check `http://fink.sourceforge.net/` for any warnings or important notes about Fink.
2. Download the Source Release from `http://fink.sourceforge.net/download/srcdist.php`. If StuffIt Expander automatically unpacks it, throw away the extracted directory; as of this writing, StuffIt Expander "expands" Fink incorrectly.
3. In Terminal, `cd` to the directory where you downloaded the tarball (called `fink-0.5.1-full.tar.gz` at the time of this writing). If downloads are saved to your Desktop folder, you would type **`cd ~/Desktop`** **<RETURN>**.
4. Use the `tar` program to extract the archive by typing **`tar xzf fink-0.5.1-full.tar.gz`** **<RETURN>**. (Remember that the name of the file you download and extract will probably be different than my example here.)
5. Change to the directory you just created: **`cd fink-0.5.1-full`** **<RETURN>**. (Again, the name of the directory may be different.)
6. Run the `bootstrap.sh` script: **`sh bootstrap.sh`** **<RETURN>**.
7. The bootstrap script asks a series of questions, showing suggested answers in square brackets. To accept the default, just press the return key. Many of these questions concern which mirror sites should be used for downloading source files—local mirrors are generally faster than remote ones, and master sites (listed first by the script), are frequently overloaded. Once it finishes gathering information, the bootstrap script will download the required software, compile it, and install the resulting files in a new `/sw` directory.
8. Among other items, Fink installs startup scripts as `/sw/bin/init.csh` and `/sw/bin/init.sh`. To activate Fink, `/sw/bin` must be added to your `PATH` environment variable; these scripts take care of that and some additional steps to activate Fink. To complete the installation, you'll have to add a line to `source` the appropriate script to a shell initialization file; the

bootstrap script instructs you on how to do this and then exits. If you have multiple users, each user should add the command to their own initialization file, or you can make the change to a shared initialization file in `/etc`, as described in "Startup and shutdown" in the `tcsh` manual page. Assuming you are using `tcsh` or `csh`, you can also activate Fink for currently running shells with **`source /sw/bin/init.csh; rehash`** <RETURN>. (The semicolon allows you to type two commands on one line; it's more compact than typing the first command, hitting return, then typing the second command and hitting return again, but accomplishes the same thing.)

NOTE When you first run the `fink` command after installation, you may get a warning that the package list is out of date; the error may suggest you type `sudo fink index` so that it can configure the appropriate privileges and update its list of packages. In normal use, you don't need to use `sudo` or `fink index`, as `fink` keeps its own package cache up to date, and can run `sudo` for you when needed.

Versions of Open Source Software

Since open source software is often worked on by large, disjointed groups of people, and the development process is much more public than that of commercial software, version numbers of open source software often mean significantly different things than they do with commercial software.

- Alpha and beta versions of open source software are often publicly available.
- Developers often encourage the use of alpha and beta versions, both because they fix known bugs, and because they get more useful feedback (feedback on released versions is likely to cover popular and already fixed bugs).
- Many open source software projects are stable and usable before the "final" release or version 1.0. The OpenSSL program, for instance, has been used to provide SSL encryption in the Apache web server and OpenSSH for years, but remains at version 0.9.*xx*.
- Development versions are generally kept in the *Concurrent Version System* (CVS) to facilitate collaboration by developers, and the CVS repository is often publicly accessible by non-developers. Apple includes the `cvs` command in OS X.
- With software stored in CVS, the latest and greatest version available in CVS is called HEAD, and developers often suggest that users "check out" the latest version from CVS and use it.

Using the *fink* Command

Fink provides several subcommands in addition to `install`, including `list` (type **`fink list -i`** <RETURN> to list installed packages, or **`fink list`** ***`name`*** <RETURN> to see packages that match *name*), and describe (type **fink describe *packagename* <RETURN>** to see details on ***packagename***). For a helpful list of `fink` subcommands, use **fink <RETURN>**. For more on the `fink` command, you can read the `fink` manual page, and the documentation at `http://fink.sourceforge.net/`.

It's also a good idea (but not absolutely necessary) to periodically type **fink selfupdate update-all <RETURN>**, which will make `fink` update its packages to the latest versions via the Internet. The `selfupdate` subcommand will even offer to get the latest version of the Fink packages from CVS, rather than the latest "released" versions (which may in fact be older).

FinkCommander

If you'd like to control Fink without using the command line, FinkCommander (`http://finkcommander.sourceforge.net/`) is just the ticket. FinkCommander is a simple program with a graphical user interface that provides a list of available packages, and lets you drive the `fink`, `dselect`, and `apt-get` programs via contextual menus or menu commands. Like `fink list`, FinkCommander can filter programs by partial name matches, but it also adds sorting and improved filtering capabilities.

Hands-On with Some Unix Programs

Apple includes hundreds of Unix programs with OS X, from the basic to the baroque. I'll mention a few here, to give you a taste.

Types of Unix Programs

There are several major types of Unix programs. The first type, which I've discussed at length in this chapter, are command-line or "interfaceless" programs. Simple ones accept instructions typed on the command line, and generally either show their results directly in Terminal, or manipulate files based on command arguments. Interactive programs, such as the `vi` and `emacs` text editors and the `more` and `less` pagers, often run in "full-screen" text mode, responding to keyboard commands until the user finishes with the program and exits. *Daemons* start up, read configuration settings from a file, and then wait in the background for service requests (frequently across a network). (See the sidebar "Daemons and Logs.")

Daemons and Logs

There are many background programs, called daemons, in Unix (try **ps -aux | grep root <RETURN>** to see some). Daemons are similar to background applications in OS 9, but are much more common and important in Unix. Many of them record important events during operation using the `syslogd` program, which saves this information in log files stored

Continued on next page

in /var/log. (I actually talked about several of these log files in Chapter 14.) The amount of information each program records is often configurable through its *configuration* file and via the /etc/syslog.conf file (see the manual pages for syslogd and syslog.conf for further info). You can find active logs by typing a command such as **ls -lt /var/log | head -5 <RETURN>**, which lists the four most recently modified logs. Or, to view the last few events in system.log, type **tail /var/log/system.log <RETURN>**. (This is actually the same content you would see by viewing the system.log file in Console or a log file utility, as discussed in the previous chapter.)

Although Unix gets a lot of mileage out of text interfaces and text manipulation—graphical interfaces are generally not as critical in Unix systems as they are under Mac OS or Windows—there are Unix programs that require (or benefit from) graphical interfaces; they have traditionally used the X11 Window System to provide that graphical display. (I talk about X Window systems below.)

Finally, in addition to traditional text and graphical Unix applications, OS X has introduced a new breed of programs—Aqua configuration tools for Darwin/Unix software. BrickHouse, SharePoints, and MacJanitor, discussed in various places in this book, are examples of third-party configuration utilities that provide a Mac OS X graphical interface to Unix programs. In fact, Apple's System Preferences application is the most familiar example—the Network pane manages Darwin's networking configuration, and the Sharing pane controls the Samba (Windows File Sharing) server, Apache (Personal Web Sharing) server, OpenSSH (Remote Login) server, FTP (FTP Access) server, and CUPS (Printer Sharing) system.

Here are a few example of useful Unix programs; some come with OS X, some are installable using fink, and others can be downloaded manually.

X Window Systems (X11 from Apple or XFree86)

I mentioned earlier that Unix is old; it's been around since long before computers had graphical interfaces. However, nowadays most people find graphical interfaces useful, so most modern Unix systems support the X Window System (also called X11). X11 provides a cross-platform toolkit for applications to display graphics on the local system or on a remote system over a network connection. X11 is primitive in many ways, but it's extremely flexible. In addition, because it's designed on a networking paradigm, X11 programs automatically have the ability to be used on a computer other than the one running them (somewhat like VNC and Timbuktu, described in Chapter 11). XFree86 has long been a popular X11 solution, and Apple provides its own package for OS X, available for free at http://www.apple.com/macosx/x11/.

NOTE The DISPLAY environment variable (type **echo $DISPLAY <RETURN>** to see your current setting) controls where X programs display their windows. This is normally set to ":0.0", which means the default display on the computer that is actually running the program (localhost). However, if you'd like to run X11 programs and display their windows on another computer, you can do so over an SSH connection. In fact, OpenSSH can set everything up for you—see "X11 and TCP forwarding" in the ssh manual page and check the X11 settings in the ssh configuration files (/etc/ssh_config and /etc/sshd_config under OS X 10.2). Note that your ssh session may stay open after logout if it is still being used for X11 forwarding, as described in the man page.

Text Editors

Because Unix is a text-based operating system, text editors are critically important for things like editing programs and configuration files, composing mail, and revising documents. Unix systems have three broad families of text editors (much like they have sh-based and csh-based shells). The vi editor and its many derivatives are one branch, the emacs editor and its variants are the second (each with its own faction of supporters, and wars between them), and all others form a third group.

The vi editor is horribly nonintuitive (although great compared to its predecessors, ed and ex, which only displayed one line at a time!); however, it has two virtues: it's extremely powerful (if you know the proper incantations) and it's ubiquitous—vi is available on just about every Unix system. (OS X includes nex/nvi, a rewrite of the ex/vi editor pair.) But if you don't know vi already, it is not worth learning just for use in OS X—use something else instead.

The emacs editor is much larger—the non-graphical version Apple includes in OS X is 4.5MB, plus 50MB of supporting files, versus 300KB for vi—but in fairness emacs is much more than a text editor: it's a full-fledged development environment, with a built-in programming language, mail and news reader, web browser, and an expansive collection of plug-ins. OS X includes emacs 21.1, and Fink can install the graphical xemacs (via fink install xemacs) if desired. However, again, if you don't know emacs, it's not worth learning just to edit text in OS X.

I say "it's not worth learning" vi or emacs mainly because if you just need to edit text, you can use one of the many graphical text editors available, including OS X's own TextEdit, but most notably the commercial BBEdit (http://www.barebones.com/), which includes a command-line bbedit program to access BBEdit from within Terminal. (If you have BBEdit 7 or later installed, try **man bbedit <RETURN>** for the command-line tool's manual page). BBEdit includes a variety of Unix integration features, including the ability to run scripts directly, syntax coloring in a variety of languages, and CVS support.

That being said, if you don't have access to Aqua programs like BBEdit, perhaps because you're logged in from another system via ssh, you can do quite a bit with pico, a simple non-graphical text editor included with OS X. To make using pico easier, it constantly shows on-screen menus, which is rare for a command-line program.

Process Management: *ps*, *top*, *kill*, and *killall* (included in OS X)

Unix is a multi-user system, with background processes running all the time, so Unix-based operating systems like OS X include several commands to see and manage what's going on. The most basic of these is ps (process status). Without options, ps isn't very useful, but ps -aux gives you a snapshot of every program running on the system at the time the command is executed, along with the owner, process ID, start time, and CPU and memory utilization of each.

NOTE Generally, programs writing to files or other programs via stdout (with “<”, “>”, or “|”) ignore the size of your Terminal (shell) window, since they aren't displaying in the window. Unfortunately, ps truncates its output to the screen width even when writing to stdout, so you may get different matches with something like **ps -aux | grep BBEdit <RETURN>** if you change the width of the Terminal window. To get the full output from ps, use -ww as an argument; ps will not truncate its output.

To see information similar to what ps provides, but updated every few seconds, use top. By default, top shows summary information on 15 programs, along with overall system status information, including how many processes (programs) are running, system load averages (see the getloadavg manual page for an explanation), and total CPU utilization; it updates its display every second. Ironically, top is so demanding that it often uses over 10 percent of CPU cycles itself, so the -s *n* argument (which tells top to update the display every *n* seconds) is often useful, as is the -u argument (which shows the top consumers of CPU cycles). With the -w (wide display) argument, top shows additional columns, and it is smart enough to show more programs if running in a taller window. For example, try typing **top -uws 5 <RETURN>**.

NOTE You may recognize a strong similarity between the output of top and the information provided by the Process Viewer utility, described in Chapter 7.

Now that you know what other processes are running, what can you do with this information? The kill command can send a *signal* to another program (using its Process ID); kill's default signal is -15 (also called SIGTERM or TERM), which tells the receiving program to terminate (like the Quit command in a Mac application). There are many other signals, but unfortunately the handling of signals is poorly standardized. The most important signal is -9 (SIGKILL), a special signal that asks the operating system to *force* the program to terminate (like using Force Quit in OS X).

To ask a process to shut down, first find its Process ID (PID) from top or ps. Typing **kill 100 <RETURN>** would ask the process PID 100 to quit (with the default SIGTERM signal). To forcefully end process 100, you would type **kill -9 100 <RETURN>** or **kill -KILL 100 <RETURN>**.

NOTE The top program runs continuously until you stop it. In order to type a command (such as a kill command), you need to either open a new Terminal window, or quit top by pressing the Q key.

WARNING At the time of this writing, SIGKILL (kill -9) doesn't always work in OS X. This is a serious bug, but it does work most of the time.

Normally the kill command requires you to provide a Process ID, which you can get from top or ps. However, Apple also provides the killall program, which allows you to kill a process by name. (killall actually searches for a matching process name, finds the PID for that process, and then sends the appropriate kill command for you.) For example, **killall Terminal <RETURN>** would kill the Terminal application. The -s option shows what killall *would* do without -s. Try typing **killall -s Terminal <RETURN>**; you'll see the actual command that would be issued had you not included the -s option. As another example, I currently have three tcsh shells running; typing **killall -s tcsh** produces the following output:

```
[g4:~] power% killall -s -9 tcsh
kill -KILL 4571
kill -KILL 4569
kill -KILL 4178
```

NOTE Like most Unix commands, the killall command is case sensitive. So "Terminal" will match Apple's Terminal program, but "terminal" won't.

Packet Analysis: *tcpdump* (included in OS X)

When you want to see what your computer is doing on the Internet, you can use a packet sniffer. There are several good commercial ones, but tcpdump is included in OS X and very capable.

For full details, see the tcpdump manual page, but to get a taste, try typing **sudo tcpdump -aN -xX -s0 -c6 host www.reppep.com and port 80 <RETURN>**. (Provide your admin password when prompted.) The -a option shows hostnames instead of IP numbers when available, and -N uses short names instead of full names. The -x and -X options show sent and received data in hexadecimal (the middle column, which you can ignore) and ASCII (the right column, which is mostly readable) formats. The -s150 option shows the first 150 bytes of each packet (-s0 would show full packets), and -c6 terminates tcpdump after 6 matching packets. To avoid mixing in other traffic, such as e-mail checking or other browser activity, including host www.reppep.com and port 80 tells tcpdump to show only web traffic to and from www.reppep.com.

Listing 15.10 **Output from `tcpdump` when visiting `http://www.reppep.com/~pepper/` in a web browser; the right column shows requests to and responses from the server.**

```
[g4:~] power% sudo tcpdump -aN -xX -s150 -c6 host www.reppep.com and port 80
tcpdump: listening on en0
15:49:40.822209 g4.49253 > www.http: S 2115499595:2115499595(0) win 32768 <mss
➥1460,nop,wscale 0,nop,nop,timestamp 3257796741 0> (DF)
0x0000   4500 003c 2333 4000 4006 c13f 425c 68c9        E..<#3@.@..?B\h.
0x0010   425c 68c8 c065 0050 7e17 f64b 0000 0000        B\h..e.P~..K....
0x0020   a002 8000 5678 0000 0204 05b4 0103 0300        ....Vx..........
0x0030   0101 080a c22e 0885 0000 0000                  ............
15:49:40.822416 www.http > g4.49253: S 2270896276:2270896276(0) ack 2115499596
➥win 57344 <mss 1460,nop,wscale 0,nop,nop,timestamp 24052699 3257796741> (DF)
0x0000   4500 003c e516 4000 4006 ff5b 425c 68c8        E..<..@.@..[B\h.
0x0010   425c 68c9 0050 c065 875b 2094 7e17 f64c        B\h..P.e.[..~..L
0x0020   a012 e000 67a6 0000 0204 05b4 0103 0300        ....g...........
0x0030   0101 080a 016f 03db c22e 0885 b8a7 fcb1        .....o..........
15:49:40.822496 g4.49253 > www.http: . ack 1 win 33304 <nop,nop,timestamp
➥3257796741 24052699> (DF)
0x0000   4500 0034 2334 4000 4006 c146 425c 68c9        E..4#4@.@..FB\h.
0x0010   425c 68c8 c065 0050 7e17 f64c 875b 2095        B\h..e.P~..L.[..
0x0020   8010 8218 5670 0000 0101 080a c22e 0885        ....Vp..........
0x0030   016f 03db                                   .o..
15:49:40.824632 g4.49253 > www.http: P 1:272(271) ack 1 win 33304
➥<nop,nop,timestamp 3257796741 24052699> (DF)
0x0000   4500 0143 2335 4000 4006 c036 425c 68c9        E..C#5@.@..6B\h.
0x0010   425c 68c8 c065 0050 7e17 f64c 875b 2095        B\h..e.P~..L.[..
0x0020   8018 8218 577f 0000 0101 080a c22e 0885        ....W...........
0x0030   016f 03db 4745 5420 2f7e 7065 7070 6572        .o..GET./~pepper
0x0040   2f20 4854 5450 2f31 2e30 0d0a 486f 7374        /.HTTP/1.0..Host
0x0050   3a20 7777 772e 7265 7070 6570 2e63 6f6d        :.www.reppep.com
0x0060   0d0a 4163 6365 7074 3a20 7465 7874 2f68        ..Accept:.text/h
0x0070   746d 6c2c 2074 6578 742f 706c 6169 6e2c        tml,.text/plain,
0x0080   2074 6578 742f 7367                            .text/sg
15:49:40.825815 www.http > g4.49253: P 1:310(309) ack 272 win 57920
➥<nop,nop,timestamp 24052699 3257796741> (DF)
0x0000   4500 0169 e517 4000 4006 fe2d 425c 68c8        E..i..@.@..-B\h.
0x0010   425c 68c9 0050 c065 875b 2095 7e17 f75b        B\h..P.e.[..~..[
0x0020   8018 e240 ab71 0000 0101 080a 016f 03db        ...@.q.......o..
0x0030   c22e 0885 4854 5450 2f31 2e31 2032 3030        ....HTTP/1.1.200
0x0040   204f 4b0d 0a44 6174 653a 204d 6f6e 2c20        .OK..Date:.Mon,.
0x0050   3137 2046 6562 2032 3030 3320 3230 3a34        17.Feb.2003.20:4
0x0060   393a 3431 2047 4d54 0d0a 5365 7276 6572        9:41.GMT..Server
0x0070   3a20 4170 6163 6865 2f32 2e30 2e34 3420        :.Apache/2.0.44.
0x0080   2855 6e69 7829 2050                            (Unix).P
15:49:40.825902 www.http > g4.49253: . 310:1758(1448) ack 272 win 57920
➥<nop,nop,timestamp 24052699 3257796741> (DF)
0x0000   4500 05dc e518 4000 4006 f9b9 425c 68c8        E.....@.@...B\h.
0x0010   425c 68c9 0050 c065 875b 21ca 7e17 f75b        B\h..P.e.[!.~..[
0x0020   8010 e240 a75d 0000 0101 080a 016f 03db        ...@.].......o..
0x0030   c22e 0885 3c21 444f 4354 5950 4520 4854        ....<!DOCTYPE.HT
```

```
0x0040   4d4c 2050 5542 4c49 4320 222d 2f2f 5733        ML.PUBLIC."-//W3
0x0050   432f 2f44 5444 2048 544d 4c20 342e 3020        C//DTD.HTML.4.0.
0x0060   5472 616e 7369 7469 6f6e 616c 2f2f 454e        Transitional//EN
0x0070   2220 2268 7474 703a 2f2f 7777 772e 7733        "."http://www.w3
0x0080   2e6f 7267 2f54 522f                            .org/TR/
15 packets received by filter
0 packets dropped by kernel
```

Network Exploration: *nmap* (available via Fink)

The `nmap` program (available via `fink`) is a powerful tool for network analysis. It offers a host of different probes, can tell what ports (network services) are available on a particular system, and can make an educated guess at what operating system that computer is running based on identifiable characteristics of network responses.

Without arguments, `nmap` prints a helpful usage message. Some particularly useful options include `-v` (verbose), `-O` (attempt to guess remote OS, requires `sudo`), `-F` (fast scan, fewer ports), and `-P0` (avoid ping tests, for scanning hosts that block ping responses). For example, after installing `nmap`, try **`typing sudo nmap -O -F www.nyu.edu <RETURN>`**; provide your admin password when prompted. This runs `nmap` against the `www.nyu.edu` web server.

NOTE Unlike most other command-line programs, `nmap` isn't flexible about combining multiple options after a single dash; you must list each option separately (e.g., `nmap -v -O -F hostname`).

WARNING Keep in mind that `nmap` is a powerful tool, used by both crackers and systems administrators to find security holes. Be very careful with it.

If you like `nmap`, the `netstat -a` command lists all open connections and listening ports (which `nmap` tries to figure out) on the *local* system (your own computer). (The `/etc/services` file lists ports that OS X knows about, and what services they are normally used to provide.)

File Transfer: *curl* (included in OS X)

The `curl` program can download and upload files using a wide variety of protocols, including HTTP, HTTPS, and FTP. In its simplest usage, `curl` goes to a URL and downloads the file to standard output; with `-o`, it downloads to the specified filename, and with `-O`, it uses the remote filename for the local file. As an example, **`curl -o index.html http://www.informinit.com/`** would download whatever file the web server `www.informinit.com` home page, and save it as a local file named `informinit.html`, while **`curl -O http://www.informinit.com/`** would fail, since there's no filename in the URL.

Directory Synchronization: *rsync* (included in OS X)

The `rsync` program does intelligent differential mirroring. It scans through master and clone directories, typically over the Internet, comparing the contents of each file in both directories and copying only the changes from the master to the clone. Using `rsync` is much more efficient for mirroring changed files than a program like `curl` can be, since it copies only the differences within files, not entire changed files.

WARNING Since `rsync` is a Unix program, it doesn't know about resource forks. This means it's great for keeping MP3 collections in sync between home and office, or backing up Word `.doc` and StuffIt `.sit` files, but not suitable for Classic applications or other files with resource forks or essential type/creator codes. If you'd like the functionality of `rsync` with the ability to work with Mac OS resource forks, check out RsyncX, available from `http://www.macosxlabs.org/rsyncx/rsyncx.html`.

Web Log Analysis: *analog* (available via Fink)

Analog is a fast and free analyzer for web server activity logs (including OS X's Apache logs). It's extremely flexible, and can crunch through huge log files in seconds, producing simple HTML charts or plain text pages. A Carbon (GUI) version of Analog is available at `http://www.summary.net/soft/analog.html`, but Fink can build a pure command-line version as well. If you like Analog, you should also take a look at DNSTran (also available from `http://www.summary.net/`), which performs hostname lookups for Analog much more quickly than Analog itself, and Report Magic (`http://www.reportmagic.org/`), which adds more and better chart options, using the `perl` language built into OS X.

Moving On...?

We've come a long way since the Introduction. If you've mastered the previous 14 chapters and this one (who am I kidding… even if you haven't mastered this one), you can surely be considered a "power user" and the master of your Mac. If you're still craving knowledge, be sure to check out Appendix A, which provides some good tips on moving from OS 9 to OS X, and switching between them, and Appendix B, which discusses using multiple volumes and disk partitions in OS X.

Appendix A

A Tale of Two Systems

(Or: Mac OS X versus Mac OS 9—transitioning and switching back and forth.)

In Chapter 8 I talked about the Classic Environment in OS X: what it is, how it works, how to best use it. What I didn't get into much was the comparison between booting *into* OS 9 versus OS X. People who are making the transition from OS 9 to OS X will notice that the latter differs significantly from the former in many ways—sometimes, in their opinion, not in good ways.

In addition, although the Classic Environment works very well, some people will need to (or, let's face it, *want* to) boot into OS 9 at times, and this itself presents challenges, because the two operating systems handle some things very differently, such as the Documents folder(s).

This appendix provides some assistance. I cover a few issues that can be confusing or troublesome when making the transition from OS 9 to OS X. I also include some tips for those who use OS X full-time, but wish that it did some things more like OS 9 (can you say, "Where's my old Apple Menu?"). Finally, I discuss problems and solutions that affect those users who tend to switch back and forth.

NOTE At this point in the book (almost the end, can you believe it?), I'm not going to spend a lot of time talking about installation and configuration when I mention a third-party software solution. I'm going to assume that you're an old pro at that by now.

Transition Technicalities

Although OS X and OS 9 are completely different operating systems under the hood, Apple has tried to make OS X's interface as similar to OS 9's as possible while still being able to add functionality and make it look "new and improved."

So if you're making the transition from OS 9, after a few hours of working in X you'll most likely be doing quite well. However, a few issues tend to be very confusing, both for users and for applications.

Documents folders Unless you used OS 9's Multiple Users feature (few people actually did), all of your Documents were stored in a folder called Documents at the root level of your hard drive. As described in Chapter 1, OS X uses a different Documents folder for each user, found inside `/Users/username`.

Unfortunately, many Classic applications (those written for OS 9) that require or access files in your Documents folder have problems with this location change. For example, as I explained in Chapter 9, if you have "Use preferences from home folder" checked in Classic preferences, the Classic Environment tells all Classic applications to use the Documents folder inside your user folder. If you haven't yet moved documents from the root level of your hard drive to your private user folder, Classic applications won't be able to find them. Conversely, if you *don't* have this option checked, Classic applications will look for documents in a folder at the root level of your hard drive (more specifically, the root level of the hard drive hosting your Classic System Folder). This presents a problem if you've moved your files into private user folder(s).

For these reasons, it's important to make sure that your Classic preferences and your Documents are set up congruently. I recommend moving documents to the appropriate user folder and then enabling the "Use preferences from home folder" option. (If you're the only user of your Mac, you can also place an alias to your personal Documents folder at the root level of your hard drive, and rename it *Desktop Folder*, so that Classic applications will always be able to locate documents.)

File comments In both OS 9 and OS X, if you use the Finder's Get Info command on a file or folder, you can enter your own comments or notes about that item. However, for some reason that is beyond my comprehension, Apple decided that OS X shouldn't recognize OS 9 file comments (at least from the very first versions of OS X to the time of this writing). The comments still *exist*; it's just that OS X can't read them. Likewise, any comments you add in OS X will exist when booted into OS 9, but OS 9 can't read them.

Fortunately, a few third-party software solutions allow you to keep your comments when transitioning to OS X. The freeware Comment Converter and the shareware File Buddy (both from `http://www.skytag.com/`) will import your OS 9 file/folder comments into OS X. In the case of Comment Converter, you simply drag files and folders onto the application's icon, and it automatically transfers comments for you. (File Buddy will also do this, but because it's a multifunction utility, it takes a couple more steps.)

In addition, if you tend to boot into OS 9 *and* OS X, the shareware Comment Synch (`http://preciousgem.dnsalias.com:90/preciousgem/index.html`) will actually synchronize comments both ways—so that you can also view your OS X file comments in OS 9. (It also makes adding and editing comments easier by allowing you to do so within its own file browser, so you don't have to use the Finder's Get Info command.)

Translated file names OS X uses the standard Unicode character encoding for naming files, and for displaying those filenames. However, OS 9 uses proprietary character sets created/provided by Apple. If you save, copy, or rename a file on an HFS Plus (a.k.a., Mac OS Extended) volume while booted into OS 9, OS 9 automatically converts its filename to Unicode so that it will also work under OS X.

Unfortunately, when you later boot into OS X, sometimes you'll find that these converted filenames contain odd characters or weren't translated properly. This is most likely to happen when the OS 9 encoding used for a filename differs from the primary language of your OS 9 installation (for example, when you use an Asian-language character set on an English version of OS 9.)

If you experience this problem, Apple provides the File Name Encoding Repair Utility, which runs under OS X, that fixes these encoding problems. You simply drop a file, or a folder of files, onto the utility, select the correct encoding from the resulting dialog, and click Repair. For more information on this utility, and/or to download it, visit `http://docs.info.apple.com/article.html?artnum=86182`.

For the Stubborn: Making OS X Work Like OS 9

User Level: any
Affects: individual user
Terminal: no

Although every day more and more users are making the switch from OS 9 to OS X, even those who are big fans of OS X (like myself) find themselves missing a few of OS 9's features and functionality. Because some of those people happen to be developers, there are a number of utilities available for OS X that bring back the most popular features of OS 9.

Bringing Back the Classic Apple Menu

As I showed you in Chapter 8, OS X's Apple Menu has some useful features, but it's not customizable like OS 9's. You can access the classic Apple Menu if the Classic Environment is running and you switch to a Classic application, but it's not quite the same. However, you can bring back Apple Menu customization using the shareware FruitMenu (`http://www.unsanity.com/`) or Classic Menu (`http://www.sigsoftware.com/`).

I've already talked about FruitMenu a couple times in the book, and discussed it extensively in the Online Bonus Chapter. Whereas FruitMenu works more like some of the other menu utilities I've discussed in the book, Classic Menu works more like the classic OS 9 Apple Menu. When it's running (you can add it to your Login Items preferences so that it always launches at login), it replaces the OS X Apple Menu with one that reflects the contents of `~/Library/Preferences/Classic Menu Items`. Much like OS 9's Apple Menu Items folder, any file or folder (or alias) you place in this folder will appear in the Apple Menu; folders will list their contents in hierarchical submenus. But unlike the classic Apple Menu, Classic Menu's Apple Menu includes shortcuts to its folder, and lets you quickly add aliases, files, and folders via an Open dialog.

In addition, unlike FruitMenu, which takes over your Apple Menu until you disable it, Classic Menu lets you access the standard OS X Apple Menu at any time by control/right-clicking on the Apple Menu icon (or using another keyboard modifier of your choosing).

Restoring the Application Menu

Speaking of menus, another one that many former OS 9 users miss when they move to OS X is the *application* menu—the one at the right side of the menu bar in OS 9 that lists all running applications (not to be confused with each application's own application menu in OS X, found on the left side of the menu bar). The reason this menu no longer exists in OS X is simple: the Dock provides all of its functionality (especially if you add the Hide option to each application's Dock menu, as described in Chapter 6). Yet many people still miss the old application menu, probably because it's so familiar to them.

If you haven't fully accepted the Dock and want your application menu back, there are a couple excellent utilities that will do just that: the shareware ASM (`http://www.vercruesse.de/software`) and the freeware X-Assist (`http://members.ozemail.com.au/~pli/x-assist/`). Both provide that familiar menu you're used to seeing, but they also provide additional features. ASM, for example, lets you add each application's Dock menu as a submenu; if an application takes advantage of its Dock menu to add functionality—for example, iTunes lets you control playback from its Dock menu—you'll be able to access those options from the application menu, as well. X-Assist adds direct access to System Preference panes, recently used applications, and the contents of its own "X-Assist Items" folder. Both also let you customize the appearance of the application menu; for example, you can have applications listed by icon, name, or both, and you can change the size of those icons. (Both applications also include another OS 9–like feature that I'll talk about in the next section.)

As a side note, I *really* missed the classic application menu when I first switched to OS X, and I used ASM to restore it. Yet the more I used OS X and the more I got used to the Dock, the less I used that menu. I eventually stopped using it altogether and haven't thought twice about it. In my conversations with other former OS 9 users, I hear similar stories. I guess this shows that either (1) the Dock is a very good substitute that just takes some getting used to; or (2) we're pretty adaptable when we're forced to be!

Making Application Windows Stick Together

One of the *most* unpopular features of OS X—at least to former OS 9 users—is the way application windows behave. In OS 9, clicking on a window in an application automatically brought *all* of that application's windows to the front. For example, if you had three Microsoft Word documents open, clicking somewhere in the window of one of them would bring all three windows to the front; likewise with Finder windows. However, in OS X, clicking on a window brings *only* that window to the front; all other windows for that application remain "layered" exactly how they are at that moment.

In some ways, OS X is actually more flexible than OS 9 in this regard. For example, in OS 9, many times you only *wanted* to view one window of an application or the Finder; bringing *all* windows forward ended up obscuring the windows of other applications that you wanted to be able to see. OS X lets you have it both ways—if you want to bring only one or two windows forward, you click on the particular window(s); however, if you want to bring *all* windows for an application forward, you click on the application's icon in the Dock.

Nevertheless, many people (myself included, much of the time) still like OS 9's way of doing things—commonly called *Classic Window Mode*—better. You can get it back via ASM or X-Assist (which I discussed in the previous section), or the shareware LiteSwitch (`http://www.proteron.com/liteswitchx/`), which I discussed in Chapter 8; in each utility, to enable this feature you simply check a box (or, in the case of LiteSwitch, select it from a pop-up menu). All three utilities also allow you to enable *Single Application Mode*, which means that when you switch to an application, all other applications are hidden.

TIP There is no utility at the time of this writing that *only* provides Classic Window Mode. However, if this is the only feature of these utilities that you want, ASM lets you turn everything else off. In addition, ASM lets you temporarily access the standard OS X window behavior by holding the shift key down as you click on a window.

If you really only want Classic Window Mode for the Finder, LiteSwitch also has a *Classic Finder Windows* option that enables Classic Window Mode for the Finder, but uses OS X's standard window behavior for all other applications. In addition, the freeware Desktop Rehab (downloadable via VersionTracker or MacUpdate) allows you to click on the Desktop to bring all Finder windows forward.

WindowShading Your Windows

Mac OS 9 offered a unique and extremely useful feature called WindowShading that let you click on a box in a window's title bar (or double-click the title bar itself) to reduce the window to *just* the title bar (it worked just like a roll-up window shade, hence the name). With OS X, Apple introduced the ability to minimize windows to the Dock, and assumed that would be an adequate substitute for the Window Shade behavior.

Many users didn't agree. Luckily, the shareware WindowShade X (`http://www.unsanity.com/`) comes to the rescue. However, it's actually much more flexible than OS 9's WindowShade functionality. It provides four different options: to WindowShade the window, to minimize the window to the Dock, to make the window transparent, or to hide the current window's application.

Each of these options can be assigned to one of four different actions: click the window's minimize button, double-click the title bar, control-double-click the title bar, or press command+M. The transparency function is especially helpful if you want to be able to view the contents of two overlapping windows at once.

As a bonus, WindowShade X includes the ability to control window shadows (those fancy shadows around the borders of windows) for both active and inactive windows. I've found that using the "No Shadows" setting (which disables all window shadows) doesn't look quite as nice, but it provides a noticeable speed boost for your Mac's interface. For example, opening, closing, scrolling, and refreshing windows happens a bit (and sometimes a *lot*) faster when shadows are disabled. And if this fancy-schmancy shadow control isn't enough, WindowShade X even brings back the "swish" sound that accompanied the collapse/expand of windows in OS 9.

Approximating Tabbed Windows

Another OS 9 feature that was very popular was *tabbed windows*. If you dragged a folder to the bottom of the screen, it was reduced to a small tab that contained the name of the folder. If you clicked on the tab, or dragged a file or folder onto it, the window would pop up to reveal its contents (and allow you to access them or to drop the file or folder into the tabbed folder). Once you clicked anywhere else in the Finder, or in another application, the tabbed window would again retreat to the bottom of the screen.

Apple did away with tabbed windows in OS X, most likely because the Dock's standard location at the bottom of the screen would have made tabbed windows very difficult to implement. OS X does provide a couple of features that resemble tabbed windows, but neither of them succeeds in giving you all of its functionality. For example, you can minimize windows to the Dock, but you lose the ability to drag files over the minimized window, and the ability to quickly view and then automatically minimize the window. OS X also has a neat feature—one that most people find on accident—that will fully reveal a partially hidden window when you want to drag a file onto it. To see this in action, open a Finder window and move it to one of the edges of your screen so that most of the window is hidden. Then drag a file into the window. If you hold the file over the window, the entire window will slide onto the screen so that it is fully revealed. If you drop the file, the window will remain visible; if you instead decide not to drop the file in the window, it will slide back to its original position off of the screen. (This feature is actually a variation of OS X's spring-loaded folders, which I discussed in Chapter 5 and its online supplement.) Likewise, if you click the green zoom button in the window's title bar, the window will resize and move so that you can view its contents; clicking it again will switch it back to its original position off of the screen.

Unfortunately, although these features are helpful, they really don't bring back tabbed windows. Even more unfortunate—if you're a big fan of tabbed windows—is that there really isn't any way to bring them back, even using third-party software. The closest things out there are the shareware DragThing (`http://www.dragthing.com/`) and Drop Drawers (`http://www.sigsoftware.com/dropdrawers/`). Both are excellent launcher and file access applications that offer drawer-like windows that open and close much like tabbed windows. Unfortunately, because these drawer windows are created *within* the applications, they don't reflect Finder windows like tabbed windows did; you have to create new drawers and then populate them with whatever files you want to appear in those drawers. However, even if they don't exactly replicate OS 9's tabbed windows, you may find them to be excellent alternatives.

If you're using OS X 10.1.*x*, the freeware DragonDrop (`http://cs.oberlin.edu/~dadamson/DragonDrop/`) also offers a good attempt at tabbed windows that actually allows you to "tab" Finder windows; unfortunately, I haven't been able to get it to work properly in OS X 10.2 or later.

Putting the Trash on the Desktop

Although in OS 9 the Trash was found on the Desktop, in OS X it's now found in the Dock. In the online supplement to Chapter 5, I showed you how to use a third-party utility to put the Trash on the Desktop and gain a good deal of additional functionality; however, what if you don't want to run a utility just to access the Trash on the Desktop? Here's another solution:

1. Create an alias of any folder in your home directory, and then move that alias to the Desktop. (It doesn't matter what the target of the alias is; we're going to change it later.) Rename the alias "Trash" (or whatever name you want your Trash to have).
2. Get Info on your new alias (File ➢ Get Info, or command+I). Click the Select New Original… button. In the dialog's "Go to" field, type **`/Users/`*`username`*`/.Trash`**, where *username* is your short username (and also the name of your home folder). Click Go and the `.Trash` folder will be highlighted, and the Go button will change to Choose. Click Choose to reassign the alias to your `.Trash` directory.
3. As of right now, your folder alias will work just like a Trash basket on your Desktop. (With one caveat—since the user-level Trash resides on the boot volume, if you drag anything into this new folder from another volume, it will be copied to the folder rather than "trashed." To throw something away that resides on a volume other than the one hosting your user folder, you'll need to use the Dock's Trash.) However, if you want it to also *look* like a Trash basket, click the Trash icon in the Dock to open the Trash folder. *Without* clicking on anything *in* the Trash folder, choose File ➢ Get Info to get info on the Trash. In the Trash Info window, select the Trash icon, and then choose Edit ➢ Copy to copy the icon to the clipboard. Switch back to the Info window for your new alias (or get info on it again if you already closed it). Click on its icon in the Info window, and then choose Edit ➢ Paste to paste the Trash icon onto the alias.

NOTE If you copy the real Trash icon when the Trash is empty, your Trash alias will always look empty. Likewise, if you copy the icon when the Trash contains files, your Trash alias will always look like it contains files. There's no way around this without using a third-party utility.

Revealing Labels

Another popular feature of OS 9 that didn't make it to OS X is Finder labels. You could use one of seven custom-colored labels on any file or folder; after being "labeled" an item's icon was highlighted with that color. Many people used labels to identify or sort items based on projects, priorities, etc.

The same developers who brought back WindowShades have also resurrected labels in OS X via Labels X (`http://www.unsanity.com/`). After installing Labels X, you can control/right-click on any file or folder to assign a label to it via contextual menus. In addition, list views in Finder windows gain a Label column that allows you to sort files by their labels. If you boot back and forth between OS X and OS 9, Labels X labels are also visible from within OS 9, and vice versa.

Restoring F-key Shortcuts

OS 9's Keyboard control panel let you assign applications, documents, and folders to your keyboard's function keys (F1-F15); pressing an F-key launched or opened the item assigned to it. Sadly, OS X's Keyboard preferences don't provide this option. If you're really missing it, and haven't found similar functionality in one of the other file launching/access tools I mentioned earlier in the book, check out the shareware FLaunch (`http://www.pariahware.com`), which lets you launch as many as four items per F-key.

Hearing What You've Been Missing (Interface Sounds)

Finally, another minor detail missing from OS X is *interface sounds*—the audible feedback that OS 9 could provide when navigating the Finder and interacting with windows, menus, etc. Once again, it's Unsanity (`http://www.unsanity.com/`) that brings a popular OS 9 feature to OS X. Xounds provides audible interface feedback just like that found in OS 9, but provides you with even more control over individual sounds than you had before. You can even import OS 9-compatible sound sets. (Custom sound sets are available from `http://www.soundsetcentral.com/`.)

For the Indecisive: Tips for Those Who Switch Back and Forth

Although many users have made the switch from OS 9 to OS X and never looked (or booted) back, others find themselves switching back and forth between the two somewhat frequently. For some users, it's an issue of important software that doesn't run in OS X and may not run properly in the Classic Environment within OS X (so they're forced to boot into OS 9 to use that software). For others it may just be a matter of evaluating OS X while they do most of their work in the familiarity of OS 9. Whatever the reason, switching back and forth between OS X and OS 9 provides some unique challenges that aren't present for those who primarily use one or the other. In this section I talk about some of these issues, as well as ways to make switching back and forth easier by using multiple OS 9 System Folders and multiple partitions or drives.

NOTE Some newer Macs can *only* boot into OS X and can only run OS 9 within the Classic Environment. If you're using one of these Macs, obviously this section won't apply to you, as you'll be using OS X exclusively. (A list of these models, updated regularly, can be found at `http://docs.info.apple.com/article.html?artnum=86209`.) Likewise, if you boot exclusively into OS X by choice, this section won't apply.

Switching Issues

Below are some of the most common issues that arise for users who frequently use both OS 9 and OS X, along with some solutions—or at least some explanations that should make dealing with these issues easier. In addition, I mentioned issues with Documents folders and file comments earlier in the chapter (under "Transition Technicalities").

Differing Desktop Folders

If you boot into OS 9, items that were on your Desktop in OS X aren't on your Desktop. Conversely, items on your OS 9 Desktop aren't visible on your OS X Desktop. If you're reading this appendix after reading Chapter 1, you may have deduced (correctly) that this has to do with each user having their own Desktop in OS X (at `~/Desktop`). However, it is likewise due to the fact that under OS 9, there is only one Desktop per *volume*; that Desktop is actually a folder at the root level of each volume called *Desktop Folder*.

What this means is that when you're booted into OS X, to access items on your OS 9 Desktop you need to open the folder called Desktop Folder at the root level of the hard drive you use for booting into OS 9. Conversely, if you're booted into OS 9, to get to files on your OS X Desktop you need to browse to `/`*`OSXvolume`*`/Users/`*`username`*`/Desktop`, where *OSXvolume* is the volume that contains your OS X system, and *username* is your OS X username.

Many users get around this inconvenience by creating an alias on each Desktop that points to the other. In fact, under OS X 10.2 and later, if there are items on the OS 9 Desktop, OS X automatically creates an alias to that Desktop for you at startup (and places it on each user's OS X Desktop). If there are no items on the OS 9 Desktop the next time you start up, the alias is removed from all OS X Desktops.

NOTE If you're using OS X 10.1.*x*, you'll need to create an alias to the OS 9 Desktop manually. The easiest way is to open Terminal and type **`ln -s '/Desktop Folder' ~/Desktop/'Desktop (Mac OS 9)'`** **<RETURN>**. If your OS 9 startup volume is different from your OS X startup volume, then instead type **`ln -s '/Volumes/`*`volumename`*`/Desktop Folder' ~/Desktop/'Desktop (Mac OS 9)'`** **<RETURN>**. An alias to the OS 9 Desktop Folder will be created on your Desktop in OS X.

The easiest way to do the opposite—create an alias to your OS X Desktop on your OS 9 Desktop—is to do it from within OS 9, since your user folder will be visible in the OS 9 Finder.

Using a Single Desktop for Both OS 9 and OS X

Although you can use the appropriate Desktop for the OS under which you're using your Mac, and access the other using an alias, there are a couple drawbacks. First, when you place documents on your OS 9 Desktop, you lose all of OS X's user security—anyone in OS 9 or OS X can access them easily. But more importantly, using two different Desktops is just plain confusing. If you're the only user of OS 9 on your Mac, you can actually force OS 9 to use your OS X Desktop as its own.

1. When booted into OS 9, move everything on your OS 9 Desktop into your OS X Desktop folder (`/Users/username/Desktop`).

WARNING If you *don't* move items *off* of your OS 9 Desktop before continuing, they will be deleted by the next step!

2. Boot into OS X, log in, and launch Terminal.
3. If your OS X boot volume and OS 9 boot volume are the same, type **`rm -rf '/Desktop Folder'`** <RETURN>. If they're different, type **`rm -rf '/Volumes/volumename/Desktop Folder'`** <RETURN>, where *volumename* is the name of your OS 9 boot volume. This step deletes your original OS 9 Desktop.
4. If your OS X boot volume and OS 9 boot volume are the same, type **`ln -s ~/Desktop '/Desktop Folder'`** <RETURN>. If they're different, type **`ln -s ~/Desktop '/Volumes/volumename/Desktop Folder'`** <RETURN>, where *volumename* is your OS 9 boot volume. This step replaces the original OS 9 Desktop with an alias to your personal OS X Desktop.

Your OS 9 Desktop will now be the same as your OS X Desktop.

NOTE The only caveat to this setup is that if anyone *else* boots into OS 9, they'll have access to everything on your Desktop. Of course, they would anyways, since permissions aren't enforced in OS 9, so they could just as easily navigate to your personal Desktop folder in the Finder.

Some users have accomplished similar functionality to the above procedure by simply changing the name of the "Desktop (Mac OS 9)" alias created by OS X (or by the user in 10.1.*x*) to "Desktop" and then replacing their personal Desktop folder with this alias. However, although the above procedure lets anyone view the contents of your Desktop by booting into OS 9, this latter procedure lets anyone view the contents of your Desktop in both OS 9 *and* OS X.

Clipping Compatibility

Like OS 9, OS X supports clipping files (I actually talked about using clippings in OS X in Chapter 7). You can create new clipping files, and you can open and use clipping files created in OS 9. However, for some reason (another mystery to me), in OS X Apple changed the creator code for clipping files from `drag` to `MACS`. Although OS X understands both of these codes, OS 9 doesn't—with the end result being that clipping files created in OS X cannot be opened in OS 9.

If you frequently boot into OS 9 and want to be able to open clipping files created in OS X, you'll need to manually change their creator codes to `drag`. I talked about creator codes and utilities for changing them in Chapter 5; any of these utilities will work just fine. However, the utility File Buddy (`http://www.skytag.com/`) lets you create "Droplets"—small utilities that can perform any function available in File Buddy by simply dropping files onto its icon. I've created a Droplet that changes the creator code of any file I drop onto it to `drag`.

Filename Formats

In Mac OS 9 and earlier, the length of file and folder names is limited to 31 characters. However, in OS X you can actually use a name of up to 256 characters. When you boot into OS 9, any file or folder name over 31 characters will be truncated; unfortunately, this truncation isn't pretty. OS 9 not only cuts characters off of the file's name; it also adds funky characters. These characters help preserve the file's name when you switch back to OS X, but they further reduce the number of "usable" characters that you see.

This means that if you switch between OS X and OS 9, you may want to be careful to keep filenames to 31 characters or less (including the file extension).

Multiple User Usernames

Although OS X is a multiple-user operating system from the ground up, OS 9 also had the (more limited) ability to accommodate more than one user via the Multiple Users control panel. In fact, from a file and folder point of view, it worked similarly to OS X—user folders were located in a folder called Users. For the most part, OS X's user directories can coexist with OS 9's. However, if you use OS 9's Multiple Users, do *not* create a new user in OS 9 that has the same username as a user in OS X; you run the risk of wiping out the OS X user. Likewise, if you somehow manage to have a user with the same name in both OS 9 and OS X, deleting that user from OS 9 will *also* delete them from OS X.

WARNING This is just a warning box to remind you that the section you just read tells you how to avoid data loss.

Why You Should Consider Multiple OS 9 System Folders

In Chapter 8, I discussed the advantages of customizing the OS 9 System Folder used for OS X's Classic Environment—slimming it down to the bare essentials. However, when you boot into OS 9, this optimized System Folder may not have all of your favorite OS 9–specific support files and system add-ons (all of the things you want when booted into OS 9 but that slow down, or are incompatible with, the Classic Environment). Likewise, some users report that the files installed into the Classic System (the one used by the Classic Environment) can actually cause problems if you use that System Folder to boot into OS 9.

Because of this, if you tend to boot into OS 9 frequently *and* use the Classic Environment, you may want to consider having two OS 9 System Folders: one optimized for the Classic Environment and one chock full of all your favorite OS 9 stuff. You can do this by installing two copies of OS 9 on your OS X boot volume (you can even name the one for Classic "Classic System Folder"), or by installing one or more copies of OS 9 on an alternate volume (a partition, second hard drive, etc.).

TIP As an alternative to having two OS 9 System Folders, you can also use Extensions Manager or Conflict Catcher to create sets of startup files, as described in Chapter 8. You can use the slim/optimized set when using OS 9 in the Classic Environment, and the full monte when actually booting into OS 9.

In addition to being able to have "slim" and "full" versions of the Classic Mac OS, having multiple System Folders also allows you to use different *versions* of the Classic Mac OS. For example, the Classic Environment requires OS 9.2.1 or later. If you prefer to use a version of the Mac OS prior to 9.2.1 when you boot into OS 9—or *need* to use an older version, even OS 8, in order to run older software—you need multiple System Folders.

Finally, if you frequently switch between booting into OS 9 and OS X, you should consider partitioning your hard drive or installing a second drive. I talk about this option next.

Why You Should Consider Having OS 9 on a Different Partition or Drives than OS X

If having multiple OS 9 System Folders sounds like something you might want to do—or even if you don't have multiple OS 9 System Folders, but tend to switch between booting into OS 9 and OS X—you should also think about partitioning your hard drive.

I discuss partitioning in detail in Appendix B, but it's basically a way of splitting a hard drive into two or more *partitions*, each of which behaves as if it's a separate hard drive or volume. In fact, if you have a single hard drive divided into three partitions, you can boot off of any of them, provided they each have a valid OS 9 System Folder or OS X installation. In the context of this discussion, you can install OS X and your Classic System Folder on one partition, and a second OS 9 System Folder—to be used when booting into OS 9—on another.

In fact, to reduce disk "clutter," some users actually place their "full" version of OS 9—the one they use when booting into OS 9—on a second drive or partition, and place their "slim" OS 9—the one used by the Classic Environment—on a disk *image* on their OS X volume. You can create a 250–300MB disk image using Disk Copy, and install OS 9 onto it. Select that System Folder in Classic preferences, and whenever you want to launch the Classic Environment, just mount the image first. The rest of the time the Classic System Folder is stored in a single file.

You may be wondering why you'd need partitions to do this, since you can simply install multiple OS 9 System Folders on your OS X volume, and then choose between them in both Classic preferences (for use in the Classic Environment) and Startup Disk preferences (for use when booting into OS 9). There are a couple additional benefits that partitions provide. The first—as I explained in Chapter 3—is that Startup Manager, accessed by holding the option key down at startup, only recognizes different bootable *volumes*. In other words, if you have your OS X and OS 9 system software installed on the same volume, you can't use the Startup Manager to choose which to boot into; you need to open the Startup Disk preferences, choose the OS to use for booting, and then restart. This means that if your computer isn't running, you need to boot up, switch OSs, and then reboot. However, with multiple partitions, you can choose which OS to boot into at startup, since OS X and OS 9 will be installed on different volumes.

The second advantage of having multiple volumes—and this is true regardless of the versions of the Mac OS you install on them—is that it provides you with an "emergency" boot volume. If one volume or OS installation gives you problems, you can boot from the other volume and run any disk utilities or perform any maintenance tasks you may need.

NOTE Most of the benefits of multiple partitions can also be attained by buying and installing a second hard drive. In fact, if you're using an older desktop Mac and buy a new hard drive, you can transfer OS X to the new drive, which will surely be much larger than your original drive, and then use the original drive for booting into OS 9.

If after reading this discussion you decide that multiple partitions is for you, be sure to read the next appendix for more information, including instructions on how to partition a drive, as well as special considerations and challenges that come with using partitions and multiple volumes.

NOTE For more information on choosing a startup OS and/or volume, see Chapter 3. For easy one-key switching between OS X and OS 9, see the ResExcellence tutorial at `http://www.resexcellence.com/hack_html_02/04-11-02.shtml`.

Appendix B

Multiple Mounts, Various Volumes, and Divided Disks

(Or: Everything you wanted to know about multiple hard drives, disk partitions, and removable volumes, but were afraid to ask.)

Although most Macs come with a single hard drive, pretty much every Mac user will at some point work with multiple mounted volumes—the technical term for hard drives, removable media, and even disk images. In addition, many users *partition* their hard drive(s), which is a way of making a single drive appear as multiple drives. Although OS X, like any modern operating system, fully supports as many volumes as you can manage to mount, working with non-boot volumes is a bit different than working with the boot volume. In fact, although the Mac OS has always been a bit confusing when it comes to working with multiple volumes—especially for new users—OS X has additional considerations that make multiple volumes a bit more challenging.

In this appendix I'm going to talk about some of the issues and quirks that arise when working with multiple volumes. I'm also going to talk about drive partitioning, including why you would want to do it, and how to actually go about it. Finally, I'll discuss a couple of ways to customize OS X when using multiple volumes, by moving user directories and/or your system swap files to non-boot volumes.

Working with Multiple Volumes in OS X

From the standpoint of the user, a *volume* is any disk, drive, partition, image, or server that appears on your computer as a location for data storage. For example, if you open a new Finder window at the Computer level, you'll see the available volumes—maybe just your hard drive, if you only have a single drive with a single partition, and no removable media or servers mounted. In fact, in many cases, a volume is the same thing as a hard drive, a CD, or a disk image.

However, from a technical standpoint—that is, the way OS X sees things—a volume is any separately identifiable unit of data storage. For example, a hard drive that has been divided into two or more partitions is seen by OS X as multiple units of storage. OS X then mounts those units as separate volumes. If you type **`sudo autodiskmount -v`** **<RETURN>** in Terminal, you'll see a list of currently mounted volumes. As an example, below are the results of this command on my computer:

```
/Users/frakes % sudo autodiskmount -v
Password:
DiskDev   FileSys Fixed Write Volume Name       Mounted On
disk0s9   hfs     yes   yes   SystemX           /
disk0s10  hfs     yes   yes   System9           /Volumes/System9
disk0s11  hfs     yes   yes   Scratch           /Volumes/Scratch
disk1s9   hfs     yes   yes   SystemXBackup     /Volumes/SystemXBackup
disk1s10  hfs     yes   yes   iTunes            /Volumes/iTunes
disk3s9   hfs     yes   yes   Backup            /Volumes/Backup
disk5     hfs     no    yes   Test Image        /Volumes/Test Image
```

The first column lists the device ID, which is a way for OS X to keep track of which disk is which. `disk0` is the first internal hard drive, `disk1` is a second internal hard drive, `disk3` is a FireWire drive, and `disk5` is a mounted disk image. In addition, some disks have multiple volumes. For example, `disk0`, the boot drive, has been partitioned into three volumes: SystemX, System9, and Scratch. The second internal hard drive, `disk1`, is also partitioned into two volumes, SystemXBackup and iTunes. The display also tells you how each volume is formatted, whether it's fixed or removable, whether it's writable, the name of the volume, and, finally, where the drive has been mounted in terms of OS X's filesystem. (I'll talk about this location in the next section.)

(In case you're wondering, SystemX is my regular OS X volume. System9 is a volume I use when I need to boot into OS 9. Scratch is a volume I use for downloads, browser caches, and temporary files in order to reduce fragmentation on my main OS X volume. SystemXBackup keeps a daily mirror of my main SystemX drive, and, the iTunes volume holds MP3s of my CD collection; we share this volume over our home network so that any of our computers can play the music.)

Although my drive setup is a bit more complex than most, as I mentioned earlier, you don't have to be a high-end user to work with multiple volumes. Any time you insert a CD, DVD, floppy, or magneto-optical disk; connect to a file server; mount your iDisk; or even mount a disk image, you're mounting a new volume, and you need to be aware of how working with files on multiple volumes differs from working with files on a single volume.

Accessing Non-Boot Volumes

Before I get into some of the issues that come with using multiple volumes, here's how you actually access files and folders that reside on non-boot volumes from the Finder, in Open/Save dialogs, and from within Terminal.

In the Finder If you've checked the boxes next to "Hard disks," "Removable media (such as CDs)," and "Connected servers" in Finder preferences, any mounted volume will show up on your Desktop. However, if you've unchecked any of these boxes, another way is to open a new Finder window and click the Computer item in the toolbar (or choose Go ➢ Computer, or press shift+command+C). This will present all mounted volumes, along with the Network icon, in a single Finder window. You can then access any volume as you would your boot volume or a folder.

In Open/Save dialogs From within Open/Save dialogs, you can access any volume via the file browser (which is probably showing by this point in the book, but, if not, is accessible by clicking the downward-pointing triangle). Click the horizontal scrollbar at the bottom of the file browser, and drag it all the way to the left. You'll see a list of all mounted volumes, which you can then browse.

From within Terminal Accessing volumes via the Finder and Open/Save dialogs is fairly intuitive, since volumes are generally hard drives, CDs, servers, etc., so it follows that you would access them at the *top* level of the Finder and file browsers. However, accessing non-boot volumes in Terminal is a bit different. If you flip back to the example I provided using the `autodiskmount` command, and look at the Mounted On column of the Terminal output, you'll see why. The boot volume is always located at `/`, whereas non-boot volumes are located in `/Volumes`. So to access a non-boot volume in Terminal, you need to use the path `/Volumes/volumename`. For example, using the volumes in that example, if I wanted to save the output of the manual page for the `mv` command to a file named `mv.txt` on the disk named Scratch, I'd type `man mv > /Volumes/Scratch/mv.txt <RETURN>`, where `/Volumes/Scratch` is the destination for the new file. (Don't worry if you don't understand this command right now; you can read Chapter 15 for some help.)

TIP You can also access non-boot volumes using any of the tips I showed you in Chapter 5, the Online Bonus Chapter, and Chapter 6.

Copying versus Moving with Multiple Volumes

User Level: any
Affects: individual user
Terminal: no

To many users this will be old hat, but users whom I consider to be quite competent have asked me about this, so it's definitely not obvious. When you drag an item (file, folder, application, etc.) from one place to another on the *same* volume, it will be moved (provided you haven't held down any modifier keys as explained in Chapter 5). However, when you drag an item from one volume to another volume, it will be *copied*. In other words, it will still exist on the first volume, but a copy of it will be made on the second.

If you want to *move* an item from one volume to another, hold down the command key as you drag it between volumes. This will copy the file to the new volume and delete it from the original volume simultaneously.

WARNING Unfortunately, the *move* command (command+drag) isn't 100% safe at the time of this writing. If you attempt to move an item and for some reason the copy cannot complete (because of a disk error, or because there's not enough room on the destination volume), the copy will fail, but the original will still be deleted, leaving you with a missing file! So be careful about using this feature until Apple fixes this bug.

Permissions on Non-Boot Volumes

I mentioned this earlier in the book, but it's worth mentioning here. The default permissions for non-boot volumes are Read & Write for Owner, Group, and Others. In other words, *everyone* has full access. This means that non-boot volumes are, by default, just like the Shared user folder.

On the other hand, items copied to a non-boot volume retain their original permissions, and you can always change the permissions on a particular document or folder to restrict access. In addition, an administrative user can also change the permissions for an entire volume. Here are a couple ways to do so.

Creating a "Private" Volume

User Level: admin
Affects: computer
Terminal: no

Consider the example I used in Chapter 1 where parents could create a group called "Parents," and then set the permissions for those items they wanted to keep private from their children to Group: Parents, Read & Write and Others: No Access. You can use a similar procedure to make an entire volume—a second hard drive, a CD-RW or DVD-R, or even a mounted disk image—private.

1. Select the mounted volume in the Finder (from the Desktop or a Finder window showing the Computer view).
2. Choose File > Get Info (or press command+I).
3. Click the triangle next to Ownership & Permissions to expand the panel.

4. For the Group setting, choose the appropriate group name, and give it Read & Write access.
5. For the Others setting, choose No Access.
6. Make sure "Ignore ownership on this volume" is *not* checked.
7. To ensure that any items already on the volume are also inaccessible to those not in your group, click the "Apply to enclosed items..." button.

Users not in your group will not even be able to view the top-level contents of the volume, but those in the group will have full access.

TIP If you want a *personal* private volume—one that no user but you can access—follow the instructions above but set the Group name to "nogroup" or "nobody." These groups have no users in them, so no one but you will have access to files on the volume. (You can also set Group Access to No Access, but this technically doesn't offer you any extra protection.)

Creating a "Universal Access" Volume

User Level: admin
Affects: computer
Terminal: no

At the opposite end of the security spectrum from a private volume, you can set up a volume where *all* users can access and modify *all* files. I call this a "universal access" volume, but some people call it a "shared" volume. (I don't like calling it a shared volume because OS X already has a Shared user folder, and that folder has different permissions.) These types of volumes are often used to share files and folders that multiple users need to edit.

To do this, simply follow Steps 1–3 above, but instead of setting any groups or permissions, check the box next to "Ignore ownership on this volume." This tells OS X to disregard ownership and permissions for any and all files on the volume.

"Ignore ownership on this volume" does just that—it allows unfettered access to any file on the volume by any user. (Technically, it's not even doing that; permissions and ownership simply do not apply.) So make sure you only use the volume for files that you are sure you want anyone to be able to modify. Just to be safe, you may want to make backup copies of files before moving them to the universal access volume.

Permissions on Removable Volumes

For the most part, permissions on removable volumes (FireWire hard drives, floppy disks, magneto-optical drives) work as described in the previous section ("Permissions on Non-Boot Volumes"), *provided* you use that volume on the computer that formatted it and/or first applied file ownership and permissions to it. However, any *other* Mac will always treat the volume as if the "Ignore ownership on this volume" box is checked in the volume's Ownership & Permissions info panel.

The reason for this is that Unix—and thus OS X—keeps track of users and groups via user IDs and group IDs; since every OS X computer uses the same ID system, there's no way for OS X to know if user ID 500 on one computer is the same person as user ID 500 on another. Thus, whenever you mount a removable volume on a computer *other* than the one used to format it, the "Ignore ownership on this volume" box will automatically be set.

Sharing a Non-Boot Volume

User Level:	admin
Affects:	computer
Terminal:	no

As I discussed in Chapter 10, by default OS X only shares user directories (to the respective user) and user Public folders (to all users). However, you can manually create additional shares using tools like SharePoints. You can use the same technique I described in Chapter 10 to share entire non-boot volumes (or just directories on a non-boot volume).

For example, as mentioned earlier in this appendix, my desktop Mac has an extra hard drive that holds all of the MP3s we've ripped from our CD collection—about 40GB worth. Rather than copy all 40GB of files to our iBook's hard drive, I've set up the iTunes music volume as a Personal File Sharing share, and then configured the iBook so that all accounts mount the iTunes music volume at login. Anyone using iTunes on the iBook can listen to all 40GB of music even though it's located on the desktop Mac.

TIP You can also combine this tip with the previous two to create private shares or universal shares that are accessible remotely.

Changing the Startup Volume

If you have OS X installed on multiple volumes, or if you have a mix of OS 9 and OS X installations on multiple volumes, you'll need to switch startup disks when you want to boot from another disk. I mention this topic here because it's a logical place for it, but I'm going to refer you to Chapter 3, where I've already covered it under "Choosing a Startup Volume or System."

Installing OS X on FireWire Volumes

User Level:	admin
Affects:	computer
Terminal:	no

You can install OS X on additional volumes using the OS X installer, or by copying an existing OS X installation using Carbon Copy Cloner, as I covered in Chapter 4. However, if you install or copy OS X to an external FireWire drive, you may initially have difficulty booting off of that drive. A possible solution is to make sure the FireWire drive is mounted and then type the following command in Terminal: **sudo bless -folder /Volumes/*volumename*/ System/Library/CoreServices <RETURN>**, where *volumename* is the name of the FireWire drive. This command *blesses* the volume, which means it forces OS X to see it as a legitimate startup volume. You should then be able to select it as a startup volume.

Using Drive Partitions

I briefly mentioned hard drive *partitions* earlier in this appendix, but I want to talk more about them here. You may already have your drive(s) partitioned, but if you don't this section should help you decide whether or not partitioning is for you. I'll also show you how to partition using OS X's built-in tools.

If you're not familiar with the procedure, partitioning is a way of taking a hard drive (or other type of volume) and dividing it up into sections (partitions) that appear to the operating system as separate volumes. For example, you can divide a 40GB drive into three partitions of 10GB, 25GB, and 5GB, and those partitions will show up in OS X as three different hard drives (on the Desktop, in Finder windows, in Terminal, etc.). You can generally partition a drive into as many segments as you want, and the partitions do not have to be of equal size.

NOTE In tech terms, hard drives are often called *physical* volumes (because they are physically a single volume), whereas partitions of a hard drive are called *logical* volumes (because they appear to the OS as separate volumes).

Benefits of Partitioning

There are, speaking generally, four benefits of partitioning. The first is that since each partition acts like a separate drive, you can install a different operating system (OS 9, OS X, Linux, etc.) on each one, and then be able to easily choose which OS to boot into (at startup using the Startup Manager, or from Startup Disk preferences). You can even install different copies or version of OS X on different partitions. If you read the previous appendix, you'll remember that I recommended this approach if you find yourself booting between OS 9 and OS X frequently.

The second reason why partitioning can be useful has to do with disk fragmentation. I mentioned fragmentation and optimization in Chapter 14, but basically it's the process through which files are stored in pieces across your hard drive instead of in contiguous segments. In theory, the more fragmented your drive, the slower its performance. (I say "in theory" because although this was very true in Mac OS 9 and earlier, it's a hotly debated topic under OS X. Some people claim the slowdown is significant, others say it's undetectable. I'm somewhere in the middle.) Some of the worst contributors to hard drive fragmentation are web browsers—which store hundreds or even thousands of cache files on your hard drive to speed up browsing—and frequent downloads and deletions. What many users do is create a small partition and relocate their browser caches, Internet downloads, and any other files that are frequently saved and deleted. This way these files don't contribute to fragmentation of your "main" volume.

Another argument for drive partitions, related to the previous one, is that many applications require large amounts of temporary disk space for working with files. For example, Adobe Photoshop requires *scratch* space on your hard drive to perform many of its functions. If you designate your main hard drive as the scratch disk, chances are Photoshop's scratch files are going to be strewn out across your drive, which can slow Photoshop's performance. Conversely, having huge Photoshop scratch files on your boot volume contributes to fragmentation of that volume. Another example is editing digital video; when you import video from a camcorder, the video data—which is significant in size—gets saved wherever there is space on your hard drive. If you save video to your boot volume, it's going to be split up into many small pieces across the drive. When you later go to work with that video, performance can suffer as your video editing application has to search for each piece. Thus it follows that if you create a dedicated partition to be used only for Photoshop scratch files, or only for digital video storage, those files are more likely to be saved in large contiguous chunks, which may increase performance (and also won't contribute to the fragmentation of your boot volume). Again, as with the previous paragraph, I should mention that because OS X handles disk fragmentation much better than OS 9 and earlier, this isn't quite the issue it used to be. However, some people still swear by it.

Another argument for partitioning is that if you do a lot of CD burning, you may want to consider creating a partition that you use exclusively for storing data to be burned. Because burning CDs requires immediate (and uninterrupted) access to the data to be copied, fragmented data can lead to unsuccessful CD burns. A dedicated CD "scratch" partition (mine is actually called CD Scratch, appropriately enough) gives you a continuous block of drive space that you can use to store files for burning. After you burn the data to CD, you can then erase the partition to ensure that it's clean and unfragmented for the next CD. As a bonus, by making it the same size as a blank CD (640MB or 695MB), you know exactly when you're out of space—when the volume is full.

Finally, another reason to consider partitioning is for easier backups. Some users like to store documents, and even their entire user directory, on a smaller, non-boot partition. Backing up is then a matter of simply backing up that partition, rather than their entire OS X volume. (If you're interested, I'll show you how to move your user folder to a non-boot partition later in the appendix.) In some situations, having all of your documents on a single partition can also improve performance, since all document access is confined to a single area of the hard drive, rather than spread out across the entire drive.

NOTE If you're not comfortable with partitioning (see the next section, "Drawbacks of Partitioning"), you can get pretty much the same benefits by simply installing a new hard drive (for a desktop Mac) or by connecting an external hard drive (for any Mac). In fact, in most cases the benefits will actually be greater, since your Mac can read data from and write data to two drives at once. Prices have gone down so much that you can get an 80GB hard drive for under $100 if you look hard enough.

Drawbacks of Partitioning

None of the benefits I described above may appeal to you; if so, great—you don't have to worry about how to go about partitioning a drive. However, if you do find partitioning tempting, keep in mind that there are also a few drawbacks.

The first, and most severe, drawback is that partitioning a drive usually requires you to first back up all the data on the drive, then *erase* the drive completely, then set up partitions, and then restore your data back to one or more of the partitions—it's not a simple procedure by any means. In fact, the best time to partition a drive is when you first get it (when you bring it home from the store, or when you first get your Mac)—that's really the only time that erasing the drive has no real drawbacks. If the drive is brand new, it's empty, or if you're just getting your new Mac, all of the software on the hard drive can be restored fairly painlessly using the Software Restore disc(s) that come with it.

The second drawback is that once you decide on your partition sizes, you're pretty much stuck with them unless you want to really get into nasty (and risky) partition resizing exercises in Terminal. So if you later realize that you made your boot partition too small, or you want to change the size of a non-boot partition, your only real recourse is to—yes—back everything up, erase the drive and set up new partitions, then restore your data. So you really need to make sure that you set up your partitions well in the beginning.

NOTE When I say that you can't partition (or re-partition) without backing up and then reformatting your hard drive, I'm not being entirely honest. There are ways to do it using Terminal, but you risk data loss if you don't know exactly what you're doing. In addition, if you boot into OS 9, FWB's Partition Toolkit (`http://www.fwb.com/`) allows you to resize, create, and delete partitions without reformatting. However, at the time of this writing, there is no OS X version of Partition Toolkit, so if you have one of the newer Macs that can't boot into OS 9, you're stuck.

Third, partitioning a drive into several volumes can actually *decrease* performance, due to the fact that the average seek time (the time it takes to move the hard drive's read/write heads from one position on the drive platters to another) is increased. For example, if you have a single volume, your system software, applications, documents, swap files, scratch files, etc. are all stored in a fairly localized group of hard drive blocks—OS X generally tries to store data as close to the beginning of the volume as is reasonable. However, if you partition a drive and split your data between partitions, you're forcing your drive's heads to move back and forth across unused drive space (the space between the end of data on one partition and the beginning of data on the next) as they retrieve and save data. The more your drive has to access data on different partitions, the longer the *average* seek time is going to be.

Finally, another drawback is that all of the issues I discussed earlier in this appendix (in the section "Working with Multiple Volumes in OS X") will apply to you and your partitions. Some of these issues are actually benefits, but a few are inconvenient at best.

Partitioning a Drive in OS X

User Level: admin
Affects: computer
Terminal: no

If after considering the pros and cons of partitions, you decide it's something you want to do, here's how to do it using OS X's Disk Utility. Note that you can't boot from the volume you're about to partition (since you're going to erase it during the process). If you have another boot volume (an additional hard drive, a FireWire drive, etc.), you can boot from that volume and then access Disk Utility in `/Applications/Utilities`. If you don't have another boot volume, you can boot from the OS X Install CD and access Disk Utility from the first screen (from the Installer menu).

WARNING As I mentioned above, to partition a drive you have to *erase* it, so *make sure* you've backed up any important data before starting this process! (And make sure it's backed up to a different drive or media, not just to somewhere else on the drive being partitioned.)

1. Double-check to make sure you've backed up any important data on the drive you're going to partition.
2. Triple-check.
3. In Disk Utility, click the Partition tab.
4. In the disk/volume window on the left, select the disk drive you want to partition. (You must select the drive itself, not any existing partitions on that drive.) You'll see a graphical representation of the disk (the volume display); if this is a new drive, it will contain one large partition, and possibly a very small partition called "free" or something similar. If you click on any part of the volume display, the Volume Information box will give you information about that partition's name, size, and format.

5. From the Volume Scheme pop-up menu, select the number of partitions into which you want to divide the drive. The volume display will automatically divide into the number of partitions you've chosen, all of equal sizes. (If you decide you want more partitions, you can select a partition and click the Split button; conversely, you can reduce the number of partitions by selecting one and clicking the Delete button.)
6. Resize each partition to the desired size. You can do this by clicking in a partition, and then typing a size in the Size field in Volume Information, or by grabbing the resize tab at the bottom of a partition in the volume display and dragging it up or down.

NOTE The Size field in the Volume Information box uses either MB or GB as the unit of size; it changes automatically to allow you to fine-tune the volume being resized.

7. Configure the volume information for each partition by clicking on a partition and then typing a name for it and choosing a drive format from the Format pop-up menu. For almost everyone, I recommend Mac OS Extended. Mac OS Standard can only be used by OS 9 and earlier, and Unix File System (also known as UFS) is not fully compatible with OS X (see `http://docs.info.apple.com/article.html?artnum=25316` for more details). Free Space has special significance that most users will never use. (If you need to format a volume as Free Space, you probably understand it and know why you need it.)
8. If you ever plan to use this disk under Mac OS 9, check the box next to "Install Mac OS 9 Disk Drivers." (It will work fine in the Classic Environment in OS X either way.)
9. Are you *absolutely* sure there is no data on this disk that you need but haven't backed up? (Sorry, I just want to make sure.)
10. Click the Partition button to partition the disk. You'll see a warning dialog reminding you how serious this procedure is (Figure B.1). If you're sure, click Partition.

The disk will be divided into separate logical partitions, each of which behaves like a separate hard drive. In Figure B.2, you can see five volumes mounted on our iBook; these are actually two hard drives divided into five partitions.

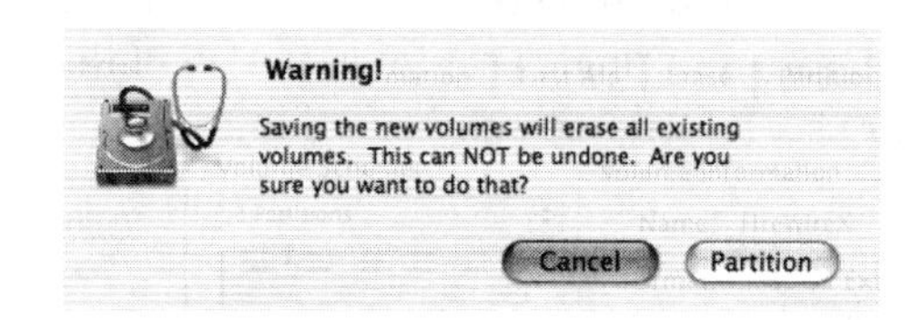

FIGURE B.1: Disk Utility warns you that partitioning erases any volumes on the disk being partitioned, and this erasure cannot be undone.

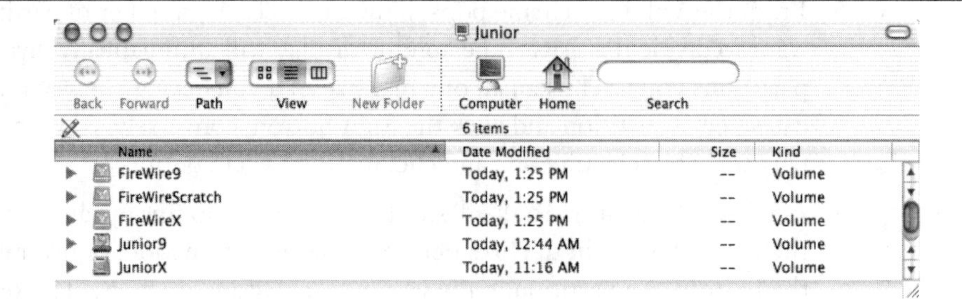

FIGURE B.2: An example of partitions: two physical drives partitioned into five volumes

Customizing OS X When Using Multiple Volumes

Besides the obvious uses for multiple volumes—storing files and alternate systems—there are a few other things you can do. In the sections that follow I'll show you how to move a user folder (or all user directories) to a non-boot volume, and how to move your system swap files to a non-boot volume.

Moving a User Folder—or All User Folders—to a Non-Boot Volume

User Level: admin
Affects: individual user or all users
Terminal: no

Although it's common in large network environments for user directories to be stored somewhere besides the local computer (e.g., on a central server), most home users have never even considered such a setup. Nevertheless, there are a few situations where you might want to consider it. For example, you can keep your user folder(s) on a separate volume from the rest of your OS X files in order to make backing up your user folder(s) easier. Or perhaps you test a lot of software—you can keep your user folder(s) on a non-boot volume, and if your OS X installation becomes unstable, you can reformat the drive and reinstall OS X, keeping your user folder(s) intact. (After you reinstall, you'll have to reassign your home directories to their location on the alternative volume.) Or maybe you have multiple OS X startup volumes—you can use a single user folder for all of them. Whatever the case, if you want to move your user folder(s) to another volume, the next two sections will show you how.

WARNING Do *not* move user folders to a removable volume. At the time of this writing, OS X does not properly handle the situation where a volume that contains user folders is not mounted. If you try to log in to an account that resides on a removable volume, and that volume is not mounted at the time, you'll not only not be able to access the account then, but you'll never be able to access it again without first using Terminal to delete a bunch of invisible files (which is too messy to get into here).

Moving a Single User Folder to a Non-Boot Volume

User Level: admin
Affects: individual or multiple users
Terminal: yes

Although it's possible to move a user directory to a different volume using a combination of Terminal and NetInfo Manager, it's easier, and quicker, to do the whole shebang using Terminal.

1. Type **`sudo ditto -rsrc /Users/`*`username`*` '/Volumes/`*`volumename`*`/Users/`*`username`*`'`** **<RETURN>**, where *username* is the short name of the user whose folder you wish to move, and *volumename* is the name of the volume to which you wish to move it; provide your admin password when prompted. The `ditto` command copies the user folder (including any hidden files); the `-rsrc` option ensures that all resource forks are copied.
2. Type **`sudo niutil -createprop / /Users/username home '/Volumes/`*`volumename`*`/Users/`*`username`*`'`** **<RETURN>**. This command uses the `niutil` command to reassign your home directory from the original location to the new location. In fact, if you were to use NetInfo Manager to make this change, you'd actually be changing the *home* property for the user *username* from `/Users/`*`username`* to `/Volumes/`*`volumename`*`/Users/`*`username`*.
3. If you moved your own account, log out and then back in, and make sure your user folder was copied and reassigned properly; otherwise have the user whose folder you moved log in and check. To do this, open a Finder window and click the Home button in the toolbar (or choose Go ➢ Home, or press shift+command+H); make sure that the path to the folder is `/Volumes/`*`volumename`*`/Users/`*`username`*.
4. Assuming everything is working properly, launch Terminal and type **`sudo rm -dr /Users/`*`username`*`/`** **<RETURN>**; provide your admin password when prompted. This command deletes your original user folder.
5. Type **`sudo ln -s '/Volumes/`*`volumename`*`/Users/`*`username`*`' /Users/`*`username`*** **<RETURN>**. This command creates a symbolic link (similar to an alias) from the Users folder on the boot volume to your new user folder on *volumename*. This step isn't absolutely necessary, but it makes it easier to access the moved user folder, since the link to the folder will show up in the standard Users directory on the boot volume.

TIP The only application that seems to have a problem with your user folder being located on a different volume than the boot volume is Microsoft Excel. If this bug affects you, locate the file called `Carbon Registration Database` from the `~/Library/Preferences/Microsoft` folder of *any* original user folder (i.e., a user folder that is still located in `/Users`). Copy this file to the same folder in any *new* user folder (i.e., a user folder on the non-boot volume). This should allow Excel to run.

Moving *All* User Folders to a Non-Boot Volume

User Level: admin
Affects: all users
Terminal: yes

If you want to move *all* user folders to another volume, the commands are similar, but not identical:

1. Type **sudo ditto -rsrc /Users '/Volumes/*volumename*/Users' <RETURN>**, where *volumename* is the name of the volume to which you wish to move the user folders; provide your admin password when prompted.
2. For *each* user, type **sudo niutil -createprop / /Users/username home '/Volumes/*volumename*/Users/*username*' <RETURN>**. (In other words, you'll need to type this command once for each user.)
3. Log out and then back in to make sure the user folders were copied and reassigned properly.
4. Assuming everything is working properly, launch Terminal and, for *each* user folder *except* the Shared user folder, type **sudo rm -dr /Users/*username*/ <RETURN>**; provide your admin password when prompted. (Again, you'll have to use this command once for each user.)
5. For each user (again, except for the Shared user folder), type **sudo ln -s '/Volumes/volumename/Users/username' /Users/*username* <RETURN>** to create a link from the Users folder on the boot volume to your new user folder on *volumename*.

NOTE The reason you need to delete each user folder and link to each separately, except for the Shared folder, is that some applications require you to have the Shared folder inside the Users folder on the boot volume. If you create a new user(s) *after* completing this procedure, you'll need to perform Steps 2-5 for that user(s).

Using a Non-Boot Volume for System Swap Files

User Level: admin
Affects: computer
Terminal: no

As mentioned earlier, one advantage of OS X is its superior memory management. Part of this memory system is the ability to use sections of the boot drive as virtual memory—hard drive space that stores less-recently-used contents of your computer's actual RAM in order to make room for data currently being used. (For the curious, this process is called *paging*.) When the data stored on the hard drive is needed, it's quickly moved back into real RAM. This memory trickery allows your computer to function as if it has far more memory than it actually does.

These sections of the hard drive used for temporary RAM offloading are called *swap files*, because the OS *swaps* data to and from them frequently. Although this process is very efficient, it has a few drawbacks. First, these swap files take up hard drive space that you may want to use for "real" files. Second, swap files themselves contribute to drive fragmentation (discussed in Chapter 14). The less free space you have on your boot volume, the worse each of these two drawbacks becomes. Finally, virtual memory works somewhat faster when swap files reside on a separate hard drive altogether, since the "swap file" drive can work independently from the system/data drive.

To get around these drawbacks, some users prefer to use a different volume altogether—one dedicated to the task—for swap files. By telling OS X to use a different volume for swap files, you don't have to worry about taking hard drive space away from other files, fragmenting your swap files, or contributing to fragmentation of your boot volume.

NOTE One of the advantages of having your swap files on a separate volume—speed—is only fully realized if the swap volume actually resides on a separate *disk* from your operating system, documents, applications, etc. Locating your swap files on a different partition of the *same* hard drive used as the boot volume will gain you benefits in terms of fragmentation, but will most likely result in a slight *decrease* in performance—the drive heads will still have to alternate between accessing swap files and other files, but will have to travel further to do so (increased average seek time, as described earlier in the chapter).

If you have an extra hard drive or driver partition, and you'd like to try this procedure, the easiest way is to use the shareware Xupport (`http://www.computer-support.ch/`) or SwapSwapVM (`http://www.sciencequest.org/support/computers/mac/repair_topics/application_specific/osx/swapswapvm.html`) Xupport is an excellent, all-around utility that provides a nice interface to *many* Unix commands—I recommend it even if you don't intend to change your swap file location. Here's how to use it to move your swap files:

1. Launch Xupport, and click the Optimize button in the Xupport toolbar. The Optimize panel will drop down.
2. At the bottom of the Optimize panel is the "Swap file" section. From the pop-up menu, choose the volume you want OS X to use for virtual memory swap files.
3. After you choose a volume, you'll see a dialog that tells you to press the Set button and restart your computer. Click OK, and then click the Set button.
4. You'll get a second dialog asking if you're sure you want to change the swap file location to the chosen volume. Click OK, and then enter your admin password when prompted.
5. Restart your Mac.

Once you restart, your Mac will store its swap files on the chosen volume. To verify this, open a new Finder window and choose Go ➢ Go to Folder… (or press shift+command+G);

type **/Volumes/*volumename*/vm** in the "Go to the folder" field (where *volumename* is the name of the volume you chose for your swap files), and then click Go. This will take you to the folder on that volume where the virtual memory swap files are stored. You should see a file named swapfile0; if you do, the procedure was successful.

WARNING As with moving user directories, *do not* move your system swap files to a removable volume, as you're asking for trouble. If you remove the volume while the system is running, or if the volume is not present when the computer boots, your computer won't have its swap space available, which is a bad thing. (OS X *should* automatically relocate its swap file storage to the boot volume, but I've heard reports that this doesn't always happen properly.)

Index

Note to the Reader: Throughout this index **boldfaced** page numbers indicate primary discussions of a topic. *Italicized* page numbers indicate illustrations.

A

B

C

D

E

F

I

J

K

L

M

N

O

P

Q

R

S

T

U

V

W

X

Z

Superb Software Solutions

Here is a list of my favorite third-party utilities and add-ons for OS X (at the time of this writing, at least). Although this list is clearly subjective, these titles warrant consideration from any aspiring power user. Included for each is a URL to get more information. In addition, a complete list of *all* of the excellent utilities and add-ons mentioned in the book, including URL links, is available online at `http://www.macosxpowertools.com/`. (All software titles are also listed, with page references for where they're mentioned in the book, in the main index.)

Software	URL
Alfred	http://www.inferiis.com/products/alfred/
BBEdit	http://www.barebones.com/
Bookit	http://www.everydaysoftware.net/bookit/
BootCD	http://www.charlessoft.com/
BrickHouse	http://personalpages.tds.net/~brian_hill/brickhouse.html
Carbon Copy Cloner	http://www.bombich.com/software/ccc.html
CronniX	http://www.koch-schmidt.de/cronnix/
Data Backup X	http://www.prosoftengineering.com/products/
Data Rescue X	http://www.prosoftengineering.com/products/
Default Folder X	http://www.stclairsoft.com/
Diablotin	http://s.sudre.free.fr/Software/Diablotin.html
DiskWarrior	http://www.alsoft.com/DiskWarrior/index.html
DocJector	http://www.monkeyfood.com/software/docJector/
File Buddy	http://www.skytag.com/filebuddy/
FileXaminer	http://www.gideonsoftworks.com/filexaminer.html
FruitMenu	http://www.unsanity.com/
Gimp-Print	http://gimp-print.sourceforge.net/
Graphic Converter	http://www.lemkesoft.com/
Horse Menu	http://www.nimatoad.com/HorseMenu/index.html
ICeCoffEE	http://web.sabi.net/nriley/software/
Keyboard Maestro	http://www.keyboardmaestro.com/